Object-Oriented Program Development Using

C++

A Class-Centered Approach

Gary J. Bronson
Fairleigh Dickinson University

THOMSON
COURSE TECHNOLOGY

Australia • Canada • Mexico • Singapore • Spain • United Kingdom • United States

Object-Oriented Program Development Using C++: A Class-Centered Approach
by Gary J. Bronson

Senior Product Manager:
Alyssa Pratt

Development Editor:
Ann Shaffer

Senior Marketing Manager:
Karen Seitz

Production Editor:
Philippa Lehar

Associate Product Manager:
Mirella Misiaszek

Editorial Assistant:
Jennifer Smith

Cover Design:
Laura Rickenbach

Interior Design:
Resa Blatman

Copy Editor:
Gary Michael Spahl

Proofreader:
Wendy Benedetto

Indexer:
Liz Cunningham

Compositor:
Pre-Press Company, Inc.

Printer:
Quebecor

Disclaimer:

Thomson Course Technology reserves the right to revise this publication and make changes from time to time in its content without notice.

ISBN 0-619-15966-9

PART IV Additional Class Capabilities   697

Chapter 11
Class Functions and Conversions   698

Chapter 12
Inheritance, Polymorphism, and Dynamic Memory Allocation   *762*

This text is designed for a first course in computer science (CS1), with an introduction to CS2. The major objectives of this book are to introduce, develop, and reinforce well-organized, object-oriented problem solving skills, and to present the C++ language as a powerful problem solving tool. Students should be familiar with fundamental algebra, but no other prerequisites are assumed.

This text is largely derived from the highly successful and well-received *Program Development and Design Using C++,* but with one very significant difference; it directly begins with an object-orientation, rather than with a structured approach. As such, this text represents the solution to a problem that has troubled many professors, including myself: specifically, how to introduce the C++ programming language within the context of a true class-centered approach in a manner that works in the classroom.

The traditional approach of introducing structured elements first and then extending these into an object orientation is certainly valid, but raises one major problem that all professors and their students have to deal with: the awkward mental leap from an algorithmic-centered approach to an object-oriented one. Having learned one way of looking at and constructing a program, students are reluctant to accept that idea that another approach is actually preferable and more useful. For most students, the switch is rather difficult and rarely ever wholly satisfactory. For this reason, many adopters of my earlier text have requested a book that begins directly with objects.

An alternate and preferable technique, and the one taken by this text, is to introduce C++ using a true class-centered approach right from day one. This reverses the conventional approach of presenting class code as a linear extension of procedural code. Presenting objects first, and then presenting procedural code as a necessary sub-set within an object-oriented framework, ensures that the student does not become attached to procedural code as their first and primary way of tackling programming problems. Presenting objects first, in a meaningful way, facilitates learning both procedural and object-oriented aspects of the language, while making the procedural aspects subservient and secondary to, rather than primary and co-equal with, the object-oriented aspects.

APPROACH

A competent C++ programmer must understand both the structural and object-oriented aspects of programming, and both are thoroughly presented in this book. However, this text reverses the conventional approach of presenting class code as a linear extension of structured code; rather, class design and development is presented first, and then structured code is dealt with as a subset under the object-oriented umbrella.

Due to the increasing importance of generic programming and the Standard Template Library (STL), a complete chapter (13) is devoted to the STL. In addition, STL classes and algorithms are discussed wherever these topics are appropriate. Thus, STL algorithms for searching and sorting are presented in Section 8.4, the STL vector class is presented in Section 8.6, and strings and STL algorithms are presented in Section 9.6.

In a similar manner, practical applications of exception handling are presented throughout the text. Thus, exception handling is first discussed in Section 7.6 as an alternative to the conventional error handling technique using functions, and then is used in both Section 10.3 (File Checking) and Appendix C.

Formally, this text is divided into five parts. Parts I and II should be covered sequentially, but the remaining three parts can then be presented in any order.

Part I presents basic computer literacy topics. It provides the foundation for understanding and directly using object-oriented development and programming techniques. This includes class structure, instance variables, and class methods.

Part II presents the basic structured elements that include assignment, input, output, selection, and repetition structures.

Part III presents functions, which are treated as a subset of class methods that are not associated with an implied object. This allows students to take the techniques for passing parameters and returning values that are described in relation to class methods in Part I and immediately apply them to functions. The remaining material in Part III deals with exception handling, arrays, strings, and data files.

Part IV covers advanced class capabilities, including operator functions, friend functions, data type conversions, inheritance, and polymorphism.

Part V provides an introduction to pointers and structures. Instructors should feel free to cover these topics in any order, and to intersperse them among any of the topics in Parts III through IV.

FEATURES

In my own teaching I've learned that, for a textbook to be effective, *it must be written so that students can read it.* The professor sets the stage for learning, but the textbook must encourage, nurture, and assist the student in acquiring and "owning" the material presented in class. Thus, my primary concern, and one of the distinctive features of this book, is that it has been written for the student.

A well-written text becomes a supporting actor to the professor, who plays the leading role. In practical terms, this means that the textbook must be sufficiently flexible so that those professors who subscribe to my objects-first approach can still mold the text to their individual preferences. After covering Parts I and II, professors are free to decide when to introduce specific topics. The following dependency chart illustrates this flexibility.

Topic Dependency Chart

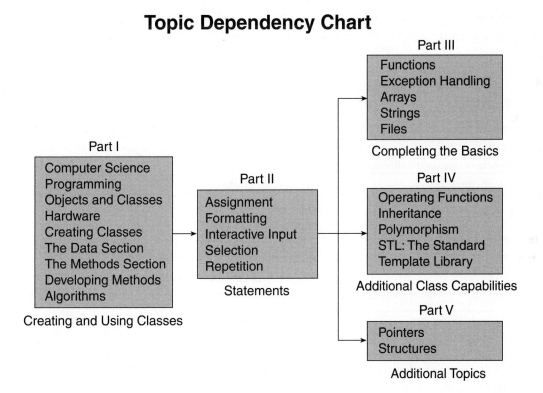

Each chapter includes the following features, which are designed to help students learn and master important programming concepts:

- Programming exercises at the end of every section

> **Exercises 7.3**
>
> 1. a. List the storage categories available to local variables.
>   b. List the storage categories available to global variables.
>
> 2. Describe the difference between a local auto variable and a local static variable.
>
> 3. What is the difference between the following functions?
>
> ```
> void init1(void)
> {
>   static int yrs = 1;
>   cout << "The value of yrs is " << yrs << endl;
>   yrs = yrs + 2;
> }
> ```

- More advanced programming exercises are included at the end of every chapter

> **Chapter Exercises**
>
> 1. a. Write a C++ program that reads a list of floating-point grades from the keyboard into an array named grade. The grades are to be counted as they are read, and entry is to be terminated when a negative value has been entered. Once all of the grades have been input, your program should find and display the sum and average of the grades. The grades should then be listed with an asterisk (*) placed in front of each grade that is below the average.
>   b. Extend the program written for Exercise 1a to display each grade and its letter equivalent. Assume the following scale:
>
>   A grade between 90 and 100 is an A.
>   A grade greater than or equal to 80 and less than 90 is a B.
>   A grade greater than or equal to 70 and less than 80 is a C.
>   A grade greater than or equal to 60 and less than 70 is a D.
>   A grade less than 60 is an F.

- Sample programs which are numbered allow for easy reference in the chapter discussion

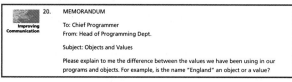

> **Program 8-1**
>
> ```
> #include <iostream>
> using namespace std;
>
> int main()
> {
>   const int MAXGRADES = 5;
>   int i, grade[MAXGRADES];
>
>   for (i = 0; i < MAXGRADES; i++)    // Enter the grades
>   {
>     cout << "Enter a grade: ";
>     cin >> grade[i];
>   }
>
>   cout << endl;
>
>   for (i = 0; i < MAXGRADES; i++)    // Display the grades
>     cout << "grade " << i << " is " << grade[i] << endl;
> ```

- Improving Communication exercises at the end of most chapters emphasize written communication

>
> **Improving Communication**
>
> 20. **MEMORANDUM**
>
> To: Chief Programmer
> From: Head of Programming Dept.
>
> Subject: Objects and Values
>
> Please explain to me the difference between the values we have been using in our programs and objects. For example, is the name "England" an object or a value?

- Working in Teams exercises at the end of chapters encourage students to solve problems as a team

> **Working in Teams**
>
> 25. Have your team list the sequence of events that occur in selecting an item from a soda vending machine. The sequence should start when a customer puts money in the machine and end when the customer removes a can of soda. From this list, complete the event trace diagram shown in Figure 7-24.

- Explanations of common programming errors

> # 9.7 COMMON PROGRAMMING ERRORS
>
> The common errors associated with defining and processing strings are:
>
> 1. Forgetting to include the string header file when using string class objects.
> 2. Forgetting to convert a string class object to a C-string when converting strings to numerical data types.
> 3. Providing insufficient space for a C-string to be stored. A simple variation of this is not providing space for the end-of-string NULL character when a string is defined as an array of characters.

- Conceptual diagrams and historical photographs that illustrate important computer science topics

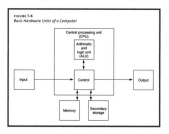

FIGURE 1-6
Basic Hardware Units of a Computer

- A review of the main topics covered in the chapter

> **SUMMARY**
>
> 1. A single-dimensional array is a data structure that can be used to store a list of values of the same data type. Such arrays must be declared by giving the data type of the values that are stored in the array as well as the array size. For example, the declaration:
>
> ```
> int num[100];
> ```
>
> creates an array of 100 integers. A preferable approach is to first use a named constant to set the array size, and then use this constant in the definition of the array. For example:
>
> ```
> const int MAXSIZE = 100;
> ```
>
> and
>
> ```
> int num[MAXSIZE];
> ```

- Bit of Background boxes, which provide interesting historical, biographical, and factual asides.

A BIT OF BACKGROUND

A Notational Inconsistency

Notice that all of the character class methods listed in Table 9-5 use the standard object-oriented notation of preceding the method's name with an object name, as in cin.get(). This is not the case with the string class's getline() method, which uses the notation getline(cin, strVar). In this notation the object, in this case cin, appears as an argument. For consistency's sake, we would have expected getline() to be called as cin.getline().

Unfortunately, this proper notation was already in use for a getline() method originally created for C-style strings (see next section). Hence, a notational inconsistency was created.

PROGRAMMING NOTE

Atomic Data

An **atomic data value** is a value that is considered a complete entity by itself and cannot be decomposed into a smaller data type. For example, although an integer can be decomposed into individual digits, C++ does not have a numerical digit type. Rather, each integer is regarded as a complete value by itself and, as such, is considered atomic data. Similarly, because the integer data type supports only atomic data values, it is said to be an **atomic data type**. As you might expect, all of the built-in data types are atomic data types.

- Programming Notes, designed to provide alternative and advanced programming techniques, such as lavalues and rvalues, values versus identities, dequeues, and stream formatting.

In the process of teaching the C++ programming language, this book presents a variety of essential computer science topics, including:

- An introduction to exception handling, with exception handling applications also presented within various sections where appropriate.
- An extensive introduction to Unified Modeling Language (UML), with UML diagrams used throughout the text to present programming solutions.
- A thorough introduction to the Standard Template Library, with STL applications integrated throughout the text.
- A thorough explanation of input data validation techniques.
- Program design and development sections that introduce and reinforce object-oriented design principles.
- A complete Date class, including Zeller's algorithm for determining the day-of-week that a date falls on, leap year determinations, and day counts.

Every C++ program in this text has been successfully compiled and run under Microsoft's Visual C++ .NET compiler. Students can use the source code provided with this text to experiment with and extend the chapter programs. The source code is also used in the end-of-section exercises.

SUPPLEMENTAL MATERIALS

The following supplemental materials are available when this book is used in a classroom setting.

Testing Center

The Testing Center. Available free with this book, Course Technology's Testing Center combines challenging assessment with helpful review material to provide students with a robust, Web-based learning tool. Utilizing the virtual compiler CodeSaw, students sharpen their programming skills through hands-on exercises, self-assessment, and interactive tutorials, all fully integrated with the text. The appendices for this book can be downloaded from the Testing Center. For instructors, the Testing Center provides a central location for review and detailed feedback on student performance. An access card with a password for the Testing Center is included in the front of this book. For more information, please visit *www.course.com/testingcenter*.

Electronic Instructor's Manual. The Instructor's Manual that accompanies this textbook includes:

- Additional instructional material to assist in class preparation, including suggestions for lecture topics.
- Solutions to all the end-of-chapter materials, including the Programming Exercises.

ExamView®. This textbook is accompanied by ExamView, a powerful testing software package that allows instructors to create and administer printed, computer (LAN-based), and Internet exams. ExamView includes hundreds of questions that correspond to the topics covered in this text, enabling students to generate detailed study guides that include page references for further review. These computer-based and Internet testing components allow students to take exams at their computers, and save the instructor time because each exam is graded automatically.

PowerPoint Presentations. This book comes with Microsoft PowerPoint slides for each chapter. These are included as a teaching aid for classroom presentations, either to make available to students on the network for chapter review, or to be printed for classroom distribution. Instructors can add their own slides for additional topics that they introduce to the class.

Distance Learning. Course Technology is proud to present online courses in WebCT and Blackboard to provide the most complete and dynamic learning experience possible. When you add online content to one of your courses, you're adding a lot: Topic Reviews, Practice Tests, Review Questions, Assignments, PowerPoint presentations, and, most of all, a gateway to the 21st century's most important information resource. For more information on how to bring distance learning to your course, contact your local Course Technology sales representative.

Source Code. The source code for this text is available at www.course.com and is also available on the Teaching Tools CD-ROM.

Solution Files. The solution files for all programming exercises are available at www.course.com, and are also available on the Teaching Tools CD-ROM.

Additional Tutorials. Step-by-step instructions on using Borland C++Builder 5.5, MetroWerks CodeWarrior 7.0, Microsoft Visual C++ 6.0, and Microsoft Visual C++ .NET are available at www.course.com.

ACKNOWLEDGMENTS

This book began as an idea. It became a reality only due to the encouragement, skills, and efforts supplied by many people. I would like to acknowledge their contribution.

First, I would like to thank my A team of editors: Alyssa, Amy, and Ann. This group of editors is one of the most superb teams that I have ever been privileged to work with. Specifically, the vision, continuous faith, encouragement, and ideas of Alyssa Pratt, Senior Product Manager at Course Technology, and Amy Yarnevich, Senior Acquisitions Editor, were instrumental in writing this text. Next, Ann Shaffer, the development editor, provided one of the most extensive and professional edits of the original manuscript that I have ever been fortunate enough to receive.

Additionally, I would like to express my gratitude to the following reviewers:

Drue Coles, Bloomsburg University

Ahmad Ghafarian, North Georgia College and State University

Kenneth Moore, Community College of Allegheny County

Ongard Sirisaengtaksin, University of Houston—Downtown

Each reviewer supplied detailed and constructive reviews of the text. Their suggestions, attention to detail, and comments were extraordinarily helpful to me as the manuscript evolved and matured throughout the editorial process.

Once the review process was completed, the task of turning the final manuscript into a textbook depended on many people. For this I especially want to thank Philippa Lehar, production editor; Gary Michael Spahl, copy editor; Wendy Benedetto, proofreader; Dan Seiter and Lisa Ruffolo, development editors who provided invaluable assistance with the page proofs; the amazing team of quality assurance testers, including Chris Scriver, Serge Palladino, Shawn Day, Burt LaFountain, and John Frietas; and once again, Ann Shaffer, the overall coordinator. Special thanks to Nicole Ashton, of Green Pen Quality Assurance for her work on the solutions. The dedication of this second team of people was incredible and very important to me. Almost from the moment the book moved to the production stage this team seemed to take personal ownership of the text and I am very grateful to them.

Special acknowledgement goes to two of my colleagues who provided material and motivation for this text. In addition to numerous contributions made by R. Kenneth Walter of Weber State University, I am especially grateful for his graciously providing the Bit of Background notes. Additionally, I want to thank one of my first mathematics instructors, Marie Bell. This exceptionally gifted individual not only taught me to enjoy mathematics, but also to understand that learning is a lifetime endeavor that must always be tinged with humour, grace, and the willingness to share what one has been given. As always, any errors in the text rest solely on my shoulders.

Finally, I gratefully acknowledge the direct encouragement and support of Fairleigh Dickinson University. Specifically, this includes the constant encouragement, support, and positive academic climate provided by Dr. Kenneth Greene, the provost; my Dean, Dr. David Steele; and my Chairperson, Dr. Paul Yoon. Without their support, this text could not have been written.

Finally, I deeply appreciate the patience, understanding, and love provided by my friend, wife, and partner, Rochelle.

Gary Bronson

Dedicated to

Rochelle,

David,

Matthew,

and

Jeremy

PART 1

CREATING AND USING C++ CLASSES

1

OBJECT-ORIENTED DESIGN AND DEVELOPMENT USING C++

This chapter provides an introduction to computer science and a brief background on programming languages. It explains the concepts of objects and classes and presents a specific structure that will be used throughout the text for constructing C++ classes and programs. Additionally, the chapter presents a specific C++ class for displaying output on a video screen. The methods of this class are used within the context of a complete program for displaying data on a video screen.

1.1 COMPUTER SCIENCE AND PROGRAMMING LANGUAGES

Our world is now almost totally dependent on and driven by the technology of gathering, processing, communicating, and using data. This technology has become a central element of our endeavors in art, science, literature, business, and engineering. It pervades our daily life, affecting transportation, medical care, grocery purchases, and almost every other aspect of our daily activities. In more formal terms, this technology both constitutes and defines what is now called the **Information Age**. The engines that drive this vast, technology-centered culture are computers. The study of these machines, including both their theoretical and practical development and applications, is referred to as **computer science**.

Because computer science is a scientific discipline, it has much in common with other areas of natural and physical science and can be approached at many different levels. The simplest level is **computer literacy**. People who are computer literate have some knowledge of computers, including their history and their possible applications (such as word processors, spreadsheet programs, the Internet, and email). Being computer literate, however, does not make you a computer scientist.

Rather than being merely a user of computer programs, a computer scientist is a problem solver who develops solutions to computer-related problems, both theoretical and practical, in the areas of:

- algorithm development
- class development and design
- programming languages
- data structures
- data collection, storage, and retrieval
- operating systems
- computer architecture
- computer applications
- social, ethical, and professional conduct and considerations

Computer scientists solve problems using the scientific method, which is common to all sciences. The **scientific method** is a research approach in which a problem is identified, relevant data are obtained, and a hypothesis is formulated from the data and then tested in a controlled and repeatable manner. Additionally, computer science requires a foundation in mathematics, model development, designing and developing theoretical and workable systems, and human communication. It also may require knowledge of other disciplines for which applications are to be developed. These additional disciplines include biology, medicine, physics, business, law, economics, geology, education, communications, psychology, robotics, image recognition, artificial intelligence, and all areas of engineering and scientific interest.

Although this all might sound daunting at first, every journey must start with the first step. It is the intention of this text to start you on your journey into computer science by focusing on fundamental concepts in the following five areas:

- Introduction to computer architecture

- The C++ programming language

- Class development and design

- Algorithm development

- Introduction to data structures

We begin this journey by considering the evolution of computers in this section, and programming languages and the development of C++ in Section 1.2.

A BRIEF HISTORY OF COMPUTERS

A BIT OF BACKGROUND

Binary ABC

In the 1930s, Dr. John V. Atanasoff struggled for several years over the design of a computing machine to help his Iowa State University graduate students solve complex equations. He considered building a machine based on binary numbers—the most natural system to use with electromechanical equipment that had one of two easily recognizable states, on and off—but feared people would not use a machine that was not based upon the familiar and comfortable decimal system. Finally, on a cold evening at a roadhouse in Illinois in 1937, he determined that it had to be done the simplest and least expensive way, with binary digits (bits). Over the next two years he and graduate student Clifford Berry built the first electronic digital computer, called the *ABC* (for Atanasoff-Berry Computer). Since that time the vast majority of computers have been binary machines.

The process of using a machine to add and subtract is almost as old as recorded history. The earliest such device was the abacus—a device as common in China today as hand held calculators are in the United States. Both of these machines, however, require direct human involvement as they are being used. To add two numbers with an abacus requires the movement of beads on the device, while adding two numbers with a calculator requires that the operator push both the number and the addition operator keys.

The first recorded attempt at creating a programmable computing machine was by Charles Babbage in England in 1822. Ada Byron, the daughter of the poet Lord Byron, developed the set of instructions that could, if the machine were ever built, be used to operate the machine. Although this mechanical machine, which Babbage called an analytical engine, was not successfully built in his lifetime, the concept of a programmable machine remained. It was partly realized in 1937 at Iowa State University by Dr. John V. Atanasoff and a graduate student named Clifford Berry, using electronic components (See Figure 1-1.). The machine was known as the ABC, which stood for Atanasoff-Berry Computer. This computer manipulated binary numbers, but required a human operator to manipulate external wiring in order to perform the desired operations. Thus, the goal of internally storing a set of instructions that could be changed had still not been achieved.

FIGURE 1-1
Charles Babbage's Analytical Engine

A BIT OF BACKGROUND

The "Turing Machine"

In the 1930s and 1940s, Alan Mathison Turing (1912–1954) and others developed a theory that described what a computing machine should be able to do. Turing's theoretical machine, known as the Turing Machine, contains the minimum set of operations for solving programming problems. Turing had hoped to prove that all problems could be solved by a set of instructions given to such a hypothetical computer. What he succeeded in proving was that some problems cannot be solved by *any* machine, just as some problems cannot be solved by any person.

Alan Turing's work formed the foundation of computer theory before the first electronic computer was built. His contributions to the team that developed the critical code-breaking computers during World War II led directly to the practical implementation of his theories.

The outbreak of World War II led to a more concentrated development of the computer, beginning in late 1939. One of the pioneers of this work was Dr. John W. Mauchly of the Moore School of Engineering at the University of Pennsylvania. Dr. Mauchly, who had visited Dr. Atanasoff and seen his ABC machine, began working with J. Presper Eckert in 1939 on a computer called ENIAC (for Electrical Numerical Integrator and Computer). Funding for this project was provided by the US government. One of the early functions performed by this machine was the calculation of trajectories for ammunition fired from large guns. When completed in 1946, ENIAC contained 18,000 vacuum tubes, weighed approximately 30 tons, and could perform 5000 additions or 360 multiplications in one second.

FIGURE 1-2
ENIAC (Courtesy IBM archives)

While work was progressing on ENIAC using vacuum tubes, work on a computer named the Mark I was being done at Harvard University using mechanical relay switches (see Figure 1-3). The Mark I was completed in 1944, but could only perform six multiplications in one second. However, both of these machines, like the Atanasoff-Berry Computer, required external wiring to perform the desired operations.

FIGURE 1-3
MARK I

The final goal of a stored program computer, where instructions as well as data are stored internally in the machine, was achieved at Cambridge University in England on May 6, 1949, with the successful operation of the EDSAC (Electronic Delayed Storage Automatic Computer) computer. In addition to performing calculations, the EDSAC could store both data and the instructions that directed the computer's operation. The EDSAC incorporated a form of memory, developed by John Von Neumann, that allowed it to retrieve an instruction and then retrieve the data needed to carry out the instruction. This same design and operating principal is still used by the majority of computers manufactured today. The only things that have significantly changed are the size and speeds of the components used to make a computer, and the type of programs that are stored in it. Collectively, the components used to make a computer are referred to as hardware, while the programs are known as software.

COMPUTER HARDWARE

Computers are constructed from physical components referred to as **hardware**. The purpose of this hardware is to facilitate the storage and processing of data under the direction of a stored program. If computer hardware could store data using the same symbols that humans do, the number 126, for example, would be stored using the symbols 1, 2, and 6. Similarly, the letter that we recognize as "A" would be stored using this same symbol. Unfortunately, a computer's internal components require a different number and letter representation. It is worthwhile to understand why computers cannot use our symbols and then see how numbers are represented within the machine. This will make it easier to understand the actual parts of a computer used to store and process this data.

Bits and Bytes

The smallest and most basic data item in a computer is a **bit**. Physically, a bit is really a switch that can be either open or closed. The convention we will follow is that the open position is represented by 0 and the closed position by 1.[1]

A single bit that can represent the values 0 and 1, by itself, has limited usefulness. All computers, therefore, group a set number of bits together both for storage and transmission. The grouping of eight bits to form a larger unit is an almost universal computer standard, and is referred to as a **byte**. A single byte, where each of the eight bits is either 0 or 1, can represent any one of 256 distinct patterns. These consist of the pattern 00000000 (all eight switches open) to the pattern 11111111 (all eight switches closed) and all possible combinations of 0s and 1s in between. Each of these patterns can be used to represent either a letter of the alphabet, other single characters (a dollar sign, comma, etc.), a single digit, or numbers containing more than one digit. The collection of patterns consisting of 0s and 1s used to represent letters, single digits, and other single characters are called **character codes** (two such codes, ASCII and Unicode, are presented in Section 2.1).

Character codes are extremely useful for such items as names and addresses, and any text that must be processed. It almost never is used, however, for arithmetic data. There are two reasons for this. First, converting a decimal number into a character code requires an individual code for each digit. For large numbers, this can waste a computer's memory space. The more basic reason, however, is that the decimal numbering system, which is based on the number 10, is inherently not supported by a computer's internal hardware. Recall that a bit, which is a computer's basic memory component, can take on only one of two possible states, open and closed, which is represented as a 0 and a 1. This would indicate that a numbering system based on these two states makes more sense, and in fact, this is the case. Section 1.6 presents the most commonly used base two numbering system.

The idea of a computer's internal numbering system differing from our decimal system should not come as a surprise. For example, you are probably already familiar with two other numbering systems, and can easily recognize the following:

Roman Numeral: XIV

Hash Mark System: ‖‖ ‖‖ ‖‖

---

[1]This convention, unfortunately, is rather arbitrary, and you will frequently encounter the reverse correspondence where the open and closed positions are represented as 1 and 0, respectively.

Components

All computers, from large super computers costing millions of dollars to smaller desk top personal computers costing hundreds of dollars, must perform a minimum set of tasks and provide the capability to:

1. Accept input, both data and instructions

2. Display output, both textural and numerical

3. Store data and instructions

4. Perform arithmetic and logic operations on either the input or stored data

5. Monitor, control, and direct the overall operation and sequencing of the system.

Figure 1-4 illustrates the computer components that support these capabilities and collectively form a computer's hardware.

FIGURE 1-4
Basic Hardware Units of a Computer

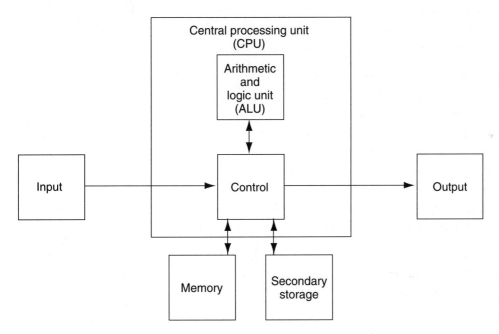

Main Memory Unit: This unit stores both data and instructions as a sequence of bytes. A program must reside in main memory if it is to operate the computer. Main memories combine one or more bytes into a single unit, referred to as a **word.** Although larger word sizes facilitate an increase in overall speed and capacity, this increase is achieved by an increase in the computer's complexity.

Early personal computers, such as the Apple IIe and Commodore machines, internally stored and transmitted words consisting of single bytes. The first IBM PCs used word sizes consisting of two bytes, while more current Pentium-based PCs store and process words consisting of four bytes each.

The arrangement of words in a computer's memory can be compared to the arrangement of suites in a large hotel, where each suite is made up of rooms of the same size. Just as each suite has a unique room number that allow patrons to locate and identify it, each word in a computer's memory has a unique numerical address. Like room numbers, word addresses are always positive unsigned whole numbers that are used for location and identification purposes. Also, like hotel rooms with connecting doors for forming larger suites, words can be combined to form larger units to accommodate different-size data types.

As a physical device, main memories are constructed as **RAM**, which is an acronym for "Random Access Memory." This means that every section of memory can be accessed randomly as quickly as any other section. Main memory is also **volatile**, which means that whatever is stored in it is lost when the computer's power is turned off. Your programs and data are always stored in RAM when your program is being executed. The size of the computer's RAM is usually specified in terms of how many bytes of RAM are available to the user. Personal Computer (PC) memories currently start at 512 million bytes (denoted as Megabytes or MB).

A second type of memory is **ROM**, which is an acronym for "Read Only Memory." ROM is **nonvolatile**; its contents are not lost when the power goes off. As such, ROM always contains fundamental instructions that cannot be lost or changed by the casual computer user. These instructions include those necessary for starting the computer's operation when the power is first turned on, and for holding any other instructions the manufacturer requires to be permanently accessible when the computer is operating.

Central Processing Unit (CPU): This unit consists of two essential sub-units, the control unit and the Arithmetic and Logic Unit (ALU). The control unit directs and monitors the overall operation of the computer. It keeps track of where in memory the next instruction resides, issues the signals needed to both read data from and write data to other units in the system, and executes all instructions. The ALU performs all of the computations, such as addition, subtraction, comparisons, and so on, that a computer provides.

The CPU is the central element of a computer and its most expensive part. Currently CPUs are constructed as a single microchip, which is referred to as a **microprocessor**. Figure 1-5 illustrates the size and internal structure of a state-of-the-art microprocessor chip used in current notebook computers. Also shown are the pins on the outside of the package that is used to house the chip.

FIGURE 1-5
A Pentium Microprocessor Chip

Input/Output (I/O) Unit: This unit provides access to the computer, allowing it to input and output data. It is the interface to which peripheral devices such as keyboards, console screens, and printers are attached.

Secondary Storage: Because main RAM memory in large quantities is still relatively expensive and volatile, it is not practical as a permanent storage area for programs and data. Secondary or auxiliary storage devices are used for this purpose. Although data have been stored on punched cards, paper tape, and other media in the past, virtually all secondary storage is now done on magnetic tape, magnetic disks, and CD-ROMS.

The surfaces of magnetic tapes and disks are coated with a material that can be magnetized to store data. Current tapes are capable of storing thousands of characters per inch of tape, and a single tape may store up to hundreds of megabytes. Tapes, by nature, are a sequential storage media, which means that they allow data to be written or read in one sequential stream from beginning to end. Should you want to access a block of data in the middle of the tape, all preceding data on the tape must be scanned to find the block. Because of this, tapes are primarily used for mass backup of historical data.

A more convenient method of rapidly accessing stored data is provided by a **direct access storage device (DASD),** which allows a computer to read or write any one file or program independent of its position on the storage medium. Until the recent advent of the CD, the most popular DASD has been the magnetic disk. A **magnetic hard disk** consists of either a single rigid platter or several platters that spin together on a common spindle. A movable access arm positions the read and write mechanisms over, but not quite touching, the recordable surfaces. Such a configuration is shown in Figure 1-6.

FIGURE 1-6
Internal Structure of a Hard Disk Drive

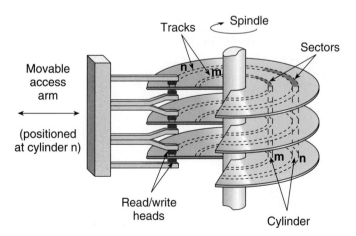

Initially, the most common magnetic disk storage device was the removable **floppy disk**. The most popular size for these is 3-1/2 inches in diameter, with a capacity of 1.44 megabytes. More recent removable disks, known as Zip disks, have capacities of 250 megabytes, with gigabyte compact disks (CDs) currently being the auxiliary storage devices of choice (one gigabyte equals 1000 megabytes).

Concurrent with the vast increase in storage capacity has been an equally significant increase in processing speed and dramatic decrease in computer size and cost. Computer hardware capabilities that cost over a million dollars in 1950 can now be purchased for less than five hundred dollars. If the same reductions occurred in the automobile industry, for example, a Rolls-Royce could now be purchased for ten dollars! The processing speeds of current computers have also increased by a factor of thousands over their 1950s predecessors, with the computational speeds of current computers being measured in both millions of instructions per second (MIPS) and billions of instructions per second (BIPS). For comparison, Figure 1-7 shows an early desktop IBM PC of the 1980s, while Figure 1-8 illustrates a current IBM notebook computer.

FIGURE 1-7
An Original (1980s) IBM Personal Computer

FIGURE 1-8
A Current IBM Notebook Computer

Exercises 1.1

1.   Define the term bit. What values can a bit assume?

2.   Define the term byte. How many distinct bit patterns can a byte assume?

3.   How is a byte used to represent characters in a computer?

4.   Define the term word. Give the word sizes for some common computers.

5.   What are the two principal parts of the CPU? What is the function of each part?

6.   a. What is the difference between RAM and ROM? What do they have in common?
     b. Why is a ROM a random access device?

7.   a. What is the input/output unit?
     b. Name three devices that would be connected to the input/output unit.

8.   Define secondary storage. Give three examples of secondary storage.

9.   What is the difference between sequential storage and direct access storage? What is the advantage of direct access storage?

10. Define a microprocessor. Name three ways microprocessors are used in everyday life.

1.2 PROGRAMMING LANGUAGES

A computer is the same as any other machine constructed of physical components, such as an airplane, automobile, or lawn mower. Like these other machines, a computer must be turned on and then piloted, driven, or controlled to perform its intended task. How this gets done is what distinguishes a computer from other types of machinery.

In an automobile, for example, control is provided by the driver, who sits inside and directs the car. In a computer, the controller is a set of instructions, called a program. Formally, a **computer program** is a self-contained set of instructions and data used to operate a computer to produce a specific result. Another term for a program or set of programs is **software**, and we will use both terms interchangeably throughout the text.

The process of developing and writing a program, or software, is called **programming**, and the set of instructions that can be used to construct a program is called a **programming language**. Available programming languages come in a variety of forms and types. Each of these different forms and types was designed to make the programming process easier, to capitalize on a special feature of the hardware, or to meet a special requirement of an application. At a fundamental level, however, all programs must ultimately be converted into a machine language program, which is the only type of program that can actually operate a computer.

MACHINE LANGUAGE

An **executable program** is a program that can operate a computer. Such programs are always written as a sequence of binary numbers, which is a computer's internal language, and are also referred to as **machine language programs**. An example of a simple machine language program containing two instructions is:

```
11000000000000000001000000000010
11110000000000000010000000000011
```

A BIT OF BACKGROUND

Ada Augusta Byron, Countess of Lovelace

Ada Byron, the daughter of the Romantic poet Lord Byron, was a colleague of Charles Babbage, who during the mid-1800s attempted to build a computing machine that he called an analytical engine. It was Ada's task to develop the algorithms—solutions to problems in the form of step-by-step instructions—that would allow the engine to compute the values of mathematical functions. Babbage's machine was not built successfully in his lifetime, primarily because the technology of the time did not allow mechanical parts to be constructed with necessary tolerances. Nonetheless, Ada is recognized as the first computer programmer. She published a collection of notes that established the basis for computer programming; the Ada programming language is named in her honor.

Each sequence of binary numbers that constitutes a machine language instruction consists of, at a minimum, two parts: an instruction part and a data part. The instruction part, which is referred to as the **opcode** (short for operation code) is usually at the beginning of each binary number and tells the computer the operation to be performed, such as add, subtract, multiply, and so on. The remaining part of the number provides information about the data.

ASSEMBLY LANGUAGE

Because each class of computer, such as IBM PCs, Apple Macintoshes, and Hewlett-Packard computers, has its own particular machine language, it is very tedious and time consuming to write machine language programs. One of the first advances in programming was the substitution of word-like symbols, such as ADD, SUB, MUL, for the binary opcodes, and both decimal numbers and labels for memory addresses. For example, in the following set of instructions, word-like symbols are used to add two numbers (referred to as `first` and `second`), multiply the result by a third number known as `factor`, and store the result as `answer`:

```
LOAD    first
ADD     second
MUL     factor
STORE   answer
```

Programming languages that use this type of symbolic notation are referred to as **assembly languages**. Since computers can only execute machine language programs, this set of assembly language instructions has to be translated into a machine language program before it can be executed by a computer. (See Figure 1-9.) Programs that convert, or translate, assembly language programs into machine language are known as **assemblers**.

FIGURE 1-9
Assembly Programs Must Be Translated

LOW- AND HIGH-LEVEL LANGUAGES

Both machine-level and assembly languages are classified as **low-level languages**. This is because both of these language types use instructions that are directly tied to one type of computer. As such, an assembly language program is limited in that it can only be used with the specific computer type for which the program is written. Such programs do, however, permit using special features of a particular computer type and generally execute at the fastest speed possible.

In contrast to low-level languages, a **high-level language** uses instructions that resemble human languages such as English, and can be run on a variety of computer types such as an IBM, Apple, and Hewlett-Packard computer. Pascal, Visual Basic, C, C++, and Java are all high-level languages. Using C++, the assembly language instructions used in the preceding section to add two numbers and multiply by a third number can be written as:

```
answer = (first + second) * factor;
```

Programs written in a computer language (high or low level) are referred to interchangeably as both **source programs** and **source code**. Once a program is written in a high-level language, it must also, like a low-level assembly program, be translated into the machine language of the computer on which it will be run. This translation can be accomplished in two ways.

When each statement in a high-level source program is translated individually and executed immediately upon translation, the programming language is called an **interpreted language**, and the program doing the translation is called an **interpreter**.

When all of the statements in a high level source program are translated as a complete unit before any individual statement is executed, the programming language is called a **compiled language**. In this case, the program doing the translation is called a **compiler**. Both compiled and interpreted versions of a single language can exist, although typically one predominates. For example, although interpreted versions of C++ exist, C++ is predominantly a compiled language.

Figure 1-10 illustrates the relationship between a C++ source code program and its compilation into a machine language executable program. As shown, the source program is entered using an editor program. This is really a word processing program that is part of the development environment supplied by the compiler. It should be understood, however, that entering the code is only begun after an application has been thoroughly analyzed, understood, and the design of the program has been carefully planned. How this is accomplished is explained in the next section.

Translation of the C++ source program into a machine language program begins with the compiler. The output produced by the compiler is called an **object** program, which is a machine language version of the source code. Almost always, your source code will make use of existing preprogrammed code, either code you have written previously or code provided by the compiler. This could include mathematical code for finding a square root, for example, or code that is being reused from another application. Additionally, a large C++ program may be stored in two or more separate program files. In all of these cases, this additional code must be combined with the object program before the program can be executed. It is the task of the **linker** to accomplish this step. The result of the linking process is a completed machine language program, containing all of the code required by your program, which is now ready for execution. The last step in the process is to load this machine language program into the computer's main memory for actual execution.

1

FIGURE 1-10
Creating an Executable C++ Program

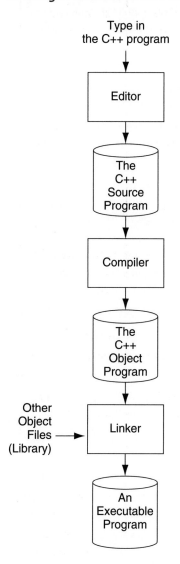

PROCEDURAL AND OBJECT ORIENTATIONS

High level languages are further classified as either procedural or object-oriented. In a **procedural language**, the available instructions are only used to create self-contained units referred to as **procedures**. The purpose of a procedure is to accept data as input and transform the data in some manner to produce a specific result as an output. Each computer language tends to refer to its procedures by a different name. For example, in Fortran, the term subprogram is used to denote a procedure; in C, a procedure is referred to as a function, in Java, a procedure is referred to as a method, while in C++, the terms method and function are both used. Until the mid-1990s, the majority of high-level languages were procedural.

Currently, a second approach, object orientation, has taken center stage. One of the motivations for **object-oriented languages** was the development of graphical screens and support for graphical user interfaces (GUIs) capable of displaying multiple windows containing both graphical shapes and text. In such an environment, each window on the screen can conveniently be considered an object with associated characteristics, such as color, position, and size. Using an object-oriented approach, a program must first define the objects it will be manipulating, which includes describing both the general characteristics of the objects themselves and specific units to manipulate them, such as changing size and position and transferring data between objects. Equally important is the fact that object-oriented languages tend to more easily support reusing existing code, which removes the necessity for revalidating and retesting new or modified code. C++, which is classified as an object-oriented language, contains features found in both procedural and object-oriented languages. In this text we will primarily design, develop, and present object-oriented code, which is how the majority of current C++ programs are written. Because object-oriented C++ code always contains some procedural code, and many extremely simple C++ programs are written entirely using only procedural code, this type of code is also extensively presented.

APPLICATION AND SYSTEM SOFTWARE

Two logical categories of computer programs are application software and system software. **Application software** consists of programs written to perform particular tasks required by the users. All of the examples in this book are of this type.

System software is the collection of programs that must be readily available to any computer system to enable the computer to operate. In the early computer environments of the 1950s and 1960s, a user had to initially load the system software by hand to prepare the computer to do anything. This was done with rows of switches on a front panel. Those initial hand-entered commands were said to **boot** the computer, a term derived from the expression "pulling oneself up by the bootstraps." Today, the so-called **bootstrap loader** is internally contained in read-only memory (ROM) and is a permanent, automatically executed component of the computer's system software.

Collectively, the set of system programs used to operate and control a computer are called the **operating system**. Tasks handled by modern operating systems include memory management; allocation of CPU time; control of input and output units such as the keyboard, screen, and printers; and the management of all secondary storage devices. Many operating systems handle very large programs, as well as multiple users concurrently, by dividing programs into segments that are moved between the disk and memory as needed. Such operating systems permit more than one user to run a program on the computer, which gives each user the impression that the computer and peripherals are his or hers alone. This is referred to as a **multi-user** system. Additionally, many operating systems, including most windowed environments, permit each user to run multiple programs. Such operating systems are referred to as both **multiprogrammed** and **multitasking** systems.

THE DEVELOPMENT OF C++

At a very basic level, the purpose of almost all application programs is to process data to produce one or more specific results. In a procedural language, a program is constructed from sets of instructions, with each set referred to as a procedure, as noted previously. Effectively, each procedure moves the data one step closer to the final desired output along the path shown in Figure 1-11.

FIGURE 1-11
Basic Procedural Operations

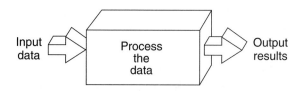

A BIT OF BACKGROUND

Niklaus Wirth

Niklaus Wirth received an M.S. degree from the University of Quebec in 1962 and a Ph.D. from the University of California at Berkeley in 1963. He then returned to his undergraduate alma mater, the Swiss Federal Institute of Technology, to teach. While serving there in 1971, he announced that he had designed a new language named *Pascal*. Pascal became very popular in the 1970s and early 1980s because of its emphasis on procedures that had to conform to specific structural requirements. This initiated a concept known as structured programming. Because all procedural code should be written in a structured form, the terms "procedural programming" and "structured programming" are frequently used as synonyms.

It is interesting to note that the programming process illustrated in Figure 1-11 directly mirrors the input, processing, and output hardware units that are used to construct a computer (see previous section). This was not accidental, because early programming languages were specifically designed to match and, as optimally as possible, directly control corresponding hardware units.

The first procedural language, named Fortran, whose name is derived from *Formula trans*lation, was introduced in 1957, and remained popular throughout the 1960s and early 1970s. (Another high-level programming language that was developed almost concurrently with Fortran, but that never achieved Fortran's overwhelming acceptance, was named Algol.) Fortran has algebra-like instructions that concentrate on the processing phase shown in Figure 1-11, and was developed for scientific and engineering applications that required high-precision numerical outputs, accurate to many decimal places. For example, calculating a rocket's trajectory or the bacterial concentration level in a polluted pond, as illustrated in Figure 1-12, requires evaluating a mathematical equation to a high degree of numerical accuracy, and is typical of Fortran-based applications.

FIGURE 1-12
Fortran Was Developed for Scientific and Engineering Applications

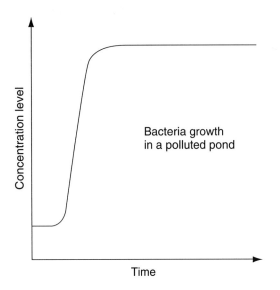

The next significant high-level application language was COBOL, which was introduced in the 1960s and remained a major procedural language through the 1980s. COBOL is an acronym for COmmon Business-Oriented Language. This language had features geared toward business applications that required simpler mathematical calculations than those needed for scientific applications. One of COBOL's main benefits is that it provided extensive output formats that made it easy to create reports (such as the one shown in Figure 1-13) containing extensive columns of neatly formatted dollar and cents numbers and totals. It also forced programmers to carefully construct well-defined, structured procedures that followed a more consistent pattern than was required in Fortran.

FIGURE 1-13
COBOL Was Developed for Business Applications

```
               INVENTORY REPORT

    Item                         In    On    Unit
    No.      Description      Stock  Order   Cost

    10365  #4  Nails, Common    20      0    1.09
    10382  #6  Nails, Common    10     50    1.14
    10420  #8  Nails, Common     2     60    1.19
    10436  #10 Nails, Common     6
    10449  #12 Nails, Common
    10486  #16 Nails, Common
```

Another language, BASIC (or Beginners All-purpose Symbolic Instruction Code), was developed at Dartmouth College about the same time as COBOL. BASIC was essentially a slightly scaled down version of Fortran that was intended as an introductory language for college students. It was a relatively straightforward, easy-to-understand language that did not require detailed knowledge of a specific application. Its main drawback was that it neither required nor enforced a consistent or structured approach to creating programs. Frequently, even a programmer could not easily figure out what her or his BASIC program did after a short lapse of time.

To remedy this and put programming on a more scientific and rational basis that made understanding and reusing code easier, the Pascal language was developed. (Pascal is not an acronym, but is named after the 17th century mathematician Blaise Pascal.) Introduced in 1971, it provided students with a firmer foundation in structured programming design than that provided by early versions of BASIC.

Structured programs are created using a set of well-defined structures that are organized into individual programming sections, each of which performs a specific task that can be tested and modified without disturbing other sections of the program. The Pascal language was so rigidly structured, however, that there were no escapes from the structured sections when such escapes would be useful. This was unacceptable for many real-world projects and is one of the reasons why Pascal did not become widely accepted in the scientific, engineering, and business fields. Instead, the structured procedural language of C, developed in the 1970s at AT&T Bell Laboratories by Ken Thompson, Dennis Ritchie, and Brian Kernighan, became the dominant applications language of the 1980s. This language has an extensive set of capabilities that permits it to be written as a high-level language, while retaining the ability to directly access the machine-level features of a computer.

C++ was developed in the early 1980s, when Bjarne Stroustrup (also at AT&T) used his simulation language background to create an object-oriented programming language. A central feature of simulation languages is that they model real-life situations as objects. This object orientation, which was ideal for graphical screen objects such as rectangles and circles, was combined with existing C features to form the C++ language. Thus, C++ retained the extensive set of structured procedural capabilities provided by C, but added its own object-orientation to become a true general-purpose programming language. As such, it can be used for everything from simple, interactive programs to highly sophisticated and complex engineering and scientific programs, within the context of a truly object-oriented structure.

Exercises 1.2

1. Define the following terms:

    a. computer program
    b. programming
    c. programming language
    d. high-level language
    e. low-level language
    f. machine language
    g. assembly language
    h. procedure-oriented language
    i. object-oriented language
    j. source program
    k. compiler
    l. assembler

2. a. Describe the difference between high and low-level languages.

    b. Describe the difference between procedure and object-oriented languages.

3. Describe the difference between assemblers, interpreters, and compilers.

4. a. Assuming the following operation codes:

    11000000   means add the 1st operand to the 2nd operand

    10100000   means subtract the 1st operand from the 2nd operand

    11110000   means multiply the 2nd operand by the 1st operand

    11010000   means divide the 2nd operation by the 1st operand

    translate the following instructions into English:

opcode	address of 1st operand	address of 2nd operand
11000000	000000000001	0000000000010
11110000	000000000010	0000000000011
10100000	000000000100	0000000000011
11010000	000000000101	0000000000011

    b. Assuming the following locations contain the following data, determine the result produced by the instructions listed in Exercise 4a.

address	initial value (in decimal) stored at this address
00000000001	5
00000000010	3
00000000011	6
00000000100	14
00000000101	4

5. Rewrite the machine level instructions listed in Exercise 4a. using assembly language notation. Use the symbolic names ADD, SUB, MUL, and DIV for addition, subtraction, multiplication, and division operations, respectively. In writing the instructions, use decimal values for the addresses.

6. Assuming that A = 10, B = 20, and C = .6, determine the numerical result of the following set of assembly language-type statements. For this exercise, assume that the LOAD instruction is equivalent to entering a value into the display of a calculator, and that ADD means add and MUL means multiply by.

    LOAD A

    ADD   B

    MUL   C

1.3 OBJECTS AND CLASSES

We live in a world full of objects—planes, trains, cars, cell phones, books, computers, and so on. It should not seem surprising then that programming languages themselves would be based on objects. The basic objects used in C++ programming are data objects. A **data object** is a set of one or more values that are packaged together as a single unit; as such it can be considered as a packet of data values. For example, a student's name and grade point average can be considered as a data object; in this case the object consists of two pieces of data. Similarly, a name, street address, city, state, and zip code can also be packaged as an object, one that would be useful for a program that must print address labels. Lastly, a multiplication table, such as the tens table, can be considered a data object, in this case a specific instance of one table out of a set of multiplication tables.

A central concept in all object-oriented programming languages is the difference between a particular object and the larger set of which it is a member. To make this clearer, consider any automobile. From an object viewpoint, a specific car is simply a particular instance, or object, of a more general class of car. Thus, a particular Ford Taurus with its own specific attributes of color, engine size, body type, and so on, can be considered as one object, in this case a car object, from the broader class of all possible Ford Tauruses that could have been built. Similarly, a BMW 525 can be considered as one object from the broader class of all possible BMW 525s that could have been built. The plan for building a particular car is held by the respective manufacturers. Only when such a plan is put into action and a car is actually built, does a specific object come into existence. The concept of creating a particular object from a larger defining set, or class, of object types is fundamental to all object-oriented programming languages, such as C++. It is from the object type, or more accurately speaking, from a class, that any one specific object is created.

In this text we will present two aspects of the C++ language: how to adapt and modify the provided object types, such as lists and tables, to create specific lists and tables and how to construct our own data object types. We will do this in reverse order, however. First, we will present the structure on which all data objects used in a C++ program are constructed, and then we will show how to use and customize C++'s pre-existing object types. As you might expect, these pre-existing types are themselves built using the same structure; thus, once we have constructed our own data objects we will have a much better grasp of how to actually use many of the supplied object types.

A CLASS IS A PLAN

When writing an object-oriented program in C++, you must create the structure, or plan, for a class of objects. In the same vein, before having a house built, you would have a detailed set of plans drawn up. Similarly, before attempting to assemble a bicycle or a backyard basketball hoop, you would want to know that a set of assembly instructions was available. In preparing a dinner, you might consult a recipe that provides a list of food ingredients and explains how they are to be assembled. Although a formal set of instructions might not exist as a written document in every situation, it has to, at least, exist in the mind of the builder, the chef, or whomever is in charge of the project. At some level, such a plan forms the basis for the construction of any object, be it a bicycle, staircase, computer, or dinner.

The same planning is required when constructing an object-oriented C++ program. The plan, which is formally called a class, must include a list of parts, as well as assembly instructions. Once the list of parts and assembly instructions that define a class are completed, specific objects can be created by a program according to the assembly instructions contained in the class. For example, we may first design a class for calculating the floor space of a room and then use the class in a program to calculate the total floor space of a house.

From a programming perspective then, a **class** is a plan with a complete set of parts and instructions needed to create objects that will be used in a program. For example, a program for simulating a card game might include an object such as a deck of cards that can be shuffled, a means of dealing individual cards from the deck, a means of displaying individual card values on a screen that can be moved under mouse control, and so forth.

To get a better understanding of the nature of a C++ class, it's useful to relate a class to a food recipe, with only one significant modification; a C++ class is a plan for assembling data objects rather than food items. Other than that, the relationship between a C++ class and a food recipe is almost one to one and extremely informative.

Consider the recipe shown in Figure 1-14. It will come as no surprise that all food recipes contain similar types of components. More surprising, however, is the fact that almost exactly the same elements are required in constructing a C++ class. Let's see what these elements are.

FIGURE 1-14
Recipe for Gary's Sardine Spread

Recipe Name: Gary's Sardine Spread
Ingredients:

Measure	*Contents*
1 can	Boneless and skinless sardines
2 stalks	Celery
1/4 medium	Red onion
1 tablespoon	Mayonnaise
1/4 cup	Parsley
dash	Olive oil
splash	Red wine vinegar
dash	Salt
dash	Pepper

Method of Preparation:
Finely shred the sardines using two forks
Finely dice the celery and onion and mix well with sardines
Add olive oil and mix well
Add mayonnaise and mix well
Add red wine vinegar and mix well
Finely dice the parsley and mix well
Salt and pepper to taste

First, notice that the recipe itself, which is listed in Figure 1-14, is not the spread; it merely provides a plan for creating the spread. The recipe can be used many times, and each time it is used a particular batch of sardine spread is produced.

Now examine the actual structure of the recipe and notice that it consists of two main sections; the top section provides a list of ingredients, while the bottom section provides a method for using these ingredients. The list of ingredients itself consists of two parts. The left side provides the type of measure, such as can, tablespoon, cup (including less precise measures, such as stalk, dash, and splash), while the right side lists the actual ingredient, such as sardines, celery, oil, vinegar, onion, and so on. This same division will hold true, with some modification, for C++ classes. For example, instead of using measures such as a teaspoon or cup, we will be dealing with measures for holding data values, such as numbers, text, and other suitable programming types.

Now we can make one addition to the top section of the recipe in Figure 1-14 by giving each ingredient and its measure a specific name, so that the ingredient section appears as in Figure 1-15. We have placed the name between the *Measure* and *Contents* columns because this is where the name is placed when constructing a C++ class. The new ingredient section appears as shown in Figure 1-15. When using our modified recipe, you could refer to each ingredient using its name. Thus, you might read the first row of the ingredient section as "sardineIngredient consists of 1 can of boneless and skinless sardines." The names used in Figure 1-15, such as `sardineIngredient`, and the fact that we have only capitalized the first letter of the word `Ingredient`, with no spaces contained within the name is, at this stage, purely a matter of choice. As we will see in the next section, this format is the convention used in naming C++ programming ingredients. Also, once we have provided each ingredient with a name, the method section can also be rewritten to make use of these names, as is illustrated in the new Method section provided in Figure 1-15.

FIGURE 1-15
Using Named Ingredients for Gary's Sardine Spread

Ingredients:

Measure	Name	Contents
1 can	sardineIngredient	Boneless and skinless sardines
2 stalks	celeryIngredient	Celery
1/4 medium	onionIngredient	Red onion
1 tablespoon	mayo	Mayonnaise
1/4 cup	parsley	Parsley
dash	dashOil	Olive oil
splash	splashVinegar	Red wine vinegar
dash	dashSalt	Salt
dash	dashPepper	Pepper

Method of Preparation:
Finely shred the sardineIngredient using two forks
Finely dice the celeryIngredient and onionIngredient, and mix well with sardineIngredient
Add dashOil and mix well
Add mayo and mix well
Add splashVinegar and mix well
Finely dice the parsley and mix well
Add dashSalt and dashPepper to taste

FROM RECIPE TO CLASS

Let us now make the almost direct connection from the recipe illustrated in Figure 1-15 to a C++ class. As we have stated before, a class can be considered the plan or recipe from which individual programming objects can be created. Like its food recipe counterpart, a class will typically contain an ingredients and method section.

Within the ingredients section, instead of measures such as a teaspoon or cup, C++ deals with measures for holding integer numbers (that is, whole numbers), real numbers (numbers that contain fractional parts), strings (text, as a sequence of characters), and other types of suitable "ingredients." These ingredients, in programming terminology are referred to as **data**. Thus, each piece of data used in C++ has a measure, such as *integer*; a specific value, such as *5*, and a name, such as `firstInteger-Number`. The description of the data used in a C++ class is, like the list of ingredients in a recipe, contained in a specific section. The description of data used in a C++ class is referred to as the **data declarations section**. At a minimum, the data declarations section should list the type of data needed and specify a name for each data item. Specific values for the data are typically assigned later. Following the data declarations section is one or more methods sections. In its simplest form, a single methods section will contain both the names and types of methods and the actual instructions for each method. More typically, however, the method sections consist of two parts: a **methods declaration section** that lists the names and types of methods, and a separate **methods implementation section**, which contains the actual code for each method declared in the methods declaration section.

As a specific example, suppose you are creating a C++ program to calculate the average of two numbers. The data elements and methods for doing this are shown in Figure 1-16.

FIGURE 1-16
A Programming Plan for Determining an Average

```
Class Name: AverageOfTwoNumbers

    data declarations section (the parts list)
        A list of the data we will use
            Type            Name
            real number     firstNumber
            real number     secondNumber
    methods section
            method 1: assign values to firstNumber and
              secondNumber
            method 2: calculate and display the average of
              firstNumber and secondNumber
```

Notice that Figure 1-16 contains the same basic two sections as those in Figure 1-15, which consist of a list of ingredients (that is, a parts sections) and an assembly section, which contains the actual instructions for using data ingredients listed in the first section. There are, however, two important modifications. The first is that the column labeled *Measure* in Figure 1-15 is relabeled as *Type* in Figure 1-16. The second modification is that the third column, labeled *Contents* in Figure 1-15, is missing in Figure 1-16. In Figure 1-16 the actual values, or contents, of the data are assigned in the methods section. Although values can be assigned in the data section, it is more typically the case that values are assigned using a method. This provides the user with the opportunity to assign values interactively while a program is being executed.

Suppose we need to create a C++ class that can be used to display a message on the screen. For this application, we can construct the preliminary class structure shown in Figure 1-17.

FIGURE 1-17
A Programming Plan for Displaying a Message

```
Class Name: DisplayMessage

   data declarations section (the parts list)
      A list of the data we will use
            Type                        Name
            string of characters        message
   methods section
            method 1: assign text to the message
            method 2: display message on the screen
```

All of the C++ classes that we design will have the same basic structure illustrated in Figures 1-16 and 1-17. This general format is summarized in Figure 1-18.

FIGURE 1-18
Basic C++ Class Syntax

Class Name
   data declarations section
      A list of the types of data to be used with a name provided for each individual data item

   methods section
      The methods that will be applied to the data

Using this basic structure, you're ready to learn how to develop a working C++ class for displaying a single line of text on a computer screen.

A C++ CLASS STRUCTURE

Understanding that a C++ class is a formal programming plan, we now present a simplified C++ class that can be used for displaying a message consisting of a single line of text on your computer's screen. Although it is necessary to know how to structure and create your own classes, part of the appeal of C++ is the very rich set of classes and functions that are provided as part of the language. This means that many programs and classes that you will write can be constructed using existing classes and functions.

Formally, a class consists of a class header line and a body. The basic class header line that we will almost exclusively use, and which is always the first line of a class, contains two words:

1. The word class

2. The name of the class

The body of a class, which always follows the header line, is enclosed within a set of braces, { and } and terminated with a semicolon. This set of braces determines the beginning and end of the class' declaration and contains the data declarations section and methods section that make up the class. Figure 1-19 illustrates the basic structure of a class that we have named ShowFirstMessage.

FIGURE 1-19
The Structure of a C++ Class Named ShowFirstMessage

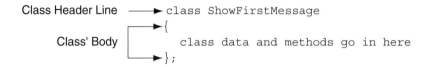

Within the class' declaration (that is, between the opening and closing braces of the class), there are typically two sections of code. The first is the data declarations section that declares the types of data that will be used, and the second is the methods section that declares and provides the procedures that will be used on the data. This is in keeping with our concept that a class can be thought of as a plan, or recipe, consisting of a list of ingredients and the methods for combining them.

Now consider the C++ class shown in Figure 1-20, which can be used to display the text Welcome to the world of C++ on your computer's screen. Although it is likely too early for you to understand this code, important basic elements can be easily identified. First, because every C++ class must contain a class header line and a body, the three initial items to notice in the figure are:

• The class header line

• The start of the class' body, which is designated by a left-facing brace, {

• The end of a class' body, which is designated by a right-facing brace, } and is terminated by a semi-colon

Be aware that braces are used elsewhere in the code, so in addition to always defining the beginning and ending of a C++ class, braces do have other uses.

Internal to the class declaration in Figure 1-20, notice that a data declarations section and a methods section are provided. Every C++ class will include either one or both of these sections. Although the methods section shown in Figure 1-20 provides the actual code for the class' methods, in many cases the actual code is provided in a separate implementations section. For the code in Figure 1-20, the data section declares a single piece of data, which can be used to hold text and is referred to as string data. The methods section provides two methods. When the first method is executed, it places the text Welcome to the world of C++ in the string named message. The second method, when executed, displays this text on the screen. The terms private and public listed in Figure 1-20 are explained more fully in the next chapter. Briefly, the private designation restricts access to the declared data so that they can only be used by the class' methods; the public designation permits, among other things, that the methods can be used by other classes.

Table 1-1 helps make the link between the class provided in Figure 1-20 and our concept of a class as a programming recipe. It summarizes the basic components of our example C++ class and the correspondence between these components and those found in the more familiar elements of a food recipe.

FIGURE 1-20
A Sample C++ Class

```
Class header line ──────────►  class ShowFirstMessage
Start of Class' body ─────────►  {
                                   // data declaration section
                                   private:
                                     string message;

                                   // methods section
                                   public:
                                    ShowFirstMessage()
                                    {
                                        message = "Welcome to the world of C++";
                                    }

                                    void displayMessage()
                                    {
                                        cout << message;
                                    }
End of Class' body ───────────►  };
```

TABLE 1-1
C++ Class Components

class component	corresponds to:
class name, such as `ShowFirstMessage`	recipe name, such as Gary's Sardine Spread
data declaration section	ingredients section
data type, such as a string	measure, such as a cup
data name, such as message	ingredient name, such as sardineIngredient
text, such as "Welcome to the world of C++"	contents, such as, 1 can of skinless and boneless sardines
methods section	procedures for combining ingredients

One additional point needs to be made here; the code shown in Figure 1-20 is not an executable C++ program. An executable C++ program must contain a special method having the name `main`. Typically, a C++ program will make use of other C++ classes, each of which has the basic structure illustrated in Figure 1-19.

Exercises 1.3

1. **a.** What are the two main sections of a C++ class?
    b. Within the first section of a C++ class, what information must be provided?
    c. What is the information provided by the second section in a C++ class?

2. Figure 1-21 presents a simplified diagram for assembling a bird house. Referring to this diagram, create a parts list and a set of instructions for constructing the bird house.

FIGURE 1-21
Building a Bird House

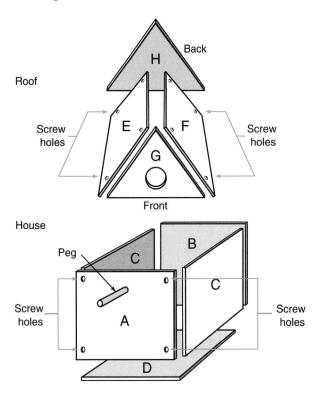

3. a. List the items that you would need to build a staircase with five steps.
    b. Write a set of instructions for assembling the items listed in Exercise 3a.

4. a. List the ingredients that you would need to create 10 peanut butter and jelly sandwiches.
    b. Write a set of instructions for assembling the items listed in Exercise 4a.

5. Obtain a set of assembly instructions from a recent item that you have built (for example, a bicycle or a backyard basketball hoop). Identify the major elements in the assembly instructions that correspond to the Ingredients and Methods sections and items listed in Figure 1-15.

6. Create a C++ class that prints out address labels in which an individual label consists of a name, two address lines, a city, state, and zip code. For this plan, list the data items and a set of methods that would be useful for such a program. Choose your own class name and data item names.

7. Create a plan for a C++ program that simulates the tossing of a single die. For this plan, list the data items and a set of methods that would be useful for such a program. Choose your own class name and data item names.

8. Create a plan for a C++ program that simulates the selection of a state lottery that randomly selects four numbers. For this plan, list the data items and a set of methods that would be useful for such a program. Choose your own class name and data item names.

9. Create a C++ program that calculates the floor space of a rectangular room. For this plan, list the data items and a set of methods that would be useful for such a program. Choose your own class name and data item names.

10. Create a C++ program that displays a rectangle on the screen. List the data items and a set of methods that would be useful for such a program. Choose your own class name and data item names.

11. Create a C++ program that calculates and displays the volume of a cylinder (volume = $\pi\, r^2\, l$, where r is the radius of the cylinder and l is the length). List the data items and a set of methods that would be useful for such a program. Choose your own class name and data item names.

12. Create a C++ program that uses dates. List the data items and a set of methods that would be useful for such a program. Choose your own class name and data item names.

13. Modify the `ShowFirstMessage` class (Figure 1-20) to display the message "Have a Great Day!"

14. For the following class, identify (a) the class name, (b) the names of data items that are used in the class, and (c) the number of methods contained within the method definition section.

```cpp
class ShowSecondMessage
{
  // data declaration section
  private:
    string message;

  // methods declaration and implementations
  public:
    ShowSecondMessage()
    {
      message = "I really prefer C!";
    }

    void changeMessage(string newMessage);
    {
      message = newMessage;
    }
      void displayMessage()
    {
      cout << message << endl;
    }
};
```

1.4 A FIRST PROGRAM IN C++

Most C++ classes are *not* executable programs, that is, they are not programs that can be executed by a user. Rather, the majority of classes serve as the source for objects that an executable program will create and use. Figure 1-22 illustrates how a typical C++ executable program could be constructed. Existing classes and individual non-class functions, which can be created by the programmer or supplied by your C++ compiler, serve as the basis for new classes, all of which can then be used by an executable program. (Recall that the terms *function* and *method* are frequently used as synonyms. Technically, a method is a procedure that is part of a class and a function is a procedure that exists independently of a class.)

FIGURE 1-22
Creating a C++ Executable Program

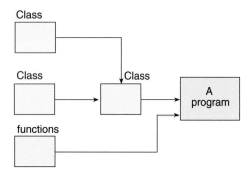

A distinct advantage of the process shown in Figure 1-22 is that the programmer can plan, in advance, for the overall objects that will be needed by an executable program, including the testing and verification of each class and function that will be included in the final program. By employing existing classes, initial design and development time is reduced, as is the time and effort required to test and verify newly created code. This allows you to focus on creating the additional classes or functions that you'll need to meet specific requirements, rather than reinventing code that has already been created and tested. C++ provides a comprehensive set of classes and functions that are collectively stored in what is known as the **standard library.** You'll be able to construct many programs based entirely on the offerings in the standard library, thereby greatly increasing your programming productivity and decreasing programming errors.

At a fundamental level, all classes and functions, which form the basis of a C++ executable program, consist of both words and special symbols, such as the brace pair, `{}`. The words permitted in C++, as in all other programming languages, are collectively referred to as identifiers. Identifiers consist of three types: reserved words, standard identifiers, and programmer-supplied words, each of which has its own special requirements. As these form the basis of all C++ code, we now consider them individually.

1

RESERVED WORDS

A **reserved word** is a word that is predefined by the programming language for a special purpose and can only be used in a specified manner for its intended purpose. Attempts to use reserved words for any other purpose will generate an error when the code is compiled. Reserved words are also referred to as **keywords** in C++, and we will use these two terms interchangeably.

Table 1-2 presents a list of the reserved words that you will initially need to become familiar with. As you progress in your programming studies, you will learn where, why, and how these words are used.

TABLE 1-2
C++ Reserved Words

auto	default	goto	public	template
break	do	if	register	this
case	double	inline	return	typedef
catch	else	int	short	union
char	enum	long	signed	unsigned
class	extern	new	sizeof	virtual
const	float	operator	static	void
continue	for	private	struct	volatile
delete	friend	protected	switch	while

Standard Identifiers

Standard identifiers are words that are predefined in C++. Standard identifiers have a predefined purpose, but this purpose can be redefined by a programmer. Generally, the term "standard identifier" refers to the names of prewritten classes and functions that that are provided in the C++ standard library. A number of these are listed in Table 1-3.

TABLE 1-3
Sample of C++ Standard Identifiers

append	container	insert	rand
assign	cout	list	size
binary_search	get	merge	sortcharAt
getline	push_back	swap	srand
cin	includes	put	vector

It is good programming practice to use standard identifiers only for their intended purpose. For example, the standard identifier rand is the name of a C++ function provided in the standard library. This function can be used to create a set of one or more random numbers, which are extremely useful in constructing simulation programs. In certain situations, however, it might be advantageous for a programmer to develop a specialized or more efficient random number generation function. In this case it would be appropriate to reuse the rand standard identifier for the function's name.

Identifiers

Reserved words and standard identifiers are examples of a broader class of words known as identifiers. Specifically an **identifier** is any combination of letters, digits, or underscores (_) subject to the following rules:

1.   The first character of the identifier must be a letter or underscore (_).

2.   Only letters, digits, or underscores may follow the initial character. Blank spaces are not allowed.

A large number of the identifiers used in a C++ program are selected by the programmer, and correspond to programmer-created classes, data, and method names. Programmer-selected identifiers must conform to C++'s identifier rules, with the additional restriction that the identifier cannot be a reserved word (see Table 1-2.)

Practically speaking, it's a good idea to limit programmer-selected identifiers to fewer than 14 characters, with 20 characters as an outside maximum. This will help prevent possible typing errors. It is often helpful to combine words to create an identifier that indicates, at a glance, the purpose of a class or method. To make such identifiers easier to read, by convention the first letter of every word after the first word is capitalized; the first word is also capitalized only if the identifier is the name of a class. Examples of valid programmer-created identifiers are:

checkItems	displayAMessage	randomNumbers	Clients
hoursWorked	tempConversion	multByTwo	Date

Following the C++ naming convention, we can see that the identifiers `Clients` and `Date`, which begin with a capital letter, are class names, while all the remaining identifiers are not. However, these identifiers could be names of data items or class methods.

PROGRAMMING NOTE

Tokens

In a computer language, a token is the smallest unit of the language that has a unique meaning. Thus, the reserved words listed in Table 1-2, programmer-defined identifiers, and all special mathematical symbols, such as + and -, are considered tokens of the C++ language.

Examples of invalid C++ programmer-created identifiers are:

   `4ab7`   (begins with a number, which violates Rule 1)
   `e*6`   (contains a special character, which violates Rule 2)
   `calculate total`   (contains a blank character, which violates Rule 2)
   `while` (this is a reserved word)

You will sometimes encounter identifiers consisting of all uppercase letters. These are usually used to indicate a symbolic constant, a topic covered in Chapter 3.

One important requirement for selecting an identifier is that it should convey some idea about how it will be used. Thus, identifiers such as `Clients` and `Date` are good choices for class names only if the classes they are used for have something to do with clients and dates. Identifiers such as:

```
Easy      duh      JustDoIt      mary      bill      TheForce
```

provide no indication of their use. They are examples of bad programming and should be avoided. Your identifiers should always be descriptive and indicate their purpose or how they will be used.

Finally, it is important to understand that C++ is a **case-sensitive** language. This means that the language distinguishes between uppercase and lowercase letters. Thus, in C++, the identifiers TOTAL, total, and TotaL represent three distinct and different identifiers.

THE main FUNCTION

Classes and functions form the building blocks of all executable C++ programs, and a true object-oriented program must use classes. An interesting holdover from the C language, upon which C++ was based, is the fact that an executable C++ program *is not* required to use any classes (in which case, the program reverts to being procedural). In its simplest form, an executable C++ program need only consist of a single special function; what makes the function special is that it must be named `main`. In fact, each executable C++ program, whether it uses a class or not, must have one and only one function named `main`. The term function is used here, in place of the term method, to reinforce the idea that the procedure named `main` typically is not a member of any class, but has its own existence, outside and independently of a class.

Figure 1-23 illustrates a structure for the `main` function. The first line of the function, in this case `int main()` is referred to as a **function header line.** A function header line, which is always the first line of a function, contains three pieces of information:

1. The type of data, if any, that is returned from the function

2. The name of the function

3. The type of data, if any, that is sent into the function

The keyword before the function name defines the type of value the function returns when it has completed its operation. When placed before the function's name, the keyword `int` (see Table 1-2) specifies that the function will return an integer value. Similarly, when the parentheses following the function name are empty, it signifies that no data will be transmitted into the function when it is run. (Data sent into a function are referred to as **arguments** of the function.) The braces, { and }, determine the beginning and end of the function body and enclose the statements making up the function. The statements inside the braces determine what the function does. Each statement inside the function must end with a semicolon (;).

FIGURE 1-23
The Structure of a `main` *Function*

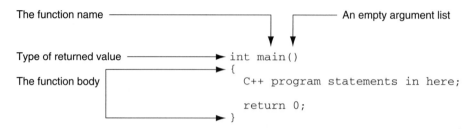

You will be naming and writing many of your own C++ functions and classes. In fact, the rest of this
book is primarily about the statements required to construct useful functions and classes, and how to
combine these into executable programs. Each executable program, however, must have one and only
one `main` function. Until we learn how to pass data into a function and return non-integer data from
a function (the topics of Chapter 3), the header line illustrated in Figure 1-23 will serve us for all the
programs we need to write. At this stage, you can regard the first two lines of the `main` function

```
int main()
{
```

as stating that "the main function begins here" and regard the last two lines,

```
    return 0;
}
```

as stating that "the function ends here." Because every C++ function and method requires parentheses
following its name, we will always include them to clearly indicate that the identifier refers to a function or method. Thus, for the rest of this text, we will always refer to the `main` function as `main()`

and to follow this practice for all other function and method names. This will make it easier for you to clearly distinguish that a procedure is being discussed. So whenever you see a name followed by parentheses, such as `displayMessage()` and `rand()`, you should understand that the name is that of a procedure, be it a function or method. Fortunately, many useful functions, methods, and classes have already been written for us. We will shortly see how to use an object created from one of these classes to create our first working C++ program.

Notice that the structure in Figure 1-23 consists of a single function named `main()` and no classes. This is the simplest structure possible for an executable C++ program and will be very useful to us when we need to quickly demonstrate how an individual C++ statement is constructed and used.

THE cout OBJECT

One of the most versatile and commonly used objects provided in C++ is named `cout` (pronounced "see out"). This object, whose name was derived from Console OUTput, is an output object that sends data given to it to the standard output display device. For most systems this display device is a video screen. The `cout` object takes whatever data is passed to it and displays it on the monitor. For example, if the data `Hello world!` is passed to `cout`, the text `Hello World!` is displayed on the monitor. Figure 1-24 shows how to write a C++ statement that passes the data `Hello world!` to the `cout` object. Note that the insertion symbol, <<, follows the object's name, coming just before the text itself. (The insertion symbol, <<, is sometimes referred to as the "put to" symbol.) The message is enclosed in quotation marks, and the statement ends in a semicolon.

FIGURE 1-24
Passing a Message to cout

```
cout << "Hello world!";
```

Now let's put all this together into a working C++ program that can be run on your computer. Consider Program 1-1.

The first four lines of program code, each of which begins with two slash symbols, //, are comments. We will have more to say about comments in the next section, but for now, it is important to understand that each source code program should begin with comments similar to those used here. These initial comment lines, at a minimum, should provide the file name under which the source code is saved, a short program description, the name of the programmer, and the date that the program was last modified. For all of the programs contained in this text, the file name refers to the name of the source code file provided with this text.

Program 1-1

```cpp
// File: pgm1-1.cpp
// Description: displays Hello World!
// Programmer: G. Bronson
// Date: 1/15/2006

#include <iostream>
using namespace std;

int main()
{
  cout << "Hello world!";

  return 0;
}
```

The sixth line (counting the blank line) of the program:

```cpp
#include <iostream>
```

is a preprocessor command that uses the reserved word `include`. Preprocessor commands begin with a pound sign, (#), and perform some action before the compiler translates the source program into machine code. Specifically, the `#include` preprocessor command causes the contents of the named file, in this case the `iostream` file, to be inserted wherever the `#include` command appears in the program. The `iostream` is a part of the standard library that contains, among other code, two classes named `istream` and `ostream`. These two classes provide the data declarations and methods used for data input and output, respectively. The `iostream` file is referred to as a **header file** because a reference to it is always placed at the top, or head, of a C++ program using the `#include` command. You may be wondering what the `iostream` file has to do with this simple program. The answer is that the `cout` object is created from the `ostream` class. Thus, the `iostream` header file must be included in all programs that use `cout`. As indicated in Program 1-1, preprocessor commands do not end with a semicolon.

PROGRAMMING NOTE

Using a Microsoft Operating System

If you are using an older Microsoft operating system, you may have to add the statement `cin.ignore();` before the `return 0;` statement in Program 1-1. The reason for this is that the operating system automatically closes an application after it has executed successfully, and the display produced by the program is lost. As a practical matter this means that the program runs, produces its output, and disappears from the screen unless there is a C++ statement that keeps the program from ending. The statement `cin.ignore()` keeps the program from ending. This statement is a request for input from the keyboard, which is then ignored. Thus, to end a program containing this statement, you will have to press any keyboard key.

Following the preprocessor `include` command is a statement containing the reserved word `using`. The statement

```
using namespace std;
```

tells the compiler where to look to find the header files in the absence of any further explicit designation. You can think of a namespace as a file directory or folder that is accessed by the compiler when it is looking for prewritten classes or functions. Because the `iostream` header file is contained within a compiler folder named `std`, the compiler will automatically use the `iostream`'s `cout` object from this namespace whenever `cout` is referenced. Using namespaces effectively permits you to create your own classes and functions with the same names as those provided by the standard library, and place them in differently named namespaces. We can then tell the program which class or function to use by indicating the namespace where we want the compiler to look for the class or function.

The `using` statement is followed by the start of the program's `main()` function. This function begins with the header line developed at the beginning of this section. The body of the function, enclosed in braces, consists of only two statements. The first statement in `main()` passes one text message to the `cout` object. The text message is the string `"Hello world!"`.

PROGRAMMING NOTE

Executable and Nonexecutable Statements

We will be introducing many C++ statements in this text that can be used to create classes, class methods, nonclass functions, and executable programs. All statements, however, belong to one or two broad categories: executable statements and nonexecutable statements.

An executable statement causes some specific action to be performed by the computer when the program is executed. For example, a statement that tells the computer to display output or add or subtract a number is an executable statement. Executable statements always must end with a semicolon.

A nonexecutable statement is one that describes some feature of the program or its data, but does not cause the computer to perform any action when a program is executed. An example of a nonexecutable statement is a function header line. This header explicitly defines the beginning of a procedure, but causes no specific action to be taken by the computer when the program is executing.

Because `cout` is an object of a prewritten class, you do not have to write it. You can employ it in your program simply by including the `iostream` header file and using the namespace `std`. Like all C++ objects, `cout` can only perform certain well defined actions; specifically, it assembles data for output display. When a string of characters is passed to `cout`, the object sees to it that the string is correctly displayed on your monitor, as shown in Figure 1-25.

FIGURE 1-25
The Output from Program 1-1

```
Hello world!
```

Formally, a **string** in C++ is any combination of letters, numbers, and special characters enclosed in double quotes (`"string in here"`). The double quotes are used to delimit (mark) the beginning and ending of the string and are not considered part of the string. Thus, the string of characters making up the text message sent to `cout` must be enclosed in double quotes, as in Program 1-1.

PROGRAMMING NOTE

The `stream` Classes

The standard library contains prewritten classes that can be used directly in a C++ program. Two of these are named `ostream` and `istream`. These classes support basic input and output services. In this regard, the `ostream` class provides functions for outputting data (formally referred to as a stream of data) from a program to a standard output device, which is usually a video screen. This connection is accomplished by an object named `cout`, which is created from the `ostream` class. This object can be used within a function or method using either the name `std::cout` or, if the `using namespace std;` statement has been included in the program, as simply `cout`.

　　　As you might expect, the `istream` class provides input functions for inputting data (again, formally referred to as a stream of data) from a standard input device into a program. This standard device is typically a keyboard, and the connection is accomplished by an object named `cin`. The use of the `cin` object is presented in Chapter 3.

To learn more about the versatility of `cout`, review Program 1-2.

Program 1-2 displays the following on the monitor:

```
Computers, computers everywhere
   as far as I can C
```

You might be wondering why `\n` (in the second `cout` statement) did not appear in the output. The two characters \ and n, when used together, are called a newline escape sequence. They tell `cout` to send instructions to the display device to move to a new line. In C++, the backslash (\\) character provides an "escape" from the normal interpretation of the character following it by altering the meaning of the next character. If the backslash was omitted from the second `cout` statement in Program 1-2, the n would be printed as the letter n and the program would print out:

1

```
Computers, computers everywheren    as far as I can C
```

Program 1-2

```cpp
// File: pgm1-2.cpp
// Description: Test program
// Programmer: G. Bronson
// Date: 1/15/2006

#include <iostream>
using namespace std;

int main()
{
  cout << "Computers, computers everywhere";
  cout << "\n    as far as I can C";

  return 0;
}
```

Newline escape sequences can be placed anywhere within the text message passed to cout. See if you can determine what is displayed on the screen as a result of Program 1-3.

Program 1-3

```cpp
// File: pgm1-3.cpp
// Description: Test program
// Programmer: G. Bronson
// Date: 1/15/2006

#include <iostream>
using namespace std;

int main()
{
  cout << "Computers everywhere\n    as far as\n\nI can see";

  return 0;
}
```

The output for Program 1-3 is:

```
Computers everywhere
   as far as

I can see
```

Exercises 1.4

1. State whether the following are valid function names. If they are valid, state whether they are descriptive names (recall that a descriptive name conveys some idea about the identifier's purpose). If they are invalid names, state why.

m1234()	newBal()	abcd()	A12345()	1A2345()
power()	absVal()	mass()	do()	while()
add_5()	taxes()	netPay()	12345()	int()
cosine()	a2b3c4d5()	payment()	amount()	$sine()
oldBalance()	nevValue()	salestax()	1stApprox()	float()

2. a. Assuming a case insensitive compiler, determine which of these identifiers are equivalent:

AVERAGE	average	MODE	BESSEL	Mode
Total	besseL	TeMp	Density	TEMP
denSITY	MEAN	total	mean	moDE

   b. Repeat Exercise 2a assuming a case sensitive compiler.

3. Which of the following identifiers could be the names of programmer-written classes and which of programmer-written functions, using the naming convention presented in this section?

NewBalance	addValues	CalculateTax
power	absVal	DisplayAMessage
invoices	SendMessage	taxes
netPay	amount	salesTax
CardGame	newBalance	ComputeGPA

4. Determine appropriate names for functions that do the following (multiple names are possible):

   a. Find the maximum value in a set of numbers.
   b. Find the minimum value in a set of numbers.
   c. Convert a lowercase letter to an uppercase letter.
   d. Convert an uppercase letter to a lowercase letter.
   e. Sort a set of numbers from lowest to highest.
   f. Alphabetize a set of names.

1

5. Just as the keyword int can be used to signify that a function will return no value, the keywords void, char, float, and double can be used to signify that a function will return no value, a character, floating point number, or double precision number, respectively. Using this information, write header lines for a main() function that will receive no arguments and will return:

a. nothing
b. a character
c. a floating point number
d. a double precision number

6. a. Using cout, write a C++ program that displays your name on one line; your street address on a second line; and your city, state, and zip code on the third line.
   b. Compile and execute the program you have written for Exercise 6a on a computer. (You may have to ask your instructor for specific details of how this is accomplished on your system.)

7. a. Write a C++ program that will display the following verse on the monitor:

```
Computers, computers everywhere
   as far as I can see
I really, really like these things,
   Oh joy, Oh joy for me!
```

   b. Compile and execute the program you have written for Exercise 7a on a computer.

8. a. How many cout statements would you use to display the following?

PART NO.	PRICE
T1267	$6.34
T1300	$8.92
T2401	$65.40
T4482	$36.99

   b. What is the minimum number of cout statements that could be used to print the table in Exercise 8a?
   c. Write a complete C++ program to produce the output illustrated in Exercise 8a.
   d. Compile and execute the program you have written for Exercise 8c on a computer.

9. In response to a newline escape sequence, cout positions the next displayed character at the beginning of a new line. This positioning of the next character actually represents two distinct operations. What are they?

Most projects, both programming and nonprogramming, can be structured into smaller subtasks or units of activity. These smaller subtasks can often be delegated to different people so that when all the tasks are finished and integrated, the project or program is completed. For exercises 10 through 15, determine a set of subtasks that, taken together, complete the required task.

(Note: The purpose of these exercises is to have you consider the different ways that complex tasks can be structured. Although there is no one correct solution to these exercises, some solutions are better than others. One solution is better than another if it more clearly or easily identifies what must be done or does it more efficiently. An incorrect solution is one that does not complete the task correctly.)

10. You are given the task of wiring and installing lights in the attic of your house. Determine a set of subtasks that, taken together, will accomplish this. (*Hint*: The first subtask would be to determine the placement of the light fixtures.)

11. You are given the job of preparing a complete meal for five people next weekend. Determine a set of subtasks that, taken together, accomplish the job of preparing the meal. (*Hint*: One subtask, not necessarily the first one, would be to buy the food.)

12. You are a sophomore in college and are planning to go on for a master's degree in computer science. List a set of major objectives that you must fulfill to meet this goal. (*Hint*: One objective is "Take the right courses.")

13. You are given the job of planting a vegetable garden. Determine a set of subtasks that accomplish this. (*Hint*: One such subtask would be to plan the layout of the garden.)

14. You are responsible for planning and arranging the family camping trip this summer. List a set of subtasks that, taken together, accomplish this objective successfully. (*Hint*: One subtask would be to select the camp site.)

15. a. A national electrical supply distribution company requires a computer system for preparing customer invoices. The system must be capable of creating each day's invoices. Additionally, the system should allow the user to retrieve and output a printed report of all invoices that meet certain criteria; for example, all invoices sent in a particular month with a net value of more than a given dollar amount, all invoices sent in a year to a particular client, or all invoices sent to firms in a particular state. Determine three or four major program units into which the system could be separated. (*Hint*: One program unit is "Prepare Invoices" to create each day's invoices.)

    b. Suppose someone enters incorrect data for a particular invoice, and that this is discovered after the data has been entered and stored by the system. Describe the program unit that would be required to correct this problem. Discuss why such a program unit might or might not be required by most business systems.

    c. Assume a program unit exists that allows a user to alter or change data that has been incorrectly entered and stored. Discuss the need for including an "audit trail" that would make it possible to determine, at a later date, what changes were made, when they were made, and who made them.

1.5 PROGRAMMING STYLE

C++ programs start executing at the beginning of the `main()` function. Since a program can have only one starting point, every C++ language program must contain one and only one `main()` function. As we have seen, all statements that make up the `main()` function are then included within the braces { } following the function name. Although the `main()` function must be present in every executable C++ program, C++ does not require that the word main, the parentheses (), or the braces { } be placed in any particular form. The form used in the last section

```
int main()
{
  program statements in here;

  return 0;
}
```

was chosen strictly for clarity and ease in reading the program. (If one of the program statements uses the `cout` object, the `iostream` header file must be included, as well as the statement `using namespace std;`). For example, the following general form of a `main()` function would also work:

```
int main
(
) { first statement;second statement;
     third statement;fourth
statement; return 0;}
```

Notice that more than one statement can be put on a line, or one statement can be written across lines. Except within strings and all identifiers, C++ ignores all white space. (The term "white space" refers to any combination of one or more blank spaces, tabs, or new lines.) For example, changing the white space in Program 1-1 and making sure not to split the string "Hello world!" across two lines results in the following valid program:

```
#include <iostream>
using namespace std;
int main
(
){
cout <<
"Hello world!";
return 0;
}
```

Although this version of `main()` does work, it is an example of poor programming style. It is difficult to read and understand. For readability, the `main()` function should always be written in standard form as:

```
int main()
{
  program statements in here;

  return 0;
}
```

In this standard form, the function name starts at the beginning of a line and is placed (along with the required parentheses) on a line by itself. The opening brace of the function body follows on the next line and is placed under the first letter of the line containing the function name. Similarly, the closing function brace is placed by itself in column 1 as the last line of the function. This structure serves to highlight the function as a single unit.

Within the function itself, all program statements are indented at least two spaces. Indentation is another sign of good programming practice, especially if the same indentation is used for similar groups of statements. Review Program 1-2 and notice that the same indentation was used for both `cout` object statements.

As you progress in your understanding and mastery of C++, you will develop your own indentation standards. Just keep in mind that the final form of your programs should be consistent and should always aid the reading and understanding of your programs.

COMMENTS

As explained earlier, comments are explanatory remarks within a program. When used carefully, comments can be very helpful in clarifying the purpose of a complete program, a specific group of statements, or an individual line. The compiler ignores all comments; they are there strictly for the convenience of anyone reading the program code and are not translated into machine language. Comments can be placed anywhere within a C++ program and have no effect on program execution. C++ supports two types of comments: line and block.

A line comment begins with two slashes (`//`) and continues to the end of the line. For example,

```
// this is a comment
// this program prints out a message
// this program calculates a square root
```

are all comment lines. The symbols `//`, with no white space between them, designate the start of the line comment. The end of the line on which the comment is written designates the end of the comment.

1

A line comment can be written either on a line by itself or at the end of a line containing a program statement. Program 1-4 illustrates the use of line comments within a program.

Program 1-4

```cpp
// this program displays a message
#include <iostream>
using namespace std;

int main()
{
   cout << "Hello world!"; // using the cout object

   return 0;
}
```

The first comment appears on a line by itself at the top of the program and describes what the program does. This is generally a good location to include a short comment describing the program's purpose. You are also free to add more comments throughout a program, one per line. If a comment is too long to be contained on one line, you can separate it into two or more line comments, with each separate comment preceded by the double slash symbol set, //. The following comment will result in a C++ error message:

```cpp
// this comment is invalid because it
   extends over two lines
```

The following shows a correct version of this comment:

```cpp
// this comment is used to illustrate a
// comment that extends across two lines
```

Comments that span across two or more lines are, however, more conveniently written as block comments rather than as multiple line comments. Block comments begin with the symbols /* and end with the symbols */. For example,

```cpp
/* This is a block comment that
   spans
   three lines */
```

A well structured C++ program should be easy for a programmer to read and understand, making extensive comments unnecessary. Choosing descriptive names for functions, classes, methods, and data items will help convey their purpose to anyone reading the program, and reduce the need for comments even further. However, if the purpose of a function, class, method, or statement is still not clear from its structure, name, or context, you should include comments for clarification. Obscure code with no comments is a sure sign of bad programming, and is the bane of programmers who have to read or maintain code written by others. Similarly, excessive comments are also a sign of bad programming, because they imply that insufficient thought was given to making the code self-explanatory.

Exercises 1.5

1. **a.** Will the following program work?

    ```
    #include <iostream>
    using namespace std;
    int main(){cout << "Hello world!"; return 0;}
    ```

    b. Is the program shown in Exercise 1a a good program? Why or why not?

2. Rewrite the following programs to conform to good programming practice.

    a.
    ```
    #include <iostream>
    using namespace std;
    int main(
    ){
    cout              <<
    "The time has come"
    ; return 0;}
    ```

    b.
    ```
    #include <iostream>
    using namespace std;
    int main
    (     ){cout << "Newark is a city\n";cout <<
    "In New Jersey\n"; cout <<
    "It is also a city\n"
    ; cout << "In Delaware\n"
    ; return 0;}
    ```

    c.
    ```
    #include <iostream>
    using namespace std;
    int main(){cout << "Reading a program\n";cout <<
    "is much easier\n"
    ;cout << "if a standard form for main is used\n"
    ;cout
    <<"and each statement is written\n";cout
    <<              "on a line by itself\n"
    ; return 0;}
    ```

    d.
    ```
    #include <iostream>
    using namespace std;
    int main
    (     ){cout << "Every C++ program"
    ;cout
    ```

```
 <<"\nmust have one and only one"
 ;
 cout << "main function"
 ;
 cout <<
 "\n the escape sequence of characters"
 ;cout <<
 "\nfor a newline can be placed anywhere"
 ;cout
 <<"\n within the message passed to cout"
 ; return 0;}
```

3. a. When included in a string displayed by cout, the backslash character will alter the meaning of the character immediately following it. Suppose you actually want cout to display the backslash character as part of the string. How would you tell cout to escape from the way it normally interprets the backslash? What character do you think is used to alter the way a single backslash character is interpreted?

    b. Using your answer to Exercise 3a, write the escape sequence for displaying a backslash.

1.6 A CLOSER LOOK: TWO'S COMPLEMENT NUMBERS

The most common number code for storing integer values inside a computer is called the **two's complement** representation. This code permits storing both positive and negative integer numbers using a binary code. For convenience, in the following discussion we will assume byte-sized bit patterns consisting of a set of eight bits each, although the procedure carries directly over to larger size bit patterns.

The easiest way to determine the integer represented by a two's complement bit pattern is first to construct a simple device called a value box. Figure 1-26 illustrates such a box for a single byte. Mathematically, each value in the box illustrated in Figure 1-26 represents an increasing power of 2. Since two's complement numbers must be capable of representing both positive and negative integers, the leftmost position, in addition to having the largest absolute magnitude, also has a negative sign.

FIGURE 1-26
An Eight-Bit Value Box

−128	64	32	16	8	4	2	1

To convert any two's complement binary number, for example 10001101, insert the bit pattern in the value box and add the values having 1s under them. Thus, as illustrated in Figure 1-27, the bit pattern 10001101 represents the integer number −115.

FIGURE 1-27
Converting 10001101 to a Base 10 Number

−128	64	32	16	8	4	2	1
1	0	0	0	1	1	0	1

−128 + 0 + 0 + 0 + 8 + 4 + 0 + 1 = −115

You can use the value box in reverse to convert a base 10 integer number into its equivalent binary bit pattern. Note that you can make some conversions by inspection. For example, the base 10 number −125 is obtained by adding 3 to −128. Thus, the binary representation of −125 is 10000011, which equals −128 + 2 + 1. Similarly, the two's complement representation of the number 40 is 00101000, which is 32 + 8.

Although the value box conversion technique is deceptively simple, it is directly related to the underlying mathematical basis of two's complement binary numbers. The two's complement code was originally called the weighted-sign code. As the name **weighted sign** implies, each bit position has a weight, or value, of 2 raised to a power and a sign. The signs of all bits except the leftmost bit are positive, and the sign of the leftmost bit is negative.

 After you work with the value box a few times, you'll begin to see that any two's complement binary number with a leading 1 represents a negative number, and any bit pattern with a leading 0 represents a positive number. Also, using the value box, you can determine the most positive and negative values that can be stored in a byte. The most negative value that can be stored in a single byte is the decimal number −128, which has the bit pattern 10000000. Any other nonzero bit will simply add a positive amount to the number. Additionally, it is clear that a positive number must have a 0 as its leftmost bit. Another thing the value box teaches us is that the largest positive eight-bit two's complement number is 01111111, or 127.

1.7 COMMON PROGRAMMING ERRORS

Part of learning any programming language is making a series of common, elementary mistakes. Each language has its own set of common programming errors waiting for the unwary, and these errors can be quite frustrating. Beginning C++ programmers commonly make the following errors:

1. Rushing to write and run a program before fully understanding what is required, including the classes needed to produce the desired result. A symptom of this haste to get a program entered into the computer is the lack of any documentation or even a program outline.

2. Forgetting to make a backup copy of all classes and programs. Almost all new programmers make this mistake until they lose a class or program that has taken considerable time to code.

3. Omitting the parentheses after `main`.

4. Omitting or incorrectly typing the opening brace { that signifies the start of a function body.

5. Omitting or incorrectly typing the closing brace } that signifies the end of a function.

6. Misspelling the name of an object or function; for example, typing `cot` instead of `cout`.

7. Forgetting to close a string sent to `cout` with a double quote symbol.

8. Forgetting to separate individual data streams passed to `cout` with an insertion ("put-to") symbol, <<.

9. Omitting the semicolon at the end of each C++ statement.

10. Adding a semicolon at the end of the `#include` preprocessor command.

11. Incorrectly typing the letter O for the number zero (0), or vice versa. Incorrectly typing the letter l, for the number 1, or vice versa.

12. Forgetting the `\n` to indicate a new line.

Except for the first two errors and the last error in this list, the remaining items all result in a compiler error message. We suggest that you write a program and specifically introduce each of these compiler errors, one at a time, to see what error messages are produced by your compiler. Then, when these error messages appear due to inadvertent errors, you will have had experience in understanding the messages and correcting them. Our experience indicates that errors 9 and 12 tend to be the most common errors. The first two errors, when they are made, result in considerable lost time and much frustration.

1.8 CHAPTER REVIEW

Key Terms

application software

assembler

assembly language

class

coding

comments

compiler

escape sequence

high-level language

low-level language

machine language

newline character

object

object-oriented

procedure-oriented

programming

programming language

software

syntax

system software

SUMMARY

1. Computer science is a discipline that is concerned with the science of computers and computing.

2. The first attempt at creating a self-operating computational machine was made by Charles Babbage in 1822. The concept became a reality with the Atanasoff-Berry Computer built in 1937 at Iowa State University, which was the first computer to use a binary numbering scheme to store and manipulate data. Two of the earliest large scale digital computers were the ENIAC, built in 1946 at the Moore School of Engineering of the University of Pennsylvania and the Mark I, built at Harvard University in 1944. All of these machines, however, required external wiring to perform the desired operations. The first computer to employ the concept of a stored program was the EDSAC, built at Cambridge University in England. The design and operating principles used in this machine, developed by the mathematician John Von Neumann, are still used by the majority of computers manufactured today.

3. The physical components used in constructing a computer are called its hardware. These components include input, processing, output, memory, and storage units.

4. The programs used to operate a computer are referred to as software.

5. Programming languages come in a variety of forms and types. Machine language programs, also known as executable programs, contain the binary codes that can be executed by a computer. Assembly languages permit the use of symbolic names for mathematical operations and memory addresses. Programs written in assembly languages must be converted to machine language, using translator programs called assemblers, before the programs can be executed. Assembly and machine languages are referred to as low-level languages.

   Compiled and interpreted languages are referred to as high-level languages. This means that they are written using instructions that resemble a written language, such as English, and can be run on a variety of computer types. Compiled languages require a compiler to translate the program into a binary language form, while interpreted languages require an interpreter to do the translation.

1

6. In a procedure-oriented language, programs are constructed using self-contained units referred to as procedures. The purpose of a procedure is to accept data as input and use it to produce a specific result as an output.

7. In an object-oriented language, the basic program unit is a class.

8. A class is effectively a plan, consisting of data and functions, out of which individual programming objects can be created and manipulated. A class may contain two sections, a class declarations section and a functions implementation section. The data items for the class are declared in a class declarations section, which also must declare all functions that will be included within the functions implementation section. The actual instructions for creating objects and manipulating their data items are contained within the functions implementation section. For each function in the implementation section, you must include a corresponding function in the declarations section. You can construct classes with no functions.

9. The simplest class structure consists of a data declaration section and a methods section, in the following structure:

```
class ClassName
{
    // data declaration section

    // methods section

};
```

In this structure the methods section contains the names, types, and actual code for each class method. Frequently, this section is divided into two parts. The first part, contained within the braces, provides the names and types of methods, while the second part, called the implementation section, provides the actual code for each method. In this two-part structure, the implementation section is placed outside of the braces and after the terminating semicolon.

10. A reserved word is a word that is predefined by the programming language for a special purpose and can only be used in a specified manner for its intended purpose. Attempts to use reserved words for any other purpose will generate an error when the code is compiled.

11. A programmer-created identifier is a word supplied by the programmer that can be made up of any combination of letters, digits, or underscores (_) selected according to the following rules:

    a. The first character cannot be a digit.
    b. Only letters (both uppercase and lowercase), digits, and underscore symbols, (_), may follow the initial character (blank spaces are not allowed).
    c. It cannot be a reserved word.

12. Classes and functions form the building blocks of an executable C++ program.

13. A C++ executable program must have a `main()` function. The general syntax of this function is:

```
int main()
{
    C++ program statements in here;

    return 0;
}
```

14. All executable C++ statements must be terminated by a semicolon.

15. The standard C++ library provides a rich set of classes and functions that can be accessed by all C++ programs.

16. A namespace identifies how predefined classes and functions can be accessed. The namespace for the classes and functions provided by the standard C++ library is named `std`.

17. The `cout` object can be used to display all of C++'s data types.

18. When the `cout` object is used within a program, the preprocessor command `#include <iostream>` must be placed at the top of the program. Preprocessor commands do not end with a semicolon.

19. A `using` statement tells the compiler to look into the referenced namespace for all predefined identifiers. In the absence of a `using` statement, each such identifier would have to be prefaced with the name of the namespace and a double colon, `::`. Thus, if the `using namespace std;` statement is not included in a program, all references to `cout` must be written as `std::cout`.

20. Comments are explanatory remarks made within a program. They are meant strictly for someone reading the program and are ignored by the compiler; thus, they have no effect on program execution.

21. C++ supports two types of comments: line and block. Line comments begin with two slashes, //, and continue to the end of the line. A block comment begins with the symbols /*, can continue over as many lines as needed, and ends with the symbol */.

Chapter Exercises

Improving Communication

1. Respond to the following request:

   MEMORANDUM

   To: U. R. Aprogrammer

   From: Head of Programming Dept.

   Subject: Preliminary Analysis Phase

1

As per our prior discussion, you will be interviewing a number of people in the company. Your goal, as we discussed, is to determine how many projects they have been involved in that have been completely specified at the start of the project. Please give me a list of questions you intend to ask and how you intend to approach the interviewees for their permission to conduct the interview.

Improving Communication

2. Respond to the following request:

MEMORANDUM

To: U. R. It

From: Head of Programming Dept.

Subject: Sampling Project

We spent a large part of the last meeting with the marketing department discussing how the input screen should look for the new Sampling Project. Jan Programmer complained to me after the meeting that she had no interest in the input screen. She said it was a boring and professionally unexciting topic, and that we should just give her the required specifications for the screen and let her do her job. Later in the day, Joan Muchsuccess, head of marketing, contacted me and said she was not impressed with Jan, did not think Jan really understood or cared about the project, and would like another programmer assigned to the task. I know Jan is one of our cracker-jack programmers and that the analysis of the data is extremely complicated and requires someone as capable as Jan. How should we handle this?

Working in Teams

3. One of the major phases of any programming project is determining what must be accomplished. Most students never get a real understanding of this phase because assignments, both programming and non-programming, are usually well defined, either by the professor or as written exercises in a text book.

   a. Discuss with each of your team members how homework has been assigned throughout their educational career. See if there is some consensus on the percentage of problems assigned where there was sufficient information to solve the problem.

   b. How might you quantify the results of your discussions with your team members?

   c. Take a moment and review how you typically react when an assignment is not totally specified; that is, when some piece of information is missing from the problem. Determine with your team members what their reactions have been. Can you determine a pattern in reactions? Which reactions do you think are most likely to yield negative results in the working world?

   d. Take a moment and review what you typically do when an assignment is not totally specified; that is, when some piece of information is missing from the problem. For example, do you:

      • Use it as an excuse not to do the assignment at all?

      • Attempt to solve the problem and stop when you reach the point where the missing information is needed?

- Make assumptions about what the missing information is, and solve the problem using your assumed data?
- Use it as a means of making the instructor wrong for not giving you all the information required?

e. Determine what your team members typically do when an assignment is not totally specified and see if the team can determine a pattern.

f. Summarize the findings of your team in a memorandum to your professor.

Working in Teams

4. a. With your team members, develop some useful questions to ask people in the working world to find out their experience with assigned projects. Specifically, you want to determine the percentage of projects that were completely specified at the start of the project and, of the remaining projects, the percentage of the project that was typically specified. Include in your discussions ways you can approach people to encourage them to speak with you, both for this exercise and for future such exercises.

   b. Ask the questions compiled for Exercise 4a to as many people in the working world that you can. Compare your results with those obtained by your team members and see if there is a pattern to your results.

   c. Summarize the finding of your team members in a memorandum to your professor.

Working in Teams

5. Computer science professionals work in a number of different environments that include academic, scientific research labs, new-venture computer companies, and commercial corporations. To be successful in each environment frequently involves a different mixture of skills.

   a. With your team members, develop some useful questions to ask people in these working environments to determine what skills they believe are required for success. Include in your discussions ways you might approach people to encourage them to speak with you, both for this project and for future projects.

   b. Ask the questions developed in Exercise 5a to as many computer professionals as you can.

   c. Ask the questions developed in Exercise 5a to supervisors of computer professionals. If possible, contact the supervisors of the people you interviewed in Exercise 5b. (*Hint*: Use both the academic departments in your college as well as the nonacademic departments.)

   d. Compare your results with those of your team members and prepare a summary of your findings in a memorandum to your professor.

Working in Teams

6. Consider the following statements: "If you think something is true, it is true" and "Just because you think something is true does not make it so." Discuss these statements with your team members and see if you can come to some consensus as to their validity. Are these statements necessarily contradictory? How might these statements be of value to you in interviewing people and determining the requirements for a new computer system?

1

**Working
in Teams**

7. Suppose you interview 10 people in an organization and all of them agree on exactly what is needed and what you must do to produce the desired system. As a programmer, can you proceed with complete confidence in designing the system? Discuss this with your team members and come up with a few examples that confirm your position. Determine if there are any examples that might indicate your conclusions are not completely correct.

**Working
in Teams**

8. Some programmers take the position that, as programmers, they should program, without question, whatever their client or supervisor requests. Discuss the pros and cons of taking this approach with your team members, assuming you are all programmers. Then discuss the pros and cons of this approach assuming you are all supervisors of programmers.

**Testing
Center**

Please visit the Testing Center at www.course.com/testingcenter for more practice on object-oriented programming in C++.

2 CREATING CLASSES

C++ programs process different types of data in different ways. For example, calculating the bacteria growth in a polluted pond requires mathematical operations on numerical data, whereas sorting a list of names requires comparison operations using alphabetical data. C++ has two fundamental categories of data: built-in types and programmer-supplied types. The latter are what we have been calling classes. In this chapter we introduce built-in data types and the operations that are built into C++ for use with them. This is followed by a presentation of variables and the construction of a class. Finally, a systematic object-oriented design and development procedure for identifying objects is presented.

2.1 BUILT-IN DATA TYPES

The objective of all programs is ultimately to process data, be it numerical, alphabetical, audio, or video. Central to this objective is the classification of data into specific types. For example, calculating the interest due on a bank balance requires mathematical operations on numerical data, while alphabetizing a list of names requires comparison operations on character-based data. Additionally, some operations are not applicable to certain types of data. For example, it makes no sense to add names together. To prevent the programmer from attempting to perform an inappropriate operation, C++ allows only certain operations to be performed on certain data types.

The types of data permitted and the appropriate operations defined for each type are referred to as a data type. Formally, a **data type** is defined as a set of values *and* a set of operations that can be applied to these values. For example, the set of all integer (whole) numbers constitutes a set of values, as does the set of all real numbers (numbers that contain a decimal point). These two sets of numbers, however, do not constitute a data type until a set of operations is also included. These operations, of course, are the familiar mathematical and comparison operations. The combination of a set of values plus operations becomes a true data type.

C++ categorizes data types into one of two fundamental groupings: built-in data types and class data types. A **class data type**, which is referred to as a class, for short, is a programmer-created data type. This means that the set of acceptable values and operations is defined by a programmer, using C++ code.

A **built-in data type** is one that is provided as an integral part of the C++ compiler and requires no external C++ code. Thus, a built-in data type can be used without recourse to supplementary language additions, such as that provided by the `iostream` header file needed for the `cout` object. Built-in data types, which are also referred to as **primitive** types, consist of the basic numerical types shown in Figure 2-1 and the operations listed in Table 2-1. As seen in this table, the majority of operations for built-in types are provided as symbols. This is in contrast to class types, where the majority of operations are provided as methods.

FIGURE 2-1
Built-In Data Types

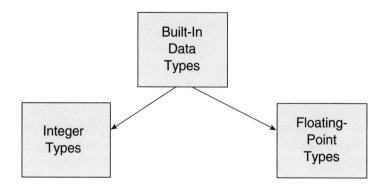

TABLE 2-1
Built-In Data Type Operations

built-in data types	operations

Integer	`+, -, *, /,`
	`%, =, ==, !=,`
	`<=, >=, sizeof(),`
	`and bit operations`
	(see Appendix C)

Floating Point	`+, -, *, /,`
	`=, ==, !=,`
	`<=, >=, sizeof()`

In introducing C++'s built-in data types, we will make use of literals. A **literal** is an acceptable value for a data type. The term "literal" reflects the fact that such a value explicitly identifies itself. (Another name for a literal is a **literal value**, or **constant**.) For example, all numbers, such as 2, 3.6, and -8.2, are referred to as literal values because they literally display their values. Text, such as `"Hello World!"` is also referred to as a literal value because the text itself is displayed. You have been using literal values throughout your life and have commonly referred to them as numbers and words. In Section 2.2 you will see some examples of non-literal values—that is, values that do not display themselves but are stored and accessed using identifiers.

2

INTEGER DATA TYPES

C++ provides nine built-in integer data types, as shown in Figure 2-2. The essential difference among the various integer data types is the amount of storage used for each type, which directly affects the range of values that each type is capable of representing. The three most important types that are used almost exclusively in the majority of applications are the int, char, and bool data types. The reason for the remaining types is essentially historical, as they were originally provided to accommodate special situations (a very small or a very large range of numbers). This permitted a programmer to maximize memory usage by selecting a data type that used the smallest amount of memory consistent with an application's requirements. When computer memories were both very small relative to today's computers and extremely expensive, this was a major concern. Although no longer a concern for the vast majority of programs, it still provides a programmer the ability to optimize memory usage when necessary. Typically these situations occur in engineering applications, such as control systems used in home appliances and automobiles.

FIGURE 2-2
C++ Integer Data Types

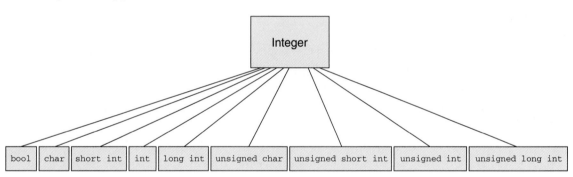

The int Data Type

The set of values supported by the int data type are whole numbers, which are mathematically known as integers. An integer value consists of digits only and can optionally be preceded by either a plus (+) or minus (-) sign. Thus, an integer value can be the number zero or any positive or negative numerical value without a decimal point. Examples of valid integers are:

    0   5   -10   +25   1000   253   -26351   +36

As these examples illustrate, integers may contain an explicit sign. No commas, decimal points, or special symbols, such as the dollar sign, are allowed. Examples of invalid integers are:

    $255.62   2,523   3.   6,243,892   1,492.89 +6.0

Different compilers have their own internal limit on the largest (most positive) and smallest (most negative) integer values that can be stored in each data type.[1] The most common storage allocation is four bytes for the `int` data type, which restricts the set of values permitted in this data type to represent integers in the range of $-2,147,483,648$ to $2,147,483,647$.[2]

PROGRAMMING NOTE

Atomic Data

An **atomic data value** is a value that is considered a complete entity by itself and cannot be decomposed into a smaller data type. For example, although an integer can be decomposed into individual digits, C++ does not have a numerical digit type. Rather, each integer is regarded as a complete value by itself and, as such, is considered atomic data. Similarly, because the integer data type supports only atomic data values, it is said to be an **atomic data type**. As you might expect, all of the built-in data types are atomic data types.

The `char` Data Type

The `char` data type is used to store individual characters. Characters include the letters of the alphabet (both uppercase and lowercase), the ten digits 0 through 9, and special symbols such as + $. , - !. A single character value is any one letter, digit, or special symbol enclosed by single quotes. Examples of valid character values are:

$$\texttt{'A'\quad '\$'\quad 'b'\quad '7'\quad 'y'\quad '!'\quad 'M'\quad 'q'}$$

Character values are typically stored in a computer using either the ASCII or Unicode codes. ASCII, pronounced AS-KEY, is an acronym for American Standard Code for Information Interchange. The ASCII code provides codes for an English-language-based character set plus codes for printer and display control, such as new line and printer paper-eject codes. Each character code is contained within a single byte, which provides for 256 distinct codes. Table 2-2 lists the ASCII byte codes for uppercase letters.

Additionally, C++ provides for the newer Unicode character set that uses two bytes per character and can represent 65,536 characters. This code is used for international applications by providing other language character sets in addition to English. As the first 256 Unicode codes have the same numerical value as the 256 ASCII codes (the additional byte is simply coded with all 0s), you need not concern yourself with which storage code is used when using English language characters.

---

[1]The limits imposed by the compiler can be found in the `limits` header file and are defined as the hexadecimal constants `int_max` and `int_min`.

[2]It is interesting to note that in all cases the magnitude of the most negative integer number is always one more than the magnitude of the most positive integer. This is due to the two's complement method of integer storage, which is described in Section 1.6.

TABLE 2-2
The ASCII Uppercase Letter Codes

letter	ASCII code	letter	ASCII code
A	01000001	N	01001110
B	01000010	O	01001111
C	01000011	P	01010000
D	01000100	Q	01010001
E	01000101	R	01010010
F	01000110	S	01010011
G	01000111	T	01010100
H	01001000	U	01010101
I	01001001	V	01010110
J	01001010	W	01010111
K	01001011	X	01011000
L	01001100	Y	01011001
M	01001101	Z	01011010

Using Table 2-2, we can determine how the characters 'A', 'N', 'D', 'R', 'E', and 'W', for example, are stored inside a computer that uses the ASCII character code. This sequence of six characters requires six bytes of storage (one byte for each letter) and would be stored as illustrated in Figure 2-3.

FIGURE 2-3
The Letters ANDREW Stored Inside a Computer

6 bytes of storage

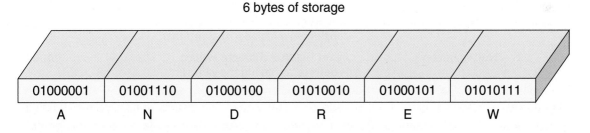

01000001	01001110	01000100	01010010	01000101	01010111
A	N	D	R	E	W

The Escape Character

One character that has a special meaning in C++ is the backslash, \, which is referred to as the **escape character**. When this character is placed directly in front of a select group of characters, it tells the compiler to escape from the way these characters would normally be interpreted. The combination of a backslash and these specific characters is called an **escape sequence**. We have already encountered an example of this in the newline escape sequence, \n, in Chapter 1. Table 2-3 lists C++'s most common escape sequences.

TABLE 2-3
Escape Sequences

escape sequence	character represented	meaning	ASCII code
\n	Newline	Move to a new line	00001010
\t	Horizontal tab	Move to next horizontal tab setting	00001001
\v	Vertical tab	Move to next vertical tab setting	00001011
\b	Backspace	Move back one space	00001000
\r	Carriage return	Carriage return (moves the cursor to the start of the current line — used for overprinting)	00001101
\f	Form Feed	Issue a form feed	00001100
\a	Alert	Issue an alert (usually a bell sound)	00000111
\\	Backslash	Insert a backslash character (this is used to place an actual backslash character within a string)	01011100
\?	Question mark	Insert a question mark character	00111111
\'	Single quotation	Insert a single quote character (this is used to place an inner single quote within a set of outer single quotes)	00100111
\"	Double quotation mark	Insert a double quote character (this is used to place an inner double quote within a set of outer double quotes)	00100010
\nnn	Octal number	The number *nnn* (*n* is a digit) is to be considered an octal number	—
\xhhhh	Hexadecimal number	The number *hhhh* (*h* is a digit) is to be considered a hexadecimal number	—
\0	Null character	Insert the Null character, which is defined as having the value 0	00000000

Although each escape sequence listed in Table 2-3 is made up of two distinct characters, the combination of the two characters, with no intervening white space, causes the compiler to create the single code listed in the ASCII code column of Table 2-3.

The bool Data Type

In C++, the bool data type is used to represent Boolean (logical) data. As such, this data type is restricted to one of two values: true or false. This data type is most useful when a program must examine a specific condition and, as a result of the condition being either true or false, take a prescribed course of action. For example, in a sales application, the condition being examined might be "is the total purchase for $100 or more." Only when this condition is true is a discount applied. The fact that the Boolean data type uses an integer storage code, however, has very useful implications that are exploited by almost all professional C++ programmers. The practical uses of Boolean conditions is considered in Chapter 5, so we defer further discussion of Boolean data until then.

Determining Storage Size

A unique feature of C++ is that it permits you to see where and how values are stored. As an example, C++ provides an operator named `sizeof()` that provides the number of bytes used to store values for any data type name included within the operator's parentheses. (Review Section 1.6 if you are unfamiliar with the concept of a byte.)   Notice that this is a built-in operator that does not use an arithmetic symbol to perform its operation. Program 2-1 uses this operator to determine the amount of storage reserved for the `int`, `char`, and `bool` data types.

PROGRAMMING NOTE

The Character '\n' and the String "\n"

Both '\n' and "\n" are recognized by the compiler as containing the newline character. The difference is in the data types being used. Formally, '\n' is a character literal, while "\n" is a string literal. From a practical standpoint both cause the same thing to happen: a new line is forced on the output display. In encountering the character value '\n', however, the compiler translates it using the single byte code 00001010 (see Table 2-3). In encountering the string value "\n", the compiler translates this string using the correct character code, but also adds additional information that includes the size of the string, which is 1, plus the initial capacity that it assigns to all strings.

      Good programming practice requires that you end the last output display with a newline escape sequence. This ensures that the first line of output from one program does not end up on the last line displayed by the previously executed program.

Program 2-1

```cpp
#include <iostream>
using namespace std;

int main()
{
  cout << "\nData Type   Bytes"
       << "\n---------   -----"
       << "\nint        " << sizeof(int)
       << "\nchar       " << sizeof(char)
       << "\nbool       " << sizeof(bool)
       << '\n';

    return 0;
}
```

In reviewing Program 2-1 notice that a single character value is inserted into cout by enclosing it within single quotes, as is the escape sequence '\n' insertion at the end of the last cout statement. Within the first five displayed lines this character is simply included within each output string. Each time the compiler encounters the newline escape sequence, either as a single character or as part of a string, it is translated as a single character that forces the display to start on a new line. Although double quotes can be used for the final newline insertion, as "\n", this would designate a string. As such, storage for the string would include not only the character code for the newline escape sequence, but also additional information, such as the size of the string and its capacity. Because only a single character is being transmitted, and to emphasize that single characters are designated using single quotes, we have used '\n' in place of "\n". From a practical standpoint, however, both notations will force a new line in the display.

The output of Program 2-1 is compiler dependent. That is to say, each compiler will correctly report the amount of storage that it provides for the data type under consideration. When run on the author's computer, which uses Microsoft's current Visual C++.net compiler, the following output was produced:

```
Data Type    Bytes
---------    -----
   int         4
   char        1
   bool        1
```

PROGRAMMING NOTE

Object-Oriented and Procedural Programs

Except for the Boolean type, all of C++'s built-in data types are direct carryovers from the C procedural language. It should not be surprising, therefore, that programs using only individual built-in types will not be object-oriented programs. Rather, as in Program 2-1, they become procedural programs; that is, a program primarily based on procedures, such as main(). It is only when built-in types are bundled together to form a packet of data, which becomes an object, can an object-oriented program come into existence. This packaging together of individual data types takes place in a class's data declaration section.

For this output, which is the typical storage provided by almost all current C++ compilers, we can determine the range of values that can be stored in each of these int data types. To do so, however, requires understanding the difference between a signed and unsigned data type.

Signed and Unsigned Data Types

A **signed data type** is defined as one that permits storing negative values in addition to zero and positive values. As such, the int data type is a signed data type. An **unsigned data type** is one that provides only for non-negative (that is, zero and positive) values. Both the char and bool data types are unsigned data types, which means that they have no codes for storing negative values.

2

There are cases, however, where an application might only require unsigned numerical values. For example, many date applications store dates in the numerical form *yearmonthday* (thus, the date 12/25/2007 would be stored as 20071225) and are only concerned with dates after 0 CE. For such applications, which will never require a negative value, an unsigned data type can be used.

All unsigned integer types, such as unsigned int, provide a range of positive values that is, for all practical purposes, double the range provided for its signed counterpart. This extra positive range is made available by using the negative range of its signed version for additional positive numbers.

With the understanding of the difference between a signed and unsigned data type, Table 2-4 can be used to determine the range of integer values supported by current C++ compilers.

TABLE 2-4
Integer Data Type Storage

name of data type	storage size (in bytes)	range of values
char	1	256 characters
bool	1	true (which is considered as any positive value) and false (which is a zero)
short int	2	-32,768 to +32,767
unsigned short int	2	0 to 65,535
int	4	-2,147,483,648 to +2,147,483,647
unsigned int	4	0 to 4,294,967,295
long int	4	-2,147,483,648 to +2,147,483,647
unsigned long int	4	0 to 4,294,967,295

One item to notice in Table 2-4 is that a long int uses the same amount of storage (four bytes) as an int. The only requirement of the ANSI C++ standard is that an int must provide at least as much storage as a short int, and that a long int must provide at least as much storage as an int. On the first desktop computer systems (1980s), which were limited in their memory capacity to thousands of bytes, a short int typically used one byte of storage, an int two bytes, and a long int four bytes. Because this storage limited the range of int values from -32,768 to +32,767, while the use of an unsigned int provided a range of values from 0 to 65,535, the doubling of possible positive values was significant. With the current range of int values in the -2 to +2 billion range, the doubling of positive values is rarely a consideration. Additionally, using a long int becomes unnecessary, because it is now uses the same storage capacity as an int.

Floating-Point Types

A **floating-point number**, which is also called a **real number**, can be the number zero or any positive or negative number that contains a decimal point. Examples of floating-point numbers are:

```
+10.625    5.    -6.2    3251.92    0.0    0.33    -6.67    +2
```

Notice that the numbers 5., 0.0, and +2. are classified as floating-point values, but the same numbers written without a decimal point (5, 0, +2) would be integer values. As with integer values, special symbols such as the dollar sign and the comma are not permitted in real numbers. Examples of invalid real numbers are:

```
5,326.25      24      6,459      $10.29      7.007.645
```

C++ supports three floating point data types: `float`, `double`, and `long double`. The difference between these data types is the amount of storage that a compiler uses for each type. Most compilers use twice the amount of storage for doubles than for floats, which allows a double to have approximately twice the precision of a `float`. For this reason, a `float` value is sometimes referred to as a **single-precision** number and a `double` value as a **double-precision** number. The actual storage allocation for each data type, however, depends on the particular compiler. The ANSI C++ standard only requires that a `double` has at least the same amount of precision as a `float` and that a `long double` has at least the same amount of storage as a `double`. Currently, most C++ compilers allocate four bytes for the `float` data type and eight bytes for both `double` and `long double` data types. This produces the range of numbers listed in Table 2-5.

TABLE 2-5
Floating-Point Data Types

type	storage	absolute range of values (+ and -)
float	4 bytes	1.40129846432481707e-45 to 3.40282346638528860e+38
double and long double	8 bytes	4.94065645841246544e-324 to 1.79769313486231570e+308

In compilers that use the same amount of storage for `double` and `long double` numbers, these two data types become identical. (The `sizeof()` operator that was used in Program 2-1 can always be used to determine the amount of storage reserved by your compiler for these data types.) A `float` literal is indicated by appending either an f or F after the number and a `long double` is created by

---

PROGRAMMING NOTE

What Is Precision?

In numerical theory, the term **precision** typically refers to numerical accuracy. In this context, a statement such as "this computation is accurate, or precise, to the fifth decimal place" is used. This means that the fifth digit after the decimal point has been rounded, and the number is accurate to within ± .00005.

In computer programming, precision can refer either to the accuracy of a number or the amount of significant digits in the number, where significant digits are defined as the number of clearly correct digits plus 1. For example, if the number 12.6874 has been rounded to the fourth decimal place, it is correct to say that this number is precise (that is, accurate) to the fourth decimal place. In other words, all of the digits in the number are accurate except the fourth decimal digit, which has been rounded. Similarly, it can be said that this same number has a precision of six digits, which means that the first five digits are correct and the sixth digit has been rounded. Another way of saying this is that the number 12.6874 has six significant digits.

Notice that the significant digits in a number need not have any relation to the number of displayed digits. For example, if the number 687.45678921 has five significant digits, it is only accurate to the value 687.46, where the last digit is assumed to be rounded. In a similar manner, dollar values in many very large financial applications are frequently rounded to the nearest hundred-thousand dollars. In such applications, a displayed dollar value of $12,400,000, for example, is not accurate to the closest dollar. If this value is specified as having three significant digits, it is only accurate to the hundred-thousands digit.

---

appending either an l or L to the number. In the absence of these suffixes, a floating-point number defaults to a `double`. For example:

9.234 indicates a double literal

9.234f indicates a float literal

9.234L indicates a long double literal

The only difference in these numbers is the amount of storage the computer may use to store them. If you require numbers having more than six significant digits to the right of the decimal point, this storage becomes important, and you should use double-precision values. Appendix E describes the binary storage format used for floating point numbers and its impact on number precision.

Exponential Notation

Floating-point numbers can also be written in exponential notation, which is similar to scientific notation and is commonly used to express both very large and very small values in compact form. The following examples illustrate how numbers with decimals can be expressed in exponential and scientific notation.

decimal notation	exponential notation	scientific notation
1625.	1.625e3	1.625×10^3
63421.	6.3421e4	6.3421×10^4
.00731	7.31e-3	7.31×10^{-3}
.000625	6.25e-4	6.25×10^{-4}

In exponential notation, the letter e stands for exponent. The number following the e represents a power of 10 and indicates the number of places the decimal point should be moved to obtain the standard decimal value. The decimal point is moved to the right if the number after the e is positive or moved to the left if the number after the e is negative. For example, the e3 in 1.625e3 means move the decimal place three places to the right so that the number becomes 1625. The e−3 in 7.31e−3 means move the decimal point three places to the left so that 7.31e−3 becomes .00731.

Exercises 2.1

1. Determine data types appropriate for the following data:

    a. the average of four grades
    b. the number of days in a month
    c. the length of the Golden Gate Bridge
    d. the numbers in a state lottery
    e. the distance from Brooklyn, N.Y. to Newark, N.J.
    f. the single-character prefix that specifies a component type

2. Convert the following numbers into standard decimal form:

    6.34e5   1.95162e2   8.395e1   2.95e-3   4.623e-4

3. Write the following decimal numbers using exponential notation:

    126.   656.23   3426.95   4893.2   .321   .0123   .006789

4. Compile and execute Program 2-1 on your computer.

5. Modify Program 2-1 to determine the storage used by your compiler for all of C++'s integer data types.

6. Using the system reference manuals for your computer, determine the character code used by your computer.

7. Show how the name KINGSLEY would be stored inside a computer that uses the ASCII code. That is, draw a figure similar to Figure 2-3 for the name KINGSLEY.

8. Repeat Exercise 7 using the letters of your own last name.

9. Modify Program 2-1 to determine how many bytes your compiler assigns to the `float`, `double`, and `long double` data types.

2

10. Since computers use different representations for storing integer, floating point, double precision, and character values, discuss how a program might alert the computer to the data types of the various values it will be using.

11. Although we have concentrated on operations involving integer and floating-point numbers, C++ allows characters and integers to be added or subtracted. This can be done because a character is stored using an integer code (it is an integer data type). Thus, characters and integers can be freely mixed in arithmetic expressions. For example, if your computer uses the ASCII code, the expression 'a' + 1 equals 'b', and 'z' - 1 equals 'y'. Similarly, 'A' + 1 is 'B', and 'Z' - 1 is 'Y'. With this as background, determine the character results of the following expressions (assume that all characters are stored using the ASCII code).

   a. 'm' - 5
   b. 'm' + 5
   c. 'G' + 6
   d. 'G' - 6
   e. 'b' - 'a'
   f. 'g' - 'a' + 1
   g. 'G' - 'A' + 1

   Note: To complete the following exercise, you need an understanding of basic computer storage concepts. Specifically, if you are unfamiliar with the concept of a byte, refer to Section 1.6 before doing the next exercise.

12. Although the total number of bytes varies from computer to computer, memory sizes of 65,536 to more than several million bytes are not uncommon. In computer language, the letter K represents the number 1,024, which is 2 raised to the 10th power, and M represents the number 1,048,576, which is 2 raised to the 20th power. Thus, a memory size of 640 K is really 640 times 1024, or 655,360 bytes, and a memory size of 4 M is really 4 times 1,048,576, which is 4,194,304 bytes. Using this information, calculate the actual number of bytes in:

   a. a memory containing 8 M bytes
   b. a memory containing 16 M bytes
   c. a memory containing 32 M bytes
   d. a memory containing 96 M bytes
   e. a memory consisting of 8 M words, where each word consists of 2 bytes
   f. a memory consisting of 16 M words, where each word consists of 4 bytes
   g. a disk that specifies 1.44 M bytes

2.2 ARITHMETIC OPERATIONS

The last section presented the data values corresponding to each of C++'s built-in data types. In this section, the set of arithmetic operations that can be applied to these values is provided.

Integers and real numbers can be added, subtracted, multiplied, and divided. Although it is usually better not to mix integers and real numbers when performing arithmetic operations, predictable results are obtained when using different data types in the same arithmetic expression. Surprisingly, you can also add character data to, or subtract it from, both character and integer data to produce useful results (for example, 'A' + 1 results in the character 'B'). This is possible because characters are stored using integer storage codes.

The operators used for arithmetic operations are called **arithmetic operators**, and are as follows:

operation	operator
Addition	+
Subtraction	-
Multiplication	*
Division	/
Modulus Division	%

Don't be concerned at this stage if you don't understand the term "modulus division." You'll learn more about this operator later in this section.

These operators are referred to as **binary operators**. This term reflects the fact that the operator requires two operands to produce a result. An **operand** can be either a literal value or an identifier that has a value associated with it. A **simple binary arithmetic expression** consists of a binary arithmetic operator connecting two literal values in the form:

```
literalValue operator literalValue
```

Examples of simple binary arithmetic expressions are:

```
3 + 7
18 - 3
12.62 + 9.8
.08 * 12.2
12.6 / 2.
```

The spaces around the arithmetic operators in these examples are inserted strictly for clarity and can be omitted without affecting the value of the expression. Notice that an expression in C++ must be entered in a straight-line form. Thus, for example, the C++ expression equivalent to 12.6 divided by 2 must be entered as 12.6 / 2 and not as the algebraic expression

$$\frac{12.6}{2}$$

2

You can use `cout` to display the value of any arithmetic expression on the console screen. To do this, the desired value must be passed to the object. For example, the statement:

```
cout << (6 + 15);
```

yields the display 21. Strictly speaking, the parentheses surrounding the expression 6 + 15 are required to indicate that the value of the expression (that is, 21) is being displayed. In practice, most compilers will accept and correctly process this statement without the parentheses.

In addition to displaying a numerical value, `cout` can display a string identifying the output, as was done in Section 1.3. For example, the statement:

```
cout << "The sum of 6 and 15 is " <<   (6 + 15);
```

causes two pieces of data to be sent to `cout`, a string and a value. Individually, each set of data sent to `cout` must be preceded by its own insertion operator symbol (<<). Here, the first data sent for display is the string `"The sum of 6 and 15 is "`, and the second item sent is the value of the expression 6 + 15. The display produced by this statement is:

```
The sum of 6 and 15 is 21
```

Notice that the space between the word "is" and the number 21 is caused by the space placed within the string passed to `cout`. As far as `cout` is concerned, its input is simply a set of characters that are then sent on to be displayed in the order they are received. Characters from the input are queued, one behind the other, and sent to the console for display. Placing a space in the input causes this space to be part of the stream of characters that is ultimately displayed. For example, the statement:

```
cout << "The sum of 12.2 and 15.754 is " <<   (12.2 + 15.754);
```

yields the display

```
The sum of 12.2 and 15.754 is 27.954
```

Note that when multiple insertions are made to `cout` the code can be spread across multiple lines. Only one semicolon, however, must be used, which is placed after the last insertion and terminates the complete statement. Thus, the prior display is also produced by the statement:

```
cout << "The sum of 12.2 and 15.754 is "
     <<   (12.2 + 15.754);
```

However, when you allow such a statement to span multiple lines, a few rules must be followed: (1) a string contained within double quotes cannot be split across lines; and (2) the terminating semicolon should appear only on the last line. Multiple insertion symbols can always be placed within a line.

Floating point numbers are displayed with sufficient decimal places to the right of the decimal place to accommodate the fractional part of the number. This is true if the number has six or fewer digits. If the number has more than six digits, the fractional part is rounded and only six digits are displayed. If the number has no decimal digits, neither a decimal point nor any decimal digits are displayed.[3]

---

[3]It should be noted that none of this output is defined as part of the C++ language. Rather, it is defined by a set of classes and routines provided with each C++ compiler.

Program 2-2 illustrates using cout to display the results of arithmetic expressions within the statements of a complete program.

Program 2-2

```
#include <iostream>
using namespace std;

int main()
{
    cout << "15.0 plus 2.0 equals "        << (15.0 + 2.0) << endl
         << "15.0 minus 2.0 equals "       << (15.0 - 2.0) << endl
         << "15.0 times 2.0 equals "       << (15.0 * 2.0) << endl
         << "15.0 divided by 2.0 equals " << (15.0 / 2.0) << endl;

    return 0;
}
```

The output of Program 2-2 is:

```
15.0 plus 2.0 equals 17
15.0 minus 2.0 equals 13
15.0 times 2.0 equals 30
15.0 divided by 2.0 equals 7.5
```

The only really new item presented in Program 2-2 is the term endl, which is an example of a C++ manipulator. A **manipulator** is an item used to manipulate how the output stream of characters is displayed. In particular, the endl manipulator first causes a newline character ('\n') to be inserted into the display and then forces all of the current insertions to be displayed immediately, rather than waiting for more data. (Section 4.2 contains a list of the more commonly used manipulators.)

Expression Types

An **expression** is any combination of operators and operands that can be evaluated to yield a value. An expression that contains only integer values as operands is called an **integer expression**, and the result of the expression is an integer value. Similarly, an expression containing only floating point values (single and double precision) as operands is called a **floating point expression**, and the result of such an expression is a floating point value (the term **real expression** is also used). An expression containing both integer and floating point values is called a **mixed-mode expression**. Although it is usually better not to mix integer and floating point values in an arithmetic operation, the data type of each operation is determined by the following rules:

1.   If both operands are integers, the result of the operation is an integer.

2.   If one operand is a real value, the result of the operation is a double precision value.

2

> PROGRAMMING NOTE
>
> **The end1 manipulator**
>
> On most systems, the end1 manipulator, which is never enclosed in quotes, and the \n escape sequence, which must always be enclosed in quotes, are processed in the same way and produce the same effect. The one exception is on those systems where the output is accumulated internally until there are sufficient characters to make it advantageous to display them all, in one burst, on the screen. In such systems, which are referred to as "buffered," the end1 manipulator forces all accumulated output to be displayed immediately, without waiting for any additional characters to fill the buffer area before being printed. As a practical matter, you would not notice a difference in the final display. Thus, as a general rule, you should use the \n escape sequence whenever it can be included within an existing string, and use the end1 manipulator whenever a \n would appear by itself or to formally signify the end of a specific group of output display.

Notice that the result of an arithmetic expression is never a single precision (float) number. This is because during execution a C++ program temporarily converts all single-precision numbers to double-precision numbers when an arithmetic expression is being evaluated.

Integer Division

The division of two integer values can produce rather strange results for the unwary. For example, the expression 15/2 yields the integer result 7. Because integers cannot contain a fractional part, a value of 7.5 cannot be obtained. The fractional part obtained when two integers are divided, that is, the remainder is always dropped (truncated). Thus, the value of 9/4 is 2, and 18/3 is 5.

Often, however, we may need to retain the remainder of an integer division. To do this, C++ provides an arithmetic operator having the symbol %. This operator, called both the **modulus** and **remainder operator**, captures the remainder when an integer number is divided by an integer (using a noninteger value with the modulus operator results in a compiler error). For example,

```
 9 % 4 is 1    (that is, the remainder when 9 is divided by 4 is 1)
17 % 3 is 2    (that is, the remainder when 17 is divided by 3 is 2)
15 % 4 is 3    (that is, the remainder when 15 is divided by 4 is 3)
14 % 2 is 0    (that is, the remainder when 14 is divided by 2 is 0)
```

More precisely, the modulus operator first determines the integer number of times that the dividend, which is the number following the % operator, can be divided into the divisor, which is the number before the % operator. It then returns the remainder.

Negation

In addition to the binary arithmetic operators, C++ also provides unary operators. A **unary operator** is one that operates on a single operand. One of these unary operators uses the same symbol as binary subtraction (-). The minus sign in front of a single numerical value negates (reverses the sign of) the number.

Table 2-6 summarizes the six arithmetic operations we have described so far and lists the data type for the result produced by each operator, based on the data type of the operands involved.

TABLE 2-6
Summary of Arithmetic Operators

operation	operator	type	operand	result
Addition	+	Binary	Both are integers	Integer
			One operand is not an integer	Double-precision
Subtraction	−	Binary	Both are integers	Integer
			One operand is not an integer	Double-precision
Multiplication	*	Binary	Both are integers	Integer
			One operand is not an integer	Double-precision
Division	/	Binary	Both are integers	Integer
			One operand is not an integer	Double-precision
Modulus	%	Binary	Both are integers	Integer
			One operand is not an integer	Double-precision
Negation	−	Unary	Integer	Integer
			Double-precision	Double-precision

OPERATOR PRECEDENCE AND ASSOCIATIVITY

In addition to such simple expressions as 5 + 12 and .08 * 26.2, more complex arithmetic expressions can be created. C++, like most other programming languages, requires you to follow certain rules when writing expressions containing more than one arithmetic operator. These rules are:

1. Two binary arithmetic operator symbols must never be placed side by side. For example, 5 * % 6 is invalid because the two operators, * and %, are placed next to each other.

2

2. Parentheses may be used to form groupings, and all expressions enclosed within parentheses are evaluated first. This permits parentheses to alter the evaluation to any desired order. For example, in the expression (6 + 4) / (2 + 3), the 6 + 4 and 2 + 3 are evaluated first to yield 10 / 5. The 10 / 5 is then evaluated to yield 2.

3. Sets of parentheses may also be enclosed by other parentheses. For example, the expression (2 * (3 + 7)) / 5 is valid and evaluates to 4. When parentheses are included within parentheses, the expressions in the innermost parentheses are always evaluated first. The evaluation continues from innermost to outermost parentheses until the expressions in all parentheses have been evaluated. The number of closing parentheses,) , must always equal the number of opening parentheses, (, so that there are no unpaired sets.

4. Parentheses cannot be used to indicate multiplication; rather, the multiplication operator, *, must be used. For example, the expression (3 + 4) (5 + 1) is invalid. The correct expression is (3 + 4) * (5 + 1).

Parentheses should specify logical groupings of operands and indicate clearly, to both the compiler and programmers, the intended order of arithmetic operations. Although expressions within parentheses are always evaluated first, expressions containing multiple operators, both within and without parentheses, are evaluated by the priority, or **precedence**, of the operators. There are three levels of precedence:

> P1—All negations are done first.

> P2—Multiplication, division, and modulus operations are computed next. Expressions containing more than one multiplication, division, or modulus operator are evaluated from left to right as each operator is encountered. For example, in the expression 35 / 7 % 3 * 4, the operations are all of the same priority, so the operations will be performed from left to right as each operator is encountered. Thus, the division is done first, yielding the expression 5 % 3 * 4. The modulus operation is performed next, yielding a result of 2. And finally, the value of 2 * 4 is computed to yield 8.

> P3—Addition and subtraction are computed last. Expressions containing more than one addition or subtraction are evaluated from left to right as each operator is encountered.

In addition to precedence, operators have an **associativity**, which is the order in which operators of the same precedence are evaluated, as described in rule P2. For example, does the expression 6.0 * 6 / 4 yield 9.0, which is (6.0 * 6)/4, or 6, which is 6.0 * (6/4)? The answer is 9, because C++'s operators use the same associativity as in general mathematics, which evaluates multiplication from left to right, as rule P2 indicates. Table 2-7 lists both the precedence and associativity of the operators considered in this section. As we have seen, the precedence of an operator establishes its priority relative to all other operators. Operators at the top of Table 2-7 have a higher priority than operators at the bottom of the table. In expressions with multiple operators of different precedence, the operator with the higher precedence is used before an operator with lower precedence. For example, in the expression 6 + 4 / 2 + 3, since the division operator has a higher precedence (P2) than addition, the division is done first, yielding an intermediate result of 6 + 2 + 3. The additions are then performed, left to right, to yield a final result of 11.

TABLE 2-7
Operator Precedence and Associativity

operator	associativity
unary -	right to left
* / %	left to right
+ −	left to right

Finally, let us use either Table 2-7 or the precedence rules to evaluate an expression containing operators of different precedence, such as 8 + 5 * 7 % 2 * 4. Because the multiplication and modulus operators have a higher precedence than the addition operator, these two operations are evaluated first (P2), using their left-to-right associativity, before the addition is evaluated (P3). Thus, the complete expression is evaluated as:

```
8 + 5 * 7 % 2 * 4 =
  8 + 35 % 2 * 4   =
       8 + 1 * 4   =
            8 + 4  = 12
```

Exercises 2.2

1. Listed below are correct algebraic expressions and incorrect C++ expressions corresponding to them. Find the errors and write corrected C++ expressions.

algebra	**C++ expression**
a. (2)(3) + (4)(5)	(2)(3) + (4)(5)
b. $\dfrac{6 + 18}{2}$	6 + 18 / 2
c. $\dfrac{4.5}{12.2 - 3.1}$	4.5 / 12.2 − 3.1
d. 4.6(3.0 + 14.9)	4.6(3.0 + 14.9)
e. (12.1 + 18.9)(15.3 − 3.8)	(12.1 + 18.9)(15.3 − 3.8)

2. Determine the value of the following integer expressions:

    a. 3 + 4 * 6
    b. 3 ^ 4 / 6 + 6
    c. 2 * 3 / 12 * 8 / 4
    d. 10 * (1 + 7 * 3)
    e. 20 - 2 / 6 + 3
    f. 20 - 2 / (6 + 3)
    g. (20 - 2) / 6 + 3
    h. (20 - 2) / (6 + 3)
    i. 50 % 20
    j. (10 + 3) % 4

3. Determine the value of the following floating point expressions:

    a. 3.0 + 4.0 * 6.0
    b. 3.0 * 4.0 / 6.0 + 6.0

2

   c. 2.0 * 3.0 / 12.0 * 8.0 / 4.0

   d. 10.0 * (1.0 + 7.0 * 3.0)

   e. 20.0 - 2.0 / 6.0 + 3.0

   f. 20.0 - 2.0 / (6.0 + 3.0)

   g. (20.0 - 2.0) / 6.0 + 3.0

   h. (20.0 - 2.0) / (6.0 + 3.0)

4. Evaluate the following mixed-mode expressions and list the data type of the result. In evaluating the expressions, be aware of the data types of all intermediate calculations.

   a. 10.0 + 15 / 2 + 4.3

   b. 10.0 + 15.0 / 2 + 4.3

   c. 3.0 * 4 / 6 + 6

   d. 3 * 4.0 / 6 + 6

   e. 20.0 - 2 / 6 + 3

   f. 10 + 17 * 3 + 4

   g. 10 + 17 / 3. + 4

   h. 3.0 * 4 % 6 + 6

   i. 10 + 17 % 3 + 4

5. Assume that `amount` stores the integer value 1, `m` stores the integer value 50, `n` stores the integer value 10, and `p` stores the integer value 5. Evaluate the following expressions:

   a. `n / p + 3`

   b. `m / p + n - 10 * amount`

   c. `m - 3 * n + 4 * amount`

   d. `amount / 5`

   e. `18 / p`

   f. `-p * n`

   g. `-m / 20`

   h. `(m + n) / (p + amount)`

   i. `m + n / p + amount`

6. Repeat Exercise 5 assuming that `amount` stores the value 1.0, `m` stores the value 50.0, `n` stores the value 10.0, and `p` stores the value 5.0.

7. Enter, compile, and run Program 2-2 on your computer system.

8. Determine the output of the following program:

```
#include <iostream>
using namespace std;

int main()   // a program illustrating integer truncation
{
   cout << "answer1 is the integer " << 9/4;
   cout << "\nanswer2 is the integer " << 17/3;

   return 0;
}
```

9. Determine the output of the following program:

```
#include <iostream>
using namespace std;

int main()  // a program illustrating the % operator
{
   cout << "The remainder of 9 divided by 4 is " << 9 % 4;
   cout << "\nThe remainder of 17 divided by 3 is " << 17 % 3;
   return 0;
}
```

10. Write a C++ program that displays the results of the expressions 3.0 * 5.0, 7.1 * 8.3 - 2.2, and 3.2 / (6.1 * 5). Calculate the value of these expressions manually to verify that the displayed values are correct.

11. Write a C++ program that displays the results of the expressions 15 / 4, 15 % 4, and 5 * 3 - (6 * 4). Calculate the value of these expressions manually to verify that the displayed values are correct.

2.3 USING VARIABLES TO CONSTRUCT A DATA DECLARATION SECTION

All integer, floating-point, and other values in a computer program are stored and retrieved from the computer's memory unit. You can think of individual locations in the memory unit as rooms in a large hotel. Each memory location has a unique address, which is analogous to a hotel room number. Before high-level languages such as C++ existed, memory locations were referenced by their addresses. For example, suppose a program stores the integer values 45 and 12 in the memory locations 1652 and 2548 (as illustrated in Figure 2-4). This would require instructions equivalent to:

Put 45 in location 1652
Put 12 in location 2548

FIGURE 2-4
Enough Storage for Two Integers

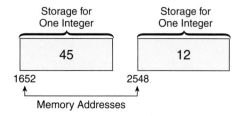

To add the two numbers stored in memory and save the result in another memory location (for example at location 3000) requires a statement comparable to:

Add the contents of location 1652 to the contents of location 2548
and store the result in location 3000

Clearly, having to spell out such detailed instructions for storage and retrieval would be cumbersome. For this reason, high-level languages such as C++ use symbolic names rather than actual memory addresses in code. For built-in data types, these symbolic names are called variables. Thus, a **variable** is a name given by the programmer that refers to computer storage locations used to store a built-in data type value. The term variable is used because the value stored in the variable can change, or vary. (As we will shortly see, one or more variables can be packaged together as an object.) The compiler keeps track of the actual memory address corresponding to the variable names specified by the programmer. Naming a variable is equivalent to putting a name on the door of a hotel room and referring to the room by this name, such as the "Blue Room," rather than by the actual room number.

In C++, you are free to choose your own variable names, as long as you follow the rules for identifiers provided in Section 1.3. In other words, the rules for selecting variable names are identical to those for selecting class and method names. These rules are repeated here for convenience:

1.   The first character of the name may only be a letter or underscore (_).
2.   Only letters, digits, or underscores may follow the initial character. Blank spaces are not allowed.

Typically there is a limit of 255 characters for a variable's name, but this is compiler dependent. As a practical matter, a variable name should always be descriptive and be limited to approximately no more than 20 characters (a more comprehensive set of naming rules is provided in this section's Programming Note). For example, a good name for a variable used to store the total of a group of grades would be `gradesSum` or `gradesTotal`. Variable names that give no indication of the value stored, such as `goForIt`, `linda`, `bill`, and `duh`, should never be selected. As with all identifiers, variable names are case sensitive.

Now assume that the first memory location illustrated in Figure 2-4, which has address 1652, is given the name `num1`. Also assume that memory location 2548 is given the variable name `num2`, and memory location 3000 is given the name `total`, as illustrated in Figure 2-5.

FIGURE 2-5
Naming Storage Locations

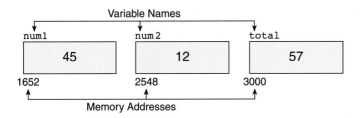

Using these variable names, the operation of storing 45 in location 1652, storing 12 in location 2548, and adding the contents of these two locations is accomplished by the C++ statements

```
num1 = 45;
num2 = 12;
total = num1 + num2;
```

Each of these three statements is called an **assignment statement** because it tells the computer to assign a value to (that is, store a value in) a variable. Assignment statements always include an equal sign, =, and one variable name immediately to the left of this sign. The value to the right of the equal sign is determined first, and this value is assigned to the variable to the left of the equal sign. The blank spaces in the assignment statements are included to make the code easier to read, but are not strictly necessary. We will have much more to say about assignment statements in Section 4.1, but for now we can use them to store values in variables.

A variable name is useful because it frees the programmer from concern over where data are physically stored inside the computer. We simply use the variable name and let the compiler worry about where in memory the data are actually stored. Before storing a value into a variable, however, C++ requires that we clearly declare the type of data to be stored in it. We must tell the compiler, in advance, the names of the variables that will be used for characters, the names that will be used for integers, and the names that will be used to store the other C++ data types.

DECLARATION STATEMENTS

Naming a variable and specifying the data type that can be stored in it is accomplished using a **declaration statement**. A declaration statement has the syntax:

> *dataType*   *variableName;*

where *dataType* designates a valid C++ data type and *variableName* is a user-selected variable name. Variables that will be used to store integer values are declared using the keyword `int` to specify the `int` data type and have the form:

> `int` *variableName;*

Thus, the declaration statement

```
int sum;
```

declares `sum` as the name of a variable capable of storing an integer value.

PROGRAMMING NOTE

Selecting Variable Names

1. Make your variable names descriptive so that you (or other program-mers) can immediately understand the purpose of each variable.
2. Limit variable names to approximately 20 characters. This prevents need-less typing and minimizes typing errors.
3. Start the variable name with a letter, rather than a numeral or other character. Underscores are frequently used as the first letter by compiler supplied variables so you *should not* use underscores as the first charac-ter in your variable names. This will avoid any potential name conflicts.
4. In a variable name consisting of several words, capitalize the first letter of each word after the first. Thus, the variable name *gradesSum* is preferable to *gradessum*.
5. Use variable names that indicate *what* the variable corresponds to, rather than *how* it is computed. Thus a variable name such as `area` is ac-ceptable, while a variable name such as *computeArea* is not.
6. Add qualifiers, such as `Avg`, `Min`, `Max`, and `Sum` to complete a vari-able's name where it is appropriate. Thus, a variable name such as `gradesAvg` is preferable to *average*, if the variable is used to store the average of a set of grades.
7. In Boolean variables, include the word *is*. For example, you could use the name `isHoliday` for a Boolean variable whose purpose is to store ei-ther a `true` or `false` value indicating whether a date is a holiday or not.
8. Use single letter variable names, such as `i`, `j`, and `k`, for loop indexes (as explained in Chapter 6).

Variables that hold single-precision, floating-point values are declared using the keyword `float`, whereas variables that hold double-precision values are declared using the keyword `double`. For ex-ample, the statement

```
float firstNumber;
```

declares `firstNumber` as a variable that will store a floating-point number. Similarly, the statement

```
double secondNumber;
```

declares that the variable `secondNumber` will store a double-precision number.

Just as integer and real variables must be declared before they can be used, a variable used to store a single character or a Boolean value must also be declared. Character variables are declared using the reserved word `char`. For example, the declaration

```
char ch;
```

declares `ch` to be a character variable. Similarly, Boolean variables are declared using the keyword `bool`.

Variables having the same data type can always be grouped together and declared using a single declaration statement. The common form of such a declaration is:

```
dataType variableList;
```

For example, the following three individual declaration statements

```
double grade1;
double grade2;
double average;
```

can be replaced by the single declaration statement

```
double grade1, grade2, average;
```

Similarly, the two Boolean declarations

```
bool isHoliday;
bool isWeekDay;
```

can be replaced with the single declaration statement

```
bool isHoliday,isWeekDay;
```

Notice that declaring multiple variables in a single declaration requires that the data type of the variables be given only once, that all the variables names be separated by commas, and that only one semicolon be used to terminate the declaration. The space after each comma is inserted for readability, and is not required.

INITIALIZATION

Declaration statements can also be used to store an initial value into declared variables. For example, the declaration statement

```
int numOne = 15;
```

both declares the variable numOne as an integer variable and provides a value of 15. This value, which is referred to as an **initial value**, will be stored in the variable when the variable is first created. When a declaration statement provides an initial value, the variable is said to be **initialized**. Thus, in this example, it is correct to say that the variable numOne will be initialized to 15 when it is created. Similarly, the declaration statements

```
double grade1 = 87.0;
double grade2 = 93.5;
double average;
```

declare three double-precision variables and provide initial values for two of them. Literals, expressions using only literals, such as 87.0 + 12 − 2, and expressions using literals and previously initialized variables can all be used as initializers within a declaration statement.

2

THE DATA DECLARATION SECTION

There are four classifications of variables: **instance**, **class**, **local**, and **global**. Although a bit confusing because one of these variable types is called a class variable, both class variables and instance variables are the types that are used to create a class's data declaration section. The difference is that a class variable is created once per class and then shared by all objects created from the class, while a separate instance variable is provided to each created object. For our immediate purposes, the only variable type that is of interest is the instance type, because it forms the basis for the vast majority of data declaration sections. For future reference purposes and completeness, Table 2-8 lists the factors that determine a variable's classification. One additional type, which acts like a variable but is formally referred to as a **parameter**, is also provided.

PROGRAMMING NOTE

Abstract Data Types (ADTs)

All of the data types that are provided as an integral part of the C++ compiler and defined by the ANSI/ISO specification are formally referred to as **built-in** or **primitive** data types (the two terms are synonyms). In contrast to built-in data types, object-oriented programming languages permit programmers to create their own data types. The general computer terminology for a user-defined data type is an **abstract data types** (**ADT**).

In C++ an abstract data type is referred to as a **class**, although the term **class data type** is actually more descriptive. The ability to create class data types, as opposed to being restricted to built-in data types, is the major enhancement provided to C by C++ (in fact, the original name for C++ was *C with Classes*).

TABLE 2-8
Determination of a Variable's Type

type	placement	comments
instance	Within a class's data declaration section.	This type of variable forms the majority of all data declaration sections. Every object that is created receives a variable of this type.
class	Within a class's data declaration section with the addition of the `static` keyword.	Each class variable is created only once per class and is shared between all objects.
local	Within a method or function.	Can only be used with code that is internal to the method or function.
global	Outside of a data declaration section, method, and function.	Can be used anywhere in the code. Rarely used.
parameter	Within the parentheses of a method or function header line. No access specification, such as private, is permitted.	Used to pass data into a method or function (See Section 3.1).

An instance variable is automatically created when a variable declaration statement is placed within a class's data declaration section. Recall that a basic class structure looks like this:

```
class className
{
  // data declaration section
  // methods declaration section
};

  // methods implementation section
```

Placing the declarations

```
double grade1;
double grade2;
double average;
```

into this class structure, and naming the class `ExampleOne`, results in the following:

```
class ExampleOne
{
  // data declaration section
  double grade1;
  double grade2;
  double average;

  // methods declaration section
};

// methods implementation section
```

By definition, due to their placement within a class structure, these declarations create variables that we have been referring to as instance variables. By default, all instance variables have what is known as **private access**. This means that these variables can only be used by methods that are also declared as part of the class. Attempting to use them in any other class or method will result in a compiler error. Even though private access is the default, the keyword `private` is almost always explicitly designated by C++ programmers. Thus, the general syntax for declaring instance variables, and the one that we shall use throughout the remainder of this text is:

```
private:
dataType variableName;
     .

     .

     .

  dataType variableName;
```

Using this general syntax, the previous three declaration statements would more typically be written as:

```
private:
   double grade1;
   double grade2;
   double total;
```

Once the keyword `private` is specified, it remains in force until it is changed. (Note the required colon after this keyword.) Also notice that each variable is declared on a line by itself. This is the general rule for declaring instance variables; multiple declarations are rarely, if ever, used for instance variables.

As a specific example of creating a data declaration section, assume that we are required to construct a program for calculating the floor area of a room, given its length and width. Assuming a rectangular floor, we can use its length and width to calculate the room's floor area. Providing for lengths and widths that can be floating-point values, a suitable set of declaration statements for a data declaration section is

```
private:
   double length;
   double width;
```

The individual declaration statements should look familiar to you. The keyword `private` explicitly designates that all subsequent variables will have a `private` access specification. This means, as has been noted, that the following variables, in this case `length` and `width`, can only be accessed using class methods (yet to be created), as well as friend methods (discussed in Section 7.2). Requiring all access to `private` variables to be made using only class methods enforces data security and restricts a user from "getting to" the data except in a manner determined by the class's creator. The variable names, `length` and `width`, are selected by the programmer. We have declared these variables to be `double`s, but clearly, if rooms having only integer-valued lengths and widths were being considered, the keyword `double` in these declarations would be changed to `int`.

You might be wondering why we did not include a declaration for the area. This is a matter of choice, and including a declaration such as

```
double area;
```

within the data declaration section is acceptable. This declaration was not included because the area is easily obtained by multiplying the length times the width; thus, whenever we need the area it can be calculated without providing a specific storage area for it.

To complete our class construction, we will name our class `RoomType`. At this stage the code for this class becomes

```
class RoomType
{
  // data declaration section
  private:
    double length;   // declare length as a double variable
    double width;    // declare width as a double variable
```

(continued on next page)

```
  //methods declaration section
};

// methods implementation section
```

Both `length` and `width` are instance variables because of their placement within the class's data declaration section.

Even though our `RoomType` class contains no methods, it is a complete class from which objects can be created. How these objects are created is presented after the next example.

As a second example of constructing a data declaration section, assume that we need to write a program to calculate the average of two integer numbers. Suitable declaration statements for this problem are

```
    private:
        int firstNumber;
        int secondNumber;
```

Here, the choice of the variable names `firstNumber` and `secondNumber` are selected by the programmer. The keyword `private` is included as noted previously and the keyword `int` is determined by the type of value that will be stored in each variable. Although the average can always be calculated as the total of the two numbers divided by 2, a specific declaration statement for the average can also be included. In this case, however, since the average of two integers can be a floating-point value, the average should be declared as a `double`. Naming our class `TwoNumbers` and including a declaration for the average, the class becomes

```
    class TwoNumbers
    {
      // data declaration section
      private:
        int firstNumber;    // this is an instance variable
        int secondNumber;   // this is an instance variable
        double average;     // this is an instance variable

      // methods declaration section
    };
    // methods implementation section
```

Creating Objects

Objects can only be created from the instance variables declared in a data declaration section. Essentially, each object becomes a packet of data, consisting of the values that get assigned to the instance variables defined for each object. For this to happen, each object receives its own copy of the declared instance variables. The creation of individual objects, the assignment of values to each individual object, and the manipulation of these values is accomplished by a class's methods. Thus, it is the job of

2

the methods that are declared in the class's methods declaration section and coded in a methods implementation section to do one of the following:

1. provide an operation that initializes an object's instance variables
2. provide operations that can be applied to objects after they have been created, or
3. provide general purpose functions that can be used independently of any one object.

Because the mechanics of creating an object are the same for all classes, we can now see how objects are created using the instance variable declared in our RoomType class.

Consider Program 2-3, which creates a single RoomType class object.

Program 2-3

```
class RoomType
{
  // data declaration section
  private:
    double length;   // declare length as a double variable
    double width;    // declare width as a double variable

  //methods declaration section
};

int main()
{
  RoomType roomOne;

  return 0;
}
```

In reviewing Program 2-3, first notice that main() is not a class method because it has not been declared within the class's declaration section. Thus, although main() follows the class declaration, it is not part of the class's implementation section.

Program 2-3 produces no output, a defect that will be remedied shortly in the next section when we add methods to our RoomType class. The program does, however, create a single object named roomOne. Let's see how this object is created.

Program 2-3's main() method consists of these two statements:

```
RoomType roomOne;
return 0;
```

The first statement in this method

```
RoomType roomOne;
```

is a declaration statement that declares a variable named `roomOne` to be of type `RoomType`. The format of this declaration statement is identical to that used for instance variables. Taking the items in reverse order and starting from the semicolon, the name of our variable is `roomOne`, which is a pro-grammer-selected identifier. The data type for this variable is `RoomType`, which is the name of the class from which we want to create an object (for convenience, this class is shown in Figure 2-6). Al-though we have called `roomOne` a variable for convenience, because it is declared for a class type rather than a built-in data type, it is more formally correct to refer to it as an object. Thus, an object can initially be considered as having the same relationship to a class as a variable does to a built-in type; it is a place that will be used to store values. In this case, the object named `roomOne` will be used to store two values; as such it can be considered as a single package containing two data values.

FIGURE 2-6
The `RoomType` *Class*

```
class RoomType
{
  // data declaration section
  private:
    double length;  // declare length as a double variable
    double width;   // declare width as a double variable
  // methods declaration section
};
// methods implementation section
```

It is important to notice that the `private` keyword must never be used within a method. This is not because we are declaring an object. Rather, it is because of the placement of the declaration statement within a method. Variables and objects declared by statements placed within a method are formally re-ferred to as **local variables** and objects (Review Table 2-8). Such variables and objects are private by def-inition, which means that they can only be used within the method that declares them. (Where a vari-able or object can be used is referred to as its *scope*, a subject that is presented in detail in Section 3.5.) Because of this, no explicit private designation within a method is either required or permitted.

The results produced by `main()`'s declaration statement is illustrated in Figure 2-7. As shown, a mem-ory storage area has been reserved for an object that is referred to as `roomOne`. Additionally, as shown in the figure, the identifier `roomOne` contains the address of where this object is located in memory. The object itself contains two variables, `length` and `width`, which are initialized with the values 0.0.

Formally, the process of creating a new object illustrated in Figure 2-7 is referred to as both **creating an instance** and **instantiating an object**. Now you can also see why the variables `length` and `width` are known as instance variables; an instance of them only comes into existence when an object is created, and each created object will contain one instance of each instance variable.

FIGURE 2-7
The Effect Produced by the Declaration Statement `RoomType roomOne;`

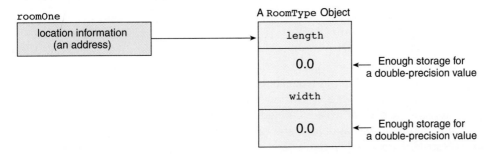

It is important to understand that the `roomOne` variable has a different use than variables declared for built-in data types, such as `length` and `width`. The `roomOne` variable, which is declared for an object type, contains a memory address; which is the address of an object. It is this stored address that is used to locate the object.

Each object created from a class always receives its own set of instance variables. For example, in Figure 2-8 each of the two objects, `roomOne` and `roomTwo`, contains its own set of the variables `length` and `width`. You might be wondering how we will distinguish between the various `length` and `width` variables shown in Figure 2-8. Effectively, this is handled by always providing an object's name. Thus, as you might expect, an object's name will have to be supplied to all methods when they are used to access an object.

FIGURE 2-8
Each Object Receives Its Own Set of Instance Variables

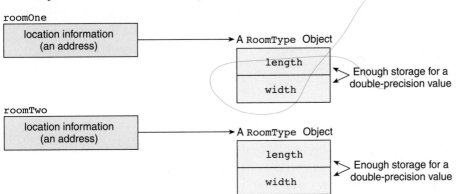

As you review Figure 2-8, note that instance variables only come into existence when an object is actually created. Whenever a built-in data type variable (`int`, `double`, `float`, `char`, or `bool`) is created, a value can be stored directly in the variable. In the absence of an explicitly assigned initial value, the default initial value stored in all numerical data types in C++ is 0. Notice that this value has been initially placed into the object's `length` and `width` variables shown in Figure 2-7.

PROGRAMMING NOTE

Variables and Objects

The relationship of an object to a class is almost identical to the relationship of a variable to a built-in type. For example, values are stored in variables, which are defined for a specific built-in data type, while values are also stored in objects, which are defined for a specific class. Similarly, variables are identifiers, just as objects are. Finally, the same terminology is used in describing how both variables and objects store values. However, although a C++ programmer will say that "this variable contains this value," and "this object contains these values," experienced C++ programmers understand that this last phrase is not strictly accurate.

    The reason for this is that, although values are stored directly into a variable, this not true for an identifier declared as an object name. Rather, an object's declared name always stores the location of where the object itself is to be found (refer to Figures 2-7 and 2-8).

Declaring instance variables as `private` imposes the restriction that once an object containing these variables is created, the variables can only be accessed by methods defined in the class. Thus, to either retrieve or modify the `length` and `width` variables in the objects shown in Figures 2-7 and 2-8, we will need to provide a set of class methods. Rather than being a hindrance, this privacy restriction is a key safety feature provided by object-oriented languages. Specifically it enforces data security by precisely requiring all access to data members using known class methods, which ensures reproducible and predicable results. This assures every programmer using the class of the variable's integrity, and removes any concern that another programmer has inadvertently altered a value in some undocumented manner. Should a programmer need to add additional methods, this is easily be done by extending the class (as explained in Section 12.1).

Memory Allocation

The declaration statements introduced in this section perform a number of distinct tasks. From a programmer's perspective, declaration statements provide a convenient list of variables and their data types. The compiler uses the list to check and control an otherwise common and troublesome error caused by the misspelling of a variable's name within a program. For example, assume that two local variables named `distance` and `gallons` are declared and initialized in a method using the statements

```
double distance = 260.5;
double gallons = 11.2
```

Now assume that the first variable is inadvertently misspelled in the statement

```
mpg = distnce / gallons;
```

In languages that do not require variable declarations, the program would treat `distnce` as a valid variable and either assign an initial value of zero to this variable or use whatever value happens to be in the variable's storage area. In either case, a value would be calculated and assigned to `mpg`, and finding the error or even knowing that an error occurred could be extremely troublesome. Such errors are impossible in C++ because the compiler flags `distnce` as an undeclared variable. The compiler cannot, of course, detect when one declared variable is typed in place of another declared variable.

In addition to these roles, declaration statements also perform a distinct role needed by the C++ compiler. Since each data type has its own storage requirements, the compiler can allocate sufficient storage for a variable only after knowing the variable's data type. Variable declarations provide this information.

In both of these roles, instance and local declarations perform in the same manner and inform the compiler about the required storage. Local variable declarations, however, serve one additional purpose. When the C++ compiler encounters a local declaration, it automatically creates the variable or object being declared. Statements that cause variables to be created are referred to as **definition statements**. Because local variables come into existence when the compiler encounters and executes them, local variable declaration statements are also definition statements.

Figure 2-9 illustrates the series of operations set in motion by local declaration statements. As the figure indicates, these declaration statements also perform a definition role. As shown, definition statements (or, if you prefer, declaration statements that also cause memory to be allocated) "tag" the first byte of each set of reserved bytes with a name. This name is, of course, the variable's name and is used by the computer to correctly locate the starting point of each variable's reserved memory area.

FIGURE 2-9A
Defining the Integer Variable Named `total`

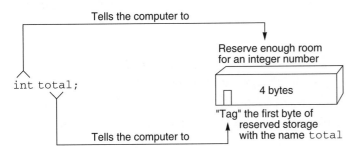

FIGURE 2-9B
Defining the Floating-Point Variable Named `firstnum`

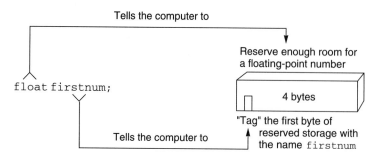

FIGURE 2-9C
Defining the Double-Precision Variable Named `secnum2`

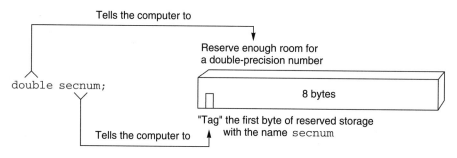

FIGURE 2-9D
Defining the Character Variable Named `ch`

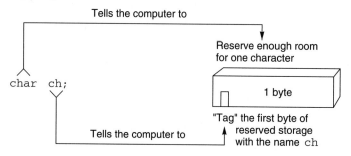

Within a method, after a variable has been declared, it is typically used by a programmer to refer to the contents of the variable (that is, the variable's value). Where in memory this value is stored is generally of little concern to the programmer. The compiler, however, must be concerned with where each value is stored and with correctly locating each variable. In this task, the computer uses the variable name to locate the first byte of storage previously allocated to the variable. Knowing the variable's data type then allows the compiler to store or retrieve the correct number of bytes.

This is not the case for the declaration of instance variables. As we have seen, storage for instance variables is only created when an object containing them comes into existence. Thus, instance variable declarations are not definition statements because they do not cause any new storage to be allocated at the time they are declared.

Exercises 2.3

1. State whether the following variable names are valid or invalid. If they are invalid, state the reason.

proda	c1234	abcd	_c3	12345
newbal	while	$total	new bal	a1b2c3d4
9ab6	sum.of	average	grade1	finGrad

2. State whether the following variable names are valid or invalid. If they are invalid, state the reason. Also indicate which of the valid variable names should not be used because they convey no information about the variable.

salestax	a243	r2d2	firstNum	cca1
harry	sue	c3p0	average	sum
maximum	okay	a	awesome	goforit
3sum	for	tot.a1	c$five	netpay

3. a. Write a declaration statement to declare that `count` will be an instance variable used to store an integer value.
    b. Write a declaration statement to declare that `grade` will be an instance variable used to store a single-precision number.
    c. Write a declaration statement to declare that `yield` will be an instance variable used to store a double-precision number.
    d. Write a declaration statement to declare that `initial` will be an instance variable used to store a character.

4. Write declaration statements for the following instance variables, assuming each set of variables is to be included in an individual data declaration section.
    a. `num1`, `num2`, and `num3` used to store integer numbers
    b. `grade1`, `grade2`, `grade3`, and `grade4` used to store single-precision numbers
    c. `tempa`, `tempb`, and `tempc` used to store double-precision numbers
    d. `ch`, `let1`, `let2`, `let3`, and `let4` used to store character types

5. Write declaration statements for the following instance variables, assuming each set of variables is to be included in an individual data declaration section.
    a. `firstNumber` and `secondNumber` used to store integers
    b. `price`, `yield`, and `coupon` used to store single-precision numbers
    c. `maturity` used to store a double-precision number

6. Create a class structure for a class named `Time`. The data declaration section should have instance variables for data consisting of an integer hour, integer minute, and integer second.

7. Create a class structure for a class named `Date`. The data declaration section should have instance variables for data consisting of an integer month, integer day, and integer year.

8. Create a class structure for a class named LongDate. The data declaration section should have an instance variable for data consisting of a long integer. For example, assume that a date is stored in the form YearMonthDay, so that a date such as 12/15/04 would be stored as 20041512. What might be the advantage of storing dates in this form?

9. Compile and execute Program 2-3.

10. Modify Program 2-3 to create an additional object named roomTwo.

11. Create a program that declares and creates two objects named firstPair and secondPair from the TwoNumbers class presented in this section.

2.4 COMPLETING THE CLASS: METHODS

Consider the RoomType class that was developed in the last section and is reproduced in Figure 2-10:

FIGURE 2-10
The RoomType *Class*

```
class RoomType
{
    // data declaration section
    private:
      double length;   // declare length as a double variable
      double width;    // declare width as a double variable

    // methods declaration section
}


// methods implementation section
```

In this section we complete the RoomType class by providing it with a methods declaration and methods implementation section. A programmer always supplies the C++ code for all class methods, the vast majority of which are placed in the implementation section; however, very short methods, consisting of one or two lines, are frequently placed directly in the methods declaration section.

When a method is coded it is said to be **defined**. Then, for each method defined in the implementation section, one and only one method declaration statement must be supplied in the methods declaration section. (For those few methods that are coded directly in the methods declaration section, a separate declaration *must not* be used.) Thus, the primary purpose of the methods declaration section is to provide a complete list of the names and types of methods that are part of the class, while the implementation section provides the actual code. Only secondarily should the declaration section contain the actual code for any methods.

This ordering, however, is arbitrary; a method may be coded first and then declared; or declared first and then coded. All C++ requires is that each class method coded in the implementations section has a corresponding declaration statement; otherwise the class will not compile.

PROGRAMMING NOTE

Defining a Method

Formally, a method is said to be defined when it is coded. One hard and fast rule in defining a method is that a method cannot be coded within another method. *Each method must be defined by itself outside of any other method.* As such, a C++ method is a separate and independent entity and nesting of methods is never permitted.

Once it has been defined (that is, coded) a method must be declared. A method declaration statement is formally known as a method prototype. Although in the vast majority of cases a class method is defined outside of and then declared within a declaration section, it can also be defined at its point of declaration.

THE IMPLEMENTATION SECTION

At a minimum, a class will typically provide three basic methods: one to initialize an object's instance variables when the object is created, one to display its values, and one to modify them. Such methods are referred to as **constructor methods**, **accessor methods**, and **mutator methods**, respectively. Other methods are then included as needed to provide additional operations appropriate to the class. The three basic types of methods are summarized in Table 2-9.

TABLE 2-9
Basic Class Method Types

type of method	purpose
Constructor	A method used to initialize an object's instance variables when the object is created.
Accessor	A method that reports one or more of the values stored in an object's variables.
Mutator	A method that modifies one or more of the values stored in an object's variables.

Each class method provided in a methods implementation section consists of two parts, a method header and a method body (Figure 2-11). The purpose of the method's header is to specify the data type of a value that can be directly returned by the method, provide the method with a name, and specify the number, order, and type of data that can be sent into the method. The purpose of the method's body is to access an object's variables, use any additional data sent into the method, operate on an object's variables, and directly return, at most, one value.

FIGURE 2-11
General Format of a C++ Method

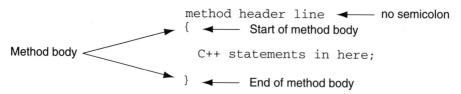

The general syntax for a member method's header line is shown in Figure 2-12. Except for constructors, which must not include a return type, this syntax is used for all other class methods. As shown, the header line contains a return type, a class name, a double set of colons, : :, a method name, and a set of parentheses that encloses a parameter list.

FIGURE 2-12
The Format of a Method Header

```
returnType className::methodName(parameterList)
```

Required parentheses

This header line should look familiar because it is almost identical to the one that we have been using for our `main()` methods. Here the *returnType* designates the data type of a value that can be returned by the method for further processing. When no value is returned, the keyword `void` must be used. (In the absence of an explicit return type, all C++ compilers assume that an integer is returned.) The *className* must be the same name as the class in which this method will be declared, and must be separated by two colons, : :, which are referred to as the **scope resolution operator**, from the method name. It is the class's name that ties the method back to a specific class. The *methodName* can be any valid identifier. Good programming practice requires that a method's name should provide some indication as to what the method does, such as `calculateSalesTax` or `setRoomWidth`. Finally, the *parameterList* provides information about data that will be sent to the method when it is used. The complete range of return types and parameter declarations is presented in Chapter 3.

All of the methods constructed in this section will return no data (`void` type) and expect no parameters. For such methods, the simplified header line syntax becomes

```
void className::methodName()
```

2

Because every class method can always gain access to an object's instance variables, very useful methods can be written using this simplified header-line syntax. A constructor method, because it performs a very specific task, is *never permitted* to designate any return type.

Constructor Methods

A **constructor** method is any method that has the same name as its class. A class can have no user-coded constructor, a single user-coded constructor, or more than one user-coded constructor, as long as each constructor has a unique parameter list.

A constructor method is automatically used each time an object is created. The purpose of the constructor is to initialize each new object's instance variables to a known set of values. If no constructor method is coded and no initial values are provided in the instance variable's declaration statement, the compiler supplies a default constructor that initializes each instance variable with the values listed in Table 2-10.

TABLE 2-10
Default Initial Values for Instance Variables

data type	default value at creation
short	0s
int	0
long	0L
float	0.0f
double	0.0d
char	NULL character, which is 00000000
boolean	false

In addition to its primary role of initializing all instance variables, a constructor can also perform other tasks, such as displaying a message, as we will see later in this section. Figure 2-13 illustrates the most commonly used format for a constructor.

FIGURE 2-13
Constructor Format

```
className::className(parameterList)
{
  C++ statements
}
```

As shown in Figure 2-13, a constructor:

1. must have the same name as the class to which it belongs.
2. must have no return type (not even `void`).

For example, consider the following constructor method for the `RoomType` class (see Figure 2-10):

```
RoomType::RoomType()
{
   length = 25.0;
   width = 12.0;
}
```

This constructor will initialize each `RoomType` object's `length` and `width` variables to 25.0 and 12.0, respectively, when an object of this class type is created.

If no constructor is coded, the compiler automatically provides a default constructor that initializes an object's instance variables using the values specified in Table 2-10. For the `RoomType` class, this default constructor is equivalent to the following:

```
RoomType::RoomType()
{
   length = 0.0;
   width = 0.0;
}
```

Although the compiler-provided default constructor may or may not be useful in a particular application, it does provide a known value for each object's data members when no other constructor is coded, and is referred to as a default constructor. More inclusively, the term **default constructor** refers to any constructor that does not require any parameters when an object is created. For example, the constructor that sets the `length` and `width` variables to 25.0 and 12.0, respectively, is also a default constructor. It is just a user-written default constructor as opposed to a compiler-supplied one. Providing a user-written default constructor permits initializing an object with programmer-selected values other than the default values listed in Table 2-10. If a user-written default constructor is supplied, the compiler will not create its own.

For our immediate purposes, and to verify that a constructor method is automatically used whenever a new object is created, we will use the following constructor:

```
RoomType::RoomType()
{
   length = 25.0;
   width = 12.0;

   cout << "Created a new room object using the default constructor.\n";
}
```

When an object is now created, in addition to the initialization of its `length` and `width` data members, the following output will also be produced:

```
Created a new room object using the default constructor.
```

PROGRAMMING NOTE

Constructors

A **constructor** is any method that has the same name as its class. A constructor is automatically called whenever an object is created and initializes its instance variables.

A compiler error results when unique identification of a constructor is not possible. If no constructor is provided, the compiler supplies a default constructor that initializes all numerical data members to 0 and all character data members to `Nulls`. Instance variables that are declared with an initial value are not affected by the compiler-provided default constructor.

Every constructor method must be declared *with no return type* (not even `void`). Even though they are methods, constructors can only be used in a statement creating an object. Additionally, a class can have multiple constructors provided that each constructor is distinguishable by having a different parameter list.

Although any legitimate C++ statement can be used within a constructor method, such as the `cout` statement used here, it is best to keep constructors simple and use them for initialization purposes only.

Accessor Methods

The purpose of an accessor method is to provide a means for reading the values stored in an object's instance variables. A true accessor method, which is also referred to as a **get()** method, will return the value stored in one instance variable. Thus, an object containing multiple instance variables would require multiple accessor methods, consisting of one `get()` method for each variable. As a practical matter, a method that either returns a combined value or simply displays one or more values is also referred to as an accessor method.

For example, if we were using a `Date` class that used `month`, `day`, and `year` instance variables, an accessor might convert the three values into a string, such as `12/25/07` and return this string value. True accessor methods would return individual `year`, `month`, and `day` values, respectively. Of course, each accessor method would have to be given a different name, such as `displayDate()`, `getYear()`, `getMonth()`, and `getDay()`.

Accessor Methods

An **accessor method**, more commonly referred to as an accessor for short, is a class method that accesses a class's private data members for the purpose of returning individual values. Such methods are also known as `get()` methods. Methods that display an object's values are also referred to as accessors, although, strictly speaking they are just display methods. Using this looser definition, the method `showRoomValues()` in the `RoomType` class is an accessor method. True accessors (that is, methods conventionally named using the word `get`, which directly return a value that can be used in a computation, for example) and methods that perform display functions are extremely important because they provide a means of retrieving and displaying an object's private data values.

When you construct a class, make sure to provide a complete set of accessor methods. Each accessor method does not have to return a data member's exact value, but it should return a useful representation of that value. For example, assume that we have created a `Date` class where a date, such as 12/25/2007, is stored as an integer in the form 20072512. Although an accessor method could display this value, a more useful representation would typically be either 12/25/07 or December 25, 2007.

Because we have not yet presented how methods can return values, we will construct a simple accessor method for our `RoomType` class that displays the values stored in an object's instance variables. Naming our accessor method `showRoomValues()`, a suitable method is:

```
void RoomType::showRoomValues()    // this is an accessor
{
  cout << "  length = " << length
       << "\n  width = " << width << endl;
}
```

Mutator Methods

The purpose of a mutator method is to provide a means for changing one or more of an object's values after the object has been created. This generally means that the user can enter new values and that these values will be passed to the object using a mutator method. Mutator methods are also known as **set()** methods.

Because we do not yet know how to pass data into a method, we will supply the `RoomType` class with a simple mutator that assigns a `RoomType` object's `length` and `width` variables with fixed values. In the next chapter we will expand this method to permit the values to be passed into the mutator.

2

Naming our mutator method setNewRoomValues(), a suitable method definition is:

```cpp
void RoomType::setNewRoomValues()    // this is a mutator
{
  length = 12.5;
  width = 9.0;
}
```

Including these constructor, accessor, and mutator methods in the RoomType class, and highlighting these additions for easier identification, yields the following, almost complete, class definition:

```cpp
#include <iostream>
using namespace std;

class RoomType
{
  // data declaration section
  private:
    double length;  // declare length as a double variable
    double width;   // declare width as a double variable

  // methods declaration section

};
```

```cpp
// methods implementation section
RoomType::RoomType()  // this is a constructor
{
  length = 25.0;
  width = 12.0;
  cout << "Created a new room object using the default constructor.\n\n";
}

void RoomType::showRoomValues()   // this is an accessor
{
  cout << "  length = " << length
       << "\n  width = " << width << endl;
}

void RoomType::setNewRoomValues()   // this is a mutator
{
  length = 12.5;
  width = 9.0;
}
```

At a minimum, and except for special situations, all classes should be provided with constructor, accessor, and mutator methods. In object-oriented terminology these methods provide a minimum set of services that objects require.

PROGRAMMING NOTE

Mutator Methods

A **mutator method**, which is more commonly referred to as a mutator, for short, is any nonconstructor class method that changes an object's data values. Mutator methods are used to alter an object's data values after the object has been created and automatically initialized by a constructor method. A class can contain multiple mutators, as long as each mutator has a unique name or parameter list. For example, in our `RoomType` class there could be a mutator for changing an object's length value, a mutator for changing an object's width value, and a third mutator that changes both values.

Constructors, whose primary purpose is to initialize an object's member variables when an object is created, are not considered to be mutator methods.

An Additional Method

In addition to constructor, accessor, and mutator methods, classes must usually provide an expanded set of methods that use an object's values in appropriate ways. For example, the purpose of the `RoomType` class is to provide a means of calculating a house's total floor area in a room-by-room manner. So before objects are created from this class, a method capable of calculating and displaying a room object's area should be implemented. The area is obtained by multiplying its length times its width, and can be displayed using `cout`. The following method accomplishes this:

```
void RoomType::calculateRoomArea()    // this performs a calculation
{
   cout << length * width;
}
```

Including the `calculateRoomArea()` method in our `RoomType` class provides a complete set of methods for calculating and displaying the floor area of a room with a rectangular floor. The completed implementation section is:

```
// methods implementation section
RoomType::RoomType()   // this is a constructor
{
   length = 25.0;
   width = 12.0;
   cout << "Created a new room object using the default constructor.\n\n";
}
```

(continued on next page)

2

```
RoomType::showRoomValues()    // this is an accessor
{
  cout << "  length = " << length
       << "\n  width = " << width << endl;
}

RoomType::setNewRoomValues()    // this is a mutator
{
  length = 12.5;
  width = 9.0;
}

RoomType::calculateRoomArea()   // this performs a calculation
{
  cout << length * width;
}
```

COMPLETING THE CLASS WITH METHOD DECLARATION STATEMENTS

Just as instance variables are declared within a class's data declaration section, all class methods must also be declared within the declaration section. The purpose of these declarations is to tell the compiler which methods are part of the class, specify access privileges for each method, and alert the compiler to the name of each method, its return data type, and the types of data that the method should accept. These latter three items are checked by the compiler for each implemented method, and if a method is missing or does not match its declaration, a compiler error is generated.

The only exception to this syntax relates to constructor methods, which *must have* the same name as their class and *must be* declared with no return data type. A method's declaration, along with supporting comments, should provide a programmer with all the information needed to successfully use the method, without the need of knowing the internal details of how the method is actually implemented.

A method declaration statement is a single line having this general syntax:

```
    returnType methodName(list of parameter data types);
```

PROGRAMMING NOTE

Method Definitions and Declarations

A **method definition** defines a method. Thus, when you write a method, a process referred to as implementing the method, you are really writing a method definition. All methods associated with a class are typically defined outside of a class's declaration sections. Each method definition begins with a method header line and ends with the closing brace that terminates the method's body. The parentheses are always required in the header line. The syntax for a class's method definition is:

```
returnType className::methodName(parameter list)
{
  C++ statements

  return value;
}
```

In addition to being defined, all class methods must be declared within the class's methods declaration section. This is accomplished using a **method declaration** statement, which is formally referred to as a **method prototype**. The syntax for this statement, which provides the return data type of the method, the method's name, and the method's parameter list (if any) is:

```
returnType methodName(list of parameter data types);
```

In this section, where all of the implemented methods return no data (`void` type) and expect no parameters, the simplified syntax that is used for all method declarations, except the constructor method, is:

```
void methodName();
```

As noted earlier, a constructor method, because it performs a very specific task, is *never permitted* to designate a return type. For the four previously defined methods named `RoomType()`, showRoomValues(), setNewRoomValues(), and calculateRoomArea(), correct method declarations statements are:

```
RoomType();  // the constructor's declaration statement
void showRoomValues();
void setNewRoomValues();
void calculateRoomArea();
```

Notice that these declarations provide the same return type as defined in the method's header line and the same data types (in this case, none) for the parameters. The compiler will verify that these items match, with an error occurring if they do not.

If these method declarations, or more formally, method prototypes, were listed immediately after the class's instance variable declarations, the private specification declared for the variables would remain in effect. As all of a class's methods are generally written to be used from outside of a class, a public specification is almost universally placed in front of these prototypes. (The last remaining designation is protected, which is presented in Chapter 12.) Doing this makes all subsequently declared methods public. Thus, for the RoomType class, a suitable methods declaration section is:

```
public:
  RoomType();  // the constructor's declaration statement
  void showRoomValues();
  void setNewRoomValues();
  void calculateRoomArea();
```

Including this declarations section in the RoomType class provides a completed class for calculating and displaying the floor area of a room that is modeled as having a rectangular-shaped floor. The completed class, which can now be compiled and used by any other class or program that we choose to write, becomes

```
#include <iostream>
using namespace std;

class RoomType
{
  // data declaration section
  private:
    double length;  // declare length as a double variable
    double width;   // declare width as a double variable
  // methods declaration section
  public:
    RoomType(); // the constructor's declaration statement
    void showRoomValues();
    void setNewRoomValues();
    void calculateRoomArea();
};
```

(continued on next page)

```cpp
// methods implementation section
RoomType::RoomType()   // this is a constructor
{
  length = 25.0;
  width = 12.0;
  cout << "Created a new room object using the default constructor.\n\n";
}

void RoomType::showRoomValues()    // this is an accessor
{
  cout << "  length = " << length
       << "\n  width = " << width << endl;
}

void RoomType::setNewRoomValues()    // this is a mutator
{
  length = 12.5;
  width = 9.0;
}

void RoomType::calculateRoomArea()   // this performs a calculation
{
  cout << length * width;
}
```

USING THE RoomType CLASS

As has been previously stated, a class by itself is not a program; it is simply a programmer-created data type. As such, it specifies a set of values in its data declarations section and a set of operations in its methods declaration section, which must then be coded. In the same manner that built-in data types are restricted to using the operations defined for them, objects created from private instance variables can only be operated on by a class's methods. To make these methods readily available to any programmer who wants to use them, they have been declared as public.

Every program (recall that a program must have a main() function), or subsequent class that makes use of another class, is restricted to using a class's public methods. Because the RoomType class's two instance variables, length and width, have been declared as private (even though a set of these variables are automatically included in each created object), they can only be retrieved or modified using the publicly available methods. Let's see how this is accomplished in practice. Consider Program 2-4, which for convenience includes the RoomType class (in lighter shading) and contains a main() method (in darker shading) that creates an object of RoomType and displays the object's internal values.[4]

---

[4]The shading used in Program 2-4 is not accidental. In practice the lighter shaded region containing the class definition would be placed in a separate file. A single #include statement would then be used to include this class definition in the program. Thus, the final program would consist of the darker shaded region consisting of a main() method with the addition of one more #include statement placed before main()'s header line.

Program 2-4

```cpp
#include <iostream>
using namespace std;

class RoomType
{
  // data declaration section
  private:
    double length;   // declare length as a double variable
    double width;    // declare width as a double variable

  // methods declaration section
  public:
    RoomType(); // the constructor's declaration statement
    void showRoomValues();
    void setNewRoomValues();
    void calculateRoomArea();
};

// methods implementation section
RoomType::RoomType()   // this is a constructor
{
  length = 25.0;
  width = 12.0;
  cout << "Created a new room object using the default constructor.\n\n";
}

void RoomType::showRoomValues()   // this is an accessor
{
  cout << "  length = " << length
       << "\n  width = " << width << endl;
}

void RoomType::setNewRoomValues()   // this is a mutator
{
  length = 12.5;
  width = 9.0;
}
```

(continued on next page)

```cpp
void RoomType::calculateRoomArea()   // this performs a calculation
{
   cout << length * width;
}

int main()
{
   RoomType roomOne;   // declare a variable of type RoomType

   cout << "The values for this room are:\n";
   roomOne.showRoomValues();        // use a class method on this object
   cout << "\nThe floor area of this room is: ";
   roomOne.calculateRoomArea();    // use another class method on this object

   roomOne.setNewRoomValues();    // call the mutator

   cout << "\n\nThe values for this room have been changed to:\n";
   roomOne.showRoomValues();
   cout << "\nThe floor area of this room is: ";
   roomOne.calculateRoomArea();

   return 0;
}
```

The first statement in the `main()` method should be familiar to you from Program 2-3. It is a declaration statement that declares the programmer selected variable name, `roomOne` to be a variable of type `RoomType`. When this statement is executed, storage space for a variable named `roomOne` and an object of the `RoomType` is allocated (as shown in Figure 2-14).

FIGURE 2-14
The Effect Produced by the Declaration Statement `RoomType roomOne;`

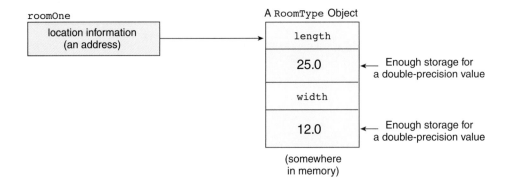

As indicated, the values of the object's `length` and `width` instance variables are initialized to 25.0 and 12.0, respectively. These initializations occur because the class's constructor is used automatically whenever an object is declared. The next statement uses a `cout` stream to display the message

```
The values for this room are:
```

The next statement, `roomOne.showRoomValues();` is new here. Notice that the notation consists of an object's name and a class method name, separated by a period. This is the standard syntax for using a class method to operate on a specific object. More formally stated, the syntax is:

```
objectName.classMethodName(parameter values);
```

The `objectName` is the name of a specific object and the `classMethodName` is the name of a class method; the period separating them is referred to as the **dot operator**. Because all class methods have been declared as `public`, they can be used outside of their defining class to access an object's `private` data members.

Using a method is formally referred to as **invoking** the method, and informally it is referred to as **calling** the method. The method being invoked is referred to as the **called** method, and the method doing the calling is referred to as the **calling method**. These terms come from standard telephone usage, where one person calls another on the telephone. Here, the person receiving the call is the called party and the person doing the calling is the calling party. For the `RoomType` class the methods being called are the class's methods, while the calling method is `main()`. In particular, the statement `roomOne.showRoomValues()` invokes the `showRoomValues()` method and tells it to operate on the object known as `roomOne`. Because we are not passing any values into the method, the parentheses do not enclose any values.

Similarly, the statement `roomOne.calculateRoomArea();` invokes the `calculateRoomArea()` method and tells it to also operate on the `roomOne` object. The mutator method is then used to change the `length` and `width` values in the `roomOne` object to 12.5 and 9.0, respectively, and the `showRoomValues()` and `calculateRoomArea()` methods are once more invoked on this specific object. The output produced by Program 2-4 is:

```
Created a new room object using the default constructor.

The values for this room are:
  length = 25
  width = 12

The floor area of this room is: 300

The values for this room have been changed to:
  length = 12.5
  width = 9

The floor area of this room is: 112.5
```

There are obvious improvements that can be made to Program 2-4. These include sending data into both the constructor and mutator, which will allow them to initialize objects and change an object's values with data supplied while the program is executing. Additionally, once we learn how to return a value from a method, we can use the accessor and calculation methods to return a value, instead of just using them for display purposes. These two modifications are presented in the next chapter. As they stand, however, the RoomType class and Program 2-4 illustrate the major issues concerned in creating and using a class.

These issues are, first and foremost, consideration of the data and methods that need to be provided. The primary concern of the main() method is in creating objects and invoking the prewritten class methods to manipulate the objects appropriately. Once an object is created, a particular method is activated, or invoked, by effectively saying "run this method on this specific object" using the dot operator.

As another example, consider Figure 2-15, which shows two objects of the RoomType type.

FIGURE 2-15
A Set of RoomType *Objects*

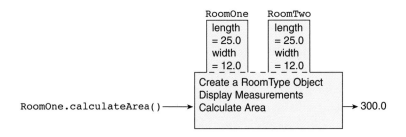

Notice that each object contains two pieces of data, the first of which is the specific room's length and the second, the room's width. In addition, the provided operations consist of creating a new room, displaying a room's measurements, and calculating a room's floor area. These methods are shared between all of the objects; that is, when a compiled class is loaded for execution, only one copy of each method defined in the class's methods implementation section is stored. Although many objects can be constructed, each of which contains its own set of instance variables, each object, when it uses a class method, uses the same copy of the class method that is loaded at execution time. Thus, to use a method we must provide both the name of the method and the name of the object that the method is to operate on. This is accomplished by separating the two pieces of information, the name of the object and the name of the method, by the dot operator, as was done in Program 2-4.

If roomOne and roomTwo have been declared as RoomType objects, the statements roomOne. calculateRoomArea() and roomTwo.calculateRoomArea();, as has been noted, both call and use the same method. That is, while an object has its own set of values, it *does not* have its own set of methods. An interesting question arises, then, as to how a called method stores the information that permits it to locate the object it is expected to currently operate on. This is handled as follows:

The object name that precedes a method's name when the method is invoked is formally referred to as both the **implied** and **implicit** object. In the first statement, the implied object is roomOne and in the second statement it is roomTwo. Information needed to locate the implied object, which is the specific object that the method is being asked to operate on, is automatically transferred to the method and stored in a special method variable named this. (The this variable is presented in detail in Section 12.3.) Essentially, the variable named this receives and automatically stores the memory address that permits it to locate the implied object.)

Using this mechanism, each method is provided with the information necessary to locate the object it is supposed to be operating on, and to access the specific set of instance variables contained in this object. It is this mechanism that permits one method to operate on any number of similarly constructed objects.

You will define your own classes and create objects as you become more fluent in C++. But you can always use any object, class, or method provided by C++, as long as you know the correct ways to activate them. Because effective object-oriented programming in C++ is based on existing classes and their methods, you will need to become very familiar with at least a subset of the available classes and their respective methods.

Exercises 2.4

1. Compile the completed RoomType class provided in this section.

2. Compile and execute Program 2-4.

3. Modify the constructor in Program 2-4 to initialize the length variable to 15.6 and the width variable to 8.2.

4. Remove the public access from the RoomType method declarations in Program 2-4 and compile the program. Determine why the compiler provides the error messages that it does.

5. a. Complete the following class by adding a constructor, accessor, and calculation method. The constructor should initialize all objects with firstNumber = 10 and secondNumber = 15. The calculation method should calculate and display the average of the two numbers.

```
class TwoNumbers
{
  // data declaration section
  private
    int firstNumber;
    int secondNumber;
    double average;

  // methods declaration section
}
methods implementation section
```

b. Include the class written for Exercise 5a within the context of a complete program. The program should create a single object and display the object's values and the average of these values.

6.   a. Construct a `Time` class containing integer instance variables `seconds`, `minutes`, and `hours`. Provide the class with a constructor that initializes each data member with a value of 10. Include an accessor method that displays the value of all data members.
     b. Include the class written for Exercise 6a within the context of a complete program.

7.   a. Construct a class named `Student` consisting of an integer student identification number and a double-precision grade point average. The constructor for this class should initialize the identification number to 111111 and the grade point average to 0.0. Included in the class should be an accessor member method to display all data values.
     b. Include the class constructed in Exercise 7a within the context of a complete program. Your program should declare two objects of type `Student` and display data for the two objects to verify operation of the class's methods.

2.5 PROGRAM DESIGN AND DEVELOPMENT: OBJECT IDENTIFICATION

When solving any problem, it's often helpful to start by creating a diagram or map, or devising some kind of theoretical analogy for the problem you are trying to solve. In other words, you need to create some kind of model. Creating a model helps you see all the parts of the problem and helps you understand what you need to do in order to solve it. The first step in constructing an object-based program is developing an object-based model of the problem. For example, the `RoomType` class developed in Section 2.3 is based on the model of a room as a rectangular object. Each class then becomes a description of the model written in C++. Thinking about a room as an object is probably not very difficult, because, in a physical sense, an object is a room. But in order to become a good object-oriented programmer, you'll need to be able to analyze more complex situations in order to think and organize programming problems as the interaction of different objects. In this section, you will explore this object-based concept in more detail. You will also learn how to develop programs systematically using object-based models. Figure 2-16 illustrates the concepts that will be presented in this section.

FIGURE 2-16
A Class Is a Programming Language Description of a Model

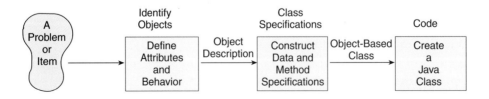

2

REPRESENTING PROBLEMS WITH MODELS

Formally, a **model** is a representation of a problem. The first step in creating an object-based model is to begin "thinking in objects." As a specific example, if the result of tossing a coin 100 times is desired, it certainly can be done by tossing a real coin. However, if a coin could be accurately modeled, the result could also be obtained by writing a program to simulate a coin toss. Similarly, a game of solitaire could be simulated if a realistic model of a deck of cards could be created, and if methods such as shuffling the deck could be coded.

Objects, such as coins, cards, and more complicated graphical objects, are well suited to a programming representation because they can all be modeled by two basic characteristics: attributes and behaviors. **Attributes** define the properties of interest, while **behaviors** define how the object reacts to its environment. When designing and developing an object-oriented program, you need to follow these two steps:

1. Identify the required objects
2. For each object:
    a. Identify the attributes of interest
    b. Identify the behaviors (operations) of interest

To make this more tangible, let us reconsider a coin-tossing experiment. Step 1 tells us to identify the required objects. For this experiment, the object under consideration is a coin. Step 2 tells us to identify the relevant attributes and behaviors. In terms of attributes, a coin has a denomination, size, weight, color, condition (tarnished, worn, proof), country of origin, and a side (head or tail). If we were purchasing a coin for collectable purposes, we would be interested in all but the last of these attributes. For the purpose of a coin-toss, however, the only attribute that is of interest is the side; whether the coin is a penny or a quarter, copper or silver colored, tarnished or not, is of no concern to us. Thus, in terms of modeling a coin for performing a coin toss, the only attribute that need initially be considered is what side is visible when the coin is tossed. It is important to understand the underlying significance of our choice of attributes—very few models are ever complete. A model typically does not reveal every aspect of the object it represents and should only include those attributes that are of relevance to the problem under consideration.

Having determined the attributes to be used in modeling a coin, the next step requires identifying the behavior that this object should exhibit. In this case, we must have a means of simulating a toss and determining the side that faces up when the toss is completed.

Figure 2-17 summarizes the initial results of the two steps required in developing our object-oriented coin toss program. That is, it identifies the required object, and lists its relevant attributes and behaviors. We will refer to the diagram in Figure 2-17 as an object description. This diagram doesn't tell everything there is to know about a coin, only what we need to know in order to create a coin toss program. For programming purposes this description will have to be translated into a programming language, be it C++ or some other object-oriented language.

FIGURE 2-17
Initial Object Diagram

Object: A coin
Attributes: Side (head or tail)
Behavior: Landing with heads up or tails up

As you expand your design for a program, you will frequently have to refine and expand the initial object description. Refinement, or improving and modifying the model, is generally always required for all but extremely simple situations.

In subsequent sections you'll learn about a more structured approach to modeling, based on a methodology known as the Unified Modeling Language (UML). This methodology, like all object-oriented design and development techniques, requires you to identify the necessary objects, and then identify the objects' attributes and behaviors. Once you build a model, you must then translate it into C++. The main point of this text is to teach you how to do just that. But your job as a beginning programmer will be much easier if you take the time first to master the techniques for properly modeling a program.

MODELING THE CLASSES

So far you have learned how to identify the objects (including their relevant attributes and behaviors) that are required for a program. But identifying the objects that will be used in a program is only the first step in the modeling process. The attributes and behavior actually define a category or type of object, out of which many individual objects can then be designated. For example, suppose we want to display a geometric object, such as a rectangle, on a screen. In its simplest representation a rectangle has a shape and location, which can be described by the object-diagram shown in Figure 2-18.

FIGURE 2-18
An Initial Object Diagram

Object: Rectangle
Attributes: shape   location

Let us now refine this model to more accurately define what is meant by shape and location. A rectangle's shape attribute can actually be broken down into two more specific attributes: length and width. As for the location attribure listed in Figure 2-18, you can also break that down into something more specific. For example, one approach might be to list the position of the upper-left corner of the rectangle relative to the upper-left corner of the screen, and then do the same for the upper-right corner of the rectangle. Those two positions, along with the length and width of the rectangle, would be enough information to allow the program to generate a rectangle. However, simply specifying one location for the rectangle may not be enough. For example, you may want to give the rectangle the ability to move its position and change either its length or width. Figure 2-19 illustrates a refined object description that takes this additional behavior into account.

FIGURE 2-19
Refined Object Diagram

Object: Rectangle
Attributes: length width top-left corner opposite corner
Behavior: move change length change width

As we have already seen, in object-based programming the category of objects defined by a given set of attributes and behavior is called a class. For example, the length and width attributes can define a general type of shape, or class, called a rectangle. Only when specific values have been assigned to these attributes have we represented a specific and particular rectangle. This distinction carries over into C++. The attributes and behavior we describe in an object diagram are used to define a general class, or type, of object. An object itself only comes into existence when we assign specific values to the attributes. The term **state** is then used to refer to how the created object appears at any one moment.

In practice, an object's state is defined by the values that have been assigned to its attributes. For example, you could completely specify the state of a rectangle by saying that its width is 1 inch, its length is 2 inches, its upper-left corner is positioned at 4 inches from the top of a video screen and 5 inches from the left side of the screen, and its opposite corner is positioned at 5 inches from the top of the screen and 7 inches from the left side of the screen. Figure 2-20 illustrates a rectangle with this state.

FIGURE 2-20
Defining the State of a Rectangle

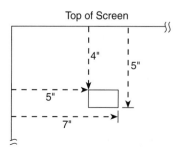

Finally, at its creation, each object must be given an identity. This means that each object, when created, must be given a name by which it can be uniquely identified within a program. This is similar to giving each automobile a vehicle identification number (VIN) when it is assembled or giving a unique name to each individual in a family. Objects are given names by declaration statements, which also create the object.

The essential difference between object-oriented and procedural programs is the model on which they are based, and as you program you should be aware of this difference. The essence of object-oriented design is constructing and testing classes that can be used by any other class or program to create as many objects as needed and provide the methods that permit manipulation of these objects in a useful manner. Thus, in object-oriented programming the emphasis is on the attributes and behavior of objects. In procedure-oriented programming no objects are created or named. The emphasis is always on the operations to be performed, such as add, multiply, and divide, and in creating methods to perform calculations using these operations.

Because procedure-oriented programs can be very helpful when learning how to use specific C++ statements, methods, or objects, such as `cout`, you will use and create such programs in this text. In fact, you already have used such programs (see, for example, Program 2-1). You may also find such programs useful for constructing output quickly for extremely simple programming problems in your professional work. But be aware that an over reliance on procedural programming can become detrimental for serious programmers, who eventually must address more complex programming situations. So even when it is convenient to create a procedural-based program, it is useful to at least contemplate how you might construct a programming solution using objects.

Exercises 2.5

1. Define the following terms:

    a. attribute
    b. behavior
    c. class
    d. identity
    e. model
    f. object
    g. object-diagram
    h. state
    i. value

2. a. Instead of specifying a rectangle's location by listing the position of two corner points, what other attributes could be used?

    b. What other attributes, besides length and width, might describe a rectangle if the rectangle is to be drawn on a color monitor?

2

c. Describe a set of attributes that could be used to define circles that are to be drawn on a black and white monitor.

d. What attributes would you add to those selected in response to Exercise 2c if the circles were to be drawn on a color monitor?

3. Classify each of the following as either classes or objects:

a. maple trees

b. Ford automobiles

c. my collie dog

d. the oak tree in your neighbor's yard

e. Boeing 767 planes

f. your Ford Taurus

g. kitchen tables

h. student desks

i. the chair you are sitting on

4. a. For each of the following, determine what attributes might be of interest to someone considering buying the item.

   i.   a book
   ii.   a can of soda
   iii. a pen
   iv.   a cassette tape
   v.   a cassette tape player
   vi.   an elevator
   vii. a car

   b. Do the attributes you used in Exercise 4a model an object or a class of objects?

5. For each of the following, what behavior might be of interest to someone considering buying the item?

a. a car

b. a boat

6. a. List five attributes of a character that could be used in a video game.

   b. List five behaviors that a character in a video game should have.

7. a. List as many attributes and behaviors that would be of interest in a program that simulates dealing a hand of playing cards. For this, assume any card game that you are familiar with.

   b. What attributes of the cards would not be of interest for purposes of the simulation?

8. a. List as many attributes and behaviors that would be of interest in a program intended to simulate an elevator that moves between floors of a building from the 1st to the 15th floor.

   b. What attributes of the elevator would not be of interest for purposes of the simulation?

2.6 A CLOSER LOOK: PROGRAMMING ERRORS

The ideal in programming is to produce readable, error-free programs that work correctly and can be modified or changed with a minimum of testing. You can work toward this ideal by keeping in mind the different types of errors that can occur, when they are typically detected, and how to correct them.

An error can be detected:

1. Before a program is compiled
2. While the program is being compiled
3. While the program is being run
4. After the program has been executed and the output is being examined

In some cases, an error may not be detected at all. Errors detected by the compiler are formally referred to as **compile-time errors**, and errors that occur while the program is running are formally referred to as **run-time errors**. Other names for compile time errors are **syntax errors** and **parse errors**, terms that emphasize the type of error being detected by the compiler.

By now, you have probably encountered numerous compile-time errors. Although beginning programmers tend to be frustrated by them, experienced programmers understand that the compiler is doing a lot of valuable checking, and that it is usually quite easy to correct any errors the compiler does detect. In addition, because these errors occur while the program is being developed, and not while a user is attempting to perform an important task, no one but the programmer ever knows they occurred; you fix them and they go away.

Run-time errors are much more troubling because they occur while a user is executing the program, and in most commercial systems the user is not the programmer. Although there are a number of error types that can cause a run-time error, such as a failure in the hardware, from a programming standpoint the majority of run-time errors are referred to as logic errors; that is faulty logic, which encompasses not fully thinking out what the program should do or not anticipating how a user can make the program fail, is at fault. For example, if a user enters data that results in an attempt to divide a number by zero, a run-time error occurs. As a programmer, the only way to protect against run-time errors is to sufficiently anticipate everything a person might do to cause errors and submit your program to rigorous testing. Although beginning programmers tend to blame a user for an error caused by entering obviously incorrect data, professionals don't. They understand that a run-time error is a flaw in the final product that additionally can cause damage to the reputation of both program and programmer.

There are ways to detect errors both before a program is compiled and after it has been executed. The method for detecting errors before a program is compiled is called **desk checking**. Desk checking,

2

which typically is performed while sitting at a desk with the code in front of you, refers to the process of checking the actual program code for syntax and logic errors. The method for detecting errors either while a program is executing or after it has executed is called **program testing**.

The terms compile-time and run-time distinguish between errors based on when the error is detected. In terms of preventing these errors, it is more fruitful to distinguish between them based on what causes them. As we have seen, compile errors are also named syntax errors, which refer to errors in either the structure or spelling of a statement. For example the statements

```
cout << "There are four syntax errors here\n
cot " Can you find tem";
```

contain four syntax errors. These errors are:

1. A closing quote is missing in line 1.
2. A terminating semicolon (;) is missing in line 1.
3. The keyword cout is misspelled in line 2.
4. The insertion symbol, <<, is missing in line 2.

All of these errors will be detected by the compiler when the program is compiled. This is true of all syntax errors because they violate the basic rules of C++; if they are not discovered by desk checking, the compiler detects them and displays an error message.[5] In some cases, the error message is clear and the error is obvious; in other cases, it takes a little detective work to understand the error message displayed by the compiler. Because syntax errors are the only type of error that can be detected at compile time, the terms compile-time errors and syntax errors are used interchangeably. Strictly speaking, however, compile-time refers to when the error was detected and syntax refers to the type of error detected.

Note that the misspelling of the word them in the second statement is not a syntax error. Although this spelling error will result in an undesirable output line being displayed, it is not a violation of C++'s syntactical rules. It is a simple case of a typographical error, commonly referred to as a "typo."

A logic error can either cause a run-time error or produce incorrect results. Such errors are characterized by erroneous, unexpected, or unintentional output that is a direct result of some flaw in the program's logic. These errors, which are never caught by the compiler, may be detected by desk checking, by program testing, by accident when a user obtains an obviously erroneous output while the program is executing, or not at all. If the error is detected while the program is executing, a run-time error can occur that results in an error message being generated, or premature program termination, or both.

The most serious logic error is caused by an incorrect understanding of the full requirements that the program is expected to fulfill. This is true because the logic contained within a program is always a reflection of the logic upon which it is coded. For example, if the purpose of a program is to calculate a mortgage payment on a house or the load bearing strength of a steel beam, and the programmer

---

[5]They may not, however, all be detected at the same time. Frequently, one syntax error masks another error, and the second error is only detected after the first error is corrected.

does not fully understand how the calculation is to be made, what inputs are needed to perform the calculation, or what special conditions exist (such as what happens when someone makes an extra payment on a mortgage or how temperature effects the beam), a logic error will occur. Because such errors are not detected by the compiler and frequently even may go undetected at run time, they are always more difficult to detect than syntax errors. If they are detected, a logic error typically reveals itself in one of two predominant ways. In one instance, the program executes to completion but produces obviously incorrect results. Generally, logic errors of this type are revealed by:

No output—This is caused either by an omission of an output statement or a sequence of statements that inadvertently bypasses an output statement.

Unappealing or misaligned output—This is caused by an error in an output statement.

Incorrect numerical results—This is caused by incorrect values assigned to the variables used in an expression, the use of an incorrect arithmetic expression, an omission of a statement, a round-off error, or the use of an improper sequence of statements.

A second way that logic errors reveal themselves is by causing a run-time error. Examples of this type of logic error are attempts to divide by zero or to take the square root of a negative number.

You should plan your program testing carefully to maximize the possibility of locating errors. Also, keep in mind that *although a single test can reveal the presence of an error, it does not verify the absence of another error*. That is, the fact that one error is revealed by testing does not indicate that another error is not lurking somewhere else in the program; furthermore, *the fact that one test revealed no errors does not mean there are no errors*.

Once you discover an error, however, the programmer must locate where the error occurs and then fix it. In computer jargon, a program error is referred to as a **bug**, and the process of isolating, correcting, and verifying the correction is called **debugging**.[6]

Although there are no hard-and-fast rules for isolating the cause of an error, some useful techniques can be applied. The first of these is a preventive technique. Frequently, many errors are introduced by the programmer in the rush to code and run a program before fully understanding what is required and how the result is to be achieved. A symptom of this haste to get a program entered into the computer is the lack of an outline of the proposed program or the lack of a detailed understanding of what is actually required. Many errors can be eliminated simply by desk checking a copy of the program before it is ever entered or compiled.

A second useful technique is to imitate the computer and execute each statement by hand, as the computer would. This means writing down each variable as it is encountered in the program and listing the value that should be stored in the variable as each input and assignment statement is encoun-

---

[6]The derivation of this term is rather interesting. When a program stopped running on the MARK I computer at Harvard University in September 1945, the malfunction was traced to a dead insect that had gotten into the electrical circuits. The programmer, Grace Hopper, recorded the incident in her logbook as, "First actual case of bug being found."

tered. Doing this also sharpens your programming skills because it requires that you fully understand what each statement in your program causes to happen. Such a check is called **program tracing**.

A third and very powerful debugging technique is to include some temporary code in your program that displays the values of selected variables. If the displayed values are incorrect, you can then determine what part of your program generated them, and make the necessary corrections.

In the same manner, you could add temporary code that displays the values of all input data. This technique is referred to as **echo printing**, and it is useful in establishing that the program is both correctly receiving and interpreting the input data.

The most powerful of all debugging and tracing techniques is to use a special program called a **debugger**. A debugger program controls the execution of a C++ program, can interrupt the C++ program at any point in its execution, and can display the values of all variables at the point of interruption.

Finally, no discussion of debugging is complete without mentioning the primary ingredient needed for successful isolation and correction of errors. This is the attitude and spirit you bring to the task. After you write a program, it's natural to assume it is correct. It is extremely difficult to back away and honestly test and find errors in your own software. As a programmer, you must constantly remind yourself that just because you think your program is correct does not make it so. Finding errors in your own programs is a sobering experience, but one that will help you to become a master programmer. It can also be exciting and fun if approached as a detection problem with you as the master detective.

2.7 COMMON PROGRAMMING ERRORS

As a general rule, it is better not to mix data types in an expression unless a specific effect is desired. In addition, the most common errors associated with the material presented in this chapter are:

1. Forgetting to declare all instance variables used in a class. When such variables are used in a class method, the compiler will issue an error message.

2. Including a return type in a constructor's header line.

3. Failing to include a return type in a nonconstructor member method's header line.

4. Defining more than one default constructor for a class.

5. Attempting to store a higher-precision value in a lower-precision data type. Thus, integer values will be accepted for both float and double variables and are automatically converted to the correct data type, but a double value cannot be stored in a float variable. This error is detected by the compiler, and an error message equivalent to "Incompatible type for declaration" is provided (the exact error message is compiler dependent).

6. Mixing data types in the same expression without clearly understanding the effect produced. Because C++ allows mixed-mode expressions, it is important to be clear about the order of evaluation and the data type of all intermediate calculations. When evaluating a numerical expression,

the following rules are applied in the order listed:

a. If either operand is a double value, the result is a double value, else

b. If either operand is a float value, the result is a float value, else

c. If either operand is a long value, the result is a long value, else

d. The result is an integer value

7. Failing to explicitly designate class methods as `public`.

8. Failing to include a method declaration statement for each implemented class method.

9. Failing to implement a class method for each declaration in the methods declaration section.

10. Failing to ensure that a class method's header line corresponds to the return type and parameter types contained in the method's declaration statement.

2.8 CHAPTER REVIEW

Key Terms

accessor method

attribute

behavior

bool

char

class

compile time error

constructor

desk checking

double

double-precision

float

floating-point literal

identity

implicit object

int

integer

integer literal

instance variable

2

logic error

model

object

object-diagram

operator associativity

operator precedence

fundamental data types

real number

run-time error

single-precision

state

value

variable

SUMMARY

1. A data type is a set of values *and* a set of operations that can be applied to these values.

2. A built-in data type is provided as an integral part of the C++ compiler, and requires no external methods; that is, it can be used without recourse to any supplementary code supplied with the compiler in header files, such as `iostream`.

3. The predominant built-in types are `char`, `bool`, and `int`, which are integer types, and `double`, which is a real number (a number with an explicit decimal point) type.

4. Built-in data type values can be displayed using the `cout` object.

5. An operand can be either a literal value or an identifier that has a value associated with it.

6. An expression is any combination of operators and operands that can be evaluated to yield a value.

7. A class is a programmer-defined data type.

8. A class is defined using a class data declaration section and a class methods implementation section. The most common syntax for defining a class is:

```
class className
{
  // data declaration section
  private:
      instance variable declarations

  // methods declaration section
  public:
      method declarations
};

// methods implementation section
```

The variables declared in a class's data declaration section are referred to as class data members, and the methods are referred to as class member methods. The terms `private` and `public` are referred to as access specifiers. The keyword `private` specifies that the class members following it are private to the class and can only be accessed by member methods. The keyword `public` specifies that the class members following it may be accessed from outside the class. Generally, all data members should be specified as `private` and all member methods as `public`.

9. Except for constructor methods, all class methods defined in the implementation section typically have the header line syntax:

    `returnType className::methodName(parameter list)`

10. A constructor method is a special method that is automatically called each time an object is declared. It must have the same name as its class and cannot have any return type. Its purpose is to initialize each declared object.

11. If no constructor is declared for a class, the compiler will supply a default constructor. The compiler-provided constructor initializes all numerical data members to zero and all string data members to a null.

12. The term default constructor refers to any constructor that does not require any arguments when it is called.

13. Each class may have only one default constructor. If a user-defined default constructor is provided, the compiler will not create its default constructor.

14. An accessor method is a member method that accesses a class's data members for the purpose of displaying or returning their values.

15. In addition to constructor and accessor methods, each class should provide a number of methods that perform appropriate calculations and operations on objects that will be constructed from the class.

16. Data passed to a method are called *arguments* of the method. Arguments are passed to a method by including each argument, separated by commas, within the parentheses following the

2

method's name. Each method has its own requirements for the number and data types of the arguments that must be provided.

17. Objects are created from a class when they are declared. When an object is created, it is also said to be instantiated.

Chapter Exercises

1. Consider the set of values defined as imaginary numbers. These numbers have the form ai, where a is any real number and i represents the square root of -1. Determine which of the arithmetic operations (addition, subtraction, multiplication, and division) can be applied to the set of values defined as imaginary numbers to form a data type.

2. Consider the set of values defined as complex numbers. These numbers have the form $a + bi$ where i represents the square root of -1, and a and b are any real numbers. Determine which of the arithmetic operations (addition, subtraction, multiplication, and division) can be applied to the set of values defined as complex numbers to form a data type.

3. a. Values defined as (a,b), where a and b can be any real numbers, are used to determine coordinates for specific points on a map. For such a set of values determine which of the arithmetic operations make sense and would practically be included to create a useful data type.

   b. Determine what additional operations, besides those determined in Exercise 3a, might be useful for operating on values of the type (a,b), (*Hint*: Consider the length and slope of a line.)

4. Create a class named `Circle`. The data declaration section should include an instance variable for data consisting of a single-precision radius.

5. Create a class named `MapPoint`. The data declaration section should have instance variables for a map coordinate consisting of a double-precision x value and a double-precision y value.

6. The class examples considered in this chapter involved inanimate objects. Do you think that animate objects such as pets and even human beings could be modeled in terms of attributes and behavior? Why or why not?

7. a. Attributes represent how objects appear to the outside world, while behavior represents how an object can respond to an external stimulus. With this in mind, what is the mechanism by which one object triggers a behavior in another object?

   b. If behavior is constructed by defining an appropriate method, how is a particular behavior activated in C++?

8. Consider the problem of adding two numbers.

    a. From a procedural orientation, what mathematical operation would you concentrate on?

    b. From an object orientation, what objects are required? What behavior should these objects have?

Improving Communication

9. Respond, in writing, to the following memorandum:

MEMORANDUM

To: U. R. It

From: Head of Programming Dept.

Subject: Object-Orientation

The terms object-oriented and procedural-oriented keep popping up in our discussions of the programming direction the firm should be pursuing. Could you please explain what the difference in these terms really means and how they are affected by our decision to base our programming effort on the C++ programming language?

Working in Teams

10. Every object has a set of attributes and a set of behaviors. For example, a radio's attributes consist of its size, color, type (AM or FM), whether it has a tape player or not, etc. Similarly, its behaviors include responding to an on-off switch, responding to a volume control, and so on. As a team, determine a list of attributes and behaviors for the following objects:

- car
- computer
- house
- computer programming class
- elevator

Working in Teams

11. **a.** Establish a criteria for names of variables and methods that will be consistently used by each member of the group in all of their programs. Some choices are:

- always consist of lowercase letters
- must always start with a lower or uppercase letter
- use uppercase letters to separate words
- use the underscore character, (_), to separate words

For example, using your rules, should a variable's name be maxnumber, max_number, maxNumber, MaxNumber or Max_number? Make a determination for both variable and method names. Check that your criteria are acceptable to your professor.

    b. After your group has come up with its recommendation, designate a representative to list your selection on the board. Then, either have all of the groups choose one of the criteria that will be common to the class, or have your professor choose one and explain his or her preference based on experience.

2

**Working
in Teams**

12. Now that you have had at least one team meeting, discuss among your team members the following issues:

   a. How did each team member feel about your last meeting? That is, did they participate in discussions or did one person tend to dominate? Was input solicited from each person and did each person feel that their input was really listened to and heard? Was it an open discussion or was the discussion more of an "I'm right, You're Wrong" type?

   b. Was a leader appointed or did a leader emerge? If not, first find out which members might have an interest in leading the group, because effective groups always have one or two people who organize and focus the discussion. Select a leader now. If more than one person wants to lead, alternate leaders on different team projects. If no one wants to lead, take time to select a leader anyway.

   c. Was someone keeping track of the time spent on each issue? Effective groups allocate time before discussing an issue and someone is designated as the time keeper. Find out who in the group is good at keeping time and is willing to be the time keeper.

   d. Discuss whether each of your team members tends to ignore or even sabotage a group decision if it is not the decision they want. Discuss the difference between agreeing on a course of action and aligning on a course of action. Aligning on a course of action means the willingness to support a course of action and make it successful, even if it is not the one you personally wanted. Make sure each member is comfortable with aligning on a course of action before closing an issue.

   e. Do you think alignment or agreement is necessary for a group of people to successfully accomplish a given task?

Please visit the Testing Center at www.course.com/testingcenter for more practice on creating classes.

**Testing
Center**

3

DEVELOPING CLASS
METHODS

The purpose of a class method is to accept an object and either use the object's values directly or modify these values in a set manner. To do this, a method may need to accept data that is not included in the object. For example, in calculating the monthly interest due on a bank balance, the actual interest rate can change from month to month; as such it would not be stored as part of an individual's bank account data, but would be sent into the interest calculation method when the calculation is actually performed.

Additionally, methods can also provide a return value that can either be displayed or sent on to the next method operating on the object. For example, when a check is deposited in an account, a portion of the deposited amount is typically made available by the bank as cash that can be immediately withdrawn. This amount can be directly returned by the method.

In this chapter, you will learn how to implement class methods that can both accept values external to the object they are operating on and return a value independently of this object. You will also learn about algorithms, the theoretical basis of all methods.

3.1 RETURNING A VALUE

It is useful to think initially of a method as a small machine that transforms an object from one state into another, much as a physical machine might take a physical object, such as a piece of wood, and transform it into a table leg. To see how a C++ method conforms to this analogy, consider the RoomType class developed in the last chapter and repeated below as Class 3-1, for convenience.

Class 3-1

```cpp
#include <iostream>
using namespace std;

class RoomType
{
  // data declaration section
  private:
    double length;            // declare length as a double variable
    double width;             // declare width as a double variable

  // methods declaration section
  public:
    RoomType();               // this will be a constructor
    void showRoomValues();    // this will be an accessor
    void setNewRoomValues();  // this will be a mutator
    void calculateRoomArea(); // an additional class method
};

// methods implementation section
RoomType::RoomType()          // this is a constructor
{
  length = 25.0;
  width = 12.0;
  cout << "Created a new room object using the default constructor.\n\n";
}
```

(continued on next page)

```
void RoomType::showRoomValues()       // this is an accessor
{
  cout << "  length = " << length << "\n  width = " << width << endl;
}


void RoomType::setNewRoomValues()     // this is a mutator
{
  length = 12.5;
  width = 9.0;
}


void RoomType::calculateRoomArea()    // this performs a calculation
{
  cout << length * width;
}
```

Each of this class's methods is restricted to operating on a `RoomType` object, (which consists of the values stored in the object's `length` and `width` instance variables) and can use any additional literal data coded within the method. Thus the constructor, as currently implemented, must always use the same literal values, 25.0 and 12.0, to initialize each newly created `RoomType` object. Additionally, the accessor and calculation methods are restricted to displaying values—rather than outputting them as numerical data to be formatted and displayed in a manner decided by the programmer using the class.

A more inclusive and useful method corresponds to that shown in Figure 3-1. Here, the method can accept additional input values and send out a value independent of the object on which it is operating. This can be compared to a machine that accepts additional raw materials and produces a second output, in addition to the object it is operating on.

In terms of the `RoomType` class, the situation shown in Figure 3-1 corresponds to setting an object's `length` and `width` values using numbers that are not coded as literals within the method; rather, they are set by data sent into the constructor and mutator when these methods are called. Thus, a hallway room could be provided with one set of values, such as 3 feet by 9 feet, and a dining room with another set, such as 6 feet by 12 feet. Additionally, using this expanded set of capabilities, the accessor and calculation methods could return a numerical value rather than just displaying it. This section explains how to write methods that return a value; the next section shows how to write methods that accept external data in addition to that provided by an object.

Independent of the changes that a class method makes to an object's instance variables, a C++ method is permitted to directly return at most one, and only one, "legitimate" value. To return a value the method must:

1. Indicate the data type of the value that it returns
2. Return a value

FIGURE 3-1
A Method as a Machine

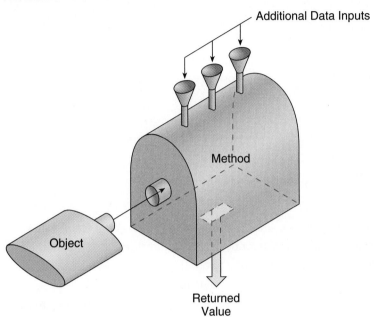

A method indicates the data type of the value it returns by specifying it as the first item listed in the method's header line. For example, in the header line for the `main()` method we have been using, `int main()`, the keyword `int` specifies that this method will return an integer value.

Similarly, the keyword `void` in the following header line specifies that no value will be returned by the `calculateRoomArea()` method.

```
void RoomType::calculateRoomArea()
```

In order to rewrite `calculateRoomArea()` so that it does return a value, you must change the header line's initial keyword to the data type of the value being returned. For example, if you wanted a double-precision value returned, you would use this method header line:

```
double RoomType::calculateRoomArea()
```

Observe that this is the same as the original method header line for `calculateRoomArea()` with the substitution of the keyword `double` for the keyword `void`. Similarly, if you want this method to return an integer value, the correct method header line becomes

```
int RoomType::calculateRoomArea()
```

and if you want the method to return a single-precision value, the header line would be

```
float RoomType::calculateRoomArea()
```

Because we want this method to return a double-precision value, corresponding to a room's floor area, the correct header line is:

```
double RoomType::calculateRoomArea()
```

Having declared the data type that `calculateRoomArea()` will return, we now alter the method's body by including a statement that forces the return of the correct value. To return a value from a method requires using a `return` statement, which has the syntax:[1]

```
return expression;
```

When the `return` statement is encountered, the *expression* is evaluated first and it is this value that is returned by the method. How this value is subsequently used is not of concern to the method returning it. It can be formatted, displayed, used as input data to another method, used as a value in an expression, or even ignored; once the method produces the value its job is completed. A relevant example is the statement `return 0;` which we have used in all of our `main()` methods. The integer value 0 returned by `main()` matches its specified `int` data type in `main's()` header line. Most oper-

---

PROGRAMMING NOTE

Program Control

Statements within a method are executed in the order that they are encountered, which corresponds to their placement in the method. Thus, the first statement within a method's body is executed first, followed by the second statement, and so on, with nonexecutable statements, such as comments, excluded. This sequential execution of one statement after another is referred to as **flow of control** or **program control.**

The normal sequential program control can be altered by either calling a method, using a selection statement (presented in Chapter 5), or using a repetition statement (presented in Chapter 6). When a method is called, execution is transferred to the first statement within the called method. After the method has finished executing, program control returns to the statement immediately following the statement that made the call.

---

[1]Some programmers place the expression within parentheses, yielding the statement `return (expression);`. The parentheses are not required, but can be used.

ating systems generally ignore this returned value, although some systems use it as a signal that the method has been successfully completed. After a `return` statement is executed, the method ceases operation and program control reverts to the point in the program immediately following the point at which the method was called.

Let us apply this to the area calculated by `calculateRoomArea()`. We want the value of the expression `length * width` (which provides the correct area) returned. To accomplish this, we need to add the statement `return length * width;` before the method's closing brace. The completed method code becomes:

```
double RoomType::calculateRoomArea()
{
   return length * width;
}
```

Pay particular attention to the fact that the data type of the expression contained in the `return` statement correctly matches the double-precision return data type declared in the method's header line. It is up to the programmer to ensure that this is true for every method returning a value. Failure to match the return value exactly with the method's declared data type may not result in an error when your class is compiled, but it may lead to undesired results because the return value is always converted to the data type declared in the method's header line. Usually this is a problem only when the fractional part of a returned floating-point or double-precision number is truncated because the method was declared to return an integer value.

The value returned by a method can be used wherever an expression is valid. For example, the expression `2 * roomOne.calculateRoomArea()` multiplies the value returned by `calculateRoomArea()` by 2. The statement

```
cout << roomOne.calculateRoomArea();
```

displays the returned value. The statement

```
area = roomOne.calculateRoomArea();
```

assigns the returned value to a variable named `area`. Before this statement can be used, the variable `area` must be declared as a double-precision value, to accept the returned value that was previously declared in the method's header line. When the newly coded `calculateRoomArea()` method is inserted into the `RoomType` class, the method's prototype (method declaration) must also be modified. A suitable prototype that correctly specifies the method's return value is:

```
double calculateRoomArea();
```

Program 3-1 uses the new `calculateRoomArea()` method within the context of a complete program.

Program 3-1

```cpp
#include <iostream>
using namespace std;

class RoomType
{
  // data declaration section
  private:
    double length;              // declare length as a double variable
    double width;               // declare width as a double variable

  // methods declaration section
  public:
    RoomType();                 // constructor declaration
    void showRoomValues();      // accessor declaration
    void setNewRoomValues();    // mutator declaration
    double calculateRoomArea(); // an additional class method
};

// methods implementation section
RoomType::RoomType()                        // this is a constructor
{
  length = 25.0;
  width = 12.0;
  cout << "Created a new room object using the default constructor.\n\n";
}


void RoomType::showRoomValues()          // this is an accessor
{
  cout << "  length = " << length << "\n  width = " << width << endl;
}


void RoomType::setNewRoomValues()        // this is a mutator
{
  length = 12.5;
  width = 9.0;
}


double RoomType::calculateRoomArea()     // this performs a calculation
{
  return length * width;
}
```

```
int main()
{
  RoomType roomOne;                    // declare a variable of type RoomType

  cout << "The values for this room are:\n";
  roomOne.showRoomValues();            // use a class method on this object
  cout << "\nThe floor area of this room is: "
       << roomOne.calculateRoomArea(); // display the returned value

  return 0;
}
```

The output produced by Program 3-1 is:

```
Created a new room object using the default constructor.

The values for this room are:
  length = 25
  width = 12

The floor area of this room is: 300
```

As you review Program 3-1, note three important points concerning the coding of the calculateRoomArea() method itself. First, the header line for the method declares that it will return a double-precision value. Secondly, the expression in the return statement evaluates to the correct data type. Thus, calculateRoomArea() is internally consistent in returning a double-precision value whenever the method is used. The output indicates that the program correctly calculates, returns, and displays the area of 300.0. The third point to note is that the declaration statement for calculateRoomArea() in the methods declaration section is consistent with the specification provided by the method's header line.

INLINE METHODS

You will frequently see methods whose bodies consist of a single statement, such as calculateRoomArea(), coded directly in a class's methods declaration section. Doing so with the calculateRoomArea() method results in the methods declaration section

```
// methods declaration section
public:
  RoomType();                // constructor declaration
  void showRoomValues();     // accessor declaration
  void setNewRoomValues();   // mutator declaration
  double calculateRoomArea(){return length * width;}  // an inline class method
```

Methods coded in this fashion are referred to as **inline methods**. Note that inline methods are not terminated with a semicolon after their closing brace.

Although any method can be coded as an inline method, only methods that can conveniently be written on a single line (or, at most, two lines) should be constructed as inline methods. For example, the mutator method can also be written as either the single line inline method

```
void setNewRoomValues(){length = 12.5; width = 9.0;}
```

or as the two-line inline method

```
void setNewRoomValues()
   {length = 12.5; width = 9.0;}
```

By limiting inline methods to two lines at most, you preserve the methods declaration section as a convenient place where you can quickly see all the methods contained in a class, the values they will return, and, as we will see in the next section, what data can be sent into them when they are called.

Exercises 3.1

1. For the following method headers, list the data type of the value returned by the method.

    a. `double RoomType::getLength()`
    b. `int Complex::getReal()`
    c. `void Bond::showPrice()`
    d. `double Bond::calculatePrice()`
    e. `double Bond::calculateYield()`
    f. `char Bond::interest()`
    g. `int SalesTax:calculateTotal()`
    h. `double Mortgage::roi()`
    i. `void Sentence::getVal()`

2. Enter and execute Program 3-1 on your computer.

3. Individually set the following prototypes and header lines in Program 3-1 and determine the error or warning message provided when a compilation is attempted.

    a. `method declaration:`   `void calculateRoomArea();`
        `method header line:`   `double RoomType::calculateRoomArea()`

    b. `method declaration:`   `int calculateRoomArea();`
        `method header line:`   `double RoomType::calculateRoomArea()`

    c. `method declaration:`   `double calculateRoomArea();`
        `method header line:`   `int RoomType::calculateRoomArea()`

    d. `method declaration:`   `calculateRoomArea();`
        `method header line:`   `void RoomType::calculateRoomArea()`

4. **a.** Replace the method `showRoomValues()` in Program 3-1 with class methods named `getLength()` and `getWidth()` that return an object's `length` and `width` values, respectively.

b. Modify Program 3-1 to verify that the methods written for Exercise 4a work correctly.

c. Convert the two methods coded for Exercise 4a into inline methods and verify that they correctly perform their intended functions.

5. Write method headers for the following:

a. A class method named `getMonth()` that accepts no parameters, returns an integer value, and is a member of a class named `Date`.

b. A class method named `getDate()` that is a member of a class named `Date`, accepts no parameters, and returns a long integer.

c. A class method named `check()` that returns a double precision value, is a member of a class named `Balance`, and expects no parameters.

d. A class method named `findAbs()` that accepts no parameters, returns a double-precision value, and is a member of a class named `MathMethods`.

e. A class method named `calculateRadius()` that accepts no parameters, returns an integer value, and is a member of a class named `Circle`.

f. A class method named `getIncrease()` that accepts no parameters, returns a double-precision value, and is a member of a class named `Economy`.

6. For each method header line created for Exercise 5, create a suitable method declaration statement.

7. **a.** Write a C++ class named `Fahrenheit` that contains a single double-precision instance variable named `temperature`. The class should include a constructor that initializes an object's temperature value to 212, and mutator method named `setFahrTemp()` that sets an object's temperature value to 72 degrees. Additionally, there should be an accessor method that returns an object's temperature value, and a class method named `convertToCelsius()` that returns the Celsius temperature corresponding to a Fahrenheit's temperature. The Celsius value can be determined using the formula

$$Celsius = 5.0/9.0 \ (Fahrenheit - 32.0).$$

b. Include the method written for Exercise 7a in a working C++ program. Make sure that all class methods are called from `main()`. Have `main()` display the value returned by `convertToCelsisus()` and verify the returned value by a hand calculation.

8. **a.** Write a C++ class named `Cylinder` that contains two double-precision instance variables named `radius` and `height`. The class should include a constructor method that initializes an object's `radius` value to 2 and its `height` to 3. The class's mutator method should set an object's `radius` value to 1.5 and its `height` to 2.5. Additionally, there should be two accessor methods that return an object's `radius` and `height`, respectively, and a class method named `volume()` that returns the volume of a `Cylinder` object. The volume of a cylinder is given by its radius squared times its height times π (r^2 x h x π). Use the value 3.1416 for π.

   b. Include the method written for Exercise 8a in a working C++ program. Make sure that all class methods are called from `main()`. Have `main()` display the value returned by `volume()` and verify the returned value by a hand calculation.

9. a. Write a C++ class named `PolyTwo` that contains three double-precision instance variables named a, b, and c, which represent the coefficients of a second-degree polynomial (a second-degree polynomial in x is given by the expression $ax^2 + bx + c$, where a, b, and c are referred to as coefficients. If the coefficient a is zero, the expression becomes a first-degree polynomial). The class should include a constructor method that initializes an object's a, b, c, and x values to 2.0, 3.0, 0.0, and 5.0, respectively. Similarly, include a mutator method that sets an object's a, b, c, and x values to 1.2, 2.2, 5.0, and 3.0, respectively. Additionally, there should be a single accessor method that displays an object's values and a class method named `polyValue()` that returns the value determined by the expression $ax^2 + bx + c$, where a, b, and c are coefficients contained in a `PolyTwo` object.

   b. Include the method written for Exercise 9a in a working C++ program. Make sure that all class methods are called from `main()`. Have `main()` display the value returned by `polyValue()` for values set by both the constructor and mutator methods. Verify the returned value by performing a hand calculation.

3.2 ACCEPTING VALUES

In addition to operating on an object and returning a value, a class method can also accept values that are not part of its implied object. This involves two distinct tasks:

1. Sending data into the method when it is called
2. Coding the method to receive, store, and process the passed data.

Sending data into a method when it is called is formally referred to as **passing** data. Figure 3-2 illustrates how this is accomplished. As shown, with the parentheses following the method's name, you must include the data passed into the method.

FIGURE 3-2
Passing Data to a Method

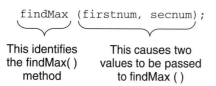

```
findMax (firstnum, secnum);
```
This identifies the findMax( ) method   This causes two values to be passed to findMax ( )

A BIT OF BACKGROUND

User-Written Procedures

The purpose of a procedure is to accept data as input and transform the data in some manner to produce a specific result. In C++, procedures that are included within a class are referred to as **methods**, while a procedure that is not part of a class is referred to as a **function**.

All programming languages use procedures, but they go by different names in different programming languages. In the C language, user-written procedures are referred to as *functions*. In Pascal they are called both *procedures* and *functions*. In Modula-2 they are called PROCEDURES. In COBOL they are called *paragraphs,* while FORTRAN and Visual Basic refer to them as both *subroutines* and *functions.*

To learn more about the process of sending data into a method, consider the following statement, which calls the class method named `setNewRoomValues()`:

```
roomOne.setNewRoomValues(10.0, 11.5);
```

In addition to telling the `setNewRoomValues()` method to operate on the `roomOne` object, this statement attempts to pass two values into the method. Assuming that `setNewRoomValues()` has been written to accept two double-precision values, the call will be successful. Thus, the parentheses permit us to pass additional data, other than the data contained in a named object, when the method is used.

The data that are passed to a method through the parentheses are referred to as **parameters**, **arguments**, and **actual arguments**. Although these terms are used interchangeably, we will generally refer to a value that is passed into a method as an argument. If no data are expected by a method, no arguments are permitted. As shown in Figure 3-3, the parentheses provide a funnel into a method through which arguments (data) can be passed. In place of literal data, arguments can also be variable names, in which case the values stored in the variables are passed into the method.

FIGURE 3-3
Passing Data to the `setNewRoomValues()` *Method*

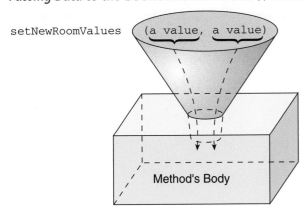

The syntax for a method header line that accepts arguments is:

```
returnType className::methodName(parameter list)
```

Here, the *parameter list* specifies the data types and names that will hold the values passed to the method. We can use this syntax to construct the following header line for a `setNewRoomValues()` mutator that returns no value and receives two double-precision values (one to set an object's `length` variable and one to set its `width` variable):

```
void RoomType::setNewRoomValues(double len, double wid)
```

The identifier names within the parentheses in the header are referred to as **formal parameters** of the method. You will also see them referred to as **formal arguments** or **parameters**. In this text the term parameter is used. Thus, the parameter `len` will store the first value passed to `setNewRoomValues()`, and the parameter `wid` will store the second value passed at the time of the method call. All parameters, such as `len` and `wid`, receive values from the calling method. The method does not know where the values come from when the call is made. The two values passed to `setNewRoomValues()` when the method is called are stored in the parameters `len` and `wid`. (See Figure 3-4.)

FIGURE 3-4
`setNewRoomValues()` *Receives Actual Values*

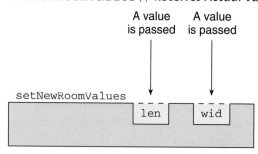

The method name and all parameter names in the header, in this case `setNewRoomValues`, `len`, and `wid`, are programmer-selected identifiers. Thus, you can use any names that follow the rules for choosing identifier names (see Section 1.4). All parameters listed in the method header line must be separated by commas and must have their individual data types declared separately.

3

A BIT OF BACKGROUND

Procedural Abstraction

The assigning of a name to a method or procedure in such a way that the method is invoked by simply using a name with appropriate arguments is formally referred to as *procedural abstraction.* In writing your own user-named methods, you are actually creating procedural abstractions.

      Notice that procedural abstraction effectively hides the implementation details of how a method actually performs its task. The ability to hide such details is one of the hallmarks and strengths of abstraction. It also alleviates the need to be concerned with all of the nitty-gritty details of the actual solution implementation. This means you can initially declare a procedure and code it to do essentially nothing, with the completion of the implementation left for another day.

When a method is called, the number, order (sequence), and data types of the arguments passed to the method *must agree* in number, order, and data type with the parameters declared in the method's header line. If the values passed to a method do not agree with the data types declared for a parameter, the result could be a possible loss of precision. (For example, attempting to send a double-precision argument into a parameter declared as an `int`, the compiler will issue a warning message such as `warning: argument: conversion from 'double' to 'int', possible loss of value.`) The compiler will not issue a warning message if a lower precision value is passed to a method that expects a higher precision parameter (for example, passing an integer value to a method that expects a double-precision parameter).

The procedure illustrated in Figure 3-4 is really a safety procedure for ensuring that a called method can not inadvertently alter any data that is sent to it from the calling method. The called method gets a copy of the data to use. It may alter its copy, of course, but this change will not affect the original values sent from the calling method. The term **pass by value** (or sometimes **call by value**) is used to refer to this situation in which only values are passed to a called method.

Having written a method header for `setNewRoomValues()`, we can now construct its body. As illustrated in Figure 3-5, a method body begins with an opening brace, {, contains any necessary declarations and other C++ statements, and ends with a closing brace, }. Again, this should look familiar to you from the structure of `main()`, which was illustrated in Chapter 1, Figure 1-23.

FIGURE 3-5
The Structure of a Method Body

```
{
   variable declarations
   and other C++ statements
}
```

In the body of the setNewRoomValues() method, we use the parameters to set an object's length and width variables. The complete definition for this method is:

```
void RoomType::setNewRoomValues(double len, double wid) // this is a mutator
{
  length = len;
  width = wid;
}
```

Having completed the method's definition, all that remains is to correctly change the method's declaration statement to indicate that two double-precision values are expected by the method. The declaration statement

```
void setNewRoomValues(double, double);   // this will be a mutator
```

accomplishes this. Notice that the keywords within a method's declaration statement only provide the data types of the values expected by the method. If these data types do not agree in order, number, and type with those specified in the method's header line, the compiler issues an error message.

Program 3-2 includes the setNewRoomValues() method and its declaration statement within the context of a complete program. Notice that the setNewRoomValues() method, its declaration, and the call to this method are highlighted with a darker shading.

Program 3-2

```
#include <iostream>
using namespace std;

class RoomType
{
  // data declaration section
  private:
    double length;   // declare length as a double variable
    double width;    // declare width as a double variable

  // methods declaration section
  public:
    RoomType();                              // this will be a constructor
    void showRoomValues();                   // this will be an accessor
    void setNewRoomValues(double, double);   // this will be a mutator
    void calculateRoomArea();                // an additional class method
};
```

(continued on next page)

```cpp
// methods implementation section
RoomType::RoomType()   // this is a constructor
{
  length = 25.0;
  width = 12.0;
  cout << "Created a new room object using the default constructor.\n\n";
}


void RoomType::showRoomValues()    // this is an accessor
{
  cout << "  length = " << length << "\n  width = " << width << endl;
}


void RoomType::setNewRoomValues(double len, double wid)    // this is a mutator
{
  length = len;
  width = wid;
}


void RoomType::calculateRoomArea()       // this performs a calculation
{
  cout << length * width;
}
```

```cpp
int main()
{
  RoomType roomOne;                    // declare a variable of type RoomType

  cout << "The values for this room are:\n";
  roomOne.showRoomValues();        // use a class method on this object
  cout << "\nThe floor area of this room is: ";
  roomOne.calculateRoomArea();     // use another class method on this object

  roomOne.setNewRoomValues(6.2,3.5);    // call the mutator

  cout << "\n\nThe values for this room have been changed to:\n";
  roomOne.showRoomValues();
  cout << "\nThe floor area of this room is: ";
  roomOne.calculateRoomArea();

  return 0;
}
```

The output display produced when this program is compiled and executed is:

```
Created a new room object using the default constructor.

The values for this room are:
  length = 25
  width = 12

The floor area of this room is: 300

The values for this room have been changed to:
  length = 6.2
  width = 3.5

The floor area of this room is: 21.7
```

As is clearly shown in this output, the `setNewRoomValues()` method successfully received and processed the arguments passed to it.

VARIABLE DECLARATION STATEMENTS

In addition to accepting and using arguments passed to a method when it is called, methods, as we have seen, can also declare variables. An example of this is the declaration statement

```
RoomType roomOne;   // declare a variable of type RoomType
```

coded as the first statement within the `main()` method in Program 3-2. Recall that variables declared within a method are formally referred to as **local variables**. (See Table 2-7.) These variables are declared in the same manner as instance variables, except they *cannot* include an access specification. The reason is that local variables can only be used within the method that declares them. Thus, they are private by default.[2] Local variables will become indispensable to us as we investigate the fundamental processing statements of C++ in the next three chapters.

The syntax for declaring a variable within a method is

where *dataType* is any valid C++ data type (int, double, char, etc.) or class type, and *variableName* is

```
dataType variableName;
```

a valid identifier selected using the same rules as those used when declaring instance variables for a class. Notice that this syntax is identical to that used for instance variables.

---

[2]Where a variable can be used is referred to as its *scope,* a subject that is presented in detail in Section 7.2.

Although declaration statements may be placed anywhere within a method, most declarations are typically grouped together and placed immediately after the method's opening brace. Using this convention, a method is typically coded using the following structure

```
method header line
{
    local declaration statements;

    other statements;

    return expression;
}
```

PROGRAMMING NOTE

Values and Identities

Apart from any behavior that an object is supplied with, a characteristic feature that objects share with variables is that they always have a unique identity. An object's identity makes it possible to distinguish one object from another. This is not true of a value, such as the number 5, because all occurrences of 5 are indistinguishable from one another. A value is simply an entity that stands for itself. As such, values are not considered objects in object-oriented programming languages such as C++.

Now consider a string such as "Chicago." As simply a string, this would be considered a value. However, Chicago could also be a specific and identifiable object of type City. Thus, the context in which the name "Chicago" is used is important. Notice that if the string "Chicago" were assigned to an object's instance variable named name, it reverts to being a value.

Local declaration statements can include initial values, just as is true with instance variables. For example, the method declaration statement

```
int firstNum = 25;
```

declares firstNum as an integer variable and assigns to it an initial value of 25.

Finally, variables with the same data type can always be grouped together and declared using a single declaration statement. Although this is almost never done for a class's instance variables, it is frequently used in declaring a method's internal, or local, variables. For example, the three separate declarations

```
double radius;
double height;
double volume;
```

can be replaced by the single declaration statement

```
double radius, height, volume;
```

As shown here, declaring multiple variables in a single declaration requires that the data type of the variables be given only once, that all the variables names be separated by commas, and that only one semicolon be used to terminate the declaration. The space after each comma is inserted for readability and is not required.

From a practical viewpoint, when arguments are passed into a called method and assigned to the method's parameters, the parameters can conveniently be considered as local variables that have been initialized from outside the method. For example, reconsider the `setNewRoomValues()` method defined in Program 3-2. As far as this method is concerned, the parameters named `len` and `wid` are dealt with exactly as any local variable declared in the method would be. The only difference between a method's parameter declarations and its variable declarations is their placement in the method. Parameter declarations are always placed within the parentheses following the method's name, while method variable declarations are placed within the method's body.

Although `setNewRoomValues()` expects arguments when it is called, it does not return a value. More generally, a method can receive arguments, declare variables, create objects, and directly return a single value. Following is the general syntax for defining a method that includes both a return type and parameter declarations:

```
returnType className::methodName(parameter declarations)
{
  object and variable declarations
  other C++ statements
  return expression;
}
```

As you learn more about C++, you will create many methods that use all of the elements included in this more general syntax. Specifically, you will create methods that use parameters, declare their own internal variables, and return a value. As you will also see in Chapter 7, this same structure can be used to create functions, such as `main()` that are not part of a class.

REUSING METHOD NAMES (OVERLOADING)[3]

C++ allows you to use the same method name for more than one method, a process known as **method overloading**. The only requirement in creating more than one method with the same name is that the compiler must be able to determine which method to use based on the data types of the parameters (not the data type of the return value, if any). Method overloading is particularly useful for constructor methods, because it allows the programmer to initialize an object in more than one way. For example, consider the following two constructor methods, both named `RoomType()`.

---

[3]This topic may be omitted on first reading without loss of subject continuity.

```
public RoomType()   // this is a constructor
{
   length = 25.0;
   width = 12.0;
   cout << "Created a new room object using the default constructor\n";
}

public RoomType(double len, double wid)   // this is a constructor
{
   length = len;
   width = wid;
}
```

Which of the two methods named `RoomType()` is called depends on the argument types supplied at the time the method is called. Thus, the declaration statement `roomOne.RoomType();` causes the default constructor to be used (recall that a default constructor is one that requires no arguments) and the statement call `RoomType.roomTwo new RoomType(6.0, 3.5);` causes the compiler to use the constructor that expects two double-precision arguments.

Notice that overloading a method's name simply means using the same name for more than one method. You must still write all the methods that use the name; each method must exist as a separate entity. The re-use of a method name does not require that the code within the methods be similar, although good programming practice dictates that methods with the same name should perform similar operations.

Clearly, overloading a method requires that the compiler be able to distinguish which method to select based on the method's name and its parameter list. The part of a header line that contains this information (that is, name and parameter list) is referred to as the **method's parameter signature**. For a class to compile correctly, each method must have a unique parameter signature. This terminology is derived from everyday usage where it is expected that each individual has a unique signature that can uniquely identify a person. From a compiler's viewpoint, unless each method has a unique parameter signature, the compiler cannot correctly determine which method is being referenced.

Exercises 3.2

1. For the following method header lines, determine the number, type, and order (sequence) of the values that must be passed to the method:

   a. `int Numbers::determineFactorial(int n)`
   b. `void Bond::calculatePrice(int type, double yield, double maturity)`
   c. `double Bond::calculateYield(int type, double price, double maturity)`
   d. `double Bond::calculateInterest(char flag, double price, double time)`
   e. `float SalesTax::total(double amount, double rate)`
   f. `boolean Mortgage::setType(int a, int b, char c, char d, double e, double f)`
   g. `void Senetence::setElements(int item, int iter, char decflag, char delim)`

2. Enter and execute Program 3-2 on your computer.

3. Add two mutator methods named `setLength()` and `setWidth()` to Program 3-2's `RoomType` class that can be used to individually set an object's `length` and `width`, respectively.

4. Modify Program 3-2 to include two constructors. The first constructor should be a default constructor that initializes an object's `length` and `width` variables to 12.0 and 9.9 respectively, while the second constructor should use two parameters, named `initLenth` and `initWidth`, that can be used to initialize an object's instance variables when the object is created.

5. Write a class declaration and implementation section for each of the following specifications. In each case, include a constructor and a mutator that use parameters to set all instance variables, and an accessor member method named `showData()` that displays an object's values.

   a. A class named `Complex` that has double-precision instance variables named `real` and `imaginary`.

   b. A class named `Circle` that has integer instance variables named `xcenter` and `ycenter` and a floating-point data member named `radius`.

   c. A class named `Computer` that has character instance variables named `compCode`, `printerCode`, and `screenCode`, and double-precision instance variables named `compPrice`, `printerPrice`, and `screenPrice`.

6. Complete the methods declaration section for the following class:

```
class RoomType
{
  // data declaration section
  private:
    double length;   // declare length as a double variable
    double width;    // declare width as a double variable

  // methods declaration section

};

  // methods implementation section
  RoomType::RoomType(double len, double wid)   // constructor
  {
    length = len;
    width = wid;
  }

  void RoomType::setNewRoomValues(double len, double wid)    // mutator
  {
    length = len;
    width = wid;
  }

  void RoomType::ShowRoomValues()    // accessor
  {
    cout << "  length = " + length + "\n  width = " + width;
  }
```

3

7. Determine the errors in the following class:

```
class Employee
{
  public:
     int empnum;
     char code;

  private:
     void showemp(int, char)
       .
       .
       .
};
```

8. Determine the errors in the following class:

```
class RoomType
{
  // data declaration section
  private:
     double length;   // declare length as a double variable
     double width;    // declare width as a double variable
  // methods declaration section
     RoomType()                          // constructor
     void setNewRoomValues(double, double)   // mutator
     void setNewRoomValues(double)        // overloaded mutator
     void ShowRoomValues()                // accessor
};
  // methods implementation section
  RoomType::RoomType   // constructor
  {
    length = 25.0;
    width = 12.0;
  }
  void RoomType::setNewRoomValues(double len, double wid)    // mutator
  {
    length = len;
    width = wid;
  }
```

(continued on next page)

```
void RoomType::setNewRoomValues(double len)   // overloaded mutator
{
  length = len;
}

void RoomType::setNewRoomValues(double wid)   // overloaded mutator
{
  width = wid;
}

void RoomType::ShowRoomValues()                    // accessor
{
  cout << "   length = " + length + "\n   width = " + width;
}
```

9. **a.** Write a C++ class named `Celsius` that contains a single double-precision instance variable named `temperature`. The class should include a constructor and mutator method that permits a programmer to set an object's temperature value to a programmer-selected value. Additionally, include an accessor method that returns an object's temperature value and a class method named `convertToFahr()` that returns the Fahrenheit temperature corresponding to a Celsius temperature. The Fahrenheit value can be determined using the formula

   Fahrenheit = 9.0/5.0 Celsius + 32.0.

   b. Include the method written for Exercise 9a in a working C++ program. Make sure that all class methods are called from `main()`. Have `main()` display the value returned by `convertToFahr()` and verify the returned value by a hand calculation.

10. **a.** Write a C++ class named `Cylinder` that contains two double-precision instance variables named `radius` and `height`. The class should include a constructor and mutator method that permit a programmer to set an object's variables to programmer-selected values. Additionally, include two accessor methods that return an object's `radius` and `height`, respectively, and a class method named `volume()` that returns the volume of a `Cylinder` object. The volume of a cylinder is given by its radius squared times its height times π (r^2 x h x π). Use the value 3.1416 for π.

    b. Include the method written for Exercise 10a in a working C++ program. Make sure that all class methods are called from `main()`. Have `main()` display the value returned by `distance()` and verify the returned value by a hand calculation.

11. **a.** Write a C++ class named `PolyTwo` that contains three double-precision instance variables named `a`, `b`, and `c`, which represent the coefficients of a second-degree polynomial (a second-degree polynomial in x is given by the expression $ax^2 + bx + c$, where a, b, and c are referred to as coefficients. If the coefficient a is zero, the expression becomes a first-degree polynomial). The class should include a constructor and mutator method that permits a programmer to set an object's variables to programmer-selected values. Additionally, there should

be a single accessor method that displays an object's values and a class method named `poly-Value()` that accepts a double-precision value as the parameter named `x`, and returns the value determined by the expression $ax^2 + bx + c$, where *a, b,* and *c* are coefficients contained in a `PolyTwo` object.

b. Include the method written for Exercise 11a in a working C++ program. Make sure that all class methods are called from `main()`. Have `main()` display the value returned by `poly-Value()` for various values of `x` that are passed into the method when it is called. Verify the returned value by performing a hand calculation.

3.3 METHOD DEVELOPMENT: ALGORITHMS

Before writing a method, a programmer must clearly understand the data that will be used, the desired result, and the programming steps that will produce this result. The steps that produce the result are referred to as an algorithm. More precisely, an **algorithm** is a step-by-step set of instructions that describes how data is to be processed to produce the desired result. In essence, an algorithm answers the question: What steps will a method use to produce the desired result?

The following simple problem illustrates the use of an algorithm: Assume you want to calculate the sum of all whole numbers from 1 through 100. Figure 3-6 shows three ways to find the required sum. Each way constitutes an algorithm.

Clearly, most people do not bother to list all possible solution alternatives in a detailed, step-by-step manner, as in Figure 3-6, and then select one of the algorithms to solve the problem. But then, most people do not think algorithmically; they tend to think heuristically. For example, if you had to change a flat tire on your car, you would not think of all the steps required; you would simply change the tire or call someone else to do the job. This is an example of heuristic thinking. Unfortunately, computers do not respond to heuristic commands. A general statement such as "add the numbers from 1 through 100" means nothing to a computer because the computer can only respond to algorithmic-like commands written in an acceptable language such as C++. To write a method that will perform a task and successfully execute, you must clearly understand this difference between algorithmic and intuitive commands. A computer is an "algorithm-responding" machine; it is not a "heuristic-responding" machine. You cannot tell a computer to change a tire or to add the numbers from 1 through 100. Instead, you must give the computer a detailed, step-by-step sequence of instructions that, collectively, forms an algorithm. The algorithm must be written in a programming language, which is called **coding the algorithm**. Typically, an algorithm is coded as a class method or a non-class function.

FIGURE 3-6
Three Ways to Sum the Numbers from 1 Through 100

A — *Columns:* Arrange the numbers from 1 to 100 in a column and add them.

$$
\begin{array}{r}
1 \\
2 \\
3 \\
4 \\
. \\
. \\
. \\
98 \\
99 \\
+\ 100 \\
\hline
5050
\end{array}
$$

B — *Groups:* Arrange the numbers in groups that sum to 101. Multiply the number of groups by 101.

$$
\begin{array}{r}
1 + 100 = 101 \\
2 + 99 = 101 \\
3 + 98 = 101 \\
4 + 97 = 101 \\
. \qquad . \\
. \qquad . \\
. \qquad . \\
49 + 52 = 101 \\
50 + 51 = 101
\end{array}
$$

50 groups → $(50 \times 101) = 5050$

C — *Formula:* Use the formula

$$
\text{Sum} = \frac{n(a + b)}{2}
$$

where

n = number of terms to be added (100)
a = first number to be added (1)
b = last number to be added (100)

$$
\text{Sum} = \frac{100(1 + 100)}{2} = 5050
$$

For example, the sequence of instructions

Set n *equal to* 100

Set a = 1

Set b *equal to* 100

Calculate sum = $\dfrac{n \times (a + b)}{2}$

3

forms a detailed series of steps, which is an algorithm for determining the sum of the numbers from 1 through 100. Notice that these instructions are not a C++ method. Unlike a method, which must be written in a language the computer can respond to, an algorithm can be written or described in various ways. When English-like phrases are used to describe the algorithm (the processing steps), the description is called **pseudocode**. When mathematical equations are used, the description is called a **formula**. When diagrams that employ the symbols shown in Figure 3-7 are used, the description is referred to as a **flowchart**. Figure 3-8 illustrates the use of these symbols in depicting an algorithm for determining the average of three numbers.

A BIT OF BACKGROUND

Al-Khowarizmi

One of the first great mathematicians was Mohammed ibn Musa al-Khowarizmi, who wrote a treatise in about 825 A.D. called *Ilm al-jabr wa'l muqabalah* ("the science of reduction and calculation"). The word *algorism* or *algorithm* is derived from al-Khowarizmi's name, and our word *algebra* is derived from the word *al-jabr* in the title of his work.

Because flowcharts are cumbersome to revise and can easily support unstructured programming practices, they have fallen out of favor among professional programmers, except for visually describing basic programming structures. In their place, pseudocode has gained increasing acceptance. In describing an algorithm using pseudocode, short English phrases are used. For example, acceptable pseudocode for describing the steps needed to compute the average of three numbers is:

> *Input the three numbers into the computer.*
> *Calculate the average by adding the numbers and dividing the sum by 3.*
> *Display the average.*

A BIT OF BACKGROUND

The Young Gauss

German mathematical genius Johann Carl Fredrich Gauss (1777–1855) professed that he could "reckon" before he could talk. At only two years old, he discovered an error in his father's business records.

One day in school, young Johann's teacher asked his class to add up the numbers between 1 and 100. To the chagrin of the teacher, who had thought the task would keep the class busy for a while, Gauss almost instantly wrote the number on his slate and exclaimed, "There it is!" He had reasoned that the series of numbers could be written forward and backward and added term-by-term to get 101 fifty times. Thus, the sum was 100(101)/2; and Gauss, at the age of 10, had discovered that $1 + 2 + \ldots + n = n(n + 1)/2$.

FIGURE 3-7
Flowchart Symbols

SYMBOL	NAME	DESCRIPTION
	Terminal	Indicates the beginning or end of an algorithm
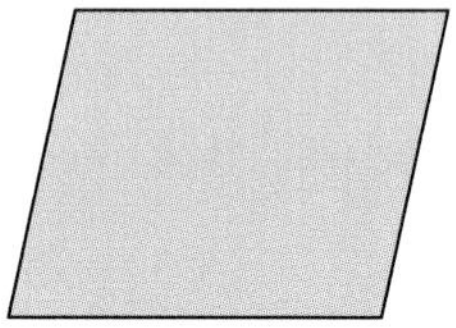	Input/Output	Indicates an input or output operation
	Process	Indicates computation or data manipulation
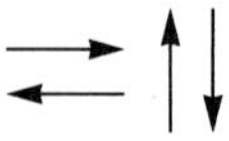	Flow Lines	Connect the flowchart symbols and indicate the logic flow
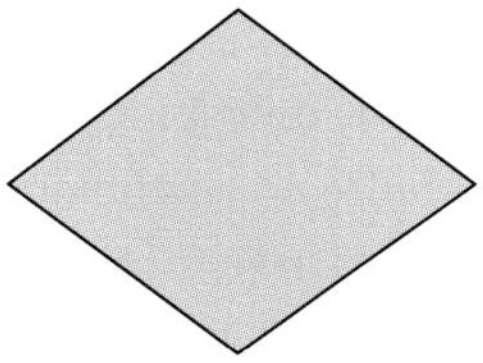	Decision	Indicates a program branch point
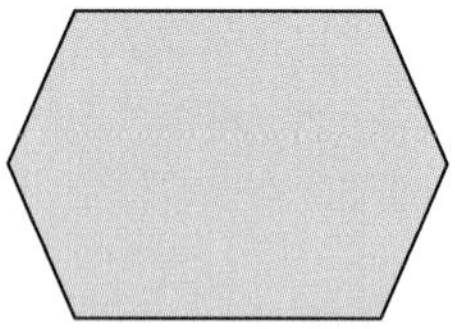	Loop	Indicates the initial, limit, and increment values of a loop
	Predefined Process	Indicates a predefined process, as in calling a method
	Connector	Indicates an entry to, or exit from, another part of the flowchart or a connection point
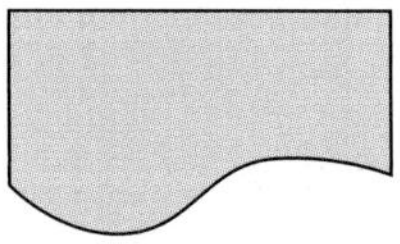	Report	Indicates a written output report

3

Only after the programmer has selected an algorithm and understands the steps required can he or she write the algorithm as a method using computer-language statements. (See Figure 3-9.)

FIGURE 3-8
Flowchart for Calculating the Average of Three Numbers

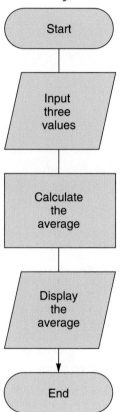

FIGURE 3-9
Coding an Algorithm

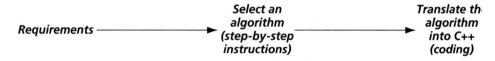

Requirements ⟶ **Select an algorithm (step-by-step instructions)** ⟶ **Translate the algorithm into C++ (coding)**

Exercises 3.3

1. a. Determine six different algorithms for painting a flower as shown in Figure 3-10. Each color must be completed before a new color can be started. (*Hint*: One of the algorithms is: Use yellow first, green second, black last.)

FIGURE 3-10
A Simple Paint-by-Number Figure

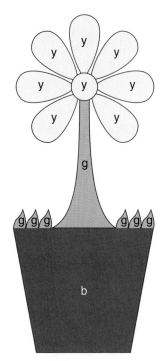

Code:
y=yellow
g=green
b=black

    b. Which of the six painting algorithms (series of steps) is best if we are limited to using one paintbrush and there is no way to clean the brush?

2. Write an algorithm for performing the following tasks. (*Note*: There is no single correct answer for each of these tasks. The exercise is designed to give you practice in converting heuristic commands into equivalent algorithms and understanding the differences in the thought processes involved in the two types of responses.)

    a. Replace a flat tire with the spare tire.
    b. Make a telephone call.
    c. Go to the store and purchase a loaf of bread.
    d. Roast a turkey.

3. Write an algorithm for interchanging the contents of two cups of liquid. Assume that a third cup is available to hold the contents of either cup temporarily. Each cup should be rinsed before any new liquid is poured into it.

4. Write an algorithm to calculate the dollar amount of money in a piggybank that contains h half-dollars, q quarters, n nickels, d dimes, and p pennies.

5. Write an algorithm to find the smallest number in a group of three integer numbers.

6. **a.** Write a set of detailed, step-by-step instructions, in English, to calculate the change remaining from a dollar after a purchase is made. Assume that the cost of the goods purchased is less than a dollar. The change received should consist of the smallest number of coins possible.
    b. Repeat Exercise 6a, but assume the change is given only in pennies.

3.4 APPLICATION: SWAPPING VALUES

It is sometimes necessary to exchange data that is either stored or referenced by two variables. Generally, this is necessary when you need to sort lists of numbers or names. In this section, we develop the basic algorithm used in swapping two values and then write this algorithm as a class method.

Swapping the values stored in two variables is similar to switching the contents of two glasses. For example, assume that the first glass in Figure 3-11a contains pink lemonade and that the second glass contains yellow lemonade. Because the children who use these glasses only want to drink from their own glass, we want to switch the contents in the glasses to give the correct drink to each child. In practice this is easily done using a third glass and following the three-step algorithm:

> *Step 1. Put the contents of the first glass into the third glass (Figure 3-11b).*
> *Step 2. Put the contents of the second glass into the first glass (Figure 3-11c).*
> *Step 3. Put the contents of the third glass into the second glass (Figure 3-11d).*

FIGURE 3-11
Switching the Contents of Two Glasses

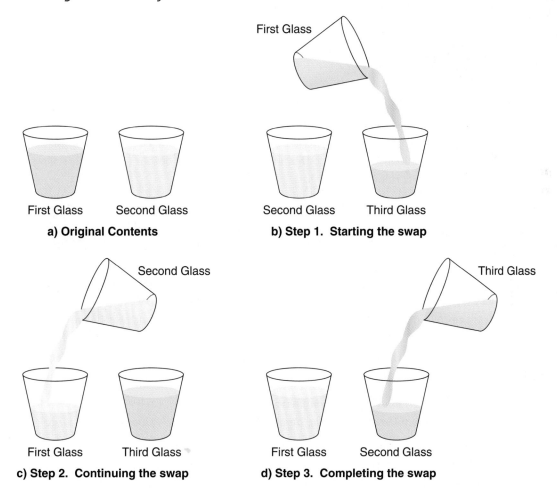

First Glass

First Glass   Second Glass
a) Original Contents

Second Glass   Third Glass
b) Step 1. Starting the swap

Second Glass

First Glass   Third Glass
c) Step 2. Continuing the swap

Third Glass

First Glass   Second Glass
d) Step 3. Completing the swap

A similar three-step algorithm is used in programming to swap the values that are either stored directly or referenced by two variables. Specifically, the swap algorithm becomes:

>**Step 1. Store the first variable's value into a temporary location (Figure 3-12A).**
>**Step 2. Store the second variable's value in the first variable (Figure 3-12B).**
>**Step 3. Store the temporary value in the second variable (Figure 3-12C).**

FIGURE 3-12A *Save the First Value*

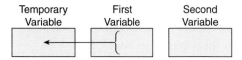

FIGURE 3-12B *Replace the First Value with the Second Value*

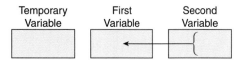

FIGURE 3-12C *Change the Second Value*

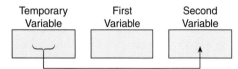

The reason for Step 1, which uses the temporary variable to hold the first variable's value, is immediately obvious once you consider what happens if this variable were not used. For example, if the value of the second variable were initially moved into the first variable (Step 2) before temporarily saving the first value (Step 1), the first value would be lost.

Now that you understand the basic swap algorithm, we can implement it within a C++ method. The key question now becomes "How should the two variables be made available to the method that will swap their values?" As illustrated in Figure 3-13, a method can receive data either as parameters (shown at the top of the figure) or as data members of a single object (shown on the figure's left side). Passing the two variables directly as parameters won't work because the method will only receive a copy of the values in the variables. Thus, switching values within the method will have no effect on the calling method's variables. The correct approach is to enclose the variables within an object as instance variables, and pass the object as an implicit parameter. Then, when the method is applied to the object, the method can directly alter the values stored in these variables. Algorithmically, this becomes:

>**Encapsulate the two variables within a single object.**
>**Use a class method to implement the swap algorithm and switch the values in the instance variables.**

3

FIGURE 3-13
A Method's Interfaces

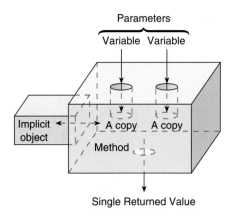

To illustrate this process, assume that we are dealing with names that must be alphabetically arranged. If two names are found to be out of order, the swapping algorithm goes into effect to switch names. This translates into creating a class that supports objects having two instance variables, each of which can reference a string value. Initially, we will supply our class with a constructor that permits us to initialize an object's two variables with the names that must be switched, accessor methods to extract and return individual names, and mutator methods to alter individual names. Next, we will add a swap() method capable of interchanging the strings referenced by an object. Class 3-2, which is named EncapsulateNames, provides the required two data members and initial class methods.

Class 3-2

```cpp
#include <iostream>
#include <string>
using namespace std;

class EncapsulateNames
{
  // data declaration section
  private:
    string nameOne;    // first name is referenced by this variable
    string nameTwo;    // second name is referenced by this variable

  // methods declaration section
  public:
    EncapsulateNames(string, string);    // constructor
    string getFirst();
    string getSecond();
```

(continued on next page)

```cpp
   void setFirstName(string);
   void setSecondName(string);
};

 // methods implementation section
 EncapsulateNames::EncapsulateNames(string s1, string s2)    // constructor
 {
   nameOne = s1;
   nameTwo = s2;
 }


   // methods to get and set individual string values
 string EncapsulateNames::getFirst()
 {
   return nameOne;
 }
 string EncapsulateNames::getSecond()
 {
   return nameTwo;
 }
 void EncapsulateNames::setFirstName(string s1)
 {
   nameOne = s1;
 }
 void EncapsulateNames::setSecondName(string s2)
 {
   nameTwo = s2;
 }
```

The class methods in Class 3-2 are relatively straightforward. The constructor permits an object to be initialized when it is created, the accessor methods return an object's nameOne and nameTwo value, and the mutator methods permit altering an object's nameOne and nameTwo values. Before testing this class's individual methods, however, we can significantly improve it by coding all of the methods as inline (refer to the end of Section 3.1). Applying the inline style to all of the class's methods yields Class 3-3. From an operational viewpoint, both classes are identical.

3

Class 3-3

```cpp
#include <iostream>
#include <string>
using namespace std;

 class EncapsulateNames
{
  // data declaration section
  private:
    string nameOne;     // first name is referenced by this variable
    string nameTwo;     // second name is referenced by this variable

  // methods declaration section
  public:
    EncapsulateNames(string s1, string s2)
      {nameOne = s1; nameTwo = s2;  }    // constructor
    string getFirst(){return nameOne;}   // accessor
    string getSecond(){return nameTwo;}  // accessor
    void setFirstName(string s1){nameOne = s1;}   // mutator
    void setSecondName(string s2){nameTwo = s2;}  // mutator

};
```

Program 3-3 verifies that all of the `EncapsulateNames` class methods are operating correctly.

Program 3-3

```cpp
#include <iostream>
#include <string>
using namespace std;

 class EncapsulateNames
{
  // data declaration section
  private:
    string nameOne;     // first name is referenced by this variable
    string nameTwo;     // second name is referenced by this variable

  // methods declaration section
  public:
    EncapsulateNames(string s1, string s2)
```

(continued on next page)

```
      {nameOne = s1; nameTwo = s2;   }    // constructor
    string getFirst(){return nameOne;}   // accessor
    string getSecond(){return nameTwo;}  // accessor
    void setFirstName(string s1){nameOne = s1;}   // mutator
    void setSecondName(string s2){nameTwo = s2;}  //  mutator
};

int main()
{
   string firstName = "Billings";
   string secName = "Ajax";
   EncapsulateNames namePair(firstName, secName);   // declare an object type

   // verify the accessors
   cout << "The first name is " << namePair.getFirst() << endl;
   cout << "The second name is " << namePair.getSecond() << endl;

   // verify the mutators
   namePair.setFirstName("Calisto");
   namePair.setSecondName("Breyer");

   // extract the two strings
   cout << "\nThe first name is " << namePair.getFirst() << endl;
   cout << "The second name is " << namePair.getSecond() << endl;

   return 0;
}
```

The output produced when Program 3-3 is executed is:

```
The first name is Billings
The second name is Ajax

The first name is Calisto
The second name is Breyer
```

As seen by this output, the created-object named `namePair` is correctly initialized, and each accessor and mutator method correctly accesses and alters the strings referenced by this object's individual internal variables. Now that we have our basic two-variable class, we can add a `swap()` method to switch the strings referenced by the two variables. The code for this method, which implements our three-step swap algorithm is:

```
public void swap()
{
  string temp; // declare a third variable for temporarily holding a double
```

```
  temp = nameOne;      // Step 1. Store the first variable's value into the temporary location
  nameOne = nameTwo;   // Step 2. Store the second variable's value into the first variable
  nameTwo = temp;      // Step 3. Store the temporary value into the second variable
}
```

In reviewing the swap() method, notice that its three assignment statements directly correspond to the three steps previously listed for the swap algorithm and illustrated in Figure 3-12. Including this method into the EncapsulateNames class results in the completed Class 3-4.

Class 3-4

```
#include <iostream>
#include <string>
using namespace std;

class EncapsulateNames
{
  // data declaration section
  private:
    string nameOne;    // first name is referenced by this variable
    string nameTwo;    // second name is referenced by this variable

  // methods declaration section
  public:
    EncapsulateNames(string s1, string s2)
      {nameOne = s1; nameTwo = s2;  }    // constructor
    string getFirst(){return nameOne;}   // accessor
    string getSecond(){return nameTwo;} // accessor
    void setFirstName(string s1){nameOne = s1;}  // mutator
    void setSecondName(string s2){nameTwo = s2;} //  mutator
    void swap();
};
// methods implementation section
void EncapsulateNames::swap()           // swap method
  {
    string temp; // declare a third variable for temporarily holding a double

    temp = nameOne;   // Step 1. Store the first variable's value in the temporary location

    nameOne = nameTwo; // Step 2. Store the second variable's value in the first variable

    nameTwo = temp;    // Step 3. Store the temporary value in the second variable
  }
```

The EncapsulateNames class permits us to create an object using any string variables. Once the object is created, the swap() method permits us to switch the values referenced by the variables, and the accessor methods permit us to return these values. Thus, we can use the EncapsulateNames class any time we are sorting string data and find values that are out of alphabetical order. In this situation, a single EncapsulateNames object would be created at the start of the sort, and then used to encapsulate two names each time a swap is needed. If we were ordering numeric data, we would use a similar class by declaring the instance variables as double-precision types rather than string types, and modifying the class methods appropriately to deal with double-precision values.

To see how the EncapsulateNames class can be used, consider Program 3-4.

Program 3-4

```cpp
#include <iostream>
#include <string>
using namespace std;

 class EncapsulateNames
{
  // data declaration section
  private:
    string nameOne;    // first name is referenced by this variable
    string nameTwo;    // second name is referenced by this variable

  // methods declaration section
  public:
    EncapsulateNames(string s1, string s2)
      {nameOne = s1; nameTwo = s2;  }    // constructor
    string getFirst(){return nameOne;}   // accessor
    string getSecond(){return nameTwo;} // accessor
    void setFirstName(string s1){nameOne = s1;}   // mutator
    void setSecondName(string s2){nameTwo = s2;} //   mutator
    void swap();
};
  // methods implementation section
  void EncapsulateNames::swap()             // swap method
  {
    string temp; // declare a third variable for temporarily holding a double
```

(continued on next page)

```
    temp = nameOne;   // Step 1. Store the first variable's value in the temporary location

    nameOne = nameTwo; // Step 2. Store the second variable's value in the first variable

    nameTwo = temp;    // Step 3. Store the temporary value in the second variable
}

int main()
{
    string firstName = "Billings";
    string secName = "Ajax";

    cout << "Before the call to swap():" << endl;
    cout << "  The string stored in firstName is " << firstName << endl;
    cout << "  The string stored in secName is " << secName << endl;

    // enclose the two strings within a single object
    EncapsulateNames namePair(firstName, secName);  // declare an object type
    // swap the string values within the object
    namePair.swap();

    // extract the two strings
    firstName = namePair.getFirst();
    secName = namePair.getSecond();

    cout << "\nAfter the call to swap():" << endl;
    cout << "  The string stored in firstName is " << firstName << endl;
    cout << "  The string stored in secName is " << secName << endl;

    return 0;
}
```

The following output was obtained using Program 3-4:

```
Before the call to swap():
  The string stored in firstName is Billings
  The string stored in secName is Ajax

After the call to swap():
  The string stored in firstName is  Ajax
  The string stored in secName is  Billings
```

As illustrated in this output, the values stored in the variables of the `main()` method have been correctly swapped from within `swap()`. This was made possible by the use of an object of type `EncapsulateNames`. In practice, the `main()` method in Program 3-4 would be modified to cycle through a complete list of names; each time names were found out of order, the two offending values would be encapsulated and swapped using an `EncapsulateNames` object. To write a program that cycles through a list of items (whether names or numbers), you'll need an understanding of repetition, selection, and arrays, which are presented in succeeding chapters. So for now, we can simply put our `EncapsulateNames` class in our own personal library of useful classes, to be used later when we have acquired additional programming skills.

Exercises 3.4

1. Compile and execute Program 3-3.

2. Compile and execute Program 3-4.

3. If a programmer attempts to modify the `swap()` method in Class 3-4 to accept an `EncapsulateNames` object as an argument, any changes to the passed object's values will have no effect outside of the method. Why is this so?

4. a. Using the `EncapsulateNames` class as a model, construct a class named `XYValues` that can be used to swap the values stored in two double-precision instance variables.
   b. Include the class written for Exercise 4a in a working C++ program. Make sure that all class methods are called from `main()`.

3.5 A CLOSER LOOK: INSIDES AND OUTSIDES

As far as the user of a class is concerned, how the class implements its methods or its objects is neither important nor relevant. For example, you neither know nor should care about how the `cout` object stores the data you send to it, or how the text in the object gets displayed on the screen. From a programming point-of-view, these are internal details of the class. If these internal, or inner workings, of the class do their job correctly, you can easily use and access objects from outside of the class in your program.

One of the major intents of object-oriented programming is to clearly separate the inner workings of a class from its outer usage. As this concept of inner workings and outer usage is central to object-oriented programming, let us explore this concept in a bit more detail.

A useful visualization of this inside-outside concept is to think about a boiled egg as shown in Figure 3-14. Notice that the egg consists of three parts: the yolk at the very center, a white surrounding the yolk, and an outer shell, which is the only part of the egg visible to the outside world. You can think of the yolk as being "very inside," and the white as being somewhat "less inside," while the shell is outside.

FIGURE 3-14
The Boiled Egg Object Model

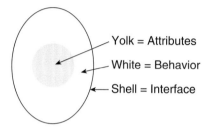

Yolk = Attributes

White = Behavior

Shell = Interface

From an inside-outside viewpoint, the protected yolk corresponds to an object's private instance variable that is surrounded by, and can only be reached via, the white—which corresponds to a class's methods. Thus, surrounding the object, in a similar manner as an egg's white surrounds its yolk, are the operations that we choose to provide for the object. Finally, in this analogy, the interface to the outside world, which is represented by the shell, represents how a user gets to invoke the class's methods on the object's instance variables.

The egg model, with its eggshell interface separating the inside of the egg from the outside, is useful precisely because it so clearly depicts the separation between what should be contained inside a class and what should be seen from the outside. From an inside-outside perspective, an object and the details of how methods are actually implemented are always hidden from the view of an object user. This separation forms an essential element in object-oriented programming.

As a practical example of this inner-outer concept, suppose you are writing a program that deals a hand of cards. From an object-oriented approach, you must start by modeling a deck of cards. The relevant attributes for the card deck is that it contains 52 cards consisting of four suits (hearts, diamonds, spades, and clubs), with each suit consisting of 13 pip values (ace to ten, jack, queen, and king).

Now consider the behavior of the deck of cards, which consists of the operations that can be applied to the deck. At a minimum, we will want the ability to shuffle the deck and deal single cards. First, consider how we might represent cards in the deck. Any of the following attributes (and there are others) could be used to represent a card:

1. Two integers, one representing a suit (a number from 1 to 4) and one representing a value (a number from 1 to 13).

2. One character value and one integer value. The character represents a card's suit, and the integer represents a card's value.

3. One integer variable having a value from 1 to 52, each of which corresponds to a unique card in the deck.

The specific way that a programmer creating the class chooses to represent a deck of cards is an inside issue. From the outside, that is to a programmer using the class, all that is of concern is that he or she have access to a deck consisting of 52 cards having the necessary suit and pip values.

The same is true for the operations that the programmer of the class decides to provide as part of the card deck class. Consider just the shuffling for now.

There are a number of algorithms for producing a shuffled deck. For example, you could use C++'s random number method, rand(), described in Section 6.7, or you could create your own random number generator. Again, the selected procedure is an inside issue to be determined by the class's designer. The specifics of the selection and how it is applied to the attributes chosen for each card in the deck are not relevant from outside the class. A user of the class need not know these internal details. For purposes of illustration, assume that you decide to use C++'s rand() method to produce a randomly shuffled deck.

If you use the first attribute set given previously, each card in a shuffled deck is produced using rand() at least twice: once to create a random number from 1 to 4 for the suit, and then again to create a random number from 1 to 13 for the card's pip value. This sequence must be done to construct 52 different attribute sets with no duplicates allowed.

If, on the other hand, you use the second attribute set given previously, a shuffled deck can be produced in exactly the same fashion just described, with one modification: The first random number (from 1 to 4) must be changed into a character to represent the suit.

Finally, if you use the third representation for a card, you will need to use rand() once for each card to produce 52 random numbers from 1 to 52 with no duplicates allowed.

The important point here is that the selection of how a deck is selected and shuffled are definition issues described in a class's data and methods section, and *definition issues are always inside issues*. A user of the card deck, who is outside, does not need to know how the shuffling is done. All the user of the deck must know is how to produce a shuffled deck. In practice, this means that the user is supplied with sufficient information to correctly instantiate a deck object and call the shuffle method. This corresponds to the interface, or outer shell of the egg.

ABSTRACTION AND ENCAPSULATION

The distinction between insides and outsides relates directly to the concepts of abstraction and encapsulation. **Abstraction** means concentrating on what an object is and does before making any decisions about how the class will be implemented. Thus, abstractly, you define a deck and the operations you want to provide. (If your abstraction is to be useful, it had better capture the attributes and operations of a real-world deck.) Once you have decided on the attributes and operations, you can actually implement, which means code, them.

Encapsulation means incorporating the implementation details of the chosen abstract attributes and behavior into a class. The external side of an object should provide only the necessary interface to users of the object for activating class methods. Imposing a strict inside-outside discipline when creating classes is really another way of saying that the class successfully encapsulates all implementation details. In our deck-of-cards example, encapsulation means that users need never be concerned with how we have internally modeled the deck or how an operation, such as shuffling, is performed; they only need to know how to activate the given operations.

CODE RE-USE AND EXTENSIBILITY

A direct advantage of an inside-outside approach is that it encourages programmers to re-use code using inheritance, which is presented in Chapter 12. This is a direct result of having all interactions between objects controlled on the outside by calling methods and restricting all implementation details within the object's inside.

For example, consider the object shown in Figure 3-15. Here any of the two class's methods can be activated by correctly stimulating either the circle or square on the outside. This stimulation is analogous to a method call. We have used a circle and square to emphasize that two different methods are provided for outside use. In our card-deck example, activation of one method might produce a shuffled deck, while activation of another method might result in a card suit and pip value being returned.

FIGURE 3-15
Using an Object's Interface

The interface

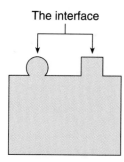

Now assume that you want to alter the implementation of an existing operation or add more functionality to your class. As long as the existing outside interface is maintained, the internal coding of any and all operations can be changed without the user ever being aware that a change took place. This is a direct result of encapsulating the attribute data and operations inside a class.

In addition, as long as the interface to existing methods is not changed, new methods can be added as they are needed. Essentially, from the outside world, all that is being added is another method call that accesses the inside attributes and modifies them in a new way.

3.6 COMMON PROGRAMMING ERRORS

1. Attempting to pass incorrect data types. This is an extremely common programming error related to methods. The values passed to a method must correspond to the data types of the parameters declared for the method. One way to verify that correct values have been received is to display all passed values within a method's body before any calculations are made. Once this verification has taken place, the display can be dispensed with.

2. Declaring the same variable locally within both the calling and called methods and assuming a change in one variable affects the other variable. Even though the variable name is the same, a change to one local variable *does not* alter the value in the other local variable.

3. Terminating a method's header line with a semicolon.

4. Forgetting to include the data type of a method's parameters within the header line.

5. Attempting to alter an object's private variables by passing the object into a nonclass method as an argument. An object type can be passed as an argument but C++'s privacy rules must still be observed.

3.7 CHAPTER REVIEW

Key Terms

algorithm	*overloading*	*state*
call by value	*parameter signature*	*swap method*
identity	*parameters*	
local variable	*pass by value*	

SUMMARY

1. A method is defined when it is written.

2. The syntax for a class method is:

```
returnType className::methodName(parameter list)
{
  declarations statements

  additional C++ statements;
  return  expression;
}
```

The first line of the method is called the method header. The opening and closing braces of the method and all statements in between these braces constitute the method's body. The parameter list is a comma-separated list of parameter declarations.

3. A method's return type declares the data type of the value returned by the method. If the method does not return a value, it should be declared as a `void` type.

4. Methods can directly return at most a single value to their calling methods. This value is the value of the expression in the `return` statement.

5. A method is called by giving its name and passing any data to it in the parentheses following the name. If a variable is one of the arguments in a method call, the called method receives a copy of the variable's value.

6. A called method cannot alter either a primitive data type argument's value or a reference variable's value by changing the value of the equivalent parameter.

7. An algorithm is a step-by-step set of instructions that describes how a single computation or task is to be performed. An algorithm is typically coded as a C++ method.

Chapter Exercises

1. **a.** Write a C++ class named `Triangle` that contains three instance variables named `sideOne`, `sideTwo`, and `angle`. The class should include a constructor and mutator method that permit a programmer to set an object's variables to programmer-selected values.

    b. Include the class written for Exercise 1a in a working C++ program. Make sure that all class methods are called from `main()`.

2. **a.** Write a C++ class named `Point` that contains two double-precision instance variables named x and y. The class should include a constructor that initializes an object's x and y variables to 3.0 and 4.0, respectively. Similarly, the class should include a mutator method that sets an object's x and y values to 4.8 and 9.2, respectively. Additionally, include an accessor method that displays the values. Also include a class method named `distance()` that returns the distance of a `Point` object from the point having coordinates (0,0). The distance, d, between a point (x,y) and (0,0) is given by the formula

    $$d = \sqrt{x^2 + y^2}$$

    (*Hint:* You must use the C++ provided method named `sqrt()`. For example, the value of `sqrt(x * x + y * y)` will return the correct value. To use this method you must include the preprocessor command `#include<cmath>`).

    b. Include the method written for Exercise 2a in a working C++ program. Make sure that all class methods are called from `main()`. Have `main()` display the value returned by `distance()` and verify the returned value by a hand calculation. For example, the distance returned for a `Point` object having x and y values of 3 and 4, respectively, should be 5.

3. a. Construct a `Time` class containing integer instance variables named `seconds`, `minutes`, and `hours`. Have the class contain two constructors: The first should be a default constructor that initializes each data member with a default value of 0. The second constructor should accept three integer arguments that will be used to set each instance variable. The class should also include a mutator that accepts three integer arguments for setting the instance variables, and an accessor method for displaying the time.

   b. Include the class written for Exercise 3a within the context of a complete program.

4. a. Construct a class named `Student` consisting of an integer instance variable for storing a student identification number, an integer instance variable for storing the number of credits completed by the student, and a double-precision value for storing a student's grade point average. The default constructor for this class should initialize all `Student` data members to 0. Additionally, an overloaded constructor should be provided to initialize a new `Student`'s instance variables to programmer-selected values, using method arguments (this second constructor would be used for transfer students). Included in the class should be mutator methods to alter a student ID number, and alter both the number of credits taken and the new GPA at the same time. Additionally, an accessor method should be provided to display all of a `Student`'s data.

   b. Include the class constructed in Exercise 4a within the context of a complete program. Your program should declare two objects of type `Student` and accept and display data for the two objects to verify operation of the member methods.

5. a. Write a set of detailed, step-by-step instructions in English for calculating the least number of dollar bills needed to pay a bill of amount `Total`. For example, if `Total` were $98, the bills would consist of one $50 bill, two $20 bills, one $5 bill, and three $1 bills. For this exercise, assume that only $100, $50, $20, $10, $5, and $1 bills are available.

   b. Repeat Exercise 5a, but assume the bill is paid only in $1 bills.

6. a. Write an algorithm to locate the first occurrence of the name "Jean" in a list of names arranged in random order.

   b. Discuss how you could improve your algorithm for Exercise 6a if the list of names was arranged in alphabetical order.

7. Determine and write an algorithm to sort three numbers in ascending (from lowest to highest) order. How would you solve this problem heuristically?

Testing Center

Please visit the Testing Center at www.course.com/testingcenter for more practice on developing class methods.

PART 2

STATEMENTS

4

ASSIGNMENT, FORMATTING, AND INTERACTIVE INPUT

In this chapter we begin an in-depth exploration of the basic statements and techniques required in the vast majority of C++ methods and functions. We begin with a more focused look at how a C++ assignment statement is used to not only initialize variables but also to obtain computational results. Next, you'll learn about C++'s formatting capabilities, which you must be able to use to produce presentable output displays. This is followed by a presentation of the standard C++ library mathematical functions, which conveniently calculate frequently needed mathematical formulas, such as square roots, exponential functions, and absolute values. Finally, you'll study a number of other basic programming techniques, including the cin object, which permits entering data interactively while a program is executing. The statements, functions, and techniques presented in this chapter form the basic foundation for all C++ programs.

4.1 ASSIGNMENT OPERATIONS

We have already encountered simple assignment statements in Section 2.2. Assignment statements are the most basic C++ statements for both assigning values to variables and performing computations. This statement has the general form:

```
variable = expression;
```

As we have seen in the last two chapters, the simplest expression in C++ is a single constant. For example, consider the following assignment statements, where the operand to the right of the assignment operator, =, is a constant:

```
length = 25;
width = 17.5;
```

In each of these assignment statements, the value of the constant to the right of the assignment operator is assigned to the variable on the left of the operator. It is important to note that the assignment operator in C++ does not have the same meaning as an equal sign in algebra. The assignment operator tells the computer to first determine the value of the operand to the right of the operator and then to store (or assign) that value in the locations associated with the variable to the left of it. In this regard, the C++ statement length = 25; is read "length is assigned the value 25." The blank spaces in the assignment statement are inserted for readability only.

As we have seen in Chapter 2, the first time a value is assigned to a variable, the variable is said to be initialized. The initial value assigned to a variable can either be explicitly designated within the declaration statement, explicitly initialized by a constructor method for instance variables, or implicitly initialized by the C++ compiler. (See Table 2-11). After a variable has been initialized, its value can subsequently be changed by an assignment statement. For example, assume that a variable named total was initialized to 3.7. A subsequent statement, such as

```
total = 6.28;
```

causes the value of 6.28 to be assigned to total. The 3.7 that was in total is overwritten with the new value of 6.28. Because a variable can store only one value at a time, it is sometimes useful to think of the variable to the left of the equal sign as a parking spot in a huge parking lot. Just as an individual parking spot can be used only by one car at a time, each individual variable can store only one value at a time. The "parking" of a new value in a variable automatically causes the computer to remove any value previously parked there.

In addition to being a literal value, the operand to the right of the assignment operator can be a variable or any other valid C++ expression. Thus, the expression to the right of the assignment operator can be used to perform calculations using the arithmetic operators introduced in Section 2.1. Examples of assignment statements using arithmetic expressions to the right of the assignment operator are:

```
sum = 3 + 7;
diff = 15 - 6;
product = 0.05 * 14.6;
tally = count + 1;
newtotal = 18.3 + total;
taxes = 0.06 * amount;
totalWeight = factor * weight;
average = sum / items;
slope = (y2 - y1) / (x2 - x1);
```

As always in an assignment statement, the value of the expression to the right of the assignment operator is evaluated first, and then this value is stored in the variable to the left of the equal sign. For example, in the assignment statement `totalWeight = factor * weight;` the arithmetic expression `factor * weight` is first evaluated to yield a result. This result, which is a number, is then stored in the variable `totalWeight`.

In writing assignment statements, you must be aware of two important considerations. Since the expression to the right of the equal sign is evaluated first, all variables used in the expression must previously have been assigned values if the result is to make sense. For example, the assignment statement `totalWeight = factor * weight;` causes a valid number to be stored in `totalWeight` only if you first take care to assign valid numbers to factor and weight. Thus, the sequence of statements

```
factor = 1.06;
weight = 155.0;
totalWeight = factor * weight;
```

ensures that we know the values being used to obtain the result that will be stored in `totalWeight`. Figure 4-1 illustrates the values stored in the variables `factor`, `weight`, and `totalWeight`.

FIGURE 4-1
Values Stored in the Variables

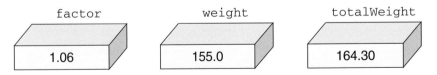

The second consideration to keep in mind is that because the value of an expression is stored in the variable to the left of the equal sign, there must be a variable listed immediately to the left of the equal sign. For example, the assignment statement

```
amount + 1892 = 1000 + 10 * 5;
```

is invalid. The expression on the right side of the equal sign evaluates to the integer 1050, which can be stored only in a variable. Because amount + 1892 is an invalid variable name, the compiler does not know where to assign the calculated value.

Program 4-1 illustrates the use of assignment statements to calculate the volume of a cylinder. As illustrated in Figure 4-2, the volume of a cylinder is determined by the formula, $Volume = \pi r^2 h$, where r is the radius of the cylinder, h is the height, and π is the constant 3.1416 (accurate to four decimal places).

FIGURE 4-2
Determining the Volume of a Cylinder

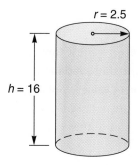

Program 4-1

```cpp
// this Program calculates the volume of a cylinder,
// given its radius and height
#include <iostream>
using namespace std;

int main()
{
   double radius, height, volume;

   radius = 2.5;
   height = 16.0;
   volume = 3.1416 * radius * radius * height;
   cout << "The volume of the cylinder is " << volume << endl;

   return 0;
}
```

When Program 4-1 is compiled and executed, the output is

```
The volume of the cylinder is 314.16
```

This output is produced by the `cout` statement within the program. As always, when a variable name is sent to `cout`, the value stored in the variable is placed on the output stream and displayed.

Consider the flow of control that the computer uses in executing Program 4-1. Execution begins with the first statement within the body of the `main()` function, which is the declarations statement, and continues sequentially, statement by statement, until the closing brace of `main()` is encountered. This flow of control is true for all programs, regardless of the language they are written in. The computer works on one statement at a time, executing that statement with no knowledge of what the next statement will be. This explains why all operands used in an expression must have values assigned to them before the expression is evaluated.

When the computer executes the assignment statement

```
volume = 3.1416 * radius * radius * height;
```

in Program 4-1, it uses whatever value is stored in the variables `radius` and `height` at the time the assignment statement is executed.[1] If no values have been specifically assigned to these variables before they are used in the assignment statement, the computer will use whatever values happen to occupy these variables when they are referenced (on some systems all variables are automatically initialized to zero). The computer does not "look ahead" to see if you assign values to these variables later in the program.

It is important to realize that in C++, the assignment operator, =, used in assignment statements is a true operator, in the same manner as all other C++ operators, such as +, - , and so on. This is *not* true in most other high-level languages. In C++ (as in C), an expression using this operator, such as `interest = principal * rate`, is an **assignment expression**. Because the assignment operator has a lower precedence than any other arithmetic operator, the value of any expression to the right of the equal sign will be evaluated first, prior to assignment. An assignment expression that is terminated with a semicolon becomes an assignment statement.

Like all expressions, assignment expressions themselves have a value. The value of the complete assignment expression is the value assigned to the variable on the left of the assignment operator. For example, the expression `a = 5` both assigns a value of 5 to the variable and results in the expression itself having a value of 5. The value of the expression can always be verified using a statement such as

```
cout << "The value of the expression is " << (a = 5) << endl;
```

Here, the value of the expression itself is displayed and not the contents of the variable a. Although both the contents of the variable and the expression have the same value, we are in fact dealing with two distinct entities.

As a programmer, you will generally only be interested in the actual assignment of a value to a variable provided when an assignment operator is used; the final value of the assignment expression itself is of little consequence. However, the fact that assignment expressions have a value has implications that you will consider when you learn how to use relational operators in C++.

---

[1]Since C++ does not have an exponentiation operator, the square of the radius is obtained by the term `radius * radius`. In Section 4.3 we introduce C++'s power function `pow()`, which allows us to raise a number to a power.

4

Because the = symbol is an operator in C++, multiple assignments are possible in the same expression or its equivalent statement. For example, in the expression a = b = c = 25, all the assignment operators have the same precedence. Since the assignment operator has a right-to-left associativity, the final evaluation proceeds in the sequence:

```
a = (b = (c = 25));
```

This evaluation has the effect of assigning the number 25 to each of the variables individually in the following sequence:

```
c = 25;
b = 25;
a = 25;
```

PROGRAMMING NOTE

lvalues and rvalues

You will encounter the terms *lvalue* and *rvalue* frequently in almost all programming languages that define assignment using an operator that permits multiple assignments in the same statement. The term lvalue refers to any quantity that is valid on the left side of an assignment operator. The term rvalue refers to any quantity that is valid on the right hand side of an assignment operator.

For example, each variable we have encountered so far can be either an lvalue or rvalue (that is, a variable, by itself, can appear on both sides of an assignment operator), while a number can only be an rvalue. More generally, any expression that yields a value can be an rvalue. Not all variables, however, can be used as either lvalues or rvalues. For example, an array type, which is introduced in Chapter 8, cannot be either an lvalue or an rvalue, while individual array elements can be both.

Now that you've learned about assignment statements, following are basic considerations and ways that you will see assignment statements used.

COERCION

One thing to keep in mind when working with assignment statements is the data type assigned to the values on both sides of the expression, because data type conversions take place across assignment operators; that is, the value of the expression on the right side of the assignment operator will be converted to the data type of the variable to the left of the assignment operator. This type of conversion is referred to as a **coercion**, because the value assigned to the variable on the left side of the assignment operator is forced into the data type of the variable it is assigned to. An example of a coercion occurs when an integer value is assigned to a real variable; this causes the integer to be converted to a real value. Similarly, assigning a real value to an integer variable converts the real value stored in the variable to an integer value, which always results in the loss of the fractional part of the number due to truncation. For example, if `temp` is an integer variable, the assignment expression `temp = 25.89` causes the integer value 25 to be stored in the integer variable `temp`.

In evaluating the expression to the right of the assignment operator, the rules for evaluating expressions previously listed in Table 2.5 (Section 2.1) are always used. As an example of this, consider the following statement, where `a` and `b` are integer variables and `d` is a floating point variable.

```
a = b * d;
```

When the mixed-mode expression `b * d` is evaluated (recall that a mixed-mode expression is any expression that contains two different data-types), the value of `d` used in the expression is converted to a double-precision number for purposes of computation. (It is important to note that the value stored in `d` remains a floating-point number.) Because one of the operands is a double-precision variable, the value of the integer variable `b` is converted to a double-precision number for the computation (again, the value stored in `b` remains an integer) and the resulting value of the expression `b * d` is a double-precision number. Finally, a data-type coercion across the assignment operator comes into play. Since the left side of the assignment operator is an integer variable, the double-precision value of the expression `(b * d)` is truncated to an integer value and stored in the variable `a`.

ASSIGNMENT VARIATIONS

Although only one variable is allowed immediately to the left of the equal sign in an assignment expression, the variable to the left of the assignment operator can also be used on the right of the operator, in the same statement. For example, the assignment statement `sum = sum + 10;` is valid. Clearly, as an algebra equation `sum` could never be equal to itself plus 10. But in C++, the statement `sum = sum + 10;` is not an equation—it is a statement that is evaluated in two major steps. The first step is to calculate the value of `sum + 10`. The second step is to store the computed value in `sum`. See if you can determine the output of Program 4-2.

Program 4-2

```cpp
#include <iostream>
using namespace std;

int main()
{
  int sum;

  sum = 25;
  cout << "The number stored in sum is " << sum << endl;
  sum = sum + 10;
  cout << "The number now stored in sum is " << sum << endl;

  return 0;
}
```

The assignment statement `sum = 25;` tells the computer to store the number 25 in `sum`, as shown in Figure 4-3.

FIGURE 4-3
The Integer 25 Is Stored in `sum`

sum

The first `cout` statement causes the value stored in `sum` to be displayed by the message `The number stored in sum is 25`. The second assignment statement, `sum = sum + 10;` causes the computer to retrieve the 25 stored in `sum` and add 10 to this number, yielding the number 35. The number 35 is then stored in the variable on the left side of the equal sign, which is the variable `sum`. The 25 previously stored in `sum` is simply overwritten by the new value of 35, as shown in Figure 4-4.

FIGURE 4-4
The Statement `sum = sum + 10;` *Causes a New Value to Be Stored in* `sum`

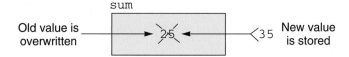

Assignment expressions like `sum = sum + 25`, which use the same variable on both sides of the assignment operator, can be written using the following **shortcut assignment operators:**

$$+= \qquad -= \qquad *= \qquad /= \qquad \%=$$

For example, the expression `sum = sum + 10` can be written as `sum += 10`. Similarly, the expression `price *= rate` is equivalent to the expression `price = price * rate`.

When using these new assignment operators, keep in mind that the variable to the left of the assignment operator is applied to the *complete* expression on the right. For example, the expression `price *= rate + 1` is equivalent to the expression `price = price * (rate + 1)`, not `price = price * rate + 1`.

ACCUMULATING

Assignment expressions like `sum += 10` or its equivalent, `sum = sum + 10`, are common in all programming languages. These expressions are required in accumulating subtotals when data is entered one number at a time, and are referred to as **accumulating statements**. For example, if we want to add the numbers 96, 70, 85, and 60 in calculator fashion, we could use the following statements

statement	value in sum
sum = 0;	0
sum = sum + 96;	96
sum = sum + 70;	166
sum = sum + 85;	251
sum = sum + 60;	311

The first statement initializes sum to 0. This removes any number stored in sum that would invalidate the final total. (Such a value is sometimes called a "garbage value.") As each number is added, the value stored in sum is increased accordingly. After the last statement is executed, sum contains the total of all the added numbers. Program 4-3 illustrates the effect of these statements by displaying the contents of sum after each addition is made.

Program 4-3

```cpp
#include <iostream>
using namespace std;

int main()
{
  int sum;

  sum = 0;
  cout << "The value of sum is initially set to " << sum << endl;
  sum = sum + 96;
  cout << "   sum is now " << sum << endl;
  sum = sum + 70;
  cout << "   sum is now " << sum << endl;
  sum = sum + 85;
  cout << "   sum is now " << sum   << endl;
  sum = sum + 60;
  cout << "   The final sum is " << sum << endl;

  return 0;
}
```

The output displayed by Program 4-3 is:

```
The value of sum is initially set to 0
  sum is now 96
  sum is now 166
  sum is now 251
  The final sum is 311
```

4

Although Program 4-3 is not really a useful program (it is easier to add the numbers by hand), it does illustrate the subtotaling effect that occurs when you repeatedly use statements having the form:

```
variable = variable + newValue;
```

We will find many uses for this type of statement when we become more familiar with the repetition statements introduced in Chapter 6.

COUNTING

Another type of assignment statement, which is very similar to the accumulating statement, is the counting statement. Counting statements have the form:

```
variable = variable + fixedNumber;
```

Examples of counting statements are:

```
i = i + 1;
n = n + 1;
count = count + 1;
j = j + 2;
m = m + 2;
kk = kk + 3;
```

In each of these examples, the same variable is used on both sides of the equal sign. After the statement is executed, the value of the respective variable is increased by a fixed amount. In the first three examples, the variables i, n, and count have all been increased by 1. In the next two examples, the respective variables have been increased by 2, and in the final example the variable kk has been increased by 3.

For the special case in which a variable is either increased or decreased by 1, C++ provides two unary operators. Using the **increment operator**[2], ++, the expression variable = variable + 1 can be replaced by either the expression variable++ or ++variable. Examples using the increment operator are:

expression	**alternative**
i = i + 1	i++ or ++i
n = n + 1	n++ or ++n
count = count + 1	count++ or ++count

Program 4-4 illustrates the use of the increment operator.

_____

[2]As an historical note, the ++ in C++ was inspired from the increment operator symbol. It was used to indicate that C++ was the next increment to the C language.

Program 4-4

```cpp
#include <iostream>
using namespace std;

int main()
{
  int count;

  count = 0;
  cout << "The initial value of count is " << count << endl;
  count++;
  cout << "   count is now " << count << endl;
  count++;
  cout << "   count is now " << count << endl;
  count++;
  cout << "   count is now " << count << endl;
  count++;
  cout << "   count is now " << count << endl;

  return 0;
}
```

The output displayed by Program 4-4 is:

```
The initial value of count is 0
count is now 1
count is now 2
count is now 3
count is now 4
```

When the ++ operator appears before a variable it is called a **prefix increment operator**; when it appears after a variable it is called **postfix increment operator**. The distinction between a prefix and postfix increment operator is important when the variable being incremented is used in an assignment expression. For example, the expression k = ++n does two things in one expression. Initially the value of n is incremented by 1 and then the new value of n is assigned to the variable k. Thus, the statement k = ++n; is equivalent to the two statements

```cpp
n = n + 1;    // increment n first
k = n;        // assign n's value to k
```

The assignment expression k = n++, which uses a postfix increment operator, reverses this procedure. A postfix increment operates after the assignment is completed. Thus, the statement k = n++; first assigns the current value of n to k and then increments the value of n by 1. This is equivalent to the two statements

```
k = n;          // assign n's value to k
n = n + 1;      // and then increment n
```

In addition to the increment operator, C++ also provides a decrement operator, --. As you might expect, the expressions variable-- and --variable are both equivalent to the expression variable = variable - 1.

Examples using the decrement operator are:

expression	alternative
i = i - 1	i-- or --i
n = n - 1	n-- or --n
count = count - 1	count-- or --count

When the -- operator appears before a variable it is called a **prefix decrement operator**. When the decrement appears after a variable it is called a **postfix decrement operator**. For example, both of the expressions n-- and --n reduce the value of n by 1. These expressions are equivalent to the longer expression n = n - 1. As with the increment operator, however, the prefix and postfix decrement operators produce different results when used in assignment expressions. For example, the expression k = --n first decrements the value of n by 1 before assigning the value of n to k, while the expression k = n-- first assigns the current value of n to k and then reduces the value of n by 1.

The increment and decrement operators can often be used advantageously to reduce storage requirements and increase execution speed. For example, consider the following three statements:

```
count = count + 1;
count += 1;
count++;
```

All perform the same function; however, when these instructions are compiled for execution on an IBM personal computer the storage requirements for the instructions are 9, 4, and 3 bytes, respectively.[3] Using the assignment operator, =, instead of the increment operator results in using three times the storage space for the instruction, with an accompanying decrease in execution speed.

Exercises 4.1

1. Write an assignment statement to calculate the circumference of a circle having a radius of 3.3 inches. The equation for determining the circumference, c, of a circle is $c = 2\pi r$, where r is the radius and π equals 3.1416.

---

[3]This is clearly a compiler dependent result.

2. Write an assignment statement to calculate the area of a circle. The equation for determining the area, a, of a circle is $a = \pi r^2$, where r is the radius and $\pi = 3.1416$.

3. Write an assignment statement to convert temperature in degrees Fahrenheit to degrees Celsius. The equation for this conversion is *Celsius = 5/9 (Fahrenheit - 32)*.

4. Write an assignment statement to calculate the round trip distance, d, in feet, of a trip that is s miles long, one way.

5. Write an assignment statement to calculate the elapsed time, in minutes, that it takes to make a trip. The equation for computing elapsed time is *elapsed time = total distance/average speed*. Assume that the distance is in miles and the average speed is in miles/hour.

6. Write an assignment statement to calculate the *n*th term in an arithmetic sequence. The formula for calculating the value, v, of the *n*th term is $v = a + (n - 1)d$, where a = the first number in the sequence and d = the difference between any two numbers in the sequence.

7. Write a C++ program that displays the results of the expressions 3.0 * 5.0, 7.1 * 8.3 - 2.2, and 3.2 / (6.1 * 5). Calculate the value of these expressions manually to verify that the displayed values are correct.

8. Write a C++ program that displays the results of the expressions 15 / 4, 15 % 4, and 5 * 3 - (6 * 4). Calculate the value of these expressions manually to verify that the display produced by your program is correct.

9. Determine the output of the following program:

```
#include <iostream>
using namespace std;

int main() // a program illustrating integer truncation
{
    int num1, num2;

    num1 = 9/2;
    num2 = 17/4;
    cout << "the first integer displayed is " << num1 << endl;
    cout << "the second integer displayed is " << num2 << endl;

    return 0;
}
```

10. Determine the output produced by the following program:

```cpp
#include <iostream>
using namespace std;

int main()
{
   double average = 26.27;

   cout << "the average is " << average << endl;
   average = 682.3;
   cout << "the average is " << average << endl;
   average = 1.968;
   cout << "the average is " << average << endl;

   return 0;
}
```

11. Determine the output produced by the following program:

```cpp
#include <iostream>
using namespace std;

int main()
{
   double sum;

   sum = 0.0;
   cout << "the sum is " << sum << endl;
   sum = sum + 26.27;
   cout << "the sum is " << sum << endl;
   sum = sum + 1.968;
   cout << "the final sum is " << sum << endl;

   return 0;
}
```

12. a. Determine what each statement causes to happen in the following program:

```cpp
#include <iostream>
using namespace std;

int main()
{
```

(continued on next page)

```
    int num1, num2, num3, total;

    num1 = 25;
    num2 = 30;
    total = num1 + num2;
    cout << num1 << " + " << num2 << " = " << total;

    return 0;
}
```

b. What is the output that is produced when the program in Exercise 12a is compiled and executed?

13. By mistake, a student reordered the statements in Program 4-2 as follows:

```
#include <iostream>
using namespace std;

int main()
{
    int sum;
    sum = 0;
    sum = sum + 96;
    sum = sum + 70;
    sum = sum + 85;
    sum = sum + 60;
    cout << "The value of sum is initially set to " << sum << endl;
    cout << "    sum is now " << sum << endl;
    cout << "    sum is now " << sum << endl;
    cout << "    sum is now " << sum << endl;
    cout << "    The final sum is " << sum << endl;

    return 0;
}
```

Determine the output produced by this program.

14. Using Program 4-1, determine the volume of cylinders having the following radii and heights.

radius (in.)	height (in.)
1.62	6.23
2.86	7.52
4.26	8.95
8.52	10.86
12.29	15.35

15. The area of an ellipse (see Figure 4-5) is given by the formula *Area* = π *a b*. Using this formula, write a C++ Program to calculate the area of an ellipse having a minor axis, *b*, of 2.5 inches and a major axis, *a*, of 6.4 inches.

FIGURE 4-5
The Minor Axis a and the Major Axis b of an Ellipse

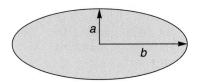

4.2 FORMATTING NUMBERS FOR PROGRAM OUTPUT

Besides displaying correct results, it is extremely important for a program to present its results attractively. Most programs are judged, in fact, on the perceived ease of data entry and the style and presentation of their output. For example, displaying a monetary result as 1.897000 is not in keeping with accepted report conventions. The display should be either $1.90 or $1.89, depending on whether rounding or truncation is used.

The format of numbers displayed by `cout` can be controlled by field width manipulators included in each output stream. Table 4-1 lists the most commonly used manipulators available for this purpose.[4]

For example, the statement `cout << "The sum of 6 and 15 is" << setw(3) <<  21;` creates this printout:

```
        The sum of 6 and 15 is 21
```

The `setw(3)` field width manipulator included in the stream of data passed to `cout` is used to set the displayed field width. The 3 in this manipulator sets the default field width for the next number in the stream to be three spaces wide. This field width setting causes the 21 to be printed in a field of three spaces, which includes one blank and the number 21. As illustrated, integers are right-justified within the specified field.

Field width manipulators are useful in printing columns of numbers so that the numbers in each column align correctly. For example, Program 4-5 illustrates how a column of integers would align in the absence of field width manipulators.

---

[4]As was noted in Chapter 2, the `endl` manipulator inserts a newline and then flushes the stream.

TABLE 4-1
Commonly Used Stream Manipulators

manipulator	action
setw(n)	Set the field width to *n*.
setprecision(n)	Set the floating-point precision to *n* places. If the fixed manipulator is designated, *n* specifies the total number of displayed digits after the decimal point; otherwise *n* specifies the total number of significant digits displayed (integer plus fractional digits).
setfill('x')	Set the default leading fill character to *x*. (The default leading fill character is a space, which is output to fill the front of an output field whenever the width of the field is larger than the value being displayed.)
setiosflags(flags)	Set the format flags (see Table 4-3 for flag settings).
scientific	Set the output to display real numbers in scientific notation.
showbase	Display the base used for numbers. A leading 0 is displayed for octal numbers and a leading 0x for hexadecimal numbers.
showpoint	Always display 6 digits in total (combination of integer and fractional parts). Fill with trailing zeros, if necessary. For larger integer values revert to scientific notation.
showpos	Display all positive numbers with a leading + sign.
boolalpha	Display Boolean values as true and false, rather than as 1 and 0.
dec	Set output for decimal display (this is the default).
endl	Output a newline character and display all characters in the buffer.
fixed	Always show a decimal point and use a default of 6 digits after the decimal point. Fill with trailing zeros, if necessary.
flush	Display all the characters in the buffer.
left	Left justify all numbers.
hex	Set output for hexadecimal display.
oct	Set output for octal display.
uppercase	Display hexadecimal digits and the exponent in scientific notation in uppercase.
right	Right justify all numbers (this is the default).
noboolalpha	Display Boolean values as 1 and 0, rather than as true and false.
noshowbase	Do not display octal numbers with a leading 0 and hexadecimal numbers with a leading 0x.
noshowpoint	Do not use a decimal point for real numbers with no fractional parts, do not display trailing zeros in the fractional part of a number, and display a maximum of 6 decimal digits only.
noshowpos	Do not display leading + signs (this is the default).
nouppercase	Display hexadecimal digits and the exponent in scientific notation in lowercase.

4

Program 4-5

```cpp
#include <iostream>
using namespace std;

int main()
{
  cout << 6 << endl
       << 18 << endl
       << 124 << endl
       << "---\n"
       << (6+18+124) << endl;

  return 0;
}
```

The output of Program 4-5 is:

```
6
18
124
---
148
```

Since no field width manipulators are included in Program 4-5, the cout object allocates enough space for each number as it is received. To force the numbers to align on the units digit requires a field width wide enough for the largest displayed number. For Program 4-5, a width of three would suffice. The use of this field width is illustrated in Program 4-6.

Program 4-6

```cpp
#include <iostream>
#include <iomanip>
using namespace std;

int main()
{
  cout << setw(3) << 6 << endl
       << setw(3) << 18 << endl
       << setw(3) << 124 << endl
       << "---\n"
       << (6+18+124) << endl;

  return 0;
}
```

The output of Program 4-6 is:

```
    6
   18
  124
  ---
  148
```

Notice that the field width manipulator must be included for each occurrence of a number inserted into the data stream sent to `cout`, and that this particular manipulator only applies to the next insertion of data immediately following it. The other manipulators remain in effect until they are changed.

When a manipulator requiring an argument is used, the `iomanip` header file must be included as part of the program. This is accomplished by the preprocessor command `#include <iomanip>`, which is listed as the second line in Program 4-6.

Formatted floating-point numbers completely requires the use of three field width manipulators. The first manipulator sets the total width of the display, the second manipulator forces the display of a decimal point, and the third manipulator determines how many significant digits will be displayed to the right of the decimal point. For example, the statement

```
cout << "|" << setw(10) << fixed << setprecision(3) << 25.67 << "|";
```

causes the printout

```
|    25.670|
```

the bar symbol, |, in the example is used to delimit (mark) the beginning and end of the display field. The `setw` manipulator tells `cout` to display the number in a total field of 10, the `fixed` manipulator explicitly forces the display of a decimal point, and the `setprecision` manipulator designates the number of digits to be displayed after the decimal point. In this case, a display of 3 digits after the decimal point is specified by `setprecision`. Without the explicit designation of a decimal point—which can also be designated as `setiosflags(ios::fixed)`—the `setprecision` manipulator specifies the total number of displayed digits (including both the integer and fractional parts of the number).

For all numbers (integers, floating point, and double precision), `cout` ignores the `setw` manipulator specification if the total specified field width is too small, and allocates enough space for the integer part of the number to be printed. The fractional part of both floating-point and double-precision numbers is displayed up to the precision set with the `setprecision` manipulator (in the absence of a `setprecision` manipulator, the default precision is set to six decimal places). If the fractional part of the number to be displayed contains more digits than called for in the `setprecision` manipulator, the number is rounded to the indicated number of decimal places; if the fractional part contains fewer digits than specified, the number is displayed with the fewer digits. Table 4-2 illustrates the effect of various format manipulator combinations. Again, for clarity, the bar symbol, |, is used to clearly delineate the beginning and end of the output fields.

TABLE 4-2
Effect of Format Manipulators

manipulators	number	display	comments
setw(2)	3	| 3|	Number fits in field
setw(2)	43	|43|	Number fits in field
setw(2)	143	|143|	Field width ignored
setw(2)	2.3	|2.3|	Field width ignored
setw(5) fixed setprecision(2)	2.366	| 2.37|	Field width of 5 with 2 decimal digits
setw(5) fixed setprecision(2)	42.3	|42.30|	Number fits in field with specified precision
setw(5) setprecision(2)	142.364	|1.4e + 002|	Field width ignored and scientific notation used with the setprecision manipulator specifying the total number of significant digits (integer plus fractional)
setw(5) fixed setprecision(2)	142.364	|142.36|	Field width ignored but precision specification used. Here the setprecision manipulator specifies the number of fractional digits
setw(5) fixed setprecision(2)	142.366	|142.37|	Field width ignored but precision specification used. Here the setprecision manipulator specifies the number of fractional digits. (Note the rounding of the last decimal digit)
setw(5) fixed setprecision(2)	142	| 142|	Field width used, fixed and setprecision manipulators irrelevant, because the number is an integer

In addition to the setw and setprecision manipulators, a field justification manipulator is also available. As we have seen, numbers sent to cout are normally displayed right-justified in the display field, while strings are displayed left-justified. To alter the default justification for a stream of data, the setiosflags manipulator can be used. For example, the statement

```
cout << "|" << setw(10) << setiosflags(ios::left) << 142 << "|";
```

causes the following left-justified display:

```
|142       |
```

PROGRAMMING NOTE

What Is a Flag?

In current programming usage the term **flag** refers to an item, such as a variable or argument, that sets a condition usually considered as either active or nonactive. Although the exact origin of this term in programming is not known, it probably originates from the use of real flags to signal a condition, such as the Stop, Go, Caution, and Winner flags commonly used at car races.

In a similar manner, each flag argument for the `setiosflags()` manipulator function activates a specific condition. For example, the `ios::dec` flag sets the display format to decimal, while the flag `ios::oct` activates the octal display format. Since these conditions are mutually exclusive (that is, only one condition can be active at a time), activating one such flag automatically deactivates the other flags.

Flags that are not mutually exclusive, such as `ios::dec`, `ios::showpoint`, and `ios::fixed` can all be set to on at the same time. This can be done using three individual `setiosflag()` calls or combining all arguments into one call as follows:

```
cout << setiosflags(ios::dec | ios::fixed | ios::showpoint);
```

As we have previously seen, since data passed to `cout` may be continued across multiple lines, the previous display would also be produced by the statement:

```
cout << "|" << setw(10)
        << setiosflags(ios::left)
        << 142 << "|";
```

As always, the field width manipulator is only in effect for the next single set of data displayed by `cout`. Right-justification for strings in a stream is obtained by the manipulator `setiosflags(ios::right)`. The symbol `ios` in both the function name and the `ios::right` argument comes from the first letters of the words "input output stream."

In addition to the left and right flags that can be used with the `setiosflags()` manipulator, other flags may also be used to affect the output. The most commonly used flags for this manipulator are listed in Table 4-3. Notice that the flags in this table effectively provide an alternate way of setting the equivalent manipulators previously listed in Table 4-1.

TABLE 4-3

Format Flags for Use with `setiosflags()`

flag	meaning
`ios::fixed`	Always show the decimal point with 6 digits after the decimal point. Fill with trailing zeros, if necessary. This flag takes precedence if it is set with the `ios::showpoint` flag.
`ios::scientific`	Use exponential display on output.
`ios::showpoint`	Always display a decimal point and 6 significant digits in total (combination of integer and fractional parts). Fill with trailing zeros after the decimal point, if necessary. For larger integer values revert to scientific notation unless the `ios::fixed` flag is set.
`ios::showpos`	Display a leading + sign when the number is positive.
`ios::left`	Left-justify output.
`ios::right`	Right-justify output.

Because the flags in Table 4-3 are used as arguments to the `setiosflags()` manipulator method, and the terms argument and parameter are synonymous, another name for a manipulator method that uses arguments is a **parameterized manipulator**. The following is an example of parameterized manipulator methods:

```
cout << setiosflags(ios::showpoint) << setprecision(4);
```

This forces all subsequent floating point numbers sent to the output stream to be displayed with a decimal point and four decimal digits. If the number has fewer than four decimal digits it will be padded with trailing zeros.

In addition to outputting integers in decimal notation, the `oct` and `hex` manipulators permit conversions to octal and hexadecimal, respectively. Program 4-7 illustrates the use of these flags. Because decimal is the default display, the `dec` manipulator is not required in the first output stream.

PROGRAMMING NOTE

Formatting cout Stream Data

Floating-point data in a `cout` output stream can be formatted in precise ways. One of the most common format requirements is to display numbers in a monetary format with two digits after the decimal point, such as 123.45. This can be done with the following statement:

```
cout << setiosflags(ios::fixed)
     << setiosflags(ios::showpoint)
     << setprecision(2);
```

The first manipulator flag, `ios::fixed`, forces all floating-point numbers placed on the cout stream to be displayed in decimal notation. This flag also prevents the use of scientific notation. The next flag, `ios::showpoint`, tells the stream to always display a decimal point. Finally, the `setprecision` manipulator tells the stream to always display two decimal values after the decimal point. Instead of using manipulators, you can also use the `cout` stream methods `setf()` and `precision()`. For example, the previous formatting can also be accomplished using the code:

```
cout.setf(ios::fixed);
cout.setf(ios::showpoint);
cout.precision(2);
```

　　Note the syntax here: the name of the object, `cout`, is separated from the method with a period. As we have already seen, this is the standard way of specifying a method and connecting it to a specific object. Which style you select is a matter of preference.

　　Additionally, the flags used in both the `setf()` method and the `setiosflags()` manipulator can be combined using the bitwise Or operator, | (explained in Appendix C). Using this operator, the following two statements are equivalent:

```
cout <<  setiosflags(ios::fixed | ios::showpoint);
cout.setf(ios::fixed | ios::showpoint);
```

Which style you select is a matter of preference.

The output produced by Program 4-7 is:

```
The decimal (base 10) value of 15 is 15
The octal (base 8) value of 15 is 017
The hexadecimal (base 16) value of 15 is 0xf
```

The display of integer values in one of the three possible number systems (decimal, octal, and hexadecimal) does not affect how the number is actually stored inside a computer. All numbers are stored using the computer's own internal codes. The manipulators sent to `cout` simply tell the object how to convert the internal code for output display purposes.

Program 4-7

```
// a program that illustrates output conversions
#include <iostream>
#include <iomanip>
using namespace std;

int main()
{
  cout << "The decimal (base 10) value of 15 is " << 15 << endl;
  cout << "The octal (base 8) value of 15 is "
       << showbase << oct << 15 <<endl;
  cout << "The hexadecimal (base 16) value of 15 is "
         << showbase << hex << 15 << endl;

  return 0;
}
```

Besides displaying integers in octal or hexadecimal form, integer constants can also be written in a program in these forms. To designate an octal integer constant, the number must have a leading zero. The number 023, for example, is an octal number in C++. Hexadecimal numbers are denoted using a leading 0x. The use of octal and hexadecimal integer constants is illustrated in Program 4-8.

Program 4-8

```
#include <iostream>
using namespace std;

int main()
{
  cout << "The decimal value of 025 is " << 025 << endl
       << "The decimal value of 0x37 is "<< 0x37 << endl;

  return 0;
}
```

The output produced by Program 4-8 is:

```
The decimal value of 025 is 21
The decimal value of 0x37 is 55
```

The relationship between the input, storage, and display of integers is illustrated in Figure 4-6.

FIGURE 4-6
Input, Storage, and Display of Integers

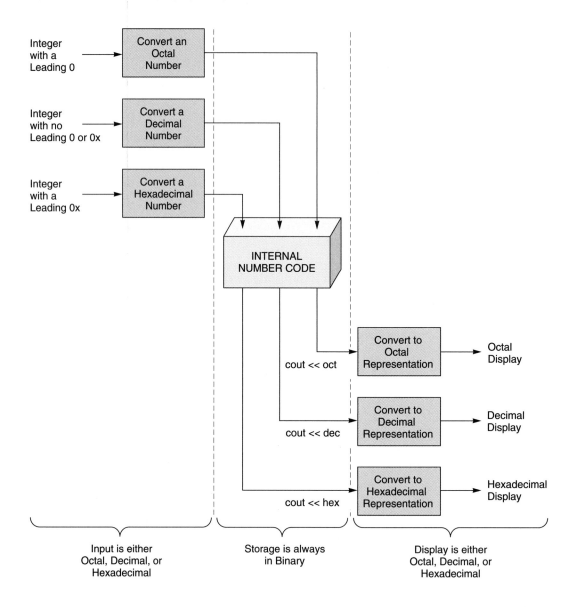

Finally, the manipulators specified in Tables 4-1 and 4-2 can also be set using the `ostream` class methods listed in Table 4-4.

4

TABLE 4-4
ostream *Class Methods*

method	comment	example
precision(*n*)	Equivalent to setprecision()	cout.precision(2)
fill('*x*')	Equivalent to setfill()	cout.fill('*')
setf(ios::fixed)	Equivalent to setiosflags (ios::fixed)	cout.setf(ios::fixed)
setf(ios::showpoint)	Equivalent to setiosflags (ios::showpoint)	cout.setf(ios::showpoint)
setf(ios::left)	Equivalent to left	cout.setf(ios::left)
setf(ios::right)	Equivalent to right	cout.setf(ios::right)
setf(ios::flush)	Equivalent to endl	cout.setf(ios::flush)

Note that in the Examples column of Table 4-4 the name of the object, cout, is separated from the method with a period. As we have already seen, this is the standard way of calling a class method and providing it with the object it is to operate on.

Exercises 4.2

1. Determine the errors in each of the following statements:

   a. cout << "\n << " 15)
   b. cout << "setw(4)" << 33;
   c. cout << "setprecision(5)" << 526.768;
   d. "Hello World!" >> cout;
   e. cout << 47 << setw(6);
   f. cout << set(10) << 526.768 << setprecision(2);

2. Determine and write out the display produced by the following statements:

   a. cout << "|" << 5 <<"|";
   b. cout << "|" << setw(4) << 5 << "|";
   c. cout << "|" << setw(4) << 56829 << "|";
   d. cout << "|" << setw(5) << setprecision(2) << 5.26 << "|";
   e. cout << "|" << setw(5) << setprecision(2) << 5.267 << "|";
   f. cout << "|" << setw(5) << setprecision(2) << 53.264 << "|";
   g. cout << "|" << setw(5) << setprecision(2) << 534.264 << "|";
   h. cout << "|" << setw(5) << setprecision(2) << 534. << "|";

3.   Write out the display produced by the following statements.

   a. cout << "The number is " << setw(6)
         << setprecision(2) << 26.27 << endl;
   cout << "The number is " << setw(6)
         << setprecision(2) << 682.3 << endl;
   cout << "The number is " << setw(6)
         << setprecision(2) << 1.968 << endl;

   b. cout << setw(6) << setprecision(2) << 26.27 << endl;
   cout << setw(6) << setprecision(2) << 682.3 << endl;
   cout << setw(6) << setprecision(2) << 1.968 << endl;
   cout << "-----\n";
   cout << setw(6) << setprecision(2)
         << 26.27 + 682.3 + 1.968 << endl;

   c. cout << setw(5) << setprecision(2) << 26.27 << endl;
   cout << setw(5) << setprecision(2) << 682.3 << endl;
   cout << setw(5) << setprecision(2) << 1.968 << endl;
   cout << "-----\n";
   cout << setw(5) << setprecision(2)
         << 26.27 + 682.3 + 1.968 << endl;

   d. cout << setw(5) << setprecision(2) << 36.164 << endl;
   cout << setw(5) << setprecision(2) << 10.003 << endl;
   cout << "-----" << endl;

4.   Write a program to verify all of the outputs listed in Table 4-2 are obtained when the listed manipulators are used.

5.   Table 4-5 lists the correspondence between the decimal numbers 1 through 15 and their octal and hexadecimal representation.

TABLE 4-5
Correspondence Between Decimal, Octal, and Hexadecimal Numbers

Decimal	1	2	3	4	5	6	7	8	9	10	11	12	13	14	15
Octal	1	2	3	4	5	6	7	10	11	12	13	14	15	16	17
Hexadecimal	1	2	3	4	5	6	7	8	9	a	b	c	d	e	f

Using the above table, determine the output of the following program:

```
#include <iostream>
#include <iomanip>
using namespace std;
```

(continued on next page)

```
int main()
{
   cout << "\nThe value of 14 in octal is " << showbase << oct << 14
        << "\nThe value of 14 in hexadecimal is " << showbase << hex << 14
        << "\nThe value of 0xa in decimal is " << dec << 0xa
        << "\nThe value of 0xa in octal is " << showbase << oct << 0xa
        << endl;

   return 0;
}
```

4.3 USING MATHEMATICAL LIBRARY FUNCTIONS

As we have seen, assignment statements can be used to perform arithmetic computations. For example, the assignment statement

```
totalPrice = unitPrice * amount;
```

multiplies the value in unitPrice times the value in amount and assigns the resulting value to totalPrice. Although addition, subtraction, multiplication, and division are easily accomplished using C++'s arithmetic operators, no such operators exist for raising a number to a power, finding the square root of a number, or determining trigonometric values. To facilitate such calculations, C++ provides standard preprogrammed functions that you can incorporate into your programs.

In order to use a mathematical function, you need to know:

- The name of the function
- What the function does
- The type of data the function requires
- The data type of the result the function returns
- How to include the section of the standard C++ library that contains the function

To illustrate the use of C++'s mathematical functions, consider the mathematical function named sqrt(), which calculates the square root of a number. The square root of a number is computed using the expression

```
sqrt(number)
```

where the function's name, in this case sqrt, is followed by parentheses containing the number for which the square root is desired. The purpose of the parentheses following the function name, as we have already seen for methods, is to pass data into the function. The items that are passed to the function through the parentheses are called the function's *arguments*; they constitute the function's input data. This concept is illustrated in Figure 4-7, for the sqrt() function.

As examples, the following expressions compute the square root of the arguments 4, 17.0, 25, 1043.29, and 6.4516, respectively:

```
sqrt(4)
sqrt(17.0)
sqrt(25)
sqrt(1043.29)
sqrt(6.4516)
```

FIGURE 4-7
Passing Data to the sqrt() *Function*

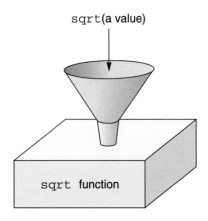

sqrt(a value)

sqrt function

Notice that the argument to the sqrt function can be either an integer or real value. This is an example of C++'s function overloading capabilities. Function overloading permits the same function name to be defined for different argument data types. In this case there are really three square root functions named sqrt()—one each defined for float, double, and long double arguments. The sqrt() function that is called depends on the type of value given it. The sqrt() function determines the square root of its argument and returns the result as a double. The values returned by the previous expressions are:

expression	value returned
sqrt(4.)	2.0
sqrt(17.0)	4.123106
sqrt(25.)	5.0
sqrt(1043.29)	32.3
sqrt(6.4516)	2.54

Table 4-6 lists the more commonly used mathematical functions provided in C++, including the sqrt function. To access these functions in a program, you need to include the header file name cmath, which contains appropriate declarations for the mathematical functions. You can do this by placing the following preprocessor statement at the top of any program using a mathematical function:

```
#include <cmath>   ← no semicolon
```

Although some of the mathematical functions listed in Table 4-6 require more than one argument, all functions, by definition, can directly return at most one value. Additionally, all of the functions listed are overloaded; in other words, the same function name can be used with integer and real arguments. Table 4-7 illustrates the value returned by selected functions using example arguments.

TABLE 4-6
Common C++ Mathematical Functions

function name	description	returned value
abs(a)	absolute value	same data type as argument
pow(a1,a2)	a1 raised to the a2 power	data type of argument a1
sqrt(a)	square root of a	double
sin(a)	sine of a (a in radians)	double
cos(a)	cosine of a (a in radians)	double
tan(a)	tangent of a (a in radians)	double
log(a)	natural logarithm of a	double
log10(a)	common log (base 10) of a	double
exp(a)	e raised to the a power	double

TABLE 4-7
Selected Function Examples

example	returned value
abs(-7.362)	7.362
abs(-3)	3
pow(2.0,5.0)	32
pow(10,3)	1000
log(18.697)	2.92836
log10(18.697)	1.27177
exp(-3.2)	0.0407622

The arguments that are passed to a function need not be single constants. Expressions can also be arguments provided that the expression can be computed to yield a value of the required data type. For example, the following arguments are valid for the given functions:

```
sqrt(4.0 + 5.3 * 4.0)          abs(2.3 * 4.6)
sqrt(16.0 * 2.0 - 6.7)         sin(theta - phi)
sqrt(x * y - z/3.2)            cos(2.0 * omega)
```

The expressions in parentheses are first evaluated to yield a specific value. Thus, values would have to be assigned to variables such as theta, phi, x, y, z, and omega before their use in the preceding expressions. After the value of the argument is calculated, it is passed to the function.

Functions may also be included as part of larger expressions. For example:

```
4 * sqrt(4.5 * 10.0 - 9.0) - 2.0 =
        4 * sqrt(36.0) - 2.0   =
                24.0 - 2.0   = 22.0
```

The step-by-step evaluation of an expression such as

```
3.0 * sqrt(5 * 33 - 13.71) / 5
```

is:

step	result
1. Perform multiplication in argument	3.0 * sqrt(165 - 13.71) / 5
2. Complete argument calculation	3.0 * sqrt(151.29) / 5
3. Return a function value	3.0 * 12.3 / 5
4. Perform the multiplication	36.9 / 5
5. Perform the division	7.38

Program 4-9 illustrates the use of the sqrt function to determine the time it takes a ball to hit the ground after it has been dropped from an 800-foot tower. The mathematical formula used to calculate the time, in seconds, that it takes to fall a given distance, in feet, is:

```
time = sqrt(2 * distance / g)
```

where g is the gravitational constant equal to 32.2 ft/sec^2.

Program 4-9

```cpp
#include <iostream>   // this line may be placed second instead of first
#include <cmath>      // this line may be placed first instead of second
using namespace std;

int main()
{
  int height;
  double time;

  height = 800;
  time = sqrt(2 * height / 32.2);
  cout << "It will take " << time << " seconds to fall "
      << height << " feet.\n";

  return 0;
}
```

The output produced by Program 4-9 is:

```
It will take 7.04907 seconds to fall 800 feet.
```

In Program 4-9, the value returned by the `sqrt()` function is assigned to the variable `time`. In addition to assigning a function's returned value to a variable, the returned value may be included within a larger expression, or even used as an argument to another function. For example, the expression

```
sqrt( pow( abs(num1),num2 ) )
```

is valid. Since parentheses are present, the computation proceeds from the inner to the outer pairs of parentheses. Thus, the absolute value of `num1` is computed first and used as an argument to the `pow()` function. The value returned by the `pow()` function is then used as an argument to the `sqrt()` function.

CASTS

We have already seen the conversion of an operand's data type within mixed-mode arithmetic expressions (Section 2.1) and across assignment operators (Section 4.1). In addition to these implicit data type conversions that are automatically made within mixed-mode arithmetic and assignment expressions, C++ also provides for explicit user-specified type conversions. The operator used to force the conversion of a value to another type is the **cast** operator. C++ provides both a compile-time and run-time cast operator.

The compile-time cast is a unary operator having the syntax

```
dataType (expression)
```

where *dataType* is the desired data type that the *expression* within parentheses will be converted to. For example, the expression

```
int (a * b)
```

ensures that the value of the expression `a * b` is converted to an integer value.[5]

In a run-time cast, the requested type conversion is checked at run-time, and is only applied if the conversion results in a valid value. Although four different types of run-time casts are available, the most commonly used cast (and the one corresponding to the compile-time cast) has the syntax

```
staticCast<dataType>(expression)
```

For example, the run-time cast `staticCast<int>(a*b)` is equivalent to the compile-time cast

```
int(a * b).
```

[5]The C type cast syntax, in this case `(int) (a*b)`, also works in C++.

Exercises 4.3

1. Write function calls to determine:

    a. The square root of 6.37.

    b. The square root of x - y.

    c. The sine of 30 degrees.

    d. The sine of 60 degrees.

    e. The absolute value of a^2 - b^2.

    f. The value of e raised to the 3rd power.

2. For a = 10.6, b = 13.9, c = -3.42, determine the value of:

    a. `int (a)`

    b. `int (b)`

    c. `int (c)`

    d. `int (a + b)`

    e. `int (a) + b + c`

    f. `int (a + b) + c`

    g. `int (a + b + c)`

    h. `float (int (a)) + b`

    i. `float (int (a + b))`

    j. `abs (a) + abs (b)`

    k. `sqrt (abs (a - b))`

3. Write C++ statements for the following:

    a. `b = sin x - cos x`

    b. `b = sin²x - cos²x`

    c. `area = (c * b * sin a)/2`

    d. $c = \sqrt{a^2 + b^2}$

    e. $p = \sqrt{|m - n|}$

    f. $sum = \dfrac{a(r^n - 1)}{r - 1}$

4. Write, compile, and execute a C++ program that calculates and returns the fourth root of the number 81.0, which is 3. When you have verified that your program works correctly, use it to determine the fourth root of 1,728.896400. Your program should make use of the `sqrt` function.

5. Write, compile, and execute a C++ program that calculates the distance between two points whose coordinates are (7, 12) and (3, 9). Use the fact that the distance between two points having coordinates (x1, y1) and (x2, y2) is *distance = sqrt([x1 - x2]² + [y1 - y2]²)*. When you have verified that your program works correctly, by calculating the distance between the two points manually, use your program to determine the distance between the points (-12, -15) and (22, 5).

6. If a 20-foot ladder is placed on the side of a building at a 85-degree angle, as illustrated in Figure 4-8, the height at which the ladder touches the building can be calculated as *height = 20 * sin 85°*. Calculate this height by hand and then write, compile, and execute a C++ program that determines and displays the value of the height. When you have verified that your program works correctly, use it to determine the height of a 25- foot ladder placed at an angle of 85 degrees.

FIGURE 4-8

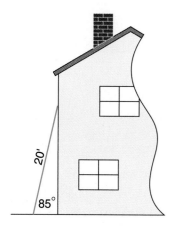

7. A model of world population, in billions of people, after 2000 is given by the equation:

$$Population = 6.0e^{.02\ [Year - 2000]}$$

Using this formula, write, compile, and execute a C++ program to estimate the world population in the year 2006. Verify the result displayed by your program by calculating the answer manually. After you have verified your program is working correctly, use it to estimate the world's population in the year 2012.

4.4 INTERACTIVE KEYBOARD INPUT

Data for programs that are only going to be executed once may be included directly in the program. For example, if you wanted to multiply the numbers 30.0 and 0.05, you could use Program 4-10.

The output displayed by Program 4-10 is:

```
30.0 times 0.05 is 1.5
```

Program 4-10

```cpp
#include <iostream>
using namespace std;

int main()
{
    double num1, num2, product;

    num1 = 30.0;
    num2 = 0.05;
    product = num1 * num2;
    cout << "30.0 times 0.05 is " << product << endl;

    return 0;
}
```

Program 4-10 can be shortened, as illustrated in Program 4-11. Both programs, however, suffer from the same basic problem in that they must be rewritten in order to multiply different numbers. The underlying problem is that both programs do not have a provision for different numbers to be entered as the program is executing.

Program 4-11

```cpp
#include <iostream>
using namespace std;
int main()
{
    cout << "30.0 times 0.05 is " << 30.0 * 0.05 << endl;

    return 0;
}
```

Except for the practice provided in writing, entering, and running the program, programs that do the same calculation only once, on the same set of numbers, are clearly not very useful. After all, it is simpler to use a calculator to multiply two numbers than to enter and run either Program 4-10 or 4-11.

This section presents the `cin` object, which is used to enter data into a program while it is executing. The process of entering data in this manner is referred to as interactive data entry, because the user is interacting with the programming while it is executing rather than passively waiting for the program to complete once it has started executing.

Just as the `cout` object displays a copy of the value stored inside a variable, the `cin` object allows the user to enter a value at the terminal (see Figure 4-9). The value is then stored directly in a variable.

4

FIGURE 4-9

cin *Is Used to Enter Data;* cout *Is Used to Display Data*

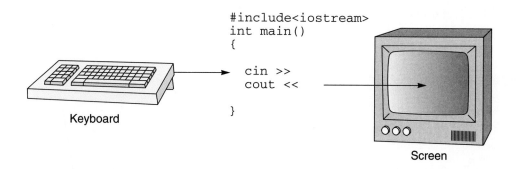

```
#include<iostream>
int main()
{

  cin >>
  cout <<

}
```

Keyboard

Screen

When a statement such as cin >> num1; is encountered, the computer stops program execution and accepts data from the keyboard. When a data item is typed, the cin object stores the item into the variable listed after the extraction operator ("get from"), >>. The program then continues execution with the statement immediately following the cin statement. To see how this works, consider Program 4-12.

Program 4-12

```cpp
#include <iostream>
using namespace std;

int main()
{
  double num1, num2, product;

  cout << "Please type in a number: ";
  cin  >> num1;
  cout << "Please type in another number: ";
  cin  >> num2;
  product = num1 * num2;
  cout << num1 << " times " << num2 << " is " << product << endl;

  return 0;
}
```

The first cout statement in Program 4-12 prints a string that tells the person at the terminal what should be typed. When an output string is used in this manner it is called a prompt. In this case, the prompt tells the user to type a number. The computer then executes the next statement, which uses the cin object. This object puts the computer into a temporary pause (or waiting) state for as long as it takes the user to type a value. Then the user signals the cin object that the data entry is finished by pressing the return key after the value has been typed. The entered value is stored in the variable to the right of the extraction symbol, and the computer is taken out of its paused state. Program execution then proceeds with the next statement, which in Program 4-12 is another `cout` statement. This statement causes the next prompt to be displayed. The second `cin` statement then puts the computer into a temporary wait state while the user types a second value. This second number is stored in the variable `num2`.

The following sample run was made using Program 4-12.

```
Please type in a number: 30
Please type in another number: 0.05
30 times 0.05 is 1.5
```

In Program 4-12, each time `cin` is used it stores one value in a variable. The `cin` object, however, can be used to enter and store as many values as there are extraction symbols, `>>`, and variables to hold the entered data. For example, the statement

```
cin >> num1 >> num2;
```

expects the user to enter two values; the first entered value is assigned to the variable `num1` and the second entered value to the variable `num2`. If the user enters this data

```
0.052 245.79
```

the variables `num1` and `num2` would contain the values 0.052 and 245.79, respectively. Notice that when you type two numbers such as 0.052 and 245.79, you must include at least one space between the numbers. The space between the entered numbers clearly indicates where one number ends and the next begins. Inserting more than one space between numbers has no effect on `cin`.

The same spacing is also applicable to entering character data; that is, the extraction operator, `>>`, will skip blank spaces and store the next nonblank character in a character variable. For example, in response to the statements

```
char ch1, ch2, ch3;   // declare three character variables
     cin >> ch1 >> ch2 >> ch3;   // accept three characters
```

the input

```
a    b   c
```

causes the letter a to be stored in the variable `ch1`, the letter b to be stored in the variable `ch2`, and the letter c to be stored in the variable `ch3`. Since a character variable can only be used to store one character, the input

```
abc
```

can also be used.

A program may include any number of statements using the `cin` object, and it may accept any number of input values via a single `cin` statement. Program 4-13 illustrates using the `cin` object to input three numbers from the keyboard. The program then calculates and displays the average of the numbers entered.

Program 4-13

```
#include <iostream>
using namespace std;

int main()
{
    int num1, num2, num3;
    double average;

    cout << "Enter three integer numbers: ";
    cin  >> num1 >> num2 >> num3;
    average =  (num1 + num2 + num3) / 3.0;
    cout << "The average of the numbers is " << average << endl;

    double 0;
}
```

The following sample run was made using Program 4-13:

```
    Enter three integer numbers: 22 56 73

    The average of the numbers is 50.3333
```

Note that the data typed at the keyboard for this sample run consists of the input:

```
    22 56 73
```

In response to this stream of input, the program stores the value 22 in the variable num1, the value 56 in the variable num2, and the value 73 in the variable num3 (see Figure 4-10). Since the average of three integer numbers can be a floating-point number, the variable average, which is used to store the average, is declared as a floating-point variable. Note also that the parentheses are needed in the assignment statement average = (num1 + num2 + num3) / 3.0;. Without these parentheses, the only value that would be divided by 3 would be the integer in num3 (because division has a higher precedence than addition).

FIGURE 4-10

Inputting Data into the Variables num1, num2, *and* num3

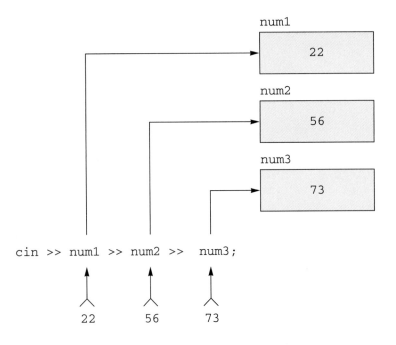

The cin extraction operation, like the cout insertion operation, is "clever" enough to make a few data type conversions. For example, if an integer is entered in place of a floating-point or double-precision number, the integer will be converted to the correct data type.[6] Similarly, if a floating-point or double-precision number is entered when an integer is expected, only the integer part of the number will be used. However, the remaining portion of the number can cause unanticipated results. For example, assume the following numbers are typed in response to the statement cin >> num1 >> num2 >> num3;, where num1 and num3 have been declared as floating point variables and num2 is an integer variable:

       56   22.879   33.923

For this input, the 56 is converted to 56.0 and stored in the variable num1. The extraction operation continues extracting data from the input stream sent to it, expecting an integer value. As far as cin is concerned, the decimal point after the 22 in the number 22.879 indicates the end of an integer. Thus, the number 22 is assigned to num2. Continuing to process its input stream, cin takes the .879 as the next floating-point number and assigns it to num3. As far as cin is concerned, 33.923 is extra input and is ignored. Conversely, if insufficient data is entered, the cin object will continue to keep the computer in a paused state until it determines that sufficient data has been entered.

---

[6]Strictly speaking, what comes in from the keyboard is not any data type, such as an int or float, but is simply a sequence of characters. The extraction operation handles the conversion from the character sequence to a defined data type.

4

A FIRST LOOK AT USER-INPUT VALIDATION

A well-constructed program should validate user input and ensure that a program does not either crash or produce nonsensical output due to unexpected input. The term **validate** means checking that the entered value matches the data type of the variable that the value is assigned to within a `cin` statement, and that the value is within an acceptable range of values appropriate to the application. Programs that detect and respond effectively to unexpected user input are formally referred to as robust programs and informally as "bullet-proof" programs. One of your jobs as a programmer is to produce such programs. As written, both Programs 4-11 and 4-12 are not robust programs. Let's see why.

The first problem with these programs becomes evident when a user enters a non-numerical value. For example, consider the following sample run using Program 4-13.

```
Enter three integer numbers: 10 20.68 20
The average of the numbers is -2.86331e+008
```

This output occurs because the conversion of the second input number results in the integer value 20 assigned to num2 and the value −858993460 assigned to num3. This last value corresponds to an invalid character, the decimal point, being assigned to an expected integer value. The average of the numbers 10, 20, and −858993460 is then computed correctly as −286331143.3, which is displayed in scientific notation with six significant digits as −2.86331e+08. As far as the average user is concerned, this will be reported as a program error. This same problem occurs whenever a noninteger value is entered for either of the first two inputs (it does not occur for any numerical value entered as the third input, because the integer part of the last input is accepted and the remaining input ignored). As a programmer your initial response may be "The program clearly asks you to enter integer values." This, however, is the response of a very inexperienced programmer. Professional programmers understand that it is their responsibility to ensure that a program anticipates and appropriately handles any and all input that a user can possibly enter. This is accomplished by both thinking about what can go wrong with your own program as you develop it and then having another person or group thoroughly test the program.

The basic approach to handling invalid data input is referred to as **user-input validation**, which means validating the entered data either during or immediately after the data have been entered, and then providing the user with a way of re-entering any invalid data. User-input validation is an essential part of any commercially viable program, and if done correctly, it will protect a program from attempting to process data that can cause computational problems. We will see how to provide this type of validation after C++'s selection and repetition statements have been presented in Chapters 5 and 6, respectively.

Exercises 4.4

1. For the following declaration statements, write a statement using the `cin` object that will cause the computer to pause while the appropriate data is typed by the user.

   a. `int firstNum;`
   b. `float grade;`
   c. `double secNum;`
   d. `char keyval;`
   e. `int month, years;`
   f. `double total, average;`
   g. `char ch;`
      `int num1, num2;`
      `double grade1, grade2;`
   h. `float interest, principal, capital;`
      `double price, yield;`
   i. `char ch, letter1, letter2;`
      `int num1, num2, num3;`
   j. `float temp1, temp2, temp3;`
      `double volts1, volts2;`

2. a. Write a C++ program that first displays the following prompt:

   `Enter the temperature in degrees Celsius:`

   Have your program accept a temperature value entered from the keyboard and convert the temperature entered to degrees Fahrenheit, using the equation *Fahrenheit = (9.0 / 5.0) * Celsius + 32.0.* Your program should then display the temperature in degrees Fahrenheit using an appropriate output message.

   b. Compile and execute the program written for Exercise 2a. Verify your program by calculating, both by hand and by program, the Fahrenheit equivalent of the following test data:

   Test data set 1: 0 degrees Celsius
   Test data set 2: 50 degrees Celsius
   Test data set 3: 100 degrees Celsius

   When you are sure your program works correctly, use it to determine the Fahrenheit temperatures for the following Celsius values:

   celsius
   45
   50
   55
   60
   65
   70

3. Write, compile, and execute a C++ program that displays the following prompt:

```
Enter the radius of a circle:
```

After accepting a value for the radius, your program should calculate and display the area of the circle. (*Hint: area = 3.1416 * radius²*.) For testing purposes, verify your program using a test input radius of 3 inches. After manually determining that the result produced by your program is correct, use your program to determine the areas for the following radius values:

radius (in.)
1.0
1.5
2.0
2.5
3.0
3.5

4. **a.** Write, compile, and execute a C++ program that displays the following prompts:

```
Enter the miles driven:
Enter the gallons of gas used:
```

After each prompt is displayed, your program should use a `cin` statement to accept data from the keyboard for the displayed prompt. After the gallons-of-gas-used number has been entered, your program should calculate and display miles-per-gallon obtained. This value should be included in an appropriate message and calculated using the equation *miles per gallon = miles / gallons used*. Verify your program using the following test data:

Test data set 1: Miles = 276, Gas = 10 gallons.
Test data set 2: Miles = 200, Gas = 15.5 gallons.

When you have completed your verification, use your program to determine the miles-per-gallon for the following data:

miles driven	gallons used
250	16.00
275	18.00
312	19.54
296	17.39

b. For the program written for Exercise 4a, determine how many verification runs are required to ensure the program is working correctly and give a reason supporting your answer.

5. **a.** Write, compile, and execute a C++ program that displays the following prompts:

```
Enter a number:
Enter a second number:
Enter a third number:
Enter a fourth number:
```

After each prompt is displayed, your program should use a `cin` statement to accept a number from the keyboard for the displayed prompt. After the fourth number has been entered, your program should calculate and display the average of the numbers. The average should be included in an appropriate message. Check the average displayed by your program using the following test data:

Test data set 1: 100, 100, 100, 100
Test data set 2: 100, 0, 100, 0

When you have completed your verification, use your program to determine the averages of the following numbers:

> 92, 98, 79, 85
> 86, 84, 75, 86
> 63, 85, 74, 82

b. Repeat Exercise 5a, making sure that you use the same variable name, `number`, for each number input. Also use the variable `sum` for the sum of the numbers. (*Hint:* To do this, you may use the statement `sum = sum + number;` after each number is accepted. Review the material on accumulating presented in Section 4.1.)

6.   Write a C++ program that displays the following prompts:

```
Enter the length of the room:
Enter the width of the room:
```

After each prompt is displayed, your program should use a `cin` object to accept data from the keyboard for the displayed prompt. After the width of the room is entered, your program should calculate and display the area of the room using the `RoomType` class presented in Program 3-2.

7.   **a.** Write a C++ program that displays the following prompts:

```
Enter the length of the swimming pool:
Enter the width of the swimming pool:
Enter the average depth of the swimming pool:
```

After each prompt is displayed, your program should use a `cin` object to accept data from the keyboard for the displayed prompt. After the depth of the swimming pool is entered, your program should calculate and display the volume of the pool. The volume should be included in an appropriate message and calculated using the equation *volume = length * width * average depth.*

b. Check the volume displayed by the program written for Exercise 7a by calculating the result manually.

8.   Write, compile, and execute a program that calculates and displays the square root value of a user-entered real number. Verify your program by calculating the square roots of the following

data: 25, 16, 0, and 2. When you have completed your verification, use your program to determine the square roots of 32.25, 42, 48, 55, 63, and 79.

9. Program 4-12 prompts the user to input two numbers, where the first value entered is stored in num1 and the second value is stored in num2. Using this program as a starting point and using the swap class method contained in Program 3-4, write a program that swaps the two entered values and displays the results.

10. Write a program that uses a class named Circle. The Circle class should have three double-precision variables named xcenter, ycenter, and radius. The constructor should accept data for these variables using its parameter list. Additionally, the class should have a method for calculating a circle's area, a method for calculating its circumference, and a method for calculating how far its center is from the origin. To do this, use the following formulas:

$$area = \pi\ (radius^2)$$
$$circumference = 2\pi\ (radius)$$
$$distance = sqrt(xcenter^2 + ycenter^2)$$

Your program should request data values for each of these variables and then display the area, circumference, and distance from the origin for the input data.

11. Write a C++ program that prompts the user to type in a number. Have your program accept the number as an integer and immediately display the integer using a cout object call. Run your program three times. The first time you run the program, enter a valid integer number, the second time enter a floating-point number, and the third time enter a character. Using the output display, see what number your program actually accepted from the data you entered.

12. Repeat Exercise 11, but have your program declare the variable (which is used to store the number) as a floating-point variable. Run the program four times. The first time enter an integer, the second time enter a decimal number with less than six decimal places, the third time enter a number having more than six decimal places, and the fourth time enter a character. Using the output display, keep track of what number your program actually accepted from the data you typed in. What happened, if anything, and why?

13. Repeat Exercise 11, but have your program declare the variable (which is used to store the number) as a double-precision variable. Run the program four times. The first time enter an integer, the second time enter a decimal number with less than six decimal places, the third time enter a number having more than six decimal places, and the fourth time enter a character. Using the output display, keep track of what number your program actually accepted from the data you typed in. What happened, if anything, and why?

14. a. Why do you think that successful applications programs contain extensive data-input validity checks? (*Hint:* Review Exercises 11, 12, and 13.)

   b. What do you think is the difference between a data-type check and a data-reasonableness check?

   c. Assume that a program requests that a month, day, and year be entered by the user. What are some checks that could be made on the entered data?

4.5 SYMBOLIC CONSTANTS

As previously described in Section 2.1, literal data is any data within a program that explicitly identifies itself. For example, the constants 2 and 3.1416 in the assignment statement

```
circumference = 2 * 3.1416 * radius;
```

are also called literals because they are literally included directly in the statement. Additional examples of literals are contained in the following C++ assignment statements. See if you can identify them.

```
perimeter = 2 * length * width;
        y = (5 * p) / 7.2;
salestax = 0.05 * purchase;
```

The literals are the numbers 2, 5 and 7.2, and 0.05 in the first, second, and third statements, respectively.

Quite frequently, literal data used within a program have a more general meaning that is recognized outside the context of the program. Examples of these types of constants include the number 3.1416, which is π accurate to four decimal places; 32.2 ft/sec^2, which is the gravitational constant; and the number 2.71828, which is Euler's number accurate to five decimal places. The meanings of certain other constants appearing in a program are defined strictly within the context of the application being programmed. For example, in a program used to determine bank interest charges, the interest rate would typically appear in a number of different places throughout the program. Similarly, in a program used to calculate taxes, the tax rate might appear in many individual instructions. Numbers such as these are referred to by programmers as magic numbers. By themselves the numbers are quite ordinary, but in the context of a particular application they have a special ("magical") meaning.

When the same magic number appears repeatedly within a program it becomes a potential source of error should the number have to be changed. For example, if either the interest rate or sales tax rate change, as rates are prone to do, the programmer would have the cumbersome task of changing the value everywhere it appears in the program. Multiple changes, however, are subject to error—if just one rate value is overlooked and not changed, the result obtained when the program is run will be incorrect and the source of the error difficult to locate.

To avoid the problem of having a magic number spread throughout a program in many places, and to permit clear identification of more universal constants such as π, C++ allows the programmer to give these constants their own symbolic name. Then, instead of using the number throughout the program, the symbolic name is used. If the number ever has to be changed, the change need only be made once at the point where the symbolic name is equated to the actual number value. Equating numbers to symbolic names is accomplished using a const variable declaration qualifier. The const qualifier specifies that the declared variable can only be read after it is initialized; it cannot be changed. Three examples using this qualifier are:

```
const double PI = 3.1416;
const float SALESTAX = 0.05f;
const int MAXNUM = 100;
```

The first declaration statement creates a double-precision variable named `PI` and initializes it with the value 3.1416, while the second declaration statement creates the floating-point variable named `SALESTAX` and initializes it to 0.05. Finally, the third declaration creates an integer variable named `MAXNUM` and initializes it with the value 100.

Once a `const` variable is created and initialized, *the value stored in the variable cannot be changed.* Thus, for all practical purposes the name of the variable and its value are linked together for the duration of the program that declares them.

Although the `const` variable names above are all uppercase, lowercase letters could have been used. It is common in C++, however, to use uppercase letters for `const` variables to make them easy to identify as `const` variables. Then, whenever a programmer sees uppercase letters in a program, he or she will know the value of the variable cannot be changed within the program.

Once declared, a `const` variable can be used in any C++ statement in place of the number it represents. For example, the assignment statements

```
circum = 2 * PI * radius;
amount = SALESTAX * purchase;
```

are both valid. These statements must, of course, appear after the declarations for all their variables. Because a `const` declaration effectively equates a constant value to a variable, and the variable name can be used as a direct replacement for its initializing constant, such variables are commonly referred to as **symbolic constants** or **named constants.** We shall use these terms interchangeably.

Because the purpose of an instance variable is to store a value that can change with each object, instance variables are never candidates to be made into symbolic constants. Rather, symbolic constants are used within methods and to fix class variables that are shared between all objects. This latter type of class variables is presented in Chapter 7. Program 4-14 illustrates the use of a symbolic constant within a `main()` function.

Program 4-14

```cpp
#include <iostream>
#include <iomanip>
using namespace std;

int main()
{
  const float SALESTAX = 0.05f;
  double amount, taxes, total;

  cout << "\nEnter the amount purchased: ";
  cin  >> amount;
  taxes = SALESTAX * amount;
  total = amount + taxes;
```

(continued on next page)

```
    // set output formats
  cout << setiosflags(ios::fixed)
       << setiosflags(ios::showpoint)
       << setprecision(2);

  cout << "The sales tax is " << setw(4) << taxes << endl;
  cout << "The total bill is " << setw(5) << total << endl;

  return 0;
}
```

The following sample run was made using Program 4-14.

```
Enter the amount purchased: 36.00
The sales tax is 1.80
The total bill is 37.80
```

Although we have used the `const` qualifier to construct symbolic constants, we will encounter this data type once again in Section 12.3, where we will show that they are useful as method arguments in ensuring that the argument is not modified within the method.

PLACEMENT OF STATEMENTS

At this stage we have introduced a variety of statement types. The general rule in C++ for statement placement is simply that a variable or named constant must be declared before it can be used. Although this rule permits both preprocessor directives and declaration statements to be placed throughout a method, the general rule is to declare the majority of variables at the top of a function or method's body; variables that are only used within a very small section of a function or method are then frequently declared within a function or method's body immediately before their use. As a matter of good programming form, the following statement ordering should be used:

```
#include statements
namespace declarations;

methodHheader
{
    symbolic constant declarations;
    variable declarations;

    other executable statements and variable declarations;

    return value;
}
```

4

As new statement types are introduced, we will expand this placement structure to accommodate them. Notice that comment statements can be freely intermixed anywhere within this basic structure.

Exercises 4.5

Determine the purpose of the programs given in Exercises 1 through 3. Then rewrite each program using a symbolic constant for the appropriate literals.

1.
```cpp
#include <iostream>
using namespace std;

int main()
{
   double radius, circum;
   cout << "Enter a radius: ";
   cin  >> radius;
   circum = 2.0 * 3.1416 * radius;
   cout << "\nThe circumference of the circle is " << circum << endl;

   return 0;
}
```

2.
```cpp
#include <iostream>
using namespace std;

int main()
{
  double prime, amount, interest;
  prime = .04;       // prime interest rate
  cout << "Enter the amount: ";
  cin >> amount;
  interest = prime * amount;
  cout << "\nThe interest earned is " << interest << " dollars." << endl;

   return 0;
}
```

3.
```cpp
#include <iostream>
  using namespace std;

  int main()
  {
    float fahren, celsius;
    cout << "Enter a temperature in degrees Fahrenheit: ";
    cin >> fahren;
```

(continued on next page)

```
        celsius = (5.0/9.0) * (fahren - 32.0);
        cout << "\nThe equivalent Celsius temperature is " << celsius << endl;

        return 0;
    }
```

4.6 A CLOSER LOOK: VARIABLE STORAGE

Every variable has three major items associated with it: its data type, the actual value stored in the variable, and the location in memory where the variable is stored. The value stored in the variable is referred to as the variable's contents; the memory location where the variable is stored is referred to as its address. This address is always the address of the first memory location used for the variable. How many locations are actually reserved for the variable, starting at its address, depends on the variable's data type. As was presented in Section 2.1, the number of bytes reserved for each data type can be determined using the sizeof() operator (shown earlier in Program 2-1). The relationship between these three items (type, contents, location) is illustrated in Figure 4-11.

FIGURE 4-11
A Typical Variable

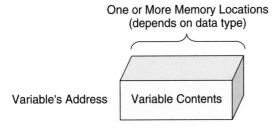

Programmers are usually concerned only with the value assigned to a variable (its contents) and give little attention to where the value is stored (its address). For example, consider Program 4-15.

Program 4-15

```
#include <iostream>
using namespace std;

int main()
{
  int num;

  num = 22;
  cout << "The value stored in num is " << num << endl;

  return 0;
}
```

The output displayed by Program 4-15 is:

```
The value stored in num is 22
```

Program 4-15 simply displays the contents of the variable num, which is 22. We can go further, however, and ask "Where is the number 22 actually stored?" Although the answer is "in num," this is only half of the answer. The variable name num is simply a convenient symbol for real, physical locations in memory, as illustrated in Figure 4-12.

FIGURE 4-12
Somewhere in Memory

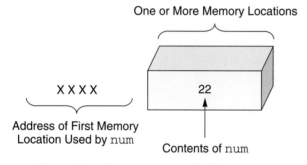

One or More Memory Locations

X X X X

22

Address of First Memory
Location Used by num

Contents of num

To determine the memory address assigned to the variable num, we can use C++'s address operator, &, which means "the address of." Except when used in a declaration statement, the address operator placed in front of a variable's name refers to the address of the variable. For example, &num means the address of num, &total means the address of total, and &price means the address of price. Program 4-16 uses the address operator to display the address of the variable num. For display purposes, the address, which is a hexadecimal number, is cast into its equivalent integer value.

Program 4-16

```cpp
#include <iostream>
#include <iomanip>
using namespace std;

int main()
{
    int num;

    num = 22;
    cout << "The value stored in num is " << num << endl;
    cout << "The address of num = " << int(&num) << endl;

    return 0;
}
```

The output of Program 4-16 is

```
The value stored in num is 22
The address of num = 1244884
```

Figure 4-13 illustrates the additional address information provided by the output of Program 4-16.

FIGURE 4-13
A More Complete Picture of the Variable num

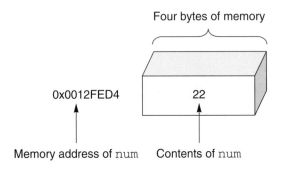

Clearly, the address displayed by Program 4-16 depends on where in memory each variable is assigned space. (This is determined when the program is loaded into the computer's memory prior to the program being executed. The program that determines these addresses is called a loader.) Every time Program 4-16 is executed, however, it displays the address of the first memory location used to store the variable num. As illustrated by Program 4-16's output, the display of addresses is in hexadecimal notation. This display has no effect on how addresses are used internally by the program; it merely provides us with a means of displaying addresses, which in turn helps us understand them. As we shall see in Chapters 10 and 12, using addresses in a program (as opposed to only displaying them) is an extremely important and powerful programming tool.

STORAGE OF INSTANCE VARIABLES

Instance variables are stored in the same manner as a method's local variables, with one important distinction: an instance variable only comes into existence when an object is created. For example, consider Program 4-17 (which uses a modified version of the RoomType class), in which the accessor method is used to display the address of each instance variable.

Within Program 4-17, the length and width members of the roomOne object are accessed when this object is provided to the showAddresses() method using the statement roomOne. showAddresses();. Calling roomOne an object is technically incorrect, but is a convention that is used by most programmers. More precisely, roomOne is a variable that contains the address of an object. Such variables are referred to as **reference variables**. Once the showAddresses() method

4

receives the address stored in roomOne, it uses this address to locate the object's instance variables. For the object created by Program 4-17, this consists of two variables named length and width. Specifically, the program reports the memory locations of these two variables as integer numbers.

Program 4-17

```cpp
#include <iostream>
using namespace std;

class RoomType
{
  // data declaration section
  private:
    double length;   // declare length as a double variable
    double width;    // declare width as a double variable

  // methods declaration section
  public:
    void showAddresses();
};

// methods implementation section
void RoomType::showAddresses()
{
  cout << "The address of length is " << int(&length) << endl;
  cout << "The address of width is " << int(&width) << endl;
}

int main()
{
  RoomType roomOne;   // declare a variable of type RoomType

  roomOne.showAddresses();

  return 0;
}
```

The output produced by Program 4-17, when it was run on the author's computer, was:

```
The address of length is 1244872
The address of width is 1244880
```

It is interesting to notice that there is an eight-byte difference between the two addresses. This provides the eight byte storage that the author's C++ compiler uses for all double-precision variables (see program 2-1).

Figure 4-14 illustrates the memory allocation provided by Program 4-17. Additionally, because the first variable stored in the object is at memory location 1244872, this same address is stored in the reference variable named roomOne. This address is actually passed to the showAddresses() method (and incidentally, stored in the variable named this, which was introduced at the end of Section 2.3).

FIGURE 4-14
Memory Storage for the roomOne *Object*

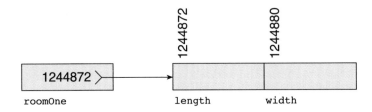

Exercises 4.6

1. Compile and execute Program 4-16.

2. Compile and execute Program 4-17.

3. Modify Program 4-17 to display the address of roomOne, using the expression &roomOne. Why do you think the address is the same as the address reported for the length variable?

4. Modify Program 4-17 to create a second object and display the address of its instance variables.

    In Exercises 5, 6, and 7, assume that a char requires one byte of storage, an int four bytes, a float four bytes, a double eight bytes, and that variables are assigned storage in the order they are declared. (Review Section 1.1 if you are unfamiliar with the concept of a byte.)

5. a. Using Figure 4-15, and assuming that the variable name rate is assigned to the byte having memory address 159, determine the addresses corresponding to each variable declared in the following statements. Also fill in the appropriate bytes with the initialization data included in the declaration statements (use letters for the characters, not the computer codes that would actually be stored).

    ```
    float rate;
    char ch1 = 'w', ch2 = 'o', ch3 = 'w', ch4 = '!';
    double taxes;
    int num, count = 0;
    ```

4

FIGURE 4-15
Memory Bytes for Exercises 5, 6, and 7

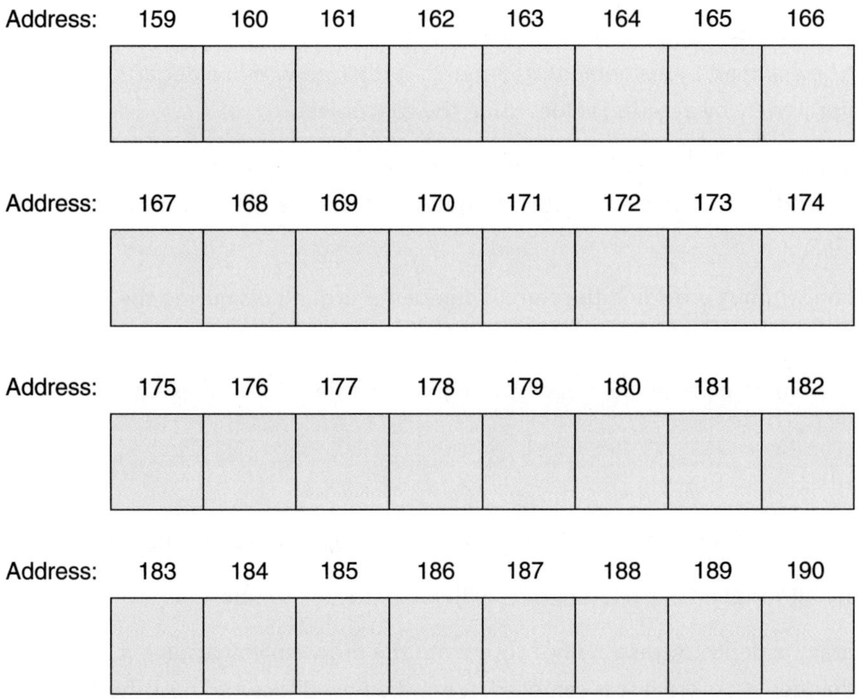

Address: 159   160   161   162   163   164   165   166

Address: 167   168   169   170   171   172   173   174

Address: 175   176   177   178   179   180   181   182

Address: 183   184   185   186   187   188   189   190

b. Repeat Exercise 5a, but substitute the actual byte patterns that a computer using the ASCII code would use to store the characters in the variables ch1, ch2, ch3, and ch4. (*Hint:* Use Table 2-2.)

6. **a.** Using Figure 4-15 and assuming that the variable named cn1 is assigned to the byte at memory address 159, determine the addresses corresponding to each variable declared in the following statements. Also fill in the appropriate bytes with the initialization data included in the declaration statements (use letters for the characters and not the computer codes that would actually be stored).

```
char cn1 = 'a', cn2 = ' ', cn3 = 'b', cn4 = 'u', cn5 = 'n';
char cn6 = 'c', cn7 = 'h', key = '\\', sch = '\'', inc = 'o';
char inc1 = 'f';
```

b. Repeat Exercise 6a, but substitute the actual byte patterns that a computer using the ASCII code would use to store the characters in each of the declared variables. (*Hint:* Use Table 2-2.)

7. Using Figure 4-15 and assuming that the variable name miles is assigned to the byte at memory address 159, determine the addresses corresponding to each variable declared in the following statements.

```
float miles;
int count, num;
double dist, temp;
```

4.7 COMMON PROGRAMMING ERRORS

In using the material presented in this chapter, be aware of these possible errors:

1. Forgetting to assign or initialize values for all variables before the variables are used in an expression. Such values can be assigned by assignment statements, initialized within a declaration statement, or assigned interactively by entering values using the `cin` object.

2. Using a mathematical library function without including the preprocessor statement `#include <cmath>` (and on a UNIX based system forgetting to include the `-lm` argument to the `cc` command).

3. Using a library function without providing the correct number or arguments having the proper data type.

4. Applying either the increment or decrement operator to an expression. For example, the expression

   ```
   (count + n)++
   ```

   is incorrect. The increment and decrement operators can only be applied to individual variables.

5. Forgetting to separate all variables expected by `cin` with an extraction symbol, `>>`.

6. Failing to test a program in depth. After all, since you wrote the program you assume it is correct or you would have changed it before it was compiled. It is extremely difficult to back away and honestly test your own software. As a programmer, you must constantly remind yourself that just because you think your program is correct does not make it so. Finding errors in your own program is a sobering experience, but one that will help you to become a master programmer.

7. Not understanding the implication of the fact that C++ does not specify the order in which operands are accessed within an expression. For example, the value assigned to result in the statement

   ```
   result = i + i++;
   ```

   is compiler dependent. If your compiler accesses the first operand, `i`, first, the above statement is equivalent to

   ```
   result = 2 * i;
   i++;
   ```

   However, if your compiler accesses the second operand, `i++`, first, the value of the first operand will be altered before it is used the second time and the value $2i + 1$ is assigned to `result`. This type of error is really quite rare and only arises when the increment and decrement operators are used with variables that appear more than once in the same expression. As a general rule, therefore, do not use either the increment or decrement operator in an expression when the variable it operates on appears more than once in the same expression.

4.8 CHAPTER REVIEW

4

Key Terms

arguments

assignment operator

assignment variation operators

cast

cin

counting

field width specifiers

hexadecimal

justification

magic numbers

mathematical header

mathematical library

named constants

octal

prompt

symbolic constants

type conversions

SUMMARY

1. An expression is a sequence of one or more operands separated by operators that can be evaluated to yield a value. An operand is a constant, a variable, a returned value from a function or method, or another expression.

2. Expressions are evaluated according to the precedence and associativity of the operators used in the expression.

3. The assignment symbol, =, is an operator. Expressions using this operator assign a value to a variable; additionally, the expression itself takes on a value. Since assignment is an operation in C++, multiple uses of the assignment operator are possible in the same expression.

4. An expression that is terminated by a semicolon becomes a statement.

5. The increment operator, ++, adds one to a variable, while the decrement operator, --, subtracts one from a variable. Both of these operators can be used as prefixes or postfixes. In prefix operation, the variable is incremented (or decremented) before its value is used. In postfix operation, the variable is incremented (or decremented) after its value is used.

6. C++ provides library functions for calculating square root, logarithmic, and other mathematical computations. To use one or more of these mathematical functions in a program, you must either include the statement `#include <cmath>` once, at the top of your program, or you must include a separate function declaration for the mathematical function before it is called. After a function has been declared, you can use it as many times as necessary following the declaration.

7. Every mathematical library function operates on its arguments to calculate a single value. To use a library function effectively, you must know what the function does, the name of the function, the number and data types of the arguments expected by the function, and the data type of the returned value.

8. Functions may be included within larger expressions.

9. The `cin` object is used for data input. This object accepts a stream of data from the keyboard and assigns the data to variables. The general form of a statement using `cin` is:

    ```
    cin >> var1 >> var2 . . . >> varn;
    ```

    The extraction symbol, >>, must be used to separate the variable names.

10. When a `cin` statement is encountered, the computer temporarily suspends further statement execution until sufficient data has been entered for the number of variables contained in the `cin` statement.

11. It is good programming practice to display a message, prior to a `cin` statement, that alerts the user as to the type and number of data items to be entered. Such a message is called a prompt.

12. Values can be equated to a single variable, using the `const` variable qualifier when the variable is declared. This makes the variable read-only after it is initialized within the declaration statement. This declaration has the form

    ```
    const dataType variableName = initial value;
    ```

and permits the variable to be used instead of the initial value anywhere in the program after the command. Generally, such declarations are placed at the top of a C++ program.

Chapter Exercises

1. For the following local variable declarations:

    ```
    int numOfApples, numOfOranges;
    int vector, digitalTemp;
    double average, distance;
    char letter, symbol;
    ```

    Determine which of the following statements are valid and which are invalid. If invalid, explain why.

    a. `average = 89.4;`
    b. `distance= 130;`
    c. `numOfOranges = (54 * numOfApples) % 3;`

d. `vector = numOfApples;`

e. `digitalTemp = double (average);`

f. `numOfApples = numOfOranges + letter;`

g. `symbol = letter;`

h. `distance = distance % average;`

i. `vector = distance / average;`

j. `numOfApples = double(average);`

k. `numOfOranges = int(distance);`

l. `average = double(vector);`

m. `distance = double(numOfApples);`

n. `numOfApples = numOfOranges - distance;`

o. `numOfOranges = -17;`

2. Determine and correct the errors in the following programs.

a.
```cpp
#include <iostream>
using namespace std;

int main()
{
    width = 15
    area = length * width;
    cout << "The area is " << area

    return 0;
}
```

b.
```cpp
#include <iostream>
using namespace std;

int main()
{
    int length, width, area;
    area = length * width;
    length = 20;
    width = 15;
    cout << "The area is " << area;

    return 0;
```

c.
```cpp
#include <iostream>
using namespace std;

int main()
{
```

```
    int length = 20; width = 15, area;
    length * width = area;
    cout << "The area is " , area;

    return 0;
}
```

3. **a.** Write a C++ program to calculate and display the value of the slope of the line connecting the two points whose coordinates are (3, 7) and (8, 12). Use the fact that the slope between two points having coordinates (x1, y1) and (x2, y2) is (y2 - y1) / (x2 - x1).

   b. How do you know that the result produced by your program is correct?

   c. Once you have verified the output produced by your program, modify it to determine the slope of the line connecting the points (2, 10) and (12, 6).

   d. What do you think will happen if you use the points (2, 3) and (2, 4), which results in a division by zero? How do you think this situation can be handled?

4. **a.** Write a C++ program to calculate and display the coordinates of the midpoint of the line segment connecting the two end points given in Exercise 3a. Use the fact that the coordinates of the midpoint between two points having coordinates (x1, y1) and (x2, y2) are ((X1+X2)/2, (Y1+Y2)/2). Your program should produce the following display:

   ```
   The x midpoint coordinate is _____
   The y midpoint coordinate is _____
   ```

   where the underlined spaces are replaced with the values calculated by your program.

   b. How do you know that the midpoint values calculated by your program are correct?

   c. Once you have verified the output produced by your program, modify it to determine the midpoint coordinates of the line connecting the points (2, 10) and (12, 6).

5. Repeat Exercise 3 but change the output produced by your program to be:

   ```
   The value of the slope is xxx.xx
   ```

   where xxx.xx denotes that the calculated value should be placed in a field wide enough for three places to the left of the decimal point, and two places to the right of it.

6. Repeat Exercise 4 but change the output produced by your program to:

   ```
   The x coordinate of the midpoint is xxx.xx
   The y coordinate of the midpoint is xxx.xx
   ```

   where xxx.xx denotes that the calculated value should be placed in a field wide enough for three places to the left of the decimal point, and two places to the right of it.

7. The change (in dollars) remaining after a restaurant check is paid can be calculated using the following C++ statements. The variable `paid` is used to store the amount the customer pays, and the variable `check` is used to store the amount of the check (that is, the amount the customer owes).

4

```
// determine the amount of pennies in the change
change = (paid - check) * 100;
// determine the number of dollars in the change
dollars = int (change/100);
```

a. Using the preceding statements as a starting point, write a C++ program that calculates the number of dollar bills, quarters, dimes, nickels, and pennies in the change when $10 is used to pay a bill of $6.07.

b. Without compiling or executing your program, manually check the effect of each statement in the program and determine what is stored in each variable as each statement is processed.

c. When you have verified that your algorithm works correctly, compile and execute your program. Verify that the result produced by your program is correct. After you have verified that your program is working correctly, use it to determine the change when a check of $12.36 is paid using a twenty dollar bill.

8. a. For display purposes, the setprecision manipulator allows the programmer to round all outputs to the desired number of decimal places. This can, however, yield seemingly incorrect results when used in financial programs that require all monetary values be displayed to the nearest penny. For example, the display produced by the program:

```
#include <iostream>
#include <iomanip>
using namespace std;

int main()
{
  double a, b, c;

  a = 1.674;
  b = 1.322;
  cout << fixed << setprecision(2) << a << endl;
  cout << fixed <<setprecision(2) << b << endl;
  cout << "------\n";
  c = a + b;
  cout << fixed << setprecision(2) << c << endl;

  return 0;
}
```

is:

```
1.67
1.32
----
3.00
```

Clearly, the sum of the displayed numbers should be 2.99 and not 3.00. The problem is that although the values in a and b have been displayed with two decimal digits, they were added internal to the program as three-digit numbers. The solution is to round the values in a and b before they are added by the statement c = a + b;. Using the int cast, devise a function to round the values in the variables a and b to the nearest hundredth (penny value) before they are added.

b. Include the function you have devised for Exercise 8a into a working program that produces the following display:

```
1.67
1.32
----
2.99
```

9. Design, write, compile, and execute a program that calculates and displays the 4th root of a number entered by the user. Recall from elementary algebra that the 4th root of a number can be found by raising the number to the 1/4 power. (Can you see why you should not use integer division?) Verify your program by calculating the 4th root of the following data: 81, 16, 1, and 0. When you have completed your verification, use your program to determine the 4th root of 42, 121, 256, 587, 1240, and 16256.

10. Using cin statements, write, compile, and execute a C++ program that accepts the x and y coordinates of two points. Have your program determine and display the midpoints of the two points (use the formula given in Exercise 4). Verify your program using the following test data:

Test data set 1: Point 1 = (0,0) and Point 2 = (16,0)
Test data set 2: Point 1 = (0,0) and Point 2 = (0,16)
Test data set 3: Point 1 = (0,0) and Point 2 = (-16,0)
Test data set 4: Point 1 = (0,0) and Point 2 = (0,-16)
Test data set 5: Point 1 = (-5,-5) and Point 2 = (5,5)

When you have completed your verification, use your program to determine the midpoints for the following data:

point 1	point 2
(4,6)	(16,18)
(22,3)	(8,12)
(-10,8)	(14,4)
(-12,2)	(14,3.1)
(3.1,-6)	(20,16)
(3.1,-6)	(-16,-18)

4

11. Design, write, compile, and execute a C++ program that calculates and displays the amount of money, A, available in N years when an initial deposit of X dollars is deposited in a bank account paying an annual interest rate of R percent. Use the relationship that $A = X(1.0 + R/100)^N$. The program should prompt the user to enter appropriate values and use `cin` statements to accept the data. In constructing your prompts use statements such as "Enter the amount of the initial deposit." Verify the operation of your program by calculating, by hand and with your program, the amount of money available for the following test cases:

> Test data set 1: $1000 invested for 10 years at 0% interest
> Test data set 2: $1000 invested for 10 years at 6% interest

When you have completed your verification, use your program to determine the amount of money available for the following cases:

a. $1000 invested for 10 years at 8% interest.
b. $1000 invested for 10 years at 10% interest.
c. $1000 invested for 10 years at 12% interest.
d. $5000 invested for 15 years at 8% interest.
e. $5000 invested for 15 years at 10% interest.
f. $5000 invested for 15 years at 12% interest.
g. $24 invested for 300 years at 4% interest.

12. Write a C++ program that prompts the user for a cost-per-item, number of items purchased, and a discount rate. The program should then calculate and print the total cost, tax due, and amount due. Use the formulas:

> total cost = number of items * cost-per-item
> total cost (discounted) = total cost - (discount rate * total cost)
> tax due = total cost * TAXRATE
> amount due = total cost + tax due

For this problem assume that the TAXRATE is 6%.

13. The roads of Kansas are laid out in a rectangular grid at exactly one-mile intervals, as shown in Figure 4-16. Lonesome farmer Pete drives his 1939 Ford pickup x miles east and y miles north to get to widow Sally's farm. Both x and y are integer numbers. Using this information, write, test, and run a C++ program that prompts the user for the values of x and y and then uses the formula

> distance = sqrt(x * x + y * y);

to find the shortest driving distance across the fields to Sally's farm. Since Pete does not understand fractions or decimals very well, the answer must be rounded to the nearest integer value before it is displayed.

FIGURE 4-16

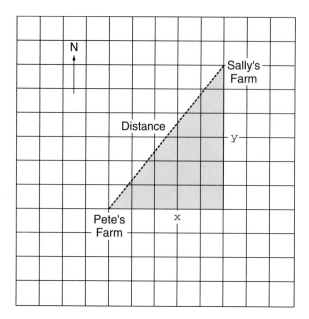

14. When a particular rubber ball is dropped from a given height (in meters) its impact speed (in meters/second) when it hits the ground is given by the formula *speed = sqrt(2 * g * height)*. The ball then rebounds to 2/3 the height from which it last fell. Using this information write, test, and run a C++ program that calculates and displays the impact speed of the first three bounces and the rebound height of each bounce. Test your program using an initial height of 2.0 meters. Run the program twice and compare the results for dropping the ball on earth (g = 9.81 meters/sec²) and on the moon (g = 1.67 meters/sec²).

Working in Teams

15. a. Have each team member make a list of their objectives in taking this course.

    b. Have each team member make a list of five attributes of the courses that they have enjoyed taking.

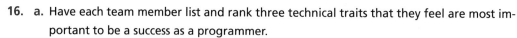

Working in Teams

16. a. Have each team member list and rank three technical traits that they feel are most important to be a success as a programmer.

    b. Have each team member list and rank three personality traits that they feel are most important for success in the programming field.

    c. Using each member's lists as a starting point, come up with three technical and three personality traits that the group, as a whole, considers most important.

    d. Put the list constructed in Exercise 16c on the board and compare lists with the other groups in the class.

    e. How could you verify that the traits you have identified are indeed valid?

4

**Working
in Teams**

17. **a.** Have each team member list three *technical* traits that they feel would be detrimental to success as a programmer.

b. Have each team member list three *personality* traits that they feel would be detrimental to success in the programming field.

c. Using each member's lists as a starting point, come up with three technical and three personality traits that the group, as a whole, agrees would be detrimental.

d. Put the list constructed in Exercise 17c on the board and compare lists with the other groups in the class.

e. How could you verify that the traits you have identified are indeed valid?

**Testing
Center**

Please visit the Testing Center at www.course.com/testingcenter for more practice on assignment, formatting, and interactive input.

5

SELECTION STRUCTURES

The term **flow of control** refers to the order in which a program's statements are executed. Unless directed otherwise, the normal flow of control for all programs is sequential. This means that each statement is executed in sequence, one after another, in the order in which they are placed within the program.

Two kinds of statements, called selection and repetition statements, allow the programmer to alter the normal flow of control. As their names imply, selection statements provide the ability to select which statement, from a well-defined set, will be executed next, whereas repetition statements provide the ability to go back and repeat a set of statements. In this chapter, we present C++'s selection statements; repetition statements are presented in Chapter 6. Since selection requires choosing between alternatives, we begin this chapter with a description of C++'s selection criteria.

5.1 RELATIONAL EXPRESSIONS

In addition to providing capabilities for addition, subtraction, multiplication, and division, all computers have the ability to compare numbers. Because many decision-making situations can be reduced to the level of choosing between two values, a computer's comparison capability can be used to create a remarkable intelligence-like facility.

Expressions that compare operands are called **relational expressions**. A **simple relational expression** consists of a relational operator connecting two variable or two constant operands (or one of each), as shown in Figure 5-1. The relational operators available in C++ are given in Table 5-1. These relational operators may be used with integer, float, double, and character data; they must be typed exactly as shown in Table 5-1. Thus, the following examples are all valid:

```
age > 40        length <= 50      temp > 98.6
  3 < 4         flag == done      idNum == 682
day != 5        2.0 < 3.3         hours > 40
```

The following are invalid:

```
length =< 50     // incorrect symbol
2.0 >> 3.3       // invalid relational operator
flag = = done    // spaces between operators are not allowed
```

FIGURE 5-1
Anatomy of a Simple Relational Expression

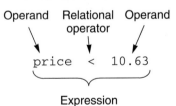

TABLE 5-1
Relational Operators for Primitive Data Types

relational operator	meaning	example
<	less than	age < 30
>	greater than	height > 6.2
<=	less than or equal to	taxable <= 20000
>=	greater than or equal to	temp >= 98.6
==	equal to	grade == 100
!=	not equal to	number != 250

Another term for a relational expression is **condition**; both terms are commonly used. Like all C++ expressions, relational expressions are evaluated to yield a result. For relational expressions, the result can only be the integer value of 1 or 0, which is interpreted as true or false, respectively. A relational expression that we interpret as true evaluates to an integer value of 1, and a false relational expression results in an integer value of 0. This is the same for the Boolean values `true` and `false`; C++ considers the Boolean value `true` as the integer value 1 and the Boolean value `false` as 0. For example, the relationship 3 < 4 is always `true` and the relationship 2.0 > 3.3 is always `false`. This can be verified using the statements

```
cout << "The value of 3 < 4 is " << (3 < 4) << endl;
cout << "The value of 2.0 > 3.0 is " << (2.0 > 3.3) << endl;
cout << "The value of true is " << true << endl;
cout << "The value of false is " << false << endl;
```

which result in the display

```
The value of 3 < 4 is 1
The value of 2.0 > 3.0 is 0
The value of true is 1
The value of false is 0
```

The value of a relational expression such as `hours > 40` depends on the value stored in the variable `hours`. In a C++ program, a relational expression such as this is typically used as part of a selection statement. In these statements, which are presented in the next section, the "selection" of which statement to execute next is based on the value obtained.

In addition to numerical operands, character data can also be compared to using relational operators. For such comparisons, the `char` values are automatically coerced to `int` values for the comparison. For example, in the Unicode code the letter 'A' is stored using a code that has a lower numerical value than the letter 'B,' the code for 'B' has a lower value than the code for 'C,' and so on. For character sets coded in this manner, the following conditions are evaluated as follows:

expression	value	interpretation
'A' > 'C'	0	false
'D' <= 'Z'	1	true
'E' == 'F'	0	false
'g' >= 'm'	0	false
'b' != 'c'	1	true
'a' == 'A'	0	false
'B' < 'a'	1	true
'b' > 'Z'	1	true

Comparing letters is essential in alphabetizing names or using characters to select a particular choice in decision-making situations. Strings of characters may also be compared. Finally, two string expressions may be compared using relational operators or the `string` class' comparison methods (Chapter 9). In the ASCII character set, a blank precedes (and is considered "less than") all letters and numbers; the letters of the alphabet are stored in order from A to Z; and the digits are stored in order from 0 to 9. In this sequence, the lowercase letters come after (are considered "greater than") the uppercase letters, and the letter codes come after (are "greater than") the digit codes (see Appendix B).

When two strings are compared, their individual characters are compared one pair at a time (both first characters, then both second characters, and so on). If no differences are found, the strings are equal; if a difference is found, the string with the first lower character is considered the smaller string. Following are examples of string comparisons:

expression	value	interpretation	comment
`"Hello" > "Good-bye"`	1	`true`	The first 'H' in Hello is greater than the first 'G' in Good-bye.
`"SMITH" > "JONES"`	1	`true`	The first 'S' in SMITH is greater than the first 'J' in JONES.
`"123" > "1227"`	1	`true`	The third character, the '3' in 123 is greater than the third character, the '2' in 1227.
`"Behop" > "Beehive"`	1	`true`	The third character, the 'h', in Behop is greater than the third character 'e' in Beehive.
`"He" == "She"`	0	`false`	The first 'H' in He is not equal to the first 'S' in She.
`"plant" < "planet"`	0	`false`	The 't' in plant is greater than the 'e' in planet.

LOGICAL OPERATORS

In addition to using simple relational expressions as conditions, you can create more complex conditions using the Boolean logical operations AND, OR, and NOT. These operations are represented by the symbols &&, ||, and !, respectively.

When the AND operator, &&, is used with two relational expressions, the condition is true only if both individual expressions are true by themselves. Thus, the logical condition

        (age > 40) && (term < 10)

is true (has a value of 1) only if age is greater than 40 and term is less than 10. Relational operators have a higher precedence than logical operators, so the parentheses in this logical expression could have been omitted. The parentheses are included here to make the relational expressions easier to read.

The logical OR operator, ||, is also applied between two expressions. When using the OR operator, the condition is satisfied if either one or both of the two expressions are true. Thus, the logical condition

        (age > 40) || (term < 10)

is `true` if `age` is greater than 40, or if `term` is less than 10, or if both conditions are true. Again, the parentheses surrounding the relational expressions are included to make the expression easier to read.

For the declarations

```
int i, j;
double a, b;
bool complete;
```

the following represent valid conditions:

```
a > b
(a/b > 5) && (i <= 20)
(i == j) || (a < b) || complete
```

Before these conditions can be evaluated, the values of `a`, `b`, `i`, `j`, and `complete` must be known. Assuming the assignments

```
a = 12.0;
b = 2.0;
i = 15;
j = 30;
complete = false;
```

the previous expressions yield the following results

expression	value	interpretation
`a > b`	1	true
`(a/b > 5) && (i <= 20)`	1	true
`(i == j) || (a < b) || complete`	0	false

The NOT operator is used to change an expression to its opposite state; that is, if the expression has any nonzero value (true), !expression produces a zero value (false). If an expression is false to begin with (has a zero value), !expression is true and evaluates to 1. For example, assuming the number 26 is stored in the variable `age`, the expression `age > 40` has a value of zero (it is false), while the expression `!(age > 40)` has a value of 1. Since the NOT operator is used with only one expression, it is a unary operator.

The `&&` and `||` operators use a "short-circuited evaluation." This means that the second operand is never evaluated if the evaluation of the first operand is sufficient to determine the final value of the logical operation. For the `&&` operator, this means that if the first condition evaluates to a nonzero (false) value, the second operand is not evaluated. The reason is that the AND logical operation can only yield a true value if both operands are true; thus if the first operand is false, the value of the operation must be false regardless of the value of the second operand. The same holds for the `||` operator. In this case, if the first operand yields a true, the complete OR operation must be true regardless of the value of the second operand, and the second operand need not be evaluated.

The relational and logical operators have a hierarchy of execution similar to the arithmetic operators. Table 5-2 lists the precedence of these operators in relation to the other operators we have encountered.

TABLE 5-2
Operator Precedence

operator	associativity
++ --	right to left
! unary -	right to left
* / %	left to right
+ -	left to right
< <= > >=	left to right
== !=	left to right
&	left to right
^	left to right
|	left to right
&&	left to right
||	left to right
= += -= *= /=	right to left

Table 5-3 illustrates the use of an operator's precedence and associativity to evaluate relational expressions, assuming the following declarations:

```
char key = 'm';
int i = 5, j = 7, k = 12;
double x = 22.5;
```

TABLE 5-3
Equivalent Expressions

expression	equivalent expression	value	interpretation
i + 2 == k - 1	(i + 2) == (k - 1)	0	false
3 * i - j < 22	((3 * i) - j) < 22	1	true
i + 2 * j > k	(i + (2 * j)) > k	1	true
k + 3 <= -j + 3 * I	(k + 3) <= ((-j) + (3*i))	0	false
'a' + 1 == 'b'	('a' + 1) == 'b'	1	true
key - 1 > 'p'	(key - 1) > 'p'	0	false
key + 1 == 'n'	(key + 1) == 'n'	1	true
25 >= x + 1.0	25 >= (x + 1.0)	1	true

A BIT OF BACKGROUND

De Morgan's Laws

Augustus De Morgan was born in Madura, India in 1806 and died in London in 1871. He became a professor of mathematics in London in 1828 and spent many years performing investigations into a variety of mathematical topics. He was a revered teacher and wrote numerous textbooks that contained a wealth of information on mathematics and its history, but which generally were very difficult for his students to understand.

De Morgan's contributions to modern computing include two laws by which AND statements can be converted to OR statements and vice versa. They are:

```
1. NOT(A AND B) = (NOT A) OR (NOT B)
2. NOT(A OR B)  = (NOT A) AND (NOT B)
```

Thus, from De Morgan's first law, the statement "Either it is not raining or I am not getting wet" says the same thing as "It is not true that it is raining and I am getting wet." Similarly, from the second law "It is not true that politicians always lie or that teachers always know the facts" becomes "Politicians do not always lie and teachers do not always know the facts."

In computer usage, De Morgan's laws are typically more useful in the following form:

```
1. A AND B = NOT((NOT A) OR (NOT B))
2. A OR B  = NOT((NOT A) AND (NOT B))
```

The ability to convert from an OR statement to an AND statement and vice versa is very useful in many programming situations.

As with all expressions, parentheses can be used to alter the assigned operator priority and improve the readability of relational expressions. By evaluating the expressions within parentheses first, the following compound condition is evaluated as:

```
(6 * 3 == 36 / 2) || (13 < 3 * 3 + 4)  && !(6 - 2 < 5)
   (18 == 18) ||    (13 < 9 + 4)  && !(4 < 5)
          1 ||    (13 < 13)     && !1
          1 ||    0             && !1
          1 ||    0
             1
```

A NUMERICAL ACCURACY PROBLEM

A problem that can occur with C++'s relational expressions is a subtle numerical accuracy issue relating to floating-point and double-precision numbers. Because of the way computers store these numbers, tests for equality of floating-point and double-precision values and variables using the relational operator == should be avoided.

The reason is that many decimal numbers, such as 0.1, cannot be represented exactly in binary using a finite number of bits. Thus, testing for exact equality for such numbers can fail. When equality of non-integer values is desired, it is better to require that the absolute value of the difference between operands be less than some extremely small value. Thus, for real operands, the general expression

        operandOne == operandTwo

should be replaced by the condition

        abs(operandOne - operandTwo) < EPSILON

where abs is the absolute value function (review Section 4.3, if necessary) and EPSILON is a named constant set to any acceptably small value, such as 0.0000001 (or any other user-selected amount).[1] Thus, if the difference between the two operands is less than the value of EPSILON, the two operands are considered essentially equal. For example, if x and y are floating-point variables, a condition such as

        x/y == 0.35

should be programmed as

        abs(x/y - 0.35)   <   EPSILON

This latter condition ensures that slight inaccuracies in representing noninteger numbers in binary do not affect evaluation of the tested condition.

Exercises 5.1

1. Determine the value of the following expressions. Assume a = 5, b = 2, c = 4, d = 6, and e = 3, and all variables are ints.

    a. a > b
    b. a != b
    c. d % b == c % b
    d. a * c != d * b
    e. d * b == c * e

    f. a * b < a % b * c
    g. a % b * c > c % b * a
    h. c % b * a == b % c * a
    i. b % c * a != a * b

2. Using parentheses, rewrite the following expressions to indicate their correct order of evaluation. Then evaluate each expression assuming a = 5, b = 2, and c = 4.

    a. a % b * c && c % b * a
    b. a % b * c || c % b * a
    c. b % c * a && a % c * b
    d. b % c * a || a % c * b

3.   Write relational expressions to express the following conditions (use variable names of your own choosing):

   a. a person's age is equal to 30
   b. a person's body temperature is greater than 98.6
   c. a person's height is less than 6 feet
   d. the current month is 12 (December)
   e. the letter input is m
   f. a person's age is equal to 30 and the person is taller than 6 feet
   g. the current day is the 15th day of the 1st month
   h. a person is older than 50 or has been employed at the company for at least 5 years
   i. a person's identification number is less than 500 and the person is older than 55
   j. a length is greater than 2 feet and less than 3 feet

4.   Determine the value of the following expressions, assuming a = 5, b = 2, c = 4, and d = 5.

   a. `a == 5`
   b. `b * d == c * c`
   c. `d % b * c > 5 || c % b * d < 7`

5.2 THE IF-ELSE STATEMENT

The `if-else` statement directs the computer to select a sequence of one or more instructions based on the result of a comparison. For example, the state of New Jersey has a two-level state income tax structure. If a person's taxable income is less than $20,000, the state tax rate is 2 percent. For incomes exceeding $20,000, a different rate is applied. The `if-else` statement can be used in this situation to determine the actual tax based on whether the gross income is less than or equal to $20,000. The general form of the `if-else` statement is:

```
if (expression)   statement1;
else   statement2;
```

The *expression* is evaluated first. If the value of the expression is true or has a nonzero value (remember that C++ considers a nonzero value as a Boolean `false`), *statement1* is executed; otherwise, the statement after the keyword `else` is executed. Thus, one of the two statements (either *statement1* or *statement2*, but not both) is always executed depending on the value of the expression. Notice that the tested expression must be put in parentheses and a semicolon is placed after each statement, and that the statement can be translated as "if the condition is true, only execute the statement following the condition; otherwise, execute the statement following the `else` keyword."

For clarity, the `if-else` statement is commonly written on four lines using the form:

```
    if (expression)    ◄──────  no semicolon here
        statement1;
    else   ◄──────────  no semicolon here
        statement2;
```

Whether a two- or four-line form of the `if-else` statement is used generally depends on the length of statements 1 and 2. However, when using the four-line form, do not put a semicolon after the parentheses or the keyword `else`. The semicolons are placed only after the ends of the statements.

The flowchart for the `if-else` statement is shown in Figure 5-2.

FIGURE 5-2
The `if-else` *Flowchart*

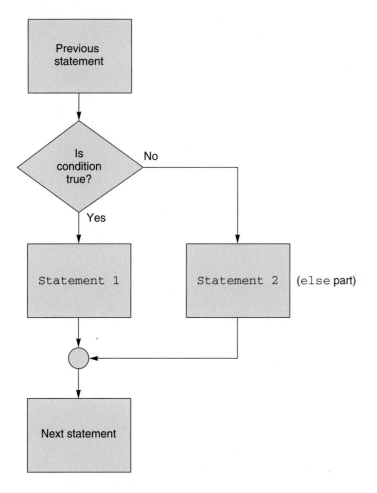

As a specific example of an `if-else` statement, we can construct a C++ program for determining New Jersey income taxes. As previously described, these taxes are assessed at 2 percent of taxable income for incomes less than or equal to $20,000. For taxable income greater than $20,000, state taxes are 2.5 percent of the income that exceeds $20,000 plus a fixed amount of $400. The expression to be tested asks whether taxable income is less than or equal to $20,000. An appropriate if-else statement for this situation is:[2]

```
if (taxable <= 20000.0)
   taxes = 0.02 * taxable;
else
   taxes = 0.025 * (taxable - 20000.0) + 400.0;
```

Here we have used the relational operator <= to represent the relation "less than or equal to." If the value of taxable is less than or equal to 20000, the condition is true (has a value of 1) and the statement taxes = .02 * taxable; is executed. If the condition is not true, the value of the expression is zero, and the statement after the keyword else is executed. Program 5-1 illustrates the use of this statement in a complete program.

Program 5-1

```
#include <iostream>
#include <iomanip>   // needed for formatting
using namespace std;

int main()
{
  double taxable, taxes;

  cout << "Please type in the taxable income: ";
  cin  >> taxable;

  if (taxable <= 20000.00)
    taxes = 0.02 * taxable;
  else
     taxes = 0.025 * (taxable - 20000.00) + 400.00;

    // set output format
  cout << setiosflags(ios::fixed)
       << setiosflags(ios::showpoint)
       << setprecision(2);

  cout << "Taxes are $ " << taxes << endl;
  return 0;
}
```

The if-else statement has been highlighted and a blank line inserted before and after it to make the statement easier to locate in the complete program. This convention will be used throughout the text to emphasize the statement being presented.

---

[2]Note that in actual practice the numerical values in this statement would be defined as symbolic constants, such as THRESHOLD, that is equated to 20000. Using this symbolic constant the tested expression becomes taxable <= THRESHOLD.

5

PROGRAMMING NOTE

The Boolean Data Type

Before the current ANSI/ISO C++ standard, C++ did not have a built-in Boolean data type with its two Boolean values, `true` and `false`. Because this data type was not originally part of the language, a tested expression could not evaluate to a Boolean value. Thus, the syntax

```
    if(Boolean expression is true)
```

was not a part of the C++ language. Rather, C++ used the more encompassing syntax

```
    if(expression)
      execute this statement;
```

where *expression* is any expression (relational, logical, or numeric) that evaluates to a numeric value. If this value were nonzero, it was considered `true`, and only a zero value was considered false.

As specified by the ANSO standard, C++ has a built-in Boolean data type, `bool`, containing the two values `true` and `false`. As currently implemented, the actual values represented by the `bool` values, `true` and `false`, are the integer values 1 and 0, respectively. For example, consider the following program, which declares two Boolean variables.

```cpp
#include <iostream>
using namespace std;

int main()
{

  bool t1, t2;
  t1 = true;
  t2 = false;

  cout << "The value of t1 is " << t1
       <<  "\n and the value of t2 is " << t2 << endl;
  return 0;
}
```

The output displayed by this method is:

```
The value of t1 is 1
 and the value of t2 is 0
```

As can be seen by this output, the Boolean values `true` and `false` are represented by the integer values 1 and 0, respectively. To see Boolean values displayed as `true` and `false`, you can insert the manipulator `boolalpha` into the `cout` stream prior to displaying Boolean values. The Boolean values have the following relationships:

```
!true  = false
!false = true
```

(continued on next page)

> **PROGRAMMING NOTE**
>
> **The Boolean Data Type** (*continued*)
>
> Additionally, applying either a postfix or prefix increment (++) operator to a variable of type `bool` sets the Boolean value to `true`. The postfix and prefix decrement operators (--) cannot be applied to a Boolean variable.
>
> Boolean values can also be compared. For example, if `flag1` and `flag2` are two Boolean variables, the relational expression `flag1 == flag2` is valid. Lastly, assigning any nonzero value to a Boolean variable results in the variable being set to `true` (that is, a value of `1`), and assigning a zero to a Boolean variable results in the variable being set to `false` (that is, a value of `0`).

To illustrate selection in action, Program 5-1 was run twice with different input data. The results are:

```
Please type in the taxable income: 10000.
Taxes are $ 200.00
```

and:

```
Please type in the taxable income: 30000.
Taxes are $ 650.00
```

Observe that the taxable income input in the first run of the program was less than $20,000, and the tax was correctly calculated as 2 percent of the number entered. In the second run, the taxable income was more than $20,000, and the else part of the `if-else` statement was used to yield a correct tax computation of

```
0.025 * ($30,000. - $20,000.) + $400. = $650.
```

Although any expression can be tested by an `if-else` statement, relational expressions are used predominantly. However, statements such as:

```
if (num)
   cout << "Bingo!";
else
   cout << "You lose!";
```

are valid. Since `num`, by itself, is a valid expression, the message `Bingo!` is displayed if `num` has any nonzero value, and the message `You lose!` is displayed if `num` has a value of zero.

COMPOUND STATEMENTS

Although only a single statement is permitted in both the if and else parts of the `if-else` statement, this statement can be a single compound statement. A **compound statement** is a sequence of statements contained between braces, as shown here:

```
            {
                statement1;
                statement2;
                statement3;

                        .

                        .

                        .

                last statement;
            }
```

The use of braces to enclose a set of individual statements creates a single block of statements, which may be used anywhere in a C++ program in place of a single statement. The next example illustrates the use of a compound statement within the general form of an `if-else` statement.

```
    if (expression)
    {
        statement1;     // as many statements as necessary
        statement2;     // can be put within the braces
        statement3;     // each statement must end with a semicolon
    }
    else
    {
        statement4;
        statement5;

            .

            .

        statementn;
    }
```

Program 5-2 checks whether the value in `tempType` is f. If the value is f, the compound statement corresponding to the `if` part of the `if-else` statement is executed. Any other letter results in execution of the compound statement corresponding to the `else` part. A sample run of Program 5-2 follows.

```
Enter the temperature to be converted: 212
Enter an f if the temperature is in Fahrenheit
 or a c if the temperature is in Celsius: f

The equivalent Celsius temperature is 100.00
```

Program 5-2

```cpp
#include <iostream>
#include <iomanip>
using namespace std;

// a temperature conversion program
int main()
{
  char tempType;
  double temp, fahren, celsius;

  cout << "Enter the temperature to be converted: ";
  cin  >> temp;
  cout << "Enter an f if the temperature is in Fahrenheit";
  cout << "\n or a c if the temperature is in Celsius: ";
  cin  >> tempType;

    // set output formats
  cout << setiosflags(ios::fixed)
       << setiosflags(ios::showpoint)
       << setprecision(2);

if (tempType == 'f')
{
  celsius = (5.0 / 9.0) * (temp - 32.0);
  cout << "\nThe equivalent Celsius temperature is "
       << celsius << endl;

}
else
{
  fahren =  (9.0 / 5.0) * temp + 32.0;
  cout << "\nThe equivalent Fahrenheit temperature is "
       << fahren << endl;
}

return 0;
}
```

5

PROGRAMMING NOTE

Placement of Braces in a Compound Statement

A common practice for some C++ programmers is to place the opening brace of a compound statement on the same line as the `if` and `else` statements. Using this convention, the `if` statement in Program 5-2 would appear as shown below. This placement is a matter of style only; both styles are used and both are acceptable.

```cpp
if (tempType == 'f') {
  celsius = (5.0 / 9.0) * (temp - 32.0);
  cout << setiosflags(ios::showpoint)
       << setprecision(2)
       << "\nThe equivalent Celsius temperature is "
       << celsius << endl;
}
else {
  fahren =  (9.0 / 5.0) * temp + 32.0;
  cout << "\nThe equivalent Fahrenheit temperature is "
       << fahren << endl;
}
```

BLOCK SCOPE

All statements contained within a compound statement constitute a single block of code. Any variable declared within such a block only has meaning between its declaration and the closing braces defining the block. For example, consider the following section of code, which consists of two blocks of code:

```cpp
{    // start of outer block
  int a = 25;
  int b = 17;

  cout << "The value of a is " << a
       <<" and b is " << b << endl;

  {    // start of inner block
    double a = 46.25;
    int c = 10;

    cout << "a is now " << a
         << " b is now " << b
         << " and c is " << c << endl;
  }    // end of inner block

  cout << "a is now " << a
       << " and b is " << b << endl;

}    // end of outer block
```

The output that is produced by this section of code is:

```
The value of a is 25 and b is 17
a is now 46.25 b is now 17 and c is 10
a is now 25 and b is 17
```

This output is produced as follows:

The first block of code, which is the outer block, defines two variables named a and b that may be used anywhere within this block after their declaration, including any block contained inside of this first block. Within the inner block, two new variables have been declared, named a and c. At this stage then, we have created four different variables, two of which have the same name. Any referenced variable first results in an attempt to access a variable correctly declared within the block containing the reference. If no variable is defined within the block, an attempt is made to access a variable in the next immediate outside block until a valid access results.

Thus, the values of the variables a and c referenced within the inner block use the values of the variables a and c declared in that block. Since no variable named b was declared inside the inner block, the value of b displayed from within the inner block is obtained from the outer block. Finally, the last cout object, which is outside of the inner block, displays the value of the variable a declared in the outer block. If an attempt was made to display the value of c anywhere in the outer block, the compiler would issue an error message stating that c is an undefined symbol.

The location within a program where a variable can be used is formally referred to as the **scope** of the variable. This subject will be covered in detail in Section 7.2.

ONE-WAY SELECTION

A useful modification of the if-else statement involves omitting the else part of the statement altogether. In this case, the if statement takes the shortened and frequently useful form:

```
if (expression)
    statement;
```

The statement following if (expression) is executed only if the expression has a nonzero value, which is interpreted as a true condition. As before, the statement may be a compound statement. The flowchart for this statement is illustrated in Figure 5-3.

FIGURE 5-3
Flowchart for the One-Way if *Statement*

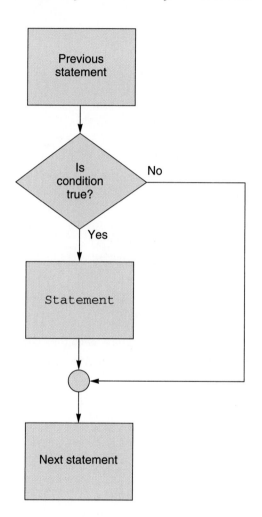

This modified form of the if statement is called a **one-way if statement**. Program 5-3 uses this statement to selectively display a message for cars that have been driven more than 3000.0 miles.

Program 5-3

```cpp
#include <iostream>
using namespace std;

int main()
{
  const double LIMIT = 3000.0;
  int idNum;
  double miles;

  cout << "Please type in car number and mileage: ";
  cin  >> idNum >> miles;

  if (miles > LIMIT)
    cout << "  Car " << idNum << " is over the limit.\n";

  cout << "End of program output.\n";

  return 0;
}
```

As an illustration of its one-way selection criteria in action, Program 5-3 was run twice, each time with different input data. Only the input data for the first run causes the message Car 256 is over the limit to be displayed.

```
Please type in car number and mileage: 256 3562.8
  Car 256 is over the limit.
End of program output.
```

and:

```
Please type in car number and mileage: 23 2562.3
End of program output.
```

PROBLEMS ASSOCIATED WITH THE if-else STATEMENT

Two of the most common problems encountered in using C++'s if-else statement are:

1. Misunderstanding the nature of an expression.
2. Using the assignment operator, =, in place of the relational operator ==.

Recall that an expression is any combination of operands and operators that yields a result. This definition is quite broad and more encompassing than is initially apparent. For example, all of the following are valid C++ expressions:

```
age + 5
age = 30
age == 40
```

Assuming that the variables are suitably declared, each of the above expressions yields a result. Program 5-4 uses the cout object to display the value of these expressions when age = 18.

Program 5-4

```
#include <iostream>
using namespace std;
int main()
{
    int age = 18;

    cout << "The value of the first expression is " << (age + 5) << endl;
    cout << "The value of the second expression is " << (age = 30) << endl;
    cout << "The value of the third expression is " << (age == 40) << endl;

    return 0;
}
```

The display produced by Program 5-4 is:

```
The value of the first expression is 23
The value of the second expression is 30
The value of the third expression is 0
```

As the output of Program 5-4 illustrates, each expression, by itself, has a value associated with it. The value of the first expression is the sum of the variable age plus 5, which is 23. The value of the second expression is 30, which is also assigned to the variable age. The value of the third expression is zero, since age is not equal to 40, and a false condition is represented in C++ with a value of zero. If the value in age had been 40, the relational expression a == 40 would be true and would have a value of 1.

Now assume that the relational expression age == 40 was intended to be used in the if statement

```
    if (age == 40)
        cout << "Happy Birthday!";
```

but was mistyped as age = 40, resulting in

```
    if (age = 40)
        cout << "Happy Birthday!";
```

Since the mistake results in a valid C++ expression, and any C++ expression can be tested by an if statement, the resulting if statement is valid and will cause the message Happy Birthday! to be printed regardless of what value was previously assigned to age. Can you see why?

The condition tested by the second if statement does not compare the value in age to the number 40, but assigns the number 40 to age. That is, the expression age = 40 is not a relational expression at all, but an assignment expression. At the completion of the assignment, the expression itself has a value of 40. Because C++ treats any nonzero value as true, the `cout` statement is executed. Another way of looking at this is to realize that the `if` statement is equivalent to the following two statements:

```
age = 40;      // assign 40 to age
if (age)       // test the value of age
   cout << "Happy Birthday!";
```

Because a C++ compiler has no means of knowing that the expression being tested is not the desired one, you must be especially careful when writing conditions.

Exercises 5.2

1. Write appropriate `if` statements for each of the following conditions:

   a. If an angle is equal to 90 degrees, print the message "The angle is a right angle"; otherwise, print the message "The angle is not a right angle".
   b. If the temperature is above 100 degrees, display the message "above the boiling point of water"; otherwise, display the message "below the boiling point of water".
   c. If the number is positive, add the number to `posTotal`; otherwise, add the number to `negsum`.
   d. If the slope is less than .5, set the variable `flag` to zero; otherwise, set `flag` to 1.
   e. If the difference between `num1` and `num2` is less than .001, set the variable `approx` to zero; otherwise, calculate `approx` as the quantity `(num1 - num2) / 2.0`.
   f. If the difference between `temp1` and `temp2` exceeds 2.3 degrees, calculate `error` as `(temp1 - temp2) * factor`.
   g. If `x` is greater than `y` and `z` is less than 20, read in a value for `p`.
   h. If `distance` is greater than 20 and it is less than 35, read in a value for `time`.

2. Write `if` statements corresponding to the conditions illustrated by each of the following flow charts.

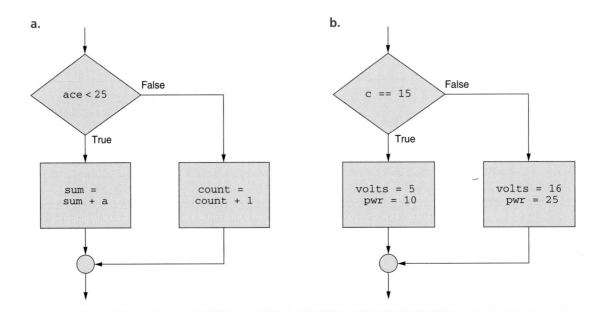

5

c.

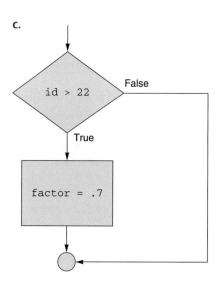

d.

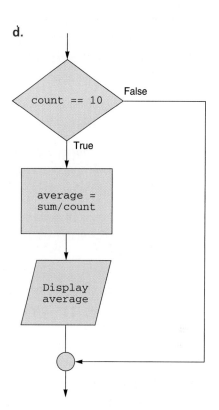

3.   Rewrite Program 5-1 using the following statements:

```
const double LIMIT = 20000;
const double REGRATE = 0.02;
const double HIGHRATE = 0.025;
const double FIXED = 400.0;
```

   (If necessary, review Section 4.5 regarding the use of symbolic constants.)

4.   Write a C++ program that asks the user to input two numbers. If the first number entered is greater than the second number, the program should print the message "The first number is greater", else it should print the message "The first number is smaller". Test your program by entering the numbers 5 and 8 and then using the numbers 11 and 2. What do you think your program will display if you enter two equal numbers? Test this case.

5. a. If money is left in a particular bank for more than two years, the interest rate given by the bank is 5.5 percent, otherwise the interest rate is 3.5 percent. Write a C++ program that uses the `cin` object to accept the number of years into the variable `nyrs` and display the appropriate interest rate depending on the input value.

    b. How many runs should you make for the program written in Exercise 5a to verify that it is operating correctly? What data should you input in each of the program runs?

6. a. In a pass/fail course, a student passes if the grade is greater than or equal to 70 and fails if the grade is lower than 70. Write a C++ program that accepts a grade and prints the message `"A passing grade"` or `"A failing grade"`, as appropriate.

    b. How many runs should you make for the program written in Exercise 6a to verify that it is operating correctly? What data should you input in each of the program runs?

5.3 NESTED IF STATEMENTS

As we have seen, an `if-else` statement can contain simple or compound statements. Any valid C++ statement can be used, including another `if-else` statement. Thus, one or more `if-else` statements can be included within either part of an `if-else` statement. The inclusion of one or more `if` statements within an existing `if` statement creates a **nested if statement**. For example, substituting the one-way `if` statement

```
if (distance > 500)
    cout << "snap";
```

for `statement1` in the following `if` statement

```
if (hours < 9)
    statement1;
else
    cout << "pop";
```

results in the nested `if` statement

```
if (hours < 9)
{
    if (distance > 500)
        cout << "snap";
}
else
    cout << "pop";
```

5

The braces around the inner one-way `if` statement are essential, because in their absence C++ associates an `else` with the closest unpaired `if`. Thus, without the braces, the above statement is equivalent to

```
if (hours < 9)
   if (distance > 500)
      cout << "snap";
   else
      cout << "pop";
```

Here the `else` is paired with the inner `if`, which destroys the meaning of the original `if-else` statement. Notice also that the indentation is irrelevant as far as the compiler is concerned. Whether the indentation exists or not, the compiler will *always* proceed by associating the last `else` with the closest unpaired `if`, unless braces are used to alter the default pairing.

The process of nesting `if` statements can be extended indefinitely, so that the `cout << "snap";` statement could itself be replaced by either a complete `if-else` statement or another one-way `if` statement.

Figure 5-4 illustrates the general form of a nested `if-else` statement when an `if-else` statement is nested (A) within the `if` part of an `if-else` statement and (B) within the `else` part of an `if-else` statement.

FIGURE 5-4A
The `if-else` Nested Within the `if` Part

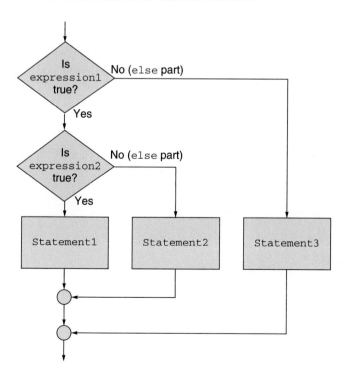

FIGURE 5-4B
The if-else *Nested Within the* else *Part*

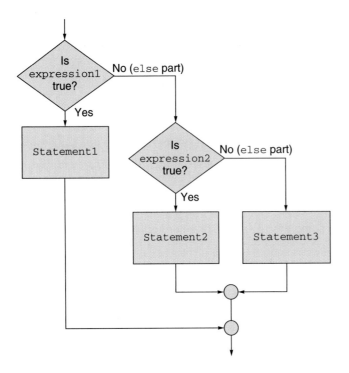

THE if-else CHAIN

In general, the nesting illustrated in Figure 5-4A tends to be confusing and is best avoided in practice. However, the following construction for the nesting illustrated in Figure 5-4B is extremely useful:

```
if (expression1)
   statement1;
else
   if (expression2)
      statement2;
   else
      statement3;
```

As with all C++ programs, since white space is ignored, the indentation shown is not required. More typically, the preceding construction is arranged as follows:

```
if (expression1)
   statement1;
else if (expression2)
   statement2;
else
   statement3;
```

This form of a nested `if` statement is very useful in practice, and is formally referred to as an **if-else chain**. Each condition is evaluated in order, and if any condition is true, the corresponding statement is executed and the remainder of the chain is terminated. The statement associated with the final `else` is only executed if none of the previous conditions is satisfied. This serves as a default or catch-all case that is useful for detecting an impossible or error condition.

The chain can be continued indefinitely by repeatedly making the last statement another `if-else` statement. Thus, the general form of an `if-else` chain is:

```
if (expression1)
    statement1;
else if (expression2)
    statement2;
else if (expression3)
    statement3;

        .
        .
        .

  else if (expressionn)
      statementn;
  else
      laststatement;
```

Each condition is evaluated in the order it appears in the statement. For the first condition that is true, the corresponding statement is executed, and the remainder of the statements in the chain are not executed. Thus, if *expression1* is true, only *statement1* is executed; otherwise *expression2* is tested. If *expression2* is then true, only *statement2* is executed; otherwise *expression3* is tested, and so on. The final `else` in the chain is optional, and *laststatement* is only executed if none of the previous expressions was true.

As a specific example, consider the following `if-else` chain:

```
if (marcode == 'm' || marcode == 'M')
   cout << "Individual is married.\n";
else if (marcode == 's' || marcode == 'S')
   cout << "Individual is single.\n";
else if (marcode == 'd' || marcode == 'D')
   cout << "Individual is divorced.\n";
else if (marcode == 'w' || marcode == 'W')
   cout << "Individual is widowed.\n";
else
   cout << "An invalid code was entered.\n";
```

Execution through this chain begins with a test of the expression marcode == 'm' || marcode == 'M'. Thus, if the value in marcode is either a lowercase or uppercase m, the message Individual is married. is displayed, no further expressions in the chain are evaluated, and execution resumes with the next statement immediately following the chain. If the value in marcode was not the letter m (lower- or uppercase) the expression marcode == 's' || marcode == 'S' is tested, and so on, until a true condition is found. If none of the conditions in the chain is true, the message An invalid code was entered. would be displayed. In all cases, execution resumes with the statement that immediately follows the chain.

Program 5-5 uses this if-else chain within a complete program.

Program 5-5

```cpp
#include <iostream>
using namespace std;

int main()
{
  char marcode;

  cout << "Enter a marital code: ";
  cin  >> marcode;

  if (marcode == 'm' || marcode == 'M')
    cout << "Individual is married.\n";
  else if (marcode == 's' || marcode == 'S')
    cout << "Individual is single.\n";
  else if (marcode == 'd' || marcode == 'D')
    cout << "Individual is divorced.\n";
  else if (marcode == 'w' || marcode == 'W')
    cout << "Individual is widowed.\n";
  else
    cout << "An invalid code was entered.\n";

  cout << "Thanks for participating in the survey.\n";

  return 0;
}
```

In reviewing Program 5-5, note that the message Thanks for participating in the survey. is always printed. This is the statement immediately after the if-else chain to which execution is transferred after the chain completes its execution. Which message is printed within the if-else chain depends on the value entered into marcode.

As a final example illustrating the `if-else` chain, let us calculate the monthly income of a computer salesperson using the following commission schedule:

monthly sales	income
greater than or equal to $50,000	$375 plus 16% of sales
less than $50,000 but greater than or equal to $40,000	$350 plus 14% of sales
less than $40,000 but greater than or equal to $30,000	$325 plus 12% of sales
less than $30,000 but greater than or equal to $20,000	$300 plus 9% of sales
less than $20,000 but greater than or equal to $10,000	$250 plus 5% of sales
less than $10,000	$200 plus 3% of sales

The following `if-else` chain can be used to determine the correct monthly income, where the variable `monthlySales` is used to store the salesperson's current monthly sales:

```
if (monthlySales >= 50000.00)
    income = 375.00 + 0.16 * monthlySales;
else if (monthlySales >= 40000.00)
    income = 350.00 + 0.14 * monthlySales;
else if (monthlySales >= 30000.00)
    income = 325.00 + 0.12 * monthlySales;
else if (monthlySales >= 20000.00)
    income = 300.00 + 0.09 * monthlySales;
else if (monthlySales >= 10000.00)
    income = 250.00 + 0.05 * monthlySales;
else
    income = 200.000 + 0.03 * monthlySales;
```

Notice that this example makes use of the fact that the chain is stopped once a true condition is found. The chain begins by first checking for the highest monthly sales. If the salesperson's monthly sales total is less than $50,000, the `if-else` chain continues checking for the next highest sales amount until the correct category is obtained.

Program 5-6 uses this `if-else` chain to calculate and display the income corresponding to the value of monthly sales input in the `cin` object.

A sample run using Program 5-6 is illustrated below.

```
Enter the value of monthly sales: 36243.89
        The income is $4674.27
```

As with all C++ statements, each individual statement within an `if-else` chain can be replaced by a compound statement bounded by the braces { and }.

Program 5-6

```cpp
#include <iostream>
#include <iomanip>
using namespace std;

int main()
{
  double monthlySales, income;

 cout <<   "Enter the value of monthly sales: ";
  cin  >> monthlySales;

  if (monthlySales >= 50000.00)
    income = 375.00 + 0.16 * monthlySales;
  else if (monthlySales >= 40000.00)
    income = 350.00 + 0.14 * monthlySales;
  else if (monthlySales >= 30000.00)
    income = 325.00 + 0.12 * monthlySales;
  else if (monthlySales >= 20000.00)
    income = 300.00 + 0.09 * monthlySales;
  else if (monthlySales >= 10000.00)
    income = 250.00 + 0.05 * monthlySales;
  else
    income = 200.00 + 0.03 * monthlySales;

    // set output format
  cout << setiosflags(ios::fixed)
       << setiosflags(ios::showpoint)
       << setprecision(2);

  cout << "The income is $" << income << endl;

  return 0;
}
```

Exercises 5.3

1.   Compile and execute Program 5-5 and verify that it responds correctly to accept both lower and uppercase letters as marriage codes.

2.   Write nested `if` statements corresponding to the conditions illustrated in each of the following flowcharts.

5

a.

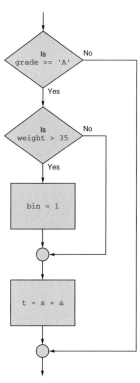

b.

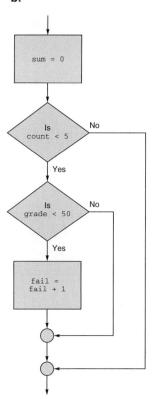

3. An angle is considered acute if it is less than 90 degrees, obtuse if it is greater than 90 degrees, and a right angle if it is equal to 90 degrees. Using this information, write a C++ program that accepts an angle, in degrees, and displays the type of angle corresponding to the degrees entered.

4. The grade level of undergraduate college students is typically determined according to the following schedule:

number of credits completed	grade level
less than 32	Freshman
32 to 63	Sophomore
64 to 95	Junior
96 or more	Senior

Using this information, write a C++ program that accepts the number of credits a student has completed, determines the student's grade level, and displays the grade level.

5. A student's letter grade is calculated according to the following schedule:

numerical grade	letter grade
greater than or equal to 90	A
less than 90 but greater than or equal to 80	B
less than 80 but greater than or equal to 70	C
less than 70 but greater than or equal to 60	D
less than 60	F

Using this information, write a C++ program that accepts a student's numerical grade, converts the numerical grade to an equivalent letter grade, and displays the letter grade.

6. The interest rate used on funds deposited in a bank is determined by the amount of time the money is left on deposit. For a particular bank, the following schedule is used:

time on deposit	interest rate
greater than or equal to 5 years	0.0475
less than 5 years but greater than or equal to 4 years	0.045
less than 4 years but greater than or equal to 3 years	0.040
less than 3 years but greater than or equal to 2 years	0.035
less than 2 years but greater than or equal to 1 year	0.030
less than 1 year	0.025

Using this information, write a C++ program that accepts the time that funds are left on deposit and displays the interest rate corresponding to the time entered.

7. Write a C++ program that accepts a number followed by one space and then a letter. If the letter following the number is an f, the program should treat the number entered as a temperature in degrees Fahrenheit, convert the number to the equivalent degrees Celsius, and print a suitable display message. If the letter following the number is a c, the program should treat the number entered as a temperature in Celsius, convert the number to the equivalent degrees Fahrenheit, and print a suitable display message. If the letter is neither an f or c, the program shoulds print a message that the data entered is incorrect and then terminate. Use an `if-else` chain in your program and make use of the conversion formulas:

$$Celsius = (5.0 / 9.0) * (Fahrenheit - 32.0)$$
$$Fahrenheit = (9.0 / 5.0) * Celsius + 32.0$$

8. Using the commission schedule from Program 5-6, the following program calculates monthly income:

```
#include <iostream>
#include <iomanip>
using namespace std;

int main()
{
```

(continued on next page)

```
   double monthlySales, income;

   cout << "Enter the value of monthly sales: ";
   cin  >> monthlySales;

   if (monthlySales >= 50000.00)
      income = 375.00 + .16 * monthlySales;
   if (monthlySales >= 40000.00 && monthlySales < 50000.00)
      income = 350.00 + .14 * monthlySales;
   if (monthlySales >= 30000.00 && monthlySales < 40000.00)
      income = 325.00 + .12 * monthlySales;
   if (monthlySales >= 20000.00 && monthlySales < 30000.00)
      income = 300.00 + .09 * monthlySales;
   if (monthlySales >= 10000.00 && monthlySales < 20000.00)
      income = 250.00 + .05 * monthlySales;
   if (monthlySales < 10000.00)
      income = 200.00 + .03 * monthlySales;

   cout << setiosflags(ios::showpoint)
        << setiosflags(ios::fixed)
        << setprecision(2)
        << "\n\nThe income is $" << income << endl;

   return 0;
}
```

a. Will this program produce the same output as Program 5-6?

b. Which program is better and why?

9. The following program was written to produce the same result as Program 5-6:

```
#include <iostream>
#include <iomanip>
using namespace std;

int main()
{
   double monthlySales, income;

   cout << "Enter the value of monthly sales: ";
   cin  >> monthlySales;

   if (monthlySales < 10000.00)
      income = 200.00 + .03 * monthlySales;
   else if (monthlySales >= 10000.00)
      income = 250.00 + .05 * monthlySales;
   else if (monthlySales >= 20000.00)
      income = 300.00 + .09 * monthlySales;
```

(continued on next page)

```
      else if (monthlySales >= 30000.00)
         income = 325.00 + .12 * monthlySales;
      else if (monthlySales >= 40000.00)
         income = 350.00 + .14 * monthlySales;
      else if (monthlySales >= 50000.00)
         income = 375.00 + .16 * monthlySales;

      cout << setiosflags(ios::showpoint)
           << setiosflags(ios::fixed)
           << setprecision(2)
           << "\n\nThe income is $" << income << endl;

      return 0;
}
```

a. Will this program run?
b. What does this program do?
c. For what values of monthly sales does this program calculate the correct income?

5.4 THE SWITCH STATEMENT

The `if-else` chain is used in programming applications where one set of instructions must be selected from many possible alternatives. The `switch` statement provides an alternative to the `if-else` chain for cases that compare the value of an integer expression to a specific value. The general form of a `switch` statement is:

```
switch (expression)
{     // start of compound statement
   case value1: ◄─────── terminated with a colon
      statement1;
      statement2;

         .

         .

      break;
   case value2: ◄─────── terminated with a colon
      statementm;
      statementn;

         .

         .

      break;

         .

         .

   case valuen: ◄─────── terminated with a colon
      statementw;
```

(continued on next page)

```
    statementx;

            .

            .

    break;
  default:              ←——— terminated with a colon
    statementaa;
    statementbb;              .

            .

}    // end of switch and compound statement
```

The `switch` statement uses four new keywords: `switch`, `case`, `default`, and `break`. The function of each keyword is described below.

The keyword `switch` identifies the start of the `switch` statement. The expression in parentheses following this word is evaluated, and the result of the expression compared to various alternative values contained within the compound statement. The expression in the `switch` statement must evaluate to an integer result, otherwise a compilation error results.

Internal to the `switch` statement, the keyword `case` is used to identify or label individual values that are compared to the value of the `switch` expression. The `switch` expression's value is compared to each of these `case` values in the order in which these values are listed until a match is found. When a match occurs, execution begins with the statement immediately following the match. Thus, as illustrated in Figure 5-5, the value of the expression determines where in the `switch` statement execution actually begins.

FIGURE 5-5
The Expression Determines an Entry Point

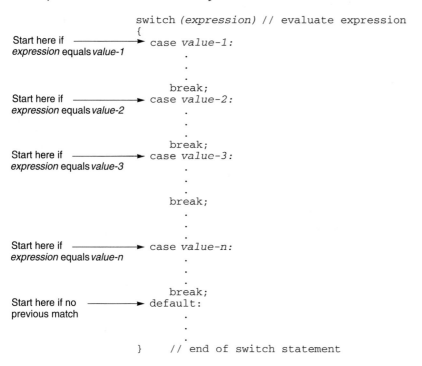

Any number of `case` labels may be contained within a `switch` statement, in any order. If the value of the expression does not match any of the case values, however, no statement is executed unless the keyword `default` is encountered. The word `default` is optional and operates the same as the last `else` in an `if-else` chain. If the value of the expression does not match any of the case values, program execution begins with the statement following the word `default`.

Once an entry point has been located by the `switch` statement, all further case evaluations are ignored and execution continues through the end of the compound statement, unless a `break` statement is encountered. This is the reason for the `break` statement, which identifies the end of a particular `case` and causes an immediate exit from the `switch` statement. Thus, just as the word `case` identifies possible starting points in the compound statement, the `break` statement determines terminating points. If the `break` statements are omitted, all cases following the matching case value, including the `default` case, are executed.

When we write a `switch` statement, we can use multiple case values to refer to the same set of statements; the `default` label is optional. For example, consider the following:

```
switch (number)
{
  case 1:
    cout << "Have a Good Morning\n";
    break;
  case 2:
    cout << "Have a Happy Day\n";
    break;
  case 3:
  case 4:
  case 5:
    cout << "Have a Nice Evening\n";
}
```

If the value stored in the variable `number` is 1, the message `Have a Good Morning` is displayed. Similarly, if the value of `number` is 2, the second message is displayed. Finally, if the value of `number` is 3 or 4 or 5, the last message is displayed. Since the statement to be executed for these last three cases is the same, the cases for these values can be "stacked together" as shown in the example. Also, since there is no default, no message is printed if the value of `number` is not one of the listed case values. Although it is good programming practice to list case values in increasing order, this is not required by the `switch` statement. A `switch` statement may have any number of case values, in any order; only the values being tested for need be listed.

Program 5-7 uses a `switch` statement to select the arithmetic operation (addition, multiplication, or division) to be performed on two numbers depending on the value of the variable `opselect`.

Program 5-7

```cpp
#include <iostream>
using namespace std;
int main()
{
  int opselect;
  double fnum, snum;

  cout << "Please type in two numbers: ";
  cin  >> fnum >> snum;
  cout << "Enter a select code: ";
  cout << "\n          1 for addition";
  cout << "\n          2 for multiplication";
  cout << "\n          3 for division : ";
  cin  >> opselect;

  switch (opselect)
  {
    case 1:
      cout << "The sum of the numbers entered is " << fnum+snum;
      break;
    case 2:
      cout << "The product of the numbers entered is " << fnum*snum;
      break;
    case 3:
      cout << "The first number divided by the second is " << fnum/snum;
      break;
  }     // end of switch

  cout << endl;

  return 0;
}
```

Program 5-7 was run twice. The resulting display clearly identifies the case selected. The results are:

```
    Please type in two numbers: 12 3
    Enter a select code:
            1 for addition
            2 for multiplication
            3 for division : 2
    The product of the numbers entered is 36
```

and:

```
    Please type in two numbers: 12 3
    Enter a select code:
```

(continued on next page)

```
1 for addition
2 for multiplication
3 for division : 3
The first number divided by the second is 4
```

In reviewing Program 5-7, notice the `break` statement in the last case. Although this break is not necessary, it is a good practice to terminate the last case in a `switch` statement with a `break`. This prevents a possible program error later, if an additional case is subsequently added to the `switch` statement. With the addition of a new case, the `break` between cases becomes necessary; having the `break` in place ensures you will not forget to include it at the time of the modification.

Since character data types are always converted to integers in an expression, a `switch` statement can also be used to "switch" based on the value of a character expression. For example, assuming that `choice` is a character variable, the following `switch` statement is valid:

```
switch (choice)
{
  case 'a':
  case 'e':
  case 'i':
  case 'o':
  case 'u':
     cout << "The character in choice is a vowel\n";
     break;
  default:
     cout << "The character in choice is not a vowel\n";
     break;    // this break is optional
}    // end of switch statement
```

Exercises 5.4

1. Rewrite the following `if-else` chain using a `switch` statement:

```
if (letterGrade == 'A')
   cout << "The numerical grade is between 90 and 100\n";
else if (letterGrade == 'B')
   cout << "The numerical grade is between 80 and 89.9\n";
else if (letterGrade == 'C')
   cout << "The numerical grade is between 70 and 79.9\n";
else if (letterGrade == 'D';
   cout << "How are you going to explain this one\n";
else
{
   cout << "Of course I had nothing to do with my grade.\n";
   cout << "It must have been the professor's fault.\n";
}
```

2. Rewrite the following `if-else` chain using a `switch` statement:

```cpp
if (resType == 1)
  {
     indata();
     check();
  }
else if (resType == 2)
{
   capacity();
   devtype();
}
else if (resType == 3)
{
   volume();
   mass();
}
else if (resType == 4)
{
   area();
   weight();
}
else if (resType == 5)
{
   files();
   save();
}
else if (resType == 6)
{
   retrieve();
   screen();
}
```

3. Each disk drive in a shipment of these devices is stamped with a code from 1 through 4, which indicates a drive of the following type:

code	disk drive type
1	360 Kilobyte Drive (5.2 inch)
2	1.2 Megabyte Drive (5.2 inch)
3	720 Kilobyte Drive (3.3 inch)
4	1.4 Megabyte Drive (3.3 inch)

Write a C++ program that accepts the code number as an input, and based on the value entered, displays the correct disk drive type.

4. Rewrite Program 5-5 using a `switch` statement.

5. Determine why the `if-else` chain in Program 5-6 cannot be replaced with a `switch` statement.

6.   Rewrite Program 5-7 using a character variable for the select code. (*Hint*: Review Section 3.4 if your program does not operate as you think it should.)

5.5 PROGRAM DESIGN AND DEVELOPMENT: INTRODUCTION TO UML

For all but extremely simple programs, you should start by creating an explicit design; after you finish the design you can begin coding. This is equivalent to designing a house using blueprints and physical models before beginning any construction. Formally, the process of designing an application is referred to as **program modeling**. In this section we introduce the Unified Modeling Language (UML), which is a program-modeling language with its own set of rules and notations. This particular modeling language has achieved wide acceptance as a primary technique for developing object-oriented programs. UML is not a part of the C++ language, but a separate language with its own set of rules and diagrams for creating an object-oriented design. If used correctly, a UML design can significantly help in understanding and clarifying a program's requirements. The finished design can serve as both a set of detailed specifications (which can easily be coded in an object-oriented programming language such as C++) and documentation for the final program.

UML uses a set of diagrams and techniques that are reasonably easy to understand and that support all of the features required for implementing an object-oriented design. Additionally, UML is currently becoming the predominate object-oriented design procedure used by professional programmers. At its most fundamental level, designing an object-oriented application requires understanding and specifying:

- The objects in the system
- What can happen to these objects
- When something can happen to these objects

In a UML analysis, each of these three items is addressed by a number of individual and separate views and diagrams. This situation is very similar to the plan for a house, which contains a number of diagrams, all required for the final construction. For example, there must be blueprints for the physical outlay; electrical, plumbing, heating, and cooling duct diagrams; and landscape and elevation diagrams. Each of these diagrams presents a different view of the completed house, and each presents different information, all of which is required for the finished product. The same is true for the diagrams specified in a UML analysis. Specifically, UML provides seven diagram types known as class, object, state, sequence, activity , use-case, component, deployment, and collaboration diagrams.

Not all of these diagram types are required for every analysis, as some provide specific details that are only needed in more advanced situations. In this text, we present the four basic UML diagram types that you should be familiar with and the rules needed to create them. Once these rules are understood, it is relatively easy to read almost any UML diagram that you will encounter. The diagrams covered in this text are the class, object, state, and sequence types.

Class and object diagrams are similar in structure, with class diagrams used to model classes and object diagrams used to model objects. As such, both diagrams include the attributes and operations for classes and objects, respectively, and the relationship between either classes or objects. A sequence diagram is used to describe the interactions between objects. Finally, a state diagram is used to describe when things happen to the objects. Although each of these diagrams may contain information present in the other three diagrams, each diagram type is intended to model and emphasize a different aspect of a system. As such, each diagram type simply views the same system from a different angle and highlights a particular characteristic of the system. Of these four diagrams, the most important and initially useful are class and object diagrams, which are described in this section. (State and sequence diagrams are described in Section 6.6.) For many systems, the description provided by class and object diagrams are more than sufficient for design and implementation purposes.

CLASS AND OBJECT DIAGRAMS

Class diagrams are used to describe classes and their relationships, while **object diagrams** are used to describe the objects and their relationships. As you already know, a class refers to a type of object, out of which many specific objects can be created, while an object always refers to a specific, single item created from a class. For example, a class of books might be described as either fiction or nonfiction, of which many specific instances, or objects, exist. The book *A History of England* is a specific object of the class nonfiction, while *Pride and Prejudice* is a specific object of the class fiction. Thus, it is always the class that is the basic plan, or recipe, from which real objects are created. It is the class that describes the properties and operations that each object must have to be a member of the class.

An **attribute**, as was described in Section 2.5, is simply a characteristic that each object in the class must have. For example, title and author are attributes of Book objects, while name, age, sex, weight, and height are attributes of Person objects. Once data values are assigned to attributes, a unique object is created. It should be noted that each and every object created from a class must also have an identity, in that one object can be distinguished from another object of the same class. This is not true of a pure data value, such as the number 5, where all occurrences of this number are indistinguishable from one another.

Both classes and objects are represented using a diagram consisting of a box. For class diagrams, the class name is centered at the top of the box and is written in bold face. For object diagrams, the class name is optional, but when it is included it is simply underlined at the top of the diagram without any boldfacing. When the class name is provided, an optional object name can precede the class name, with a mandatory colon separating the two names. Alternatively, an object diagram may contain only the object's name, underlined, with no class name provided. For example, Figure 5-6 illustrates the representation of a Person class, along with one Person object named Janet.

FIGURE 5-6
A Class and Object Representation

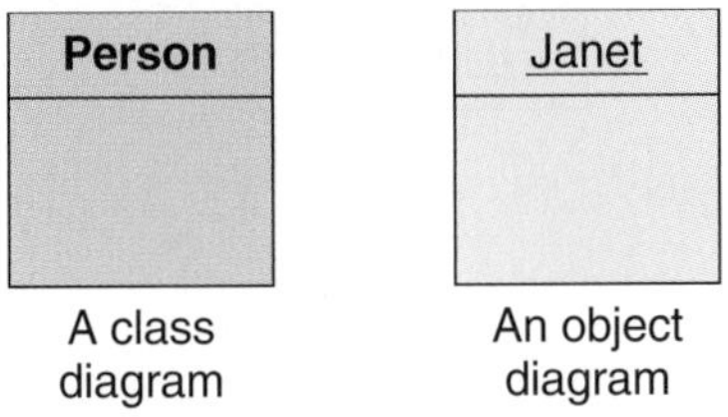

A class
diagram

An object
diagram

The basic symbols and notations used in constructing class and object diagrams are presented in Figure 5-7.

FIGURE 5-7
Basic UML Symbols and Notation

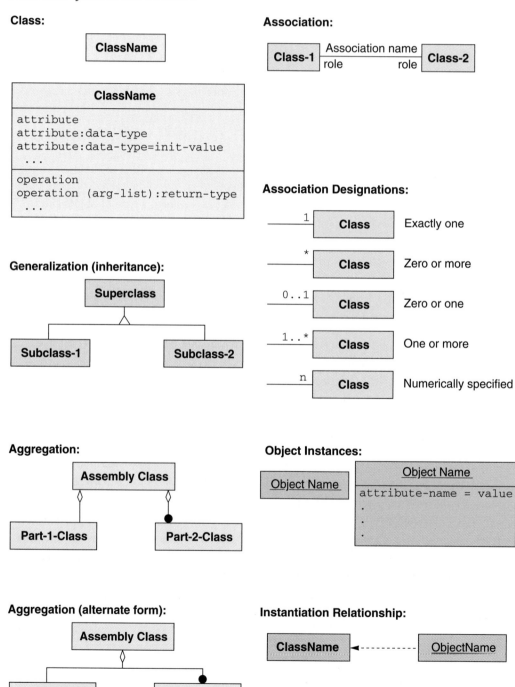

Once the attributes of a class have been identified, they are listed in a class diagram below the class name, separated by a line. Specific objects are shown in a similar manner, with data values provided for all attributes. For example, Figure 5-8 shows the attributes and values associated with the class Country. As you might expect, the attributes listed in a class diagram will become, in C++, the instance variables declared in a class's data declaration section.

FIGURE 5-8
Including Attributes in UML Class and Object Diagrams

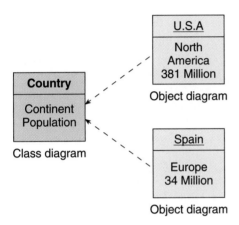

Attributes have two qualities, *type* and *visibility*. An attribute's **type** is either a primitive data type, such as integer, real, boolean, or character, or a class type, such as a string. Type is required in a class diagram and is indicated by following an attribute name with a mandatory colon and the data type.

Visibility defines where an attribute can be seen—that is, whether the attribute can be used in other classes or is restricted to the class defining it. If an attribute has a private visibility, it can only be used within its defining class and cannot be directly accessed by other classes. An attribute with public visibility can be used directly in any other class. In UML, public visibility is expressed by placing a plus sign (+) in front of the attribute's name within the class diagram. A minus sign (-) in front of the attribute's name designates the attribute as private. Protected visibility means that an attribute can be passed along to a derived class and is indicated by including neither a plus nor minus sign. In a class diagram, an attribute's name and type are required; all other information is optional. Figure 5-9 illustrates the class diagram for a class named RoomType, that contains two private attributes, named length and width. Notice that we have also included default values that the class is expected to provide to its attributes.

FIGURE 5-9
A Class with Attributes

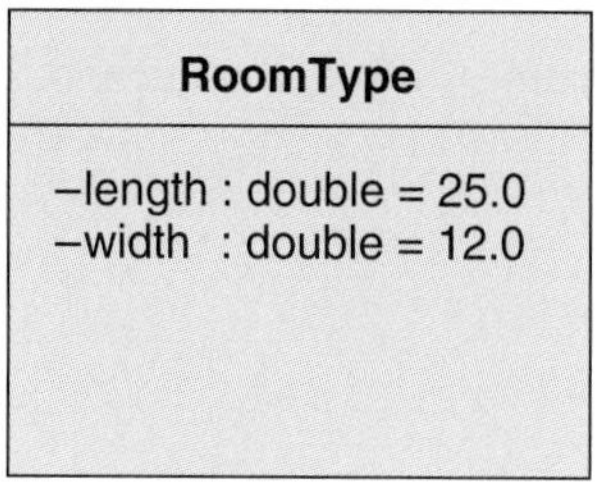

RoomType
−length : double = 25.0 −width : double = 12.0

Just as attributes are designated within a class diagram, so are operations. **Operations** are transformations that can be applied to attributes, and it is the operations that will ultimately be coded as C++ methods. Operation names are listed in a class box below the attributes and separated from them by a line. Figure 5-10 illustrates two class diagrams that include operations.

FIGURE 5-10
Including Operations in Class Diagrams

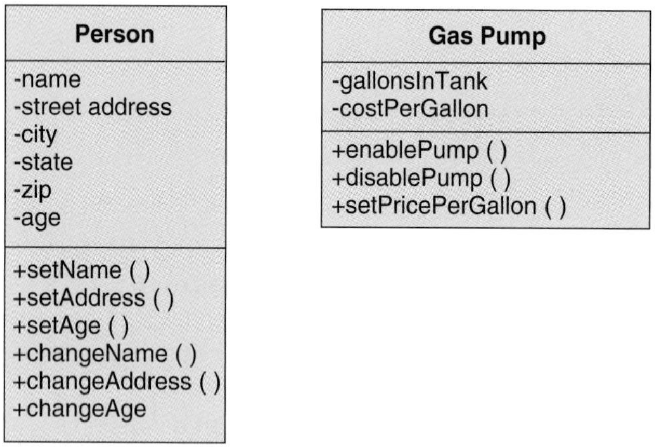

Person
-name -street address -city -state -zip -age
+setName ( ) +setAddress ( ) +setAge ( ) +changeName ( ) +changeAddress ( ) +changeAge

Gas Pump
-gallonsInTank -costPerGallon
+enablePump ( ) +disablePump ( ) +setPricePerGallon ( )

RELATIONSHIPS

In addition to graphically describing classes and objects, UML class and object diagrams present the relationships existing between classes and objects. The three basic relationships are association, aggregation, and generalization.

Associations between classes are typically signified by phrases such as "is related to," "is associated with," "has a," "is employed by," "works for," etc. This type of association is indicated by a straight line connecting two classes or two objects, where the type of association is listed above or below the line. For example, Figure 5-11 shows an association between a Person and a Company. As indicated, a Person is "employed by" a Company, and a Company "employs" zero or more Persons. The designation of "zero or more," which is referred to as the multiplicity of the relationship, is indicated by the notation * in the diagram. Table 5-4 lists the symbols used to indicate an association's multiplicity. These symbols can be placed either above or below the line connecting two classes or objects.

FIGURE 5-11
An Association

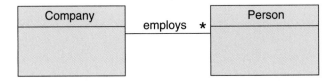

TABLE 5-4
UML Association Notation

symbol	relationship
1	One and only one
n	Exactly the specified number (n an integer)
0..1	Zero or one
m..n	From m to n (m and n integers)
* or 0..*	From zero to any positive integer
1..*	From one to any positive integer

An **aggregation** is a particular type of an association where one class or object, referred to as the whole element, "consists of" or, alternatively, "is composed of," other classes or objects, which are referred to as parts. For example, a sentence consists of words, which consists of characters. Thus, characters are parts of words, which are themselves parts of sentences. This type of association is indicated by a diamond symbol. Figures 5-12, 5-13, and 5-14 illustrate three aggregation associations. Reading each of these object diagrams is much easier if you replace the diamond with either the words "consists of" or "is composed of." When the diamond symbol is hollow, as it is in Figure 5-12, it indicates that the parts can still exist independent of the whole to which they belong. Thus, even if a team is broken up or destroyed, its individual members can still exist. When the diamond symbol is solid, as it is in Figures 5-13 and 5-14, it indicates that the component parts are intrinsic members of the whole. As such, if the central, or whole, class or object is removed, its aggregated parts will also be destroyed. Therefore, as indicated in Figure 5-13, if a sentence is removed, all of its associated words are removed. Similarly, erasing a word causes the erasure of the characters within the word. As indicated in all three figures, the diamond symbol always attaches to the whole, or central, class or object.

FIGURE 5-12
Single-Level Aggregation

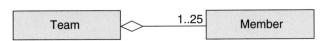

FIGURE 5-13
Another Single-Level Aggregation

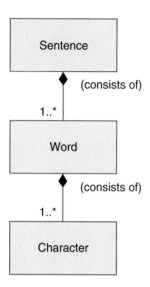

FIGURE 5-14
Multi-Level Aggregation

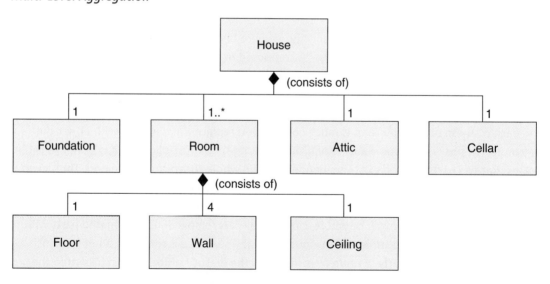

The last type of relationship that we will consider is generalization, which is more commonly referred to as inheritance. **Generalization** is a relationship between a class and a refined version of the class.

For example, a refinement of the object type Vehicle can be either a Land, Space, or Water version. In this case, Vehicle would be the base class, and Land, Space, and Water are the refined classes. Figure 5-15 shows how this generalization relationship is illustrated using a class diagram.

FIGURE 5-15
A Generalization Relationship

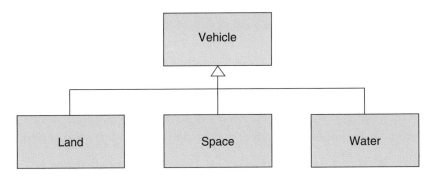

Exercises 5.5

1. Define the following terms:

   a. attribute
   b. aggregation
   c. association
   d. class
   e. class diagram
   f. generalization
   g. multiplicity
   h. program model
   i. object
   j. object diagram
   k. operation

2. Construct a class diagram for a country class, in which each country has a capital city. The attributes of interest for each country are its population, size, main agricultural product, and main manufactured product.

3. a. Construct a class diagram for a single gas tank that is connected to one or more gas pumps. The attributes of interest for the tank are its capacity, current level, and grade of gas. The attributes of interest for a pump are the amount of gallons dispensed and the cost per gallon. Additionally, the pump responds to being enabled and disabled.

   b. Modify the class diagram constructed in Exercise 3a to account for the fact that a gas pump may be associated with more than one gas tank.

4. Construct a class diagram for a book consisting of one or more chapters, each of which consists of one or more sections.

5. a. Construct a class diagram for a computer that consists of a monitor, keyboard, mouse, printer, and system box.

b. Modify the class diagram constructed in Exercise 5a to account for the fact that one or more monitors and keyboards may be attached to the system box and that the system may have no mouse or may have multiple mice.

c. Extend the class diagram constructed for Exercise 5b to denote that the system box is composed of a CPU chip, a memory board containing zero or more RAM chips, and one case.

6. Construct a class diagram for a class of circles that is the base class to a class of spheres and a class of cylinders.

7. Construct a class diagram for a collection of cards that consists of zero or more individual cards. The collection of cards forms a base class for both a deck of cards and an individual hand of cards.

8. Determine a car's major subsystems, such as brakes, steering, etc. Then, considering these subsystems as classes, construct a class diagram for a Car class that simply shows the associations between classes (no attributes or operations). Then determine a set of attributes and operations appropriate to each subsystem. Finally, modify the original class diagram to include the additional information.

9. Determine a cellular telephone's major subsystems, such as keypad, antenna, etc. Then, considering these subsystems as classes, construct a class diagram for a Cellular class that simply shows the associations between classes (no attributes or operations). Then determine a set of attributes and operations appropriate to each subsystem. Finally, modify the original class diagram to include the additional information.

5.6 APPLICATION: A DATE CLASS

As a specific example of developing a class using UML, suppose that we need to develop a date class. This type of class is very important in financial programs, where the calculations of settlement dates, accrued interest, and dividend payments all depend on date determinations. When creating a date class, you need to keep in mind important questions such as: Does a date fall on a weekend or holiday? If one day is added to today's date, does this put us into another month or a new year? How many days are there between two dates, taking into account the actual number of days in each month? Does the date fall in a leap year, where February has 29 days instead of the usual 28? Let us see how we might go about designing and developing this class. The first stage in any design is to identify the type of objects we will be dealing with. In this situation the object is a date. Assuming that we name our class Date, we can now draw the initial class diagram shown in Figure 5-16.

FIGURE 5-16
Initial Date *Class Diagram*

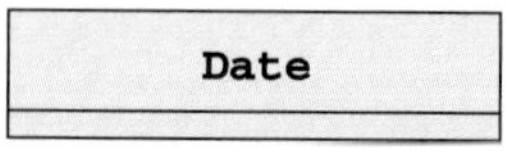

Date

The next step is to decide how we will internally represent each Date object that will be constructed from the Date class. At a practical level, this means identifying the attributes of a Date object. Although there are actually a number of ways to represent a date (see Exercise 6 at the end of this section), we will store a date using three integers: one for the month, day, and year, respectively, with the year stored as a four-digit number. Thus, for example, we will store the year 1999 as '1999' and not as '99'. Making sure to store all years with their correct century designation will eliminate a multitude of problems that can crop up if only the last two digits, such as 99, are stored. For example, the number of years between 2005 and 1999 can be quickly calculated as 2005 - 1999 = 6 years, but this same answer is not so easily obtained if only the year values 05 and 99 are used. In addition, using four digits ensures that we are certain what year 2005 refers to; a two-digit value (such as 05) could refer to either 1905 or 2005. So at this stage, our initial class diagram can be refined to that shown in Figure 5-17. Notice that we have also preceded each attribute name with a minus sign (-) to indicate that these attributes are to be private. This is in keeping with the basic convention that, unless there is some overriding reason for making an attribute public, all attributes are private. To ensure that we do not later forget that each year will be stored as a four-digit value, we have included a class diagram with specific initial values (Figure 5-18).

FIGURE 5-17
*First Refinement—*Date *Class Diagram*

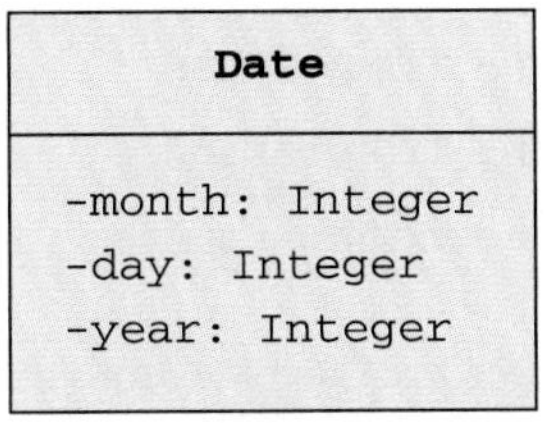

Date
-month: Integer -day: Integer -year: Integer

FIGURE 5-18
A Date *Object Diagram*

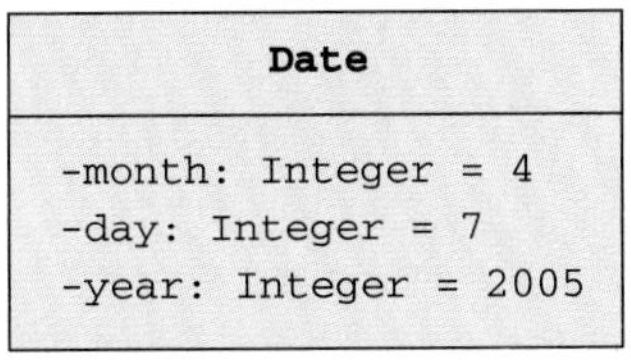

Date
-month: Integer = 4 -day: Integer = 7 -year: Integer = 2005

Notice that, even at this early stage, we can directly translate the Date class into C++ code as follows:

```
class Date
{
  // data declaration section
  private:
    int month;
    int day;
    int year;
}
```

Having identified the class's attributes (and these can be modified or added to as new information becomes available), we now need to identify an initial set of operations. Table 5-5 lists the operations that we initially determine are appropriate for our Date class.

TABLE 5-5
Required Operations for the Date *Class*

operation	returned value	comments
Initialize	None	Constructor
Modify	None	Mutator
Display	None	Accessor
Is the year a leap year	Boolean	Requires a comparison
Is the date a weekday	Boolean	Requires a comparison
Is the day a holiday	Boolean	Requires a comparison and file access of holidays
Are two dates the same	Boolean	Requires a comparison
Is one date before a second date	Boolean	Requires a comparison
Is one date after a second date	Boolean	Requires a comparison
Determine the day of the week	Integer	Requires a comparison
Determine next day's date	Date	Requires a comparison
Determine prior day's date	Date	Requires a comparison
Day difference between two dates	Integer	Requires a comparison

As can be seen in Table 5-4, the majority of the operations require comparisons. Because we have not yet presented the C++ statements required for accessing a file (see Chapter 12), we will not be able to actually code the operation for determining if a date is a holiday or not. Nonetheless, we can include the requirement for this method in the refinement of our Date class diagram (Figure 5-19). In fact, this is

FIGURE 5-19
*Second Refinement—*Date *Class Diagram*

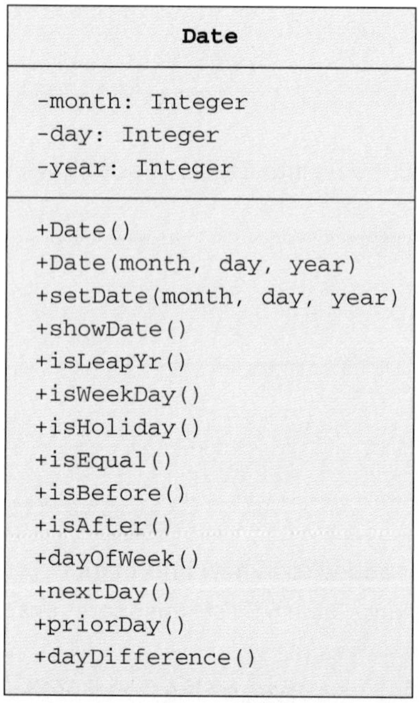

```
                    Date

      -month: Integer
      -day: Integer
      -year: Integer

      +Date()
      +Date(month, day, year)
      +setDate(month, day, year)
      +showDate()
      +isLeapYr()
      +isWeekDay()
      +isHoliday()
      +isEqual()
      +isBefore()
      +isAfter()
      +dayOfWeek()
      +nextDay()
      +priorDay()
      +dayDifference()
```

one of the useful features provided in a UML analysis; it alerts us to the capabilities we will need to eventually develop in order to complete a class. Notice also that, by preceding all method names with a +, we have indicated that these methods will have public visibility.

The first four methods shown in Figure 5-19 consist of constructor, accessor, and mutator methods. As we have seen, these methods form the basis for almost every class we will develop. Class 5-1 presents a basic `Date` class that contains these four methods.

Class 5-1

```cpp
#include <iostream>
#include <iomanip>   // needed for formatting
using namespace std;

class Date
{
   // data declaration section
   private:
      int month;
      int day;
      int year;

   // methods declaration section
public:
      Date();                                  // default constructor
      Date(int, int, int);                     // overloaded constructor
      void setDate(int mm, int dd, int yyyy);  // mutator
      void showDate();                         // accessor
};

// methods implementation section
   Date::Date()     // this is a constructor method because it has the same
   {                          // name as the class
      month = 7;
      day = 4;
      year = 2005;
      cout << "From the default constructor:"
           << "\n  Created a new Date object with data values"
           << "\n    month = " << month << "  day = " << day
           << "  year = " << year << "\n\n";
   }

   Date::Date(int mm, int dd, int yyyy)   // this is an overloaded constructor
   {
      month = mm;
      day = dd;
```

(continued on next page)

```
    year = yyyy;
    cout << "From the overloaded constructor:"
         << "\n  Created a new Date object with data values"
         << "\n    month = " << month << "  day = " << day
         << "  year = " << year << "\n\n";
}

void Date::setDate(int mm, int dd, int yyyy)
{
  month = mm;
  day = dd;
  year = yyyy;
}

void Date::showDate()
{

  cout << "The date is " << setfill('0')
       << setw(2) << month << '/'
       << setw(2) << day << '/'
       << setw(2) << year % 100; // extract the last 2 year digits
  cout << endl;

}
```

EXPLANATION OF THE BASIC Date CLASS

Although by now you should be comfortable discussing the constructor, accessor, and mutator methods provided in the Date class, we will take a moment to analyze them.

The default constructor, repeated below for convenience, initializes the instance variables named month, day, and year with the values 7, 4, and 2005, respectively. In addition, a cout object has been included to display the initialized values.

```
Date::Date()    // this is a constructor method because it has the same
{               // name as the class
  month = 7;
  day = 4;
  year = 2005;
  cout << "From the default constructor:"
       << "\n  Created a new Date object with data values"
       << "\n    month = " << month << "  day = " << day
       << "  year = " << year << "\n\n";
}
```

Instead of always accepting the values provided by the default constructor, the second constructor provides the capability of initializing a Date object with values selected at the time of an object's creation. This is made possible by first declaring three integer parameters in its header line. The code for this constructor is:

```
Date::Date(int mm, int dd, int yyyy)   // this is an overloaded constructor
{
   month = mm;
   day = dd;
   year = yyyy;
   cout << "From the overloaded constructor:"
        << "\n  Created a new Date object with data values"
        << "\n    month = " << month << "  day = " << day
        << "  year = " << year << "\n\n";
}
```

Here the overloaded constructor is declared as receiving three integer arguments, which are then used to initialize the month, day, and year data members. As with the default constructor, a cout object has been included to display the initialized values.

The next method header line

```
        void Date::setDate(int mm, int dd, int yyyy)
```

defines this as the setDate() method. This mutator method is almost identical to the overloaded constructor. It expects three integer parameters, mm, dd, and yyyy and assigns the data members month, day, and year with the values of its parameters, respectively.

Finally, the last method header line in the definition section defines an accessor method named showDate(). This method has no parameters and returns no value. The body of this method, however, needs a little more explanation.

Although we have chosen to internally store all years as four-digit values that retain century information, users are accustomed to seeing dates with the year represented as a two-digit value, such as 12/15/99. To display the last two digits of the year value, the expression year % 100 is initially used. For example, if the year is 1999, the expression 1999 % 100 yields the value 99, and if the year is 2006, the expression 2006 % 100 yields the value 6. Notice that if we had used an assignment such as year = year % 100; we would actually be altering the stored value of year to correspond to the last one or two digits of the year. Since we want to retain the year as a four-digit number, we must be careful only to manipulate the displayed value using the expression year % 100. The formatting ensures that the displayed values correspond to conventionally accepted dates. For example, a date such as December 9, 2004, will appear as 12/09/04 and not as 12/9/4.

USING THE BASIC Date CLASS

To see how our basic Date class can be used within the context of a complete program, consider Program 5-8, which constructs and manipulates objects of the Date class. For ease of reading, the Date class has been lightly shaded and included within the program itself. (In Section 7.6 you will see how the class itself can be stored in one file and the executing program, consisting of the darker shaded region in Program 5-8, is stored separately from the Date class.)

Program 5-8

```cpp
#include <iostream>
#include <iomanip>  // needed for formatting
using namespace std;

class Date
{
  // data declaration section
  private:
    int month;
    int day;
    int year;

  // methods declaration section
  public:
    Date();                               // default constructor
    Date(int, int, int);                  // overloaded constructor
    void setDate(int mm, int dd, int yyyy);  // mutator
    void showDate();                      // accessor
};

// methods implementation section
  Date::Date()    // this is a constructor method because it has the same
  {               // name as the class
    month = 7;
    day = 4;
    year = 2005;
    cout << "From the default constructor:"
         << "\n  Created a new Date object with data values"
         << "\n    month = " << month << "   day = " << day
         << "   year = " << year << "\n\n";
  }

  Date::Date(int mm, int dd, int yyyy)   // this is an overloaded constructor
  {
    month = mm;
    day = dd;
    year = yyyy;
    cout << "From the overloaded constructor:"
         << "\n  Created a new Date object with data values"
         << "\n    month = " << month << "   day = " << day
```

(continued on next page)

```
            << "   year = " << year << "\n\n";
}

void Date::setDate(int mm, int dd, int yyyy)
{
  month = mm;
  day = dd;
  year = yyyy;
}

void Date::showDate()
{

  cout << "The date is " << setfill('0')
       << setw(2) << month << '/'
       << setw(2) << day << '/'
       << setw(2) << year % 100; // extract the last 2 year digits
  cout << endl;
}
```

```
int main()
{
  Date firstDate;  // declare an object using the default constructor
  Date secondDate(5,1,2006);  // declare another object using the
                              // overloaded constructor

    // display the Date objects
  firstDate.showDate();
  secondDate.showDate();
    // reset and display one Date
  secondDate.setDate(12,25,2007);
  secondDate.showDate();

  return 0;
}
```

The output displayed by Program 5-8 is:

```
From the default constructor:
  Created a new Date object with data values
    month = 7   day = 4   year = 2005

From the overloaded constructor:
  Created a new Date object with data values
    month = 5   day = 1   year = 2006

The date is 07/04/05
The date is 05/01/06
The date is 12/25/07
```

Let us see how this output is produced. Two objects are created in Program 5-8's `main()` method. The first object, which is referenced by the variable named `firstDate`, is initialized using the default constructor. The second object, which is initialized with the arguments 5, 1, and 2006, uses the second, overloaded, constructor. The compiler knows to use this second constructor because three integer arguments are specified, and there is only one constructor that accepts three integer arguments. Notice that a compiler error would occur if the two constructors had the same number and types of parameters because the compiler would not be able to determine which constructor to use.

It is also worth noting that objects have the same relationship to classes as variables do to C++'s built-in data types. For example, in a declaration, such as

```
int firstNumber;
```

`firstNumber` is said to be a variable, while in Program 5-8's declaration

```
Date firstDate;
```

`firstDate` is said to be a reference variable. A variable for a built-in data type contains an actual data value, whereas a reference variable will either store the memory address of an object or a `null` address if no object is referenced.

PROGRAMMING NOTE

User Interfaces, Definitions, and Information Hiding

The terms "user interface" and "definition" are employed extensively in the object-oriented programming literature. Each of these terms can be equated to specific parts of a class's declaration and definition sections.

A user interface consists of a class's public methods' declarations and any supporting comments. Thus, the interface should be all that is required to tell a programmer how to use the class.

The definition consists of both the class's definition section, which consists of both private and public member definitions, *and* the class's private data members that are contained in a class declaration section.

The definition is the essential means of providing information hiding. In its most general context, information hiding refers to *how* a class is internally constructed and is not relevant to any programmer who wishes to use the class. That is, the class code can and should be hidden from all class users precisely to ensure that the class is not altered or compromised in any way. All that a programmer needs to know to use the class correctly should be provided by the interface.

The first date object, named `firstDate`, in Program 5-8, is created by the declaration statement `Date firstDate;`. Because we have included a `cout` object in this constructor, the call to it produces this initial output:

```
From the default constructor:
  Created a new Date object with data values
    month = 7   day = 4   year = 2005
```

For our purposes, this display verifies that the default constructor was in fact called. The real work done by a default constructor is to put an object into a known and meaningful state when it is created. In this case the `Date()` constructor assigns the values 7, 4, and 2005 to the created object's `month`, `day`, and `year` variables, respectively. In a similar manner, when the object named `secondDate` is defined, the overloaded constructor is called, resulting in the initialization of `secondDate`'s data members with `month`, `day`, and `year` values of 5, 1, and 2006, respectively. (Although `secondDate` is referred to as an object, it is important again to keep in mind that `secondDate` is really a reference to the object and not the object itself.) Because a `cout` object was included in the overloaded constructor, the following output is produced:

```
From the overloaded constructor:
  Created a new Date object with data values
    month = 5   day = 1   year = 2006
```

The next two statements in Program 5-8 call the `showDate()` method to operate on the `firstDate` and `secondDate` objects. The first call results in the display of `firstDate`'s data values, and the second call results in the display of `secondDate`'s data values, producing the output:

```
The date is 7/4/05
The date is 5/1/06
```

The statement `secondDate.setDate(12,25,2007);` then calls the `setDate()` mutator method to operate on the `secondDate` object, which uses the argument values 12, 25, 2007 to reset `secondDate`'s data members.

Finally, the last statement `secondDate.showDate();` causes the values in the `secondDate` object to be displayed once again. Because these values were reset, the output becomes:

```
The date is 12/25/07
```

Notice that a statement such as `cout << secondDate;` *cannot* be used, because the `cout` object does not know how to handle an object of class `Date`. Instead, we have supplied our class with an accessor method that can be used to display an object's internal values.

SIMPLIFYING THE CODE

Assuming that you understand what each `Date` class method accomplishes, the first useful modification is to remove the displays from the constructors and `setDate()` methods. The next modification is to have the two constructors call the `setDate()` method to initialize all of the instance variables, rather than repeating each sequence of three assignment statements within these methods. These modifications result in the following simpler constructor methods:

```
Date::Date()    // default constructor
{
  setDate(7,5,2005);
}


Date::Date(int mm, int dd, int yyyy)  // overloaded constructor
{
  setDate(mm, dd, yyyy);
}
```

Finally, each of these single-line constructors can be written as inline constructors. Doing so permits both methods to be implemented within the class's declaration section. If this is done, the two methods would appear as:

```
Date() {setDate(7,5,2005);}  // default constructor
Date(int mm, int dd, int yyyy) {setDate(7,5,2005);}  // overloaded constructor
```

These modifications result in the simpler listing presented as Class 5-2.

Class 5-2

```
#include <iostream>
#include <iomanip>  // needed for formatting
using namespace std;

class Date
{
  // data declaration section
  private:
      int month;
    int day;
    int year;

  // methods declaration
public:
    Date() {setDate(7,5,2005);}  // default constructor
    Date(int mm, int dd, int yyyy) {setDate(mm, dd, yyyy);}  // overloaded constructor
    void setDate(int mm, int dd, int yyyy);  // mutator
    void showDate();                          // accessor
};

// methods implementation section
  void Date::setDate(int mm, int dd, int yyyy)
  {
    month = mm;
    day = dd;
    year = yyyy;
```

(continued on next page)

```
   }

void Date::showDate()
{
   cout << "The date is " << setfill('0')
        << setw(2) << month << '/'
        << setw(2) << day << '/'
        << setw(2) << year % 100; // extract the last 2 year digits
   cout << endl;
}
```

ADDING ADDITIONAL CLASS METHODS

Having constructed and tested our basic Date class, we can now begin to add the class methods specified in Figure 5-19. Specifically, we will implement the two methods named isLeapYear() and dayOfWeek() and leave the remaining methods for you to implement in the Exercises. We begin with the isLeapYear() method.

A leap year is any year that is evenly divisible by 4 but not evenly divisible by 100, with the exception that all years evenly divisible by 400 are leap years. For example, the year 1996 was a leap year because it is evenly divisible by 4 and not evenly divisible by 100. The year 2000 was a leap year because it is evenly divisible by 400. Thus, the algorithm for determining a leap year is:

> **Leap Year Algorithm**
>   **If the year is divisible by 4 with a remainder of 0 And the year is divisible by 100 with a**
>   **nonzero remainder or the year is divisible by 400 with no remainder**
>   **then the year is a leap year**
> **Else**
>   **the year is not a leap year**
> **EndIf**

This algorithm can be coded as a C++ method as follows:

```
bool Date::isLeapYear()
{
   if ( (year % 4 == 0 && year % 100 != 0) || (year % 400 == 0) )
      return true;    // is a leap year
   else
      return false;   // is not a leap year
}
```

There are two items to notice in this code. First, notice that the AND operation (&&) and the OR operation (||) correspond to the And and Or specified in the algorithm. Next, it is not necessary for you to personally develop each algorithm that you code. In this case, the algorithm is provided, and your job as a C++ programmer is to understand that you require an algorithm that is capable of determining if a year is a leap year and then to correctly code the algorithm.

Now let us code the `dayOfWeek()` method. To do this, we require an algorithm that can determine the day of the week for any date that is provided. Again, you can either create your own algorithm or find one that appropriately solves the required task. In this case, a commonly used algorithm for determining the day of the week, known as **Zeller's algorithm,** is the following:

> **Zeller's Algorithm**
>> **If the month is less than 3**
>>> *month = month +12*
>>> *year = year - 1*
>> **EndIf**
>> **Set century = int(year/100)**
>> **Set year = year % 100**
>> **Set T = day + int(26*(month + 1)/10) + year + int(year/4) + int(century/4) - 2 * century**
>> **Set dd = T % 7**
>> **If dd is less than 0**
>>> **Set dd = dd + 7**
>> **EndIf**

Using this algorithm, the variable `dd` will have a value of 0 if the date is a Saturday, 1 if the date is a Sunday, 2 if a Monday, and so on. C++ code that implements this algorithm is:

```cpp
// methods implementation section
/* This method acts on a Date object to determine the Date's day
//of the week
   Parameters: none
   Return value: an integer representing a day of the week, as follows
      0 if the date is a Saturday,
      1 if the date is a Sunday,
      2 if a Monday, and so on, with a 6 being a Friday.
*/
int Date::dayOfWeek()
{
   int T, mm, dd, yy, cc;

   mm = month;
   yy = year;
   if (mm < 3)
   {
      mm = mm + 12;
      yy = yy - 1;
   }
   cc = int(yy/100);
   yy = yy % 100;
   T = day + int(26 * (mm + 1)/10) + yy;
   T = T + int(yy/4) + int(cc/4) - 2 * cc;
   dd = T % 7;
   if (dd < 0) dd = dd + 7;;
   return dd;
}
```

We leave it as an exercise (see Exercise 4, below) for you to include the `isLeapYear()` and `dayOfWeek()` methods into the `Date` class in Program 5-8 and then verify that both methods work correctly.

Exercises 5.6

1. List any additional operations that you think could be included in Figure 5-19. (*Hint*: Consider additional mutator and accessor operations.)

2. List a set of operations that are appropriate for a complex-number class that consists of two attributes: a real double-precision value and an imaginary double-precision value.

3. Enter and execute Program 5-8.

4. **a.** Include the `isLeapYear()` and `dayOfWeek()` methods into Program 5-7's `Date` class and then modify the program to test these methods. For testing purposes, use the fact that the years 1996 and 2004 are both leap years, that March 12, 2003 was a Wednesday and March 15, 2003 was a Saturday.
    b. Use the updated `Date` class written for Exercise 4a to determine the day of the week you were born and whether this was a weekday or not.

5. Rewrite Program 5-8 to include user-entered input for the day, month, and year.

6. **a.** Add another member method named `convert()` to the `Date` class used in Program 5-8 that does the following: The method should access the `month`, `year`, and `day` data members and return a long integer that is calculated as `year * 10000 + month * 100 + day`. For example, if the date is 4/1/2002, the returned value is 20020401 (dates in this form are useful when performing sorts, because placing the numbers in numerical order automatically places the corresponding dates in chronological order).
    b. Include the modified `Date` class constructed for Exercise 6a in a complete program that tests the `convert()` method.

7. Add a method named `isWeekday()` to Program 5-8's `Date` class that returns a boolean value of `true` if the date is a weekday; otherwise, it should return a Boolean value of `false`. The method should call `dayOfWeek()` and then use the returned integer value to determine if the day is a weekday. A weekday is any day between 2 and 6, inclusive, which corresponds to the days Monday through Friday.

8. Add a method named `nameOfDay()` to Program 5-8's `Date` class that returns the name of the day of week, as a string. Thus, one of the strings `Sunday`, `Monday`, `Tuesday`, `Wednesday`, `Thursday`, `Friday`, or `Saturday` should be returned by the method. The method should call `dayOfWeek()` and then use the returned integer value to determine the name of the day of the week.

9.   Modify Program 5-8 so that the only instance variable of the class is a long integer named `yyyymmdd`. Do this by substituting the declaration

```
private:
    long yyyymmdd;
```

for the existing declarations

```
private:
    int month;
    int day;
    int year;
```

Then, rewrite each class method to correctly initialize the single class data member.

10. Modify Program 5-8's `Date` class to include an `isLarger()` method. This method should compare two `Date` objects and return a Boolean value of `true` if the first date is larger than the second; otherwise it should return a `false` value. The header for this method should be `bool isLarger(Date second)`, and should be written according to the following algorithm:

Comparison method
 Accept one date as the current object being evaluated and a second date as an argument
 Determine the later date using the following procedure:
 Convert each date into a long integer value having the form yyyymmdd. This can be accom-plished using the algorithm described in Exercise 6.
 Compare the corresponding integers for each date.
 If the first date's long integer value is larger than the second date's long integer value, return true; otherwise return false

11. Modify Program 5-8's `Date` class to include an `isEqual()` method. This method should compare two `Date` objects and return a Boolean value of `true` if the two dates are equal. The header for this method should be `bool isEqual(Date second)`.

12. Modify Program 5-8's `Date` class to include a `nextDay()` method that increments a date by one day. Test your method to ensure that it correctly increments days into a new month and into a new year.

13. Modify Program 5-8's `Date` class to include a `priorDay()` method that decrements a date by one day. Test your method to ensure that it correctly decrements days into a prior month and into a prior year.

14. a. Construct a class named `Rectangle` that has floating-point data members named `length` and `width`. The class should have a member method named `perimeter()` and `area()` to calculate the perimeter and area of a rectangle, a member method named `getData()` to set a rectangle's length and width, and a member method named `showData()` to display a rectangle's length, width, perimeter, and area.
     b. Include the `Rectangle` class constructed in Exercise 14a within a working C++ program.

15. Construct a class named `Light` that simulates a traffic light. The class should contain a single instance variable having a `string` data type. When a new `Light` object is created, its initial color should be red. Additionally, there should be a method that changes the state of a `Light` object and an accessor method that returns the color currently stored in a `Light` object's instance variable.

16. a. Construct a class definition that can be used to represent an employee of a company. Each employee is defined by an integer ID number, a floating-point pay rate, and the maximum number of hours the employee should work each week. The services provided by the class should be the ability to enter data for a new employee, the ability to change data for a new employee, and the ability to display the existing data for a new employee.

    b. Include the class definition created for Exercise 16a in a working C++ program that asks the user to enter data for three employees and displays the entered data.

5.7 A CLOSER LOOK AT PROGRAM TESTING

In theory, a comprehensive set of test runs would reveal all possible program errors and ensure that a program will work correctly for any and all combinations of input and computed data. In practice, this requires checking all possible combinations of statement execution. Due to the time and effort required, this is an impossible goal except for very simple programs. Let us see why this is so. Consider Program 5-9.

Program 5-9

```cpp
#include <iostream>
using namespace std;
int main()
{
  int num;

  cout << "Enter a number: ";
  cin  >> num;
  if (num == 5)
    cout << "Bingo!\n";
  else
    cout << "Bongo!\n";

  return 0;
}
```

Program 5-9 has two paths that can be traversed from when the program is run to when the program reaches its closing brace. The first path, which is executed when the input number is 5, follows this sequence:

```
cout << "Enter a number";
cin  >> num;
cout << "Bingo!\n";
```

The second path, which is executed whenever any number except 5 is input, follows this sequence:

```
cout << "Enter a number";
cin  >> num;
cout << "Bongo!\n";
```

To test each possible path through Program 5-9 requires two runs of the program, with a judicious selection of test input data to ensure that both paths of the `if` statement are exercised. The addition of one more `if` statement in the program increases the number of possible execution paths by a factor of two and requires four (2^2) runs of the program for complete testing. Similarly, two additional `if` statements increase the number of paths by a factor of four and requires eight (2^3) runs for complete testing, and three additional `if` statements would produce a program that required sixteen (2^4) test runs.

Now consider a modestly sized application program consisting of only ten modules, each module containing five `if` statements. Assuming the modules are always called in the same sequence, there are 32 possible paths through each module (2 raised to the fifth power) and more than 1,000,000,000,000,000 (2 raised to the fiftieth power) possible paths through the complete program (all modules executed in sequence). The time needed to create individual test data to exercise each path and the actual computer run time required to check each path make the complete testing of such a program impossible to achieve.

The inability to fully test all combinations of statement execution sequences has led to the programming saying "There is no error-free program." It has also led to the realization that any testing that is done should be well thought out to maximize the possibility of locating errors. At a minimum, test data should include appropriate values for input values, illegal input values that the program should reject, and limiting values that are checked by selection statements within the program.

5.8 COMMON PROGRAMMING ERRORS

The following are programming errors to watch for when you use C++ selection statements:

1. Using the assignment operator, =, in place of the relational operator, ==. This can cause an enormous amount of frustration, because any expression can be tested by an `if-else` statement. For example, the statement:

```
if (opselect = 2)
  cout << "Happy Birthday\n";
else
  cout << "Good Day\n";
```

5

always results in the message `Happy Birthday` being printed, regardless of the initial value in the variable `opselect`. The reason is that the assignment expression `opselect = 2` has a value of 2, which is considered a true value in C++. The correct expression to determine the value in `opselect` is `opselect == 2`.

2. Assuming the `if-else` statement is selecting an incorrect choice when the problem is really the values being tested. This is a typical debugging problem in which the programmer mistakenly concentrates on the tested condition as the source of the problem rather than the values being tested. For example, assume that the following correct `if-else` statement is part of your program:

```
if (keyCode == 'F')
{
   contemp = (5.0/9.0) * (intemp - 32.0);
   cout << "Conversion to Celsius was done";
}
else
{
   contemp = (9.0/5.0) * intemp + 32.0;
   cout << "Conversion to Fahrenheit was done";
}
```

This statement always displays `Conversion to Celsius was done` when the variable `keyCode` contains an `F`. Therefore, if this message is displayed when you believe `keyCode` does not contain an `F`, investigation of `keyCode`'s value is called for. As a general rule, whenever a selection statement does not act as you think it should, make sure to test your assumptions about the values assigned to the tested variables by displaying their values. If an unanticipated value is displayed, you have at least isolated the source of the problem to the variables themselves, rather than the structure of the `if-else` statement. From there, you will have to determine where and how the incorrect value was obtained.

3. Using nested `if` statements without including braces to clearly indicate the desired structure. When braces are not used, the compiler defaults to pairing `else`s with the closest unpaired `if`s, which sometimes destroys the original intent of the selection statement. To avoid this problem and to create code that is readily adaptable to change, it is useful to write all `if-else` statements as compound statements in the form

```
if (expression)
{
  one or more statements in here
}
else
{
  one or more statements in here
}
```

By using this form, no matter how many statements are added later, the original integrity and intent of the `if` statements are maintained.

4. Forgetting to use a `break` statement to close off a `case` within a `switch` statement. This can be especially troubling when additional cases are added later. For example, consider the following statement:

```
switch(code)
{
   case 1: price = 2.00;
           break;
   case 2: price = 2.50;
}
```

Here, not having a `break` for the last `case` does not immediately cause any problem. It is, however, a potential source of error later if a `case` is subsequently added. With the addition of another `case`, a `break` is necessary to prevent the new `case` 3 from always overriding `case` 2. For example, consider the following code without the `break`:

```
switch(code)
{
   case 1: price = 2.00;
           break;
   case 2: price = 2.50;
   case 3: price = 3.00;
}
```

Because there is no `break` between `cases` 2 and 3, whenever `case` 2 is selected the code not only starts execution with this statement but continues execution through the end of the `switch` statement. Thus the `price` assignment for `case` 3 is also executed. This is referred to as "falling through" the `switch` statement until the end of the `switch` statement is reached. To prevent this error, it is good programming practice to terminate all cases with a `break` (except where the stacking of cases is consciously desired).

5.9 CHAPTER REVIEW

Key Terms

aggregation

association

class diagram

compound statement

condition

false condition

generalization

if-else chain

if-else statement

nested if statements

object diagram

one-way if statements

one-way selection

simple relational expression

switch statement

true condition

type

Unified Modeling Language (UML)

visibility

SUMMARY

1. Relational expressions, which are also called **simple conditions**, are used to compare operands. If a relational expression is true, the value of the expression is the integer 1. If the relational expression is false, it has an integer value of 0. Relational expressions are created using the following relational operators:

relational operator	meaning	example
<	less than	age < 30
>	greater than	height > 6.2
<=	less than or equal to	taxable <= 20000
>=	greater than or equal to	temp >= 98.6
==	equal to	grade == 100
!=	not equal to	number != 250

2. More complex conditions can be constructed from relational expressions using C++'s logical operators, && (AND), || (OR), and ! (NOT).

3. An `if-else` statement is used to select between two alternative statements based on the value of an expression. Although relational expressions are usually used for the tested expression, any valid expression can be used. In testing an expression, `if-else` statements interpret a nonzero value as true and a zero value as false. The most commonly used form of an `if-else` statement is:

```
if (expression)
   statement1;
else
   statement2;
```

This is a two-way selection statement. If the expression has a nonzero value it is considered as true, and `statement1` is executed; otherwise `statement2` is executed.

4. An `if-else` statement can contain other `if-else` statements. In the absence of braces, each `else` is associated with the closest unpaired `if`.

5. The `if-else` chain is a multiway selection statement having the general form:

```
if (expression1)
   statement1;
else if (expression2)
   statement2;
else if (expression3)
   statement3;

         .

         .

         .

else if (expressionm)
   statementm;
else
   statementn;
```

Each *expression* is evaluated in the order it appears in the chain. Once an expression having a nonzero value is detected, only the statement between that expression and the next *else if* or *else* is executed, and no further expressions are tested. The final *else* is optional, and the statement corresponding to the final *else* is only executed if none of the previous expressions is true (has a nonzero value).

6. A compound statement consists of any number of individual statements enclosed within the brace pair { and }. Compound statements are treated as a single block and can be used anywhere a single statement is called for.

7. The `switch` statement is a multiway selection statement. The general syntax of a `switch` statement is:

```
switch (expression)
{                                  // start of compound statement
  case value1:      ◄────── terminated with a colon
    statement1;
    statement2;
        .
        .
    break;
  case value2:      ◄────── terminated with a colon
    statementm;
    statementn;
        .
        .
    break;
        .
        .
  case valuen:      ◄────── terminated with a colon
      statementw;
      statementx;
        .
        .
    break;
  default:      ◄────── terminated with a colon
      statementaa;
      statementbb;
        .
        .
} // end of switch and compound statement
```

For this statement, the value of an integer expression is compared to a number of integer constants, character constants, or expressions containing only constants and operators. Program execution is transferred to the first matching case and continues through the end of the `switch` statement unless an optional `break` statement is encountered. The cases in a `switch` statement can appear in any order, and an optional `default` case can be included. The `default` case is executed if none of the other `cases` is matched.

Chapter Exercises

1. Write C++ code sections to make the following decisions:

    a. Ask for two integer temperatures. If their values are equal, display the temperature; otherwise, do nothing.

    b. Ask for character values `letter1` and `letter2`, representing capital letters of the alphabet, and display them in alphabetical order.

    c. Ask for three integer values, `num1`, `num2`, and `num3`, and display them in decreasing order.

2. **a.** Write a C++ program to compute and display a person's weekly salary as determined by the following conditions:

    If the hours worked are less than or equal to 40, the person receives $8.00 per hour; otherwise, the person receives $320.00 plus $12.00 for each hour worked over 40 hours. The program should request the hours worked as input and should display the salary as output.

    b. How many runs should you make for the program written in Exercise 2a to verify that it is operating correctly? What data should you input in each of the program runs?

3. **a.** Write a program that displays either the message `"I FEEL GREAT TODAY!"` or `"I FEEL DOWN TODAY."` depending on the input. If the character 'u' is entered in the variable code, the first message should be displayed; otherwise the second message should be displayed. (Do not include the quotation marks in the message.)

    b. How many runs should you make for the program written in Exercise 3a to verify that it is operating correctly? What data should you input in each of the program runs?

4. **a.** A senior computer analyst is paid $1500 a week and a junior analyst $900 a week. Write a C++ program that accepts as input an analyst's status in the character variable status. If status equals 'S', the senior person's salary should be displayed, otherwise the junior person's salary should be output.

    b. How many runs should you make for the program written in Exercise 4a to verify that it is operating correctly? What data should you input in each of the program runs?

5. Write a C++ program that accepts a character as input data and determines if the character is an uppercase letter. An uppercase letter is any character that is greater than or equal to 'A' and less than or equal to 'Z'. If the entered character is an uppercase letter, display the message "The character just entered is an uppercase letter." If the entered letter is not uppercase, display the message "The character just entered is not an uppercase letter." (Do not include the quotation marks in the message.)

6. Repeat Exercise 5 to determine if the character entered is a lowercase letter. A lowercase letter is any character greater than or equal to 'a' and less than or equal to 'z'.

7. The following program displays the message "Hello there!" regardless of the letter input. Find the error.

```cpp
#include <iostream>
using namespace std;
int main()
{
   char letter;
   cout << "Enter a letter: ";
   cin  >> letter;
   if (letter = 'm')
      cout << "Hello there!\n";
   return 0;
}
```

8. **a.** Write, run, and test a C++ program that accepts a user-input integer number and determines whether it is even or odd. The program should display the entered number and a message indicating whether the number is even or odd.

  b. Modify the program written for Exercise 8a to determine if the entered number is exactly divisible by a value specified by the user. That is, is it divisible by 3, 7, 13, or any other user-specified value.

9. As a part-time student, you took two courses last term. Write, run, and test a C++ program that calculates and displays your grade point average (GPA) for the term. Your program should prompt the user to enter the grade and credit hours for each course. The program should then display the grades, with the lower grade first. The grade point average for the term should be calculated and displayed. A warning message should be printed if the GPA is less than 2.0 and a congratulatory message if the GPA is 3.5 or above.

10. Write a program that will give the user only three choices: Convert from Fahrenheit to Celsius, Convert from Celsius to Fahrenheit, or Quit. If the third choice is chosen, the program stops. If one of the first two choices is selected, the program should prompt the user for either a Fahrenheit or Celsius temperature, as appropriate, and then calculate and display the corresponding temperature. Use the conversion equations:

$$F \;=\; (9/5)\; C \;+\; 32$$
$$C \;=\; (5/9)\; (F \;-\; 32)$$

11. Write a program that displays the following two prompts:

```
Enter a month (use a 1 for Jan, etc.):
Enter a day of the month:
```

  a. Have your program accept and store a number in the variable month in response to the first prompt, and accept and store a number in the variable day in response to the second prompt. If the month entered is not between 1 and 12 inclusive, the program should print a message informing the user that an invalid month has been entered. If the day entered is not between 1 and 31, the program should print a message informing the user that an invalid day has been entered.

  b. What will your program do if the user types a number with a decimal point for the month? How can you ensure that your if statements check for an integer number?

  c. In a nonleap year, February has 28 days; the months January, March, May, July, August, October, and December have 31 days; and all other months have 30 days. Using this information, modify the program written in Exercise 11a to display a message when an invalid day is entered for a month entered by the user. For this program, ignore leap years.

12. **a.** As shown in the following table, the angle that a line makes with the positive x-axis tells you the quadrant in which the line resides:

angle from the positive x-axis	quadrant
Between 0 and 90 degrees	I
Between 90 and 180 degrees	II
Between 180 and 270 degrees	III
Between 270 and 360 degrees	IV

Using this information, write a C++ program that accepts the angle of the line as user input and determines and displays the quadrant appropriate to the input data. (*Note*: If the angle is exactly 0, 90, 180, or 270 degrees, the corresponding line does not reside in any quadrant but lies on an axis.)

b. Modify the program written for Exercise 12a so that a message is displayed that identifies an angle of zero degrees as the positive x-axis, an angle of 90 degrees as the positive y-axis, an angle of 180 degrees as the negative x-axis, and an angle of 270 degrees as the negative y-axis.

13. Based on an automobile's model year and weight, the state's motor vehicle department determines the car's weight class and registration fee using the following schedule:

model year	weight	weight class	registration fee
1970 or earlier	Less than 2,700 lbs	1	$16.50
	2,700 to 3,800 lbs	2	25.50
	More than 3,800 lbs	3	46.50
1971 to 1979	Less than 2,700 lbs	4	27.00
	2,700 to 3,800 lbs	5	30.50
	More than 3,800 lbs	6	52.50
1980 or later	Less than 3,500 lbs	7	19.50
	3,500 or more lbs	8	52.50

Using this information, write a C++ program that accepts the year and weight of an automobile and determines and displays the weight class and registration fee for the car.

Improving Communication

14.   MEMORANDUM

To: Chief Programmer
From: Head of Programming Dept.

Subject: OOP Course

Now that you have returned from a course in OOP, could you please describe the difference between a class diagram and an object diagram. Why do we need both?

Improving Communication

15.   MEMORANDUM

To: U. R. It
From: Chief Programmer

Subject: OOP Approach

Our latest project will require us to use dates extensively by comparing a beginning date to an ending date and determining the actual number of days between the two dates. Why can't we just implement this using a method that compares two numbers, rather than using two Date objects, as you have proposed?

5

**Working
in Teams**

16. Your team is responsible for analyzing a gas station pumping system. The pump itself consists of a gun, holster, pump display, and meter. Connected to the pump is the main gas tank. The tank supplies gas to the pump. The attributes of the tank are its capacity, current level, and grade of gas. The pump's attributes are the amount it dispenses and its cost. The tank is enabled when the gun is removed from the holster and is disabled when the gun is replaced.

    As a team, identify potential objects in the problem. Typically, objects are identified by locating the nouns, such as pump, tank, etc., in the problem statement.

    Next, assign one object to each team member. Each member should then write a paragraph describing what the object does, and how it interacts with other objects.

**Working
in Teams**

17. Your team is responsible for developing a software simulation program to model the operation of a single elevator. The elevator is capable of moving from the basement of the building it is housed in to the sixth floor, which is at the top of the building. The elevator responds to the external up and down buttons as follows:

    • If the elevator is moving down and a down button is activated on a lower floor, the elevator will stop at the designated floor.

    • If the elevator is moving up and an up button is activated on a higher floor, the elevator will stop at the designated floor.

    • The external buttons are pushed by people, who arrive randomly at any floor.

    • Internally, the elevator responds to an activated floor button by turning on the button's light and then stopping at the next floor in the direction it is moving. When it reaches the designated floor it opens the doors and turns off the internal floor button.

    As a team, identify potential objects in the problem. Typically, objects are identified by locating the nouns, such as people, button, etc., in the problem statement.

    Next, assign one object to each team member. Each member should then write a paragraph describing what the object does, and how it interacts with other objects.

Please visit the Testing Center at www.course.com/testingcenter for more practice on selection structures.

**Testing
Center**

REPETITION STATEMENTS

This chapter presents C++ statements that repeat sections of code. A section of code that is repeated is commonly referred to as a **loop** because after the last statement in the code is executed, the program loops back to the first statement and starts another repetition through the code. Each repetition is referred to as an iteration of the loop, or sometimes a pass through the loop.

In addition to learning how to create such statements, in this chapter you will learn about the programming situations that require a repetition capability. These situations include continual checking of user data entries until an acceptable entry, such as a valid password, is entered; counting and accumulating running totals; and accepting input data and recalculating output values that only stop upon entry of a predetermined sentinel value.

6.1 BASIC LOOP STRUCTURES

The real power of a program is realized when the same type of operation must be performed over and over. Repetition statements allow you to type a set of instructions once and then have this same set of instructions repeated continuously until some preset condition is met.

Constructing a repeating section of code requires four elements. The first necessary element is a repetition statement. This statement both defines the boundaries containing the repeating section of code and controls whether the code will be executed or not. In general, there are three different forms of repetition statements, all of which are provided in C++:

a. `while`
b. `for`
c. `do-while`

The second required element for constructing repeating sections of code is a condition that must be evaluated. This condition is necessary for all three types of repetition statements listed above. Valid conditions are identical to those used in selection statements (as described in Chapter 5). If the condition is true, the code is executed; otherwise, it is not.

The third required element is a statement that sets the initial state of the condition being tested. This statement must always be placed before the condition is first evaluated, to ensure correct loop execution the first time the condition is evaluated.

Finally, there must be a statement within the repeating section of code that allows the condition to become false. This is necessary to ensure that, at some point, the repetitions stop.

Repetition statements are also categorized based on where in the overall loop they are tested (at the top or bottom). They are also be categorized based on the type of condition being tested. These distinctions are covered in the following section.

PRETEST AND POSTTEST LOOPS

The condition being tested can be evaluated at either the beginning or the end of the repeating section of code. Figure 6-1 illustrates the case where the test occurs at the beginning of the loop. This type of loop is referred to as a **pretest loop** because the condition is tested before any statements within the loop are executed. If the condition is true, the executable statements within the loop are executed. If the initial value of the condition is false, the executable statements within the loop are never executed, and control transfers to the first statement after the loop. To avoid infinite repetitions, the condition must be updated within the loop. Pretest loops are also referred to as **entrance-controlled loops**. Both the `while` and `for` loop structures are examples of such loops.

FIGURE 6-1
A Pretest Loop

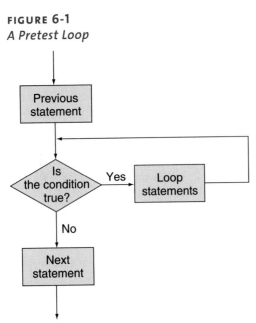

A loop that evaluates a condition at the end of the repeating section of code, as illustrated in Figure 6-2, is referred to as a **posttest loop** or **exit-controlled** loop. These loops always execute the loop statements at least once before the condition is tested. Since the executable statements within the loop are continually executed until the condition becomes false, there always must be a statement within the loop that updates the condition and permits it to become false. The do-while construct is an example of a posttest loop.

FIGURE 6-2
A Posttest Loop

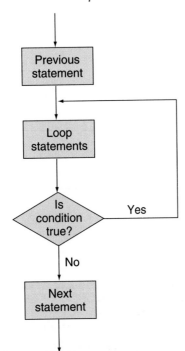

6

FIXED-COUNT VERSUS VARIABLE-CONDITION LOOPS

In addition to categorizing loops based on where the condition is tested (pretest or posttest), loops are categorized based on the type of condition being tested. In a **fixed-count loop**, the condition is used to keep track of how many repetitions have occurred. For example, we might want to produce a table of 10 numbers, including their squares and cubes, or a fixed design such as:

```
* * * * * * * * * * * * * * * * * * * * * * * *
* * * * * * * * * * * * * * * * * * * * * * *
* * * * * * * * * * * * * * * * * * * * * * * *
* * * * * * * * * * * * * * * * * * * * * *
```

In each of these cases, a fixed number of calculations are performed or a fixed number of lines are printed, at which point the repeating section of code is exited. All of C++'s repetition statements can be used to produce fixed-count loops.

In many situations, the exact number of repetitions is not known in advance or the items are too numerous to count beforehand. For example, when entering a large amount of market research data, we might not want to take the time to count the number of actual data items to be entered. In cases like this, a variable-condition loop is used. In a **variable-condition loop**, the tested condition does not depend on a count being achieved but rather on a variable that can change interactively with each pass through the loop. When a specified value is encountered, regardless of how many iterations have occurred, repetitions stop. All of C++'s repetition statements can be used to create variable-condition loops.[1] In this chapter, we will encounter examples of both fixed-count and variable-condition loops.

Exercises 6.1

1. List the three repetition structures that are provided in C++.

2. List the four elements that must be present in a repetition structure.

3. a. What is an entrance-controlled loop?
    b. Which of C++'s repetition statements produce entrance-controlled loops?

4. a. What is an exit-controlled loop?
    b. Which of C++'s repetition statements produce exit-controlled loops?

---

[1]In this case, C++ differs from most other languages such as BASIC, FORTRAN, and Pascal. In each of these languages, a `for` loop (which is implemented using a DO statement in FORTRAN) can only be used to produce fixed-count loops. C++'s `for` loop, as we will see shortly, is virtually interchangeable with a `while` loop.

5. a. What is the difference between a pretest loop and posttest loop?
    b. If the condition being tested in a pretest loop is false to begin with, how many times will statements internal to the loop be executed?
    c. If the condition being tested in a posttest loop is false to begin with, how many times will statements internal to the loop be executed?

6. What is the difference between a fixed-count and variable-condition loop?

6.2 WHILE LOOPS

In C++, a while loop is constructed using a while statement. The general form of this statement is:

```
while (expression)
    statement;
```

The *expression* contained within parentheses is the condition that is tested to determine if the statement following the parentheses is executed. The *expression* is evaluated in exactly the same manner as that contained in an if-else statement; the difference is in how the *expression* is used. As we have seen, when the *expression* is true (has a nonzero value) in an if-else statement, the statement following the *expression* is executed once. In a while statement, the statement following the *expression* is executed repeatedly as long as the *expression* evaluates to a nonzero value. Considering just the *expression* and the statement following the parentheses, the process used by the computer in evaluating a while statement is:

1. Test the expression

2. If the expression has a nonzero (true) value

    a. execute the statement following the parentheses
    b. go back to step 1
    else
       exit the while statement and execute the next
        executable statement following the while statement

Notice that step 2b forces program control to be transferred back to step 1. This transfer of control back to the start of a while statement in order to re-evaluate the expression is what forms the program loop. The while statement literally loops back on itself to recheck the expression until it evaluates to zero (becomes false). This naturally means that somewhere in the loop a statement must be able to alter the value of the tested expression. As we will see, this is indeed the case.

This looping process produced by a while statement is illustrated in Figure 6-3. A diamond shape is used to show the two entry and two exit points required in the decision part of the while statement.

6

FIGURE 6-3
Structure of a while *Loop*

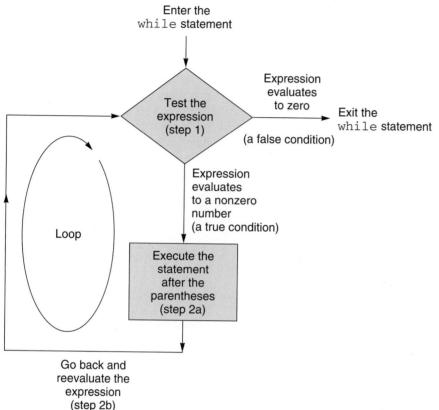

To make this concept a little more tangible, consider the relational expression count <= 10 and the following statement:

cout << count; . Using these, we can write the following valid while statement:

```
while (count <= 10)
    cout << count;
```

Although the preceding statement is valid, the alert reader will realize that we have created a situation in which the cout object either is called forever (or until we stop the program) or is not called at all. Let us see why this happens.

If count has a value less than or equal to 10 when the expression is first evaluated, the cout statement is executed. The while statement then automatically loops back on itself and retests the expression. Since we have not changed the value stored in count, the expression is still true and another call to cout is made. This process continues forever, or until the program containing this statement is prematurely stopped by the user. However, if count starts with a value greater than 10, the expression is false to begin with and the cout object is never used.

A BIT OF BACKGROUND

Comptometer Arithmetic

In the early 1900s, mechanical calculators, called *comptometers*, performed only addition. Because multiplication is simply a quick method of addition (for example, 5 x 4 is really 5 added 4 times), producing multiplication results presented no problems—the answers were obtained using repeated additions. Subtraction and division, however, initially did present a problem. Clever accountants soon discovered that subtraction and division were possible. Subtraction was accomplished by writing the nine's complement on each numeric key. That is, 9 was written on the 0 key, 8 on the 1 key, 7 on the 2 key, and so on. Subtraction was then performed by adding the nine's complement numbers, then adding 1 to the result. For example, consider the subtraction problem

    637 - 481 = 156
The nine's complement of 481 is 518, and

    637 + 518 + 1 = 1,156

which gives the answer (156) to the problem when the leftmost carry digit is ignored.

It did not take the accountants long to solve division problems using repeated subtractions—all on a machine designed to handle only additions.

Early computers, which could only perform addition, used similar algorithms for performing subtraction, multiplication, and division. These computers, however, used two's complement numbers rather than nine's complement (See Section 1.8 for an introduction to two's complement numbers).

Although many computers now come with special purpose hardware, called floating-point processors, to perform multiplication and division directly, they still use two's complement number representation internally and perform subtraction using two's complement addition. And when a floating-point processor is not used, sophisticated software algorithms are employed that perform multiplications and divisions based on repeated additions and subtractions.

How do we set an initial value in `count` to control what the `while` statement does the first time the expression is evaluated? The answer, of course, is to assign values to each variable in the tested expression before the `while` statement is encountered. For example, the following sequence of instructions is valid:

```
count = 1;
while (count <= 10)
   cout << count;
```

Using this sequence of instructions, we have ensured that count starts with a value of 1. We could assign any value to count in the assignment statement—the important thing is to assign some value. In practice, the assigned value depends on the application.

We must still change the value of count so that we can finally exit the while statement. To do this requires an expression such as count = count + 1 to increment the value of count each time the while statement is executed. The fact that a while statement provides for the repetition of a single statement does not prevent us from including an additional statement to change the value of count. All we have to do is replace the single statement with a compound statement. For example:

```
count = 1;              // initialize count
while (count <= 10)
{
  cout << count;
  count++;              // increment count
}
```

Note that, for clarity, we have placed each statement in the compound statement on a different line. This is consistent with the convention adopted for compound statements in the last chapter. Let us now analyze the above sequence of instructions.

The first assignment statement sets count equal to 1. The while statement is then entered and the expression is evaluated for the first time. Since the value of count is less than or equal to 10, the expression is true and the compound statement is executed. The first statement in the compound statement uses to the cout object to display the value of count. The next statement adds 1 to the value currently stored in count, making this value equal to 2. The while statement now loops back to retest the expression. Since count is still less than or equal to 10, the compound statement is again executed. This process continues until the value of count reaches 11. Program 6-1 illustrates these statements in an actual program.

Program 6-1

```
#include <iostream>
using namespace std;

int main()
{
  int count;

  count = 1;                 // initialize count
  while (count <= 10)
  {
    cout << count << "   ";
    count++;                 // increment count
  }

  return 0;
}
```

The output for Program 6-1 is:

```
1   2   3   4   5   6   7   8   9   10
```

There is nothing special about the name count used in Program 6-1. Any valid integer variable could have been used.

Before we consider other examples of the while statement, two comments concerning Program 6-1 are in order. First, the statement count++ can be replaced with any statement that changes the value of count. A statement such as count = count + 2, for example, would cause every second integer to be displayed. Second, it is the programmer's responsibility to ensure that count is changed in a way that ultimately leads to a normal exit from the while loop. For example, if we replace the expression count++ with the expression count--, the value of count will never exceed 10 and an infinite loop will be created. An **infinite loop** is a loop that never ends. The computer will not reach out, touch you, and say, "Excuse me, you have created an infinite loop." It just keeps displaying numbers until you realize that the program is not working as you expected.

Now that you have some familiarity with the while statement, see if you can read and determine the output of Program 6-2.

Program 6-2

```cpp
#include <iostream>
using namespace std;

int main()
{
  int i;

  i = 10;
  while (i >= 1)
  {
    cout << i << "   ";
    i--;                    // subtract 1 from i
  }

  return 0;
}
```

The assignment statement in Program 6-2 initially sets the int variable i to 10. The while statement then checks to see if the value of i is greater than or equal to 1. While the expression is true, the value of i is displayed by the cout object and the value of i is decremented by 1. When i finally reaches zero, the expression is false (has a zero value) and the program exits the while statement. Thus, the following display is obtained when Program 6-2 is run:

```
10   9   8   7   6   5   4   3   2   1
```

To illustrate the power of the while statement, consider the task of printing a table of numbers from 1 to 10 with their squares and cubes. This can be done with a simple while statement as illustrated by Program 6-3.

Program 6-3

```cpp
#include <iostream>
#include <iomanip>  // needed for formatting
using namespace std;

int main()
{
    int num;

    cout << "NUMBER    SQUARE    CUBE\n"
         << "------    ------    ----\n";

    num = 1;
    while (num < 11)

    {
        cout << setw(3) << num << "        "
             << setw(3) << num * num      << "      "
             << setw(4) << num * num * num << endl;
        num++;            // increment num
    }

    return 0;
}
```

When Program 6-3 is run, the following display is produced:

NUMBER	SQUARE	CUBE
------	------	----
1	1	1
2	4	8
3	9	27
4	16	64
5	25	125
6	36	216
7	49	343
8	64	512
9	81	729
10	100	1000

Note that the expression used in Program 6-3 is num < 11. For the integer variable num, this expression is exactly equivalent to the expression num <= 10. The choice of which to use is entirely up to you.

If we want to use Program 6-3 to produce a table of 1000 numbers, all we do is change the expression in the while statement from num < 11 to num < 1001. Changing the 11 to 1001 produces a table of 1000 lines—not bad for a simple five-line while statement.

All the program examples illustrating the while statement we have shown so far are examples of fixed-count loops, because the tested condition is a counter that checks for a fixed number of repetitions. A variation on the fixed-count loop can be made where the counter is not incremented by one each time through the loop, but by some other value. For example, consider the task of producing a Celsius to Fahrenheit temperature conversion table. Assume that Fahrenheit temperatures corresponding to Celsius temperatures ranging from 5 to 50 degrees are to be displayed in increments of five degrees. The desired display can be obtained with the series of statements:

```
celsius = 5;       // starting Celsius value
while (celsius <= 50)
{
   fahren = (9.0/5.0) * celsius + 32.0;
   cout << celsius
        << fahren << endl;
   celsius = celsius + 5;
}
```

As before, the while statement consists of everything from the word while through the closing brace of the compound statement. Prior to entering the while loop, we have made sure to assign a value to the counter being evaluated, and there is a statement to alter the value of the counter within the loop (in increments of 5) to ensure an exit from the while loop. Program 6-4 illustrates the use of this code in a complete program.

The display obtained when Program 6-4 is executed is:

```
DEGREES      DEGREES
CELSIUS      FAHRENHEIT
-------      ----------
   5           41.00
  10           50.00
  15           59.00
  20           68.00
  25           77.00
  30           86.00
  35           95.00
  40          104.00
  45          113.00
  50          122.00
```

6

Program 6-4

```cpp
#include <iostream>
#include <iomanip>   // needed for formatting
using namespace std;

// a program to convert Celsius to Fahrenheit
int main()
{
  const int MAX_CELSIUS = 50;
  const int START_VAL = 5;
  const int STEP_SIZE = 5;

  int celsius;
  double fahren;

  cout << "DEGREES    DEGREES\n"
       << "CELSIUS   FAHRENHEIT\n"
       << "-------    ----------\n";

  celsius = START_VAL;

    // set output formats for floating point numbers only
  cout << setiosflags(ios::fixed)
       << setiosflags(ios::showpoint)
       << setprecision(2);

  while (celsius <= MAX_CELSIUS)
  {
    fahren = (9.0/5.0) * celsius + 32.0;
    cout << setw(4)  << celsius
         << setw(13) << fahren << endl;
    celsius = celsius + STEP_SIZE;
  }

  return 0;
}
```

Exercises 6.2

1. Rewrite Program 6-1 to print the numbers 2 to 10 in increments of two. The output of your program should be:

    2   4   6   8   10

2. Rewrite Program 6-4 to produce a table that starts at a Celsius value of -10 and ends with a Celsius value of 60, in increments of 10 degrees.

3.   a. For the following program, determine the total number of items displayed. Also determine the
         first and last numbers printed.

```
#include <iostream>
using namespace std;
int main()
{
    int num = 0;
    while (num <= 20)
    {
        num++;
        cout << num << " ";
    }

    return 0;
}
```

      b. Enter and run the program from Exercise 3a on a computer to verify your answers to the
         exercise.
      c. How would the output be affected if the two statements within the compound statement
         were reversed (that is, if the cout object statement was placed before the ++n statement)?

4.   Write a C++ program that converts gallons to liters. The program should display gallons from 10
      to 20 in 1-gallon increments and the corresponding liter equivalents. Use the relationship:
      liters = 3.785 * gallons.

5.   Write a C++ program to produce the following display:

```
0
 1
  2
   3
    4
     5
      6
       7
        8
         9
```

6.   Write two C++ programs to produce the following displays:
      a. ****   b.   ****
            ****   ****
              ****   ****
                ****   ****

7. Write a C++ program that converts feet to meters. The program should display feet from 3 to 30 in 3-foot increments and the corresponding meter equivalents. Use the relationship: *meters = feet / 3.28.*

8. A machine purchased for $28,000 is depreciated at a rate of $4000 a year for seven years. Write and run a C++ program that computes and displays a depreciation table for seven years. The table should have the form:

Year	Depreciation	End-of-year Value	Accumulated Depreciation
1	4000	24000	4000
2	4000	20000	8000
3	4000	16000	12000
4	4000	12000	16000
5	4000	8000	20000
6	4000	4000	24000
7	4000	0	28000

9. An automobile travels at an average speed of 55 miles per hour for four hours. Write a C++ program that displays the distance driven, in miles, that the car has traveled after 1, 2, 3, and 4 hours.

10. a. An approximate conversion formula for converting Fahrenheit to Celsius temperatures is:

$$Celsius\ 5\ (Fahrenheit - 30)\ /\ 2$$

Using this formula, and starting with a Fahrenheit temperature of zero degrees, write a C++ program that determines when the approximate equivalent Celsius temperature differs from the exact equivalent value by more than four degrees. (*Hint:* Use a while loop that terminates when the difference between approximate and exact Celsius equivalents exceeds four degrees.)

b. Using the approximate Celsius conversion formula given in Exercise 10a, write a C++ program that produces a table of Fahrenheit temperatures, exact Celsius equivalent temperatures, approximate Celsius equivalent temperatures, and the difference between the correct and approximate equivalent Celsius values. The table should begin at zero degrees Fahrenheit, use two-degree Fahrenheit increments, and terminate when the difference between exact and approximate values differs by more than four degrees.

11. Write a C++ program to find the sum, sum of squares, and the sum of cubes of the first n integers, beginning with 1 and ending with $n = 100$. Verify that in each case:

$$1 + 2 + 3 + ... + n = n(n+1)/2$$
$$1^2 + 2^2 + 3^2 + ... + n^2 = n(n+1)(2n+1)/6$$
$$1^3 + 2^3 + 3^3 + ... + n^3 = n^2(n+1)^2/4$$

12. Write a C++ program to find the sum of the first 100 terms in the series

$$1/(1 * 2) + 1/(2 * 3) + 1/(3 * 4) + ... + 1/[n * (n+1)]$$

Verify that the sum equals $n/(n + 1)$. Determine the value that the sum approaches as n gets infinitely large.

6.3 INTERACTIVE WHILE LOOPS

Combining interactive data entry with the repetition capabilities of the `while` statement produces very adaptable and powerful programs. To understand the concept involved, consider Program 6-5, where a `while` statement is used to accept and then display four numbers entered, one at a time, by the user. Although it is based on a very simple idea, the program highlights the flow-of-control concepts needed to produce more useful programs.

The following is a sample run of Program 6-5. The italicized items were input in response to the appropriate prompts.

```
This program will ask you to enter 4 numbers.

Enter a number: 26.2
The number entered is 26.200
Enter a number: 5
The number entered is 5.000
Enter a number: 103.456
The number entered is 103.456
Enter a number: 1267.89
The number entered is 1267.890
```

Let us review the program so we clearly understand how the output was produced. The first message displayed is caused by execution of the first `cout` object call. This call is outside and before the `while` statement, so it is executed once before any statement in the `while` loop.

Once the `while` loop is processed, the statements within the compound statement are executed while the tested condition is true. The first time through the compound statement, the message "`Enter a number:`" is displayed. The program then calls `cin`, which forces the computer to wait for a number to be entered at the keyboard. Once a number is typed and the Enter key is pressed, the cout object that displays the number is executed. The variable count is then incremented by one. This process continues until four passes through the loop have been made and the value of count is 5. Each pass causes: (1) the message "Enter a number:" to be displayed; (2) one call to cin to be made; and (3) the message "The number entered is" to be displayed. Figure 6-4 illustrates this flow of control.

Program 6-5

```
#include <iostream>
#include <iomanip>
using namespace std;

int main()
{
  const int MAXNUMS = 4;
  int count;
  double num;

  cout << "\nThis program will ask you to enter "
       << MAXNUMS << " numbers.\n";
  count = 1;

  cout << setiosflags(ios::fixed) << setprecision(3);
  while (count <= MAXNUMS)
  {
    cout << "\nEnter a number: ";
    cin  >> num;
    cout << "The number entered is " << num;
    count++;
  }
  cout << endl;

  return 0;
}
```

FIGURE 6-4
Flow of Control for Program 6–5

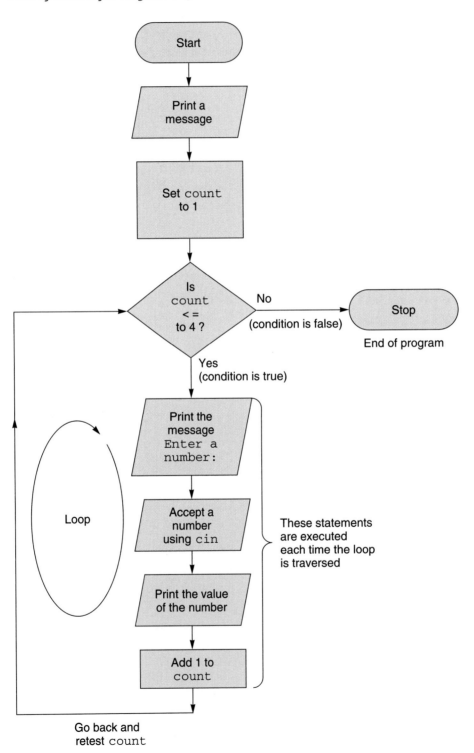

6

Rather than simply displaying the entered numbers, Program 6-5 can be modified to use the entered data. For example, let us add the numbers entered and display the total. To do this, we must be very careful about how we add the numbers, since the same variable `num` is used for each number entered. As a result, the entry of a new number in Program 6-5 automatically causes the previous number stored in `num` to be lost. Thus, each number entered must be added to the total before another number is entered. The required sequence is:

> ***Enter a number***
> ***Add the number to the total***

How do we add a single number to a total? A statement such as `total = total + num` does the job perfectly. (You may recognize this as the accumulating statement introduced in Section 4.1.) After each number is entered, the accumulating statement adds the number to the total, as illustrated in Figure 6-5. The complete flow of control required for adding the numbers is illustrated in Figure 6-6.

FIGURE 6-5
Accepting and Adding a Number to a Total

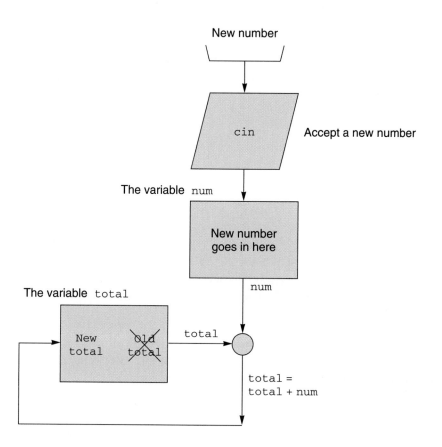

FIGURE 6-6
Accumulation Flow of Control

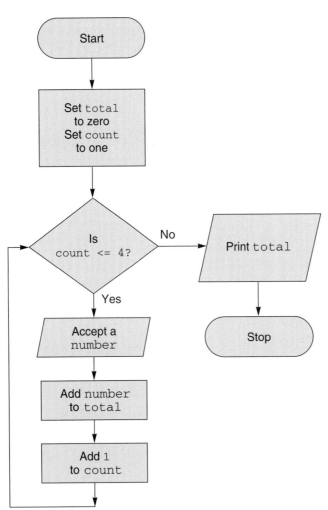

In reviewing Figure 6-6, observe that we have made a provision for initially setting the total to zero before the while loop is entered. If we were to clear the total inside the while loop, it would be set to zero each time the loop was executed and any value previously stored would be erased.

Program 6-6 incorporates the necessary modifications to Program 6-5 to total the numbers entered. As indicated in the flow diagram shown in Figure 6-6, the statement total = total + num; is placed immediately after the cin object call. Putting the accumulating statement at this point in the program ensures that the entered number is immediately "captured" into the total.

Let us review Program 6-6. The purpose of the variable total is to store the total of the numbers entered. Before the while statement, the value of total is set to zero. This ensures that any previous value present in the storage location(s) assigned to the variable total is overwritten. Within the while loop, the statement total = total + num; is used to add the value of the entered number to total. As each value is entered, it is added to the existing value in total to create a new total. Thus, total becomes a running subtotal of all the values entered. Only when all numbers are entered does `total` contain the final sum of all the numbers. After the `while` loop is finished, the last `cout` statement is used to display this sum.

Program 6-6

```cpp
#include <iostream>
#include <iomanip>
using namespace std;

int main()
{
  const int MAXNUMS = 4;
  int count = 1;
  double num;
  double total = 0;

  cout << "\nThis program will ask you to enter "
       << MAXNUMS << " numbers.\n";

  cout << setiosflags(ios::fixed) << setprecision(3);
  while (count <= MAXNUMS)
  {
    cout << "\nEnter a number: ";
    cin  >> num;
    total = total + num;
    cout << "The total is now " << total;
    count++;
  }

  cout << "\n\nThe final total is " << total << endl;

  return 0;
}
```

Using the same data we entered in the sample run for Program 6-5, the following sample run of Program 6-6 was made:

```
This program will ask you to enter 4 numbers.

Enter a number: 26.2
The total is now 26.200
Enter a number: 5
The total is now 31.200
Enter a number: 103.456
The total is now 134.656
Enter a number: 1267.89
The total is now 1402.546

The final total is 1402.546
```

Having used an accumulating assignment statement to add the numbers entered, we can now go further and calculate the average of the numbers. Where do we calculate the average—within the `while` loop or outside of it?

In the case at hand, calculating an average requires that both a final sum and the number of items in that sum be available. The average is then computed by dividing the final sum by the number of items. At this point, we must ask, "At what point in the program is the correct sum available, and at what point is the number of items available?" In reviewing Program 6-6 we see that the correct sum needed for calculating the average is available after the `while` loop is finished. In fact, the sole purpose of the `while` loop is to ensure that the numbers are entered and added correctly to produce a correct sum. After the loop is finished, we also have a count of the number of items used in the sum. However, due to the way the `while` loop was constructed, the number in `count` (5) when the loop is finished is 1 more than the number of items (4) used to obtain the total. Knowing this, we simply subtract one from `count` before using it to determine the average. With this as background, see if you can read and understand Program 6-7.

Program 6-7

```cpp
#include <iostream>
#include <iomanip>
using namespace std;

int main()
{
  const int MAXNUMS = 4;
  int count;
  double num, total, average;

  cout << "\nThis program will ask you to enter "
       << MAXNUMS << " numbers.\n";
  count = 1;
  total = 0;

  cout << setiosflags(ios::fixed) << setprecision(3);

  while (count <= MAXNUMS)
  {
    cout << "Enter a number: ";
    cin  >> num;
    total = total + num;
    count++;
  }

  count--;
  average = total / count;
  cout << "\nThe average of the numbers is " << average << endl;

  return 0;
}
```

Program 6-7 is almost identical to Program 6-6, except for the calculation of the average. We have also removed the constant display of the total within and after the `while` loop. The loop in Program 6-7 is used to enter and add four numbers. Immediately after the loop is exited, the average is computed and displayed.

A sample run of Program 6-7 follows:

```
This program will ask you to enter 4 numbers.
Enter a number: 26.2
Enter a number: 5
Enter a number: 103.456
Enter a number: 1267.89

The average of the numbers is 350.637
```

SENTINELS

All of the loops we have created thus far have been examples of fixed-count loops, where a counter has been used to control the number of loop iterations. However, you can also use a `while` statement to construct variable-condition loops. For example, when entering grades we may not want to count the number of grades that will be entered, but would prefer to enter the grades continuously and, at the end, type in a special data value to signal the end of data input.

In computer programming, data values used to signal either the start or end of a data series are called **sentinels**. The sentinel values must, of course, be selected so as not to conflict with legitimate data values. For example, if we were constructing a program to process a student's grades, and assuming that no extra credit is given that could produce a grade higher than 100, we could use any grade higher than 100 as a sentinel value. Program 6-8 illustrates this concept. In Program 6-8, data is continuously requested and accepted until a number larger than 100 is entered. Entry of a number higher than 100 alerts the program to exit the `while` loop and display the sum of the numbers entered.

A sample run of Program 6-8 is shown below. As long as grades less than or equal to 100 are entered, the program continues to request and accept additional data. When a number less than or equal to 100 is entered, the program adds this number to the total. When a number greater than 100 is entered, the `while` loop is exited and the sum of the grades that were entered is displayed.

```
To stop entering grades, type in any number greater than 100.

Enter a grade: 95
Enter a grade: 100
Enter a grade: 82
Enter a grade: 101

The total of the grades is 277
```

Program 6-8

```cpp
#include <iostream>
using namespace std;

int main()
{
  const int HIGHGRADE = 100;
  double grade = 0;
  double total = 0;

  cout << "\nTo stop entering grades, type in any number";
  cout << " greater than 100.\n\n";

  while (grade <= HIGHGRADE)
  {
    total = total + grade;
    cout << "Enter a grade: ";
    cin  >> grade;
  }

  cout << "\nThe total of the grades is " << total << endl;

  return 0;
}
```

break AND continue STATEMENTS

Two useful statements in connection with repetition statements are the break and continue statements. We have encountered the break statement in relation to the switch statement. The general
form of this statement is:

```cpp
break;
```

A break statement, as its name implies, forces an immediate break, or exit, from the switch and
while statements (which you've already encountered) and the for and do-while statements (which
are presented in upcoming sections).

For example, execution of the following while loop is immediately terminated if a number greater
than 76 is entered.

The break statement violates pure structured programming principles because it provides a second,
nonstandard exit from a loop. Nevertheless, the break statement is very useful for breaking out of
loops when an unusual condition is detected. The break statement is also used to exit from a switch
statement, but this is because the desired case has been detected and processed.

```
while(count <= 10)
{
  cout << "Enter a number: ";
  cin  >> num;
  if (num > 76)
  {
    cout << "You lose!\n";
    break;        // break out of the loop
  }
  else
    cout << "Keep on trucking!\n";
  count++;
}
// break jumps to here
```

The `continue` statement is similar to the `break` statement, but applies only to loops created with `while`, `do-while`, and `for` statements. The general format of a `continue` statement is:

$$continue;$$

When a `continue` is encountered in a loop, the next iteration of the loop immediately begins. For `while` loops, this means that execution is automatically transferred to the top of the loop and re-evaluation of the tested expression is initiated. Although the `continue` statement has no direct effect on a `switch` statement, it can be included within a `switch` statement that itself is contained in a loop. Here the effect of `continue` is the same: the next loop iteration begins.

As a general rule, the `continue` statement is less useful than the `break` statement, but it is convenient for skipping over data that should not be processed while remaining in a loop. For example, invalid grades are simply ignored in the following section of code and only valid grades are added to the total:[2]

```
while (count < 30)
{
  cout << "Enter a grade: ";
  cin >> grade;
  if(grade < 0 || grade > 100)
    continue;
  total = total + grade;
  count++;
}
```

---

[2]The `continue` statement is not essential, however, and the selection could have been written as:
```
if (grade >= 0 && grade <= 100)
{
  total = total + grade;
  count++;
}
```

THE NULL STATEMENT

All statements must be terminated by a semicolon. A semicolon with nothing preceding it is also a valid statement, called the **null statement**. Thus, the statement

;

is a null statement. You can think of this as a do-nothing statement that is used where a statement is syntactically required, but no action is called for. Null statements typically are used with either `while` or `for` statements. An example of a `for` statement using a null statement is found in Program 6-9 in the next section.

Exercises 6.3

1. Rewrite Program 6-6 to compute the total of eight numbers.

2. Rewrite Program 6-6 to display the prompt `"Please type in the total number of data values to be added: "`. In response to this prompt, the program should accept a user-entered number and then use this number to control the number of times the `while` loop is executed. Thus, if the user enters a 5 in response to the prompt, the program should request the input of five numbers and display the total after five numbers have been entered.

3. a. Write a C++ program to convert Celsius degrees to Fahrenheit. The program should request the starting Celsius value, the number of conversions to be made, and the increment between Celsius values. The display should have appropriate headings and list the Celsius value and the corresponding Fahrenheit value. Use the relationship *Fahrenheit = (9.0 / 5.0) * Celsius + 32.0.*

    b. Run the program written in Exercise 3a on a computer. Verify that your program starts at the correct starting Celsius value and contains the exact number of conversions specified in your input data.

4. a. Modify the program written in Exercise 3a to request the starting Celsius value, the ending Celsius value, and the increment. Thus, instead of the condition checking for a fixed count, the condition will check for the ending Celsius value.

    b. Run the program written in Exercise 4a on a computer. Verify that your output starts at the correct beginning value and ends at the correct ending value.

5. Rewrite Program 6-7 to compute the average of ten numbers.

6. Rewrite Program 6-7 to display the prompt: `"Please type in the total number of data values to be averaged: "`. In response to this prompt, the program should accept a user-entered number and then use this number to control the number of times the `while` loop is executed. Thus, if the user enters a 6 in response to the prompt, the program should request the input of six numbers and display the average of the next six numbers entered.

7. By mistake, a programmer put the statement `average = total / count;` within the `while` loop immediately after the statement `total = total + num;` in Program 6-7. Thus, the `while` loop becomes:

```
while (count <= MAXNUMS)
{
   cout << "Enter a number: ";
   cin  >> num;
   total = total + num;
   average = total / count;
   count++;
}
```

Will the program yield the correct result with this `while` loop?

From a programming perspective, which `while` loop is better ? Why?

8. An arithmetic series is defined by

$$a + (a + d) + (a + 2d) + (a + 3d) + ... + (a + (n-1)d)$$

where a is the first term, d is the "common difference," and n is the number of terms to be added. Using this information, write a C++ program that uses a `while` loop to both display each term and determine the sum of the arithmetic series having $a = 1$, $d = 3$, and $n = 100$. Make sure that your program displays the value it has calculated.

9. A geometric series is defined by

$$a + ar + ar^2 + ar^3 + ... + ar^{n-1}$$

where a is the first term, r is the "common ratio," and n is the number of terms in the series. Using this information, write a C++ program that uses a `while` loop to both display each term and determine the sum of a geometric series having $a = 1$, $r = 0.5$, and $n = 100$. Make sure that your program displays the value it has calculated.

10. In addition to the arithmetic average of a set of numbers, both a geometric and harmonic mean can be calculated. The geometric mean of a set of n numbers x_1, x_2, ... x_n is defined as

$$\sqrt[n]{x_1 \cdot x_2 \cdot ... \cdot x_n}$$

and the harmonic mean as

$$\frac{n}{\dfrac{1}{x_1} + \dfrac{1}{x_2} + ... + \dfrac{1}{x_n}}$$

Using these formulas, write a C++ program that continues to accept numbers until the number 999 is entered, and then calculates and displays both the geometric and harmonic means of the entered numbers. (*Hint*: It will be necessary for your program to correctly count the number of values entered.)

11. a. The following data were collected on a recent automobile trip.

	Mileage	Gallons
Start of trip:	22495	Full tank
	22841	12.2
	23185	11.3
	23400	10.5
	23772	11.0
	24055	12.2
	24434	14.7
	24804	14.3
	25276	15.2

Write a C++ program that accepts a mileage and a gallons value and calculates the miles-per-gallon (mpg) achieved for that segment of the trip. The miles-per-gallon is obtained as the difference in mileage between fill-ups divided by the number of gallons of gasoline used in the fill-up.

b. Modify the program written for Exercise 11a to additionally compute and display the cumulative mpg achieved after each fill-up. The cumulative mpg is calculated as the difference between each fill-up mileage and the mileage at the start of the trip divided by the sum of the gallons used to that point in the trip.

12. a. A bookstore summarizes its monthly transactions by keeping the following information for each book in stock:

    Book identification number
    Inventory balance at the beginning of the month
    Number of copies received during the month
    Number of copies sold during the month

Write a C++ program that accepts this data for each book and then displays the book identification number and an updated book inventory balance using the relationship:

New balance   = *Inventory balance at the beginning of the month*
       + *Number of copies received during the month*
       − *Number of copies sold during the month*

Your program should use a `while` loop with a fixed-count condition so that information on only three books is requested.

b. Run the program written in Exercise 12a on a computer. Review the display produced by your program and verify that the output produced is correct.

13. Modify the program you wrote for Exercise 12a to keep requesting and displaying results until a sentinel identification value of 999 is entered. Run the program on a computer.

6.4 FOR LOOPS

In C++, a `for` loop is constructed using a `for` statement. This statement performs the same functions as the `while` statement, but uses a different form. In many situations, especially those that use a fixed-count condition, the `for` statement format is easier to use than its `while` statement equivalent. The general syntax of the `for` statement is:

```
for (initializing list; expression; altering list)
   statement;
```

Although the `for` statement looks a little complicated, it is really quite simple if we consider each of its parts separately.

Within the parentheses of the `for` statement are three items, separated by semicolons. Each of these items is optional, but *the semicolons must be present.*

In its most common form, the *initializing list* consists of a single statement used to set the starting (initial) value of a counter, the *expression* contains the maximum or minimum value the counter can have and determines when the loop is finished, and the *altering list* provides the increment value that is added to or subtracted from the counter each time the loop is executed. Examples of simple `for` statements having this form are:

```
for (count = 1; count < 10; count = count + 1)
   cout << count;
```

and

```
for (i = 5; i <= 15; i = i + 2)
   cout <<  i;
```

In the first `for` statement, the counter variable is named `count`, the initial value assigned to `count` is 1, the loop continues as long as the value in `count` is less than 10, and the value of `count` is incremented by 1 each time through the loop. In the next `for` statement, the counter variable is named `i`, the initial value assigned to `i` is 5, the loop continues as long as `i`'s value is less than or equal to 15, and the value of `i` is incremented by 2 each time through the loop. In both cases, a `cout` statement is used to display the value of the counter. Another example of a `for` loop is given in Program 6-9.

When Program 6-9 is executed, the following display is produced:

```
NUMBER    SQUARE ROOT
------    -----------
   1         1.00000
   2         1.41421
   3         1.73205
   4         2.00000
   5         2.23607
```

Program 6-9

```cpp
#include <iostream>
#include <iomanip>
#include <cmath>
using namespace std;

const int MAXCOUNT = 5;

int main()
{
    int count;

    cout << "NUMBER     SQUARE ROOT\n";
    cout << "------     -----------\n";

    cout << setiosflags(ios::showpoint);
    for (count = 1; count <= MAXCOUNT; count++)
      cout << setw(4) << count
           << setw(15) << sqrt(double(count)) << endl;

    return 0;
}
```

The first two displayed lines are produced by the two cout statements placed before the for statement. The remaining output is produced by the for loop. This loop begins with the for statement and is executed as follows.

The initial value assigned to the counter variable count is 1. Since the value in count does not exceed the final value of 5, the execution of the cout statement within the loop produces the display:

```
1    1.000000
```

Control is then transferred back to the for statement, which then increments the value in count to 2, and the loop is repeated, producing the display:

```
2    1.414214
```

This process continues until the value in count exceeds the final value of 5, producing the complete output table. For comparison purposes, a while loop equivalent to the for loop contained in Program 6-9 is:

```cpp
count = 1;
while (count <= MAXCOUNT)
{
    cout << setw(4) << count
         << setw(15) << setiosflags(ios::showpoint)
         << sqrt(double(count)) << endl;
    count++;
}
```

6

As seen in this example, the difference between the `for` and `while` loops is the placement of the initialization, condition test, and incrementing items. The grouping of these items in the `for` statement is very convenient when fixed-count loops must be constructed. See if you can determine the output produced by Program 6-10.

Program 6-10

```cpp
#include <iostream>
using namespace std;

int main()
{
  int count;

  for (count = 2; count <= 20; count = count + 2)
    cout << count << "   ";

  return 0;
}
```

Did you figure it out? The loop starts with a `count` initialized to 2, stops when `count` exceeds 20, and increments `count` in steps of 2. The output of Program 6-10 is:

```
2   4   6   8   10   12   14   16   18   20
```

The `for` statement does not require that any of the items in parentheses be present or that they be used for initializing or altering the values in the expression statements. However, the two semicolons must be present within the `for` statement's parentheses. For example, the construction `for ( ; count <= 20 ;)` is valid.

If the initializing list is missing, the initialization step is omitted when the `for` statement is executed. This, of course, means that the programmer must provide the required initializations before the `for` statement is encountered. Similarly, if the altering list is missing, any expressions needed to alter the evaluation of the tested expression must be included directly within the statement part of the loop. The `for` statement only ensures that all expressions in the initializing list are executed once, before evaluation of the tested expression, and that all expressions in the altering list are executed at the end of the loop before the tested expression is rechecked. Thus, Program 6-10 can be rewritten in any of the three ways shown in Programs 6-10a, 6-10b, and 6-10c.

Program 6-10a

```cpp
#include <iostream>
using namespace std;

int main()
{
  int count;

  count = 2;     // initializer outside for statement
  for ( ; count <= 20; count = count + 2)
    cout << count << "   ";

  return 0;
}
```

Program 6-10b

```cpp
#include <iostream>
using namespace std;

int main()
{
  int count;

  count = 2;                         // initializer outside for loop
  for( ; count <= 20; )
  {
    cout << count << "   ";
    count = count + 2;        // alteration statement
  }

  return 0;
}
```

Program 6-10c

```cpp
#include <iostream>
using namespace std;

int main()    // all expressions within the for statement's parentheses
{
  int count;

  for (count = 2; count <= 20; cout << count << "   ", count = count + 2);

  return 0;
}
```

In Program 6-10a, `count` is initialized outside the `for` statement and the first list inside the parentheses is left blank. In Program 6-10b, both the initializing list and the altering list are removed from within the parentheses. Program 6-10b also uses a compound statement within the `for` loop, with the expression-altering statement included in the compound statement. Finally, Program 6-10c has included all items within the parentheses, so there is no need for any useful statement following the parentheses. Here the null statement satisfies the syntactical requirement of one statement to follow the `for`'s parentheses.

PROGRAMMING NOTE

Where to Place the Opening Braces

Two styles of `for` loops are used by professional C++ programmers. These styles only come into play when the `for` loop contains a compound statement. The style illustrated and used in the text takes the form:

```
for (expression)
{
    compound statement in here
}
```

An equally acceptable style that is used by many programmers places the initial brace of the compound statement on the first line. Using this style, a `for` loop appears as:

```
for (expression) {
    compound statement in here
}
```

The advantage of the first style is that the braces line up under one another, making it easier to locate brace pairs. The advantage of the second style is that it makes the code more compact and saves a display line, permitting more code to be viewed in the same display area. Both styles are used but are almost never intermixed. Select whichever style appeals to you or is specified by your professor or employer, and be consistent in its use. As always, the indentation you use within the compound statement (two or four spaces, or a tab) should also be consistent throughout all of your programs. The combination of styles that you select becomes a "signature" for your programming work.

Observe also in Program 6-10c that the altering list (the last set of items in parentheses) consists of two items, and that a comma has been used to separate these items. The use of commas to separate items in both the initializing and altering lists is required if either of these two lists contains more than one item. Lastly, note that Programs 6-10a, 6-10b, and 6-10c are all inferior to Program 6-10 and, although you may encounter them in your programming career, you should not use them. Including items other than loop control variables and their updating conditions within the for statement makes the for statement hard for you and other programmers to read, and can introduce unwanted effects. Keeping the loop control structure "clean," as is done in Program 6-10, is an important good programming practice.

Although the initializing and altering lists can be omitted from a for statement, omitting the tested expression results in an infinite loop. For example, such a loop is created by the statement:

```
for (count = 2;  ; count = count + 1)
    cout << count;
```

As with the while statement, both break and continue statements can be used within a for loop. The break forces an immediate exit from the for loop, as it does in the while loop. A continue statement, however, forces control to be passed to the altering list in a for statement, after which the tested expression is re-evaluated. This differs from the action of continue in a while statement, where control is passed directly to the re-evaluation of the tested expression.

To understand the enormous power of for loops, consider the task of printing a table of numbers from 1 to 10, including their squares and cubes, using a for statement. Such a table was previously produced using a while loop in Program 6-3. You may wish to review Program 6-3 and compare it to Program 6-11 to get a further sense of the equivalence of for and while loops. Figure 6-7 illustrates the internal workings of a for loop.

Program 6-11

```
#include <iostream>
#include <iomanip>
using namespace std;

int main()
{
const int MAXNUMS = 10;
   int num;
   cout << "NUMBER     SQUARE      CUBE\n"
        << "------     ------      ----\n";

 for (num = 1; num <= MAXNUMS; num++)
     cout << setw(3) << num << "          "
          << setw(3) << num * num << "         "
          << setw(4) << num * num * num << endl;

   return 0;
 }
```

6

FIGURE 6-7
for Loop Control

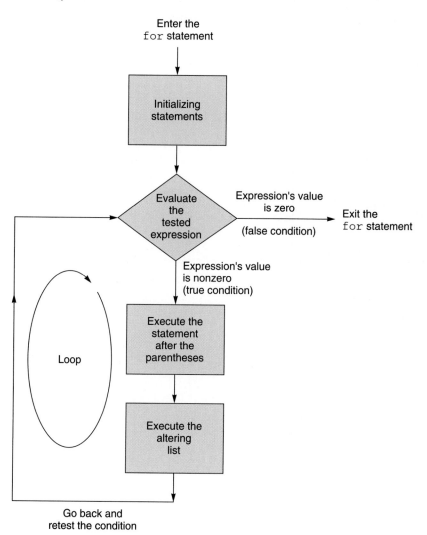

When the `for` loop is completed control is transferred to the first executable statement following the loop. To avoid the necessity of always illustrating these steps, a simplified set of flowchart symbols is available for describing `for` loops. A `for` statement can be represented by the following flowchart symbol:

Using this symbol, complete `for` loops can also be illustrated as shown in Figure 6-8.

FIGURE 6-8
Simplified `for` *Loop Flowchart*

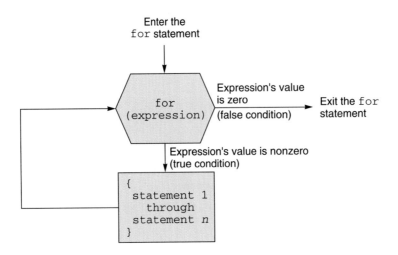

Running Program 6-11 produces the following display:

NUMBER	SQUARE	CUBE
------	------	----
1	1	1
2	4	8
3	9	27
4	16	64
5	25	125
6	36	216
7	49	343
8	64	512
9	81	729
10	100	1000

In the `for` statement of Program 6-11, simply changing the number 10 to a 1000 creates a loop that is executed 1000 times and produces a table of numbers from 1 to 1000. As with the `while` statement, this small change produces an immense increase in the processing and output provided by the program. Notice also that the expression `num++` was used in the altering list in place of the usual `num = num + 1`.

Do You Use a `for` or a `while` Loop?

Beginning programmers often wonder which loop structure they should use. Is a `for` loop or a `while` loop preferable? This is a good question, because both loop structures are pretest loops that, in C++, can be used to construct both fixed-count and variable-condition loops.

In almost all other computer languages, including Visual Basic and Pascal, the answer is relatively straightforward, because the `for` statement can only be used to construct fixed-count loops. Thus, in these languages, `for` statements are used to construct fixed-count loops and `while` statements are generally used only when constructing variable-condition loops.

In C++, this easy distinction does not hold, since each statement can be used to create each type of loop. The answer in C++, then, is really a matter of style. Since a `for` and `while` loop are interchangeable in C++, either loop is appropriate. Some professional programmers always use a `for` statement for every pretest loop they create and almost never use a `while` statement. Others always use a `while` statement and rarely use a `for` statement. Still a third group tends to retain the convention used in other languages—a `for` loop is generally used to create fixed count loops and a `while` loop is used to create variable condition loops. In C++ it is all a matter of style, and you will encounter all three styles in your programming career.

NESTED LOOPS

In many situations it is convenient to use a loop contained within another loop. Such loops are called **nested loops**. A simple example of a nested loop is:

```
for(i = 1; i <= 5; i++)        // start of outer loop
{                                  //
   cout << "\ni is now " << i << endl;  //
                                   //
   for(j = 1; j <= 4; j++)         // start of inner loop
     cout << "  j = " << j;        // end of inner loop
}                               // end of outer loop
```

The first loop, controlled by the value of i, is called the outer loop. The second loop, controlled by the value of j, is called the inner loop. Notice that all statements in the inner loop are contained within the boundaries of the outer loop and that we have used a different variable to control each loop. For each single trip through the outer loop, the inner loop runs through its entire sequence. Thus, each time the i counter increases by 1, the inner `for` loop executes completely. This situation is illustrated in Figure 6-9.

FIGURE 6-9
For Each Pass Through i , j *Loops*

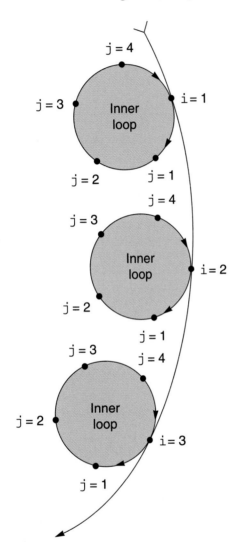

Program 6-12 includes the preceding code in a working program.

Program 6-12

```cpp
#include <iostream>
using namespace std;

int main()
{
```

(continued on next page)

6

```cpp
const int MAXI = 5;
const int MAXJ = 4;
int i, j;

for(i = 1; i <= MAXI; i++)     // start of outer loop
{                                          //
  cout << "\ni is now " << i << endl;   //
                                          //
  for(j = 1; j <= MAXJ; j++)             // start of inner loop
    cout << "  j = " << j;               // end of inner loop
}                                  // end of outer loop

cout << endl;

return 0;
}
```

The output of a sample run of Program 6-12 is:

```
i is now 1
  j = 1  j = 2  j = 3  j = 4
i is now 2
  j = 1  j = 2  j = 3  j = 4
i is now 3
  j = 1  j = 2  j = 3  j = 4
i is now 4
  j = 1  j = 2  j = 3  j = 4
i is now 5
  j = 1  j = 2  j = 3  j = 4
```

To illustrate the usefulness of a nested loop, we will use one to compute the average grade for each student in a class of 20 students. Each student has taken four exams during the course of the semester. The final grade is calculated as the average of these examination grades. The pseudocode describing how this computation can be done is:

> **For 20 times**
>   **Set the student grade total to zero**
>   **For 4 times**
>   **Input a grade**
>   **Add the grade to the total**
>   **EndFor // end of inner for loop**
>   **Calculate student's average grade**
>   **Print the student's average grade**
> **EndFor // end of outer for loop**

As described by the pseudocode, an outer loop consisting of 20 passes will be used to compute the average grade for each student. The inner loop will consist of four passes. One examination grade is entered in each inner loop pass. As each grade is entered it is added to the total for the student, and at the end of the loop the average is calculated and displayed. Since both outer and inner loops are fixed-count loops of 20 and 4, respectively, we will use for statements to create these loops (see Programming Note on the use of for and while statements in this section). Program 6-13 provides the C++ code corresponding to the pseudocode.

Program 6-13

```cpp
#include <iostream>
using namespace std;

int main()
{
  const int NUMGRADES = 4;
  const int NUMSTUDENTS = 20;
  int i,j;
  double grade, total, average;

  for (i = 1; i <= NUMSTUDENTS; i++) // start of outer loop
  {
    total = 0;                          // clear the total for this student
    for (j = 1; j <= NUMGRADES; j++)  // start of inner loop
    {
      cout << "Enter an examination grade for this student: ";
      cin >> grade;
      total = total + grade;          // add the grade into the total
    }                                   // end of the inner for loop
    average = total / NUMGRADES;     // calculate the average
    cout << "\nThe average for student " << i
        << " is " << average << "\n\n";
  }                                     // end of the outer for loop

  return 0;
}
```

In reviewing Program 6-13, pay particular attention to the initialization of total within the outer loop, before the inner loop is entered. As you can see, total is initialized 20 times, once for each student. Also notice that the average is calculated and displayed immediately after the inner loop is finished. Since the statements that compute and print the average are also contained within the outer loop, 20 averages are calculated and displayed. The entry and addition of each grade within the inner loop use techniques that should now be familiar to you.

A BIT OF BACKGROUND

The Blockhead

One mathematician of the Middle Ages who has had a profound influence on modern science is Leonardo of Pisa (1170–1250). In his youth he was called *Filus Bonacci,* which means "son of (Guglielmo) Bonacci," and the name stuck. Hence, he is commonly known today as Fibonacci. He traveled widely, met with scholars throughout the Mediterranean area, and produced four very significant works on arithmetic and geometry. One of his discoveries is the sequence of numbers that bears his name: 0,1, 1,2,3,5,8,13,.... After the first two values, 0 and 1, each number of the Fibonacci sequence is obtained from the sum of the preceding two numbers.

Fibonacci often referred to himself as Leonardo Bigollo, probably because *bigollo* is Italian for "traveler." However, another meaning of *bigollo* in Italian is "blockhead." Some people suspect he may have adopted this name to show the professors of his time what a blockhead—a person who had not been educated in their schools—could accomplish.

Some blockhead! The Fibonacci sequence alone describes such natural phenomena as the spiraling pattern of nautilus shells, elephant tusks, sheep horns, bird's claws, pineapples, and branching patterns of plants *and* the proliferation of rabbits.

The ratio of successively higher adjacent terms in the sequence also approaches the "golden section," a ratio that describes an aesthetically pleasing proportion used in the visual arts.

Exercises 6.4

1. Write individual `for` statements for the following cases:

    a. Use a counter named `i` that has an initial value of 1, a final value of 20, and an increment of 1.

    b. Use a counter named `icount` that has an initial value of 1, a final value of 20, and an increment of 2.

    c. Use a counter named `j` that has an initial value of 1, a final value of 100, and an increment of 5.

    d. Use a counter named `icount` that has an initial value of 20, a final value of 1, and an increment of -1.

    e. Use a counter named `icount` that has an initial value of 20, a final value of 1, and an increment of -2.

    f. Use a counter named `count` that has an initial value of 1.0, a final value of 16.2, and an increment of 0.2.

    g. Use a counter named `xcnt` that has an initial value of 20.0, a final value of 10.0, and an increment of -0.5.

2. Determine the number of times that each `for` loop is executed for the `for` statements written for Exercise 1.

3. Determine the value in total after each of the following loops is executed.

   a.
   ```
   total = 0;
   for (i = 1; i <= 10; i = i + 1)
     total = total + 1;
   ```

   b.
   ```
   total = 1;
   for (count = 1; count <+ 10; count = count + 1)
     total = total * 2;
   ```

   c.
   ```
   total = 0;
   for (i = 10; i <= 15; i = i + 1)
     total = total + i;
   ```

   d.
   ```
   total = 50;
   for (i = 1; i <=10; i = i + 1)
     total = total - i;
   ```

   e.
   ```
   total = 1;
   for (icnt = 1; icnt <= 8; ++icnt)
     total = total * icnt;
   ```

   f.
   ```
   total = 1.0;
   for (j = 1; j <= 5; ++j)
     total = total / 2.0;
   ```

4. Determine the output of the following program.

   ```
   #include <iostream>
   using namespace std;

   int main()
   {
       int i;

       for (i = 20; i >= 0; i = i - 4)
           cout << i << " ";

       return 0;
   }
   ```

5. Modify Program 6-11 to produce a table of the numbers zero through 20 in increments of 2, with their squares and cubes.

6. Modify Program 6-11 to produce a table of numbers from 10 to 1, instead of 1 to 10 as it currently does.

7. Write and run a C++ program that displays a table of 20 temperature conversions from Fahrenheit to Celsius. The table should start with a Fahrenheit value of 20 degrees and be incremented in values of 4 degrees. Recall that Celsius = (5.0/9.0) * (Fahrenheit - 32).

6

8. Modify the program written for Exercise 7 to initially request the number of conversions to be made.

9. A programmer starts with a salary of $25,000 and expects to receive a $1500 raise each year.

    a. Write a C++ program to compute and print the programmer's salary for each of the first 10 years and the total amount of money the programmer would receive over the 10-year period.

    b. Write a C++ program to compute and print the programmer's salary for 10 years if the programmer begins at $25,000 and receives a 5% raise each year.

10. The probability that an individual telephone call will last less than t minutes can be approximated by the exponential probability function

    Probability that a call lasts less than t minutes = 1 - e^{-t/a}

    where a is the average call length and e is Euler's number (2.71828). For example, assuming that the average call length is 2 minutes, the probability that a call will last less than 1 minute is calculated as $1 - e^{-1/2} = 0.3297$.

    Using this probability function, write a C++ program that calculates and displays a list of probabilities of a call lasting less than 1 to less than 10 minutes, in 1-minute increments.

11. a. The arrival rate of customers in a busy New York bank can be estimated using the Poisson probability function

    $$P(x) = \frac{\lambda^x e^{-\lambda}}{x!}$$

    where x = the number of customer arrivals per minute; λ = the average number of arrivals per minute; and e = Euler's number (2.71828). For example, if the average number of customers entering the bank is three customers per minute, then λ is equal to 3. Thus,

    Probability of one customer arriving in any one minute =

    $$P(x = 1) = \frac{3^1 e^{-3}}{1!} = 0.149561$$

    and

    probability of two customers arriving in any one minute =

    $$P(x = 2) = \frac{3^2 e^{-3}}{2!} = 0.224454$$

    Using the Poisson probability function, write a C++ program that calculates and displays the probability of 1 to 10 customer arrivals in any one minute when the average arrival rate is three customers per minute.

    b. The formula given in Exercise 11a is also applicable for estimating the arrival rate of planes at a busy airport (here, an arriving "customer" is an incoming airplane). Using this same formula, modify the program written in Exercise 11a to accept the average arrival rate as an input data item. Then run the modified program to determine the probability of zero to 10 planes attempting to land in any one-minute period at an airport during peak arrival times. Assume that the average arrival rate for peak arrival times is two planes per minute.

12. Write and run a program that calculates and displays the amount of money available in a bank account that initially has $1000 deposited in it and that earns 8% interest a year. Your program should display the amount available at the end of each year for a period of 10 years. Use the fact that the money available at the end of each year equals the amount of money in the account at the start of the year plus 0.08 times the amount available at the start of the year.

13. The Fibonacci sequence is 0, 1, 1, 2, 3, 5, 8, 13, ... where the first two terms are 0 and 1, and each term thereafter is the sum of the two preceding terms; that is $Fib[n] = Fib[n-1] + Fib[n-2]$. Using this information, write a C++ program that calculates the nth number in a Fibonacci sequence, where n is interactively entered into the program by the user. For example, if $n = 6$, the program should display the value 5.

14. A machine purchased for $28,000 is depreciated at a rate of $4000 a year for seven years. Write and run a C++ program that computes and displays a depreciation table for seven years. The table should have the form:

```
                    Depreciation Schedule
              ------------------------

                          End-of-year      Accumulated
    Year     Depreciation    value         depreciation
    ----     ------------  ----------      ------------

     1           4000        24000             4000
     2           4000        20000             8000
     3           4000        16000            12000
     4           4000        12000            16000
     5           4000         8000            20000
     6           4000         4000            24000
     7           4000            0            28000
```

15. A well-regarded manufacturer of widgets has been losing 4% of its sales each year. The annual profit for the firm is 10% of sales. This year the firm has had $10 million in sales and a profit of $1 million. Determine the expected sales and profit for the next 10 years. Write a program that produces the following display:

6

```
            Sales and Profit Projection
            --------------------------------

       Year            Expected sales        Projected profit
       ----            --------------         ----------------
        1              $10000000.00            $1000000.00
        2              $ 9600000.00            $ 960000.00
        3                    .                       .
        .                    .                       .
        .                    .                       .
        .                    .                       .
       10                    .                       .
            --------------------------------------------------
       Totals:         $     .                 $     .
```

16. Four experiments are performed, each producing six test results. The results for each experiment are given below. Write a program using a nested loop to compute and display the average of the test results for each experiment.

```
Experiment 1 results:   23.2   31      16.9   27      25.4   28.6
Experiment 2 results:   34.8   45.2    27.9   36.8    33.4   39.4
Experiment 3 results:   19.4   16.8    10.2   20.8    18.9   13.4
Experiment 4 results:   36.9   39      49.2   45.1    42.7   50.6
```

17. Modify the program written for Exercise 16 so that the number of test results for each experiment is entered by the user. Write your program so that a different number of test results can be entered for each experiment.

18. a. A bowling team consists of five players. Each player bowls three games. Write a C++ program that uses a nested loop to enter each player's individual scores and then computes and displays the average score for each bowler. Assume that each bowler has the following scores:

	game 1	game 2	game 3
bowler 1:	286	252	265
bowler 2:	212	186	215
bowler 3:	252	232	216
bowler 4:	192	201	235
bowler 5:	186	236	272

b. Modify the program written for Exercise 18a to calculate and display the average team score. (*Hint*: Use a second variable to store the total of all the players' scores.)

19. Rewrite the program written for Exercise 18a to eliminate the inner loop. To do this, you will have to input three scores for each bowler rather than one at a time.

20. Write a program that calculates and displays values for y when

$$y = xz/(x - z)$$

Your program should calculate y for values of x ranging between 1 and 5 and values of z ranging between 2 and 6. Use x to control the outer loop and increment x in steps of 0.2. Use z to control the inner loop and increment z in steps of 1. Your program should also display the message `"function undefined"` when the x and z values are equal.

21. Write a program that calculates and displays the yearly amount available if $1000 is invested in a bank account for 10 years. Your program should display the amounts available for interest rates from 6% to 12% inclusively, in 1% increments. Use a nested loop, with the outer loop controlling the interest rate and the inner loop controlling the years. Use the fact that the money available at the end of each year equals the amount of money in the account at the start of the year, plus the interest rate times the amount available at the start of the year.

6.5 DO-WHILE LOOPS

As you have learned, the `while` and `for` statements evaluate an expression at the start of the repetition loop; that's why they are always used to create pretest loops. Now it's time to turn our attention to posttest loops, or exit-controlled loops . In C++, you create such a loop by constructing a `do-while` loop as illustrated in Figure 6-10. Notice that a `do-while` loop continues iterations through the loop while the condition is `true`, and ends when the condition is `false`.

FIGURE 6-10
The do-while *Loop Structure*

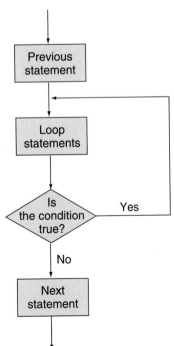

In C++, a posttest loop is created using a do-while statement. As its name implies, this statement allows us to do some statements before an expression is evaluated at the end of the loop. The general form of C++'s do-while statement is:

```
do
    statement;
while (expression);
```

As with all C++ programs, the single statement within the do-while may be replaced with a compound statement. A flow-control diagram illustrating the operation of the do-while statement is shown in Figure 6-11.

FIGURE 6-11
The do-while *Statement's Flow of Control*

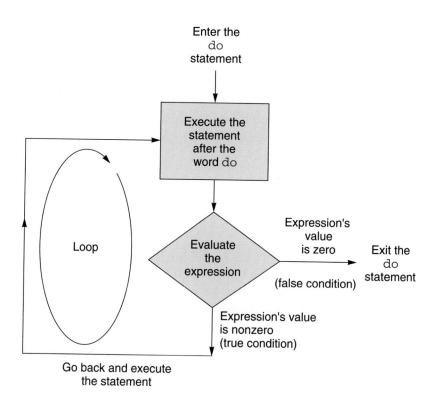

As illustrated, all statements within the do-while statement are executed at least once before the expression is evaluated. Then, if the expression has a nonzero value, the statements are executed again. This process continues until the expression evaluates to zero (becomes false). For example, consider the following do statement:

```
do
{
  cout << "\nEnter a price: ";
  cin  >> price;
  if (fabs(price - SENTINEL) < 0.0001)
    break;
  salestax = RATE * price;
  cout << setiosflags(ios::showpoint)
       << setprecision(2)
       << "The sales tax is $ " << salestax;
}
while (price != SENTINEL);    // don't forget the final semi-colon
```

Observe that only one prompt and cin statement are used here, because the tested expression is evaluated at the end of the loop.

As with all repetition statements, the do statement can always replace or be replaced by an equivalent while or for statement. The choice of which statement to use depends on the application and the style preferred by the programmer. In general, the while and for statements are preferred because they clearly let anyone reading the program know what is being tested "right up front" at the top of the program loop.

VALIDITY CHECKS

The do statement is particularly useful in examining user-entered input for specific values, which is referred to as filtering the data, and providing data validation checks. For example, assume that an operator is required to enter a valid customer identification number between the numbers 1000 and 1999. A number outside this range is to be rejected and a new request for a valid number made. The following section of code provides the necessary data filter to verify the entry of a valid identification number:

```
do
{
  cout << "\nEnter an identification number: ";
  cin  >> idNum;
}
while (idNum < 1000 || idNum > 1999);
```

Here, a request for an identification number is repeated until a valid number is entered. This section of code is "bare bones" in that it neither alerts the operator to the cause of the new request for data nor allows premature exit from the loop if a valid identification number cannot be found. Clearly, both of these conditions are less than optimal for a well-functioning program. Alternative code that removes the first drawback is:

```
do
{
  cout << "\nEnter an identification number: ";
  cin  >> idNum;
  if (idNum < 1000 || idNum > 1999)
  {
    cout << "An invalid number was just entered\n";
    cout << "Please check the ID number and re-enter\n";
  }
  else
    break;    // break if a valid id num was entered
} while(1);   // this expression is always true
```

Here we have used a break statement to exit from the loop. Since the expression evaluated by the do statement is always 1 (true), an infinite loop has been created that is only exited when the break statement is encountered.

Exercises 6.5

1. a. Using a do-while statement, write a program to accept a grade. The program should request a grade continuously as long as an invalid grade is entered. An invalid grade is any grade less than 0 or greater than 100. After a valid grade has been entered, your program should display the value of the grade entered.

    b. Modify the program written for Exercise 1a so that the user is alerted when an invalid grade has been entered.

    c. Modify the program written for Exercise 1b so that it allows the user to exit the program by entering the number 999.

    d. Modify the program written for Exercise 1b so that it automatically terminates after five invalid grades are entered.

2. a. Write a program that continuously requests a grade to be entered. If the grade is less than 0 or greater than 100, your program should print an appropriate message informing the user that an invalid grade has been entered, else the grade should be added to a total. When a grade of 999 is entered, the program should exit the repetition loop and compute and display the average of the valid grades entered.

    b. Run the program written in Exercise 2a on a computer and verify the program using appropriate test data.

3. a. Write a program to reverse the digits of a positive integer number. For example, if the number 8735 is entered, the number displayed should be 5378. (*Hint*: Use a do statement and continuously strip off and display the units digit of the number. If the variable num initially contains the number entered, the units digit is obtained as num % 10. After a units digit is displayed, dividing the number by 10 sets up the number for the next iteration. Thus, 8735 % 10 is 5 and 8735 / 10 is 873. The do statement should continue as long as the remaining number is not zero).

    b. Run the program written in Exercise 3a on a computer and verify the program using appropriate test data.

4. Repeat any of the exercises in Section 6.3 using a do-while statement rather than a while statement.

5. Given a number *n,* and an approximation for its square root, a closer approximation to the actual square root can be obtained using the formula:

$$\text{new approximation} = \frac{(n/\text{previous approximation}) + \text{previous approximation}}{2}$$

Using this information, write a C++ program that prompts the user for a number and an initial guess at its square root. Using this input data, your program should calculate an approximation to the square root that is accurate to 0.00001. (*Hint*: Stop the loop when the difference between the two approximations is less than 0.00001.)

6. This is a challenging problem for those who know a little calculus. The Newton-Raphson method can be used to find the roots of any equation $y(x) = 0$. In this method the $(i + 1)^{st}$ approximation, $x_{i+1},$ to a root of $y(x) = 0$ is given in terms of the ith approximation, $x_i,$ by the formula

$$x_{i+1} = x_i - y(x_i) / y'(x_i)$$

For example, if $y(x) = 3x^2 + 2x - 2$, then $y'(x) = 6x + 2$, and the roots are found by making a reasonable guess for a first approximation $x_1,$ and iterating using the equation

$$x_{i+1} = x_i - (3x_i^2 + 2x_i - 2) / (6x_i + 2)$$

    a. Using the Newton-Raphson method, find the two roots of the equation $3x^2 + 2x - 2 = 0$. (*Hint*: There is one positive root and one negative root.)

    b. Extend the program written for Exercise 6a so that it will find the roots of any function $y(x) = 0$, when the function for $y(x)$ and the derivative of $y(x)$ are placed in the code.

6.6 PROGRAM DESIGN AND DEVELOPMENT: UML STATE DIAGRAMS

The UML object diagrams presented in Section 5.5 are considered static models because they portray objects and classes at a fixed point in time, in the same manner that a photograph captures a scene in a single moment. State diagrams present the transition of an object's state over time, and are

6

therefore considered dynamic models. A state diagram shows the different states that an object can have and the events that cause these states to appear. In effect, a state diagram describes how an object's attributes change over time.

The most important part of creating state diagrams is clearly specifying the events that can cause a change in an object's state. Each event then becomes associated with a method that is included in the class model. Figure 6-12 illustrates that an event becomes coded as a class method. It is a method that permits a change in an object's state to occur.

FIGURE 6-12
The State Model Identifies Operations to Be Included in the Class Diagram

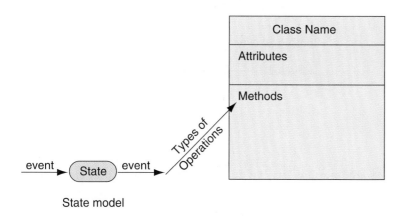

A state diagram consists of events and states. An **event** is defined as an individual signal (sometimes called a stimulus) from one object to another. For example, turning the key in a car's ignition is a signal to the electrical system to turn on or off. In object terms, turning the key is an event. Similarly, pushing the button on an elevator is considered an event. The press of the button is a signal to the elevator to move to another floor.

In contrast to events are states. An object's **state**, in its simplest form, is defined by the values of an object's attributes. For example, a switch that can be either on or off has two states: on and off. Similarly, if a rectangle is described by three attributes—length, width, and position—giving values to these attributes defines a single state for a rectangle object.

In a state diagram, each object has a clearly defined set of states. For example, if the system being programmed has three objects, then you will typically have three state diagrams, one for each object, each with its own set of states. Each state diagram, then, is a structured network of events and states. Figure 6-13 illustrates the basic symbols and notation used in a state diagram. As shown, the two primary symbols are a flow line, which denotes an event, and a rectangle with rounded corners, which denotes a state. Each event shown in a state diagram can be augmented by a guard, attribute, or action, which are explained later in this section. Similarly, each state can have an optional state name listed in the state rectangle, as well as activity information.

FIGURE 6-13
State Diagram Notation

Event causes transition between states:

State-1 —*event*→ State-2

Event with attribute:

State-1 —*event (attribute)*→ State-2

Initial and final states:

●→ Initial State → Intermediate State → ◉ *result*

Action on a transition:

State-1 —*event / action*→ State-2

Guarded transition:

State-1 —*event [guard]*→ State-2

Output event on a transition:

State-1 —*event1 / event2*→ State-2

Actions and activity while in a state:

> **State Name**
> *entry* / entry-action
> do: activity-A
> *event-1* / action-1
> . . .
> *exit* / exit-action

Sending an event to another object:

State-1 —*event1*→ State-2
        ⋮ *event2*
      Class-3

Notice in Figure 6-13 that events separate states. A state has duration in that it exists over an interval of time and only changes in response to an event, which is assumed to occur in zero time. For example, turning a car's ignition key to start the engine is an event. Once the car's engine is started the state of the engine, which is running, is assumed to continue until an event occurs that turns the engine off. Figure 6-14 illustrates a state diagram for a car's ignition system.

FIGURE 6-14
A Car's Ignition System State Diagram

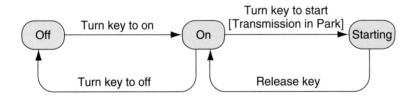

As shown, the ignition system consists of three states: On, Off, and Starting. The events associated with these states are "Turn key to on," "Turn key to start," "Release key," and "Turn key to off." Notice that the event "Turn key to start" has the precondition "Transmission in Park." Preconditions, which are also referred to as guards, are listed within square brackets after or under the event's name. A precondition specifies that the event cannot take place unless the precondition is satisfied. In this case, the "Turn key to start" will not force a change in state unless the transmission is in Park.

Events are always one-way messages from one object to another. If the message also provides data values to an object, the data values are listed in parentheses following the event name. As we have seen, these data values are referred to as an event's attributes. Since each event eventually defines an operation, which in C++ is coded as a method, an event's attributes become the method's arguments. As one-way signals, however, events never receive a return value from the implemented method. Any reply from the receiving object is considered a separate event to the sending object, which must be realized using another method.

In addition to conditions and attributes, an event may also be associated with some instantaneous action. For example, pressing the right button on a mouse may cause a pop-up menu to appear, while the state of the original menu item becomes highlighted. Such actions are listed after the event and are separated by a forward slash (/) from the event description, as shown in Figure 6-15. These actions form the basis for events that interact with other objects.

FIGURE 6-15
An Example of an Event Activity

Just as events may have actions associated with them, states may have activities. The difference between an action and an activity is the time needed to accomplish them. Actions, as we have noted, are assumed to be accomplished in zero-time (instantaneously), while activities take time to complete. As such, activities are associated with states. The notation *do: activity* within a state rectangle denotes that the activity begins when the state is entered and terminates when the state is left. For example, as illustrated in Figure 6-16, if the state of a house bell-chime system is ringing in response to the event "Push bell button," the action is "ring the chimes."

FIGURE 6-16
A State with an Activity

A state diagram can either represent a continuously operating system or a finite, one-time, lifecycle. For example, making one phone call, or filling a car with a tank of gas, can be modeled as a finite, one-time, activity. The operation of the phone or the gas pump, however, (where the system goes from idle to active) is a continuous operation. One-time activities are typically modeled by a state diagram where the initial state, which represents the creation of an object, is shown by a solid circle. The final state, which represents the end of the cycle and the destruction of an object, is shown by a bull's eye circle, as illustrated in Figure 6-17.

FIGURE 6-17
A State Diagram of a Water Sprinkler

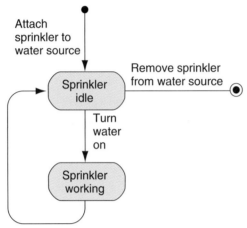

Although state diagrams almost always have an initial state, they may have one or more final states, or no final state. For example, Figure 6-18 illustrates a state diagram for an elevator. As shown, the elevator initially begins at the first floor, but once in operation it can be positioned at any other floor. Its activity is restricted to moving either up or down between floors, and remains at its last destination until a new activity takes place. In the next section, we will create a C++ class that implements these activities and states.

FIGURE 6-18
A State Diagram for an Elevator

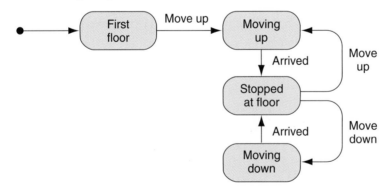

Exercises 6.6

1. Describe the differences between a class and state diagram.

2. Why are state diagrams referred to as dynamic models?

3. Construct a state diagram for a game of checkers.

4. Construct a state diagram for using the brakes on a car.

5.   Construct a state diagram for shifting a car's transmission. Assume that there are six gears; Park, Reverse, Neutral, Drive, Drive-1, and Drive-2.

6.   The control switch on a thermostat has three positions; Cool, Off, and Heat. Construct a state diagram for the switch.

7.   Draw a state diagram for a traffic light that can be in one of three states: green, yellow, or red.

8.   List the sequence of events that occur when you select an item from a soda vending machine. The sequence should start when a customer puts money in the machine and end when the customer removes a can of soda. Using this list, complete the sequence diagram shown in Figure 6-19.

FIGURE 6-19

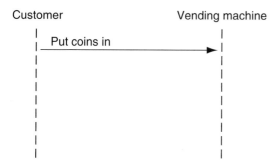

Each vertical line on the sequence diagram corresponds to an object, while the horizontal lines correspond to events. The arrow head on the event line corresponds to the event receiver, while the line's tail corresponds to the event sender. Although time is assumed to increase from the top of the diagram to the bottom, the spacing between events is not drawn to time scale. The sequence of events, from first to last, however, is indicated on the diagram starting with the first event shown and ending with the last event.

Once you have completed the sequence diagram, use it to create a state diagram for the vending machine.

9.   List the sequence of events that occur in using an ATM machine. The sequence should start when the customer inserts the ATM card and end when the card is returned. From this list, complete the sequence diagram shown in Figure 6-20.

FIGURE 6-20

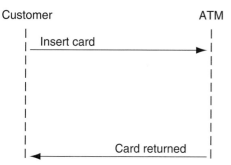

Each vertical line on the sequence diagram corresponds to an object, while the horizontal lines correspond to events. The arrow head on the event line corresponds to the event receiver, while the line's tail corresponds to the event sender. Although time is assumed to increase from the top of the diagram to the bottom, the spacing between events is not drawn to time scale. The sequence of events, from first to last, however, is indicated on the diagram starting with the first event shown and ending with the last event.

Once you have completed the sequence diagram, use it to create a state diagram for the ATM machine.

10. List the sequence of events that occur in the making of a phone call. The sequence should start when the caller picks up the phone and end when the caller hangs up. From this list, complete the sequence diagram shown in Figure 6-21.

FIGURE 6-21

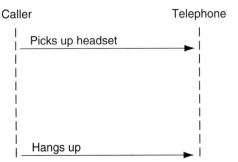

Each vertical line on the sequence diagram corresponds to an object, while the horizontal lines correspond to events. The arrow head on the event line corresponds to the event receiver, while the line's tail corresponds to the event sender. Although time is assumed to increase from the top of the diagram to the bottom, the spacing between events is not drawn to time scale. The sequence of events, from first to last, however, is indicated on the diagram starting with the first event shown and ending with the last event.

Once you have completed the sequence diagram, use it to create a state diagram for the phone system.

6.7 APPLICATIONS: RANDOM NUMBERS AND SIMULATIONS

There are many commercial and scientific problems in which probability must be considered or statistical sampling techniques must be used. For example, in simulating automobile traffic flow or telephone usage patterns, statistical models are required. In addition, applications such as simple computer games and more involved gaming scenarios can only be described statistically. All of these statistical

6

models require the generation of **random numbers**—that is, a series of numbers whose order cannot be predicted.

In practice, it is hard to find truly random numbers. Dice are never perfect, cards are never shuffled completely randomly, and digital computers can handle numbers only within a finite range and with limited precision. The best one can do in most cases is generate **pseudorandom numbers**, which are sufficiently random for the task at hand.

Some computer languages contain a library method that produces random numbers; others do not. All C++ compilers provide a general-purpose method for creating random numbers named rand() that is defined in the Math class. This method produces a series of double-precision random numbers in the range 0.0 up to, but not including, 1.0.

The general procedure for creating a series of N random numbers in C++ is illustrated in Program 6-14, which uses the rand() method to generate a series of 10 random numbers.

Program 6-14

```cpp
#include <iostream>
#include <ctime>
#include <cmath>
using namespace std;

int main()
{
  double randValue;
  int i;

  srand(time(NULL));   // this generates the first "seed" value

  for (i = 1; i <= 10; i++)
  {
    randValue = rand();
    cout << randValue << endl;
  }

  return 0;
}
```

The following is the output produced by one run of Program 6-14:

```
25140
17626
21997
657
31803
29419
```

(continued on next page)

31873
3263
13106
24521

Each time Program 6-14 is executed, it will create a different series of ten random numbers.

Scaling

In practice, you'll typically need to make one modification to the random numbers produced by the rand() method. In most applications, the random numbers must be integers within a specified range, such as 1 to 100. The method for adjusting the random numbers produced by a random-number generator to reside within such ranges is called **scaling**.

Scaling random numbers to reside within the range 0.0 to 1.0 is easily accomplished by dividing the returned value of rand() by RAND_MAX.[3] Thus, the expression double(rand())/RAND_MAX produces a floating-point random number between 0.0 and 1.0.

Scaling a random number as an integer value between 0 and N - 1 is accomplished using either of the expressions int(double(rand())/RAND_MAX * N) or rand() % N. For example, the expression int(double(rand())/RAND_MAX * 100) produces a random integer between 0 and 99, as does the expression rand() % 100.

To produce an integer random number between 1 and N, you can use the expression:

1 + int(double(rand())/RAND_MAX * N) or the expression 1 + rand() % N.

For example, in simulating the roll of a die, the expression 1 + int(double(rand())/RAND_MAX * 6) produces a random integer between 1 and 6, as does the expression 1 + rand() % 6. In general, to produce a random integer between the numbers a and b, you can use the expression a + int(double(rand())/RAND_MAX * (b + 1 - a)) or the expression a + rand() % (b + 1 - a).

SIMULATIONS

A common use of random numbers is to simulate events, rather than going through the time and expense of constructing a real-life experiment. In this section, we present two examples that illustrate the general concepts and techniques frequently encountered in constructing simulations.

Coin Toss Simulation

The probability of having a single tossed coin turn up heads is 50%. Similarly, there is a 50% probability of having a single tossed coin turn up tails. Using these probabilities, we would expect a single coin that is tossed 1000 times to turn up heads 500 times and tails 500 times. In practice, however, this is never exactly realized for a single experiment consisting of 1000 tosses. Instead of actually tossing a

---

[3] RAND_MAX is the maximum number returned by rand(), and is compiler dependent.

coin 1000 times, we can use a random number generator to simulate these tosses. In particular, we will use the random number method developed in the previous application.

Figure 6-22 illustrates the class diagram for a coin that can be used in a coin toss simulation. As described by this diagram, each `CoinToss` object will contain a `heads` instance variable and a `tosses` instance variable. The `tosses` variable will be used to keep track of how many times the coin has been tossed, while the `heads` variable will keep track of how many times the head side came up. We do not need to keep count of the number of tails that appear because this number can always be calculated as `tosses-heads`.

The `flip()` method will be used to simulate tossing the coin as many times as indicated by the parameter `numTimes`. To determine the number of heads and tails, we will have to simulate random numbers in a manner that permits us to define a result of "heads" or "tails" from each generated number in a statistically correct way. There are a number of ways to do this.

FIGURE 6-22
A Class Diagram for a `CoinToss` *Class*

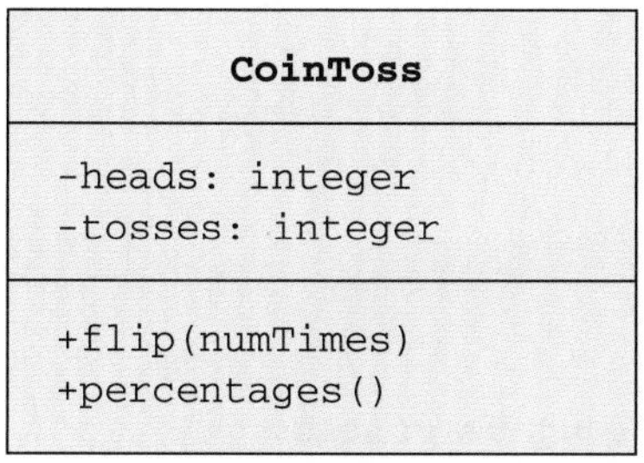

CoinToss
-heads: integer -tosses: integer
+flip(numTimes) +percentages()

One way is to scale the numbers generated by the `random()` method to make them integers between 1 and 100. Knowing that any single toss has a 50% chance of being either a head or a tail, we could then designate a "head" as an even random number and a "tail" as an odd random number. Another approach would be to use the generated values as is, and simply define a "head" as any number equal to or greater than 0.5 and any other result as a "tail." This is the approach we will adopt.

Having defined how we will create a single toss that has a 50% chance of turning up heads or tails, the generation of a sequence of tosses is rather simple: we use a fixed-count loop to generate the desired number of random numbers. For each random number generated, we identify the result as either a head or tail and increment the `heads` variable each time a head is indicated. We will initialize the `heads` and `tosses` variables to zero when a `CoinToss` object is created using the default values supplied by a default constructor. Given this initialization, the coin toss algorithm becomes:

> *Coin Toss Algorithm*
> > *For numTimes times*
> > > *Generate a random number between 0 and 1*
> > > *If the random number is equal to or greater than .5, increment the heads count*
> > > *Increment the tosses count*
> > *End For*

The implementation of this algorithm into a method named `flip()` is:

```
// this method tosses the coin numTimes
// and records the number of tosses and the number of heads
void CoinToss::flip(int numTimes)
{
  double randValue;
  int i;

  srand(time(NULL));   // this generates the first "seed" value

  for (i = 1; i <= numTimes; i++)
  {
    randValue = (double(rand())/RAND_MAX);
    if (randValue >= 0.5) heads++;
    tosses++;
  }
}
```

The algorithm for calculating the percentages of heads and tails for the `percentages()` method is:

> **Percentage Algorithm**
> **If the number of tosses equals zero**
>   **Display a message indicating that no tosses were made**
> **Else**
>   **Calculate the number of tails as the number of tosses minus the number of heads**
>   **Display the number of tosses, number of heads, and number of tails**
>   **Calculate the percentage of heads as the number of heads divided by the number of tosses x 100%**
>   **Calculate the percentage of tails as the number of tails divided by the number of tosses x 100%**
>   **Print the percentage of heads and tails**
> **EndIf**

Class 6-1 includes the code for this algorithm within the context of a complete class.

Class 6-1

```
#include <iostream>
#include <iomanip>
#include <ctime>
using namespace std;

class CoinToss
```

(continued on next page)

```cpp
{
  // data declaration section
private:
  int heads;
  int tosses;
  // methods declaration section
public:
  CoinToss(){heads = 0; tosses = 0;}  // in-line constructor
  void flip(int);
  void percentages();
};
  // methods implementation section

  // this method tosses the coin numTimes
  // and records the number of tosses and the number of heads
  void CoinToss::flip(int numTimes)
  {
    double randValue;
    int i;

    srand(time(NULL));  // this generates the first "seed" value

    for (i = 1; i <= numTimes; i++)
    {
      randValue = (double(rand())/RAND_MAX);
      if (randValue >= 0.5) heads++;
      tosses++;
    }
  }

  // this method calculates the percentages of heads
  // and tails, and displays the results
  void CoinToss::percentages()
  {
    int tails;
    double perheads, pertails;

    if (tosses == 0)
      cout << "There were no tosses, so no percentages"
           << "can be calculated.";
    else
```

(continued on next page)

```
  {
    tails = tosses - heads;
    cout << "Number of coin tosses: " << tosses;
    cout << "\n    " << heads << " Heads      " << tails << " Tails";
    perheads = double(heads)/double(tosses) * 100.0;
    pertails = double(tosses - heads)/double(tosses) * 100.0;

    cout << "\nHeads came up " << perheads
         << " percent of the time.";
    cout << "\nTails came up " << pertails
         << " percent of the time.\n";
  }
}
```

Having created a suitable class for a coin toss simulation, we can now perform a simulation by creating a coin object, tossing it the desired number of times, and displaying the resulting percentages. This is accomplished by Program 6-15, which simulates the tossing of a coin 1000 times.

Program 6-15

```cpp
#include <iostream>
#include <iomanip>
#include <ctime>
using namespace std;

class CoinToss
{
  // data declaration section
 private:
   int heads;
   int tosses;

  // methods declaration section
 public:
   CoinToss(){heads = 0; tosses = 0;}  // in-line constructor
   void flip(int);
   void percentages();
};
  // methods implementation section

  // this method flips the coin numTimes
  // and records the number of tosses and the number of heads
  void CoinToss::flip(int numTimes)
```

(continued on next page)

```cpp
{
  double randValue;
  int i;

  srand(time(NULL));   // this generates the first "seed" value

  for (i = 1; i <= numTimes; i++)
  {
    randValue = (double(rand())/RAND_MAX);
    if (randValue >= 0.5) heads++;
    tosses++;
  }
}

// this method calculates the percentages of heads
// and tails, and displays the results
void CoinToss::percentages()
{
  int tails;
  double perheads, pertails;

  if (tosses == 0)
   cout << "There were no tosses, so no percentages"
        << "can be calculated.";
  else
  {
    tails = tosses - heads;
    cout << "Number of coin tosses: " << tosses;
    cout << "\n   " << heads << " Heads        " << tails << " Tails";
    perheads = double(heads)/double(tosses) * 100.0;
    pertails = double(tosses - heads)/double(tosses) * 100.0;

    cout << "\nHeads came up " << perheads
         << " percent of the time.";
    cout << "\nTails came up " << pertails
         << " percent of the time.\n";
  }
}

int main()
{
  CoinToss coinOne;        // create a CoinToss object
  coinOne.flip(1000);      // flip the coin 1000 times
  coinOne.percentages();   // display the results

  return 0;
}
```

Following are two sample runs using Program 6-15:

```
Number of coin tosses: 1000
    497 Heads        503 Tails
Heads came up 49.7 percent of the time
Tails came up 50.3 percent of the time
```

and

```
Number of coin tosses: 1000
    504 Heads        496 Tails
Heads came up 50.4 percent of the time
Tails came up 49.6 percent of the time
```

A BIT OF BACKGROUND

Monte Carlo Techniques

Monte Carlo is a city within the principality of Monaco on the Mediterranean coast of France. Monte Carlo's fame as a gambling resort is responsible for its name being adopted for mathematical methods involving random numbers.

Monte Carlo techniques involve creating random numbers within given limits and determining what percentage of those numbers meet certain criteria. This technique can be used to calculate the area between curves, to estimate the arrival of airplanes at an airport, to predict the percentage of manufactured parts that will be defective, to project the growth and decline of populations with fixed resources, to specify the needed thickness of nuclear-reactor shielding, and so forth.

Monte Carlo calculations were not feasible before the development of high-speed computers. In many cases, billions of random numbers must be generated in order to achieve statistically accurate results. If, on an early personal computer, one random number selection and test calculation required a microsecond, then a billion calculations would take about 1000 seconds (roughly 17 minutes). Clearly, then, the speed and capacity of a computer are critical for effective application of Monte Carlo techniques. With newer parallel-processing machines, which can handle many operations concurrently, the time required for Monte Carlo calculations using large data samples has been reduced to the point that Monte Carlo simulations are now routine.

Writing and executing Class 6-1 is certainly easier than manually tossing a coin 1000 times. Notice how simple the simulation program becomes once the `CoinToss` class has been created. This is typical of programs that use objects and is the essence of object-oriented programming; the design process is front-loaded with the requirement that careful consideration of the class—its data declarations and method definitions—be given. Any program that subsequently creates and uses an object does not have to repeat the coding contained in a class's methods. The subsequent program, in this case

6

Program 6-15, need only address sending messages to its objects to activate them appropriately. How the method is implemented and how the state of the object is retained is not `main()`'s concern—these details are hidden within the class's construction.

Elevator Simulation

In this application, we will simulate the operation of an elevator. The state diagram for an elevator object was provided in Figure 6-18 and is repeated as Figure 6-23 for convenience.

FIGURE 6-23
A State Diagram for an Elevator

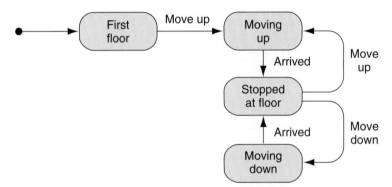

For this application, the only attribute of interest is the location of the elevator. This location, which corresponds to the elevator's current floor position, can be represented by an integer instance variable. The value of this variable, which we will name `currentFloor`, for the elevator's current location, effectively represents the current state of the elevator. We will also provide each object with a maximum floor that it can travel to. This will be useful for simulating multiple elevators in larger buildings. For initialization purposes we will set this maximum floor to 15. In actuality, any value will do, as long as we explicitly set some value to override the default of zero that would be provided by the compiler. The services that we will provide for changing the state of the elevator will be an initialization method to set the initial floor position when a new elevator is put in service, a method to set the highest floor that the elevator can rise to, and a request method to change the elevator's position (state) to a new floor. Figure 6-24 presents the class diagram for our elevator object.

FIGURE 6-24
A Class Diagram for an `Elevator` *Class*

Elevator
`-currentFloor: integer = 1` `-maxFloor: integer = 15`

`+Elevator()`
`+setMaxFloor()`
`+request(newFloor)`

The actual data declarations for this class and the constructor and mutator methods will be relatively simple. The request() method, however, is more complicated and provides the class's primary service. An algorithm that describes this service is:

> *If a request is made for either a nonexistent floor or the current floor,*
>> *Do nothing*
>
> *ElseIf the request is for a floor above the current floor*
>> *Display the current floor number*
>> *While not at the designated floor*
>>> *Increment the floor number*
>>> *Display the new floor number*
>>
>> *EndWhile*
>> *Display the ending floor number*
>
> *Else   // the request must be for a floor below the current floor*
>> *Display the current floor number*
>> *While not at the designated floor*
>>> *Decrement the floor number*
>>> *Display the new floor number*
>>
>> *EndWhile*
>> *Display the ending floor number*
>
> *EndIf*

This algorithm consists of an if-else statement having three parts: If an incorrect service is requested, no action is taken; if a floor above the current position is selected, the elevator moves up; and if a floor below the current position is selected, the elevator moves down. For movement up or down, a while loop can be used to increment or decrement the elevator's position one floor at a time and report the movement using a cout statement. This algorithm can be coded as follows:

```cpp
void Elevator::request(int newfloor)
{
  if (newfloor < 1 || newfloor > maxFloor || newfloor == currentFloor)
    ;// do nothing
  else if (newfloor > currentFloor)  // move elevator up
  {
    cout << "\nStarting at floor " << currentFloor << endl;
    while (newfloor > currentFloor)
    {
      currentFloor++;     // add one to current floor
      cout << "  Going Up - now at floor " << currentFloor << endl;
    }
    cout << "Stopping at floor " << currentFloor << endl;
  }
  else  // move elevator down
```

(continued on next page)

```cpp
{
  cout << "\nStarting at floor " << currentFloor << endl;
  while (newfloor < currentFloor)
  {
    currentFloor--;     // subtract one from current floor
    cout << "   Going Down-- now at floor " << currentFloor << endl;
  }
  cout << "Stopping at floor " << currentFloor << endl;
  }
}
```

Class 6-2 includes this method within the context of a complete class. The remaining methods in this class are straightforward. When an elevator object is created it can either be initialized to a specified floor by the overloaded constructor or, if no floor is explicitly given, a default value of 1 will be used. In both constructors, a default value of 15 is provided for the highest floor. This value can be explicitly altered by the setMaxFloor() method.

Class 6-2

```cpp
#include <iostream>
using namespace std;

class Elevator
{
  // data declaration section
  private:
    int maxFloor;
    int currentFloor;
  // methods declaration section
  public:
    Elevator();                    // default constructor
    Elevator(int);                 // overloaded constructor
    void setMaxFloor(int);
    void request(int);
};
  // methods implementation section
  Elevator::Elevator()             // this is the default constructor
  {
    currentFloor = 1;
    maxFloor = 15;
  }
```

(continued on next page)

```cpp
Elevator::Elevator(int cfloor)   // an overloaded constructor
{
  currentFloor = cfloor;
  maxFloor = 15;
}

void Elevator::setMaxFloor(int max)
{
  maxFloor = max;
}

void Elevator::request(int newfloor)
{
  if (newfloor < 1 || newfloor > maxFloor || newfloor == currentFloor)
    ;                                   // do nothing
  else if ( newfloor > currentFloor)    // move elevator up
  {
    cout << "\nStarting at floor " << currentFloor << endl;
    while (newfloor > currentFloor)
    {
      currentFloor++;                   // add one to current floor
      cout << "  Going Up - now at floor " << currentFloor << endl;
    }
    cout << "Stopping at floor " << currentFloor << endl;
  }
  else                                  // move elevator down
  {
    cout << "\nStarting at floor " << currentFloor << endl;
    while (newfloor < currentFloor)
    {
      currentFloor--;                   // subtract one from current floor
      cout << "  Going Down - now at floor " << currentFloor << endl;
    }
    cout << "Stopping at floor " << currentFloor << endl;
  }
```

Using the `Elevator` class requires putting an elevator into service and then requesting various floors and seeing that the elevator responds appropriately. Putting an elevator in service is accomplished by creating an object of type `Elevator`, while requesting a new floor position is equivalent to pushing an elevator button. This is done within Program 6-16.

Program 6-16

```cpp
#include <iostream>
using namespace std;

class Elevator
{
  // data declaration section
  private:
    int maxFloor;
    int currentFloor;
  // methods declaration section
  public:
    Elevator();                          // default constructor
    Elevator(int);                       // overloaded constructor
      void setMaxFloor(int);
      void request(int);
};
  // methods implementation section
  Elevator::Elevator()                   // this is the default constructor
  {
    currentFloor = 1;
    maxFloor = 15;
  }

  Elevator::Elevator(int cfloor)         // an overloaded constructor
  {
    currentFloor = cfloor;
    maxFloor = 15;
  }

void Elevator::setMaxFloor(int max)
{
  maxFloor = max;
}

void Elevator::request(int newfloor)
{
  if (newfloor < 1 || newfloor > maxFloor || newfloor == currentFloor)
    ;                                    // do nothing
  else if ( newfloor > currentFloor)  // move elevator up
  {
    cout << "\nStarting at floor " << currentFloor << endl;
    while (newfloor > currentFloor)
```

(continued on next page)

```
        {
            currentFloor++;       // add one to current floor
            cout << "   Going Up - now at floor " << currentFloor << endl;
        }
        cout << "Stopping at floor " << currentFloor << endl;
    }
    else                          // move elevator down
    {
        cout << "\nStarting at floor " << currentFloor << endl;
        while (newfloor < currentFloor)
        {
            currentFloor--;       // subtract one from current floor
            cout << "   Going Down - now at floor " << currentFloor << endl;
        }
        cout << "Stopping at floor " << currentFloor << endl;
    }
}
```

```
int main()
{
    Elevator a;                   // declare 1 object of type Elevator

    a.request(16);                // try to go above the highest floor
    a.setMaxFloor(6);             // set the highest floor for this elevator
    a.request(7);                 // try to go above the new maximum floor

    a.request(6);
    a.request(3);

    return 0;

}
```

The first statement in Program 6-16's main() method creates an object of type Elevator that can be accessed using the reference variable named a. Since no explicit floor has been given, this elevator will begin at floor 1, which is provided by the default constructor. A request is then made to move the elevator to floor 16. Because this floor number exceeds the highest floor that this elevator can travel to, no elevator movement will be displayed. This sequence of no movement is repeated by setting the maximum floor value to 6 and then requesting that the elevator travel to the 7th floor. The next two statements, however, will cause the elevator to move. This is accomplished by a request to move to the 6th floor, followed by a request to move to the 3rd floor. The output produced by Program 6-16 is:

```
Starting at floor 1
   Going Up - now at floor 2
   Going Up - now at floor 3
   Going Up - now at floor 4
```

```
   Going Up - now at floor 5
   Going Up - now at floor 6
Stopping at floor 6

Starting at floor 6
   Going Down - now at floor 5
   Going Down - now at floor 4
   Going Down - now at floor 3
Stopping at floor 3
```

In Program 6-16 notice the control provided by the `main()` method. This control, which is sequential, with subsequent calls made to various class methods using different argument values, is suitable for testing purposes. However, by incorporating calls to `request()` within a `while` loop and using the random number method `Math.random()` to generate random floor requests, a continuous simulation of the elevator's operation is possible (see Exercise 5 in the following set of exercises).

Exercises 6.7

1. Enter and execute Program 6-15 on your computer.

2. Modify Program 6-15 so that it requests the number of tosses from the user. (*Hint*: Make sure to have the program correctly determine the percentages of heads and tails obtained.)

3. Enter and execute Program 6-16 on your computer.

4. a. Modify the `main()` method in Program 6-16 to put a second elevator in service starting at the 5th floor. Have this second elevator move to the 1st floor and then move to the 12th floor.
   b. Verify that the constructor method is called by adding a message within the constructor that is displayed each time a new object is created. Run your program to ensure its operation.

5. Modify the `main()` method in Program 6-16 to use a `while` loop that calls the `Elevator`'s request method with a random number between 1 and 15. If the random number is the same as the elevator's current floor, generate another request. The `while` loop should terminate after five valid requests have been made and satisfied by movement of the elevator.

6. a. Construct a class definition of a `Person` object type. The class should have no attributes, a single constructor method, and two additional member methods named `arrive()` and `request()`. The constructor method should be an empty, do-nothing method. The `arrive()` method should provide a random number between 1 and 10 as a return value, while the `request()` method should provide a random number between 1 and 15.
   b. Test the `Person` class methods written for Exercise 6a in a complete working program.
   c. Use the `Person` class method to simulate a random arrival of a person and a random request for a floor to which the elevator should take this person.

7. Construct a class named `Light` that simulates a traffic light. The color attribute of the class should change from green to yellow to red and then back to green by the class's `change()` method. When a new `Light` object is created, its initial color should be red.

6.8 COMMON PROGRAMMING ERRORS

Beginning C++ programmers commonly make five errors when using repetition statements.

1. Creating a loop that is "off by one," where the loop executes either one too many or one too few times. For example, the loop created by the statement `for(i = 1; i < 11; i++)` executes 10 times, not 11, even though the number 11 is used in the statement. Thus, an equivalent loop can be constructed using the statement `for(i = 1; i <= 10; i++)`. However, if the loop is started with an initial value of `i = 0`, using the statement `for(i = 0; i < 11; i++)`, the loop will be executed 11 times, as will a loop constructed with the statement `for(i = 0; i <= 10; i++)`. Thus, in constructing loops, you must pay particular attention to both initial and tested conditions that control the loop, to ensure that the number of loop repetitions is not off by one too many or one too few executions.

2. Testing for equality when testing floating-point or double-precision operands. For example, the condition `fnum == 0.01` should be replaced by a test requiring that the absolute value of `fnum − 0.01` be less than an acceptable amount. One reason is that all numbers are stored in binary form. Using a finite number of bits, decimal numbers such as 0.01 have no exact binary equivalent, so tests requiring equality with such numbers can fail.

3. Placing a semicolon at the end of either the `while` or `for` statement's parentheses, which frequently produces a do-nothing loop. For example, consider the statements:

```
for(count = 0; count < 10; count++);
    total = total + num;
```

Here the semicolon at the end of the first line of code is a null statement. This has the effect of creating a loop that is executed 10 times with nothing done except the incrementing and testing of `count`. This error tends to occur because C++ programmers are accustomed to ending most lines with a semicolon.

4. Using commas rather than the required semicolons to separate the items in a `for` statement. An example is the statement:

```
for (count = 1, count < 10, count++)
```

Commas are used to separate items within the initializing and altering lists, and semicolons must be used to separate these lists from the tested condition.

5. Omitting the final semicolon from the `do-while` statement. This error is usually made by programmers who have learned to omit the semicolon after the parentheses of a `while` statement and who then carry over this habit when the reserved word `while` is encountered at the end of a `do-while` statement.

6.9 CHAPTER REVIEW

6

Key Terms

counter

data validation

do-while statement

fixed-count loop

for statement

infinite-loop

iteration

nested loop

posttest loop

pretest loop

pseudorandom numbers

random numbers

repetition

sentinel

simulation

variable-condition loop

while statement

SUMMARY

1. A section of repeating code is referred to as a loop. The loop is controlled by a repetition statement that tests a condition to determine whether the code will be executed. Each pass through the loop is referred to as a repetition or iteration. The tested condition must always be explicitly set prior to its first evaluation by the repetition statement. Within the loop there must always be a statement that permits altering of the condition so that the loop, once entered, can be exited.

2. There are three basic types of repetition statements used to create loops. These statements are:

    a. `while`
    b. `for`
    c. `do-while`

    Loops created from these statements are referred to as `while` loops, `for` loops, and `do-while` loops, respectively. The `while` and `for` loops are pretest or entrance-controlled loops. In this type of loop, the tested condition is evaluated at the beginning of the loop, which requires that the tested condition be explicitly set prior to loop entry. If the condition is true, loop repetitions begin; otherwise the loop is not entered. Iterations continue as long as the condition remains true. In C++, while and for loops are constructed using while and for statements, respectively.

The do-while loop is a posttest or exit-controlled loop, where the tested condition is evaluated at the end of the loop. This type of loop is always executed at least once. A do-while loop continues to execute as long as the tested condition remains true.

3.   Loops are also classified as to the type of tested condition. In a fixed-count loop, the condition is used to keep track of the number of repetitions that have occurred. In a variable-condition loop, the tested condition is based on a variable that can change interactively with each pass through the loop.

4.   In C++, a while loop is constructed using a while statement. The most commonly used form of this statement is:

```
while (expression)
{
    statements;
}
```

The expression contained within parentheses is the condition tested to determine if the statement following the parentheses, which is generally a compound statement, is executed. The expression is evaluated in the same manner as that contained in an if-else statement; the difference is how the expression is used. In a while statement, the statement following the expression is executed repeatedly as long as the expression retains a nonzero value, rather than just once, as in an if-else statement. An example of a while loop is:

```
count = 1;                    // initialize count
while (count <= 10)
{
    cout << count << "   ";
    count++;                  // increment count
}
```

The first assignment statement sets count equal to 1. The while statement is then entered and the expression is evaluated for the first time. Since the value of count is less than or equal to 10, the expression is true and the compound statement is executed. The first statement in the compound statement uses the cout object to display the value of count. The next statement adds 1 to the value currently stored in count, making this value equal to 2. The while statement now loops back to retest the expression. Since count is still less than or equal to 10, the compound statement is again executed. This process continues until the value of count reaches 11.

The while statement always checks its expression at the top of the loop. This requires that any variables in the tested expression must have values assigned before the while is encountered. Within the while loop there must be a statement that alters the tested expression's value.

6

5. In C++, a `for` loop is constructed using a `for` statement. This statement performs the same functions as the `while` statement, but uses a different form. In many situations, especially those that use a fixed-count condition, the `for` statement format is easier to use than its while statement equivalent. The most commonly used form of the `for` statement is:

    ```
    for (initializing list; expression; altering list)
    {
       statements;
    }
    ```

    Within the parentheses of the `for` statement are three items, separated by semicolons. Each of these items is optional, but the semicolons must be present.

    The initializing list is used to set any initial values before the loop is entered; generally it is used to initialize a counter. Statements within the initializing list are only executed once. The expression in the `for` statement is the condition being tested: it is tested at the start of the loop and prior to each iteration. The altering list contains loop statements that are not contained within the compound statement: generally it is used to increment or decrement a counter each time the loop is executed. Multiple statements within a list are separated by commas. An example of a `for` loop is:

    ```
    for (total = 0, count = 1; count < 10; count++)
    {
       cout << "Enter a grade: ";
       total = total + grade;
    }
    ```

    In this `for` statement, the initializing list is used to initialize both `total` and `count`. The expression determines that the loop will execute as long as the value in `count` is less than 10, and the value of `count` is incremented by 1 each time through the loop.

6. The `for` statement is very useful in creating fixed-count loops. This is because the initializing statements, the tested expression, and statements affecting the tested expression can all be included in parentheses at the top of a `for` loop for easy inspection and modification.

7. The `do-while` statement is used to create posttest loops because it checks its expression at the end of the loop. This ensures that the body of a `do` loop is executed at least once. Within a `do` loop there must be at least one statement that alters the tested expression's value.

Chapter Exercises

1. Write sections of C++ code to do the following:

    a. Display the multiples of 3 backward from 33 to 3, inclusive.
    b. Display the capital letters of the alphabet backward from Z to A.

2. Write, run, and test a C++ program to find the value of 2^n using a `for` loop where n is an integer value entered by the user at the keyboard. (*Hint*: Initialize `result = 1`. Accumulate `result = 2 * result`.)

3. The value of Euler's number e, can be approximated using the formula

$$e = 1 + 1/1! + 1/2! + 1/3! + 1/4! + 1/5! + \ldots$$

Using this formula, write a C++ program that approximates the value of e using a `while` loop that terminates when the difference between two successive approximations differs by less than 1.0e-6.

4. Using the formula provided in Exercise 3, determine how many terms are needed to approximate the value returned by the intrinsic `exp()` function with an error less than 1.0e-6. (*Hint:* Use a `while` loop that terminates when the difference between the value returned by the `exp()` function and the approximation is less than 1.0e-6.)

5. a. The outstanding balance on Rhona Karp's car loan is $8000. Each month Rhona is required to make a payment of $300, which includes both interest and principal repayment of the car loan. The monthly interest is calculated as 0.10/12 of the outstanding balance of the loan. After the interest is deducted, the remaining part of the payment is used to pay off the loan. Using this information, write a C++ program that produces a table indicating the beginning monthly balance, the interest payment, the principal payment, and the remaining loan balance after each payment is made. Your output should resemble and complete the entries in the following table until the outstanding loan balance is zero.

Beginning Payment	Interest Payment	Principal Balance	Ending Loan Balance
----------	----------	----------	----------
8000.000000	66.666667	233.333333	7766.666667
7766.666667	64.722223	235.277777	7531.388889
7531.388889	.	.	.
.	.	.	.
.	.	.	.
.	.	.	0.000000

b. Modify the program written in Exercise 5a to display the total of the interest and principal paid at the end of the table produced by your program.

6. The monthly payment due on an outstanding car loan is typically calculated using the formula:

$$\text{Monthly payment} = \frac{(\text{loan amount})(\text{monthly interest rate})}{1.0 - (1.0 + \text{monthly interest rate})^{-(\text{number of months})}}$$

where

$$MonthlyinterestRate = AnnualpercentageRate/(12.0 * 100)$$

Using these formulas, write, run, and test a C++ program that prompts the user for the amount of the loan, the annual percentage rate, and the number of years of the loan. From this input data, produce a loan amortization table similar to the one shown below:

```
What is the amount of the loan? $ 1500.00
What is the annual percentage rate? 14.0
How many years will you take to pay back the loan? 1.0
```

Amount	Annual % Interest	Years	Monthly Payment
1500.00	14.00	1	134.68

Payment Number	Interest Paid	Principal Paid	Cumulative Interest	Total Paid to Date	New Balance Due
1	17.50	117.18	17.50	134.68	1382.82
2	16.13	118.55	33.63	269.36	1264.27
3	14.75	119.93	48.38	404.04	1144.34
4	13.35	121.33	61.73	538.72	1023.01
5	11.94	122.75	73.67	673.40	900.27
6	10.50	124.18	84.17	808.08	776.09
7	9.05	125.63	93.23	942.76	650.46
8	7.59	127.09	100.81	1077.45	523.37
9	6.11	128.57	106.92	1212.13	394.79
10	4.61	130.07	111.53	1346.81	264.72
11	3.09	131.59	114.61	1481.49	133.13
12	1.55	133.13	116.16	1616.16	0.00

In constructing the loop necessary to produce the body of the table, the following initializations must be made:

New balance due = Original loan amount
Cumulative interest = 0.0
Paid to date = 0.0
Payment number = 0

Within the loop, the following calculations and accumulations should be used:

Payment number = Payment number + 1
Interest paid = New balance due * Monthly interest rate
Principal paid = Monthly payment - Interest paid
Cumulative interest = Cumulative interest + Interest paid
Paid to date = Paid to date + Monthly payment
New balance due = New balance due - Principal paid

7. Modify the program written for Exercise 6 to prevent the user from entering an illegal value for the interest rate. That is, write a loop that asks the user repeatedly for the annual interest rate until a value between 1.0 and 25.0 is entered.

8. A model of worldwide population, in billions of people, is given by the equation

$$Population = 6.0(e^{0.02*t})$$

where t is the time in years ($t = 0$ represents January 2000 and $t = 1$ represents January 2001). Using this formula, write a C++ program that displays a yearly population table for the years January 2005 though January 2010.

9. The height, as a function of time t, of a projectile fired with an initial velocity v straight into the air is given by

$$height = vt - 2\ gt^2$$

where g is the gravitational constant equal to 32.2 ft/sec². Using these formulas, write a C++ program that displays a table of heights for a projectile fired with an initial velocity of 500 ft/sec. The table should contain values corresponding to the time interval 0 to 10 seconds in increments of one-half seconds.

10. In the hypothetical Republic of Dwump, the basic unit of currency is the dwork, and the exchange rate at present is 27 dworks per US dollar. Develop, run, and test a C++ program to create a table of dollars versus dworks in steps of $0.25 from `MinDollars` to `MaxDollars`, where values for these two variables will be entered by the user at the keyboard. The exchange rate (27 dworks per dollar) and the step value (0.25) should be declared as named constants, so that they can be found and changed easily. The exchange rate should be displayed at the head of the output table, and the columns Dollars and Dworks should be labeled.

11. Develop, test, and execute a C++ program that uses a `while` loop to determine the smallest integer power of 3 that exceeds 30,000. That is, find the smallest value of n such that $3^n > 30,000$. (*Hint*: Initialize `PowerOfThree = 1` and then let `PowerOfThree = 3 * PowerOfThree`.)

12. A prime integer number is one that has exactly two different divisors, namely 1 and the number itself. Write, run, and test a C++ program that finds and prints all the prime numbers less than 100. (*Hint*: 1 is a prime number.) For each number from 2 to 100, find `Remainder = Number % n`, where n ranges from 2 to `sqrt(number)`. If n is greater than `sqrt(number)`, then the number is not equally divisible by n. (Why?) If any `Remainder` equals 0, then the number is not a prime number.

13. Print the decimal, octal, and hexadecimal values of all characters between the start and stop characters entered by a user. For example, if the user enters an 'a' and a 'z', the program should print all the characters between a and z and their respective values. Make sure that the second character entered by the user occurs later in the alphabet than the first character. If it does not, write a loop that asks the user repeatedly for a valid second character.

14. Create a table of selling price versus purchase price. Have the user enter the range of purchase prices (from lowest to highest), the percent markup, and the increment between purchase prices. Display the table of purchase prices and selling prices on the screen, with appropriate headings. The formulas for calculating the selling price from the purchase price are:

$$Markup\ fraction = Percent\ markup\ /\ 100.0$$
$$Selling\ price = (1.0 + Markup\ fraction) * Purchase\ price$$

15. The quotient in long division is the number of times the divisor can be subtracted from the dividend. The remainder is what is left over after the last subtraction. Write a C++ program that performs division using this method.

16. Write a C++ program that uses iteration to accumulate the sum $1 + 2 + 3 + ... + n$, where n is a user-entered integer number. Then evaluate the expression $n(n + 1)/2$ to verify that this expression yields the same result as the iteration.

17. a. An old Arabian legend has it that a fabulously wealthy but unthinking king agreed to give a beggar one cent and double the amount for 64 days. Using this information, write, run, and test a C++ program that displays how much the king must pay the beggar on each day. The output of your program should appear as follows:

```
Day             Amount Owed
---             -----------
  1                0.01
  2                0.02
  3                0.04
  .                 .
  .                 .
  .                 .
 64                 .
```

    b. Modify the program you wrote for Exercise 17a to determine on which day the king will have paid a total of one million dollars to the beggar.

18. According to legend, the island of Manhattan was purchased by the Dutch from the Manhattan Indians in 1626 for $24. Assuming that this money was invested in a Dutch bank paying 5% simple interest per year, construct a table showing how much money the Indians would have at the end of each 20-year period starting in 1626 and ending in 2006.

Improving Communication

19.   MEMORANDUM

       To: Chief Programmer
       From: Head of Programming Dept.

       Subject: Object-Oriented Analysis

Please detail the concept of state, as it refers to an object. This term has come up a few times in our meetings and a number of nonprogrammers have requested a clarification of what is being discussed.

**Improving
Communication**

20.   MEMORANDUM

To: Chief Programmer
From: Head of Programming Dept.

Subject: Objects and Values

Please explain to me the difference between the values we have been using in our programs and objects. For example, is the name "England" an object or a value?

**Working
in Teams**

21. As a team, make a list of a car's major subsystems, such as brakes, steering, etc. Then, considering these subsystems as classes, construct an object diagram for a Car class that simply shows the associations between classes (no attributes or operations). Assign each subsystem to individual team members. Each member should determine a set of attributes and operations appropriate to their assigned subsystem. When each member has completed his or her task, modify the original object diagram to include the additional information.

22. As a team, make a list of a cellular telephone's major subsystems, such as keypad, antenna, etc. Then, considering these subsystems as classes, construct an object diagram for a Cellular class that simply shows the associations between classes (no attributes or operations). Assign each subsystem to individual team members. Each member should determine a set of attributes and operations appropriate to their assigned subsystem. When each member has completed his or her task, modify the original object diagram to include the additional information.

**Testing
Center**

Please visit the Testing Center at www.course.com/testingcenter for more practice on repetition statements.

PART 3

COMPLETING THE BASICS

7

FUNCTIONS

C++ was created as an extension to the procedural C language, and consequently retains and supports procedural elements. This means that you can, and sometimes must, include C++'s procedural and nonclass features within a new C++ program. For example, the requirement that every executable C++ program must contain a main() function, which is a nonclass procedure, is a holdover from the C language. Additionally, we found it useful to use nonclass code within the programs in Part Two that emphasized a particular statement or programming technique.

The basis of C++'s procedural code is a function, which can be visualized as a nonclass method that cannot accept, and therefore is never called by using, an implicit object. You learned about the main() function, as well as a number of standard library mathematical functions, in Section 4.3. In many situations, however, you will find it useful to create your own functions. You'll learn how to do that in this chapter.

7.1 FUNCTION DECLARATIONS AND DEFINITIONS

Unlike a method, which is always a member of a class, a function is a nonclass procedure. This distinction means that a function cannot accept, and never operates on, an implied object, while a method must always accept an implied object when it is called.[1] However a function can accept data, including objects, as arguments and, like a method, directly return a single value. As such, functions are extremely useful for performing general-purpose tasks that are independent of any particular class. Examples of this are the mathematical procedures presented in Section 4.3, all of which are constructed as functions.

As illustrated in Figure 7-1, a function can be considered as a special-purpose machine, designed to complete a specific programming task. Comparing Figure 7-1 with Figure 3-1 reveals that a function is identical to a class method except that it does not receive nor operate on an implied object.

FIGURE 7-1
A Function as a Machine

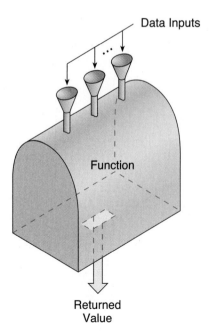

<hr />

[1]The technical distinction is that a method always has a `this` argument, while a function does not (this is described in detail in Section 12.3).

In creating C++ functions, you must be concerned with both the function itself, how it interacts with other functions, such as main(), and how it interacts with class methods. This means that when a function requires data inputs, these inputs are passed into the function correctly when it is called, and when a function returns a value, it corresponds to the data type declared for the function.

As we have already seen with mathematical functions, you call a function by giving the function's name and passing data to it, if any are required, as arguments within the parentheses following the function name (see Figure 7-2). The called function must be able to accept the data passed to it by the function doing the calling. Only after the called function successfully receives the data can the data be manipulated to produce a useful result.

FIGURE 7-2
Calling and Passing Data to a Function

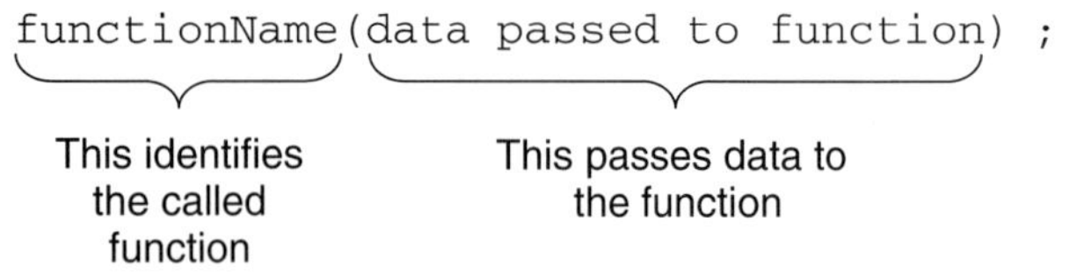

```
functionName(data passed to function);
```

This identifies   This passes data to
the called   the function
function

To clarify the process of sending and receiving data, consider Program 7-1, which calls a function named findMax(). The program, as shown, is not yet complete. Once the function findMax() is written and included in Program 7-1, the completed program, consisting of the functions main() and findMax(), can be compiled and executed.

Program 7-1

```cpp
#include <iostream>
using namespace std;

int main()
{
  int findMax(int, int);   // function declaration (prototype)
  int firstnum, secnum;

  cout << "\nEnter a number: ";
  cin  >> firstnum;
  cout << "Great! Please enter a second number: ";
  cin  >> secnum;

  cout << "\nThe maximum of these two values is "
       << findMax(firstnum, secnum) << endl; // the function is called here
  return 0;
}
```

Let us examine the declaration and calling of the function findMax() within main(). We will then write the function findMax() to accept the data passed to it and return the largest value of the two passed values.

Within `main()`, the called function, in this case `findMax()`, is declared as a function that expects to receive two integer numbers and to return an `int` data type to `main()`. This declaration is identical to the declarations made for class methods. The function is then called by the expression `findMax(firstnum, secnum)` contained in the last `cout` statement. Except for the lack of a preceding object name, this function invocation is the same as that used in calling class methods.

FUNCTION PROTOTYPES

Before a function can be called, it must be declared to the function that will do the calling. The declaration statement for a function is referred to as a **function prototype**, and is identical to the method declarations included within a class's declaration section. As a declaration statement, the function prototype tells the calling function the type of value that will be formally returned, if any, and the data type and order of the values that the calling function should transmit to the called function. For example, the function prototype previously used in Program 7-1:

```
int findMax(int, int);
```

declares that the function `findMax()` expects two integer values to be sent to it, and that this particular function formally returns an `int` data type. Function prototypes may be placed with the variable declaration statements of the calling function, as in Program 7-1; above the calling function name; or in a separate header file that is included using a `#include` preprocessor statement. Thus, the function prototype for `findMax()` could have been placed either before or after the statement `#include <iostream>`, prior to `main()`, or within `main()`, as in Program 7-1. (The reasons for the choice of placement are presented in Section 7.3.) The general form of function prototype statements is:

```
returnDataType     functionName(list of argument data types);
```

As with method declarations, the `returnDataType` specifies the data type of the value that will be directly returned by the function. Examples of function prototypes are:

```
void fmax(int, int);
bool swap(int, char, char, double);
double display(double, double);
```

The function prototype for `fmax()` declares that this function expects to receive two integer arguments and will formally return no value (`void`). Such a function might be used to display the results of a computation directly, without returning any value to the called function. The function prototype for `swap()` declares that this function requires four arguments consisting of an integer, two characters, and a double-precision argument (in this order) when it is called, and will formally return a Boolean value. Finally, the function prototype for `display()` declares that this function requires two double-precision arguments when it is called and returns a double-precision value.

The use of function prototypes permits error checking of data types by the compiler. If the function prototype does not agree with data types defined when the function is written, an error message (typically `TYPE MISMATCH`) will occur. The prototype also serves another task; it ensures conversion of all arguments passed to the function to the declared argument data type when the function is called.

CALLING A FUNCTION

Calling a function is identical to calling a class method, except that no object is specified as an implied object in the call statement. All that is required is the name of the function and any data passed to the function, enclosed within the parentheses following the function name. The data must correspond to the same order and type as declared in the function prototype. As with class methods, the data enclosed within the parentheses are referred to as **actual arguments**, with the terms arguments, actual parameters, and parameters all acceptable as synonyms.

If a variable is one of the actual arguments in a function call, the called function receives a copy of the value stored in the variable. For example, the expression `findMax(firstnum, secnum)` calls the function `findMax()` and causes the values currently residing in the variables `firstnum` and `secnum` to be passed to `findMax()`. The variable names in parentheses are actual arguments that provide values to the called function. After the values are passed, control is transferred to the called function.

As illustrated in Figure 7-3, the function `findMax()` *does not receive the variable names* `firstnum` *and* `secnum` *and has no knowledge of these variable names.*[2] The function simply receives the values in these variables, and must itself determine where to store these values before it does anything else. This procedure, as with class methods, is referred to as a **call-by-value**, and ensures that a called function does not inadvertently change data stored in a variable. The function gets a copy of the data to use. It may change its copy and, of course, change any variables or arguments declared inside itself. However, unless specific steps are taken to do so, a function is not allowed to change the contents of variables declared in other functions.

FIGURE 7-3
`findMax()` *Receives Actual Values*

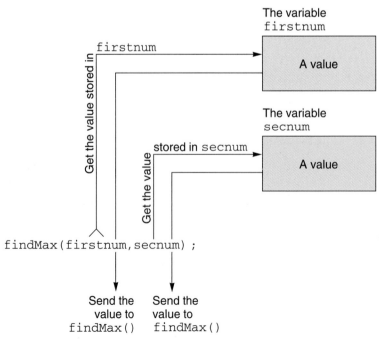

---

[2]Using reference variables to provide direct access to a calling function's variables is presented in Section 7.4.

In the next section, we will begin writing the function `findMax()` to process the values passed to it in Program 7-1 and return an appropriate value.

DEFINING A FUNCTION

As with class methods, a function is defined when it is written. Like the `main()` function, every C++ function consists of two parts, a function header and a function body, as illustrated in Figure 7-4. The purpose of the function header is to identify the data type of the value returned by the function, provide the function with a name, and specify the number, order, and type of arguments expected by the function. The purpose of the function body is to operate on the passed data and directly return, at most, one value back to the calling function. (You will see in Section 7.4 how a function can be made to return multiple values through the parameter list.)

FIGURE 7-4
General Format of a Function

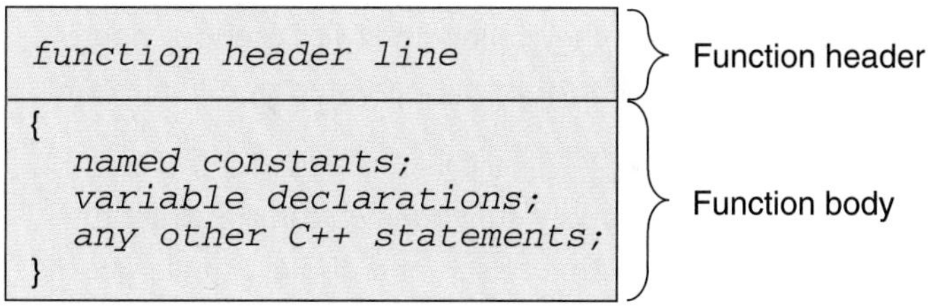

The function header is always the first line of a function and contains the function's returned value type, its name, and the names and data types of its arguments. Because `findMax()` will formally return an integer value and is to receive two integer arguments, the following header line can be used:

$$\text{int findMax(int x, int y)} \quad \longleftarrow \quad \text{no semicolon}$$

The argument names in the header line act in an identical manner as a method's arguments, and can be referred to as either **formal parameters** or **formal arguments** (the terms are used interchangeably).[3] Thus, the argument x will be used to store the first value passed to `findMax()` and the argument y will be used to store the second value passed at the time of the function call. The function does not know where the values come from when the call is made from `main()`. The first part of the call procedure executed by the computer involves going to the variables `firstnum` and `secnum` and retrieving the stored values. These values are then passed to `findMax()` and ultimately stored in the formal parameters x and y (see Figure 7-5).

---

[3]The portion of the function header that contains the function name and parameters is formally referred to as a *function declarator.*

FIGURE 7-5
Storing Values into Parameters

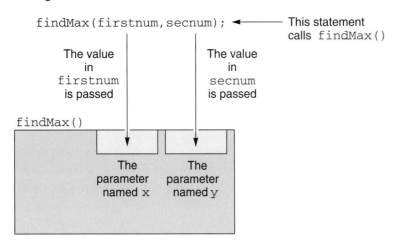

The function name and all parameter names in the header line, in this case findMax, x, and y, are chosen by the programmer. Any names can be used, provided they follow the rules used to choose variable names. All parameters listed in the function header line must be separated by commas and must have their individual data types declared separately.

Now that we have written the function header for the findMax() function, we can construct the body of this function. Let us assume that the findMax() function selects and displays the larger of the two numbers passed to it.

As shown in Figure 7-6, a function's body is constructed in an identical manner as that of a class method; it begins with an opening brace, {; contains any necessary variable declarations and other C++ statements; and ends with a closing brace, }. This structure is also the same as that used in the main() function, which should come as no surprise because main() is itself a function that must adhere to the rules required for constructing all legitimate functions.

FIGURE 7-6
Structure of a Function Body

```
{
    named constants
    variable declarations
    other C++ statements
}
```

PROGRAMMING NOTE

Function Definitions and Function Prototypes

When you write a function, you are formally creating a function definition. A **function definition** begins with a header line that includes a formal parameter list, if any, enclosed in parentheses and ends with the closing brace that terminates the function's body. The parentheses are required whether or not the function uses any arguments. The syntax for a function definition is:

```
returnDataType functionName(parameter list, if any)
{
  variable declarations

  other C++ statements

  return value;
}
```

A **function prototype** declares a function. The syntax for a function prototype, which provides the return data type of the function, the function's name, and the function's parameter list, is:

```
returnDataType functionName(list of parameter data types, if any);
```

As such, the prototype (along with pre- and postcondition comments, as described in the next Programming Note in this section) should provide a user with all the programming information needed to successfully call the function.

Generally, all function prototypes are placed at the top of the program, and all definitions are placed after the `main()` function. However, this placement can be changed. The only requirement in C++ is that a function cannot be called before it has been either declared or defined.

In the body of the function `findMax()`, a variable, named `maxnum`, will be declared to store the maximum of the two numbers passed to it. An `if-else` statement is then used to find the maximum of the two numbers and assign this value to `maxnum`. Finally, a return statement is used to return `maxnum`'s value to the calling function. The following code performs these tasks.

```
int findMax(int x, int y)
{                       // start of function body
 int maxnum;            // variable declaration

  if (x >= y)           // find the maximum number
    maxnum = x;
  else
    maxnum = y;

  return (maxnum);   // return statement
}
```

In this code for findMax(), note that the data type of the expression contained within the return statement's parentheses correctly matches the data type in the function's header line. The programmer must ensure that this is so for every function returning a value. Failure to match exactly the return value with the function's declared data type may not result in an error when your program is compiled, but it may lead to undesired results, because the return value is always converted to the data type declared in the function declaration. Usually this is a problem only when the fractional part of a returned floating-point or double-precision number is truncated, because the function was declared to return an integer value.

To use a returned value in the calling method or function, we must either use the returned value directly, as is done in Program 7-1, or provide a variable to store the returned value. Storing the returned value in a variable is accomplished using a standard assignment statement. For example, the assignment statement

```
max = findMax(firstnum, secnum);
```

can be used to store the value returned by findMax() in the variable named max. This assignment statement does two things. First, the right side of the assignment statement calls findMax(), then the returned value is stored in the variable max. Since the value returned by findMax() is an integer, the variable max must also be declared as an integer variable within the calling function's variable declarations.

The value returned by a function need not be stored directly in a variable, but can be used wherever an expression is valid. For example, the expression 2 * findMax(firstnum, secnum); multiplies the value returned by findMax() by 2, and the statement cout << findMax(firstnum, secnum); displays the returned value.

Program 7-2 illustrates findMax() used within the context of a complete program. In keeping with our convention of placing the main() function first, we have placed the findMax() function after main().

Program 7-2 can be used to select and print the maximum of any two integer numbers entered by the user. Following is a sample run using Program 7-2:

```
Enter a number: 25
Great! Please enter a second number: 5

The maximum of the two values is 25
```

In reviewing Program 7-2, it is important to note the following items. The first item is the prototype for findMax() within main(). This statement, which ends with a semicolon as all declaration statements do, alerts main() to the data type that findMax() will be returning. The parentheses after the name findMax inform main() that findMax is a function rather than a variable.

Program 7-2

```cpp
#include <iostream>
using namespace std;

int main()
{
  int findMax(int, int);   // function declaration (prototype)
  int firstnum, secnum;

  cout << "\nEnter a number: ";
  cin  >> firstnum;
  cout << "Great! Please enter a second number: ";
  cin  >> secnum;

  cout << "\nThe maximum of these two values is "
       << findMax(firstnum, secnum) << endl; // the function is
                                             //called here

  return 0;
}

int findMax(int x, int y)
{                       // start of function body
  int maxnum;           // variable declaration

  if (x >= y)           // find the maximum number
    maxnum = x;
  else
    maxnum = y;

  return (maxnum);      // return statement
}
```

The next item to note is the value returned by findMax(), which must match the return type declared in the function's header line. Thus, findMax() is internally consistent in returning an integer value to main(), and main() has been correctly alerted to receive and use the returned integer.

You must always keep these items in mind when writing your own functions. To get some practice, see if you can identify these items in Program 7-3.

PROGRAMMING NOTE

Preconditions and Postconditions

Preconditions are any set of conditions required by a function to be true if the function is to operate correctly. For example, if a function uses the symbolic constant MAXCHARS, which must have a positive value, a precondition is that MAXCHARS be declared with a positive value before the function is called.

Similarly, a postcondition is a condition that will be true after the function is executed, assuming that the preconditions are met.

Pre- and postconditions are typically written as user comments. For example, consider the following declaration and comments:

```
bool leapyr(int)
// Precondition:
//    The year must represent a year in a four-digit form,
//    such as 2006
// Postcondition:
//    A value of true is returned if the year is a leap
//    year; otherwise false is returned
```

Pre- and postcondition comments should be included with both function prototypes and function definitions whenever clarification is needed.

In reviewing Program 7-3, let us first analyze the function `tempvert()`. The complete definition of the function begins with the function's header line and ends with the closing brace after the `return` statement. The function is declared as a double; this means the expression in the function's `return` statement must evaluate to a double-precision number, which it does. Because a function header line is not a statement but the start of the code defining the function, the function header line does not end with a semicolon.

On the receiving side, `main()` has a prototype for the `tempvert()` that agrees with the function's header line. As with all declaration statements, multiple declarations of the same type may be made within the same statement. Thus, we could have used the same declaration statement to declare both the variable `fahren` and the function `tempvert()` as double-precision data types. If we had done so, the single declaration statement `double fahren, tempvert(double);` could have been used to replace the two individual declarations for `fahren` and `tempvert()`. For clarity, however, we will always keep function prototype statements apart from variable declaration statements. No additional variable is declared in `main()` to store the returned value from `tempvert()` because the returned value is immediately passed to `cout` for display.

One further point is worth mentioning here. One of the purposes of declarations, as we learned in Section 2.3, is to alert the computer to the amount of internal storage reserved for the data. The prototype within `main()` for `tempvert()` performs this task, telling the computer how much storage area must be accessed by `main()` when the returned value is retrieved. Had we placed the `tempvert()` function before `main()`, however, the function header line for `tempvert()` would suffice to alert the compiler to the type of storage needed for the returned value. In this case, the function prototype for `tempvert()`, within `main()`, could be eliminated. Since we have chosen always to list `main()` as the first function in a file, we must include function prototypes for all functions called by `main()`. This style also serves to document what functions will be called by `main()`.

Program 7-3

```
#include <iostream>
using namespace std;

int main()
{
  double tempvert(double);   // function prototype

  const int CONVERTS = 4;    // number of conversions to be made
  int count;                 // start of variable declarations
  double fahren;

  for(count = 1; count <= CONVERTS; count++)
  {
    cout << "\nEnter a Fahrenheit temperature: ";
    cin >> fahren;
    cout << "The Celsius equivalent is "
         << tempvert(fahren) << endl;
  }


  return 0;
}

// convert fahrenheit to celsius
double tempvert(double inTemp)
{
  return ( (5.0/9.0) * (inTemp - 32.0) );
}
```

The placement of the `findMax()` function after the `main()` function in Program 7-2 is a matter of choice. Some programmers prefer to put all called functions at the top of a program and make `main()` the last function listed. We prefer to list `main()` first because it is the driver function that should give anyone reading the program an idea of what the complete program is about before encountering the details of each function. Either approach is acceptable, and you will encounter both styles in your programming work. In no case, however, can the definition of `findMax()` be placed inside `main()`. This is true for all C++ functions, which must be defined by themselves outside any other function. Each C++ function is a separate and independent entity with its own arguments and variables; *nesting of functions is never permitted.*

PLACEMENT OF STATEMENTS

C++ does not impose a rigid statement ordering structure on the programmer. The general rule for placing statements in a C++ program is simply that all preprocessor commands, variables, named constants, and function calls must be either declared or defined before they can be used. As we have noted previously, although this rule permits both preprocessor commands and declaration statements to be placed throughout a program, doing so generally results in a very poor program structure.

As a matter of good programming practice, the following statement ordering should form the basic structure around which all of your C++ programs are constructed.

```
preprocessor commands

int main()
{
   function declarations;
   symbolic constants;
   variable declarations;

   other C++ statements;

   return value;
}
```

As always, comment statements can be freely intermixed anywhere within this basic structure.

VARIATIONS[4]

There are a number of useful variations to defining and declaring functions. One of these, overloading, we have encountered before in constructing multiple versions of a class's constructor method. Additionally, all of the other variations introduced here for functions are also applicable to class methods.

Function Stubs

An alternative to completing each function required in a complete program is to write the main() function first, and then add the required functions later, as they are developed. The problem that arises with this approach, however, is the same problem that occurred with Program 7-1; that is, the program cannot be run until all of the functions are included. For illustration, the code for Program 7-1 is reproduced below.

---

[4]All of these variations may be omitted on first reading without loss of subject continuity.

```
#include <iostream>
using namespace std;

int main()
{
   int findMax(int, int);   // function declaration (prototype)
   int firstnum, secnum;

   cout << "\nEnter a number: ";
   cin  >> firstnum;
   cout << "Great! Please enter a second number: ";
   cin  >> secnum;

   cout << "\nThe maximum of these two values is "
        << findMax(firstnum, secnum) << endl; // the function is called here

   return 0;
}
```

This program would be complete if there were a function definition for findMax(). But we really don't need a *correct* findMax() function to test and run what has been written, we just need a function that *acts* as if it is correct. That is, a "fake" findMax() that accepts the proper number and types of arguments—and returns values of the proper form for the function call—is all we need to allow initial testing. This fake function is called a stub. A **stub** is the beginning of a final function that can be used as a placeholder for the final unit until the unit is completed. A stub for findMax() is as follows:

```
int findMax(int x, int y)
{
   cout << "In findMax()\n";
   cout << "The value of x is " << x << endl;
   cout << "The value of x is " << y << endl;

   return 0;
}
```

This stub function can now be compiled and linked with the previously completed code to obtain an executable program. The code for the function can then be further developed, with the "real" code, when it is completed, replacing the stub portion. As illustrated, a stub should always display the name of the function that it represents.

The minimum requirement of a stub function is that it compile and link with its calling module. In practice, it is a good idea to have a stub display a message that it has been invoked and then display the value(s) of its received arguments, as in the stub for findMax().

As the function is refined, you let it do more and more, perhaps allowing it to return intermediate or incomplete results. This incremental refinement is an important concept in efficient program development that provides you with the means to run a program that does not yet meet all of its final requirements.

Functions with Empty Parameter Lists

Although useful functions having an empty parameter list are quite limited (one such function is provided in Exercise 11), they can occur. The function prototype for such a function requires either writing the keyword `void` or putting nothing at all between the parentheses following the function's name. For example, both prototypes

        int display();

and

        int display(void);

indicate that the `display()` function takes no arguments and returns an integer value. A function with an empty parameter list is called by its name with nothing written within the required parentheses following the function's name. For example, the statement `display();` correctly calls the `display()` function whose prototype was given above.

PROGRAMMING NOTE

Isolation Testing

One of the most successful software testing methods is to embed the code being tested within an environment of working code. For example, assume you have two untested functions that are called in the order shown below, and the result returned by the second function is incorrect.

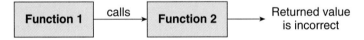

From the information shown on this figure, one or possibly both of the functions could be operating incorrectly. The first order of business is to isolate the problem to a specific function.

One of the most powerful methods of performing this code isolation is to decouple the functions. This is done by either testing each function individually or by testing one function first, and only when you know it is operating correctly, reconnecting it to the second function. Then if an error occurs, you have isolated the error to either the transfer of data between functions or the internal operation of the second function.

This specific procedure is an example of the *basic rule of testing*, which states that each function should only be tested in a program in which all other functions are known to be correct. This means that one function must first be tested by itself, using stubs if necessary for any called functions; that a second tested function should be tested either by itself or with a previously tested function; and so on. This ensures that each new function is isolated within a test bed of correct functions, with the final program effectively built of tested function code.

Default Arguments

A convenient feature of C++ is the flexibility of providing default arguments in a function call. The primary use of default arguments is to extend the parameter list of existing functions without requiring any change in the calling argument lists already in place within a program.

Default argument values are listed in the function prototype and are automatically transmitted to the called function when the corresponding arguments are omitted from the function call. For example, the function prototype

```
void example(int, int = 5, double = 6.78);
```

provides default values for the last two arguments. If any of these arguments are omitted when the function is actually called, the C++ compiler will supply these default values. Thus, all of the following function calls are valid:

```
example(7, 2, 9.3)   // no defaults used
example(7, 2)        // same as example(7, 2, 6.78)
example(7)           // same as example(7, 5, 6.78)
```

Four rules must be followed when using default parameters. First, default values can only be assigned in the function prototype. Second, if any parameter is given a default value in the function prototype, all parameters following it must also be supplied with default values. The third rule is that if one argument is omitted in the actual function call, then all arguments to its right must also be omitted. These rules make it clear to the C++ compiler which arguments are being omitted, and permit the compiler to supply correct default values for the missing arguments, starting with the rightmost argument and working in toward the left. The last rule specifies that the default value used in the function prototype may be an expression consisting of both constants and previously declared variables. If such an expression is used, it must pass the compiler's check for validly declared variables, even though the actual value of the expression is evaluated and assigned at run time.

Default arguments are useful when extending an existing function to include more features that require additional arguments. Adding the new arguments to the right of the existing arguments and providing each new argument with a default value permits all existing function calls to remain as they are. Thus, the effects of the new changes are conveniently isolated from existing code in the program.

Reusing Function Names (Overloading)

As with class methods, functions can also be overloaded. This permits the same name to be used for functions that perform the same task, regardless of the differences in parameter and return value types (in fact, the parameter list *must be* different for overloaded functions). For example, consider determining and displaying the absolute value of a number. If the number passed into the function can be an integer, a long integer, or a double-precision value, three distinct functions must be written to correctly handle each case. As was done in C, we could give each of these functions a unique name, such as abs(), labs(), and dabs(), respectively, having the function prototypes:

```
void abs(int);
void labs(long);
void dabs(double);
```

Clearly, each of these three functions performs essentially the same operation, but on different argument data types. In C++, as long as the compiler can determine which function to use based on the data types of the arguments (not the data type of the return value, if any), the same function name can be used for more than one function. Using the same function name for more than one function is referred to as **function overloading.**

Applying function overloading to our absolute value functions permits us to write three C++ functions that all have the same name. Using the function name showabs() for these functions, they can be written as follows:

```cpp
void showabs(int x)   // display the absolute value of an integer
{
  if ( x < 0 )
    x = -x;
  cout << "The absolute value of the integer is  " << x << endl;
}

void showabs(long x)   // display the absolute value of a long integer
{
  if ( x < 0 )
    x = -x;
  cout << "The absolute value of the long integer is  " << x << endl;
}

void showabs(double x)   // display the absolute value of a double
{
  if ( x < 0 )
    x = -x;
  cout << "The absolute value of the double is  " << x << endl;
}
```

The argument types supplied at the time of the call determine which of the three functions named abs() is actually called. Thus, the function call showabs(10); would cause the compiler to use the function named abs that expects an integer argument, and the function call abs(6.28); would cause the compiler to use the function named abs that expects a double-valued argument.[5]

Notice that overloading a function's name simply means using the same name for more than one function. Each function that uses the name must still be written and exists as a separate entity. The use of the same function name does not require that the code within the functions be similar, although good programming practice dictates that functions with the same name should perform essentially the same operations. All that is formally required in using the same function name is that the compiler can distinguish which function to select, based on the data types of the arguments when the function is called.

---

[5]This is accomplished by a process referred to as *name mangling*. Using this process, the function name actually generated by the C++ compiler differs from the function name used in the source code. The compiler appends information to the source code function name depending on the type of data being passed, and the resulting name is said to be a mangled version of the source code name.

Inline Functions

Calling a function places a certain amount of overhead on a computer. This consists of placing argument values in a reserved memory region that the function has access to (this memory region is referred to as the *stack*), passing control to the function, providing a reserved memory location for any returned value (again, using the stack region of memory), and finally returning to the proper point in the calling program. Paying this overhead is well justified when a function is called many times, because it can significantly reduce the size of a program. Rather than repeating the same code within a function each time it is needed, the code is written once, as a function, and called whenever it is needed.

For small functions that are not called many times, however, paying the overhead for passing and returning values may not be warranted. It still would be convenient, though, to group repeating lines of code together under a common function name and have the compiler place this code directly into the program wherever the function is called. This capability is provided by inline functions.

Telling the C++ compiler that a function is *inline* causes a copy of the function code to be placed in the program at the point the function is called. For example, consider the function tempvert() defined in Program 7-3. Since this is a relatively short function, it is an ideal candidate to be an inline function.

To make this, or any other function, inline simply requires placing the reserved word inline before the function name, and defining the function before any calls are made to it. This is done for the tempvert() function in Program 7-4.

Program 7-4

```cpp
#include <iostream>
using namespace std;

inline double tempvert(double inTemp)   // an inline function
{
   return( (5.0/9.0) * (inTemp - 32.0) );
}

int main()
{
    const int CONVERTS = 4;                // number of conversions to be made
   int count;                             // start of declarations
   double fahren;

   for(count = 1; count <= CONVERTS; count++)
   {
     cout << "\nEnter a Fahrenheit temperature: ";
     cin  >> fahren;
     cout << "The Celsius equivalent is "
          << tempvert(fahren) << endl;
   }

   return 0;
}
```

Observe in Program 7-4 that the inline function is placed ahead of any calls to it. This is a requirement of all inline functions and obviates the need for a function prototype within any subsequent function calling it. Since the function is now an inline one, its code will be expanded directly into the program wherever it is called.

The advantage of using an inline function is an increase in execution speed. Since the inline function is directly expanded and included in every expression or statement calling it, there is no execution time loss due to the call and return overhead required by a non-inline function. The disadvantage is the increase in program size when an inline function is called repeatedly. Each time an inline function is referenced, the complete function code is reproduced and stored as an integral part of the program. A non-inline function, however, is stored in memory only once. No matter how many times the function is called, the same code is used. Therefore, inline functions should only be used for small functions that are not extensively called in the program.

Making a class method inline simply means defining the method in the class's declaration section. In this case, however, the keyword `inline` is not required because class methods defined within a declaration section are constructed as `inline` by default.

Function Templates

In most high-level languages, including C++'s immediate predecessor, C, each function requires its own unique name. In theory, this makes sense, but in practice it can lead to a profusion of function names, even for functions that perform essentially the same operations. For example, consider determining and displaying the absolute value of a number. If the number passed into the function can be either an integer, a long integer, or a double-precision value, three distinct functions must be written to handle each case correctly. Certainly, we could use function overloading or give each of these functions a unique name, such as `abs()`, `labs()`, and `dabs()`, respectively, having the function prototypes:

```
void abs(int);
void labs(long);
void dabs(double);
```

Clearly, each of these three functions performs essentially the same operation but on different parameter data types. A much cleaner and more elegant solution is to write a general function that handles all cases, but whose parameters, variables, and even return type can be set by the compiler based on the actual function call. This is possible in C++ using function templates.

A **function template** is a single, complete function that serves as a model for a family of functions. Subsequent function calls determine which function from the family is actually created. To make this more concrete, consider a function template that computes and displays the absolute value of a passed argument.

An appropriate function template is:

```
template <class T>
void showabs(T number)
{
  if (number < 0)
    number = -number;
```

(continued on next page)

```
        cout << "The absolute value of the number "
             << " is " << number << endl;
        return;
    }
```

For the moment, ignore the first line `template <class T>`, and look at the second line, which consists of the function header `void showabs (T number)`. Notice that this header line has the same syntax that we have been using for all of our function definitions, except for the `T` where a data type is usually placed. For example, if the header line were `void showabs(int number)`, you should recognize this as a function named `showabs` that expects one integer argument to be passed to it and that returns no value. Similarly, if the header line were `void showabs(double number)`, you should recognize it as a function that expects one double-precision argument to be passed when the function is called.

The advantage in using the `T` within the function template header line is that it represents a general data type that is replaced by an actual data type, such as `int`, `float`, `double`, etc., when the compiler encounters an actual function call. For example, if a function call with an integer argument is encountered, the compiler uses the function template to construct the code for a function that expects an integer parameter. Similarly, if a call is made with a floating-point argument, the compiler constructs a function that expects a floating-point parameter. As a specific example of this, consider Program 7-5.

Program 7-5

```cpp
#include <iostream>
using namespace std;

template <class T>
void showabs (T number)
{
   if (number < 0)
     number = -number;
   cout << "The absolute value of the number is "
        << number << endl;

   return;
}

int main()
{
   int num1 = -4;
   long num2 = -423456L;
   double num3 = -4.23456;
   showabs(num1);
   showabs(num2);
   showabs(num3);

   return 0;
}
```

First notice the three function calls made in the `main()` function shown in Program 7-4, which call the function `showabs()` with an integer, long, and double value, respectively. Now review the function template for `showabs()` and let us consider the first line, `template <class T>`. This line, which is called a **template prefix**, is used to inform the compiler that the function immediately following is a template that uses a data type named `T`. Within the function template, `T` is used in the same manner as any other data type, such as `int`, `long`, `double`, etc. Then, when the compiler encounters an actual function call for `showabs()`, the data type of the argument passed in the call is substituted for `T` throughout the function. In effect, the compiler creates a specific function, using the template that expects the argument type in the call. Since Program 7-5 makes three calls to `showabs`, each with a different argument data type, the compiler creates three separate `showabs()` functions.

The compiler knows which function to use based on the arguments passed at the time of the call. The output displayed when Program 7-5 is executed is:

```
The absolute value of the number is 4
The absolute value of the number is 423456
The absolute value of the number is 4.23456
```

The letter `T` used in the template prefix `template <class T>` is simply a placeholder for a data type that is defined when the function is invoked. Any letter or nonkeyword identifier can be used instead. Thus, the `showabs()` function template could have been defined as:

```
template <class DTYPE>
void showabs (DTYPE number)
{
  if (number < 0)
    number = -number;
  cout << "The absolute value of the number is "
      << number << endl;

  return;
}
```

In this regard, it is sometimes simpler and clearer to read the word `class` in the template prefix as `data type`. Thus, the template prefix `template <class T>` can be read as "we are defining a function template that has a data type named `T`." Then, within both the header line and body of the defined function, the data type `T` (or any other letter or identifier defined in the prefix) is used in the same manner as any built-in data type, such as `int`, `float`, `double`, etc.

Now suppose we want to create a function template to include both a return type and an internally declared variable. For example, consider the following function template:

```
template <class T>   // template prefix
abs (T value)        // header line
{
  T absnum;          // variable declaration
```

(continued on next page)

```
        if (value < 0)
          absnum = -value;
        else
          absnum = value;

        return absnum;
      }
```

In this template definition, we have used the data type T to declare three items: the return type of the function, the data type of a single function parameter named value, and one variable declared within the function. Program 7-6 illustrates how this function template could be used within the context of a complete program. Because we have placed the function's definition prior to its call main(), a function prototype is not required within main().

Program 7-6

```cpp
#include <iostream>
using namespace std;

template <class T>  // template prefix
T abs (T value)      // header line
{
  T absnum;          // variable declaration
  if (value < 0)
      absnum = -value;
  else
      absnum = value;

  return absnum;
}

int main()
{
  int num1 = -4;
  long num2 = -423456L;
  double num3 = -4.23456;

  cout << "The absolute value of " << num1
          << " is " << abs(num1) << endl;
  cout << "The absolute value of " << num2
        << " is " << abs(num2) << endl;
  cout << "The absolute value of " << num3
          << " is " << abs(num3) << endl;

  return 0;
}
```

In the first call to abs() made within main(), an integer value is passed as an argument. In this case, the compiler substitutes an int data type for the T data type in the function template and creates the following function:

```
int showabs(int value) // header line
{
   int absnum;              // variable declaration
   if (value < 0)
     absnum = -value;
   else
     absnum = value;

   return absnum;
}
```

Similarly, in the second and third function calls, the compiler creates two more functions, one in which the data type T is replaced by the keyword float and one in which the data type T is replaced by the keyword double. The output produced by Program 7-6 is:

```
The absolute value of -4 is 4
The absolute value of -4.23 is 4.23
The absolute value of -4.23456 is 4.23456
```

The value of using the function template is that one function definition effectively has been used to create three different functions, each of which uses the same logic and operations but operates on different data types. (The compiler only retains one copy, however, of the function, and adjusts it accordingly, based on the passed data types.)

Finally, although both Programs 7.5 and 7.6 define a function template that uses a single placeholder data type, function templates with more than one data type can be defined. For example, the template prefix

```
template <class DTYPE1, class DTYPE2, class DTYPE3>
```

can be used to create a function template that requires three different data types. As before, within the header and body of the function template, the data types DTYPE1, DTYPE2, and DTYPE3 are used in the same manner as any built-in data type, such as int, float, double, etc. Additionally, as noted previously, the names DTYPE1, DTYPE2, and DTYPE3 can be any identifier that is not a keyword. Conventionally, the letter T followed by zero or more digits would be used, such as T, T1, T2, T3, etc.

Exercises 7.1

1. For the following function headers, determine the number, type, and order (sequence) of values that should be passed to the function when it is called, and the data type of the value returned by the function.

   a. int factorial(int n)
   b. double price(int type, double yield, double maturity)

c. `double yield(int type, double price, double maturity)`
d. `char interest(char flag, double price, double time)`
e. `int total(double amount, double rate)`
f. `double roi(int a, int b, char c, char d, double e, double f)`
g. `void getVal(int item, int iter, char decflag)`

2. a. Write a function named `check()` that has three parameters. The first parameter should accept an integer number, the second parameter a floating-point number, and the third parameter a double-precision number. The body of the function should only display the values of the data passed to the function when it is called.

    (*Note:* When tracing errors in functions, it is helpful to have the function display the values it has been passed. Quite frequently, the error is not in the function but in the data received and stored.)

    b. Include the function written in Exercise 2a in a working program. Make sure your function is called from `main()`. Test the function by passing various data to it.

3. a. Write a function named `findAbs()` that accepts a double-precision number passed to it, computes its absolute value, and returns its absolute value. The absolute value of a number is the number itself if the number is positive, and the negative of the number if the number is negative.

    b. Include the function written in Exercise 3a in a working program. Make sure your function is called from `main()`. Test the function by passing various data to it.

4. a. Write a function called `mult()` that accepts two floating-point numbers as parameters, multiplies these two numbers, and returns the result.

    b. Include the function written in Exercise 4a in a working program. Make sure your function is called from `main()`. Test the function by passing various data to it.

5. a. Write a function named `sqrIt()` that computes and returns the square of the integer value passed to it.

    b. Include the function written in Exercise 5a in a working program. Make sure your function is called from `main()`. Test the function by passing various data to it.

6. a. Write a function named `powFun()` that raises an integer number passed to it to a positive integer power (also passed as an argument) and returns the result. Declare the variable used to store the result as a long-integer data type to ensure sufficient storage for the result.

    b. Include the function written in Exercise 6a in a working program. Make sure your function is called from `main()`. Test the function by passing various data to it.

7. a. Write a function named `hypotenuse()` that accepts the lengths of two sides of a right triangle as the parameters a and b, respectively. This function should determine and return the hypotenuse, c, of the triangle. (*Hint:* Use Pythagoras's theorem that $c^2 = a^2 + b^2$.)

    b. Include the function written in Exercise 7a in a working program. Make sure your function is called from `main()` and correctly returns a value to `main()`. Have `main()` display the value returned. Test the function by passing various data to it.

8. Write a function that produces a table of the numbers from 1 to 10, their squares, and cubes. The function should produce the same display as that produced by Program 6.3.

9. a. Modify the function written for Exercise 8 to accept the starting value of the table, the number of values to be displayed, and the increment between values.
    If the increment is not explicitly sent, the function should use a default value of 1. Name your function `selTab()`. A call to `selTab(6,5,2);` should produce a table of five lines, the first line starting with the number 6 and each succeeding number increasing by 2.

    b. Include the function written in Exercise 9a in a working program. Make sure your function is called from `main()`. Test the function by passing various data to it.

10. a. Write a C++ program that accepts an integer argument and determines whether the passed integer is even or odd. (*Hint:* Use the % operator.)

    b. Enter, compile, and execute the program written for Exercise 10a.

11. A useful function with an empty parameter list can be constructed to return a value for π that is accurate to the maximum number of decimal places allowed by your computer. This value is obtained by taking the arcsine of 1.0, which is $\pi/2$, and multiplying the result by 2. In C++, the required expression is 2.0 * *asin(1.0)*, where the `asin()` function is provided in the standard C++ mathematics library (remember to include `cmath`). Using this expression, write a C++ function named `Pi()` that calculates and displays the value of π.

12. Rewrite Program 7-2 so that the function `findMax()` accepts two floating-point arguments and returns a floating-point value to `main()`.

13. A second-degree polynomial in x is given by the expression $ax^2 + bx + c$, where a, b, and c are known numbers and a is not equal to zero. Write a C++ function named `polyTwo(a,b,c,x)` that computes and returns the value of a second-degree polynomial for any passed values of a, b, c, and x.

14. a. Rewrite the function `tempvert()` in Program 7-3 to accept a temperature and a character as arguments. If the character passed to the function is the letter f, the function should convert the passed temperature from Fahrenheit to Celsius, or else the function should convert the passed temperature from Celsius to Fahrenheit.

    b. Modify the `main()` function in Program 7-3 to call the function written for Exercise 14a. Your `main()` function should ask the user for the type of temperature being entered and pass the type (f or c) into `tempvert()`.

15. a. Write a function named `totamt()` that accepts four actual integer arguments named `quarters`, `dimes`, `nickels`, and `pennies`, which represent the number of quarters, dimes, nickels, and pennies in a piggy bank. The function should determine the dollar value of the number of quarters, dimes, nickels, and pennies passed to it and display the calculated value.

    b. Include the `totamt()` function written for Exercise 15a in a working program. The `main()` function should correctly call and pass the values of 26 quarters, 80 dimes, 100 nickels, and 216 pennies to `totamt()`. Make sure you do a hand calculation to verify the result displayed by your program.

16. **a.** A useful programming algorithm for rounding a real number to n decimal places is:

   Step 1: Multiply the number by 10^n.
   Step 2: Add 0.5.
   Step 3: Delete the fractional part of the result.
   Step 4: Divide by 10^n.

   For example, using this algorithm to round the number 78.374625 to three decimal places yields:

   Step 1: 78.374625 $x10^3$ = 78374.625
   Step 2: 78374.625 + 0.5 = 78375.125
   Step 3: Retaining the integer part = 78375
   Step 4: 78375 divided by 10^3 = 78.375

   Use this information to write a C++ function named `round()` that rounds the value of its first parameter to the number of decimal places specified by its second parameter. Incorporate the `round()` function into a program that accepts a user-entered value of money, multiplies the entered amount by an 8.675% interest rate, and displays the result rounded to two decimal places.

   b. Enter, compile, and execute the program written for Exercise 16a.

17. **a.** Write a function template named `display()` that displays the value of the single argument passed to it when the function is called.

   b. Include the function template created in Exercise 17a within a complete C++ program that calls the function four times: once with a character argument, once with an integer argument, once with a floating-point argument, and once with a double-precision argument.

18. **a.** Write a function template named `maximum()` that returns the maximum value of three arguments passed to the function when it is called. Assume that all three arguments are of the same data type.

   b. Include the function template created for Exercise 18a within a complete C++ program that calls the function with three integers and then with three floating-point numbers.

19. **a.** Write a function template named `square()` that computes and returns the square of the single argument passed to the function when it is called.

   b. Include the function template created for Exercise 19a within a complete C++ program.

7.2 VARIABLE SCOPE

Now that we have begun to write programs containing more than one function, we can look more closely at the variables declared within each function and their relationship to variables in other functions and class methods.

By their very nature, C++ functions are independent modules. As we have seen, values are passed to a function using the function's parameter list and a value is returned from a function using a return statement. Seen in this light, a function can be thought of as a closed box, with slots at the top to receive values and a single slot at the bottom of the box to return a value (see Figure 7-7).

FIGURE 7-7
A Function Can Be Considered a Closed Box

Values into the function

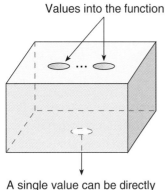

A single value can be directly
returned by the function

The metaphor of a closed box is useful because it emphasizes the fact that what goes on inside the function, including all variable declarations within the function's body, are hidden from the view of all other functions. Since the variables created inside a function are conventionally available only to the function itself, they are said to be local to the function, or local variables. This term refers to the **scope** of a variable, where scope is defined as the section of the program where the variable is valid or "known." This section of the program is also referred to as the area where the variable is visible. A function's variable can have either a local scope or a global scope. A variable with a local scope is simply one that has had storage locations set aside for it by a declaration statement made within a function body. Local variables are only meaningful when used in expressions or statements inside the function that declared them. This means that the same variable name can be declared and used in more than one function. For each function that declares the variable, a separate and distinct variable is created.

All the variables used in this chapter have been local variables. This is a direct result of placing their declaration statements inside functions and using them as definition statements that cause the computer to reserve storage for the declared variable. As we shall see, declaration statements can be placed outside functions and need not act as definitions that cause new storage areas to be reserved for the declared variable.

A variable with **global scope**, more commonly termed a **global variable**, is one whose storage has been created for it by a declaration statement located external to all functions and classes. These variables can be used by all functions that are physically placed after the global variable declaration. This is shown in Program 7-7, where we have purposely used the same variable name inside both functions contained in the program.

7

Program 7-7

```cpp
#include <iostream>
using namespace std;

int firstnum;           // create a global variable named firstnum

int main()
{
  void valfun(void);    // function prototype (declaration)
  int secnum;           // create a local variable named secnum

  firstnum = 10;        // store a value into the global variable
  secnum = 20;          // store a value into the local variable

  cout << "From main(): firstnum = " << firstnum << endl;
  cout << "From main(): secnum =  " << secnum << endl;

  valfun();             // call the function valfun

  cout << "\nFrom main() again: firstnum = " << firstnum << endl;
  cout << "From main() again: secnum = " << secnum << endl;

  return 0;
}

void valfun(void)       // no values are passed to this function
{
  int secnum;           // create a second local variable named secnum

  secnum = 30;          // this only affects this local variable's value

  cout << "\nFrom valfun(): firstnum = " << firstnum << endl;
  cout << "From valfun(): secnum = " << secnum << endl;

  firstnum = 40;        // this changes firstnum for both functions

  return;
}
```

The variable `firstnum` in Program 7-7 is a global variable because its storage is created by a definition statement located outside a function. Since both functions, `main()` and `valfun()`, follow the definition of `firstnum`, both of these functions can use this global variable with no further declaration needed.

Program 7-7 also contains two separate local variables, both named `secnum`. Storage for the `secnum` variable named in `main()` is created by the definition statement located in `main()`. A different storage area for the `secnum` variable in `valfun()` is created by the definition statement located in the `valfun()` function. Figure 7-8 illustrates the three distinct storage areas reserved by the three definition statements found in Program 7-7.

FIGURE 7-8
The Three Storage Areas Created by Program 7-7

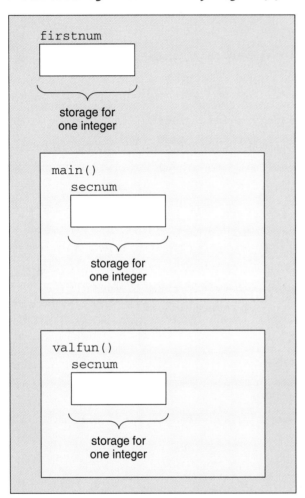

Each of the variables named secnum is local to the function in which its storage is created, and each of these variables can only be used from within the appropriate function. Thus, when secnum is used in main(), the storage area reserved by main() for its secnum variable is accessed, and when secnum is used in valfun(), the storage area reserved by valfun() for its secnum variable is accessed. The following output is produced when Program 7-7 is run:

```
From main(): firstnum = 10
From main(): secnum = 20

From valfun(): firstnum = 10
From valfun(): secnum = 30

From main() again: firstnum = 40
From main() again: secnum = 20
```

7

Let's analyze this output. Because `firstnum` is a global variable, both the `main()` and `valfun()` functions can use and change its value. Initially, both functions print the value of 10 that `main()` stored in `firstnum`. Before returning, `valfun()` changes the value of `firstnum` to 40, which is the value displayed when the variable `firstnum` is next displayed from within `main()`.

Because each function only "knows" its own local variables, `main()` can only send the value of its `secnum` to the `cout` object, and `valfun()` can only send the value of its `secnum` to the `cout` object. Thus, whenever `secnum` is obtained from `main()` the value of 20 is displayed, and whenever `secnum` is obtained from `valfun()` the value 30 is displayed.

C++ does not confuse the two `secnum` variables, because only one function can execute at a given moment. While a function is executing, only those variables and arguments that are "in scope" for that function (global and local) can be accessed.

The scope of a variable in no way influences or restricts the data type of the variable. Just as a local variable can be a character, integer, Boolean, double, or any of the other data types (long/short) we have introduced, so can global variables be of these data types, as illustrated in Figure 7-9. The scope of a variable is determined by the placement of the definition statement that reserves storage for it and, optionally, by a declaration statement that makes it visible, whereas the data type of the variable is determined by using the appropriate keyword (`char`, `int`, `bool`, `double`, etc.) before the variable's name in a declaration statement.

FIGURE 7-9
Relating the Scope and Type of a Variable

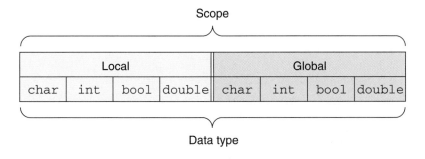

SCOPE RESOLUTION OPERATOR

When a local variable has the same name as a global variable, all references to the variable name made within the scope of the local variable refer to the local variable. This situation is illustrated in Program 7-8, where the variable `number` is defined as both a global and local variable.

Program 7-8

```cpp
#include <iostream>
using namespace std;

double number = 42.8;        // a global variable named number

int main()
{
    double number = 26.4;    // a local variable named number

    cout << "The value of number is " << number << endl;

    return 0;
}
```

When Program 7-8 is executed, the following output is displayed.

```
The value of number is 26.4
```

As shown by this output, the local variable name takes precedence over the global variable. In such cases, we can still access the global variable by using C++'s scope resolution operator. This operator, which has the symbol ::, must be placed immediately before the variable name, as in :: number. When used in this manner the :: tells the compiler to use the global variable. As an example, the global resolution operator is used in Program 7-8a.

Program 7-8a

```cpp
#include <iostream>
using namespace std;

double number = 42.5;        // a global variable named number

int main()
{
    double number = 26.4;    // a local variable named number

    cout << "The value of number is " << ::number << endl;

    return 0;
}
```

The output produced by Program 7-8a is:

```
The value of number is 42.5
```

As indicated by this output, the global resolution operator causes the global variable, rather than the local variable, to be accessed.

Misuse of Globals

Global variables allow the programmer to "skirt around" the normal safeguards provided by functions. Rather than passing variables to a function, it is possible to make all variables global. *Do not do this.* By indiscriminately making all variables global, you instantly destroy the safeguards C++ provides to make functions independent and insulated from each other, including the necessity of carefully designating the type of arguments needed by a function, the variables used in the function, and the value returned.

Using only global variables can be especially disastrous in larger programs that have many user-created functions. Since all variables in a function must be declared, creating functions that use global variables requires that you remember to write the appropriate global declarations at the top of each program using the function; they no longer come along with the function. An even greater problem is the horror of trying to track down an error in a large program using global variables. Since a global variable can be accessed and changed by any function following the global declaration, it is a time-consuming and frustrating task to locate the origin of an erroneous value.

Global variables, however, are sometimes useful in creating variables that must be shared between many functions. Rather than passing the same variable to each function, it is easier to define the variable once as a global. Doing so also alerts anyone reading the program that many functions use the variable. Most large programs almost always make use of a few global variables. Smaller programs containing a few functions, however, should almost never contain globals.

CLASS SCOPE

In addition to local and global variable scopes, variables can also have a **class scope**. That is, the names of the data and function members are local to the scope of their class. Thus, if a global variable name is re-used within a class, the global variable is hidden by the class data member in the same manner as a local function variable hides a global variable of the same name. Similarly, member function names are local to the class they are declared in, and can only be used by objects declared for the class. Additionally, local function variables also hide the names of class data members having the same name. Figure 7-10 illustrates the scope of the variables and functions for the following declarations:

```
class Test
{
  // data declaration section
  private:
    double amount;   //these variables have class scope
    double price;
    double total;
  // methods declaration section
  public:
    double extend(float, float);   // this method has class scope
};
```

FIGURE 7-10
Example of Class Scopes

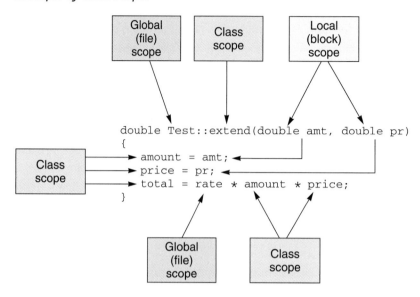

Exercises 7.2

1. a. For the following section of code, determine the data type and scope of all declared variables. To do this, create a table on a piece of paper with the column headings Variable Name, Data Type, and Scope. The entries for the first variable are filled in here to get you started:

Variable Name	Data Type	Scope
price	int	global to `main`, `roi`, and `step`

```cpp
#include <iostream>
using namespace std;

int price;
long int years;
double yield;

int main()
{
   int bondType;
   double interest, coupon;

      .

      .

   return 0;
}

double roi(int mat1, int mat2)
```

```
{
    int count;
    double effectiveInterest;

        .

        .

    return(effectiveInterest);
}

int step(double first, double last)
{
    int numofyrs;
    double fracpart;

        .

        .

    return(10*numofyrs);
}
```

b. Draw boxes around the appropriate section of the preceding code to enclose the scope of each variable.

c. Determine the data type of the arguments that the functions `roi` and `step` expect, and the data type of the value returned by these functions.

2. **a.** For the following section of code, determine the data type and scope of all declared variables. To do this, create a table on a piece of paper with the column headings Variable Name, Data Type, and Scope. The entries for the first variable are filled in here to get you started:

variable name	data type	scope
key	char	global to main, func1, and func2

```
#include <iostream>
using namespace std;

char key;
long int number;

int main()
{
    int a,b,c;
    double x,y;

        .

        .

    return 0;
}

double secnum;
```

(continued on next page)

```
int func1(int num1, int num2)
{
    int o,p;
    double q;
        .

        .
    return(p);
}

double func2(double first, double last)
{
    int a,b,c,o,p;
    double r;
    double s,t,x;
        .

        .
    return(s * t);
}
```

b. Draw a box around the appropriate section of the code above to enclose the scope of the variables key, secnum, y, and r.

c. Determine the data type of the arguments that functions func1 and func2 expect, and the data type of the value returned by these functions.

3. In addition to speaking about the scope of a variable, we can also apply the term to the arguments declared inside a function. What do you think is the scope of all function arguments?

4. Consider the following program structure:

```
#include <iostream>
using namespace std;

int a, b;

int main()
{
    int c, d;
    double e, f;
    double One(double);
        .

        .
    return 0;
}

double One(double p2)
{
    char m, n;
```

7

```
    void Two(void);
        .
        .
        .
}

void Two(void)
{
    int p, d;
    double q, r;
        .
        .
        .
}
```

Define the scope of the argument p2 and the variables a, b, c, d, m, n, p, d, q, and r.

5.   Determine the values displayed by each cout statement in the following program:

```
#include <iostream>
using namespace std;

int firstnum = 10;      // declare and initialize a global variable

int main()
{
    int firstnum = 20;     // declare and initialize a local variable
    void display(void);    // function prototype
    cout << "\nThe value of firstnum is " << firstnum << endl;
    display();

    return 0;
}

void display(void)
{
    cout << "The value of firstnum is now " << firstnum << endl;
    return;
}
```

7.3 VARIABLE STORAGE CATEGORIES

The scope of a variable defines the location within a program where that variable can be used. Given a program, you could take a pencil and draw a box around the section of the program where each variable is valid. The space inside the box would represent the scope of the variable. From this viewpoint, scope can be thought of as the space within the program where the variable is valid.

In addition to the space dimension represented by its scope, variables also have a time dimension. The time dimension refers to the length of time that storage locations are reserved for the variable. This time dimension is referred to as both a variable's lifetime and duration. (The two terms are synonymous.) The final lifetime of all variable storage locations is determined by the point at which a program has completed execution, because all variable storage locations used by a program are released back to the computer when the program is finished running. However, while a program is still executing, interim variable storage areas are reserved and subsequently released back to the computer. Where and how long a variable's storage locations are kept before they are released can be determined by the **storage class** of the variable.

Besides having a data type and scope, every variable also has a storage category. The four available storage categories are called `auto`, `static`, `extern`, and `register`. If one of these keywords is used, it must be placed before the variable's data type in a declaration statement. Examples of declaration statements that include a storage category designation are:

```
auto int num;          // auto storage category and int data type
static int miles;      // static storage category and int data type
register int dist;     // register storage category and int data type
extern int price;      // extern storage category and int data type
auto double coupon;    // auto storage category and double data type
static double years;   // static storage category and double data type
extern double yield;   // extern storage category and double data type
auto char inKey;       // auto storage category and char variable
```

To understand what a variable's storage category is, we will first consider local variables (those variables created inside a function) and then global variables (those variables created outside a function).

LOCAL VARIABLE STORAGE CATEGORIES

Local variables can only be members of the `auto`, `static`, or `register` storage categories. If no category description is included in the declaration statement, the variable is automatically assigned to the `auto` category. Thus, `auto` is the default category used by C++. All the local variables we have used, since the storage category designation was omitted, have been `auto` variables.

The term `auto` is short for **automatic.** Storage for automatic local variables is automatically reserved or created each time a function declaring automatic variables is called. As long as the function has not returned control to its calling function, all automatic variables local to the function are alive—that is, storage for the variables is available. When the function returns control to its calling function, its local automatic variables "die"—that is, the storage for the variables is released back to the computer. This process repeats itself each time a function is called. For example, consider Program 7-9, where the function `testauto()` is called three times from `main()`.

Program 7-9

```cpp
#include <iostream>
using namespace std;

int main()
{
  void testauto(void);      // function prototype
  int count;                // count is a local auto variable

  for(count = 1; count <= 3; count++)
    testauto();

  return 0;
}

void testauto(void)
{
  int num = 0;              // num is a local auto variable
                            // and initialize to zero
  cout << "The value of the automatic variable num is "
       << num << endl;
  num++;

  return;
}
```

The output produced by Program 7-9 is:

```
The value of the automatic variable num is 0
The value of the automatic variable num is 0
The value of the automatic variable num is 0
```

Each time `testauto()` is called, the local automatic variable `num` is created and initialized to zero. When the function returns control to `main()`, the variable `num` is destroyed along with any value stored in `num`. Thus, the effect of incrementing `num` in `testauto()`, before the function's `return` statement, is lost when control is returned to `main()`.

For most applications, the use of automatic variables works just fine. There are cases, however, where we would like a function to remember values between function calls. This is the purpose of the `static` storage category. A local variable that is declared as static causes the program to keep the variable and its latest value even when the function that declared it is through executing. Examples of local static variable declarations are:

```cpp
static int rate;
static double taxes;
static double amount;
static char inKey;
static long years;
```

A local static variable is not created and destroyed each time the function declaring the static variable is called. Once created, local static variables remain in existence for the life of the program. This means that the last value stored in the variable when the function is finished executing is available to the function the next time it is called.

Because local static variables retain their values, they are not initialized within a declaration statement in the same way as automatic variables. To understand why, consider the automatic declaration int num = 0;, which causes the automatic variable num to be created and set to zero each time the declaration is encountered. This is called a **run-time initialization** because initialization occurs each time the declaration statement is encountered. This type of initialization would be disastrous for a static variable, because resetting the variable's value to zero each time the function is called would destroy the very value we are trying to save.

The initialization of static variables (both local and global) is done only once, when the program is first compiled. At compilation time, the variable is created and any initialization value is placed in it.[6] Thereafter, the value in the variable is kept without further initialization each time the function is called. To see how this works, consider Program 7-10.

Program 7-10

```cpp
#include <iostream>
using namespace std;

int main()
{
  void teststat(void);     // function prototype
  int count;               // count is a local auto variable

  for(count = 1; count <= 3; count++)
    teststat();
  return 0;
}

void teststat(void)
{
  static int num = 0;     // num is a local static variable
  cout << "The value of the static variable num is now "
       << num << endl;
  num++;

  return;
}
```

---

[6]Some compilers initialize static local variables the first time the definition statement is executed, rather than when the program is compiled.

The output produced by Program 7-10 is:

```
The value of the static variable num is now 0
The value of the static variable num is now 1
The value of the static variable num is now 2
```

As illustrated by this output, the static variable num is set to zero only once. The function teststat() then increments this variable just before returning control to main(). The value that num has when leaving the function teststat() is retained and displayed when the function is next called.

Unlike automatic variables that can be initialized by either constants or expressions (using both constants and previously initialized variables), static variables can only be initialized using constants or constant expressions, such as 3.2 + 8.0. Also, unlike automatic variables, all static variables are set to zero when no explicit initialization is given. Thus, the specific initialization of num to zero in Program 7-10 is not required.

The remaining storage category available to local variables, the register category, is not used as extensively as either automatic or static variables. Examples of register variable declarations are:

```
register int time;
register double diffren;
register double coupon;
```

Register variables have the same time duration as automatic variables; that is, a local register variable is created when the function declaring it is entered, and is destroyed when the function completes execution. The only difference between register and automatic variables is the storage location for the variable.

Storage for all variables (local and global), except register variables, is reserved in the computer's memory area. Most computers have a few additional high-speed storage areas located directly in the computer's processing unit that can also be used for variable storage. These special high-speed storage areas are called registers. Since registers are physically located in the computer's processing unit, they can be accessed faster than the normal memory storage areas located in the computer's memory unit. Also, computer instructions that reference registers typically require less space than instructions that reference memory locations, because there are fewer registers that can be accessed than there are memory locations. Use of the registers, however, is typically only used by systems software and special purpose utility programs. For example, the UNIX operating system, written in C and C++, makes use of registers. Besides decreasing the size of a compiled C++ program, using register variables can also increase the execution speed of a C++ program if the computer you are using supports this data type. Applications programs that are intended to be executed on a variety of computers should not use registers. Attempts to do so will generally be foiled by the compiler by automatically switching variables declared with the register storage category to the auto storage category.

The only restriction in using the `register` storage category is that the address of a register variable, using the address operator `&`, cannot be taken. This is easily understood when you realize that registers do not have standard memory addresses.

GLOBAL VARIABLE STORAGE CATEGORIES

There are two types of global variables—those that are members of a class and those that are not. We will introduce each of these types separately, as they serve two distinct tasks.

Nonclass Global Variables

Nonclass global variables are created by definition statements external to both a function and a class. By their nature, these externally defined variables do not come and go with the calling of any function. Once such a global variable is created, it exists until the program in which it is declared is finished executing. Thus, global variables cannot be declared as either auto or register variables that are created and destroyed as the program is executing. However, such variables may additionally be declared as members of the `static` or `extern` storage categories (but not both). Examples of declaration statements including these two category descriptions are:

```
extern int sum;
extern double price;
static double yield;
```

The `static` and `extern` categories affect only the scope, not the time duration, of global variables. As with static local variables, all numeric global variables are initialized to zero at compile time. Similarly, uninitialized global character and Boolean data types are, by default, intiailized to a `NULL` and `false` value, respectively.

The purpose of the `extern` storage category is to extend the scope of a global variable beyond its normal boundaries. To understand this, we must first note that all of the programs we have written so far have always been contained together in one file. Thus, when you have saved or retrieved programs, you have only needed to give the computer a single name for your program. This is not required by C++.

Larger programs typically consist of many functions and classes that are stored in multiple files. An example of this is shown in Figure 7-11, where the three functions `main()`, `func1()`, and `func2()` are stored in one file and the two functions `func3()` and `func4()` are stored in a second file.

FIGURE 7-11
A Program May Extend Beyond One File

File 1

```
int price;
float yield;
static double coupon;



int main( )
{
    func1( );
    func2( );
    func3( );
    func4( );
}
int func1( )
{



}
int func2( )
{



}
```

File 2

```
double interest;
int func3( )
{



}
int func4( )
{



}
```

For the files illustrated in Figure 7-11, the global variables `price`, `yield`, and `coupon` declared in File 1 can only be used by the functions `main()`, `func1()`, and `func2()` in this file. The single global variable `interest`, declared in File 2, can only be used by the functions `func3()` and `func4()` in File 2.

Although the variable `price` has been created in File 1, we may want to use it in File 2. Placing the declaration statement `extern int price;` in File 2, as shown in Figure 7-12, allows us to do this. Putting this statement at the top of File 2 extends the scope of the variable `price` into File 2 so that it may be used by both `func3()` and `func4()`. Thus, the `extern` designation simply declares a global variable that is defined in another file. So placing the statement `extern float yield;` in `func4()` extends the scope of this global variable, created in File 1, into `func4()`, and the scope of the global variable `interest`, created in File 2, is extended into `func1()` and `func2()` by the declaration statement `extern double interest;` placed before `func1()`. Notice that `interest` is not available to `main()`.

FIGURE 7-12
Extending the Scope of a Global Variable

File 1

```
int price;
float yield;
static double coupon;



int main( )
{
    func1( );
    func2( );
    func3( );
    func4( );
}
extern double interest;
int func1( )
{



}
int func2( )
{



}
```

File 2

```
double interest;
extern int price;
int func3( )
{



}
int func4( )
{
    extern float yield;



}
```

PROGRAMMING NOTE

Storage Categories

Variables of type `auto` and `register` are always local variables. Only non-static global variables may be declared using the `extern` keyword. Doing so extends the variable's scope into another file or function.

Making a global variable `static` makes the variable private to the file in which it is declared. Thus, static variables cannot use the `extern` keyword. Except for `static` variables, all variables are initialized each time they come into scope. Static variables are only initialized once, when they are defined.

A declaration statement that specifically contains the word `extern` is different from every other declaration statement, in that it does not cause the creation of a new variable by reserving new storage for the variable. An `extern` declaration statement simply informs the computer that a global variable already exists and can now be used. The actual storage for the variable must be created somewhere else in the program using one, and only one, global declaration statement in which the word `extern` has not been used. Initialization of the global variable can, of course, be made with the original declaration of the global variable. Initialization within an `extern` declaration statement is not allowed and will cause a compilation error.

The existence of the `extern` storage category is the reason we have been so careful to distinguish between the creation and declaration of a variable. Declaration statements containing the word `extern` do not create new storage areas; they only extend the scope of existing global variables.

The last global category, `static` global variables, is used to prevent the extension of a global variable into a second file. Global `static` variables are declared in the same way as local `static` variables, except that the declaration statement is placed outside any function.

The scope of a global static variable cannot be extended beyond the file in which it is declared. This provides a degree of privacy for static global variables. Since they are only "known" and can only be used in the file in which they are declared, other files cannot access or change their values. Static global variables cannot be subsequently extended to a second file using an `extern` declaration statement. Trying to do so will result in a compilation error.

Global Class Variables

As each class object is created, it gets its own block of memory for its data members. In some cases, however, it is convenient for every instantiation of a class to share the same memory location for a specific variable. For example, consider a class consisting of employee payment information, where each employee is subject to the same social security tax rate. Clearly we could make the tax rate a non-class global variable, but this is not very safe. Such data could be modified anywhere in the program, could conflict with an identical variable name within a function, and certainly violates C++'s principle of data hiding.

This type of situation is handled in C++ by declaring a class variable to be `static`. Static class data members share the same storage space for all objects created from the class; as such, they act as global variables for the class and provide a means of communication between objects. Such variables *are not* part of any instantiated objects, but exist outside of all objects and can be created even if no object is created.

C++ requires that such static variables be declared within the class's declaration section. To actually create such variables, the declared static variable must be redeclared, with or without an intitial value (this defines the variable, in contrast to a formal declaration statement that does not physically allocate storage for the variable) outside of the class's declaration sections.

For example, assuming the class declaration

```
//class declaration

class Employee
{
  private:
    static double taxRate;
```

(continued on next page)

```
            int idNum;
        public:
            Employee(int);    //constructor
            void display();
      };
```

the definition and initialization of the static variable taxRate are accomplished using a statement
such as:

```
      double Employee::taxRate = 0.07;   // this defines taxRate
```

Here the scope resolution operator, : :, is used to identify taxRate are a member of the class
Employee and the keyword static is not included. Program 7-11 uses this definition within the context of a complete program.

Program 7-11

```
#include <iostream>
using namespace std;

class Employee
{
  // data declaration section
  private:
    static double taxRate;
    int idNum;

  // method declarations
  public:
    Employee(int = 0);      // constructor
    void display();         // access function
};

// static member definition
double Employee::taxRate = 0.07;    // this defines taxRate

// implementation section

Employee::Employee(int num)
{
  idNum = num;
}

void Employee::display()
{
  cout << "Employee number " << idNum
       << " has a tax rate of " << taxRate << endl;
}
```

```
int main()
{
    Employee emp1(11122), emp2(11133);

    emp1.display();
    emp2.display();

    return 0;
}
```

The output produced by Program 7-11 is:

```
Employee number 11122 has a tax rate of 0.07
Employee number 11133 has a tax rate of 0.07
```

Once the definition (as opposed to the declaration) of a static class variable is made, any other definition will result in an error. Thus, the actual definition of a `static` member remains the responsibility of the class creator. A compiler error will occur if this definition is omitted. The storage sharing produced by the `static` data member and the objects created in Program 7-11 is illustrated in Figure 7-13.

FIGURE 7-13
Sharing the Static Class Variable `taxRate`

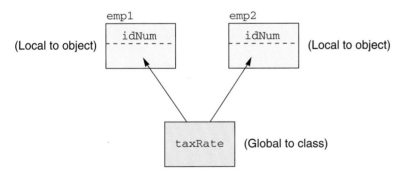

In addition to `static` data members, `static` member methods can also be created. Such methods apply to a class as a whole rather than for individual class objects and can only access `static` data members and other `static` member methods of the class.[7] An example of such a method is provided by Program 7-12.

Program 7-12

```
#include <iostream>
using namespace std;

class Employee
{
    // data declaration section
```

---

[7]The reason is that the pointer named `this`, which is discussed next, is not passed to static member functions.

```cpp
  private:
    static double taxRate;
    int idNum;

  // method declarations
  public:
    Employee(int = 0);     // constructor
    void display();        // access function
    static void disp();    // static function
};

// static member definition
double Employee::taxRate = 0.07;    // this defines taxRate

// implementation section

Employee::Employee(int num)
{
  idNum = num;
}

void Employee::display()
{
  cout << "Employee number " << idNum
       << " has a tax rate of " << taxRate << endl;
}

void Employee::disp()
{
  cout << "The static tax rate is " << taxRate << endl;
}
```

```cpp
int main()
{
  Employee::disp();    // call the static functions
  Employee emp1(11122), emp2(11133);

  emp1.display();
  emp2.display();

  return 0;
}
```

The output produced by Program 7-12 is:

```
The static tax rate is 0.07
Employee number 11122 has a tax rate of 0.07
Employee number 11133 has a tax rate of 0.07
```

In reviewing Program 7-12, notice that the keyword static is used only when static variables and methods are declared; it is not included in the definition of these members. Also notice that the static method is called using the resolution operator with the method's class name. Finally, since static methods access only static variables that are created prior to, and are not contained within, any instantiated objects, such methods can be called before any instantiations are declared.

Exercises 7.3

1. a. List the storage categories available to local variables.
    b. List the storage categories available to global variables.

2. Describe the difference between a local auto variable and a local static variable.

3. What is the difference between the following functions?

```
void init1(void)
{
   static int yrs = 1;
   cout << "The value of yrs is " << yrs << endl;
   yrs = yrs + 2;
}

void init2(void)
{
   static int yrs;
   yrs = 1;
   cout << "The value of yrs is " << yrs << endl;
   yrs = yrs + 2;
}
```

4. a. Describe the difference between a static global variable and an extern global variable.
    b. If a variable is declared as an extern, what other declaration statement must be present somewhere in the program?

5. The declaration statement static double years; can be used to create either a local or global static variable. What determines the scope of the variable years?

6. For the function and variable declarations illustrated in Figure 7-14, write seven new extern declarations to accomplish the following:

    a. Extend the scope of the global variable choice into all of File 2.
    b. Extend the scope of the global variable flag into the function production() only.
    c. Extend the scope of the global variable date into the functions production() and bid().
    d. Extend the scope of the global variable date into the function roi() only.
    e. Extend the scope of the global variable coupon into the function roi() only.
    f. Extend the scope of the global variable bondType into all of File 1.
    g. Extend the scope of the global variable maturity into both price() and yield().

FIGURE 7-14
Files for Exercise 6

File 1

```
char choice;
int flag;
long date, time;
int main( )
{
    .
    .
    .
}
double coupon;
double price( )
{
    .
    .
    .
}
double yield( )
{
    .
    .
    .
}
```

File 2

```
char bondType;
double maturity;
double roi( )
{
    .
    .
    .
}
double production( )
{
    .
    .
    .
}
double bid( )
{
    .
    .
    .
}
```

7. a. Enter and execute Program 7-11.

b. Remove the definition statement for taxRate within Program 7-11 and attempt to compile it. What is the error message telling you about this variable?

8. a. Enter and execute Program 7-12.

b. Alter the definition of taxRate in Program 7-12 to remove the explicit initialization, so that the definition reads double Employee::taxRate; and execute the modified program. From the output, determine the default value that the compiler uses to initialize taxRate.

9. a. Rewrite Program 7-12 to include a static data member named numemps. This variable, which should be an integer, should act as a counter that is initialized to zero and is incremented by the class constructor each time a new object is declared. Rewrite the static function disp() to display the value of this counter.

b. Test the program written for Exercise 9a. Have the main() function call disp() after each Employee object is created.

7.4 PASS BY REFERENCE USING REFERENCE PARAMETERS

In a typical function invocation, the called function receives values from its calling function, stores and manipulates the passed values, and directly returns at most one single value. As we have seen, this method of calling a function and passing values to it is referred to as a function call by value.

The ability to call a function by value is a distinct advantage of C++. It allows functions to be written as independent entities that can use any variable name without concern that other functions may also be using the same name. It also alleviates any concern that altering an argument or local variable in one function may inadvertently alter the value of a variable in another function. Under this approach, formal (receiving) parameters can be considered as either initialized variables or variables that will be assigned values when the function is executed. At no time, however, does the called function have direct access to any local variable contained in the calling function.

There are times, however, when it is necessary to alter this approach by giving a called function direct access to the local variables of its calling function. This allows one function, which is the called function, to use and change the value of another function's local variable. To do this requires that the address of the variable be passed to the called function. Once the called function has the variable's address, it "knows where the variable lives," so to speak, and can access and change the value stored there directly.

The process of passing addresses into a function is referred to as a **call by reference**, because the called function can reference, or access, the variable using the passed address. C++ provides two types of arguments that can accept addresses: references and pointers. In this section we describe the method that uses reference arguments (pointers are presented in Chapter 14).

As always, in exchanging data between two functions we must be concerned with both the sending and receiving sides of the data exchange. From the sending side, however, calling a function and passing an address as an actual argument that will be accepted as a reference parameter on the receiving side is exactly the same as calling a function and passing a value: the called function is summoned into action by giving its name and a list of arguments. For example, the statement newval(firstnum, secnum); both calls the function named newval and passes two arguments to it. Whether a value or an address is actually passed depends on the function header line for newval(). Let us now write the newval function and prototype so that it receives the addresses of the variables firstnum and secnum, which we will assume to be floating-point variables, rather than their values.

One of the first requirements in writing newval() is to declare two reference arguments for accepting passed addresses. In C++ a reference argument is declared using the syntax

```
dataType&    referenceName
```

For example, the reference declaration

```
double& num1;
```

declares that num1 is a reference argument that will be used to store the address of a double. Similarly, the declaration int& secnum; declares that secnum is a reference to an integer and the declaration char& key; declares that key is a reference to a character.

Recall from Section 2.4 that the ampersand (&) symbol in C++ means "the address of." Additionally, when an & symbol is used within a declaration, it refers to "the address of" the preceding data type. Using this information, declarations such as double& num1 and int& secnum are sometimes more clearly understood if they are read backwards. Reading the declaration double& num1 in this manner yields the information that "num1 is the address of a double-precision value."

Because newval() needs to accept two addresses, the declarations double& num1, double& num2 are appropriate for the parameters num1 and num2. Including these declarations within the parameter list for newval(), and assuming that the function returns no value (void), the function header for newval() becomes:

```
void newval(double& num1, double& num2)
```

For this function header line, an appropriate function prototype is:

```
void newval(double&, double&);
```

This prototype and header line are included in Program 7-13, which includes a completed newval() function body that both displays and directly alters the values stored in these reference variables from within the called function.

Program 7-13

```cpp
#include <iostream>
using namespace std;

int main()
{
  void newval(double&, double&); // prototype with two references arguments
  double firstnum, secnum;

  cout << "Enter two numbers: ";
  cin  >> firstnum >> secnum;
  cout << "\nThe value in firstnum is: " << firstnum << endl;
  cout << "The value in secnum is: " << secnum << "\n\n";

  newval(firstnum, secnum);   // call the function

  cout << "The value in firstnum is now: " << firstnum << endl;
  cout << "The value in secnum is now: " << secnum << endl;


  return 0;
}

void newval(double& xnum, double& ynum)
{
   cout << "The value in xnum is: " << xnum << endl;
```

(continued on next page)

```
  cout << "The value in ynum is: " << ynum << "\n\n";
  xnum = 89.5;
  ynum = 99.5;

  return;
}
```

In Program 7-13, it is important to understand the connection between the actual arguments, `first-num` and `secnum`, used in the `newval()` function call and the formal parameters, `xnum` and `ynum`, used in the function header. *Both reference the same data items.* The significance of this is that the values in the actual arguments `firstnum` and `secnum` can now be altered from within `newval()` by using the formal parameter names `xnum` and `ynum`. Thus, the formal parameters `xnum` and `ynum` do not store copies of the values in `firstnum` and `secnum`, but directly access the locations in memory set aside for these two arguments. The equivalence of argument names in Program 7-13, which is the essence of a call by reference, is illustrated in Figure 7-15. As illustrated in this figure, both actual argument names and their matching formal parameter names are simply different names referring to the same memory storage areas. In `main()` these memory locations are referenced by the names `firstnum` and `secnum`, respectively, while in `newval()` the same locations are referenced by the formal parameter names `xnum` and `ynum`, respectively.

FIGURE 7-15
The Equivalence of Actual and Formal Arguments in Program 7-13

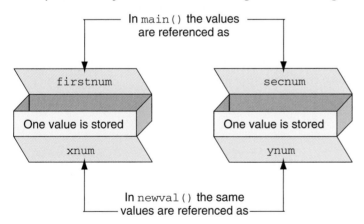

The following sample run was obtained using Program 7-13:

```
Enter two numbers: 22.5 33.6

The value in firstnum is: 22.5
The value in secnum is:   33.6

The value in xnum is: 22.5
The value in ynum is: 33.6

The value in firstnum is now: 89.5
The value in secnum is now: 99.5
```

In reviewing this output, notice that the values initially displayed for the formal arguments xnum and ynum are the same as those displayed for the actual arguments firstnum and secnum. Since xnum and ynum are reference variables, however, newval() now has direct access to the arguments firstnum and secnum. Thus, any change to xnum within newval() directly alters the value of firstnum in main() and any change to ynum directly changes secnum's value. As illustrated by the final displayed values, the assignment of values to xnum and ynum within newval() is reflected in main() as the altering of firstnum's and secnum's values.

The equivalence (illustrated in Program 7-13) between actual calling arguments and formal function parameters provides the basis for returning multiple values from within a function. For example, assume that a function is required to accept three values, compute these values' sum and product, and return these computed results to the calling routine. Naming the function calc() and providing five formal parameters (three for the input data and two references for the returned values), the following function can be used:

```
void calc(double num1, double num2, double num3, double& total, double& product)
{
  total = num1 + num2 + num3;
  product = num1 * num2 * num3;
  return;
}
```

This function has five formal parameters, named num1, num2, num3, total, and product, of which only the last two are declared as references. Within the function, only the last two parameters are altered. The value of the fourth parameter, total, is calculated as the sum of the first three arguments and the last parameter, product, is computed as the product of the arguments num1, num2, and num3. Program 7-14 includes this function in a complete program.

Program 7-14

```
#include <iostream>
using namespace std;

int main()
{
  void calc(double, double, double, double&, double&);  // function
                                                         // prototype
  double firstnum, secnum, thirdnum, sum, product;

  cout << "Enter three numbers: ";
  cin  >> firstnum >> secnum >> thirdnum;

  calc(firstnum, secnum, thirdnum, sum, product);        // function call

  cout << "\nThe sum of the numbers is: " << sum << endl;
  cout << "The product of the numbers is: " << product << endl;
```

(continued on next page)

```
    return 0;
}

void calc(double num1, double num2, double num3, double& total, double&
    product)
{
    total = num1 + num2 + num3;
    product = num1 * num2 * num3;
    return;
}
```

Within `main()`, the function `calc()` is called using the five actual arguments `firstnum`, `secnum`, `thirdnum`, `sum`, and `product`. As required, these arguments agree in number and data type with the formal parameters declared by `calc()`. Of the five actual arguments passed, only `firstnum`, `secnum`, and `thirdnum` have been assigned values when the call to `calc()` is made. The remaining two arguments have not been initialized and will be used to receive values back from `calc()`. Depending on the compiler used in compiling the program, these arguments will initially contain either zeros or "garbage" values. Figure 7-16 illustrates the relationship between actual and formal parameter names and the values they contain after the return from `calc()`.

FIGURE 7-16
Relationship Between Arguments and Parameters

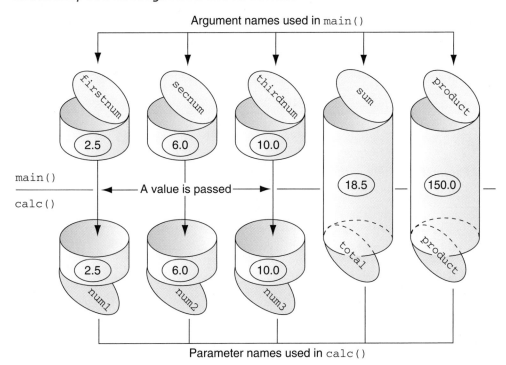

Once `calc()` is called, it uses its first three arguments to calculate values for `total` and `product` and then returns control to `main()`. Because of the order of its actual calling arguments, `main()`

knows the values calculated by calc() as sum and product, which are then displayed. Following is a sample run using Program 7-14.

```
Enter three numbers: 2.5 6.0 10.0
The sum of the entered numbers is: 18.5
The product of the entered numbers is: 150
```

As a final example of passing references to a called function, we will construct a function named swap() that exchanges the values of two of main()'s floating-point variables. Because the value of more than a single variable is affected, swap() cannot be written as a call-by-value function that returns a single value. The desired exchange of main()'s variables by swap() can only be obtained by giving swap() access to main()'s variables. One way of doing this is using reference variables.

We have already seen how to pass references to two variables in Program 7-14. We will now construct a function to exchange the values in the passed reference arguments. Exchanging values in two variables is accomplished using the swap algorithm provided in Section 3.4. Briefly, this algorithm consists of the three steps:

1. Save the first parameter's value in a temporary location (Figure 7-17A).

2. Replace the first parameter's value with the second parameter's value (Figure 7-17B).

3. Change the second parameter's value (Figure 7-17C).

FIGURE 7-17A
Save the First Parameter's Value in a Temporary Location

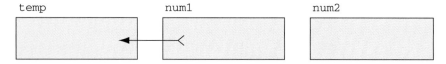

FIGURE 7-17B
Replace the First Parameter's Value with the Second Parameter's Value

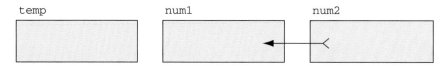

FIGURE 7-17C
Change the Second Parameter's Value

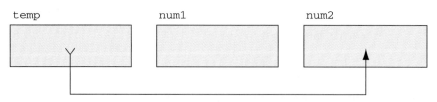

7

Following is the function `swap` written according to these specifications:

```
void swap(double& num1, double& num2)
{
  double temp;

  temp = num1;      // save num1's value
  num1 = num2;      // store num2's value in num1
  num2 = temp;      // change num2's value

  return;
}
```

Notice that the use of references in `swap()`'s header line gives `swap()` access to the equivalent arguments in the calling function. Thus, any changes to the two reference parameters in `swap()` automatically changes the values in the calling function's arguments. Program 7-15 contains `swap()` in a complete program.

The following sample run was obtained using Program 7-15:

```
The value stored in firstnum is: 20.5
The value stored in secnum is: 6.25

The value stored in firstnum is now: 6.25
The value stored in secnum is now: 20.5
```

As illustrated in this output, the values stored in `main()`'s variables have been modified from within `swap()`, which was made possible by the use of reference parameters. If a call by value had been used instead, the exchange within `swap()` would only affect `swap()`'s parameters and would accomplish nothing with respect to `main()`'s variables. Thus, as a function, `swap()` can only be written using references or some other means that provides access to `main()`'s variables (this other means is by pointers, the topic of Chapter 14). Clearly, `swap()` can be written as a class method, which avoids the use of references altogether. However, at times it is easier and more concise to use a swap procedure as a function. As always, C++ provides a vast set of programming tools and it is up to the programming team to decide which tool is more appropriate for any given circumstance.

Finally, in using reference parameters two cautions need to be mentioned. The first is that reference parameters *cannot* be used to change constants. For example, calling `swap()` with two constants, such as in the call `swap(20.5, 6.5)`, passes two constants to the function. Although `swap()` may execute, it will not change the values of these constants.[8]

The second caution to note is that a function call itself gives no indication that the called function will be using reference parameters. The default in C++ is to make calls by value rather than calls by reference, precisely to limit a called function's ability to alter variables in the calling function. This calling procedure should be followed whenever possible, which means that reference parameters should only

---

[8]Most compilers will catch this error.

be used in very restricted situations that actually require multiple return values, such as in the `swap()` function illustrated in Program 7-15. The `calc()` function, included in Program 7-14, while useful for illustrative purposes, can be written as two separate functions, each returning a single value.

Program 7-15

```cpp
#include <iostream>
using namespace std;

int main()
{
  void swap(double&, double&);    // function receives two references
  double firstnum = 20.5, secnum = 6.25;

  cout << "The value stored in firstnum is: " << firstnum << endl;
  cout << "The value stored in secnum is: "<< secnum << "\n\n";

  swap(firstnum, secnum);         // call the function with references

  cout << "The value stored in firstnum is now: "
       << firstnum << endl;
  cout << "The value stored in secnum is now: "
       << secnum << endl;


  return 0;
}
void swap(double& num1, double& num2)
{
  double temp;

  temp = num1;     // save num1's value
  num1 = num2;     // store num2's value in num1
  num2 = temp;     // change num2's value

  return;
}
```

Exercises 7.4

1. Write parameter declarations for:

   a. a formal parameter named `amount` that will be a reference to a floating-point value

   b. a formal parameter named `price` that will be a reference to a double-precision number

   c. a formal parameter named `minutes` that will be a reference to an integer number

d. a formal parameter named `key` that will be a reference to a character

e. a formal parameter named `yield` that will be a reference to a double-precision number

2. Three integer arguments are to be used in a call to a function named `time()`. Write a suitable function header for `time()`, assuming that `time()` accepts `sec`, `min`, and `hours` as reference parameters and returns no value to its calling function.

3. Rewrite the `findMax()` function in Program 7-2 so that the variable `max`, declared in `main()`, is used to store the maximum value of the two passed numbers. The value of `max` should be set directly from within `findMax()`. (*Hint*: A reference to `max` will have to be accepted by `findMax()`.)

4. Write a function named `change()` that has a floating-point argument and four integer reference arguments named `quarters`, `dimes`, `nickels`, and `pennies`, respectively. The function is to consider the floating-point passed value as a dollar amount and convert the value into an equivalent number of quarters, dimes, nickels, and pennies. Using the references, the function should directly alter the respective actual arguments in the calling function.

5. Write a function named `time()` that has an integer argument named `seconds` and three integer reference arguments named `hours`, `min`, and `sec`. The function is to convert the passed number of seconds into an equivalent number of hours, minutes, and seconds. Using the references, the function should directly alter the respective actual arguments in the calling function.

6. Write a function named `yearCalc()` that has a long-integer argument representing the total number of days from the turn of the century and reference parameters named `year`, `month`, and `day`. The function is to calculate the current year, month, and day for the given number of days passed to it. Using the references, the function should directly alter the respective actual arguments in the calling function. For this problem, assume that each year has 365 days and each month has 30 days.

7. Write a function named `liquid()` that has an integer number argument and reference parameters named `gallons`, `quarts`, `pints`, and `cups`. The passed integer represents the total number of cups, and the function is to determine the number of gallons, quarts, pints, and cups in the passed value. Using the references, the function should directly alter the respective actual arguments in the calling function. Use the relationships of two cups to a pint, four cups to a quart, and 16 cups to a gallon.

8. The following program uses the same argument names in both the calling and called function. Determine if this causes any problem for the compiler, or if the compiler correctly detects that two distinct sets of variables are being used.

```
#include <iostream>
using namespace std;

int main()
{
  void time(int&, int&);  // function prototype
```

(continued on next page)

```cpp
    int min, hour;

    cout << "Enter two numbers :";
    cin >> min >> hour;
    time(min, hour);

    return 0;
}

void time(int& min, int& hour)    // accept two references
{
    int sec;

    sec = (hour * 60 + min) * 60;
    cout << "The total number of seconds is " << sec << endl;

    return;
}
```

7.5 RECURSION[9]

Because C++ allocates new memory locations for arguments and local variables each time a function is called, it is possible for a function to call itself. Functions that do so are referred to as **self-referential** or **recursive** functions. The process of a function invoking itself is called **direct recursion**. Similarly, a function can invoke a second function, which in turn invokes the first function. This type of recursion is referred to as **indirect** or **mutual recursion**.

MATHEMATICAL RECURSION

In 1936 Alan Turing showed that, although not every possible problem can be solved by computer, those problems that have recursive solutions also have computer solutions, at least in theory. The basic concept at work here is that the solution to a problem can be stated in terms of recurring versions of the same algorithm. Some problems can be solved using an algebraic formula that shows recursion explicitly. For example, consider finding the factorial of a number n, denoted as $n!$, where n is positive. This is defined as:

$0! = 1$
$1! = 1*1 = 1*0! = 1$
$2! = 2 * 1 = 2 * 1!$
$3! = 3 * 2 * 1 = 3 * 2!$
$4! = 4 * 3 * 2 * 1 = 4 * 3!$
and, so on

---

[9]This topic may be omitted on first reading with no loss of subject continuity.

A BIT OF BACKGROUND

The Universal Algorithm Machine

In the 1930s and 1940s, Alan Mathison Turing (1912–1954) and others studied in considerable depth the theory of what a computing machine should
be able to do. Turing invented a theoretical, pencil-and-paper computer—
now appropriately called a Turing machine—that he hoped would be a
"universal algorithm machine." That is, he hoped to prove theoretically that
all problems could be solved by a set of instructions to a hypothetical computer. What he succeeded in proving was that some problems cannot be
solved by *any* machine, just as some problems cannot be solved by any person. However, he did show that algorithms that can be defined recursively
can indeed be solved by machine, though it may not be possible to predict
how long it will take the machine to find the solution.

     Alan Turing's work formed the foundation of computer theory be-
fore the first electronic computer was built. His contribution to the team
that developed the critical code-breaking computers during World War II
led directly to the practical implementation of his theories.

For consistency, the definition for *n*! can be summarized by the following statements:

```
0! = 1
n! = n * (n-1)!    for n >= 0
```

This definition illustrates the two questions you must ask when constructing a recursive algorithm:

1.   What is the first case?

2.   How is the *n*th case related to the *(n-1)* case?

Although the definition seems to define a factorial in terms of a factorial, the definition is valid, because it can always be computed. For example, using the definition, 3! is first computed as:

    3! = 3 * 2!

The value of 2! is determined from the definition as:

    2! = 2 * 1!

Substituting this expression for 2! in the determination of 3! yields:

    3! = 3 * 2 * 1!

Finally, substituting the expression 1* 0! for 1! yields:

    3! = 3 * 2 * 1 * 0!

0! is not defined in terms of the recursive formula, but is simply defined as being equal to 1. Substituting this value into the expression for 3! gives us

        3! = 3 * 2 * 1* 1 = 6

To see how a recursive function is defined in C++, we construct the function `factorial`. In pseudocode, the processing required of this function is:

> **If n = 0**
>   **factorial = 1**
> **Else**
>   **factorial = n * factorial(n - 1)**

Notice that this algorithm is simply a restatement of the recursive definition previously given. In C++, this can be written as:

```cpp
int factorial(int n)
{
   if (n == 0)
      return (1);
   else
      return (n * factorial(n - 1));
}
```

Program 7-16 illustrates this code in a complete program.

Program 7-16

```cpp
#include <iostream>
using namespace std;

int main()
{
   int factorial(int);    // function prototype
   int n, result;

   cout << "Enter a number: ";
   cin  >> n;
   result = factorial(n);
   cout << "\nThe factorial of " << n << " is " << result << endl;

   return 0;
}

int factorial(int n)
{
```

(continued to next page)

7

```
    if (n == 0)
        return (1);
    else
        return (n * factorial(n-1));
}
```

Following is a sample run of Program 7-16:

```
        Enter a number: 3
        The factorial of 3 is 6
```

HOW THE COMPUTATION IS PERFORMED

The sample run of Program 7-16 invoked the `factorial` function from `main()` using the call statement `result = factorial(n);`, where n has previously been assigned a value of 3.

Let's see how the computer actually performs the computation. The mechanism that makes it possible for a C++ function to call itself is that C++ allocates new memory locations for all function arguments and local variables as each function is called. This allocation is made dynamically, as a program is executed, in a memory area referred to as the memory stack.

A **memory stack** is an area of memory used for rapidly storing and retrieving data. It is conceptually similar to a stack of trays in a cafeteria, where the last tray placed on top of the stack is the first tray removed. This last-in/first-out mechanism provides the means for storing information in order of occurrence. Each function call simply reserves memory locations on the stack for its arguments, its local variables, a return value, and the address where execution is to resume in the calling program when the function has completed execution. Thus, when the function call `factorial(n)` is made, the stack is initially used to store the address of the instruction being executed, a space for the value to be returned by the function, and the argument value for n, which is 3. At this stage the stack can be envisioned as shown in Figure 7-18. From a program execution standpoint, the function that made the call to `factorial()`, in this case `main()`, is suspended and the compiled code for the `factorial()` function starts executing.

FIGURE 7-18
The Stack for the First Call to `factorial()`

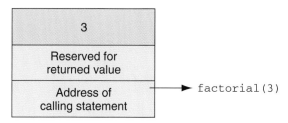

Within the `factorial()` function itself, another function call is made. That this call is to `factorial()` is irrelevant as far as C++ is concerned. The call simply is another request for stack space. In this case, the stack stores the address of the instruction being executed in `factorial()`, a space for the value to be returned by the function, and the number 2. The stack can now be envisioned as shown in Figure 7-19. At this point a second version of the compiled code for `factorial()` begins execution, while the first version is temporarily suspended.

FIGURE 7-19
The Stack for the Second Call to `factorial()`

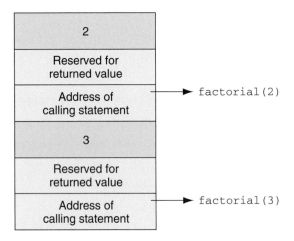

Once again, the currently executing code, which is the second invocation of `factorial`, makes a function call. That this call is to itself is irrelevant in C++. The call is once again handled in the same manner as any function call and begins with allocation of the stack's memory space. Here the stack stores the address of the instruction being executed in the calling function, which happens to be `factorial()`, a space for the value to be returned by the function, and the number 1. The stack can now be envisioned as shown in Figure 7-20. At this point, the third version of the compiled code for `factorial()` begins execution, while the second version is temporarily suspended.

7

FIGURE 7-20
The Stack for the Third Call to `factorial()`

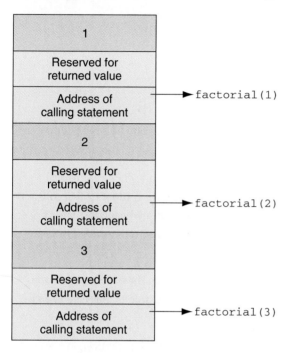

The next call, which is the fourth call to `factorial`, continues in the same fashion, except, rather than resulting in another call, it results in a returned value of 1 being placed on the stack. This completes the set of recursive calls and permits the suspended calling functions to resume execution and be completed in reverse order. The value of 1 is used by the third invocation of `factorial()` to complete its operation and place a return value of 1 on the stack. This value is then used by the second invocation of `factorial()` to place a return value of .2 on the stack. Finally, this value is then used by the first invocation of `factorial()` to complete its operation and place a return value of 6 on the stack, with execution now returning to `main()`. The original calling statement within `main()` stores the return value of its invocation of `factorial()` into the variable result.

RECURSION VERSUS ITERATION

The recursive method can be applied to any problem in which the solution is represented in terms of solutions to simpler versions of the same problem. The most difficult tasks in implementing recursion are deciding how to create the process and visualizing what happens at each successive invocation. Any recursive function can always be written in a nonrecursive manner using an iterative solution. For example, the `factorial` function can be written using an iteration algorithm as:

```
int factorial(int n)
{
   int fact;

   for(fact = 1; n > 0; n--)
      fact = fact * n;
   return (fact);
}
```

Recursion is usually a difficult concept for beginning programmers. One difficulty lies in determining the conditions in which you would use recursion rather than a repetitive solution. The answer is rather simple.

If a problem solution can be expressed iteratively or recursively with equal ease, the iterative solution is preferable because it executes faster (there are no additional function calls, which consumes processing time) and uses less memory (the stack is not used for the multiple function calls needed in recursion). There are times, however, when recursive solutions are preferable.

First, some problems are simply easier to visualize using a recursive algorithm than a repetitive one. The Towers of Hanoi problem, which is a classic recursion problem, is an example of this (see Exercise 24 at the end of this chapter).

A second reason for using recursion is that it sometimes provides a much simpler solution. In these situations, obtaining the same result using repetition requires extremely complicated coding that can be avoided by using recursion. An example of this is the quicksort sorting algorithm presented in Section 8.7.

Exercises 7.5

1. The Fibonacci sequence is 0, 1, 1, 2, 3, 5, 8, 13,... such that the first two terms are 0 and 1, and each term thereafter is defined recursively as the sum of the two preceding terms; that is,

   $Fib(n) = Fib(n-1) + Fib(n-2)$

   Write a recursive function that returns the nth number in a Fibonacci sequence when n is passed to the function as an argument. For example, when $n = 8$, the function returns the 8th number in the sequence, which is 13.

2. The sum of a series of consecutive numbers from 1 to n can be defined recursively as:

   $sum(1) = 1;$
   $sum(n) = n + sum(n - 1)$

   Write a recursive C++ function that accepts n as an argument and calculates the sum of the numbers from 1 to n.

3. **a.** The value of x^n can be defined recursively as:

$$x^0 = 1$$
$$x^n = x * x^{n-1}$$

Write a recursive function that computes and returns the value of x^n.

b. Rewrite the function written for Exercise 3a so that it uses a repetitive algorithm for calculating the value of x^n.

4. **a.** Write a function that recursively determines the value of the nth term of a geometric sequence defined by the terms

$$a, ar, ar^2, ar^3, ... ar^{n-1}$$

The argument to the function should be the first term, a, the common ratio, r, and the value of n.

b. Modify the function written for Exercise 4a so that the sum of the first n terms of the sequence is returned.

5. **a.** Write a function that recursively determines the value of the nth term of an arithmetic sequence defined by the terms

$$a, a+d, a+2d, a+3d, ... a+(n-1)d$$

The argument to the function should be the first term, a, the common difference, d, and the value of n.

b. Modify the function written for Exercise 5a so that the sum of the first n terms of the sequence is returned. (*Note:* This is a more general form of Exercise 2.)

7.6 EXCEPTION HANDLING

One of the latest features added to C++ was the introduction of exception handling for dealing with error conditions. The traditional approach that was initially used in C++, and is still available and used quite frequently, is that a function, such as `main()`, returns a specific value to indicate specific operations. Typically, a return value of 0 or 1 is used to indicate a successful completion of the function's task, while a negative value is used to indicate an error condition. For example, if a function were used to divide two numbers, a return value of -1 could be used to indicate that the denominator was zero, and the division could not be performed. When multiple error conditions can occur, different return values are used to indicate specific errors.

A number of problems can occur with this traditional approach. First, it requires that the programmer actually check the return value to detect if an error did occur. Next, the error handling code that checks the return value frequently becomes intermixed with normal processing code, so it sometimes can be difficult to clearly determine which part of the code is handling errors as opposed to handling normal program processing. Finally, returning an error condition from a method means that the condition must be of the same data type as a valid returned value; hence, the error code must be a specially identified value that can be identified as an error alert. Thus, the error code is effectively embedded as one of the possible nonerror values that may be required from the function, and is only available at the point where the method returns a value. Finally, a function that returns a Boolean value has no additional values that can be used to report an error condition.

None of this is insurmountable, and many times this approach is simple and effective. However, in its latest versions, most C++ compilers have now added an additional technique specifically designed for error detection and handling., which is referred to as exception handling.

In **exception handling,** when an error occurs while a method is executing, the method creates either a value, variable, or object (which is referred to as an **exception**) at the point the error occurs, and which contains information about the error. This exception is then immediately passed, again at the point it was generated, to code that is referred to as the **exception handler,** which is designed to correctly deal with the exception. The process of generating and passing the exception at the point the error was detected is referred to as **throwing an exception**. Notice that the exception is thrown from within the method while it is still executing. This permits handling the error and returning control back to the method so that it can complete its assigned task correctly.

In general, there are two fundamental types of errors that can cause C++ exceptions: those that result from an inability of the program to obtain a required resource and those that result from flawed data. Examples of the first error type are attempts to obtain a system resource, such as finding a file for input. These types of errors are the result of external resources over which the programmer has no control.

Examples of the second type of error can occur when a program prompts the user to enter an integer, and the user enters a string, such as e234, that cannot be converted to a numerical value. Another example is the attempt to divide two numbers when the denominator has a value of 0. This latter condition is referred to as a divide-by-zero error. Each of these errors can always be checked and handled in a manner that does not result in a program crash. Before seeing how this is accomplished using exception handling, review Table 7-1 to familiarize yourself with the terminology that is used in relation to the processing of exceptions.

TABLE 7-1
Exception Handling Terminology

terminology	description
Exception	A value, variable, or object that identifies a specific error that has occurred while a program is executing
Throw an exception	Send the exception to a section of code that processes the detected error
Catch or handle an exception	Receive a thrown exception and process it
Catch clause	The section of code that processes the error
Exception handler	The code used to throw and catch an exception

7

The general syntax of the code required to throw and catch an exception is:

```
try
{
  // one or more statements,
  // at least one of which should
  // be capable of throwing an exception;
}
catch(exceptionDataType parameterName)
{
  // one or more statements
}
```

This code uses two new keywords: `try` and `catch`. Let's see what each of these words does.

The keyword `try` identifies the start of an exception-handling block of code. At least one of the statements within the braces defining this block of code should be capable of throwing an exception. For example, the `try` block in the following section of code

```
try
{
  cout << "Enter the numerator (whole numbers only): ";
  cin  >> numerator;
  cout << "Enter the denominator (whole numbers only): ";
  cin  >> denominator;
  result = numerator/denominator;
}
```

contains five statements, three of which may result in an error that we want to catch. In particular, in a professionally written program we would want to ensure that valid integers were entered in response to both prompts, and that the second entered value was not a zero. For demonstration purposes, we will initially only check that this second value entered is not zero (in Section 16.5 you will find the exception-handling code that can be used to validate both inputs to ensure that the entered data are integers).

Thus, from the standpoint of the `try` block, it is only the value of the second number that is now of concern. Essentially, the `try` block will be altered to say "try all of the statements within me to see if an exception, which in this particular case is a zero second value, occurs." This is accomplished by adding a `throw` statement within the `try` block, as follows:

```
try
{
  cout << "Enter the numerator (whole numbers only): ";
  cin  >> numerator;
  cout << "Enter the denominator (whole numbers only): ";
  cin  >> denominator;
```

(continued on next page)

```
    if (denominator == 0)
        throw denominator;
    else
        result = numerator/denominator;
}
```

Two points need to be understood with respect to this `try` block. First, the item that is thrown is an integer literal. We could just as easily have thrown a string literal, a variable, or an object; but only one of these items can be thrown by any single `throw` statement. Secondly, the first three statements in the `try` block need not have been included in the code; however, doing so keeps all of the relevant statements together. This will also facilitate adding `throw` statements within the same `try` block to ensure that the two input values are integer values, so it is more convenient to have all the relevant code available within the same `try` block.

A `try` block must be followed by one or more `catch` blocks, which serve as exception handlers for any exceptions thrown by the statements in the `try` block. Here is a `catch` block that appropriately handles the thrown exception, which is an integer:

```
catch(int e)
{
    cout << "A denominator value of " << e << " is invalid." << endl;
    exit (1);
}
```

The exception handling provided by this `catch` block is simply an output statement that identifies the particular exception that has been caught and terminates program execution. Notice the parentheses following the `catch` keyword. Listed within the parentheses is the data type of the exception that is thrown and a parameter name used to receive it, which we have named e. This identifier, which is programmer-selected but conventionally uses the letter e for exception, is used to hold the exception value generated when an exception is thrown.

Although we have provided a single `catch` block, multiple `catch` blocks can be provided, as long as each block `catch`es a unique data type. All that is required is that at least one `catch` block be provided for each `try` block. Naturally, the more exceptions that can be caught with the same `try` block, the better. Program 7-17 provides a complete program that includes a `try` and `catch` block to detect a divide-by-zero error.

Program 7-17

```
#include <iostream>
using namespace std;

int main()
{
    int numerator, denominator;
```

(continued on next page)

```
  try
  {
    cout << "Enter the numerator (whole number only): ";
    cin  >> numerator;
    cout << "Enter the denominator(whole number only): ";
    cin  >> denominator;
    if (denominator == 0)
      throw denominator;  // an integer value is thrown
    else
        cout << numerator <<'/' << denominator
             << " = " << double(numerator)/ double(denominator) << endl;
  }
  catch(int e)
  {
    cout << "A denominator value of " << e << " is invalid." << endl;
    exit (1);
  }

  return 0;
}
```

Following are two sample runs using Program 7-17. As seen, the second output indicates that an attempt to divide by a zero denominator has been successfully detected before the operation is performed.

```
    Enter the numerator (whole number only): 12
    Enter the denominator(whole number only): 3
    12/3 = 4
```

and

```
    Enter the numerator (whole number only): 12
    Enter the denominator(whole number only): 0
    A denominator value of 0 is invalid.
```

Having detected a zero denominator, rather than terminating program execution, a more robust program would provide the user with the opportunity to re-enter a nonzero value. This can be accomplished by including the try block within a while statement, and then having the catch block return program control to the while statement after informing the user that a zero value has been entered. The code in Program 7-18 accomplishes this.

In reviewing this code, notice that it is the continue statement within the catch block that returns control to the top of the while statement (see Section 6.3 for a review of the continue statement).

Program 7-18

```cpp
#include <iostream>
using namespace std;

int main()
{
  int numerator, denominator;
  bool needDenominator = true;

  cout << "Enter a numerator (whole number only): ";
  cin  >> numerator;

  cout << "Enter a denominator (whole number only): ";
  while (needDenominator)
  {
    cin  >> denominator;
    try
    {
      if (denominator == 0)
        throw denominator;  // an integer value is thrown
    }
    catch(int e)
    {
      cout << "A denominator value of " << e << " is invalid." << endl;
      cout << "Please re-enter the denominator (whole number only): ";
      continue;  // this sends control back to the while statement
    }
    cout << numerator <<'/' << denominator
         << " = " << double(numerator)/ double(denominator) << endl;
    needDenominator = false;
  }

  return 0;
}
```

Following is a sample run using Program 7-18:

```
Enter a numerator (whole number only): 12
Enter a denominator (whole number only): 0
A denominator value of 0 is invalid.
Please re-enter the denominator (whole number only): 5
12/5 = 2.4
```

One caution should be mentioned when throwing string literals as opposed to numeric values. As an example, consider that rather than throwing the value of the `denominator` variable in both Programs 7-17 and 7-18, the following statement was used:

```
throw "***Invalid input - A denominator value of zero is not permitted***";
```

Whenever a string literal is thrown, it is a C-string, not a string class object that is thrown. This means that the catch statement must declare the received argument as a C-string, which is a character array, rather than as a string. Thus, a correct catch statement for the preceding throw statement is:

```
catch(char e[])
```

An attempt to declare the exception as a string class variable will result in a compiler error.

Exercises 7.6

1. Define the following terms:

exception	exception handler
try block	throw an exception
catch block	catch an exception

2. Enter and execute Program 7-17.

3. Replace the statement

    ```
    cout << numerator <<'/' << denominator
         << " = " << double (numerator)/ double (denominator) <<
    endl;
    ```

    in Program 7-17 with the statement

    ```
    cout << numerator <<'/' << denominator
         << " = " << numerator/denominator << endl;
    ```

    and execute the modified program. Enter the values 12 and 5, and explain why the result is incorrect from the user's viewpoint.

4. a. Modify Program 7-17 to throw an exception when a negative number is entered. The exception handler should provide the user with the number entered and then display a message that the factorial of a negative number is not defined.

    b. Modify the program written for Exercise 4a to have the program continuously request a non-negative number until a valid value is entered. Additionally, if the user enters the number 999, the program should terminate. Use an if statement to detect the input of this number.

5. Modify Program 7-17 so that it throws and correctly catches the message ***Invalid input - A denominator value of zero is not permitted***. (*Hint:* Review the caution presented at the end of this section.)

6. Enter and execute Program 7-18.

7. Modify Program 7-18 so that it continues to divide two numbers until the user enters the number 999 (either as a numerator or denominator) to terminate program execution.

7.7 PROGRAM DESIGN AND DEVELOPMENT: CREATING A PERSONAL LIBRARY

Until the introduction of personal computers in the early 1980s, with their extensive use of integrated circuits and microprocessors, both the speed of computers and their available memory were severely restricted. For example, the most advanced computers of the time had speeds measured in milliseconds (one-thousandth of a second), whereas current computers have speeds measured in nanoseconds (one-billionth of a second) and higher. Similarly, the memory capacity of early personal computers (1980s) consisted of 32,000 locations, with each location consisting of 8 bits. Today's computer memories consist of millions of memory locations, each consisting of 32 to 64 bits.

These early hardware restrictions made it imperative that programmers use every possible trick to save memory space and make programs run more efficiently. Almost every program was handcrafted and included what was referred to as "clever-code" to minimize run time and maximize the use of memory storage. Unfortunately, this individualized code, over time, became a liability. New programmers had to expend considerable time understanding existing code, and frequently even the original programmer had trouble figuring out code that was written only months before. This made modifications time-consuming and costly, and precluded cost-effective use of existing code for new installations.

The inability to re-use code efficiently, combined with expanded hardware capabilities, provided the incentive for discovering more efficient ways of programming. Initially this led to the structured-programming concepts incorporated into procedural languages such as Pascal, and currently to the object-oriented techniques that form the basis of C++. One of the early criticisms of C++, however, was that it did not provide a comprehensive library of classes. This has changed dramatically with the finalization of the ANSI/ISO standard and the inclusion of a rather extensive C++ library.

Although many useful classes and functions are provided with the C++ compiler, these classes and functions may not be sufficient for all the applications you will be asked to create. Financial, marketing, engineering, and scientific applications have their own specialized requirements. For example, C++ provides rather good date and time functions in its `ctime` header file. For specialized needs, such as those encountered in the financial industry, however, these functions must be expanded. Thus, a more complete set of functions would include finding the number of business days between two dates that took into account both weekends and holidays. It would also require functions that implemented prior and next-day algorithms that take into account leap years and the actual days in each month. These could either be provided as part of a more complete `Date` class or as nonclass functions.

In situations like this, professional programmers create and share their own libraries of classes and functions with other programmers working on the same or similar projects. Once the classes and functions have been tested, they can be incorporated in any program without further expenditures of coding time.

At this stage in your programming career you can begin to build your own library of specialized classes. To show how this is accomplished in practice, we will use Section 5.6's `Date` class, which is reproduced for convenience as Class 7-1.

Class 7-1

```cpp
#include   <iostream>
#include <iomanip>          // needed for formatting
using namespace std;

class Date
{
  // data declaration section
  private:
    int month;
    int day;
    int year;

  // methods declaration
  public:
    Date();                   // default constructor
    Date(int, int, int);   // overloaded constructor
    void setDate(int mm, int dd, int yyyy);  // mutator
    void showDate();       // accessor
};

// methods implementation section
  Date::Date()    // this is a constructor method because it has the
  {               // same name as the class
    month = 7;
    day = 4;
    year = 2005;
    cout << "From the default constructor:"
        << "\n  Created a new Date object with data values"
        << "\n    month = " << month << "  day = " << day
        << "  year = " << year << "\n\n";
  }

  Date::Date(int mm, int dd, int yyyy)  // overloaded constructor
  {
    month = mm;
    day = dd;
    year = yyyy;
    cout << "From the overloaded constructor:"
        << "\n  Created a new Date object with data values"
        << "\n    month = " << month << "  day = " << day
        << "  year = " << year << "\n\n";
  }
```

(continued on next page)

```cpp
void Date::setDate(int mm, int dd, int yyyy)
{
  month = mm;
  day = dd;
  year = yyyy;
}

void Date::showDate()
{
  cout << "The date is " << setfill('0')
       << setw(2) << month << '/'
       << setw(2) << day << '/'
       << setw(2) << year % 100; // extract the last 2 year digits
  cout << endl;
}
```

The first step in creating a library is to optionally encapsulate all of the desired classes and functions into one or more namespaces and then store the complete code (with or without using a namespace) into one or more files. For our example, we create one namespace named finDates and save it in the file named financialDate.cpp. It is important to note that the file name under which the namespace is saved *need not* be the same as the namespace name used in the code.

The syntax for creating a namespace is:

```
namespace name
{
  class declaration and/or class definitions and/or
  functions in here
}  // end of namespace
```

Including Class 7-1 within a namespace named finDates and adding the appropriate include files and using declaration statement needed by the new namespace yields the following code. For convenience, the syntax required to create the namespace has been highlighted.

```cpp
#include <iostream>
#include <iomanip>  // needed for formatting
using namespace std;

namespace finDates
{
  class Date
  {
    // data declaration section
    private:
```

(continued on next page)

```
    int month;
    int day;
    int year;

  // methods declaration
  public:
    Date();                   // default constructor
    Date(int, int, int);   // overloaded constructor
    void setDate(int mm, int dd, int yyyy);   // mutator
    void showDate();          // accessor
};

// methods implementation section
  Date::Date()     // this is a constructor method because it has the
  {                // same name as the class
    month = 7;
    day = 4;
    year = 2005;
    cout << "From the default constructor:"
         << "\n  Created a new Date object with data values"
         << "\n    month = " << month << "  day = " << day
         << "  year = " << year << "\n\n";
  }

  Date::Date(int mm, int dd, int yyyy)   // overloaded constructor
  {
    month = mm;
    day = dd;
    year = yyyy;
    cout << "From the overloaded constructor:"
         << "\n  Created a new Date object with data values"
         << "\n    month = " << month << "  day = " << day
         << "  year = " << year << "\n\n";
  }

  void Date::setDate(int mm, int dd, int yyyy)
  {
    month = mm;
    day = dd;
    year = yyyy;
  }

  void Date::showDate()
  {
    cout << "The date is " << setfill('0')
         << setw(2) << month << '/'
```

(continued on next page)

```
               << setw(2) << day << '/'
               << setw(2) << year % 100; // extract the last 2 year digits
        cout << endl;

    }
}   // end of finDates namespace
```

Once the namespace has been created and stored in a file, it can be included within another file by supplying a preprocessor directive informing the compiler where the desired namespace is to be found, and including a `using` directive instructing the compiler as to which particular namespace in the file to use. For our namespace, which has been stored in a file named `financialDates` located in a folder named `mylibrary`, this is accomplished by the statements:

```
        #include <c::\\mylibrary\\financialDates>
        using namespace finDates;
```

The first statement provides the full path name for the source code file. Notice that a full path name has been used and that two slashes are used to separate path names. The double slashes are required whenever providing either a relative or full path name. The only time that slashes are not required is when the library code resides in the same directory as the program being executed. As indicated, on the author's computer the `financialDates` source file has been saved within a folder named `mylibrary`. The second statement tells the compiler to use the `finDates` namespace within the designated file. Program 7-19 includes these two statements within an executable program.

Program 7-19

```
#include <c:\\mylibrary\\financialDates>
using namespace finDates;

int main()
{
  Date firstDate;   // declare an object using the default constructor
  Date secondDate(5,1,2006);     // declare another object using the
                                 // overloaded constructor

  // display the Date objects
  firstDate.showDate();
  secondDate.showDate();
  // reset and display one Date
  secondDate.setDate(12,25,2007);
  secondDate.showDate();

  return 0;
}
```

The only requirement for the `include` statement in Program 7-19 is that file name and location must correspond to an existing file having the same name in the designated path; otherwise a compiler error will occur. Should you wish to name the source code file using an extension, any extension can be used, as long as the following rules are maintained:

1. The file name under which the code is stored includes the extension.

2. The same file name, including extension, is used in the `include` statement.

Thus, if the file name used to store the `Date` class were `financialDates.cpp`, the include statement in Program 7-19 would be `#include <c::\\mylibrary\\financialDates.cpp>`. Additionally, a namespace is not required within the file. Using a namespace lets us isolate the `Date` class code into one area and, at some future time, permits us to add namespaces to our file for code that is unrelated to the `Date` class. The designation of a namespace in the `using` statement tells the compiler to only include the code in the specified namespace, rather than all of the code in the file. If the `Date` class code was not enclosed within a namespace, the `using` statement for the `finDates` namespace in Program 7-19 would have to be omitted.

Including the previously written and tested `Date` class within Program 7-19 as a separate file allows you to focus on the code within the program that uses this class, rather than being concerned with the class code itself. This permits you to concentrate on correctly using the class as opposed to re-examining or even seeing the previously written and tested `Date` class code. In Program 7-19, the `main()` method simply exercises the `Date` class's methods and produces the same output as Program 5-8 (if necessary, refer to Program 5-8 for an explanation of how this display is produced):

```
From the default constructor:
  Created a new Date object with data values
    month = 7   day = 4   year = 2005

From the overloaded constructor:
  Created a new Date object with data values
    month = 5   day = 1   year = 2006

The date is 07/04/05
The date is 05/01/06
The date is 12/25/07
```

In creating the `finDates` namespace we have included source code for the `Date` class. This is not required and a compiled version of the source code can be saved instead. Finally, additions to a namespace defined in one file can be made in another file by using the same namespace name in the new file and including a `using` statement for the first file's namespace.

Exercises 7.7

1. Enter and compile Program 7-19. (*Hint:* Both the namespace header file `financialDates` and the program file are available with the source code provided for this text.)

2. Why would a programmer supply a namespace file in its compiled form rather than as source code?

3.   a. What is an advantage of namespaces?
     b. What is a possible disadvantage of namespaces?

4.   What types of classes and functions would you include in a personal library? Why?

5.   a. Write a C++ function named `whole()` that returns the integer part of any number passed to the function. (*Hint:* Assign the passed argument to an integer variable.)
     b. Include the function written in Exercise 5a in a working program. Make sure your function is called from `main()` and correctly returns a value to `main()`. Have `main()` use a `cout` statement to display the value returned. Test the function by passing various data to it.
     c. When you are confident that the `whole()` function written for Exercise 5a works correctly, save it in a namespace and a personal library of your choice.

6.   a. Write a C++ function named `fracpart()` that returns the fractional part of any number passed to the function. For example, if the number 256.879 is passed to `fracpart()`, the number .879 should be returned. Have the function `fracpart()` call the function `whole()` that you wrote in Exercise 5. The number returned can then be determined as the number passed to `fracpart()` less the returned value when the same argument is passed to `whole()`. The completed program should consist of `main()` followed by `fracpart()` followed by `whole()`.
     b. Include the function written in Exercise 6a in a working program. Make sure your function is called from `main()` and correctly returns a value to `main()`. Have `main()` use a `cout` statement to display the value returned. Test the function by passing various data to it.
     c. When you are confident that the `fracpart()` function written for Exercise 6a works correctly, save it in the same namespace and personal library selected for Exercise 5c.

7.8 COMMON PROGRAMMING ERRORS

The following list summarizes some errors to watch out for when you write code that uses functions:

1.   Passing incorrect data types—This is a very common programming error related to functions. The values passed to a function must correspond to the data types of the parameters declared for the function. One way to verify that correct values have been received is to display all passed values within a function's body before any calculations are made. Once this verification has taken place, you can dispense with the display.

2.   Giving a local variable the same name as a global variable—Within the function declaring the variable, the use of the variable's name only affects the local variable's contents unless the scope resolution operator, `::`, is used.

3.   Omitting the called function's prototype either within or before the calling function—The called function must be alerted to the type of value that will be returned, and this information is pro-

vided by the function prototype. The prototype can be omitted if the called function is physically placed in a program before its calling function. The actual value returned by a function can be verified by displaying it both before and after it is returned.

4. Terminating a function's header line with a semicolon.

5. Forgetting to include the data type of a function's parameters within the header line.

6. Throwing a string literal and catching it as a string class object. When a string literal is thrown, C++ creates the literal as a C-string.

7.9 CHAPTER REVIEW

Key Terms

actual arguments	*function body*	*parameters*
call by value	*function header*	*scope*
catch statement	*function prototype*	*static*
exception	*global scope*	*throw an exception*
exception handler	*global variable*	*stub function*
extern	*local scope*	*variable scope*
formal arguments	*local variable*	

SUMMARY

1. A function is called by giving its name and passing any data to it in the parentheses following the name. If a variable is one of the arguments in a function call, the called function receives a copy of the variable's value.

2. The commonly used form of a user-written function is:

```
returnType functionName(formal parameter list)
{
    declaration statements;
    other C++ statements;
    return expression;
}
```

The first line of the function is called the function header. The opening and closing braces of the function and all statements inside these braces constitute the function's body. The returned data type is, by default, an integer when no returned data type is specified. The formal parameter list is a comma -separated list of parameter declarations.

3.   A function's return type is the data type of the value returned by the function. If no type is declared, the function is assumed to return an integer value. If the function does not return a value, it should be declared as a void type.

4.   Functions can directly return at most a single data type value to their calling functions. This value is the value of the expression in the return statement.

5.   You can use reference parameters to pass the address of a variable to a function. If a called function is passed an address, the function has the capability of directly accessing the respective calling function's variable. Using passed addresses permits a called function to effectively return multiple values.

6.   Functions can be declared to all calling functions by means of a function prototype. The prototype provides a declaration for a function that specifies the data type returned by the function, its name, and the data types of the arguments expected by the function. As with all declarations, a function prototype is terminated with a semicolon and may be included within local variable declarations or as a global declaration. The most common form of a function prototype is:

   returnDataType functionName(argument data type list);

If the called function is placed physically above the calling function, no further declaration is required, since the function's definition serves as a global declaration to all following functions.

7.   Every variable used in a program has a scope, which determines where in the program the variable can be used. The scope of a variable is either local or global. The scope of a variable is determined by where the variable's definition statement is placed. A local variable is defined within a function and can only be used within its defining function or block. A global variable is defined outside a function and can be used in any function following the variable's definition. All numeric global variables that are not explicitly initialized are initialized by the compiler to zero, while the default for character data is a NULL and Boolean data is a false. Global variables can be shared between files using the keyword extern.

8.   Every variable has a storage category. The storage category of a variable determines how long the value in the variable will be retained. auto variables are local variables that exist only while their defining function is executing. register variables are similar to auto variables but are stored in a computer's internal registers rather than in memory. Static local variables can be either global or local and retain their values for the duration of a program's execution. static local variables are set by the compiler to the default values 0, NULL, or false, for numerical, character, and Boolean data type, respectively, whenever they are defined but not explicitly initialized by the user.

9.   A recursive solution is one in which the solution can be expressed in terms of a recurring version of the basic solution algorithm. A recursive algorithm must always specify:

   • the first case or cases
   • how the nth case is related to the (n-1) case

10. If a problem solution can be expressed repetitively or recursively with equal ease, the repetitive solution is preferable because it executes faster and uses less memory. In many advanced applications, recursion is simpler to visualize and the only practical means of implementing a solution.

11. An exception is a value, variable, or object that contains information about an error that occurs while a program is executing. The following terminology is used in processing exceptions:

terminology	description
Exception	A value, variable, or object that identifies a specific error that has occurred while a program is executing.
Throw an exception	Send the exception to a section of code that processes the detected error.
Catch or handle an exception	Receive a thrown exception and process it.
Catch clause	The section of code that processes the error.
Exception handler	The code used to throw and catch an exception.

12. The general syntax of the code required to throw and catch an exception is:

```
try
{
   // one or more statements,
   // at least one of which should
   // be capable of throwing an exception;
}
catch(exceptionDataType parameterName)
{
    // one or more statements
}
```

The keyword `try` identifies the start of the statement. One of the statements within the braces defining this block of code should be capable of throwing an exception.

A `try` block must be followed by at least one `catch` block, which serves to process a specific exception thrown by one of the statements in the `try` block. Additional `catch` blocks are optional. Listed within the parentheses are the data type of the exception being caught and a user-selectable parameter name. This parameter is used to hold the exception value or object generated when the exception occurs.

Chapter Exercises

1. A function is defined by the following code:

```
double fractionToDecimal(double numerator, double denominator)
{
   return numerator/denominator;
}
```

Write the shortest driver program module you can to test this function and check the passing of parameters.

2. A formula to raise a real number *a* to the real power *b* is given by the formula

$$a^b = e^{(b \, * \, \ln(a))}$$

where *a* must be positive and *b* must be positive or zero. Using this formula, write a function named power() that accepts *a* and *b* as real values and returns a^b.

3. A fraction-handling program contains this menu:

```
A. Add two fractions
B. Convert a fraction to decimal
C. Multiply two fractions
Q. Quit
```

a. Write C++ code for the program with stub functions for the choices.
b. Insert the function fractionToDecimal() from Exercise 1 into the code with appropriate commands to pass and display the parameters.
c. Complete the program by replacing the stub functions with functions that perform appropriate operations.

4. a. The time in hours, minutes, and seconds is to be passed to a function named totsec(). Write totsec() to accept these values, determine the total number of seconds in the passed data, and return the calculated value.
b. Include the totsec() function written for Exercise 4a in a working program. The main() function should correctly call totsec and display the value returned by the function. Use the following test data to verify your program's operation: hours = 10, minutes = 36, and seconds = 54. Make sure to do a hand calculation to verify the result displayed by your program.

5. A value that is sometimes useful is the greatest common divisor of two integers *n*1 and *n*2. A famous mathematician, Euclid, discovered an efficient method to do this over two thousand years ago. Right now, however, we'll settle for a stub. Write the integer function stub gcd(n1, n2). Simply have it return a value that suggests it received its arguments correctly. (*Hint:* n1 + n2 is a good choice of return values. Why isn't n1 / n2 a good choice?)

6. Euclid's method for finding the greatest common divisor (GCD) of two positive integers consists of the following steps:

a. Divide the larger number by the smaller and retain the remainder.
b. Divide the smaller number by the remainder, again retaining the remainder.
c. Continue dividing the prior remainder by the current remainder until the remainder is zero, at which point the last non-zero remainder is the greatest common divisor.

For example, assuming the two positive integers are 84 and 49, we have:

Step 1: 84/49 yields a remainder of 35
Step 2: 49/35 yields a remainder of 14
Step 3: 35/14 yields a remainder of 7
Step 4: 14/7 yields a remainder of 0

Thus, the last nonzero remainder, which is 7, is the greatest common divisor of 84 and 49.

Using Euclid's algorithm, replace the stub function written for Exercise 5 with an actual function that determines and returns the GCD of its two integer arguments.

7. **a.** Write a function named `tax()` that accepts a dollar amount and a tax rate as formal parameters, and returns the tax due on the dollar amount. For example, if the numbers 100.00 and .06 are passed to the function, the value returned should be 6.00, which is 100.00 times .06.

   b. Include the `tax()` function written for Exercise 7a in a working program. The `main()` function should correctly call `tax()` and display the value returned by the function.

8. **a.** Write a function named `daycount()` that accepts a month, day, and year as its input parameters, calculates an integer representing the total number of days from the turn of the century corresponding to the passed date, and returns the calculated integer to the calling function. For this problem, assume that each year has 365 days and each month has 30 days. Test your function by verifying that the date 1/1/00 returns a day count of 1.

   b. Include the `daycount()` function written for Exercise 8a in a working program. The `main()` function should correctly call `daycount()` and display the integer returned by the function.

9. **a.** A clever and simple method of preparing to sort dates into either ascending (increasing) or descending (decreasing) order is to first convert a date having the form month/day/year into an integer number using the formula *date = year * 10000 + month * 100 + day*. For example, using this formula the date 12/6/1999 converts to the integer 19991206 and the date 2/28/2006 converts to the integer 20060228. Sorting the resulting integer numbers automatically puts the dates into the correct order. Using this formula, write a function named `convertdays()` that accepts a month, day, and year; converts the passed data into a single date integer; and returns the integer to the calling function.

   b. Include the `convertdays()` function written for Exercise 9a in a working program. The `main()` function should correctly call `convertdays()` and display the integer returned by the function.

10. The following program uses the same variable names in both the calling and called function. Determine if this causes any problem for the compiler.

```cpp
#include <iostream>
using namespace std;

int main()
{
   int time(int, int);   // function prototype
   int min, hour, sec;

   cout << "Enter two numbers: ";
   cin  >> min, hour;
   sec = time(min, hour);
   cout << "The total number of seconds is " << sec << endl;

   return 0;
}

int time(int min, int hour)
{
   int sec;
   sec = (hour * 60 + min) * 60;
   return (sec);
}
```

11. Write a program that reads a key pressed on the keyboard and displays its code on the screen. Use the program to determine the code for the Enter key. Then write a function named readOneChar() that reads a character and ignores any succeeding characters until the Enter key is pressed. The entered character should be returned by the function.

12. a. Write and test a C++ function makeMilesKmTable() to display a table of miles converted to kilometers. The arguments to the function should be the starting and stopping values of miles and the increment. The output should be a table of miles and their equivalent kilometer values. Use the relationship that one mile is 1.61 kilometers.

   b. Modify the function written for Exercise 12a so that two columns are printed. For example, if the starting value is 1 mile, the ending value 20 miles, and the increment is 1, the display should look like:

```
   Miles  =  Kilometers      Miles = Kilometers
     1           1.61         11        17.71
     2           3.22         12        19.32
     .            .            .          .
     .            .            .          .
    10          16.10         20        32.20
```

   (*Hint*: Find split = (start + stop)/2. Let a loop execute from miles = start to split, and calculate and print across one line the values of miles and kilometers for both miles and (miles - start + split + 1).)

13. Heron's formula for the area *A* of a triangle with sides of length *a, b,* and *c* is
A = sqrt([s(s-a)(s-b)(s-c)], where *s* = (*a* + *b* + *c*)/2. Write, test, and execute a function that
accepts the values of *a, b,* and *c* as parameters from a calling function, and then calculates the values of *s* and *s(s - a)(s - b)(s - c)*. If this quantity is positive, the function calculates *A*. If the quantity is negative, *a, b,* and *c* do not form a triangle, and the function
should set *A* = -1. The value of *A* should be returned by the function.

14. Write and test two functions `enterData()` and `printCheck()` to produce the sample
paycheck illustrated in Figure 7-21 on the screen (not including the boxed outline). The
items in parentheses should be accepted by `enterData()` and passed to
`printCheck()` for display.

FIGURE 7-21

Zzyz Corp.   Date: (today's date)
1164 Sunrise Avenue
Kalispell, Montana

Pay to the order of: (first and last name) $ (amount)

UnderSecurity Bank
Missoula, MT
                                                    _____
                                                    Authorized Signature

15. Your company will soon open a new office in France. So that they can do business there,
they have asked you to prepare a comprehensive package that will perform the following conversions on demand:

measure	American	metric	conversion
distance	inch	centimeter	2.54 cm/in
	foot	meter	0.305 m/ft
	yard	meter	0.9144 m/yd
	mile	kilometer	1.6093 km/mi
temperature	Fahrenheit	Celsius	C = (5/9)(F - 32)
weight	pound	kilogram	0.454 kg/lb
	ounce	gram	28.35 gm/oz
Currency	Dollar	Euro	entered by the user
			about 1 Euro/Dollar
capacity	quart	liter	0.946 liter/qt
	teaspoon	milliliter	4.9 ml/tsp
math	degree	radian	rad = (π/180)(degree)
	degree	grad	grad = (200/180)(degree)

16. **a.** Write a function named `date()` that accepts a long integer of the form yyyymmdd, such as 20060412; determines the corresponding month, day, and year; and returns these three values to the calling function. For example, if `date` is called using the statement:

    ```
    date(20060412, month, day, year)
    ```

    the number 4 should be returned in `month`, the number 12 in `day`, and the number 2006 in `year`.

    b. Include the date subroutine written for Exercise 16a in a working program. The `main()` function should correctly call `date` and display the three values returned by the function.

17. Write a function named `payment()` that has three arguments: `principal`, which is the amount financed; `rate`, which is the monthly interest rate; and `months`, which is the number of months the loan is for. The function should return the monthly payment according to the following formula:

    $$payment = \frac{principal}{\left[\dfrac{1 - (1 + interest)^{-months}}{interest}\right]}$$

    Note that the interest value used in this formula is a monthly rate, as a decimal. Thus, if the yearly rate is 10%, the monthly rate is (.10/12). Test your function. What argument values cause it to malfunction (and should not be input)?

18. The volume of a right circular cylinder is given by the following formula:

    $$volume = \pi\, r^2\, h$$

    Write a function that accepts two floating-point arguments (the radius of a cylinder and the cylinder's height) and returns the cylinder's volume. Use the function `Pi()` developed in the text in your function.

19. Write a function that calculates the area *a* of a circle when its circumference, *c*, is given. This function should call a second function that returns the radius, *r*, of the circle, given *c*. The relevant formulas are:

    $$r = c/2\pi \text{ and } a = \pi r^2$$

20. **a.** A recipe for making enough acorn squash for four people requires the following ingredients:

    2 acorn squashes
    2 teaspoons of lemon juice
    ¼ cup of raisins
    1½ cups of applesauce

¼ cup of brown sugar

3 tablespoons of chopped walnuts

Using this information, write and test six functions that each accept the number of peo-ple that must be served and return the amount of each ingredient, respectively, that is required.

b. Include the functions written for Exercise 20a in a complete program .

21. The owner of a strawberry farm has told a group of students they may pick all the strawberries they want. When they are through picking, the strawberries will be weighed; the farm will retain 50% of the strawberries and the students will divide the remainder evenly among them. Using this information, write and test a C++ function named `straw()` that accepts the number of students and the total pounds picked as input arguments, and returns the approximate number of strawberries each receives. Assume that a strawberry weighs approximately one ounce. There are 16 ounces to a pound. Include the `straw()` function in a working C++ program.

22. The determinant of the 2 by 2 matrix

$$\begin{vmatrix} a_{11} & a_{12} \\ a_{21} & a_{22} \end{vmatrix}$$

is $a_{11}a_{22} - a_{21}a_{12}$

Similarly, the determinant of a 3 by 3 matrix

$$\begin{vmatrix} a_{11} & a_{12} & a_{13} \\ a_{21} & a_{22} & a_{23} \\ a_{31} & a_{32} & a_{33} \end{vmatrix} =$$

$$a_{11}\begin{vmatrix} a_{22} & a_{23} \\ a_{32} & a_{33} \end{vmatrix} - a_{21}\begin{vmatrix} a_{12} & a_{13} \\ a_{32} & a_{33} \end{vmatrix} + a_{31}\begin{vmatrix} a_{12} & a_{13} \\ a_{22} & a_{23} \end{vmatrix}$$

Using this information, write and test two functions, named `det2()` and `det3()`. The `det2()` function should accept the four coefficients of a 2 by 2 matrix and return its determinant. The `det3()` function should accept the nine coefficients of a 3 by 3 matrix and return its determinant by calling `det2()` to calculate the required 2 by 2 determinants.

23. Assume that we must write a C++ program to convert the Cartesian (x, y) coordinates of a point into polar form. That is, given an x and y position on a Cartesian coordinate sys-tem, as illustrated in Figure 7-22, we must calculate the distance from the origin, r, and the angle from the x-axis, θ, specified by the point. The values of r and θ are referred to as the point's polar coordinates.

FIGURE 7-22
Correspondence Between Polar (Distance and Angle) and Cartesian (x, y) Coordinates

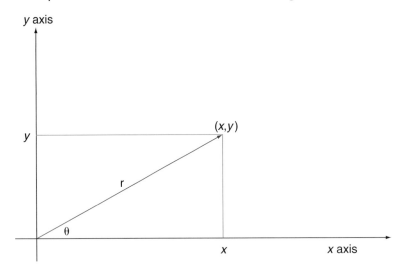

When the *x* and *y* coordinates of a point are known, the equivalent *r* and θ coordinates can be calculated using the formulas:

$$r = \sqrt{x^2 + y^2}$$

$$\theta = \tan^{-1}(y/x), \quad x \neq 0$$

Using these formulas, write a function named `polar()` that returns the *r* and θ values, respectively, for a point having rectangular coordinates *x* and *y*.

24. A classic recursion problem is represented by The Towers of Hanoi puzzle, which consists of three pegs and a set of disks initially set up as shown in Figure 7-23.

FIGURE 7-23
The Towers of Hanoi Puzzle

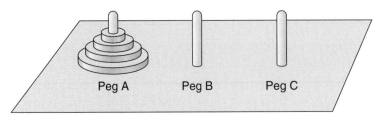

The object of the puzzle is to move all the disks from Peg A to Peg C, using Peg B as needed, with the following constraints:

1. Only one disk may be moved at a time.

2. A larger disk can never be placed on a smaller disk.

The legend associated with this problem is that it was initially given, with 64 disks, to ancient monks in a monastery with the understanding that when the task was completed and all 64 disks reached Peg C in the correct order, the world would end.

The solution to this puzzle is easily expressed as a recursive procedure where each *n* disk solution is defined in terms of an *n*-1 disk solution. To see how this works, first consider a 1-disk puzzle. Clearly this has a simple solution, where we move the disk from Peg A to Peg C.

Now consider the 2-disk problem. The solution to this puzzle is:

1. Use a 1-disk solution to move the first disk to Peg B.

2. Move the second disk to Peg C.

3. Use a 1-disk solution to move the disk on Peg B to Peg C.

The 3-disk problem is slightly more complicated, but can be solved in terms of the 2- and 1-disk puzzle. The solution is:

1. Use a 2-disk solution to get the first two disks in the right order on Peg B.

2. Move the third disk to Peg C.

3. Use a 2-disk solution to correctly move the two disks from Peg B to Peg C.

Notice how the 3-disk solution uses the 2-disk solution and the 2-disk solution uses the 1-disk solution. Let's see if this same recursive reference holds for a 4-disk puzzle.

The solution to the 4-disk puzzle is:

1. Use a 3-disk solution to get the first three disks in the right order on Peg B.

2. Move the fourth disk to Peg C.

3. Use a 3-disk solution to move the three disks from Peg B to Peg C.

At this stage we are ready to generalize the solution to *n* disks, which is:

1. Use an *n*-1-disk solution to get the first *n*-1 disks in the right order on Peg B.

2. Move the *n*th disk to Peg C.

3. Use the *n*-1 solution to move the *n*-1 disks from Peg B to Peg C.

Using this information, write a C++ program that asks the user how many disks to use and then prints the individual moves that must be made to solve the puzzle. For example, if the user responded with 3 for the number of disks, the program should display the following:

```
Move a disk from Peg A to Peg C
Move a disk from Peg A to Peg B
Move a disk form Peg C to Peg B
```

```
Move a disk from Peg A to Peg C
Move a disk from Peg B to Peg A
Move a disk from Peg B to Peg C
Move a disk from Peg A to Peg C
```

Working in Teams

25. Have your team list the sequence of events that occur in selecting an item from a soda vending machine. The sequence should start when a customer puts money in the machine and end when the customer removes a can of soda. From this list, complete the event trace diagram shown in Figure 7-24.

FIGURE 7-24

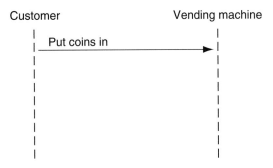

Each vertical line on the event trace diagram corresponds to an object, while the horizontal lines correspond to events. The arrow head on the event line corresponds to the event receiver, while the line's tail corresponds to the event sender. Although time is assumed to increase from the top of the diagram to the bottom, the spacing between events is not drawn to time scale. The sequence of events, from first to last, however, is indicated on the diagram starting with the first event shown and ending with the last event.

Once your team has completed the event trace diagram, use it to create a state diagram for the vending machine.

Working in Teams

26. Have your team list the sequence of events that occur in using an ATM machine. The sequence should start when the customer inserts a card and end when the card is returned. From this list, complete the event trace diagram shown in Figure 7-25.

FIGURE 7-25

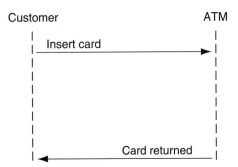

Each vertical line on the event trace diagram corresponds to an object, while the horizontal lines correspond to events. The arrow head on the event line corresponds to the event receiver, while the line's tail corresponds to the event sender. Although time is assumed to increase from the top of the diagram to the bottom, the spacing between events is not drawn to time scale. The sequence of events, from first to last, however, is indicated on the diagram starting with the first event shown and ending with the last event.

Once your team has completed the event trace diagram, use it to create a state diagram for the ATM machine.

Working in Teams

27. Have your team list the sequence of events that occur in the making of a phone call. The sequence should start when the caller picks up the phone and end when the caller hangs up. From this list, complete the event trace diagram shown in Figure 7-26.

FIGURE 7-26

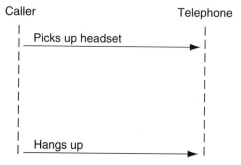

Each vertical line on the event trace diagram corresponds to an object, while the horizontal lines correspond to events. The arrow head on the event line corresponds to the event receiver while the line's tail corresponds to the event sender. Although time is assumed to increase from the top of the diagram to the bottom, the spacing between events is not drawn to time scale. The sequence of events, from first to last, however, is indicated on the diagram starting with the first event shown and ending with the last event.

Once your team has completed the event trace diagram, use it to create a state diagram for the phone system.

Please visit the Testing Center at www.course.com/testingcenter for more practice on functions.

Testing Center

ARRAYS

The built-in data types that we have used so far have all had a common characteristic: Each variable of a given data type can only be used to store a single value at a time. For example, although the variables key, count, and grade declared in the statements

```
char key;
int count;
double grade;
```

are of different data types, each variable can only store one value of the declared data type. These types of variables are called scalar variables. A **scalar** variable, which is also referred to as an **atomic** variable, is a variable whose value cannot be further subdivided or separated into a legitimate data type.

Frequently we may have a set of values, all of the same data type, that form a logical grouping. For example, Figure 8-1 illustrates three groups of items. The first group is a list of five floating-point temperatures, the second group is a list of four character codes, and the last group is a list of six integer grades.

FIGURE 8-1
Three Lists of Items

Temperatures	Codes	Grades
95.75	Z	98
83.0	C	87
97.625	K	92
72.5	L	79
86.25		85
		72

A simple list containing individual items of the same data type is called a one-dimensional array. In this chapter we describe how one-dimensional arrays are declared, initialized, stored, and processed. Additionally, a number of useful algorithms from C++'s Standard Template Library (STL) are presented for sorting and searching arrays. Procedures for declaring and using multidimensional arrays are presented, as is a special data type called a vector that can be declared directly from C++ STL. In addition to providing all of the features of individually declared arrays, vectors provide an extensive set of useful methods for manipulating and operating on individual vector elements, ranges of elements, and the data structure as a complete unit.

8.1 ONE-DIMENSIONAL ARRAYS

A **one-dimensional array**, which is also referred to as a **single-dimensional array**, is a list of related values with the same data type that is stored using a single group name.[1] In C++, as in other computer languages, the group name is referred to as the array name. For example, consider the list of temperatures illustrated in Figure 8-2.

---

[1]Note that lists can be implemented in a variety of ways, some of which are further described in Chapter 13. An array is simply one implementation of a list in which all of the list elements are of the same type and each element is stored consecutively in a set of contiguous memory locations.

FIGURE 8-2
A List of Temperatures

Temperatures
―――――――――
95.75
83.0
97.625
72.5
86.25

All the temperatures in the list are floating-point numbers and must be declared as such. However, the individual items in the list do not have to be declared separately. The items in the list can be declared as a unit and stored under a single array name. For convenience, we will choose `temp` as the name for the list shown in Figure 8-2. To specify that `temp` is an array capable of storing five individual floating-point values requires the declaration statement `double temp[5]`. Notice that this declaration statement gives the array (or list) name, the data type of the items in the array, and the number of items in the array. Good programming practice requires defining the number of array items as a constant before declaring the array. Thus, the previous array declaration would, in practice, be declared using two statements, such as:

```
const int NUMELS = 5;
double temp[NUMELS];
```

Further examples of array declarations are:

```
const int NUMELS = 6;
int grade[NUMELS];

const int ARRAYSIZE = 4;
char code[ARRAYSIZE];

const int SIZE = 100;
double amount[SIZE];
```

In these declaration statements, each array is allocated sufficient memory to hold the number of data items given in the declaration statement. Thus, the array named `grade` has storage reserved for six integers, the array named `code` has storage reserved for four characters, and the array named `amount` has storage reserved for 100 double-precision numbers. The constant identifiers NUMELS, ARRAYSIZE, and SIZE are programmer-selected symbolic constant names.

Figure 8-3 illustrates the storage reserved for the `grade` and `code` arrays.

FIGURE 8-3
The code *and* grade *Arrays in Memory*

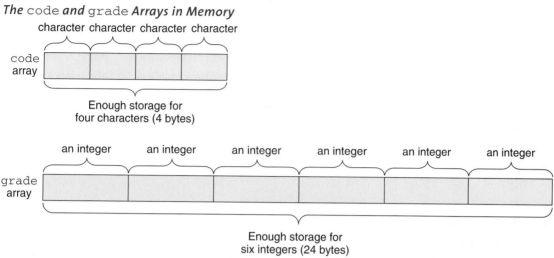

Each item in an array is called an **element** or **component** of the array. The individual elements stored in the arrays illustrated in Figure 8-3 are stored sequentially, with the first array element stored in the first reserved location, the second element stored in the second reserved location, and so on until the last element is stored in the last reserved location. This contiguous storage allocation is a key feature of arrays because it provides a simple mechanism for easily locating any single element in the array.

Because elements in the array are stored sequentially, any individual element can be accessed by giving the name of the array and the element's position. This position is called the element's **index** or **subscript value** (the two terms are synonymous). For all single-dimensional arrays, the first element has an index of 0, the second element has an index of 1, and so on. In C++, the array name and index of the desired element are combined by listing the index in braces after the array name. For example, given the declaration double temp[5],

temp[0] refers to the first temperature stored in the temp array
temp[1] refers to the second temperature stored in the temp array
temp[2] refers to the third temperature stored in the temp array
temp[3] refers to the fourth temperature stored in the temp array
temp[4] refers to the fifth temperature stored in the temp array

Figure 8-4 illustrates the temp array in memory with the correct designation for each array element. Each individual element is referred to as an **indexed variable** or a **subscripted variable**, because both a variable name and an index or subscript value must be used to reference the element. Remember that the index or subscript value designates the position of the element in the array.

FIGURE 8-4
Identifying Individual Array Elements

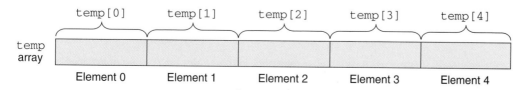

The subscripted variable, temp[0], is read as "temp sub zero" and "temp-zero." This is a shortened way of saying "the temp array subscripted by zero." Similarly, temp[1] is read as either "temp sub one" or "temp-one," temp[2] as either "temp sub two" or "temp-two," and so on.

Although it may seem unusual to reference the first element with an index of zero, doing so increases the computer's speed when it accesses array elements. Internally, the computer uses the index as an offset from the array's starting position. As illustrated in Figure 8-5, the index tells the computer how many elements to skip, starting from the beginning of the array, to get to the desired element.

FIGURE 8-5
Accessing an Individual Array Element—Element 3

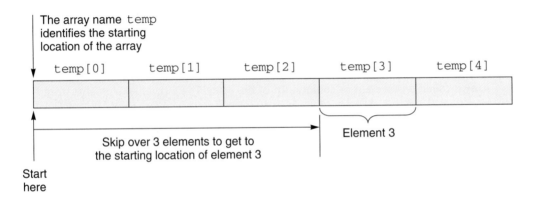

Subscripted variables can be used anywhere that scalar variables are valid. Examples using the elements of the temp array are:

```
temp[0] = 95.75;
temp[1] = temp[0] - 11.0;
temp[2] = 5.0 * temp[0];
temp[3] = 79.0;
temp[4] = (temp[1] + temp[2] - 3.1) / 2.2;
sum = temp[0] + temp[1] + temp[2] + temp[3] + temp[4];
```

The subscript contained within brackets need not be an integer constant; any expression that evaluates to an integer may be used as a subscript.[2] In each case, of course, the value of the expression must be within the valid subscript range defined when the array is declared. For example, assuming that i and j are int variables, the following subscripted variables are valid:

```
temp[i]
temp[2*i]
temp[j-i]
```

---

[2]*Note:* Some compilers permit floating-point variables as subscripts; in these cases the floating-point value is truncated to an integer value.

8

One important advantage of using integer expressions as subscripts is that it allows sequencing through an array by using a loop. This makes statements like

```
sum = temp[0] + temp[1] + temp[2] + temp[3] + temp[4];
```

unnecessary. The subscript values in this statement can be replaced by a `for` loop counter to access each element in the array sequentially. For example, the code

```
sum = 0;                      // initialize the sum to zero
for (i = 0; i < 5; i++)
    sum = sum + temp[i];      // add in a value
```

sequentially retrieves each array element and adds the element to `sum`. Here the variable `i` is used both as the counter in the `for` loop and as a subscript. As `i` increases by one each time through the loop, the next element in the array is referenced. This procedure for adding the array elements within the `for` loop is similar to the accumulation procedure we have used many times before.

The advantage of using a `for` loop to sequence through an array becomes apparent when working with larger arrays. For example, if the `temp` array contained 100 values rather than just five, simply changing the number 5 to 100 in the `for` statement is sufficient to sequence through the 100 elements and add each temperature to the sum.

As another example of using a `for` loop to sequence through an array, assume that we want to locate the maximum value in an array of 1000 elements named `grade`. The procedure we will use to locate the maximum value is to assume initially that the first element in the array is the largest number. Then, as we sequence through the array, the maximum is compared to each element. When an element with a higher value is located, that element becomes the new maximum. The following code does the job.

```
const int NUMELS = 1000;

maximum = grade[0];                 // set the maximum to element zero
for (i = 1; i < NUMELS; i++)        // cycle through the rest of the array
    if (grade[i] > maximum)         // compare each element to the maximum
        maximum = grade[i];         // capture the new high value
```

In this code the `for` statement consists of one `if` statement. The search for a new maximum value starts with element 1 of the array and continues through the last element. Each element is compared to the current maximum, and when a higher value is encountered it becomes the new maximum.

INPUT AND OUTPUT OF ARRAY VALUES

Individual array elements can be assigned values interactively using the `cin` object. Examples of individual data entry statements are:

```
cin >> temp[0];
cin >> temp[1] >> temp[2] >> temp[3];
cin >> temp[4] >> grade[6];
```

In the first statement a single value is read and stored in the variable named `temp[0]`. The second statement causes three values to be read and stored in the variables `temp[1]`, `temp[2]`, and `temp[3]`, respectively. Finally, the last `cin` statement will read values into the variables `temp[4]` and `grade[6]`.

Alternatively, a `for` loop can be used to cycle through the array for interactive data input. For example, the code

```
const int NUMELS = 5;

for (i = 0; i < NUMELS; i++)
{
  cout << "Enter a temperature: ";
  cin  >> temp[i];
}
```

prompts the user for five temperatures. The first temperature entered is stored in `temp[0]`, the second temperature entered in `temp[1]`, and so on until five temperatures have been input.

One caution should be mentioned about storing data in an array. C++ does not check the value of the index being used (called a **bounds check**). If an array has been declared as consisting of 10 elements, for example, and you use an index of 12, which is outside the bounds of the array, C++ will not notify you of the error when the program is compiled. The program will attempt to access element 12 by skipping over the appropriate number of bytes from the start of the array. Usually this results in a program crash, but not always. If the referenced location itself contains a value of the correct data type, the new value will be accessed. This can lead to more errors, which are particularly troublesome to locate when the retrieved value is processed.

During output, individual array elements can be displayed using the `cout` object or complete sections of the array can be displayed by including a `cout` statement within a `for` loop. Examples of this are:

```
cout << grade[6];
```

and

```
cout << "The value of element " << i << " is " << temp[i];
```

and

```
const int NUMELS = 20;

for (k = 5; k < NUMELS; k++)
   cout <<  k << amount[k] << endl;
```

The first statement displays the value of the subscripted variable `grade[6]`. The second statement displays the value of the subscript `i` and the value of `temp[i]`. Before this statement can be executed, `i` would have to have an assigned value. Finally, the last example includes a `cout` object within a `for` loop. Both the value of the index and the value of the elements from 5 to 19 are displayed.

Program 8-1 illustrates these input and output techniques using an array named `grade` that is defined to store five integer numbers. Included in the program are two `for` loops. The first `for` loop is used to cycle through each array element and allows the user to input individual array values. After five values have been entered, the second `for` loop is used to display the stored values.

Program 8-1

```cpp
#include <iostream>
using namespace std;

int main()
{
  const int MAXGRADES = 5;
  int i, grade[MAXGRADES];

  for (i = 0; i < MAXGRADES; i++)      // Enter the grades
  {
    cout << "Enter a grade: ";
    cin  >> grade[i];
  }

  cout << endl;

  for (i = 0; i < MAXGRADES; i++)      // Display the grades
    cout << "grade " << i << " is " << grade[i] << endl;

  return 0;
}
```

A sample run of Program 8-1 follows:

```
Enter a grade: 85
Enter a grade: 90
Enter a grade: 78
Enter a grade: 75
Enter a grade: 92

grade 0 is 85
grade 1 is 90
grade 2 is 78
grade 3 is 75
grade 4 is 92
```

In reviewing the output produced by Program 8-1, pay particular attention to the difference between the index value displayed and the numerical value stored in the corresponding array element. The index value refers to the location of the element in the array, while the subscripted variable refers to the value stored in the designated location.

In addition to simply displaying the values stored in each array element, the elements can also be processed by appropriately referencing the desired element. For example, in Program 8-2, the value of each element is accumulated in a total, which is displayed upon completion of the individual display of each array element.

Program 8-2

```
#include <iostream>
using namespace std;

int main()
{
  const int MAXGRADES = 5;
  int i, grade[MAXGRADES], total = 0;

  for (i = 0; i < MAXGRADES; i++)      // Enter the grades
  {
    cout << "Enter a grade: ";
    cin  >> grade[i];
  }

  cout << "\nThe total of the grades";

  for (i = 0; i < MAXGRADES; i++)      // Display and total the grades
  {
    cout << "   " << grade[i];
    total =  total + grade[i];
  }

  cout << " is " << total << endl;

  return 0;
}
```

A sample run of Program 8-2 follows:

```
Enter a grade: 85
Enter a grade: 90
Enter a grade: 78
Enter a grade: 75
Enter a grade: 92

The total of the grades 85   90   78   75   92 is 420
```

Notice that in Program 8-2, unlike in Program 8-1, only the values stored in each array element are displayed. Although the second `for` loop was used to accumulate the total of each element, the accumulation could also have been accomplished in the first loop by placing the statement `total = total + grade[i];` after the `cin` statement used to enter a value. Also notice that the `cout` statement used to

> **PROGRAMMING NOTE**
>
> **Structured Data Types**
>
> Atomic data types, such as integers and floating-point built-in types, cannot be decomposed into simpler types. In contrast, structured types *can* be decomposed into simpler types that are related within a defined structure. (Another term used for a structured type is a data structure.) Because a structured type consists of one or more simpler types, operations must be available for retrieving and updating the individual types that make up a data structure.
>
> Single-dimensional arrays are examples of a structured type. In a single-dimensional array, such as an array of integers, the array is composed of individual integer values, where the values are related by their position in the array. For arrays, index values provide the means of accessing and modifying individual values.

display the total is made outside of the second `for` loop, so that the total is displayed only once, after all values have been added to the total. If this `cout` statement were placed inside of the `for` loop, five totals would be displayed, with only the last displayed total containing the sum of all of the array values.

Exercises 8.1

1. Write array declarations for the following:

    a. a list of 100 single-precision grades
    b. a list of 50 double-precision temperatures
    c. a list of 30 characters, each representing a code
    d. a list of 100 integer years
    e. a list of 32 single-precision velocities
    f. a list of 1000 double-precision distances
    g. a list of 6 integer code numbers

2. Write appropriate notation for the first, third, and seventh elements of the following arrays:

    a `int grade[20]`
    b. `double grade[10]`
    c. `double amps[16]`
    d. `int dist[15]`
    e. `double velocity[25]`
    f. `double time[100]`

3. a. Write individual `cin` statements that can be used to enter values into the first, third, and seventh elements of each of the arrays declared in Exercises 2a through 2f.
    b. Write a `for` loop that can be used to enter values for the complete array declared in Exercise 2a.

4. a. Write individual `cout` statements that can be used to print the values from the first, third, and seventh elements of each of the arrays declared in Exercises 2a through 2f.
    b. Write a `for` loop that can be used to display values for the complete array declared in Exercise 2a.

5. List the elements that will be displayed by the following sections of code:

    a. `for (m = 1; m <= 5; m++)`
        `cout << a[m] << " ";`
    b. `for (k = 1; k <= 5; k = k + 2)`
        `cout <<  a[k] << " ";`
    c. `for (j = 3; j <= 10; j++)`
        `cout << b[j] << " ";`
    d. `for (k = 3; k <= 12; k = k + 3)`
        `cout << b[k] << " ";`
    e. `for (i = 2; i < 11; i = i + 2)`
        `cout << c[i] << " ";`

6. a. Write a program to input the following values into an array named `prices`: 10.95, 16.32, 12.15, 8.22, 15.98, 26.22, 13.54, 6.45, 17.59. After the data have been entered, have your program output the values.
    b. Repeat Exercise 6a, but after the data have been entered, have your program display it in the following form:

    ```
    10.95   16.32   12.15
     8.22   15.98   26.22
    13.54    6.45   17.59
    ```

7. Write a program to input eight integer numbers into an array named `temp`. As each number is input, add the numbers into a total. After all numbers are input, display the numbers and their average.

8. a. Write a program to input 10 integer numbers into an array named `fmax` and determine the maximum value entered. Your program should contain only one loop and the maximum should be determined as array element values are being input. (*Hint*: Set the maximum equal to the first array element, which should be input before the loop used to input the remaining array values.)
    b. Repeat Exercise 8a, keeping track of both the maximum element in the array and the index number for the maximum. After displaying the numbers, your program should print these two messages:

    ```
    The maximum value is: ____ .
    This is element number ____ in the list of numbers.
    ```

    Have your program display the correct values in place of the underlines in the messages.
    c. Repeat Exercise 8b, but have your program locate the minimum of the data entered.

8

9. **a.** Write a program to input the following integer numbers into an array named `grade`: 89, 95, 72, 83, 99, 54, 86, 75, 92, 73, 79, 75, 82, 73. As each number is input, add the numbers to a total. After all numbers are input and the total is obtained, calculate the average of the numbers and use the average to determine the deviation of each value from the average. Store each deviation in an array named `deviation`. Each deviation is obtained as the element value minus the average of all the data. Have your program display each deviation alongside its corresponding element from the grade array.

   b. Calculate the variance of the data used in Exercise 9a. The variance is obtained by squaring each individual deviation and dividing the sum of the squared deviations by the number of deviations.

10. Write a program that specifies three one-dimensional arrays named `prices`, `quantity`, and `amount`. Each array should be capable of holding 10 elements. Using a `for` loop, input values for the `prices` and `quantity` arrays. The entries in the `amount` array should be the product of the corresponding values in the `prices` and `quantity` arrays (thus, `amount[i] = price[i] * quantity[i]`). After all of the data have been entered, display the following output:

```
   Price          Quantity       Amount
   -----          --------       ------
```

   Under each column heading display the appropriate value.

11. **a.** Write a program that inputs 10 double numbers into an array named `raw`. After 10 user-input numbers are entered into the array, your program should cycle through `raw` 10 times. During each pass through the array, your program should select the lowest value in `raw` and place the selected value in the next available slot in an array named `sorted`. Thus, when your program is complete, the `sorted` array should contain the numbers in `raw` in sorted order from lowest to highest. (*Hint*: Make sure to reset the lowest value selected during each pass to a very high number so that it is not selected again. You will need a second `for` loop within the first `for` loop to locate the minimum value for each pass.)

   b. The method used in Exercise 11a to sort the values in the array is very inefficient. Can you determine why? What might be a better method of sorting the numbers in an array?

8.2 ARRAY INITIALIZATION

Array elements can be initialized within their declaration statements in the same manner as scalar variables, except that the initializing elements must be included in braces. Examples of such initializations are:

```
const int NUMGRADES = 5;
int grade[NUMGRADES] = {98, 87, 92, 79, 85};

const int NUMCODES = 6;
char codes[NUMCODES] = {'s', 'a', 'm', 'p', 'l', 'e'};
```

```
const int SIZE = 7;
double width[SIZE] = {10.96, 6.43, 2.58, .86, 5.89, 7.56, 8.22};
```

Initializers are applied in the order they are written, with the first value used to initialize element 0, the second value used to initialize element 1, and so on, until all values have been used. Thus, in the declaration

```
int grade[NUMGRADES] = {98, 87, 92, 79, 85};
```

grade[0] is initialized to 98, grade[1] is initialized to 87, grade[2] is initialized to 92, grade[3] is initialized to 79, and grade[4] is initialized to 85.

Because white space is ignored in C++, initializations may be continued across multiple lines. For example, the declaration

```
const int NUMGALS = 20;
int gallons[NUMGALS] = {19, 16, 14, 19, 20, 18,   // initializing values
                        12, 10, 22, 15, 18, 17,   // may extend across
                        16, 14, 23, 19, 15, 18,   // multiple lines
                                        21,  5};
```

uses four lines to initialize all of the array elements.

If the number of initializers is less than the declared number of elements listed in square brackets, the initializers are applied starting with array element zero. Thus, in the declaration

```
const int ARRAYSIZE = 7;
double length[ARRAYSIZE] = {7.8, 6.4, 4.9, 11.2};
```

only length[0], length[1], length[2], and length[3] are initialized with the listed values. The other array elements are initialized to zero. Unfortunately, there is no method of either indicating repetition of an initialization value or initializing later array elements without first specifying values for earlier elements.

A unique feature of initializers is that the size of an array may be omitted when initializing values are included in the declaration statement. For example, the declaration

```
int gallons[] = {16, 12, 10, 14, 11};
```

reserves enough storage room for five elements. Similarly, the following two declarations are equivalent:

```
char codes[6] = {'s', 'a', 'm', 'p', 'l', 'e'};
char codes[] = {'s', 'a', 'm', 'p', 'l', 'e'};
```

A BIT OF BACKGROUND

Handling Lists with LISP

Methods of handling lists have been especially important in the development of computer science and applications. In fact, in 1958 John McCarthy developed a language at the Massachusetts Institute of Technology specifically for manipulating lists. This language was named *LISP*, the acronym for *LISt Processing*. It has proved valuable for handling problems based on mathematical logic and is used extensively in artificial intelligence and pattern recognition projects.

One simple language related to LISP is named Logo, and has been made particularly user-friendly. It incorporates a technique called "turtle graphics," by which a pointer is moved around the screen to plot geometric figures. Logo has been used widely to teach programming fundamentals to children.

Both of these declarations set aside six character locations for an array named `codes`. An interesting and useful simplification can also be used when initializing character arrays. For example, the declaration

```
char codes[] = "sample";    // no braces or commas
```

uses the string `"sample"` to initialize the `codes` array. Recall that a string is any sequence of characters enclosed in double quotes. This last declaration creates a character array named `codes` having seven elements and fills the array with the seven characters illustrated in Figure 8-6. The first six characters, as expected, consist of the letters s, a, m, p, l, and e. The last character, which is the escape sequence \0, is called the **NULL character**. The NULL character is automatically appended to all strings that are used to initialize a character array, and is what distinguishes a C-string from a string class value. The NULL character has an internal storage code that is numerically equal to zero (the storage code for the zero character has a numerical value of decimal 48, so the two cannot be confused by the computer), and is used as a marker, or sentinel, to mark the end of a C-string. As we shall see in Chapter 12, this marker is invaluable when manipulating arrays of characters, which is the way C-strings are stored in C++. Another technique is to use the string class, which is presented in Chapter 9.

FIGURE 8-6
Initializing a Character Array with a String Adds a Terminating \0 Character

codes[0]	codes[1]	codes[2]	codes[3]	codes[4]	codes[5]	codes[6]
s	a	m	p	l	e	\0

Once values have been assigned to array elements, either through initialization within the declaration statement or using interactive input, the array elements can be processed as described in the previous section. For example, Program 8-3 illustrates the initialization of array elements within the declaration of the array and then uses a `for` loop to locate the maximum value stored in the array.

Program 8-3

```cpp
#include <iostream>
using namespace std;

int main()
{
    const int MAXELS = 5;
    int nums[MAXELS] = {2, 18, 1, 27, 16};
    int i, max;

    max = nums[0];

    for (i = 1; i < MAXELS; i++)
        if (max < nums[i])
            max = nums[i];

    cout << "The maximum value is " << max << endl;

    return 0;
}
```

The output produced by Program 8-3 is:

```
The maximum value is 27
```

Exercises 8.2

1. Write array declarations, including initializers, for the following:

    a. a list of 10 integer grades: 89, 75, 82, 93, 78, 95, 81, 88, 77, 82
    b. a list of five double-precision amounts: 10.62, 13.98, 18.45, 12.68, 14.76
    c. a list of 100 double-precision interest rates; the first six rates are 6.29, 6.95, 7.25, 7.35, 7.40, 7.42
    d. a list of 64 double-precision temperatures; the first 10 temperatures are 78.2, 69.6, 68.5, 83.9, 55.4, 67.0, 49.8, 58.3, 62.5, 71.6
    e. a list of 15 character codes; the first seven codes are f, j, m, q, t, w, z

2. Write an array declaration statement that stores the following values in an array named `prices`: 16.24, 18.98, 23.75, 16.29, 19.54, 14.22, 11.13, 15.39. Include these statements in a program that displays the values in the array.

3. Write a program that uses an array declaration statement to initialize the following numbers in an array named `slopes`: 17.24, 25.63, 5.94, 33.92, 3.71, 32.84, 35.93, 18.24, 6.92. Your program should locate and display both the maximum and minimum values in the array.

4. Write a program that stores the following prices in an array named `prices`: 9.92, 6.32, 12.63, 5.95, 10.29. Your program should also create two arrays named `units` and `amounts`, each

capable of storing five double-precision numbers. Using a `for` loop and a `cin` statement, have your program accept five user-input numbers into the `units` array when the program is run. Your program should store the product of the corresponding values in the `prices` and `units` arrays in the `amounts` array (for example, `amounts[1] = prices[1] * units[1]`) and display the following output (fill in the table appropriately):

```
      Price        Units        Amount
      -----        -----        ------
       9.92          .             .
       6.32          .             .
      12.63          .             .
       5.95          .             .
      10.29          .             .
                                 ------
      Total:                       .
```

5. The string of characters `"Good Morning"` is to be stored in a character array named `goodstr1`. Write the declaration for this array in three different ways.

6. a. Write declaration statements to store the string of characters `"Input the Following Data"` in a character array named `messageOne`, the string `"----------------------"` in a character array named `messageTwo`, the string `"Enter the Date: "` in a character array named `messageThree`, and the string `"Enter the Account Number: "` in the character array named `messageFour`.

   b. Include the array declarations written in Exercise 6a in a program that uses the `cout` object to display the messages. For example, the statement `cout << messageOne;` causes the string stored in the `messageOne` array to be displayed. Your program will require four such statements to display the four individual messages. Using the `cout` object to display a string stored in a character array requires the last character in the array to be the null character, `'\0'`.

7. a. Write a declaration to store the string `"This is a test"` into a character array named `strtest`. Include the declaration in a program to display the message using the following loop:

```
for (i = 0; i < NUMDISPLAY; i++)
   cout << strtest[i];
```

   where `NUMDISPLAY` is a symbolic constant for the number 14.

   b. Modify the `for` statement in Exercise 7a to display only the array characters t, e, s, and t.

   c. Include the array declaration written in Exercise 7a in a program that uses the `cout` object to display characters in the array. For example, the statement `cout << strtest;` causes the characters stored in the `strtest` array to be displayed. Using this statement requires that the last character in the array is the end of string marker `'\0'`.

   d. Repeat Exercise 7a using a `while` loop. (Hint: Stop the loop when the `\0` escape sequence is detected. The expression `while (strtest[i] != '\0')` can be used.)

8.3 ARRAYS AS ARGUMENTS

Individual array elements are passed to a called function in the same manner as individual scalar variables; they are simply included as subscripted variables when the function call is made. For example, the function call `findMin(grade[2], grade[6]);` passes the values of the elements `grade[2]` and `grade[6]` to the function `findMin()`.

Passing a complete array of values to a function is in many respects an easier operation than passing individual elements. The called function receives access to the actual array, rather than a copy of the values in the array. For example, if `grade` is an array, the function call `findMax(grade);` makes the complete `grade` array available to the `findMax()` function. This is different from passing a single variable to a function.

Recall that when a single scalar argument is passed to a function, the called function only receives a copy of the passed value, which is stored in one of the function's parameters. If arrays were passed in this manner, a copy of the complete array would have to be created. For large arrays, making duplicate copies of the array for each function call would waste storage space and frustrate the effort to return multiple element changes made by the called program. (Recall that a function returns at most one value.) To avoid these problems, the called function is given direct access to the original array.[3] Thus, any changes made by the called function are made directly to the array itself. For the following specific examples of function calls, assume that the arrays `nums`, `keys`, `units`, and `prices` are declared as:

```
int nums[5];                    // an array of five integers
char keys[256];                 // an array of 256 characters
double units[500], prices[500]; // two arrays of 500 doubles
```

For these arrays, the following function calls can be made:

```
        findMax(nums);
        findChar(keys);
        calcTotal(nums, units, prices);
```

In each case, the called function receives direct access to the named array.

On the receiving side, the called function must be alerted that an array is being made available. For example, suitable function header lines for the previous functions are:

```
int findMax(int vals[5])
char findChar(char inKeys[256])
void calcTotal(int arr1[5], double arr2[500], double arr3[500])
```

---

[3]This is accomplished because the starting address of the array is actually passed as an argument. The formal parameter receiving this address argument is referred to as a pointer. The intimate relationship between array names and pointers is presented in Chapter 14.

In each of these function header lines, the names in the parameter list are chosen by the programmer. However, the parameter names used by the functions still refer to the original array created outside the function. This is made clear in Program 8-4.

Program 8-4

```cpp
#include <iostream>
#include <string>
using namespace std;
const int MAXELS = 5;

int main()
{
  int findMax(int []);        // function prototype

  int nums[MAXELS] = {2, 18, 1, 27, 16};

  cout << "The maximum value is " << findMax(nums) << endl;

  return 0;
}

// find the maximum value
int findMax(int vals[])
{
  int i, max = vals[0];

  for (i = 1; i < MAXELS; i++)
    if (max < vals[i]) max = vals[i];

  return max;
}
```

The output displayed by Program 8-4 is:

```
The maximum value is 27
```

Notice that the function prototype for findMax() within main() declares that findMax() will return an integer and expects an array of integers as an actual argument. It is also important to know that only one array is created in Program 8-4. In main() this array is known as nums, and in findMax() the array is known as vals. As illustrated in Figure 8-7, both names refer to the same array. Thus, in Figure 8-7 vals[3] is the same element as nums[3]. The declaration of MAXELS as a global symbolic constant permits its use in both main() and findMax().

FIGURE 8-7
Only One Array Is Created

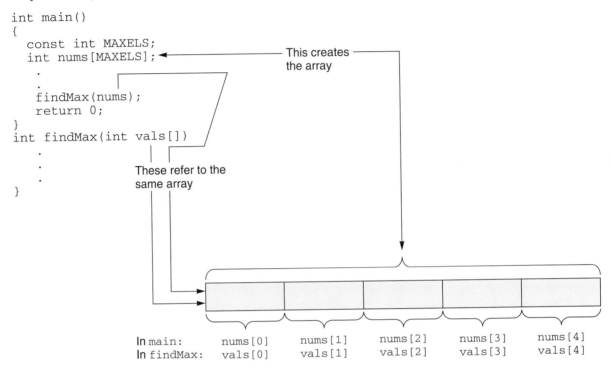

```
int main()
{
    const int MAXELS;
    int nums[MAXELS];
    .
    .
    .
    findMax(nums);
    return 0;
}
int findMax(int vals[])
    .
    .
    .
}
```

This creates the array

These refer to the same array

| In main: | nums[0] | nums[1] | nums[2] | nums[3] | nums[4] |
| In findMax: | vals[0] | vals[1] | vals[2] | vals[3] | vals[4] |

Also notice that the parameter declaration in findMax()'s header line is not required to specify the number of elements in the array argument. Because the array has been created in main() and no additional storage space is needed in findMax(), the declaration for vals can omit the size of the array. This makes more sense when you realize that only one item is actually passed to findMax() when the function is called, which is the starting address of the nums array. This is illustrated in Figure 8-8.

FIGURE 8-8
The Starting Address of the Array Is Passed

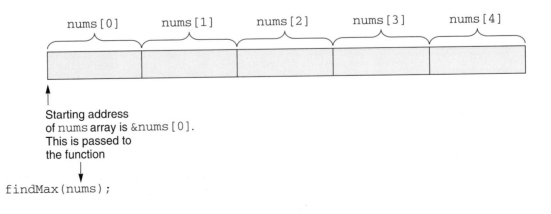

| nums[0] | nums[1] | nums[2] | nums[3] | nums[4] |

Starting address
of nums array is &nums[0].
This is passed to
the function

```
findMax(nums);
```

Because only the starting address of `vals` is passed to `findMax()`, the number of elements in the array need not be included in the declaration for `vals`.[4] In fact, it is generally advisable to omit the size of the array in the function header line, because, as written, `findMax()` can be used to find the maximum value of an integer array of arbitrary size simply by redefining the value stored in `MAXELS`.

Internally, once `findMax()` is called, the function uses the number of elements, passed as the argument `MAXELS`, as the boundary for its search. The `for` loop causes each array element to be examined in sequential order and determines the maximum number in the array.

Exercises 8.3

1. The following declaration was used to create the `prices` array:

   ```
   const int NUMGRADES = 500;
   double prices[NUMGRADES];
   ```

   Write two different function header lines for a function named `sortArray()` that accepts the `prices` array as an argument named `inArray`.

2. The following declaration was used to create the `Keys` array:

   ```
   const int NUMKEYS = 256;
   char Keys[NUMKEYS];
   ```

   Write two different function header lines for a function named `findKey()` that accepts the `Keys` array as an argument named `select`.

3. The following declaration was used to create the `rates` array:

   ```
   const int NUMRATES = 10;
   double rates[NUMRATES];
   ```

   Write two different function header lines for a function named `prime()` that accepts the `rates` array as an argument named `rates`.

4. a. Modify the `findMax()` function in Program 8-4 to locate the minimum value of the passed array.
   b. Include the function written in Exercise 4a in a complete program and run the program on a computer.

5. Write a program that has a declaration in `main()` to store the following numbers into an array named `rates`: 6.5, 7.2, 7.5, 8.3, 8.6, 9.4, 9.6, 9.8, 10.0. There should be a function call to `show()` that accepts the `rates` array as an argument named `rates` and then displays the numbers in the array.

---

[4]An important consequence of this is that `findMax()` has direct access to the passed array. This means that any change to an element of the `vals` array actually is a change to the `nums` array. This is significantly different than the situation with scalar variables, where the called function does not receive direct access to the passed variable.

6. a. Write a program that has a declaration in `main()` to store the string `"Vacation is near"` into an array named `message`.

    There should be a function call to `display()` that accepts a message in an argument named `string` and then displays the message.

    b. Modify the `display()` function written in Exercise 6a to display the first eight elements of the `message` array.

7. Write a program that declares three single-dimensional arrays named `price`, `quantity`, and `amount`. Each array should be declared in `main()` and should be capable of holding 10 double-precision numbers. The numbers that should be stored in `price` are 10.62, 14.89, 13.21, 16.55, 18.62, 9.47, 6.58, 18.32, 12.15, 3.98. The numbers that should be stored in `quantity` are 4, 8.5, 6, 7.35, 9, 15.3, 3, 5.4, 2.9, 4.8. Your program should pass these three arrays to a function called `extend()`, which should calculate the elements in the `amount` array as the product of the corresponding elements in the `price` and `quantity` arrays (for example, `amount[1] = price[1] * quantity[1]`). After `extend()` has put values into the `amount` array, the values in the array should be displayed from within `main()`.

8. Assume the following letters are stored in an array named `alphabet`: B, J, K, M, S, Z. Write and test a function named `addLetter()`, which accepts both the `alphabet` array and a new letter as arguments, and inserts the new letter in the correct alphabetical order in the `alphabet` array.

9. Write a program that includes two functions named `calcAverage()` and `variance()`. The `calcAverage()` function should calculate and return the average of the values stored in an array named `testvals`. The array should be declared in `main()` and include the values 89, 95, 72, 83, 99, 54, 86, 75, 92, 73, 79, 75, 82, 73. The `variance()` function should calculate and return the variance of the data. The variance is obtained by subtracting the average from each value in `testvals`, squaring the values obtained, adding them, and dividing by the number of elements in `testvals`. The values returned from `calcAverage()` and `variance()` should be displayed using `cout` statements in `main()`.

8.4 USING STL ALGORITHMS FOR SEARCHING AND SORTING[5]

At some time in their career, programmers find that they need to both sort and search arrays of data items. For example, experimental results might have to be arranged in either increasing (ascending) or decreasing (descending) order for statistical analysis; an array of names, as string data, may have to be sorted in alphabetical order; or an array of dates may have to be rearranged in ascending date order. Similarly, an array of names may have to be searched to find a particular name in the list, or a list of dates may have to be searched to locate a particular date.

Sorting and searching arrays can be accomplished either by using a prewritten function or by writing the code from scratch (referred to in programming as "rolling your own"). C++'s Standard Template

---
[5] This topic is optional and may be omitted without loss of subject continuity.

Library (STL) provides a set of generic capabilities that can be applied to both STL data structures, such as the `vector` type presented in Section 8.6, as well as non-STL data structures, such as an array. Table 8-1 lists three of these capabilities (a more complete list is provided in Section 8.6) that are directly applicable to searching and sorting arrays. These capabilities are provided as methods and are formally referred to as STL algorithms.

TABLE 8-1
Standard Template Library (STL) Search and Sort Algorithms

algorithm name	description
binary_search (start, end, value)	Returns a Boolean value of `true` if the specified value exists within the specified range; otherwise returns `false`. Can only be used on a sorted set of values.
find (start, end, value)	Returns the position of the first occurrence of an element in a specified range having a specified value, if the value exists. Performs a linear search, starting with the first element in a specified range, and proceeds one element at a time until the complete range has been searched or the specified element has been found.
sort (start, end)	Sorts elements in the specified range into an ascending order.

The basics underlying the search and sort functions listed in Table 8-1 are presented in Section 8.7. You will need to understand these concepts in order to create a specialized sort or search function. This section presents sorting and searching array elements using the STL functions, which is the preferred technique because it relies on tested and reliable code. In general it is not necessary to sort a list before searching it, although, in many cases, much faster searches can be performed if an array's elements are in sorted (either ascending or descending) order.

Notice that all of the STL algorithms listed in Table 8-1 operate on elements within a designated range. This range is always specified by providing the first element in the range and one element beyond the last desired element. When used with arrays, these first and last elements are easily specified as offsets using the array's name as the starting point. Examples of various ranges, assuming an array named `names`, are:

first element	last element	specified range
names + 0	names + 3	names[0] through names[2], inclusive.
names	names + 3	same as above, because a 0 offset for the first element can be omitted.
names + 1	names + 11	names[1] through names[10], inclusive.

This notation permits the first and last elements to be passed to the selected algorithm using the same procedure in which arrays were passed into a called function (that is, by the array's name, as presented in the last section). For example, the statement `sort(names, names + 11);` calls the `sort` algorithm and specifies that the elements from `names[0]` to `names[10]` should be replaced in a sorted order. Notice that in all cases the specified range starts at the first element and ends at one element less than the last specified element.

The function prototypes for each of the algorithms listed in Table 8-1 are provided in a header file named `algorithm`; thus, this file must be included in any program that uses these algorithms. This is accomplished by including the statement `#include <algorithm>`.

The `sort()` method uses a modified quicksort algorithm (described in Section 8.7) to arrange an array's elements into an ascending (increasing) order, while the `binary_search()` method (also described in Section 8.7) requires a sorted list for its search. Thus, in practice, the `sort()` method is almost always called immediately before the `binary_search()` method is invoked, unless the array is known to be in a sorted order to begin with. The `find()` method not only searches for a designated value, but returns the position of the first match. Because this method performs a linear search, starting at the first element in the specified range and moving sequentially, element by element, through the list, it does not require the list to be in a sorted order. However, for large lists it will frequently save time if the list is first sorted and a `binary_search()` performed to establish that a desired element is present, before invoking the slower `find()` method to sequentially search each item in the list.

As a specific example of this, and to see how each of the algorithms listed in Table 8-1 can be used, consider Program 8-5. This program first permits keyboard entry of five names that are entered into an array. The `sort()` method is then called to rearrange the elements into ascending order. Once the sort has been completed, the program requests the entry of a name that is subsequently used as an argument to the `binary_search()` method. This method returns a Boolean `true` value if the specified name is contained in the array; otherwise, it returns a `false` value. Then, and only if the `binary_search()` method determines that the value is in the array, the `find()` method is called to determine where the name is actually located. The statements in Program 8-5 that use the `sort()`, `binary_search()`, and `find()` methods have been highlighted for easy identification.

Program 8-5

```
#include <iostream>
#include <string>
#include <algorithm>   // needed to access STL algorithms
using namespace std;

int main()
{
  const int NUMELS = 5;
  string names[NUMELS];   //an array of string values
  string value;
  int i, offset;
  bool found;

  // read the array values
  for (i = 0; i < NUMELS; i++)
  {
    cout << "Enter name " << (i+1) << ": ";
    cin  >> names[i];
  }
```

(continued on next page)

```
// sort the array
sort(names, names + NUMELS);

cout << "\nEnter the name you are looking for: ";
cin  >> value;

found = binary_search(names, names + NUMELS, value);
if (found)
{
   offset = find(names, names + NUMELS, value) - names;
   cout << "\nThe name " << value << " is located at position "
        << offset + 1 << " in the sorted array." << endl;
}
else
   cout << "\nThe name " << value << " is not in the array." << endl;

// display the sorted array
cout << "\nThe values in sorted order are:";
for (i = 0; i < NUMELS; i++)
   cout << "  " << names[i];
cout << endl;

return 0;
}
```

Following is a sample run using Program 8-5, where the user enters five names into the array and then requests that the sorted array names be searched for the name Menning.

```
Enter name 1: Williams
Enter name 2: Menning
Enter name 3: Able
Enter name 4: Jones
Enter name 5: Smith

Enter the name you are looking for: Menning
```

The name Menning is located at position 3 in the sorted array.

```
The values in sorted order are:  Able  Jones  Menning  Smith  Williams
```

In reviewing Program 8-5, notice that the sort() method arranges array elements into alphabetical order for string elements and in increasing numerical order for primitive data types. In addition, when the binary_search() method is used to locate a specified value, the method returns either a Boolean true (1) or false (0) value; it does not return the location of the value. Also notice that all three functions use the array's name as their first argument, and the name plus an offset as their second argument, while the binary_search() and find() functions require an additional third argument, which is the searched-for value. If only a section of the array is desired to be sorted or searched, the first two arguments in all three function calls can be specified with offsets. For example, if only the third through fifth array elements were to be sorted, the appropriate method call would be sort(nums + 2, nums + 4).

Finally, the `find()` method returns the location of the designated element, which is equivalent to the array's name plus an offset to the element. The offset to the element is then determined by subtracting the array's name from the returned value, which is done in the statement:

```
offset = find(names, names + NUMELS, value) - names;
```

Adding one to this value converts this offset to the exact position of the located element.

Exercises 8.4

1. Enter and run Program 8-5 on your computer.

2. Execute Program 8-5, but enter names with both lowercase and uppercase letters and determine if the correct alphabetical order is produced. What does this tell you about the `sort()` function?

3. Execute Program 8-5, entering all names in the array with an initial capital letter. Then enter the searched-for name in all lowercase letters. What does the output display tell you about the `binary_search()` function?

4. Modify Program 8-5 to enter and sort an array of integers.

5. Modify Program 8-5 to enter and sort an array of characters.

6. Using either the Internet or the online documentation provided with your compiler, obtain documentation on the STL and the list of algorithms provided by this library.

8.5 TWO-DIMENSIONAL ARRAYS

A **two-dimensional array**, which is sometimes referred to as a table, consists of both rows and columns of elements. For example, the array of numbers

$$
\begin{array}{cccc}
8 & 16 & 9 & 52 \\
3 & 15 & 27 & 6 \\
14 & 25 & 2 & 10
\end{array}
$$

is called a two-dimensional array of integers. This array consists of three rows and four columns. To reserve storage for this array, both the number of rows and the number of columns must be included in the array's declaration. Calling the array `val`, the correct specification for this two-dimensional array is:

```
const int NUMROWS = 3;
const int NUMCOLS = 4;
int val[NUMROWS][NUMCOLS];
```

8

Similarly, the declarations

```
const int NUMROWS = 10;
const int NUMCOLS = 5;
double prices[NUMROWS][NUMCOLS];

const int NUMROWS = 5;
const int NUMCOLS = 26
char code[NUMROWS][NUMCOLS];
```

declare that the array `prices` consists of 10 rows and 5 columns of double-precision numbers and that the array `code` consists of 5 rows and 26 columns, with each element capable of holding one character. Again, notice that we have used symbolic constants in declaring each array's size. As with single-dimensional arrays, two-dimensional arrays can also be declared directly, without using symbolic constants. Thus, the previous three arrays can also be declared as:

```
int val[3][4];
double prices[10][5];
char code[5][26];
```

The advantage of using symbolic constants, however, becomes evident when processing array elements with `for` and `while` loops that use the constants as counters. Each element in a two-dimensional array is located by identifying its position in the array. As illustrated in Figure 8-9, the term `val[1][3]` uniquely identifies the element in row 1, column 3. As with single-dimensional array variables, double-dimensional array variables can be used anywhere that scalar variables are valid. Examples using elements of the `val` array are:

```
amount = val[2][3];
val[0][0] = 62;
newnum = 4 * (val[1][0] - 5);
sumRow = val[0][0] + val[0][1] + val[0][2] + val[0][3];
```

FIGURE 8-9
Each Array Element Is Identified by Its Row and Column Position

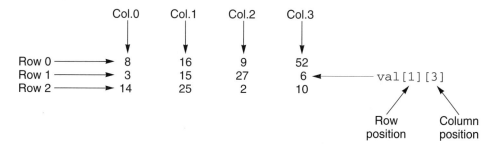

The last statement causes the values of the four elements in row 0 to be added and the sum to be stored in the scalar variable `sumRow`.

As with single-dimensional arrays, two-dimensional arrays can be initialized from within their declaration statements. This is done by listing the initial values within braces and separating them by commas. Additionally, braces can be used to separate individual rows. For example, the declaration

```
const int NUMROWS = 3;
const int NUMCOLS = 4;
int val [NUMROWS][NUMCOLS] = { {8,16,9,52},
                              {3,15,27,6},
                              {14,25,2,10} };
```

declares val to be an array of integers with three rows and four columns, with the initial values given in the declaration. The first set of internal braces contains the values for row 0 of the array, the second set of internal braces contains the values for row 1, and the third set of braces the values for row 2.

Although the commas in the initialization braces are always required, the inner braces can be omitted. Thus, the initialization for val may be written as

```
int val[NUMROWS][NUMCOLS] = {8,16,9,52,
                             3,15,27,6,
                             14,25,2,10};
```

The separation of initial values into rows in the declaration statement is not necessary since the compiler assigns values beginning with the [0][0] element and proceeds row by row to fill in the remaining values. Thus, the initialization

```
int val[NUMROWS][NUMCOLS] = {8,16,9,52,3,15,27,6,14,25,2,10};
```

is equally valid but does not clearly illustrate to another programmer where one row ends and another begins.

As illustrated in Figure 8-10, the initialization of a two-dimensional array is done in row order. First, the elements of the first row are initialized, then the elements of the second row are initialized, and so on, until the initializations are completed. This row ordering is also the same ordering used to store two-dimensional arrays. That is, array element [0][0] is stored first, followed by element [0][1], followed by element [0][2], and so on. Following the first row's elements are the second row's elements, and so on for all the rows in the array.

FIGURE 8-10
Storage and Initialization of the val *Array*

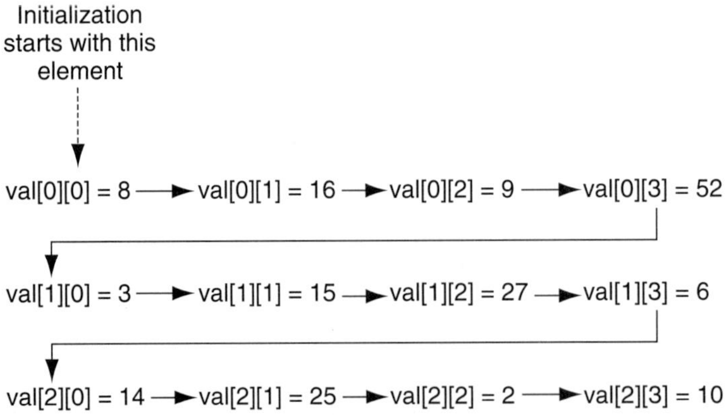

Initialization
starts with this
element

val[0][0] = 8 ⟶ val[0][1] = 16 ⟶ val[0][2] = 9 ⟶ val[0][3] = 52

val[1][0] = 3 ⟶ val[1][1] = 15 ⟶ val[1][2] = 27 ⟶ val[1][3] = 6

val[2][0] = 14 ⟶ val[2][1] = 25 ⟶ val[2][2] = 2 ⟶ val[2][3] = 10

8

As with single-dimensional arrays, two-dimensional arrays may be displayed by individual element notation or by using loops (either `while` or `for`). This is illustrated by Program 8-6, which displays all of the elements of a 3 by 4 two-dimensional array using two different techniques. Notice in Program 8-6 that we have used symbolic constants to define the array's rows and columns.

Program 8-6

```cpp
#include <iostream>
#include <iomanip>
using namespace std;

int main()
{
  const int NUMROWS = 3;
  const int NUMCOLS = 4;
  int val[NUMROWS][NUMCOLS] = {8,16,9,52,3,15,27,6,14,25,2,10};
  int i, j;

  cout << "\nDisplay of val array by explicit element"
       << '\n' << setw(4) << val[0][0] << setw(4) << val[0][1]
       << setw(4) << val[0][2] << setw(4) << val[0][3]
       << '\n' << setw(4) << val[1][0] << setw(4) << val[1][1]
       << setw(4) << val[1][2] << setw(4) << val[1][3]
       << '\n' << setw(4) << val[2][0] << setw(4) << val[2][1]
       << setw(4) << val[2][2] << setw(4) << val[2][3];

  cout << "\n\nDisplay of val array using a nested for loop";

  for (i = 0; i < NUMROWS; i++)
  {
    cout << endl;       // print a new line for each row
    for (j = 0; j < NUMCOLS; j++)
      cout << setw(4) <<  val[i][j];
  }

  cout << endl;

  return 0;
}
```

The display produced by Program 8-6 follows:

```
Display of val array by explicit element
   8  16   9  52
   3  15  27   6
  14  25   2  10
```

```
Display of val array using a nested for loop
    8   16    9   52
    3   15   27    6
   14   25    2   10
```

The first display of the val array produced by Program 8-6 is constructed by explicitly designating each array element. The second display of array element values, which is identical to the first, is produced using a nested for loop. Nested loops are especially useful when dealing with two-dimensional arrays because they allow the programmer to designate and cycle through each element easily. In Program 8-6, the variable i controls the outer loop and the variable j controls the inner loop. Each pass through the outer loop corresponds to a single row, with the inner loop supplying the appropriate column elements. After a complete row is printed, a new line is started for the next row. The effect is a display of the array in a row-by-row fashion.

Once two-dimensional array elements have been assigned, array processing can begin. Typically, for loops are used to process two-dimensional arrays because, as was previously noted, they allow the programmer to designate and cycle through each array element easily. For example, the nested for loop illustrated in Program 8-7 is used to multiply each element in the val array by the scalar number 10 and display the resulting value.

Program 8-7

```cpp
#include <iostream>
#include <iomanip>
using namespace std;

int main()
{
  const int NUMROWS = 3;
  const int NUMCOLS = 4;
  int val[NUMROWS][NUMCOLS] = {8,16,9,52,
                               3,15,27,6,
                               14,25,2,10};
  int i, j;

  // multiply each element by 10 and display it
  cout << "\nDisplay of multiplied elements";
  for (i = 0; i < NUMROWS; i++)
  {
    cout << endl;    // start each row on a new line
    for (j = 0; j < NUMCOLS; j++)
    {
      val[i][j] = val[i][j] * 10;
      cout << setw(5) << val[i][j];
```

(continued on next page)

```
    }   // end of inner loop
  }     // end of outer loop

  cout << endl;

  return 0;
}
```

Following is the output produced by Program 8-7.

```
Display of multiplied elements
        80   160    90   520
        30   150   270    60
       140   250    20   100
```

Passing two-dimensional arrays into a function is a process identical to passing single-dimensional arrays. The called function receives access to the entire array. For example, the function call display(val); makes the complete val array available to the function named display(). Thus, any changes made by display() will be made directly to the val array. Assuming that the following two-dimensional arrays named test, code, and stocks are declared as:

```
int test[7][9];
char code[26][10];
double stocks[256][52];
```

the following function calls are valid:

```
findMax(test);
obtain(code);
price(stocks);
```

On the receiving side, the called function must be alerted that a two-dimensional array is being made available. For example, assuming that each of the previous functions returns an integer, suitable function header lines for the functions are:

```
int findMax(int nums[7][9])
int obtain(char key[26][10])
int price(double names[256][52])
```

In each of these function header lines, the argument names chosen are local to the function. However, the internal local names used by the function still refer to the original array created outside the function. Program 8-8 illustrates passing a local, two-dimensional array into a function that displays the array's values.

Both symbolic constants, ROWS and COLS, in Program 8-8 have a global scope throughout the source code, which is created by placing their declarations outside and above the first function. This is, perhaps, one of the few legitimate uses of a global variable because it makes the same constant available to all functions in the file, and avoids the necessity of passing the same constant value as an argument when the function is called.

Program 8-8

```cpp
#include <iostream>;
#include <iomanip>
using namespace std;

const int ROWS = 3;
const int COLS = 4;

int main()
{
  void display(int [ROWS][COLS]);     // function prototype
  int val[ROWS][COLS] = {8,16,9,52,
                         3,15,27,6,
                         14,25,2,10};

  display(val);

  return 0;
}

void display(int nums[ROWS][COLS])
{
  int rowNum, colNum;
  for (rowNum = 0; rowNum < ROWS; rowNum++)
  {
    for(colNum = 0; colNum < COLS; colNum++)
      cout << setw(4) <<nums[rowNum][colNum];
    cout << endl;
  }

  return;
}
```

Only one array is created in Program 8-8. This array is known as val in main() and as nums in display(). Thus, val[0][2] refers to the same element as nums[0][2].

Notice the use of the nested for loop in Program 8-8 for cycling through each array element. In Program 8-8, the variable rowNum controls the outer loop and the variable colNum controls the inner loop. For each pass through the outer loop, which corresponds to row, the inner loop makes one pass through the column elements. After a complete row is printed, the endl manipulator causes a new line to be started for the next row. The effect is a display of the array in a row-by-row fashion:

```
   8   16    9   52
   3   15   27    6
  14   25    2   10
```

8

The argument declaration for `nums` in `display()` contains extra information that is not required by the function. The declaration for `nums` can omit the row size of the array. Thus, an alternative function declaration is:

```
display(int nums[][4])
```

The reason why the column size must be included while the row size is optional becomes obvious when you consider how the array elements are stored in memory. Starting with element `val[0][0]`, each succeeding element is stored consecutively, row by row, as `val[0][0]`, `val[0][1]`, `val[0][2]`, `val[0][3]`, `val[1][0]`, `val[1][1]`, and so on, as illustrated in Figure 8-11.

FIGURE 8-11
Storage of the `val` *Array*

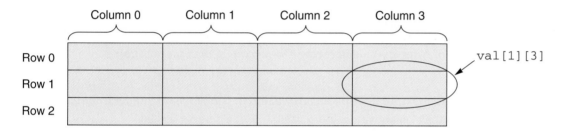

As with all arrays accessed, an individual element of the `val` array is obtained by adding an offset to the starting location of the array. For example, element `val[1][3]` of the `val` array illustrated in Figure 8-11 is located at an offset of 28 bytes from the start of the array (assuming four bytes per `int`). Internally, the compiler determines this offset using the calculation shown in Figure 8-12. The column size is necessary in the offset calculation so that the compiler can determine the number of positions to skip over in order to get to the desired row.

FIGURE 8-12
Calculating the Offset for `val [1] [3]`

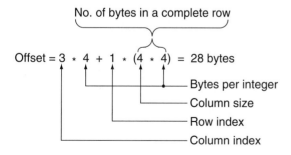

INTERNAL ARRAY ELEMENT LOCATION ALGORITHM[6]

Internally, each individual element in an array is obtained by adding an offset to the starting address of the array. Thus, the memory address of the *i*th array element is internally calculated as:

Address of element i = starting array address + the offset

For single-dimensional arrays the offset to the element with index *i* is calculated as:

*Offset = i * the size of an individual element*

For two-dimensional arrays the same address calculation is made, except that the offset is determined as follows:

*Offset = Column Index Value * the size of an individual element*
*+ Row Index value * number of bytes in a complete row*

where the number of bytes in a complete row is calculated as:

*number of bytes in a complete row = maximum column specification ** *the size of an individual element*

For example, as illustrated in Figure 8-13, for an array of integers where each integer is stored using four bytes, the offset to the element whose index value is 5 would be 5 * 4 = 20.

FIGURE 8-13
The Offset of the Element with an Index Value of 5

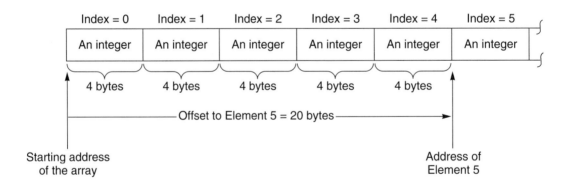

Using the address operator, &, we can check this address algorithm. For example, consider Program 8-9.

Program 8-9

```
#include <iostream>
using namespace std;
```

(continued on next page)

[6]This topic is optional and may be omitted without loss of subject continuity.

8

```cpp
int main()
{
  const int NUMELS = 20;
  int arr[NUMELS];

  cout << "The starting address of the arr array is: "
       << int(&arr[0]) << endl;
  cout << "The storage size of each array element is: "
       << sizeof(int) << endl;
  cout << "The address of element number 5 is: "
       << int(&arr[5]) << endl;
  cout << "The starting address of the array, "
       << "\ndisplayed using the notation arr, is: "
       << int(arr) << endl;

  return 0;
}
```

The output produced by executing Program 8-9 is:

```
The starting address of the arr array is: 1244796
The storage size of each array element is: 4
The address of element number 5 is: 1244816
The starting address of the array,
displayed using the notation arr, is: 1244796
```

Notice that the addresses have been displayed in decimal form and the address of element 5 is 20 bytes beyond the starting address of the array. Also notice that the starting address of the array is the same as the address of the zero element, which is coded as `&arr[0]`. Alternatively, as illustrated by the displayed line, the starting array address can also be obtained as `arr`, which is the name of the array. This is because an array name is itself an address. (The close association of array names and pointers is explained in depth in Chapter 14.)

LARGER-DIMENSIONAL ARRAYS

Although arrays with more than two dimensions are not commonly used, C++ does allow any number of dimensions to be declared. This is done by listing the maximum size of all dimensions for the array. For example, the declaration `int response [4][10][6];` declares a three-dimensional array. The first element in the array is designated as `response [0][0][0]` and the last element as `response [3][9][5]`.

Conceptually, as illustrated in Figure 8-14, a three-dimensional array can be viewed as a book of data tables. Using this visualization, the first index can be thought of as the location of the desired row in a table, the second index value as the desired column, and the third index value, which is often called the "rank," as the page number of the selected table. Similarly, arrays of any dimension can be declared. Conceptually, a four-dimensional array can be represented as a shelf of books, where the fourth dimension is used to declare a desired book on the shelf, and a five-dimensional array can be viewed as a bookcase filled with books where the fifth dimension refers to a selected shelf in the bookcase. Using the same analogy, a six-dimensional array can be considered as a single row of book-cases where the sixth dimension references the desired bookcase in the row; a seven-dimensional array can be considered as multiple rows of bookcases where the seventh dimension references the desired row, and so on. Alternatively, three, four, five, six, etc., dimensional arrays can be viewed as mathe-matical *n*-tuples of order three, four, five, six, etc., respectively.

FIGURE 8-14
Representation of a Three-Dimensional Array

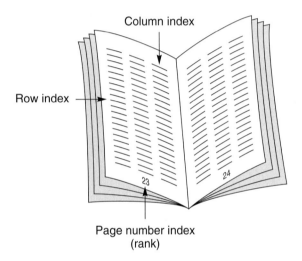

Exercises 8.5

1.   Write appropriate specification statements for:

   a. an array of integers with 6 rows and 10 columns
   b. an array of integers with 2 rows and 5 columns
   c. an array of characters with 7 rows and 12 columns
   d. an array of characters with 15 rows and 7 columns
   e. an array of double-precision numbers with 10 rows and 25 columns
   f. an array of double-precision numbers with 16 rows and 8 columns

2.   Determine the output produced by the following program:

```
#include <iostream>
using namespace std;

int main()
{
   const int ROWS = 3;
```

```
     const int COLS = 4;

     int i, j, val[ROWS][COLS]  =  {8,16,9,52,3,15,27,6,14,25,2,10};

     for (i = 0; i < 3; ++i)
       for (j = 0; j < 4; ++j)
         cout << val[i][j] << "   ";

     return 0;
   }
```

3. **a.** Write a C++ program that adds the values of all elements in the `val` array used in Exercise 2 and displays the total.

b. Modify the program written for Exercise 3a to display the total of each row separately.

4. Write a C++ program that adds equivalent elements of the two-dimensional arrays named `first` and `second`. Both arrays should have two rows and three columns. For example, element `[1][2]` of the resulting array should be the sum of `first[1][2]` and `second[1][2]`. The `first` and `second` arrays should be initialized as follows:

	first			second	
16	18	23	24	52	77
54	91	11	16	19	59

5. **a.** Write a C++ program that finds and displays the maximum value in a two-dimensional array of integers. The array should be declared as a 4 by 5 array of integers and initialized with the data:

`16,22,99,4,18,-258,4,101,5,98,105,6,15,2,45,33,88,72,16,3`

b. Modify the program written in Exercise 5a so that it also displays the maximum value's row and column subscript numbers.

6. Write a C++ program to select the values in a 4 by 5 array of integers in increasing order, and store the selected values in the single-dimensional array named `sort`. Use the data statement given in Exercise 5a to initialize the two-dimensional array.

7. **a.** A professor has constructed a two-dimensional array of double numbers having 3 rows and 5 columns. This array currently contains the test grades of the students in the professor's advanced compiler design class. Write a C++ program that reads 15 array values and then determine the total number of grades in the ranges less than 60, greater than or equal to 60 and less than 70, greater than or equal to 70 and less than 80, greater than or equal to 80 and less than 90, and greater than or equal to 90.

b. Entering 15 grades each time the program written for Exercise 7a is run is cumbersome. What method, therefore, is appropriate for initializing the array during the testing phase?

c. How might the program you wrote for Exercise 7a be modified to include the case of no grade being present? That is, what grade could be used to indicate an invalid grade and how would your program have to be modified to exclude counting such a grade?

8. a. Write a function that finds and displays the maximum value in a two-dimensional array of integers. The array should be declared as a 10-row by 20-column array of integers in `main()` and the starting address of the array should be passed to the function.

    b. Modify the function written in Exercise 8a so that it also displays the row and column number of the element with the maximum value.

    c. Can the function you wrote for Exercise 8a be generalized to handle any size two-dimensional array?

8.6 THE STL VECTOR CLASS

Many programming applications require lists that must constantly be expanded and contracted as items are added to and removed from the list. Although expanding and contracting an array can be accomplished by creating, copying, and deleting arrays, this solution tends to be costly in terms of initial programming, maintenance, and testing time. To meet the need of providing a completely tested and generic set of data structures that can be easily modified, expanded, and contracted, C++ provides a useful set of classes in its Standard Template Library (STL).

Each STL class is coded as a template (see Section 7.1) that permits the construction of a generic type of data structure, which is referred to as a **container**. The terms **list** and **collection** are frequently used as synonyms for a container, with each term referring to a set of data items that form a natural unit or group. Using this definition, an array is also a container; however, it is a container that is provided as a built-in type as contrasted to the containers created using STL. Figure 8-15 illustrates the container types provided by the STL.

FIGURE 8-15
The STL Container Types

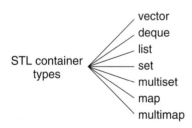

This section presents the vector container class, along with the most commonly used algorithms for this class and the arguments, known as iterators, required for these algorithms. You have already encountered three of these algorithms (`sort`, `find`, and `binary_search`) and their required iterator arguments in Section 8.4.

A vector is similar to an array in that it stores elements that can be accessed using an integer index that starts at zero, but dissimilar in that a vector will automatically expand as needed, and is provided by a number of useful class methods for operating on the vector. Table 8-2 lists these vector class methods, with highlighting used to identify the methods that we will use in our demonstration program.

8

TABLE 8-2
Summary of Vector Class Methods and Operations

methods and operations	type	description
`vector<DataType> name`	constructor	Creates an empty vector with compiler-dependent initial size
`vector<DataType> name(source)`	constructor	Creates a copy of the source vector
`vector<DataType> name(n)`	constructor	Creates a vector of size *n*
`vector<DataType> name(n, elem)`	constructor	Creates a vector of size *n* with each element initialized as `elem`
`vector<DataType> name(src.beg, src.end)`	constructor	Creates a vector initialized with elements from a source container beginning at `src.beg` and ending at `src.end`
`~vector<DataType>()`	destructor	Destroys the vector and all elements it contains
`name[index]`	accessor	Returns the element at the designated index, with no bounds checking
`name.at(index)`	accessor	Returns the element at the specified index argument, with bounds checking on the index value
`name.front()`	accessor	Returns the first element in the vector
`name.back()`	accessor	Returns the last element in the vector
`dest = src`	mutator	Assigns all elements of `src` vector to `dest` vector
`name.assign(n, elem)`	mutator	Assigns *n* copies of `elem`
`name.assign(src.begin, src.end)`	mutator	Assigns the elements of the `src` container (need not be a vector) between the range `src.begin` and `src.end`, to the `name` vector
`name.insert(pos, elem)`	mutator	Inserts `elem` at position `pos`
`name.insert(pos, n, elem)`	mutator	Inserts *n* copies of `elem` starting at position `pos`
`name.insert(pos, src.begin, src.end)`	mutator	Inserts starting at position `pos`, a copy of the elements that start at `src.begin`, and stop at `src.end`
`name.push_back(elem)`	mutator	Appends `elem` at the end of the vector
`name.erase(pos)`	mutator	Removes the element at the specified position

(continued on next page)

TABLE 8-2
Summary of Vector Class Methods and Operations (Continued)

methods and operations	type	description
erase(begin, end)	mutator	Removes the elements within the specified range
resize(value)	mutator	Resizes the vector to a larger size, with new elements instantiated using the default constructor
resize(value, elem)	mutator	Resizes the vector to a larger size, with new elements instantiated as elem
clear()	mutator	Removes all elements from the vector
swap(nameB)	mutator	Swaps the elements of nameA and nameB vectors; can be performed using the swap() algorithm
nameA == nameB	relational	Returns a Boolean true if nameA elements all equal nameB elements; otherwise, returns false
nameA != nameB	relational	Returns a Boolean false if nameA elements all equal nameB elements; otherwise, returns true; same as !(nameA == nameB)
nameA < nameB	relational	Returns a Boolean true if nameA is less than nameB; otherwise, returns false
nameA > nameB	relational	Returns a Boolean true if nameA is greater than nameB; otherwise, returns false; same as nameB < nameA
nameA <= nameB	relational	Returns a Boolean true if nameA is less than or equal to nameB
nameA >= nameB	relational	Returns a Boolean true if nameA is greater than or equal to nameB
name.size()	capacity	Returns the size of the vector as an int
name.empty()	capacity	Returns a Boolean true if vector is empty; otherwise, returns false
name.max_size()	capacity	Returns the maximum possible elements as an integer
name.capacity()	capacity	Returns the maximum possible elements, as an integer, without relocation of the vector

In addition to the specific vector class methods listed in Table 8-2, vectors also have access to the complete set of generic STL algorithms, three of which were presented in Section 8.4. Table 8-3 summarizes the most commonly used STL algorithms.

TABLE 8-3
Commonly Used Standard Template Library (STL) Algorithms

algorithm name	description
accumulate	Returns the sum of the numbers in a specified range
binary_search	Returns a Boolean value of `true` if the specified value exists within the specified range; otherwise returns `false`. Can only be used on a sorted set of values
copy	Copies elements from a source range to a destination range
copy_backward	Copies elements from a source range to a destination range in a reverse direction
count	Returns the number of elements in a specified range that match a specified value
equal	Compares the elements in one range of elements, element by element, to the elements in a second range
fill	Assigns every element in a specified range to a specified value
find	Returns the position of the first occurrence of an element in a specified range having a specified value, if the value exists. Performs a linear search, starting with the first element in a specified range, and proceeds one element at a time until the complete range has been searched or the specified element has been found
max_element	Returns the maximum value of the elements in the specified range
min_element	Returns the minimum value of the elements in the specified range
random_shuffle	Randomly shuffles element values in a specified range
remove	Removes a specified value within a specified range without changing the order of the remaining elements
replace	Replaces each element in a specified range having a specified value with a newly specified value
reverse	Reverses elements in a specified range
search	Finds the first occurrence of a specified value or sequence of values within a specified range
sort	Sorts elements in a specified range into an ascending order
swap	Exchanges element values between two objects
unique	Removes duplicate adjacent elements within a specified range

Notice that there is both a swap algorithm (Table 8-3) and a swap vector class method (Table 8-2). Because a class method is targeted to work specifically with its container type and generally will execute faster, whenever a container class provides a method with the same name as an algorithm, you should use the class method.

PROGRAMMING NOTE

When to Use an Array or a Vector

An array is the data structure of first choice whenever you have a list of primitive data types or objects that does not have to be expanded or contracted.

A vector is the data structure of first choice whenever you have a list of primitive data types or objects that can be grouped as an array, but must be expanded or contracted.

Whenever possible, always use STL algorithms to operate on both arrays (see Section 8.4) and vectors (described in this section). Both STL classes and algorithms provide verified and reliable code that can significantly shorten program development time.

Finally, a number of additional items, referred to as iterators, are also provided by the STL. Iterators provide the means of specifying which elements in a container are to be operated on when an algorithm or method is called.

Two of the most useful iterators are returned by the STL iterator functions named `begin()` and `end()`. These are general purpose functions that return the positions of the first and last elements in a container, respectively.

To make this more tangible and provide a meaningful introduction to using an STL container class, we will use the vector container class to create a vector for holding a list of names. As we shall see, a vector is very similar to a C++ array, except that it can automatically expand as needed.

Program 8-10 initially constructs a vector and initializes it with names stored in a string array. Once it is initialized, various vector methods and STL algorithms are used to operate on the vector. Specifically, one method is used to change an existing name, another to insert a name within the vector, and a third method to append a name to the end of the list of names. After each method and algorithm is applied, a `cout` object is employed to display the results.

Program 8-10

```cpp
#include <iostream>
#include <string>
#include <vector>
#include <algorithm>
using namespace std;

int main()
{
  const int NUMELS = 4;
  string n[] ={"Donavan", "Michaels", "Smith", "Jones"};
```

(continued on next page)

```cpp
  int i;

  // instantiate a vector of strings using the n[] array
  vector<string> names(n, n + NUMELS);
  cout << "\nThe vector initially has a size of "
       << names.size() << ",\n and contains the elements:\n";
  for (i = 0; i < names.size(); i++)
    cout << names[i] << "    ";

  // modify the element at position 3 (i.e. index = 2) in the vector
  names[2] = "Farmer";
  cout << "\n\nAfter replacing the third element, the vector has a size of "
       << names.size() << ",\n and contains the elements:\n";
  for (i = 0; i < names.size(); i++)
    cout << names[i] << "    ";

  // insert an element into the vector at position 2 (i.e. index = 1)
  names.insert(names.begin()+1, "Williams");
  cout << "\n\nAfter inserting an element into the second position,"
       << "\n the vector has a size of " << names.size() << ","
       << " and contains the elements:\n";
  for (i = 0; i < names.size(); i++)
   cout << names[i] << "    ";

  // add an element to the end of the vector
  names.push_back("Adams");
  cout << "\n\nAfter adding an element to the end of the list,"
       << "\n  the vector has a size of " << names.size() << ","
       << " and contains the elements:\n";
  for (i = 0; i < names.size(); i++)
   cout << names[i] << "    ";

  // sort the vector
  sort(names.begin(), names.end());
  cout << "\n\nAfter sorting, the vector's elements are:\n";
  for (i = 0; i < names.size(); i++)
   cout << names[i] << "    ";

  cout << endl;

  return 0;
}
```

In reviewing Program 8-10, first notice the inclusion of the four header files <iostream>, <string>, <vector>, and <algorithm> and the using namespace std; statement. The <iostream>

header is needed to create and use the `cout` stream; the `<string>` header is required for construct-ing strings; the `<vector>` header to create one or more `vector` objects; and the `<algorithm>` header is required for the `sort` algorithm that is applied after we have completed adding and replac-ing `vector` elements.

The statement in Program 8-10 that is used to create and initialize the vector named `names` is:

```
vector<string> names(n, n + NUMELS);
```

Here, the vector `names` is declared as a vector of type `string` and is initialized with elements from the *n* array, starting with the first element of the array (element `n[0]`), and ending with the last array element, which is located at position `n + NUMELS`. Thus, the vector `names` now has a size sufficient for four string values and has been initialized with the strings `"Donavan"`, `"Michaels"`, `"Smith"`, and `"Jones"`. The next set of statements in Program 8-10 display the initial values in the vector, using standard subscripted vector notation that is identical to the notation used for accessing array ele-ments. Displaying the vector values in this manner, however, requires knowing how many elements each vector contains. As we insert and remove elements, we would like the vector itself to keep track of where the first and last elements are; this capability is, in fact, automatically provided by two itera-tor methods furnished for each STL container, named `begin()` and `end()`.

The next major set of statements, consisting of:

```
// modify the element at position 3 (i.e. index = 2) in the vector
names[2] = "Farmer";
```

and

```
// insert an element into the vector at position 2 (i.e. index = 1)
names.insert(names.begin()+1, "Williams");
```

are used to both modify an existing vector value and insert a new value into the vector. Specifically, the `names[2]` notation uses standard indexing, while the `insert()` method requires an iterator and the value to be inserted, as arguments. Thus, `names[2]` specifies the third element in the vector will be changed (remember that vectors, like arrays, begin at index position 0). The `insert()` method is then used to insert the string literal `Williams` in the second position of the vector. Notice that itera-tor arithmetic is allowed. Thus, because the `begin()` method returns the iterator value corresponding to the start of the vector, adding 1 to it designates the second position in the vector. It is at this posi-tion the new value is inserted with all subsequent values moved up by one position in the vector, with the vector automatically expanding to accept the inserted value. At this point in the program, the vec-tor `names` now contains the elements:

```
Donavan   Williams   Michaels   Farmer   Jones
```

This arrangement of values was obtained by replacing the original value `Smith` with `Farmer` and then inserting the string `Williams` into the second position, which automatically moves all subse-quent elements up by one position and increases the total vector size to accommodate 5 strings.

Next the statement `names.push_back("Adams");` is used to append the string literal `Adams` to the end of the vector, which results in the elements:

```
Donavan  Williams  Michaels  Farmer  Jones  Adams
```

Finally, the last section of code used in Program 8-10 uses the `sort` algorithm to sort the elements in each vector. Notice that this algorithm uses iterator values to determine the sequence of elements to be operated upon. After the algorithm is applied, the values in the vector are once again displayed. Following is the complete output produced by Program 8-10:

```
The vector initially has a size of 4,
 and contains the elements:
Donavan   Michaels   Smith   Jones

After replacing the third element, the vector has a size of 4,
 and contains the elements:
Donavan  Michaels  Farmer  Jones

After inserting an element into the second position,
 the vector has a size of 5, and contains the elements:
Donavan  Williams  Michaels  Farmer  Jones

After adding an element to the end of the list,
 the vector has a size of 6, and contains the elements:
Donavan  Williams  Michaels  Farmer  Jones  Adams

After sorting, the vector's elements are:
Adams   Donavan  Farmer  Jones  Michaels  Williams
```

Program 8-10 is useful in illustrating the construction and maintenance of a vector. From a practical standpoint, however, one important element is missing from the program, which is the inclusion of a programmer-designed record type. For example, assume a list of employee records must be maintained where each record consists of an employee's name and pay rate (Figure 8-16).

FIGURE 8-16
A NameRate *UML Class Diagram*

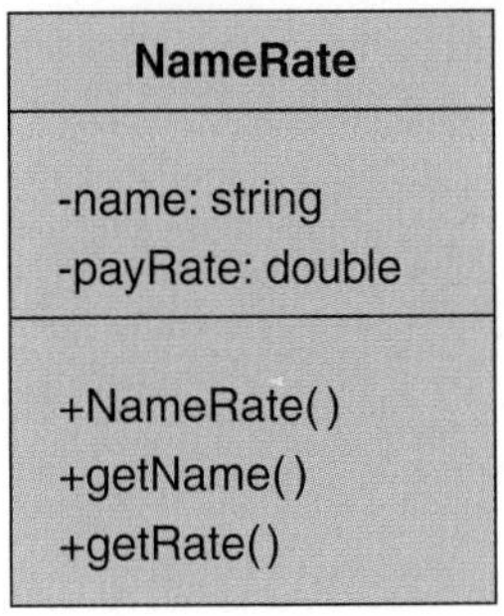

NameRate
-name: string -payRate: double
+NameRate() +getName() +getRate()

For this UML description, a class must first be created, from which individual programmer-defined objects can be constructed and added into the list. Once the desired class has been constructed and compiled, a vector for objects constructed from this class can be created.

Class 8-1 provides the code for Figure 8-16's class diagram.

Class 8-1

```
#include <string>
using namespace std;

class NameRate
{
  // data declarations
  private:
    string name;
    double payRate;

  // method definitions
  public:
    NameRate(string nn, double rate)    // constructor
        {name = nn; payRate = rate;};
    string getName(){return name;};      // accessor
    double getRate(){return payRate;}; // accessor
};
```

In reviewing Class 8-1, make special note that all of the class's data members have been declared as public. This is necessary because we will be placing them into a vector in which we specifically want anyone with access to the list to be able to change, remove, and add instantiated objects. Having developed a class for our employee records, we can now construct a vector container for storing objects created from this class. This, of course, requires two distinct operations: instantiating actual objects and then storing each object within the vector.

Program 8-11 shows how this can be accomplished. Initially, four records of the NameRate type are created. Each of these records is created individually and added into the list using the vector class's push_back() method.

Program 8-11

```
#include <iostream>
#include <string>
#include <vector>
#include <algorithm>
```

```cpp
using namespace std;

class NameRate
{
  // data declarations
  private:
    string name;
    double payRate;

  // method definitions
  public:
    NameRate(string nn, double rate)  // constructor
        {name = nn; payRate = rate;};
    string getName(){return name;};      // accessor
    double getRate(){return payRate;}; // accessor

};

int main()
{

  NameRate a("Bender, Jim", 18.55);
  NameRate b("Acme, Sam", 26.58);
  NameRate c("Mening, Stephen", 15.85);
  NameRate d("Zeman, Harold", 17.92);

  vector<NameRate> empRecords; // create a vector

  cout << "The size of the instantiated vector is "
       << empRecords.size() << endl << "  and its capacity is "
       << empRecords.capacity() << endl << endl;
  empRecords.push_back(a);
  empRecords.push_back(b);
  empRecords.push_back(c);
  empRecords.push_back(d);

  cout << "After adding four objects, the size of the list is "
       << empRecords.size() << endl << "  and its capacity is "
       << empRecords.capacity() << endl << endl;

  cout << "The data stored in the vector is:" << endl << endl;
  cout << "     Name              Pay Rate\n";
  cout << "--------------      ---------------\n";

  // use accessor methods to extract the name and pay rate
  for(int i = 0; i < empRecords.size(); i++)
  {
```

(continued on next page)

```
    cout << empRecords[i].getName()
        << "\t\t" << empRecords[i].getRate() << endl;
  }

  return 0;
}
```

In reviewing Program 8-11 note that the statement

```
    vector<NameRate> empRecords;
```

creates an empty vector named empRecords. After the list has been created, the program inserts four NameRate objects into the list. This is one of the distinguishing advantages of vectors over arrays: elements can be inserted, appended, and removed from the list without the programmer having to explicitly write the code underlying all of these operations, as is required by arrays.

Now review the for loop coded at the end of Program 8-11. Specifically, notice that the loop is terminated by the expression empRecords.size(), which uses the vector class's size() method to determine the actual number of elements in the vector. The individual data items in each retrieved NameRate object are then accessed using NameRate's accessor methods. In Program 8-11 this is restricted to accessing the name and payRate data using the getName() and getRate() accessors. That this is successfully accomplished is verified by the following output produced by the program:

```
    The size of the instantiated vector is 0
      and its capacity is 0

    After adding four objects, the size of the list is 4
      and its capacity is 4

    The data stored in the vector is:

          Name                   Pay Rate
    ---------------         ---------------
    Bender, Jim                   18.55
    Acme, Sam                     26.58
    Mening, Stephen               15.85
    Zeman, Harold                 17.92
```

PARALLEL ARRAYS

Consider the data provided in Table 8-4. Clearly, it is possible to store this information using three individual arrays, where one array is used for storing the integer employee numbers, one for the string names, and one for the double-precision pay rates (Figure 8-17). Such arrays, where corresponding data in a record resides in the same position in more than one array, are referred to as **parallel arrays**. The separation of an individual record into parallel arrays was required in earlier programming languages that only supported array data structures. Unfortunately, it sometimes also becomes the first choice of beginning programmers who are familiar with arrays and how to program them.

TABLE 8-4
A Table of Employee Data

employee number	employee name	employee pay rate
12479	Adams, C.	15.72
13623	Brenner, D.	17.54
14145	Dunson, P.	16.55
15987	Franklin, S.	18.43
16203	Jamason, T.	15.72
16417	Kline, H.	19.64
17634	Opper, G.	17.29
18321	Smith, S.	18.67
19435	Voelmer, L.	15.50
19567	Wilson, R.	17.35

If you find yourself thinking in terms of parallel arrays, use them only as a design aid to help you structure the data as an object. For example, using an object approach, each record that is divided across the three arrays in Figure 8-17 can be combined into an object, which accurately encapsulates each employee's data as a single record. (See Figure 8-18.) Once you have correctly captured a record's structure, the usefulness of the parallel array as a design aid is completed. Except for very simple or specialized applications, you should rarely ever code a set of parallel arrays.

FIGURE 8-17
Employee Records Represented Using Three Parallel Arrays

employee number	employee name	employee pay rate
12479	ADAMS, C.	15.72
13623	BRENNER, D.	17.54
14145	DUNSON, P.	16.56
15987	FRANKLIN, S.	18.43
16203	JAMASON, T.	15.72
16417	KLINE, H.	19.64
17634	OPPER, G.	17.29
18321	SMITH, S.	18.67
19435	VOELMER, L.	15.50
19567	WILSON, R.	17.35

FIGURE 8-18

Employee Records Represented as Objects

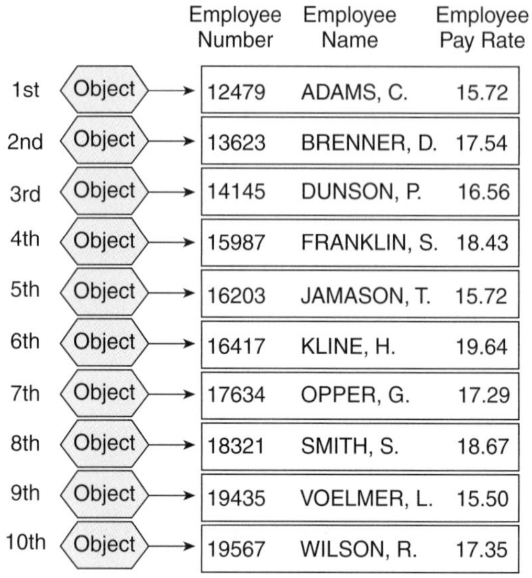

Exercises 8.6

1. Define the terms "container" and "Standard Template Library."

2. What `include` statements should be included with programs that use the Standard Template Library?

3. Enter and execute Program 8-10.

4. Modify Program 8-10 so that the initial set of names is input by the user when the program executes. Either have the program first request the number of initial names that will be entered or terminate name entry with a sentinel value.

5. Modify Program 8-10 to use and display the results reported by the vector class's `capacity()` and `max_size()` methods.

6. Modify Program 8-10 to use the `random_shuffle()` algorithm.

7. Modify Program 8-10 to use the `binary_search()` and `find()` algorithms. Have your program request the name that is to be searched and found.

8. Using Program 8-10 as a starting point, create an equivalent program that uses a vector of integers. Initialize the vector using the array `int values[]` = `{10, 14, 98, 64, 88, 2, 20, 17}`.

9. Use the `max_element()` and `min_element()` algorithms to determine the maximum and minimum values in the vector created for Exercise 8. (*Hint*: Use the expression `max_element(vectorName.begin(), vectorName.end())` to determine the maximum value stored in the vector. Then use the same arguments for the `min_element()` algorithm.)

10. Enter and execute Program 8-11.

8

11. What vector class methods can you use to explicitly set a vector's capacity, both when the vector is instantiated and after it has been created?

12. For the following class:

```
public class Inventory
{
  public:
    string description;
    int prodnum;
    int quantity;
    double price;
}
```

Write the following:

a. An accessor method for each instance variable.
b. A declaration for a vector of `Inventory` objects, named `invRecords`.
c. A statement that reads and displays the price of the 15th `Inventory` object stored in the vector.

13. Define a vector for factory employee objects, in which each object contains the name, age, social security number, hourly wage, and number of years an employee has been with the company. Write the following:

a. An accessor method for each instance variable.
b. Statements that display the name and number of years with the company for the 25th employee in the vector.
c. A loop that, for every employee, adds 1 to the number of years with the company and that adds 50 cents to the hourly wage.

8.7 A CLOSER LOOK: SEARCHING AND SORTING

In this section we introduce the fundamentals of sorting and searching lists. Note that it is not necessary to sort a list before searching it, although, as we shall see, much faster searches are possible if the list is in sorted order.

SEARCH ALGORITHMS

A common requirement of many programs is to search a list for a given element. For example, in a list of names and telephone numbers, we might search for a specific name so that the corresponding telephone number can be printed, or we might wish to search the list simply to determine if a name is there. The two most common methods of performing such searches are the linear and binary search algorithms.

Linear Search Algorithm

In a **linear search**, which is also known as a sequential search, each item in the list is examined in the order in which it occurs in the list until the desired item is found or the end of the list is reached. This is analogous to looking at every name in the phone directory, beginning with Aardvark, Aaron, until you find the one you want or until you reach Zzxgy, Zora. Obviously, this is not the most efficient way to search a long alphabetized list. However, a linear search has these advantages:

1. The algorithm is simple.
2. The list need not be in any particular order.

In a linear search, the search begins at the first item in the list and continues sequentially, item by item, through the list. The pseudocode for a function performing a linear search is:

> *For all the items in the list*
>   *Compare the item with the desired item*
>   *If the item was found*
>   *Return the index value of the current item*
>   *Endif*
> *EndFor*
> *Return −1 because the item was not found*

Notice that the function's return value indicates whether the item was found or not. If the return value is −1, the item was not in the list; otherwise, the return value within the `for` loop provides the index of where the item is located within the list.

The function `linearSearch()` illustrates this procedure as a C++ function:

```cpp
// this function returns the location of key in the list
// a -1 is returned if the value is not found
int linearSearch(int list[], int size, int key)
{
   int i;

   for (i = 0; i < size; i++)
   {
     if (list[i] == key)
       return i;
   }

   return -1;
}
```

In reviewing `linearSearch()` notice that the `for` loop is simply used to access each element in the list, from first element to last, until a match is found with the desired item. If the desired item is located, the index value of the current item is returned, which causes the loop to terminate; otherwise, the search continues until the end of the list is encountered.

8

To test this function we have written a main() driver function to call it and display the results returned by linearSearch(). The complete test program is illustrated in Program 8-12.

Program 8-12

```cpp
#include <iostream>
using namespace std;

int main()
{
  int linearSearch(int [], int, int);  // function prototype

  const int NUMEL = 10;
  int nums[NUMEL] = {5,10,22,32,45,67,73,98,99,101};
  int item, location;

  cout << "Enter the item you are searching for: ";
  cin  >> item;

  location = linearSearch(nums, NUMEL, item);

  if (location >= 0)
    cout << "The item was found at index location " << location
         << endl;
  else
    cout << "The item was not found in the list\n";

  return 0;
}

// this function returns the location of key in the list
// a -1 is returned if the value is not found
int linearSearch(int list[], int size, int key)
{
  int i;

  for (i = 0; i < size; i++)
  {
    if (list[i] == key)
      return i;
  }

  return -1;
}
```

Sample runs of Program 8-12 follow:

```
Enter the item you are searching for: 101
The item was found at index location 9
```

and

```
Enter the item you are searching for: 65
The item was not found in the list
```

As has already been pointed out, an advantage of linear searches is that the list does not have to be in sorted order to perform the search. Another advantage is that if the desired item is toward the front of the list, only a small number of comparisons will be done. The worst case, of course, occurs when the desired item is at the end of the list. On average, however, and assuming that the desired item is equally likely to be anywhere within the list, the number of required comparisons will be $N/2$, where N is the list's size. Thus, for a 10-element list, the average number of comparisons needed for a linear search is 5, and for a 10,000-element list, the average number of comparisons needed is 5000. As we show next, this number can be significantly reduced using a binary search algorithm.

Binary Search Algorithm

In a **binary search** the list must be in sorted order. Starting with an ordered list, the desired item is first compared to the element in the middle of the list (for lists with an even number of elements, either of the two middle elements can be used). Three possibilities present themselves once the comparison is made: the desired item may be equal to the middle element, it may be greater than the middle element, or it may be less than the middle element.

In the first case, the search has been successful, and no further searches are required. In the second case, since the desired item is greater than the middle element, if it is found at all it must be in the upper part of the list. This means that the lower part of the list, consisting of all elements from the first to the midpoint element, can be discarded from any further search. In the third case, since the desired item is less than the middle element, if it is found at all it must be found in the lower part of the list. For this case, the upper part of the list, containing all elements from the midpoint element to the last element, can be discarded from any further search.

The algorithm for implementing this search strategy is illustrated in Figure 8-19 and defined by the following pseudocode:

> *Set the lower index to 0*
> *Set the upper index to one less than the size of the list*
> *Begin with the first item in the list*
> *While the lower index is less than or equal to the upper index*
>   *Set the midpoint index to the integer average of the lower and upper index values*
>   *Compare the desired item to the midpoint element*
>   *If the desired element equals the midpoint element*
>   *Return the index value of the current item*
>   *Else if the desired element is greater than the midpoint element*
>   *Set the lower index value to the midpoint value plus 1*
>   *Else if the desired element is less than the midpoint element*
>   *Set the upper index value to the midpoint value less 1*
>   *Endif*
> *EndWhile*
> *Return −1 because the item was not found*

FIGURE 8-19
The Binary Search Algorithm

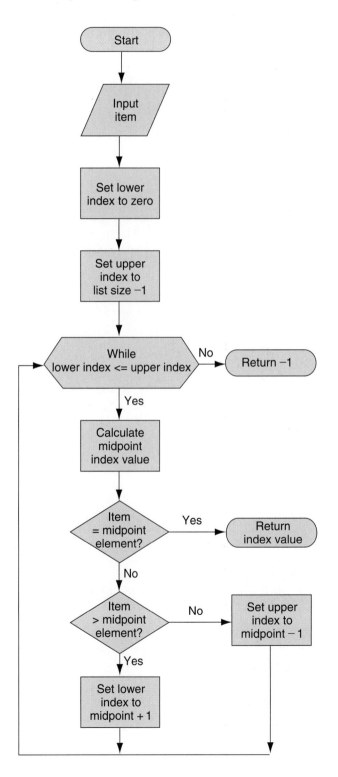

As illustrated by both the preceding pseudocode and the flowchart in Figure 8-19, a while loop is used to control the search. The initial list is defined by setting the lower index value to 0 and the upper index value to one less than the number of elements in the list. The midpoint element is then taken as the integer average of the lower and upper values. Once the comparison to the midpoint element is made, the search is subsequently restricted by moving either the lower index to one integer value above the midpoint, or by moving the upper index one integer value below the midpoint. This process is continued until the desired element is found or the lower and upper index values become equal. The function binary_search() presents the C++ version of this algorithm.

```cpp
// this function returns the location of key in the list
// a -1 is returned if the value is not found
int binary_search(int list[], int size, int key)
{
    int left, right, midpt;

    left = 0;
    right = size - 1;

    while (left <= right)
    {
        midpt = (int) ((left + right) / 2);
        if (key == list[midpt])
        {
            return midpt;
        }
        else if (key > list[midpt])
            left = midpt + 1;
        else
            right = midpt - 1;
    }

    return -1;
}
```

Program 8-13 employs this function.

Program 8-13

```cpp
#include <iostream>
using namespace std;

int main()
{
    int binary_search(int [], int, int);// function prototype
```

(continued on next page)

```cpp
   const int NUMEL = 10;
   int nums[NUMEL] = {5,10,22,32,45,67,73,98,99,101};
   int item, location;

   cout << "Enter the item you are searching for: ";
   cin  >> item;
   location = binary_search(nums, NUMEL, item);
   if (location >= 0)
     cout << "The item was found at index location "
        << location << endl;
   else
     cout << "The item was not found in the array\n";

   return 0;
}

// this function returns the location of key in the list
// a -1 is returned if the value is not found
int binary_search(int list[], int size, int key)
{
   int left, right, midpt;

   left = 0;
   right = size - 1;

   while (left <= right)
   {
     midpt = (int) ((left + right) / 2);
     if (key == list[midpt])
     {
       return midpt;
     }
     else if (key > list[midpt])
       left = midpt + 1;
     else
       right = midpt - 1;
   }

   return -1;
}
```

A sample run using Program 8-13 yielded the following:

```
Enter the item you are searching for: 101
The item was found at index location 9
```

The value of using a binary search algorithm is that the number of elements that must be searched is cut in half each time through the while loop. Thus, the first time through the loop N elements must be searched; the second time through the loop N/2 of the elements have been eliminated and only N/2 remain. The third time through the loop another half of the remaining elements have been eliminated, and so on.

In general, after p passes through the loop, the number of values remaining to be searched is $N/(2^p)$. In the worst case the search can continue until there is less than or equal to 1 element remaining to be searched. Mathematically, this can be expressed as $N/(2^p) \le 1$. Alternatively, this may be rephrased as follows: p is the smallest integer such that $2^p \ge N$. For example, for a 1000-element array, N is 1000 and the maximum number of passes, p, required for a binary search is 10. Table 8-5 compares the number of loop passes needed for a linear and binary search for various list sizes.

TABLE 8-5

A Comparison of while *Loop Passes for Linear and Binary Searches*

Array Size	10	50	500	5,000	50,000	500,000	5,000,000	50,000,000
Average Linear Search Passes	5	25	250	2,500	25,000	250,000	2,500,000	25,000,000
Maximum Linear Search Passes	10	50	500	5,000	50,000	500,000	5,000,000	50,000,000
Maximum Binary Search Passes	4	6	9	13	16	19	23	26

As illustrated in Table 8-5, the maximum number of loop passes for a 50-item list is almost 10 times more for a linear search than for a binary search, and even more spectacular for larger lists. As a rule of thumb, 50 elements are usually taken as the switchover point: For lists smaller than 50 elements, linear searches are acceptable; for larger lists, a binary search algorithm should be used.

Big O Notation

On average, over a large number of linear searches with N items in a list, we would expect to examine half (N/2) of the items before locating the desired item. In a binary search, the maximum number of passes, p, occurs when $N/(2)^p = 1$. This relationship can be algebraically manipulated to $2^p = N$, which yields $p = \log_2 N$, which approximately equals $3.33 - \log_{10} N$.

For example, finding a particular name in an alphabetical directory with $N = 1000$ names would require an average of 500 (N/2) comparisons using a linear search. With a binary search, only about 10 ($-3.33 * \log_{10} 1000$) comparisons would be required.

A common way to express the number of comparisons required in any search algorithm using a list of *N* items is to give the order of magnitude of the number of comparisons required, on average, to locate a desired item. Thus, the linear search is said to be of order N and the binary search of order $\log_2 N$. Notationally, this is expressed as O(N) and O($\log_2 N$), where the O is read as "the order of," and is referred to as the Big O.

8

SORT ALGORITHMS

For sorting data, two major categories of sorting techniques exist: internal and external sorts. Internal sorts are used when the data list is not too large and the complete list can be stored within the computer's memory, usually in an array. External sorts are used for much larger data sets that are stored in large external disk or tape files and cannot be accommodated within the computer's memory as a complete unit.

Here we present three internal sort algorithms that range from the simple and slow to the complex and fast. The first two algorithms presented are all quite commonly used when sorting lists with less than approximately 50 elements. For larger lists, more sophisticated sorting algorithms, such as the quicksort algorithm, are typically employed.

Selection Sort

One of the simplest sorting techniques is the selection sort. In a **selection sort** the smallest value is initially selected from the complete list of data and exchanged with the first element in the list. After this first selection and exchange, the next smallest element in the revised list is selected and exchanged with the second element in the list. Since the smallest element is already in the first position in the list, this second pass need only consider the second through last elements. For a list consisting of N elements, this process is repeated N−1 times, with each pass through the list requiring one less comparison than the previous pass.

For example, consider the list of numbers illustrated in Figure 8-20. The first pass through the initial list results in the number 32 being selected and exchanged with the first element in the list. The second pass, made on the reordered list, results in the number 155 being selected from the second through fifth elements. This value is then exchanged with the second element in the list. The third pass selects the number 307 from the third through fifth elements in the list and exchanges this value with the third element. Finally, the fourth and last pass through the list selects the remaining minimum value and exchanges it with the fourth list element. Although each pass in this example resulted in an exchange, no exchange would have been made in a pass if the smallest value were already in the correct location.

FIGURE 8-20
A Sample Selection Sort

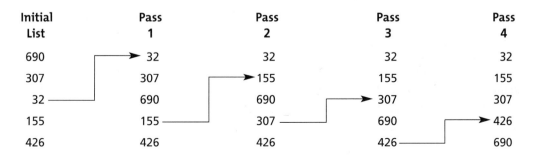

Initial List	Pass 1	Pass 2	Pass 3	Pass 4
690	32	32	32	32
307	307	155	155	155
32	690	690	307	307
155	155	307	690	426
426	426	426	426	690

In pseudocode, the selection sort is described as:

> *Set interchange count to zero (not required, but done just to keep track of the interchanges)*
> *For each element in the list from first to next-to-last*
> *Find the smallest element from the current element being referenced to the last element by:*
> *Setting the minimum value equal to the current element*
> *Saving (storing) the index of the current element*
> *For each element in the list from the current element 1 + 1 to the last element in the list*
> *If element[inner loop index] < minimum value*
> *Set the minimum value = element[inner loop index]*
> *Save the index to the new found minimum value*
> *Endif*
> *EndFor*
> *Swap the current value with the new minimum value*
> *Increment the interchange count*
> *EndFor*
> *Return the interchange count*

The function `selectionSort()` incorporates this procedure into a C++ function.

```cpp
int selectionSort(int num[], int numel)
{
  int i, j, min, minidx, temp, moves = 0;

  for ( i = 0; i < (numel - 1); i++)
  {
    min = num[i];    // assume minimum is the first array element
    minidx = i;      // index of minimum element
    for(j = i + 1; j < numel; j++)
    {
      if (num[j] < min)    // if we've located a lower value
      {                    // capture it
        min = num[j];
        minidx = j;
      }
    }
    if (min < num[i])   // check if we have a new minimum
    {                   // and if we do, swap values
      temp = num[i];
      num[i] = min;
      num[minidx] = temp;
      moves++;
    }
  }

  return moves;
}
```

8

The `selectionSort()` function expects two arguments, the list to be sorted and the number of elements in the list. As specified by the pseudocode, a nested set of `for` loops performs the sort. The outer `for` loop causes one less pass through the list than the total number of data items in the list. For each pass, the variable `min` is initially assigned the value `num[i]`, where `i` is the outer `for` loop's counter variable. Since `i` begins at 0 and ends at one less than `numl`, each element in the list, except the last, is successively designated as the current element.

The inner loop used in the function cycles through the elements below the current element to select the next smallest value. Thus, this loop begins at the index value `i+1` and continues through the end of the list. When a new minimum is found, its value and position in the list are stored in the variables named `min` and `minidx`, respectively. Upon completion of the inner loop, an exchange is made only if a value less than that in the current position was found.

For purposes of testing `selectionSort()`, Program 8-14 was constructed. This program implements a selection sort for the same list of 10 numbers that was previously used to test our search algorithms. For later comparison to the other sorting algorithms that will be presented, the number of actual moves made by the program to get the data into sorted order is counted and displayed.

Program 8-14

```
#include <iostream>
using namespace std;

int main()
{
  int selectionSort(int [], int);   // function prototype

  const int NUMEL = 10;
  int nums[NUMEL] = {22,5,67,98,45,32,101,99,73,10};
  int i, moves;

  moves = selectionSort(nums, NUMEL);

  cout << "The sorted list, in ascending order, is:\n";
  for (i = 0; i < NUMEL; i++)
    cout << "   " <<nums[i];

  cout << endl << moves << " moves were made to sort this list\n";

  return 0;
}

int selectionSort(int num[], int numel)
```

(continued on next page)

```
{
  int i, j, min, minidx, temp, moves = 0;

  for ( i = 0; i < (numel - 1); i++)
  {
    min = num[i];    // assume minimum is the first array element
    minidx = i;      // index of minimum element
    for(j = i + 1; j < numel; j++)
    {
      if (num[j] < min)    // if we've located a lower value
      {                    // capture it
      min = num[j];
      minidx = j;
      }
    }
    if (min < num[i])   // check if we have a new minimum
    {                   // and if we do, swap values
      temp = num[i];
      num[i] = min;
      num[minidx] = temp;
      moves++;
    }
  }

  return moves;
}
```

The output produced by Program 8-14 is as follows:

```
The sorted list, in ascending order,  is:
  5   10   22   32   45   67   73   98   99   101
8 moves were made to sort this list
```

Clearly, the number of moves displayed depends on the initial order of the values in the list. An advantage of the selection sort is that the maximum number of moves that must be made is N−1, where N is the number of items in the list. Further, each move is a final move that results in an element residing in its final location in the sorted list.

A disadvantage of the selection sort is that N(N−1)/2 comparisons are always required, regardless of the initial arrangement of the data. This number of comparisons is obtained as follows: the last pass always requires one comparison, the next-to-last pass requires two comparisons, and so on, to the first pass, which requires N−1 comparisons. Thus, the total number of comparisons is:

$$1 + 2 + 3 + \ldots + N-1 = N(N-1)/2 = N^2/2 - N/2$$

For large values of N the N^2 dominates, and the order of the selection sort is $O(N^2)$.

8

Exchange (Bubble) Sort

In an **exchange sort** elements of the list are exchanged with one another in such a manner that the list becomes sorted. One example of such a sequence of exchanges is provided by the **bubble sort**, where successive values in the list are compared, beginning with the first two elements. If the list is to be sorted in ascending (from smallest to largest) order, the smaller value of the two being compared is always placed before the larger value. For lists sorted in descending (from largest to smallest) order, the smaller of the two values being compared is always placed after the larger value.

For example, assuming that a list of values is to be sorted in ascending order, if the first element in the list is larger than the second, the two elements are interchanged. Then the second and third elements are compared. Again, if the second element is larger than the third, these two elements are interchanged. This process continues until the last two elements have been compared and exchanged, if necessary. If no exchanges were made during this initial pass through the data, the data is in the correct order and the process is finished; otherwise, a second pass is made through the data, starting from the first element and stopping at the next-to-last element. The reason for stopping at the next-to-last element on the second pass is that the first pass always results in the most positive value "sinking" to the bottom of the list.

As a specific example of this process, consider the list of numbers illustrated in Figure 8-21. The first comparison results in the interchange of the first two element values, 690 and 307. The next comparison, between elements two and three in the revised list, results in the interchange of values between the second and third elements, 690 and 32. This comparison and possible switching of adjacent values is continued until the last two elements have been compared and possibly switched. This process completes the first pass through the data and results in the largest number moving to the bottom of the list. As the largest value sinks to its resting place at the bottom of the list, the smaller elements slowly rise, or "bubble," to the top of the list. This bubbling effect of the smaller elements is what gave rise to the name "bubble sort" for this sorting algorithm.

FIGURE 8-21
The First Pass of a Bubble Sort

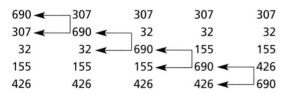

Because the first pass through the list ensures that the largest value always moves to the bottom of the list, the second pass stops at the next-to-last element. This process continues with each pass stopping at one higher element than the previous pass, until either N−1 passes through the list have been completed or no exchanges are necessary in any single pass. In both cases the resulting list is in sorted order. The pseudocode describing this sort is:

> ***Set interchange count to zero (not required, but done just to keep track of the interchanges)***
> ***For the first element in the list to one less than the last element (i index)***
> ***For the second element in the list to the last element (j index)***

> *If num[j] < num[j − 1]*
> *{*
>   *swap num[j] with num[j − 1]*
>   *increment interchange count*
> *}*
> *EndFor*
> *EndFor*
> *Return interchange count*

This sort algorithm is coded in C++ as the function bubbleSort, which is included within Program 8-15 for testing purposes. This program tests bubbleSort with the same list of 10 numbers used in Program 8-14 to test selectionSort. For comparison to the earlier selection sort, the number of adjacent moves (exchanges) made by bubbleSort is also counted and displayed.

Program 8-15

```cpp
#include <iostream>
using namespace std;

int main()
{
    int bubbleSort(int [], int);

    const int NUMEL = 10;
    int nums[NUMEL] = {22,5,67,98,45,32,101,99,73,10};
    int i, moves;

    moves = bubbleSort(nums, NUMEL);

    cout << "The sorted list, in ascending order, is:\n";
    for (i = 0; i < NUMEL; ++i)
        cout << "   " <<nums[i];

    cout << endl << moves << " moves were made to sort this list\n";

    return 0;
}

int bubbleSort(int num[], int numel)
{
    int i, j, temp, moves = 0;

    for ( i = 0; i < (numel - 1); i++)
    {
        for(j = 1; j < numel; j++)
        {
            if (num[j] < num[j-1])
```

(continued on next page)

```
        {
            temp = num[j];
            num[j] = num[j-1];
            num[j-1] = temp;
            moves++;
        }
    }
}

    return moves;
}
```

Here is the output produced by Program 8-15:

```
The sorted list, in ascending order, is:
  5   10   22   32   45   67   73   98   99   101
18 moves were made to sort this list
```

As with the selection sort, the number of comparisons using a bubble sort is $O(N^2)$ and the number of required moves depends on the initial order of the values in the list. In the worst case, when the data is in reverse sorted order, the selection sort performs better than the bubble sort. Here both sorts require $N(N-1)/2$ comparisons, but the selection sort needs only $N-1$ moves while the bubble sort needs $N(N-1)/2$ moves. The additional moves required by the bubble sort result from the intermediate exchanges between adjacent elements to "settle" each element into its final position. In this regard the selection sort is superior, because no intermediate moves are necessary. For random data, such as that used in Programs 8-14 and 8-15, the selection sort generally performs equal to or better than the bubble sort.

A modification to the bubble sort (see Exercise 4 at the end of this section) which causes the sort to terminate when the list is in order regardless of the number of passes made, can make the bubble sort operate as an $O(N)$ sort in specialized cases.

Quicksort

The selection and exchange sorts both require $O(N^2)$ comparisons, which make them very slow for long lists. The **quicksort algorithm**, which is also called a **partition sort**, divides a list into two smaller sublists and sorts each sublist by partitioning into smaller sublists, and so on.[7] The order of a quicksort is $N\log_2 N$. Thus, for a 1000-item list, the total number of comparisons for a quicksort is in the order of $1000(3.3 \log_{10} 1000) = 1000(10) = 10,000$, compared to $1000(1000) = 1,000,000$ for a selection or exchange sort.

The quicksort algorithm puts a list into sorted order by a partitioning process. At each stage the list is partitioned into sublists so that a selected element, called the pivot, is placed in its correct position in the final sorted list. To learn more about the process, review the list illustrated in Figure 8-22.

---

[7]This algorithm was developed by C.A.R. Hoare and first described by him in an article entitled "QuickSort" in *Computer Journal* (vol. 5, pp10-15) in 1962. This sorting algorithm was so much faster than previous algorithms that it became known as *the* Quicksort.

FIGURE 8-22
A First Quicksort Partition

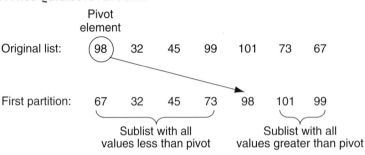

The original list shown consists of seven numbers. Designating the first element in the list, 98, as the pivot element, the list is rearranged as shown in the first partition. Notice that this partition results in all values less than 98 residing to its left and all values greater than 98 to its right. For now, disregard the exact order of the elements to the left and right of the 98 (in a moment we will see how the arrangement of the numbers came about).

The numbers to the left of the pivot constitute one sublist and the numbers to the right another sublist, which individually must be reordered by a partitioning process. The pivot for the first sublist is 67 and the pivot for the second sublist is 101. Figure 8-23 shows how each of these sublists is partitioned using their respective pivot elements. The partitioning process stops when a sublist has only one element. In the case illustrated in Figure 8-23, a fourth partition is required for the sublist containing the values 45 and 32, since all other sublists have only one element. Once this last sublist is partitioned, the quicksort is completed and the original list is in sorted order.

FIGURE 8-23
Completing the Quicksort

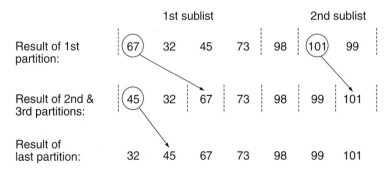

As we have illustrated, the key to the quicksort is its partitioning process. An essential part of this process is that each sublist is rearranged in place; that is, elements are rearranged within the existing list. This rearrangement is facilitated by first saving the value of the pivot, which frees its slot to be used by another element. The list is then examined from the right, starting with the last element in the list, for a value less than the pivot; when one is found it is copied to the pivot slot. This copy frees a slot at the right of the list for use by another element. The list is now examined from the left for any value greater than the pivot; when one is found it is copied to the last freed slot. This right-to-left and left-to-right scan is continued until the right and left index values meet. The saved pivot element is then copied into this slot. At that point all values to the left of the index are smaller than the pivot value and all values to the right are greater. Before providing the pseudocode for this process, we will show all of the steps required to complete one partition using our previous list of numbers.

Consider Figure 8-24, which shows the original list from Figure 8-22 and the positions of the initial left and right indexes. As shown in Figure 8-24, the pivot value has been saved into a variable named pivot, and the right index points to the last list element and is the active index. Using this index, the scan for elements less than the pivot value of 98 begins.

FIGURE 8-24
Start of the Scanning Process

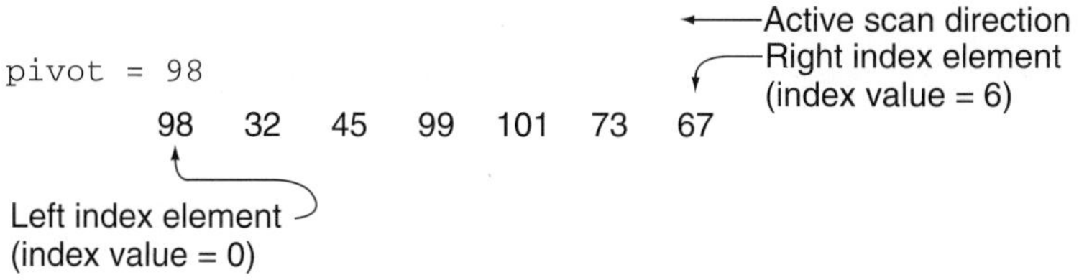

pivot = 98

98   32   45   99   101   73   67

Active scan direction
Right index element
(index value = 6)

Left index element
(index value = 0)

Because 67 is less than the pivot value of 98, the 67 is moved into the pivot slot (the pivot value is not lost because it has been assigned to the variable pivot) and the left index is incremented. This results in the arrangement shown in Figure 8-25.

FIGURE 8-25
The List After the First Copy

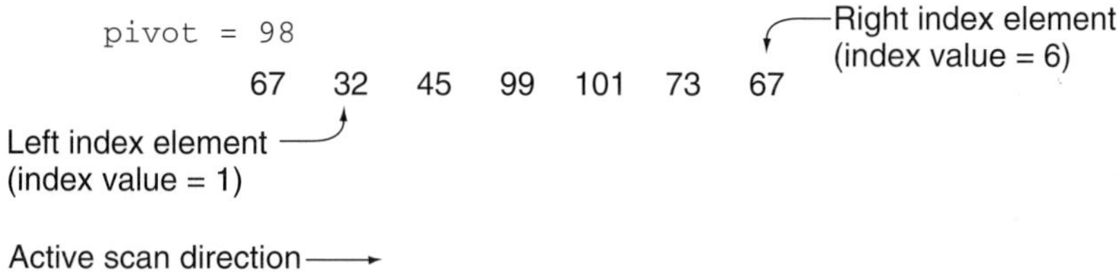

pivot = 98

67   32   45   99   101   73   67

Right index element
(index value = 6)

Left index element
(index value = 1)

Active scan direction

Notice in Figure 8-25 that the element pointed to by the right index is now available for the next copy, since its value, 67, has been reproduced as the first element. (This will always be the case; when a scan stops, its index will indicate the position available for the next move.)

Scanning of the list shown in Figure 8-25 continues from the left for a search of all values greater than 98. This occurs when the 99 is reached. Since 99 is greater than the pivot value of 98, the scan stops and the 99 is copied into the position indicated by the right index. The right index is then decremented, which produces the situation illustrated in Figure 8-26.

FIGURE 8-26
Start of the Second Right-Side Scan

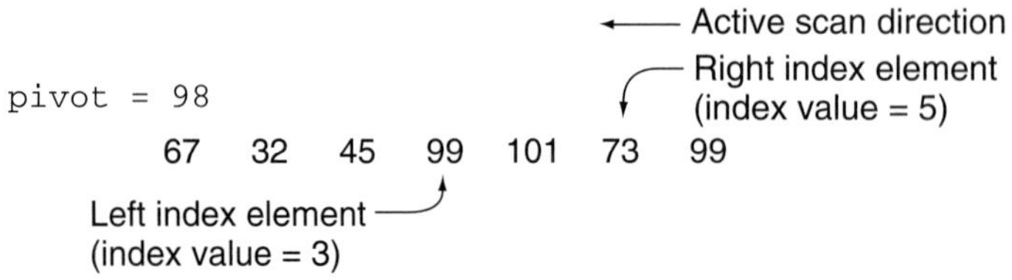

Scanning of the list shown in Figure 8-26 now continues from the right in a search for values less than the pivot. Since 73 qualifies, the right scan stops, the 73 is moved into the position indicated by the left index, and the left index is incremented. This results in the list shown in Figure 8-27.

FIGURE 8-27
Start of the Left-Side Scan

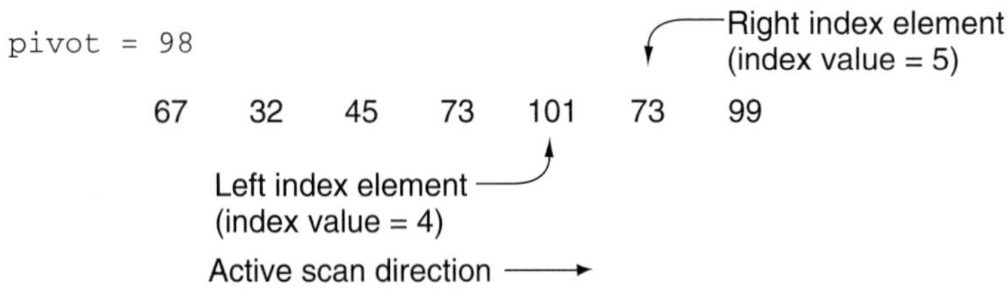

Scanning of the list shown in Figure 8-27 now resumes from the left in a search for values greater than 98. Since 101 qualifies, this scan stops and the 101 is moved into the slot indicated by the right index, and the right index is decremented. This results in the list illustrated in Figure 8-28.

FIGURE 8-28
The Position of List Elements After the 101 Is Moved

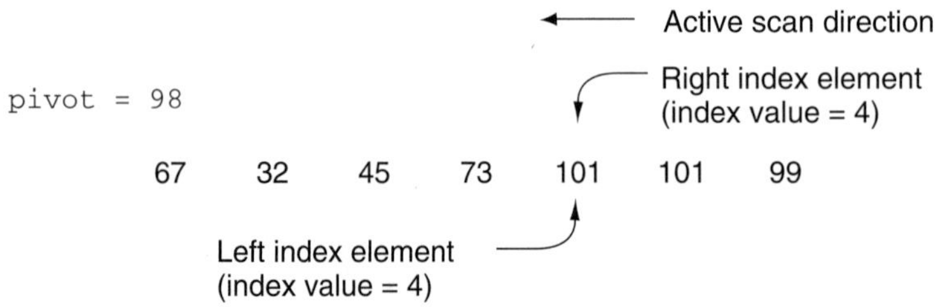

Notice in this figure that left and right indices are equal. This is the condition that stops all scanning and indicates the position where the pivot should be placed. Doing so results in completion of this partition with the list in the order:

67 32 45 73 98 101 99

Compare this list with the one previously shown for the first partition in Figure 8-22; they are the same. Here the pivot has been placed so that all elements less than it are to its left and all values greater than it are to its right. The same partitioning process would now be applied to the sublists on either side of the partition.

The pseudocode describing this partitioning process is:

> *Set the pivot to the value of the first list element*
> *initialize the left index to the index of the first list element*
> *initialize the right index to the index of the last list element*
> *While (left index ≠ right index)*
>   *// scan from the right, skipping over larger values*
>   *While (right index element >= pivot) // skip over larger values*
>   *decrement right index*
>   *EndWhile*
>   *If (right index <= left index)*
>   *move the lower value into the slot indicated by the left index*
>   *increment the left index*
>   *EndIf*
>   *// scan from the left, skipping over smaller values*
>   *While (left index element ≠ pivot) // skip over smaller values*
>   *increment left index*
>   *EndWhile*
>   *If (left index ≠ right index)*
>   *move the higher value into the slot indicated by the right index*
>   *decrement the right index*
>   *EndIf*
> *EndWhile*
> *Move the pivot into the slot indicated by the left or right index (they are equal here)*
> *Return the left (or right) index*

The function partition, contained within Program 8-16, codes this algorithm in C++.

Program 8-16

```cpp
#include <iostream>
using namespace std;

int main()
{
  int partition(int [], int, int); // function prototype

  const int NUMEL = 7;
  int nums[NUMEL] = {98,32,45,99,101,73,67};
  int i, pivot;
```

```
  pivot = partition(nums, 0, NUMEL-1);

  cout << "\nThe returned pivot index is " << pivot;
  cout << "\nThe list is now in the order:\n";
  for (i = 0; i < NUMEL; i++)
    cout << "   " << nums[i];
  cout << endl;

  return 0;
}

int partition(int num[], int left, int right)
{
  int pivot;

  pivot = num[left];   // "capture" the pivot value, which frees up one slot
  while (left < right)
  {
      // scan from right to left
    while(num[right] >= pivot && left < right)  // skip over larger or equal values
      right--;
    if (right != left)
    {
      num[left] = num[right];    // move the higher value into the available slot
      left++;
    }
      // scan from left to right
    while (num[left] <= pivot && left < right) // skip over smaller or equal values
      left++;
    if (right != left)
    {
      num[right] = num[left];   // moves lower value into the available slot
      right--;
    }
  }
  num[left] = pivot;   // move pivot into correct position

  return left;       // return the pivot index
}
```

Program 8-16 is simply used to test the function. Notice that it contains the same list that we used in our hand calculation. A sample run using Program 8-16 produced this output:

```
The returned pivot index is 4
The list is now in the order:
  67   32   45   73   98   101   99
```

8

Notice that this output produces the result previously obtained by our hand calculation. The importance of the returned pivot index is that it defines the sublists that will be subsequently partitioned. The first sublist consists of all elements from the first list element to the element whose index is 3 (one less than the returned pivot index) and the second sublist consists of all elements starting at index value 5 (one more than the returned pivot index) and ending at the last list element.

The quicksort uses the returned pivot value in determining whether additional calls to partition are required for each sublist defined by the list segments to the left and right of the pivot index. This is done using the following recursive logic:

> *quicksort(list, lower index, upper index)*
>   *calculate a pivot index calling partition(list, lower index, upper index)*
>   *If (lower index < pivot index)*
>   *quicksort(list, lower index, pivot index − 1)*
>   *If (upper index > pivot index)*
>   *quicksort(list, upper index, pivot index + 1)*

The C++ code for this logic is described by the quicksort function contained within Program 8-17. As indicated, quicksort requires a partition both to rearrange lists and return its pivot value.

Program 8-17

```cpp
#include <iostream>
using namespace std;

int main()
{
  void quicksort(int [], int, int);  // function prototype

  const int NUMEL = 7;
  int nums[NUMEL] = {67,32,45,73,98,101,99};
  int i;

  quicksort(nums, 0, NUMEL-1);

  cout << "\nThe sorted list, in ascending order, is:\n";
  for (i = 0; i < NUMEL; i++)
    cout << "  " <<nums[i];
  cout << endl;

  return 0;
}

void quicksort(int num[], int lower, int upper)
{
  int i, j, pivot;
  int partition(int [], int, int);
```

(continued on next page)

```
   pivot = partition(num, lower, upper);

   if (lower < pivot)
      quicksort(num, lower, pivot - 1);
   if (upper > pivot)
      quicksort(num, pivot + 1, upper);

   return;
}

int partition(int num[], int left, int right)
{
   int pivot, temp;

   pivot = num[left];  // "capture" the pivot value, which frees up one slot
   while (left < right)
   {
       // scan from right to left
     while(num[right] >= pivot && left < right)  // skip over larger or equal values
        right--;
     if (right != left)
     {
       num[left] = num[right];    // move the higher value into the available slot
       left++;
     }
       // scan from left to right
     while (num[left] <= pivot && left < right) // skip over smaller or equal values
        left++;
     if (right != left)
     {
       num[right] = num[left];  // move lower value into the available slot
       right--;
     }
   }
   num[left] = pivot;  // move pivot into correct position

   return left;        // return the pivot index
}
```

Here is the output produced by Program 8-17:

```
The sorted list, in ascending order, is:
   32   45   67   73   98   99   101
```

As indicated by this output, quicksort correctly sorts the test list of numbers. Figure 8-29 shows the sequence of calls made to quicksort by Program 8-17. In this figure, left-pointing arrows indicate calls made because the first `if` condition (lower < pivot) was true, and right-pointing arrows indicate calls made because the second `if` condition (upper > pivot) was true.

FIGURE 8-29
The Sequence of Call Made by Program 8-17

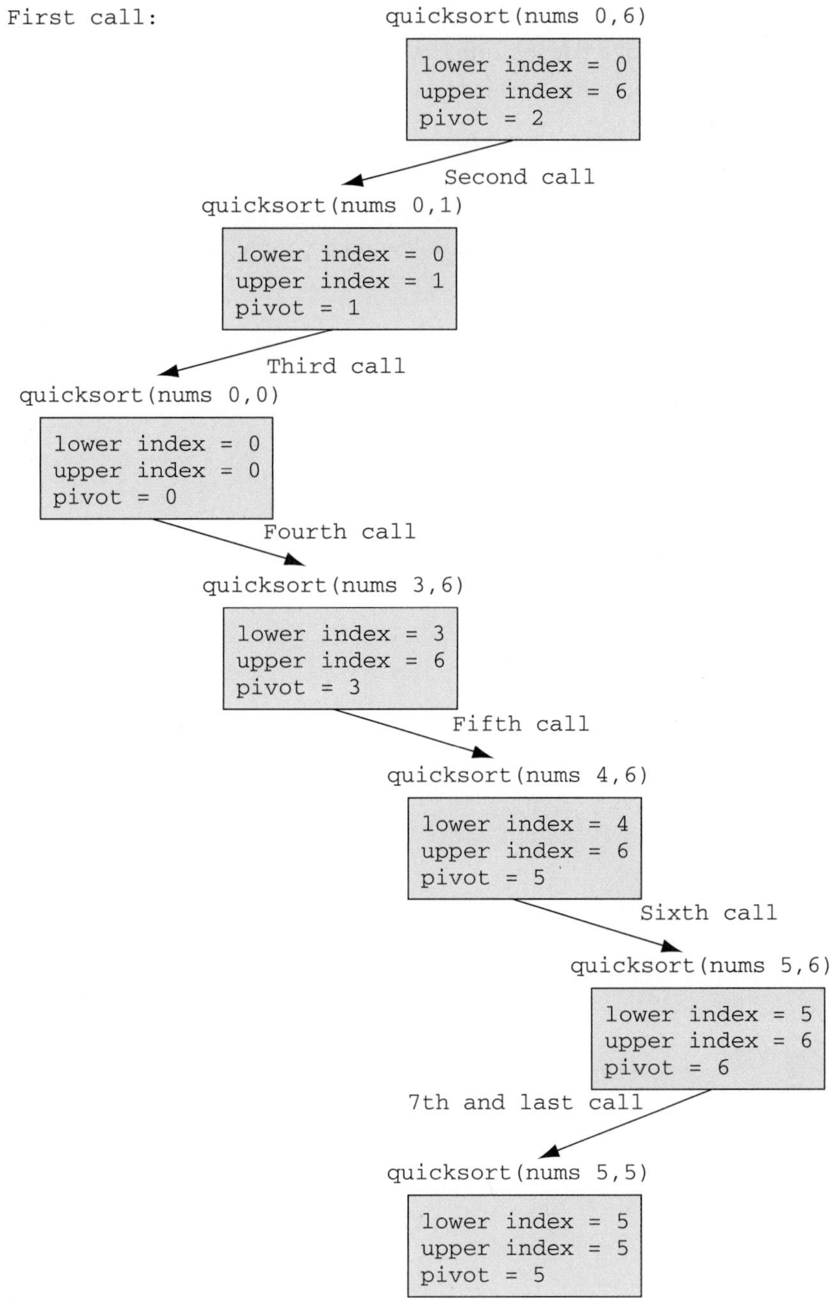

```
First call:                        quicksort(nums 0,6)

                                   lower index = 0
                                   upper index = 6
                                   pivot = 2

                        Second call
           quicksort(nums 0,1)

              lower index = 0
              upper index = 1
              pivot = 1

                  Third call
    quicksort(nums 0,0)

       lower index = 0
       upper index = 0
       pivot = 0

                    Fourth call
           quicksort(nums 3,6)

              lower index = 3
              upper index = 6
              pivot = 3

                      Fifth call
                quicksort(nums 4,6)

                   lower index = 4
                   upper index = 6
                   pivot = 5

                           Sixth call
                    quicksort(nums 5,6)

                       lower index = 5
                       upper index = 6
                       pivot = 6

        7th and last call

    quicksort(nums 5,5)

       lower index = 5
       upper index = 5
       pivot = 5
```

Exercises 8.7

1. **a.** Modify Program 8-14 to use a list of 100 randomly generated numbers and determine the number of moves required to put the list in order using a selection sort. Display both the initial list and the reordered list.

   b. Redo Exercise 1a using a bubble sort.

2. For the functions `selectionSort()`, `bubbleSort()`, and `quicksort()`, the sorting can be done in decreasing order by a simple modification. In each case, identify the required changes and then rewrite each function to accept a flag indicating whether the sort should be in increasing or decreasing order. Modify each routine to correctly receive and use this flag argument.

3. Describe why the quicksort function does not require the swapping algorithm used by the selection and bubble sorts.

4. An alternate form of the bubble sort is presented in the following program:

```cpp
#include <iostream>
using namespace std;
const int TRUE = 1;
const int FALSE = 0;
int main()
{
   int nums[10] = {22,5,67,98,45,32,101,99,73,10};
   int i, temp, moves, npts, outord;

   moves = 0;
   npts = 10;
   outord = TRUE;
   while (outord && npts > 0)
   {
     outord = FALSE;
     for ( i = 0; i < npts - 1; i++)
       if (nums[i] > nums[i+1])
       {
          temp = nums[i+1];
          nums[i+1] = nums[i];
          nums[i] = temp;
          outord = TRUE;
          moves++;
       }
     npts--;
   }
   cout << "The sorted list, in ascending order, is:\n";
```

(continued on next page)

```
for (i = 0; i < 10; i++)
  cout << "  " << nums[i];
cout << endl << moves
     << " moves were made to sort this list" << endl;

return 1;
}
```

An advantage of this version of the bubble sort is that processing is terminated whenever a sorted list is encountered. In the best case, when the data is in sorted order to begin with, an exchange sort requires no moves (the same for the selection sort) and only $N-1$ comparisons (the selection sort always requires $N(N-1)/2$ comparisons).

After you have run this program to convince yourself that it correctly sorts a list of integers, rewrite the sort algorithm it contains as a function named `newBubble()`, and test your function using the driver function contained in Program 8-15.

5. **a.** Modify Program 8-15 to use a larger test list consisting of 20 numbers.
    b. Modify Program 8-15 to use a list of 100 randomly selected numbers.

6. A company currently maintains two lists of part numbers, where each part number is an integer. Write a C++ program that compares these lists of numbers and displays the numbers, if any, that are common to both. (*Hint*: Sort each list prior to making the comparison.)

7. Redo Exercise 6, but display a list of part numbers that are only on one list, but not both.

8. Rewrite the binary search algorithm to use recursion rather than iteration.

8.8 COMMON PROGRAMMING ERRORS

Four common errors are associated with arrays:

1. Forgetting to declare an array. This error results in a compiler error message equivalent to "invalid indirection" each time a subscripted variable is encountered within a program. The exact meaning of this error message will become clear in Chapter 14, when the correspondence between arrays and pointers is established.

2. Using a subscript that references a nonexistent array element. For example, declaring the array to be of size 20 and using a subscript value of 25. This error is not detected by most C++ compilers. It will, however, result in a run-time error that results either in a program crash or a value that has no relation to the intended element being accessed from memory. In either case, the error is usually difficult to locate. The only solution to this problem is to make sure, either by specific programming statements or by careful coding, that each subscript references a valid array element.

3. Not using a large enough conditional value in a `for` loop counter to cycle through all the array elements. This error usually occurs when an array is initially specified to be of size *n* and there is a `for` loop within the program of the form `for (i = 0; i < n; i++)`. The array size is then expanded, but the programmer forgets to change the interior `for` loop parameters. Declaring an array's size using a named constant and consistently using the named constant throughout the function in place of the variable *n* eliminates this problem.

4. Forgetting to initialize an array. Although many compilers automatically set all elements of integer and real valued arrays to zero, and all elements of character arrays to blanks, it is up to the programmer to ensure that each array is correctly initialized before processing of array elements begins.

8.9 CHAPTER REVIEW

Key Terms

container

index

indexed variable

linear (sequential) search

NULL character ('\0')

one-dimensional array

single-dimensional array

Standard Template Library

subscript

subscripted variable

two-dimensional array

vector

8

SUMMARY

1. A single-dimensional array is a data structure that can be used to store a list of values of the same data type. Such arrays must be declared by giving the data type of the values that are stored in the array as well as the array size. For example, the declaration:

    ```
    int num[100];
    ```

    creates an array of 100 integers. A preferable approach is to first use a named constant to set the array size, and then use this constant in the definition of the array. For example:

    ```
    const int MAXSIZE = 100;
    ```

    and

    ```
    int num[MAXSIZE];
    ```

2. Array elements are stored in contiguous locations in memory and referenced using the array name and a subscript, for example, `num[22]`. Any nonnegative integer value expression can be used as a subscript, and the subscript 0 always refers to the first element in an array.

3. A two-dimensional array is declared by listing both a row and a column size with the data type and name of the array. For example, the declaration:

    ```
    int mat[5][7];
    ```

    creates a two-dimensional array consisting of five rows and seven columns of integer values.

4. Two-dimensional arrays may be initialized when they are declared. This is accomplished by listing the initial values, in a row-by-row manner, within braces and separating them with commas. For example, the declaration:

    ```
    int vals[3][2] = { {1, 2},
                       {3, 4},
                       {5, 6} };
    ```

    produces the following three-row by two-column array:

    ```
    1   2
    3   4
    5   6
    ```

    As C++ uses the convention that initialization proceeds in row-wise order, the inner braces can be omitted. Thus, an equivalent initialization is provided by the statement:

    ```
    int vals[3][2] = { 1, 2, 3, 4, 5, 6};
    ```

5. Arrays are passed to a function by passing the name of the array as an argument. The value actually passed is the address of the first array storage location. Thus, the called function receives direct access to the original array and not a copy of the array elements. Within the called function,

a formal parameter must be declared to receive the passed array name. The declaration of the formal parameter can omit the row size of the array.

6. The linear search is an *O(N)* search. It examines each item in a list until the searched item is found or until it is determined that the item is not in the list.

7. The binary search is an $O(\log_2 N)$ search. It requires that a list be in sorted order before it can be applied.

8. The selection and exchange sort algorithms require an order of magnitude of N^2 comparisons for sorting a list of *N* items.

9. The quicksort algorithm requires an order of magnitude of $N \log_2 N$ comparisons to sort a list of *N* items.

Chapter Exercises

1. a. Write a C++ program that reads a list of floating-point grades from the keyboard into an array named grade. The grades are to be counted as they are read, and entry is to be terminated when a negative value has been entered. Once all of the grades have been input, your program should find and display the sum and average of the grades. The grades should then be listed with an asterisk (*) placed in front of each grade that is below the average.

   b. Extend the program written for Exercise 1a to display each grade and its letter equivalent. Assume the following scale:

   A grade between 90 and 100 is an A.
   A grade greater than or equal to 80 and less than 90 is a B.
   A grade greater than or equal to 70 and less than 80 is a C.
   A grade greater than or equal to 60 and less than 70 is a D.
   A grade less than 60 is an F.

2. Define an array named `PeopleTypes` that can store a maximum of 50 integer values that will be entered at the keyboard. Enter a series of 1s, 2s, 3s, and 4s into the array, where a 1 represents an infant, a 2 represents a child, a 3 represents a teenager, and a 4 represents an adult who was present at a local school function. Any other integer value should not be accepted as valid input, and data entry should stop when a negative value has been entered.

   Your program should count the number of each 1, 2, 3, and 4 in the array and output a list of how many infants, children, teenagers, and adults were at the school function.

3. Given a one-dimensional array of integer numbers, write and test a function that prints the elements in reverse order.

4. Write and test a function that returns the position of the largest and smallest values in an array of floating-point numbers.

5. Read a set of numerical grades from the keyboard into an array. The maximum number of grades is 50 and data entry should be terminated when a negative number has been entered. Have your program sort and print the grades in *descending* order.

6. a. Define an array with a maximum of 20 integer values and either fill the array with numbers input from the keyboard or assigned by the program. Then write a function named `split()` that reads the array and places all zero or positive numbers into an array named `positive` and all negative numbers into an array named `negative`. Finally, have your program call a function that displays the values in both the `positive` and `negative` arrays.

   b. Extend the program written for Exercise 6a to sort the `positive` and `negative` arrays into ascending order before they are displayed.

7. Using the `srand()` and `rand()` C++ library functions, fill an array of 1000 floating-point numbers with random numbers that have been scaled to the range 1 to 100. Then determine and display the number of random numbers having values between 1 and 50 and the number having values greater than 50. What do you expect the output counts to be?

8. In many statistical analysis programs, data values that are considerably outside the range of the majority of values are simply dropped from consideration. Using this information, write a C++ program that accepts up to 10 floating-point values from a user and determines and displays the average and standard deviation of the input values. All values that are more than four standard deviations away from the computed average are to be displayed and dropped from any further calculation, and a new average and standard deviation should be computed and displayed.

9. Given a one-dimensional array of floating-point numbers named `num`, write a function that determines the sum of the numbers:

   a. Using repetition.
   b. Using recursion. (*Hint:* If $n = 1$, then the sum is `num[0]`; otherwise, the sum is `num[n]` plus the sum of the first $(n - 1)$ elements.)

10. Your professor has asked you to write a C++ program that can be used to determine grades at the end of the semester. Each student is identified by an integer number between 1 and 5. Four examination grades must be kept for each student. Additionally, two final grade averages must be computed. The first grade average is simply the average of all four grades. The second grade average is computed by weighting the four grades as follows: the first grade gets a weight of 0.2, the second grade gets a weight of 0.3, the third grade a weight of 0.3 and the fourth grade a weight of 0.2; that is, the final grade is computed as:

```
0.2 * grade1 + 0.3 * grade2 + 0.3 * grade3 + 0.2 * grade4
```

Using this information, construct a 50 by 7 two-dimensional array, in which the first column is used for the student number, the next four columns for the grades, and the last two columns for the computed final grades. The output of the program should be a display of the data in the completed array. For test purposes, the professor has provided the following data:

student	grade 1	grade 2	grade 3	grade 4
1	100	100	100	100
2	100	0	100	0
3	82	94	73	86
4	64	74	84	94
5	94	84	74	64

11. Modify the program written for Exercise 10 by adding an eighth column to the array. The grade in the eighth column should be calculated by computing the average of the top three grades only.

12. a. You are to create a two-dimensional list of integer part numbers and quantities of each part in stock, and write a function that displays the data in the array in decreasing quantity order. Assume that no more than 100 different parts are being tracked, and that data input should stop when a negative part number is entered. Test your program with the following data:

part no.	quantity
1001	62
949	85
1050	33
867	125
346	59
1025	105

b. Modify the function written in Exercise 12a to display the data in part number order.

13. Assume that the answers to a true-false test are as follows: T T F F T. Given a two-dimensional answer array where each row corresponds to the answers provided on one test, write a function that accepts the two-dimensional array and the number of tests as arguments, and returns a one-dimensional array containing the grades for each test (assume each question is worth 5 points, so that the maximum possible grade is 25). Test your function using the following data:

Test 1: T F T T T
Test 2: T T T T T
Test 3: T T F F T
Test 4: F T F F F
Test 5: F F F F F
Test 6: T T F T F

14. Modify the function that you wrote for Exercise 13 so that each test is stored in column order rather than row order.

15. Write a function that can be used to sort the elements of a 3 by 4 two-dimensional array of integers so that the lowest value is in element position [0][0], the next highest value in element position [0][1], and the highest value in element position [2][3].

16. A magic square is a square of numbers with *N* rows and *N* columns in which each of the integer values from 1 to (*N* * *N*) appears exactly once, and in which the sum of each column, each row, and each diagonal is the same value. For example, Figure 8-30 shows a magic square in which *N* = 3 and the sum of the rows, columns, and diagonals is 15. Write a program that constructs and displays a magic square for any given odd number *N*. The algorithm is:

Insert the value 1 in the middle of the first row (element [0][N/2])
After a value, x, has been placed, move up one row and to the right one column. Place the next number, x + 1, there, unless:
*   (1) You move off the top (row = −1) in any column. Then move to the bottom row and place the next number, x + 1, in the bottom row of that column.*
*   (2) You move off the right end (column = N) of a row. Then place the next number, x + 1, in the first column of that row.*
*   (3) You move to a position that is already filled or out of the upper-right corner. Then place the next number, x + 1, immediately below x.*
Stop when you have placed as many elements as there are in the array.

FIGURE 8-30
A Magic Square

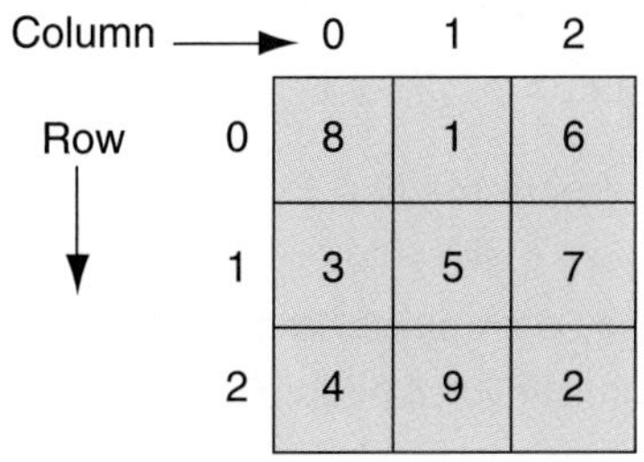

Column →	0	1	2
Row 0	8	1	6
1	3	5	7
2	4	9	2

17. Among other applications, Pascal's triangle (see Figure 8-31) provides a means of determining the number of possible combinations of *n* things taken *r* at a time. For example, the number of possible combinations of five people ($n = 5$) taken two at a time ($r = 2$) is 10.

FIGURE 8-31
Pascal's Triangle

			r				
n	**0**	**1**	**2**	**3**	**4**	**5**	**• • •**
0	1						
1	1	1					
2	1	2	1				
3	1	3	3	1			
4	1	4	6	4	1		
5	1	5	10	10	5	1	
• • •							

Each row of the triangle begins and ends with 1. Every other element in a row is the sum of the element directly above it with the element to the left of the one above it. That is,

$$\text{Element}[n][r] = \text{Element}[n-1][r] + \text{Element}[n-1][r-1]$$

Using this information, write and test a C++ program to create the first 11 rows of a two-dimensional array representing Pascal's triangle. For any given value of *n* less than 11 and *r* less than or equal to *n*, the program should display the appropriate element. Use your program to determine in how many ways a committee of 8 people can be selected from a group of 10 people.

18. A three-dimensional weather array for the first two weeks of January 2005 uses the first index, which can take on a value of 0 or 1, to represent the first and second week, respectively. The second index is numbered 0 through 6 and represents the days, and the last index is 0 and 1, which represents the day's high and low temperatures, respectively.

8

Use this information to write a C++ program that either prompts for or assigns the high and low temperatures for each element of the arrays. Then allow the user to request

- Any day's high and low temperature
- Average high and low temperatures for a given week
- Week and day with the highest temperature
- Week and day with the lowest temperature

**Testing
Center**

Please visit the Testing Center at www.course.com/testingcenter for more practice on arrays.

9

STRINGS AND CHARACTERS

A **string literal**, as we have already seen, is any sequence of characters enclosed in double quotation marks. As has been noted throughout the text, a string literal is also referred to as a string value, a string constant, and more conventionally, simply as a string. Examples of strings are `"This is a string"`, `"Hello World!"`, and `"xyz 123 *!#@&"`. The double quotation marks are used to mark the beginning and ending points of the string and are never stored with the string.

Each computer language has its own way of storing and processing strings. Some languages, such as C++, have a rich set of string manipulation functions and capabilities. Other languages, such as FORTRAN, which was predominantly used for numerical calculations, added string handling capabilities with later versions of the compiler. Java provides strings only as objects of a string class, while languages such as LISP, which are targeted for list-handling applications, provide an exceptional string manipulation capability.

C++ provides two different ways of storing and manipulating strings. Originally, strings could only be stored as arrays of characters that were terminated by a sentinel value. (The sentinel character was the escape sequence `'\0'`.) This representation permitted strings to be manipulated using standard element-by-element array-processing techniques. Strings stored in this manner are now referred to as character strings, or C-strings, for short. In addition, a `cstring` class is now available that provides a number of useful methods for operating on C-strings, such as inserting, deleting, and extracting individual characters from the string.

With the new ANSI/ISO C++ standard, a second approach to storing and processing strings, which in many ways is simpler and easier to use than C-strings, has been added. This second approach creates strings as objects of a class named `string`. The `string` class provides a greatly expanded set of methods that include easy insertion and removal of characters from a string, automatic string expansion whenever its original capacity is exceeded, automatic string contraction when characters are removed from the string, and range checking to detect invalid index values. Additionally, the `string` class was designed so that string objects could easily use the Standard Template Library's (STL) algorithms.

This chapter presents both forms of string representation and manipulation, including conversion between the two string representations. Additionally, character-based methods that can be applied to individual elements of both string types are provided.

9.1 THE STRING CLASS

Figure 9-1 shows the programming representation of the string `Hello` whenever this string is created as an object of the `string` class. By convention, the first character in a string is always designated as position 0. This position value is also referred to as both the character's index value and its offset value.

FIGURE 9-1
The Storage of a String as a Sequence of Characters

Position:	0	1	2	3	4
	H	e	l	l	o

string CLASS CONSTRUCTORS

The Standard Template Library's `string` class provides a number of constructor methods for creating and initializing a string. As was described in Section 2.4, the process of creating a new object is referred to as instantiating an object, which in this case becomes instantiating a string object, or creating a string, for short. Table 9-1 lists the constructor methods for creating and initializing a string object.

TABLE 9-1
string Class Constructors
(Required header file is string)

constructor	description	examples

`string objectName = value`	Creates and initializes a string object to `value`, which can be a string literal, previously declared string object, or an expression containing both string literals and string objects	`string str1 = "Good Morning";`
		 `string str2 = str1;`
		 `string str3 = str1 + str2;`

`string objectName(string-value)`	Produces the same initialization as above	`string str1("Hot");` `string str1(str1 + " Dog");`
`string objectName(str, n)`	Creates and initializes a string object with a substring of string object `str`, starting at index position n of `str`	`string str1(str2, 5)` If `str2` contains the string `Good Morning`, then `str1` becomes the string `Morning`
`string objectName(str, n, p)`	Creates and initializes a string object with a substring of string object `str`, starting at index position n of `str` and containing p characters	`string str1(str2, 5,2)` If `str2` contains the string `Good Morning`, then `str1` becomes the string `Mo`

TABLE 9-1
string *Class Constructors (Continued)*

`string objectName( n, char)`	Creates and initializes a string object and initializes it with n copies of char	`string str1(5,'*')` This makes `str1 = "*****"`
`string objectName;`	Creates and initializes a string object to represent an empty character sequence. Same as string `objectName = "";` the length of the string is 0	`string message;`

Program 9-1 illustrates examples of each of the constructor types provided by the string class.

Program 9-1

```cpp
#include <iostream>
#include <string>
using namespace std;

int main()
{
   string str1; // an empty string
   string str2("Good Morning");
   string str3 = "Hot Dog";
   string str4(str3);
   string str5(str4, 4);
   string str6 = "linear";
   string str7(str6, 3, 3);

   cout << "str1 is: " << str1 << endl;
   cout << "str2 is: " << str2 << endl;
   cout << "str3 is: " << str3 << endl;
   cout << "str4 is: " << str4 << endl;
   cout << "str5 is: " << str5 << endl;
   cout << "str6 is: " << str6 << endl;
   cout << "str7 is: " << str7 << endl;

   return 0;
}
```

The output created by Program 9-1 is:

```
str1 is:
str2 is: Good Morning
str3 is: Hot Dog
str4 is: Hot Dog
```

```
str5 is: Dog
str6 is: linear
str7 is: ear
```

Although this output is straightforward, two comments are in order. First, notice that `str1` is an empty string consisting of no characters. Next, because the first character in a string is designated as position zero, not position one, the character position of the D in the string `Hot Dog` is located at position four, which is shown in Figure 9-2.

FIGURE 9-2
The Character Positions of the String `Hot Dog`

Character Position:	0	1	2	3	4	5	6
	H	o	t		D	o	g

string INPUT AND OUTPUT

In addition to initializing a string using the constructors in Table 9-1, strings can be input from the keyboard and displayed on the screen. Table 9-2 lists the basic `string` input and output methods.

TABLE 9-2
string *Input and Output Routines*

C++ routine	description
cout	General purpose screen output
cin	General purpose keyboard input that stops reading when a whitespace is encountered
getline(cin, strObj)	General purpose keyboard input that inputs all characters entered into the string named `strObj` and stops accepting characters when it receives a newline character (`'\n'`)

As listed in Table 9-2, in addition to the standard `cout` and `cin` streams, the `string` class provides the `getline()` method for string input. For example, the expression `getline(cin, message)` will continuously accept and store characters typed at the keyboard until the Enter key is pressed. Pressing the Enter key at the keyboard generates a newline character, `'\n'`, which is interpreted by `getline()` as the end-of-line entry. All the characters encountered by `getline()`, except the newline character, are stored in the string named `message`, as illustrated in Figure 9-3.

FIGURE 9-3
Inputting a String with `getline()`

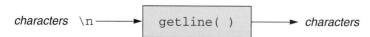

Program 9-2 illustrates using the `getline()` method and `cout` stream to input and output a string, respectively, that is entered at the user's keyboard.

Program 9-2

```cpp
#include <iostream>
#include <string>
using namespace std;

int main()
{
  string message;       // declare a string object

  cout << "Enter a string:\n";

  getline(cin, message);

  cout << "The string just entered is:\n"
       << message << endl;

  return 0;
}
```

The following is a sample run of Program 9-2:

```
Enter a string:
This is a test input of a string of characters.
The string just entered is:
This is a test input of a string of characters.
```

Although the `cout` stream object is used in Program 9-2 for string output, the `cin` stream input object generally cannot be used in place of `getline()` for string input. This is because the `cin` object reads a set of characters up to either a blank space or a newline character. Thus, attempting to enter the characters `This is a string` using the statement `cin >> message;` only results in the word `This` being assigned to `message`.

The fact that a blank terminates a `cin` extraction operation restricts `cin`'s usefulness for entering string data and is the reason for using `getline()`.

In its most general form, the `getline()` method has the syntax

```
getline(cin, strObj, terminatingChar)
```

where `strObj` is a string variable name, and `terminatingChar` is an optional character constant or variable specifying the terminating character. For example, the expression `getline(cin, message,`

'!') will accept all characters entered at the keyboard, including a newline character, until an exclamation point is entered. The exclamation point will not be stored as part of the string.

If the optional third argument is omitted when `getline()` is called, the default terminating character is the newline (`'\n'`) character. Thus, the statement `getline(cin, message, '\n');` can be used in place of the statement `getline(cin, message);`. Both of these statements stop reading characters when the Enter key is pressed. In all future programs we will assume that input is terminated by the Enter key, which generates a newline character. As such, the optional third argument passed to `getline()`, which is the terminating character, will be omitted.

CAUTION: THE PHANTOM NEWLINE CHARACTER

Seemingly strange results can be obtained when the `cin` input stream and `getline()` method are used together to accept data, or when the `cin` input stream is used to accept individual characters. To see how this can occur, consider Program 9-3, which uses `cin` to accept an integer entered at the keyboard, storing it in the variable named `value`, followed by a `getline()` method call.

Program 9-3

```
#include <iostream>
#include <string>
using namespace std;

int main()
{
  int value;
  string message;

  cout << "Enter a number: ";
  cin  >> value;
  cout << "The number entered is: " << value << endl;

  cout << "Enter text:\n";
  getline(cin, message);
  cout << "The text entered is: " << message << endl;


  return 0;
}
```

When Program 9-3 is run, the number entered in response to the prompt `Enter a number:` is stored in the variable named `value`. At this point, everything seems to be working fine. Notice, however, that in entering a number, you actually enter a number and press the Enter key. On almost all computer systems this entered data is stored in a temporary holding area called a buffer immediately after the characters are entered, as illustrated in Figure 9-4.

FIGURE 9-4
Typed Keyboard Characters Are First Stored in a Buffer

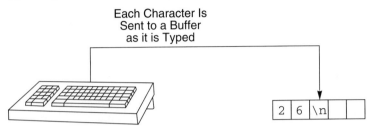

Each Character Is
Sent to a Buffer
as it is Typed

| 2 | 6 | \n | | |

The `cin` input stream in Program 9-3 first accepts the typed number, but leaves the `'\n'` in the buffer. The next input statement, which is a call to `getline()`, will automatically pick up the code for the Enter key as the next character, and immediately terminate any further input. Following is a sample run for Program 9-3:

```
Enter a number: 26
The number entered is: 26
Enter text:
The text entered is:
```

Notice in this output that no text is accepted in response to the prompt `Enter text:`. This occurs because after the number 26 has been accepted by the program, the code for the Enter key, which is a newline escape sequence, remains in the buffer and is picked up and interpreted by the `getline()` method as the end of its input. This will occur whether an integer, as in Program 9-3, or a string, or any other input is accepted by `cin`, and then followed by a `getline()` method call.

There are three separate solutions to this "phantom" Enter key problem:

- Do not mix `cin` with `getline()` inputs in the same program.
- Follow the `cin` input with the call to `cin.ignore()`.
- Accept the Enter key into a character variable and then ignore it.

PROGRAMMING NOTE

The `string` and `char` Data Types

A string can consist of zero or more characters. When it has no characters, it is said to be an empty string and has a length of zero. A string with a single character, such as `"a"`, is a string of length one and is stored differently than a `char` data type such as `'a'`. However, for many practical purposes a string of length one and a `char` respond in the same manner. For example, `cout >> "\n"` and `cout >> '\n'` both produce a new line on the screen, yet it is important to understand that they are different data types. For example, both declarations

```
string s1 = 'a';  // INVALID INITIALIZATION
char key = "\n"; // INVALID INITIALIZATION
```

produce a compiler error because they attempt to initialize one data type with literal values of another type.

The preferred solution is the first one. All solutions, however, center on the fact that the Enter key is a legitimate character input and must be recognized as such. We will encounter this problem once again when we consider accepting `char` data types in the next section.

STRING PROCESSING

Strings can be manipulated using either `string` class methods or the character-at-a-time methods described in the next section. Table 9-3 lists the most commonly used `string` class methods. These include accessor and mutator methods, plus additional methods and operator functions that use the standard arithmetic and comparison operators.

The most commonly used method in Table 9-3 is the `length()` method. This returns the number of characters in the string, which is referred to as the string's length. For example, the value returned by the method call `"Hello World!".length()` is 12. As always, the double quotes surrounding a string value are not considered part of the string. Similarly, if the string referenced by `string1` contains the value `"Have a good day."`, the value returned by the call `string1.length()` is 16.

Notice that two string expressions may be compared for equality using the standard relational operators. Each character in a string is stored in binary using either the ASCII or UNICODE code. Although these codes are different, they have some characteristics in common: in each of them, a blank precedes (is less than) all letters and numbers; the letters of the alphabet are stored in order from A to Z; and the digits are stored in order from 0 to 9. In both character codes the digits come before (that is, are less than) the uppercase characters, which are then followed by the lowercase characters. Thus, the uppercase characters are mathematically less than the lowercase characters. When two strings are compared, their individual characters are compared a pair at a time (both first characters, then both second characters, and so on). If no differences are found, the strings are equal; if a difference is found, the string with the first lower character is considered the smaller string. Thus,

- `"Hello"` is greater than `"Good Bye"` because the H in `Hello` is greater than the G in `Good Bye`

- `"Hello"` is less than `"hello"` because the H in `Hello` is less than the h in `hello`

- `"SMITH"` is greater than `"JONES"` because the S in `SMITH` is greater than the J in `JONES`

- `"123"` is greater than `"1227"` because the third character, the 3 in `123`, is greater than the third character, the 2 in `1227`

- `"Behop"` is greater than `"Beehive"` because the third character, the h in `Behop`, is greater than the third character, the e in `Beehive`

TABLE 9-3
The string *Class Methods*
(Require the header file string*)*

method/operation	description	example
int length()	Returns the length of the implicit string	string.length()
int size()	Same as above	string.size()
at(int index)	Returns the character at the specified index, and throws an exception if the index is non existent	string.at(4)
int compare (string)	Compares two strings; returns a negative value if the implied string is less than str, 0 if they are equal, and a positive value if the implied string is less than str	string1.compare (string2);
c_str()	Returns the string as a NULL terminated C-string	s1 = string1.c_str();
empty()	Returns true if the implied string is empty; otherwise, returns false	string1.empty();
erase(ind,n);	Removes n characters from the implied string, starting at index ind	string1.erase(2,3);
erase(ind)	Removes all characters from the implied string, starting from index ind until the end of the string. The length of the remaining string becomes ind	string1.erase(4);
int find(str)	Returns the index of the first occurrence of str within the implied object	string1.find ("the")
int find(str, ind)	Returns the index of the first occurrence of str within the implied object, with the search beginning at index ind	string1.find ("the", 5);
int find_first_of(str, ind)	Returns the index of the first occurrence of any character in str within the implied object, with the search starting at index ind	string1.find_first_of("lt", 6)
int find_first_not_of(str, ind)	Returns the index of the first occurrence of any character not in str within the implied object, with the search starting at index ind	string1.find_first_not_of ("lt",6)
void insert(ind, str)	Inserts the string str into the implied string, starting at index ind	string.insert(4, "there");
void replace(ind, n, str)	Removes n characters in the implied object, starting at index position ind, and inserts the string str at index position ind	string1.replace(2,4,"okay");
string substr(ind,n)	Returns a string consisting of n characters extracted from the implied string starting at index ind. If n is greater than the remaining number of characters, the rest of the implied string is used.	string2 = string1.substr(0,10);
void swap(str)	Swaps characters in str with the implied object	string1.swap(string2);
[ind]	Returns the character at index x, without checking if ind is a valid index	

(continued on next page)

TABLE 9-3
The string *Class Methods (Continued)*

method/operation	description	example
=	Assignment (also converts a C-string to a string)	string1 = string
+	Concatenates two strings	string1 + string2
+=	Concatenation and assignment	string2 += string1
== != < <= > >=	Relational operators. Return true if the relation is satisfied; otherwise return false.	string1 == string2 string1 <= string2 string1 > string2

Program 9-4 uses length() and several relational expressions within the context of a complete program.

Program 9-4

```cpp
#include <iostream>
#include <string>
using namespace std;

int main()
{
  string string1 = "Hello";
  string string2 = "Hello there";

  cout << "string1 is the string:" <<  string1 << endl;
  cout << "The number of characters in string1 is " <<  string1.length()
       << endl << endl;

  cout << "string2 is the string:" <<  string2 << endl;
  cout << "The number of characters in string2 is " <<  string2.length()
       << endl << endl;

  if (string1 < string2)
    cout << string1 <<  " is less than " <<  string2 << endl << endl;
  else if (string1 == string2)
    cout << string1 <<  " is equal to " <<  string2 << endl << endl;
  else
    cout << string1 <<  " is greater than " <<  string2 << endl << endl;

  string1 = string1 + " there world!";
  cout << "After concatenation, string1 contains the characters: " << string1 << endl;
  cout << "The length of this string is " <<  string1.length() << endl;

  return 0;
}
```

Following is a sample output produced by Program 9-4:

```
string1 is the string: Hello
The number of characters in string1 is 5

string2 is the string: Hello there
The number of characters in string2 is 11

Hello is less than Hello there

After concatenation, string1 contains the characters: Hello there world!
The length of this string is 18
```

In reviewing this output, refer to Figure 9-5, which shows how the characters in `string1` and `string2` are stored in memory. Note that the length of each string refers to the total number of characters in the string, and that the first character in each string is located at index position 0. Thus, the length of a string is always one more than the index number of the last character's position in the string.

FIGURE 9-5
The Initial Strings Used in Program 9-4

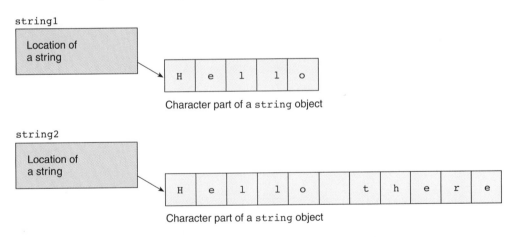

Although you will mostly use the concatenation operator and the `length()` method, there are times when you will find the other string methods in Table 9-3 useful. One of the more useful of these is the `at()` method, which permits you to retrieve individual characters in a string. Program 9-5 uses this method to select one character at a time from the string, starting at string position zero and ending at the index of the last character in the string. This last index value is always one less than the number of characters (that is, the string's length) in the string.

Program 9-5

```cpp
#include <iostream>
#include <string>
using namespace std;

int main()
{

   string str = "Counting the number of vowels";
   int i, numChars;
   int vowelCount = 0;

   cout << "The string:" <<  str << endl;

   numChars = str.length();
   for (i = 0; i < numChars; i++)
   {
     switch(str.at(i))    // here is where a character is retrieved
     {
       case 'a':
       case 'e':
       case 'i':
       case 'o':
       case 'u':
          vowelCount++;
     }
   }
   cout << "has " <<  vowelCount <<  " vowels." << endl;

   return 0;
}
```

The expression str.at(i) in Program 9-5's switch statement retrieves the character at position i in the string. This character is then compared to five different character values. The switch statement uses the fact that selected cases "drop through" in the absence of break statements. Thus, all selected cases result in an increment to vowelCount. The output displayed by Program 9-5 is:

```
The string: Counting the number of vowels
has 9 vowels.
```

As an example of insertion and replacement methods listed in Table 9-3, assume that we start with a string created by the statement:

```
string str = "This cannot be";
```

Figure 9-6 illustrates how this string is stored in the buffer created for it. As indicated, the initial length of the string is 14 characters.

FIGURE 9-6
Initial Storage of a String Object

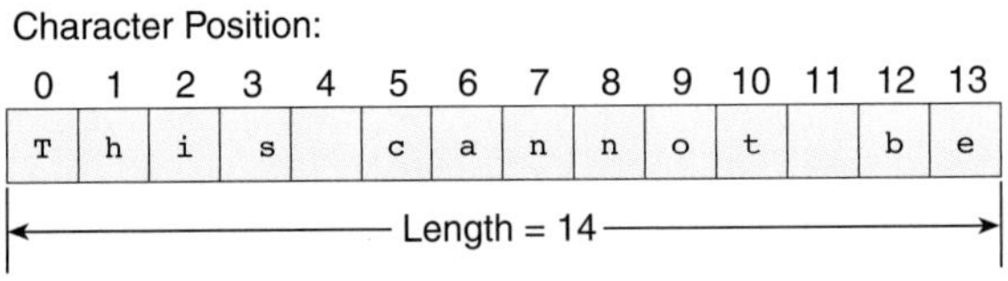

Character Position:

0	1	2	3	4	5	6	7	8	9	10	11	12	13
T	h	i	s		c	a	n	n	o	t		b	e

|←———————— Length = 14 ————————→|

Now assume that the following statement is executed:

```
str.insert(4," I know");
```

This statement causes the designated seven characters, beginning with a blank, to be inserted starting at index position four in the existing string. The resulting string, after the insertion, is as shown in Figure 9-7.

FIGURE 9-7
The String After the Insertion

Character Position:

0	1	2	3	4	5	6	7	8	9	10	11	12	13	14	15	16	17	18	19	20
T	h	i	s		I		k	n	o	w		c	a	n	n	o	t		b	e

|←——————————— Length = 21 ———————————→|

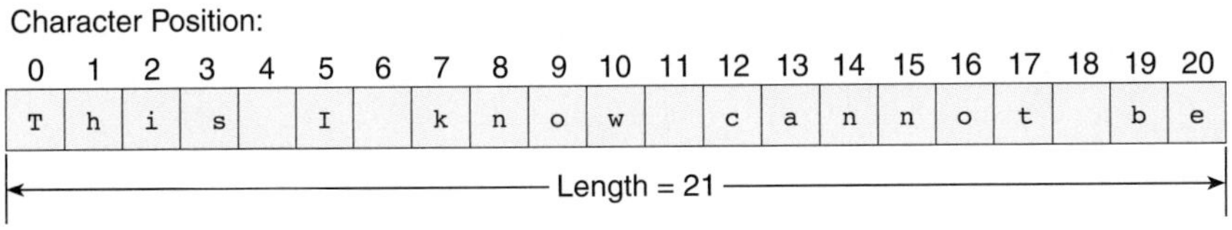

If the statement `str.replace(12, 6, "to");` is now executed, the existing characters in index positions 12 through 17 will be deleted and the two characters `to` inserted starting at index position 12. Thus, the net effect of the replacement is as shown in Figure 9-8. It is worthwhile noting that the number of replacement characters, which in this case is two, can be less than, equal to, or greater than the characters that are being replaced, which in this case is six.

FIGURE 9-8
The String After the Replacement

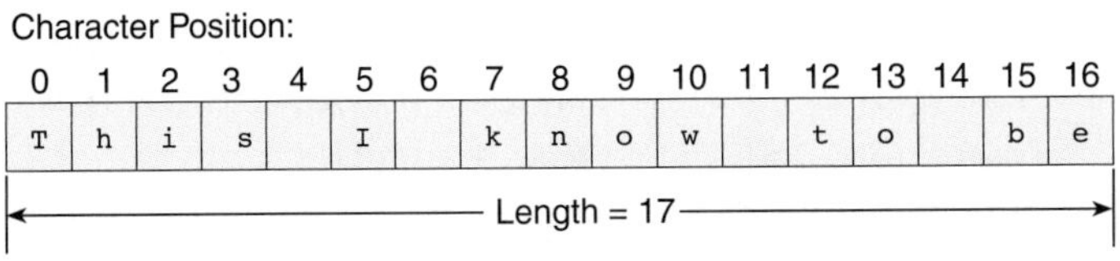

Character Position:

0	1	2	3	4	5	6	7	8	9	10	11	12	13	14	15	16
T	h	i	s		I		k	n	o	w		t	o		b	e

|←————————— Length = 17 —————————→|

Finally, if we append the string `"correct"` to the string shown in Figure 9-8 using the concatenation operator, + the string illustrated in Figure 9-9 is obtained.

FIGURE 9-9
The String After the Append

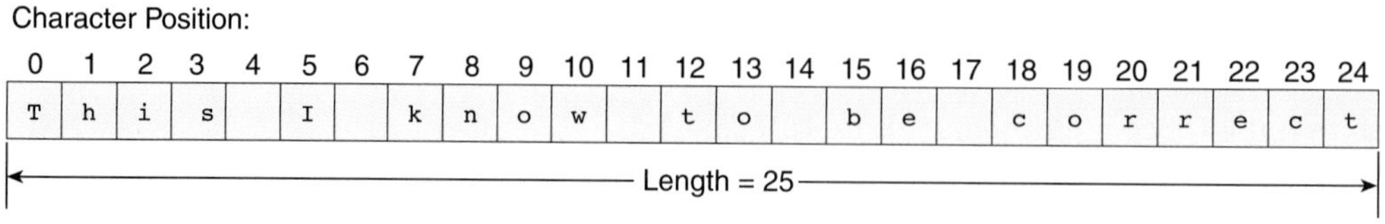

Character Position:

0	1	2	3	4	5	6	7	8	9	10	11	12	13	14	15	16	17	18	19	20	21	22	23	24
T	h	i	s		I		k	n	o	w		t	o		b	e		c	o	r	r	e	c	t

Length = 25

Program 9-6 illustrates using the statements we have just examined within the context of a complete program.

Program 9-6

```cpp
#include <iostream>
#include <string>
using namespace std;

int main()
{
    string str = "This cannot be";
    int i, numChars;

    cout << "The original string is: " << str << endl
         << "   and has " << str.length() << " characters." << endl;
    // insert characters
    str.insert(4," I know");
    cout << "The string, after insertion, is: " << str << endl
         << "   and has " << str.length() << " characters." << endl;
    // replace characters
    str.replace(12, 6, "to");
    cout << "The string, after replacement, is: " << str << endl
         << "   and has " << str.length() << " characters." << endl;
    // append characters
    str = str + " correct";
```

(continued on next page)

```
cout << "The string, after appending, is: " << str << endl
     << "  and has " << str.length() << " characters." << endl;

   return 0;
}
```

The following output, produced by Program 9-6, matches the strings shown in Figures 9-6 to 9-9:

```
The original string is: This cannot be
   and has 14 characters.
The string, after insertion, is: This I know cannot be
   and has 21 characters.
The string, after replacement, is: This I know to be
   and has 17 characters.
The string, after appending, is: This I know to be correct
   and has 25 characters.
```

Of the remaining string methods listed in Table 9-3, the most commonly used are those that locate specific characters in a string and create substrings. Program 9-7 presents examples of how some of these other methods are used.

Program 9-7

```
#include <iostream>
#include <string>
using namespace std;

int main()
{
   string string1 = "LINEAR PROGRAMMING THEORY";
   string s1, s2, s3;
   int j, k, l;

   cout << "The original string is " <<  string1 << endl;

   j = string1.find('I');
   cout << "  The first position of an 'I' is " <<  j << endl;

   k = string1.find('I', (j+1));
   cout << "  The next position of an 'I' is " <<  k << endl;

   j = string1.find("THEORY");
   cout << "  The first location of \"THEORY\" is " <<  j << endl;

   k = string1.find("ING");
   cout << "  The first index of \"ING\" is " <<  k << endl;
```

```
    s1 = string1.substr(2,5);
    s2 = string1.substr(19,3);
    s3 = string1.substr(6,8);

    cout << s1 + s2 + s3 << endl;

    return 0;
}
```

The output produced by Program 9-7 is:

```
The original string is LINEAR PROGRAMMING THEORY
  The first position of an 'I' is 1
  The next position of an 'I' is 15
  The first location of "THEORY" is 19
  The first index of "ING" is 15
NEAR THE PROGRAM
```

The main point illustrated in Program 9-7 is that both individual characters and sequences of characters can be located and extracted from a string.

Exercises 9.1

1. Enter and execute Program 9-2 on your computer.

2. Determine the value of `text.at(0)`, `text.at(3)`, and `text.at(10)`, assuming that `text` is, individually, each of the following strings:

   a. `now is the time`
   b. `rocky raccoon welcomes you`
   c. `Happy Holidays`
   d. `The good ship`

3. Enter and execute Program 9-5 on your computer.

4. Modify Program 9-5 to count and display the individual numbers of each vowel contained in the string.

5. Modify Program 9-5 to display the number of vowels in a user-entered string.

6. Using the `at()` method, write and execute a C++ program that reads in a string using `getline()` and then displays the string in reverse order. (*Hint*: Once the string has been entered and saved, retrieve and display characters starting from the end of the string.)

7. Write a C++ program that accepts both a string and a single character from the user. The program should then determine how many times the character is contained in the string. (*Hint*: Search the string using the `find(str, ind)` method. This method should be used in a loop that starts the index value at zero, and then changes the index to one value past the index of where the character was last found.)

9

8. Enter and execute Program 9-6 on your computer.

9. Enter and execute Program 9-7 on your computer.

10. Write a C++ program that accepts a string from the user and then replaces all occurrences of the letter e with the letter x.

11. Modify the program written for Exercise 10 to search for the first occurrence of a user-entered sequence of characters and replace this sequence, when it is found in the string, with a second set of a user-entered sequence. For example, if the entered string is `Figure 4-4 illustrates the output of Program 4-2` and the user enters that `4-` is to be replaced by `3-`, the resulting string will be `Figure 3-4 illustrates the output of Program 4-2`. (Note that only the first occurrence of the searched-for sequence has been changed.)

12. Modify the program written for Exercise 11 to replace all occurrences of the designated sequence of characters with the new sequence of characters. For example, if the entered string is `Figure 4-4 illustrates the output of Program 4-2` and the user enters that `4-` is to be replaced by `3-`, the resulting string will be `Figure 3-4 illustrates the output of Program 3-2`.

9.2 CHARACTER MANIPULATION METHODS

In addition to the string methods provided by the string class, the C++ language provides a number of very useful `character` class functions. These functions are listed in Table 9-4. The function declarations (prototypes) for each of these routines are contained in the header `cctype`.

TABLE 9-4
Character Library Functions
(Defined in the `cctype` *header file)*

function prototype	description	example
`int isalpha(charExp)`	Returns a `true` (nonzero integer) if `charExp` evaluates to a letter; otherwise, it returns a `false` (zero integer)	`isalpha('a')`

`int isalnum(charExp)`	Returns a `true` (nonzero integer) if `charExp` evaluates to a letter or a digit; otherwise, it returns a `false` (zero integer)	`char key;`
		`cin >> key;`
		`isalnum(key);`

`int isupper(charExp)`	Returns a `true` (nonzero integer) if `charExp` evaluates to an uppercase letter; otherwise it returns a `false` (zero integer)	`isupper('a')`

(continued on next page)

TABLE 9-4
Character Library Functions (Continued)

function prototype	description	example
`int islower(charExp)`	Returns a `true` (nonzero integer) if `charExp` evaluates to a lowercase letter; otherwise it returns a `false` (zero integer)	`islower('a')`
`int isdigit(charExp)`	Returns a `true` (nonzero integer) if `charExp` evaluates to a digit (0 through 9); otherwise it returns a `false` (zero integer)	`isdigit('a')`
`int isascii(charExp)`	Returns a `true` (nonzero integer) if `charExp` evaluates to an ASCII character; otherwise returns a `false` (zero integer)	`isascii('a')`
`int isspace(charExp)`	Returns a `true` (nonzero integer) if `charExp` evaluates to a space; otherwise, returns a `false` (zero integer)	`isspace(' ')`
`int isprint(charExp)`	Returns a `true` (nonzero integer) if `charExp` evaluates to a printable character; otherwise, returns a `false` (zero integer)	`isprint('a')`
`int isctrl(charExp)`	Returns a `true` (nonzero integer) if `charExp` evaluates to a control character; otherwise, it returns a `false` (zero integer)	`isctrl('a')`
`int ispunct(charExp)`	Returns a `true` (nonzero integer) if `charExp` evaluates to a punctuation character; otherwise, returns a `false` (zero integer)	`ispunct('!')`
`int isgraph(charExp)`	Returns a `true` (nonzero integer) if `charExp` evaluates to a printable character other than whitespace; otherwise returns a `false` (zero integer)	`isgraph(' ')`
`int toupper(charExp)`	Returns the uppercase equivalent if `charExp` evaluates to a lowercase character; otherwise it returns the character code without modification	`toupper('a')`
`int tolower(charExp)`	Returns the lowercase equivalent if `charExp` evaluates to an uppercase character; otherwise it returns the character code without modification	`tolower('A')`

Because all of the `istype( )` functions listed in Table 9-4 return a nonzero integer (which is interpreted as a Boolean `true` value) when the character meets the desired condition, and a zero integer (or Boolean `false` value) when the condition is not met, these functions are typically used directly within an `if` statement. For example, consider the following code segment, which assumes that `ch` is a character variable:

```
if(isdigit(ch))
   cout << "The character just entered is a digit" << endl;
else if(ispunct(ch))
   cout << "The character just entered is a punctuation mark" << endl;
```

Here, if `ch` contains a digit character, the first `cout` statement is executed; if the character is a letter, the second `cout` statement is executed. In both cases, however, the character to be checked is included as an argument to the appropriate method. Program 9-8 illustrates this type of code within a program that counts the number of letters, digits, and other characters in a string. The individual characters to be checked are obtained using the `string` class's `at()` method. Here, this method is used in a `for` loop that cycles through the string from the first character to the last.

Program 9-8

```
#include <iostream>
#include <string>
#include <cctype>
using namespace std;

int main()
{
  string str = "This -123/ is 567 A ?<6245> Test!";
  char nextChar;
  int i;
  int numLetters = 0, numDigits = 0, numOthers = 0;

  cout << "The original string is: " <<  str
       << "\nThis string contains " <<  str.length()
       << " characters," <<   " which consist of" << endl;

  // check each character in the string
  for (i = 0; i < str.length(); i++)
  {
    nextChar = str.at(i);   // get a character
    if (isalpha(nextChar))
      numLetters++;
    else if (isdigit(nextChar))
      numDigits++;
    else
      numOthers++;
  }
```

(continued on next page)

```
    cout << "        " <<  numLetters <<  " letters" << endl;
    cout << "        " <<  numDigits <<  " digits" << endl;
    cout << "        " <<  numOthers <<  " other characters." << endl;

    return 0;
}
```

The output produced by Program 9-8 is:

```
The original string is: This -123/ is 567 A ?<6245> Test!
This string contains 33 characters, which consist of
     11 letters
     10 digits
     12 other characters.
```

As indicated by this output, each of the 33 characters in the string has correctly been categorized as either a letter, digit, or other character.

Typically, as in Program 9-8, each of the functions in Table 9-4 is used in a character-by-character manner on each character in a string. This is again illustrated in Program 9-9, where each lowercase string character is converted to its uppercase equivalent using the toupper() function. This function only converts lowercase letters, leaving all other characters unaffected.

Program 9-9

```cpp
#include <iostream>
#include <string>
#include <cctype>
using namespace std;

int main()
{
  int i;
  string str;

  cout << "Type in any sequence of characters: ";
  getline(cin,str);

  // cycle through all elements of the string
  for (i = 0; i < str.length(); i++)
    str[i] = toupper(str[i]);

  cout << "The characters just entered, in uppercase, are: "
       << str << endl;

  return 0;
}
```

9

A sample run of Program 9-9 produced the following output:

```
Type in any sequence of characters: this is a test of 12345.
The characters just entered, in uppercase, are: THIS IS A TEST OF 12345.
```

Pay particular attention in Program 9-9 to the statement `for (i = 0; i < str.length(); i++)` that is used to cycle through each of the characters in the string. This is typically how each element in a string is accessed, using the `length()` method to determine when the end of the string has been reached (review Program 9-8 to see that it is used in the same way). The only real difference is that in Program 9-9, each element is accessed using the subscript notation `str[i]`, while in Program 9-8 the `at()` method was used. Although these two notations are interchangeable, and which you use is a matter of choice, for consistency the two notations should not be mixed in the same program.

CHARACTER I/O

Although we have used `cin` and `getline()` to accept data entered from the keyboard in a more or less "cookbook" manner, it is useful to understand what data are actually being sent to the program and how the program must react to process the data correctly. At a very fundamental level, all input (as well as output) is done on a character-by character basis.

PROGRAMMING NOTE

Why the `char` Data Type Uses Integer Values

In C++, a character is stored as an integer value, which is sometimes confusing to beginning programmers. The reason is that, in addition to the standard English letters and characters, a program needs to store special characters that have no printable equivalents. One of these is the end-of-file sentinel, which all computer systems use to designate the end of a file of data. These end-of-file sentinels can also be transmitted from the keyboard. For example, on Unix-based systems it is generated by pressing the Ctrl and D keys at the same time, while on Windows-based systems it is generated by simultaneously pressing the Ctrl and Z keys. Both of these sentinels are stored as the integer number -1, which has no equivalent character value. (You can check this by displaying the integer value of each entered character—see Program 9-10—and typing either Ctrl+D or Ctrl+Z, depending on the system you are using.)

Additionally, by using a 16-bit integer value, over 64,000 different characters can be represented. This provides sufficient storage for multiple character sets that can include Arabic, Chinese, Hebrew, Japanese, Russian, and almost all known language symbols. Thus, storing a character as an integer value has a very practical value.

A very important consequence of using integer codes for string characters is that characters can easily be compared for alphabetical ordering. For example, as long as each subsequent letter in an alphabet has a higher value than its preceding letter, the comparison of character values is reduced to the comparison of numeric values. Additionally, if characters are stored in sequential numerical order, it ensures that adding 1 to a letter will produce the next letter in the alphabet.

The entry of every piece of data, be it a string or a number, consists of typing individual characters. For example, the entry of the string `Hello` consists of pressing and releasing the six keys H, e, 1, 1, o, and Enter. Similarly, the output of the number `26.95` consists of the display of the five characters 2, 6, ., 9, and 5. Although the programmer typically doesn't think of data in this manner, the program is always restricted to this character-by-character I/O, and all of C++'s higher-level I/O methods and streams are based on lower-level character I/O methods. These more elemental character methods, which can also be used directly by a programmer, are listed in Table 9-5.

TABLE 9-5
Basic Character I/O Methods
(Requires the header file `cctype`*)*

method	description	example
`cout.put(charExp)`	Places the character value of `charExp` on the output stream	`cout.put('A');`
`cin.get(charVar)`	Extracts the next character from the input stream and assigns it to the variable `charVar`	`cin.get(key);`
`cin.peek(charVar)`	Assigns the next character from the input stream to the variable `charVar` *without* extracting the character from the stream	`cin.peek(nextKey);`
`cin.putback(charExp)`	Pushes a character value of `charExp` back onto the input stream	`cin.putback(cKey);`
`cin.ignore(n, char)`	Ignores a maximum of the next n input characters, up to and including the detection of `char`. If no arguments are specified, ignores the next single character on the input stream	`cin.ignore(80,'\n');` `cin.ignore();`

The `get()` function reads the next character in the input stream and assigns it to the function's character variable. For example, a statement such as

```
cin.gct(nextChar);
```

causes the next character entered at the keyboard to be stored in the character variable `nextChar`. This function is useful for inputting and checking individual characters before they are assigned to a complete string or other C++ data type.

A BIT OF BACKGROUND

A Notational Inconsistency

Notice that all of the `character` class methods listed in Table 9-5 use the standard object-oriented notation of preceding the method's name with an object name, as in `cin.get()`. This is not the case with the `string` class's `getline()` method, which uses the notation `getline(cin, strVar)`. In this notation the object, in this case `cin`, appears as an argument. For consistency's sake, we would have expected `getline()` to be called as `cin.getline()`.

Unfortunately, this proper notation was already in use for a `getline()` method originally created for C-style strings (see next section). Hence, a notational inconsistency was created.

The character output function corresponding to `get()` is `put()`. This function expects a single character argument and displays the character passed to it on the console monitor. For example, the statement `cout.put('A')` causes the letter A to be displayed on the screen.

Of the last three functions listed in Table 9-5, the `cin.ignore()` function is the most useful. This function permits skipping over input until a designated character such as `'\n'` is encountered. For example, the statement `cin.ignore(80, '\n')` will skip up to a maximum of the next 80 characters, or stop the skipping if the newline character is encountered. Such a statement can be useful in skipping all further input on a line, up to a maximum of 80 characters, or until the end of the current line is encountered. Input would then begin with the next line.

The `peek()` function returns the next character on the stream, but does not remove it from the stream's buffer. For example, the expression `cin.peek(nextChar)` returns the next character input by the keyboard, but leaves it in the buffer. This is sometimes useful for "peeking" ahead and seeing what the next character is, while leaving it in place for the next input.

Finally, the `putback()` function places a character back on the stream so that it will be the next character read. The argument passed to `putback()` can be any character expression that evaluates to a legitimate character value, and need not be the last input character.

THE PHANTOM NEWLINE REVISITED

As we saw in the previous section, seemingly strange results are sometimes obtained when a `cin` stream input is followed by a `getline()` method call. This same result can occur when characters are input using the `get()` character method. To see how this can occur, consider Program 9-10, which uses the `get()` method to accept the next character entered at the keyboard and stores the character in the variable `fkey`.

Program 9-10

```
#include <iostream>
#include <cctype>
using namespace std;

int main()
{
  char fkey, skey;

  cout << "Type in a character: ";
  cin.get(fkey);
  cout << "The key just accepted is " << int(fkey) << endl;

  return 0;
}
```

When Program 9-10 is run, the character entered in response to the prompt `Type in a character:` is stored in the character variable `fkey` and the decimal code for the character is displayed by explicitly casting the character into an integer, to force its display as an integer value. The following sample run illustrates this:

```
Type in a character: m
The key just accepted is 109
```

At this point, everything seems to be working just fine, although you might be wondering why we displayed the decimal value of `m` rather than the character itself. The reason for this will soon become apparent.

In typing `m`, two keys are usually pressed, the `m` key and the Enter key. On almost all computer systems these two characters are stored in a temporary holding area called a buffer immediately after they are pressed, as illustrated in Figure 9-10.

9

FIGURE 9-10
Accepting Keyboard-Entered Data

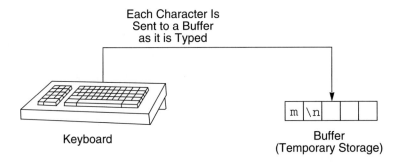

The first key pressed, m in this case, is taken from the buffer and stored in fkey. This, however, still leaves the code for the Enter key in the buffer. Thus, a subsequent call to get() for a character input will automatically pick up the code for the Enter key as the next character. For example, consider Program 9-11.

Program 9-11

```cpp
#include <iostream>
#include <cctype>
using namespace std;

int main()
{
  char fkey, skey;

  cout << "Type in a character: ";
  cin.get(fkey);
  cout << "The key just accepted is " << (int)fkey << endl;

  cout << "Type in another character: ";
  cin.get(skey);
  cout << "The key just accepted is " << (int)skey << endl;

  return 0;
}
```

The following is a sample run for Program 9-11:

```
Type in a character: m
The key just accepted is 109
Type in another character: The key just accepted is 10
```

Let us review what has happened. In entering m in response to the first prompt, the Enter key is also pressed. From a character standpoint, this represents the entry of two distinct characters. The first character is m, which is coded and stored as the integer 109. The second character also gets stored in the buffer with the numerical code for the Enter key. The second call to get() picks up this code immediately, without waiting for any additional key to be pressed. The last cout stream displays the code for this key. The reason for displaying the numerical code rather than the character itself is because the Enter key has no printable character associated with it that can be displayed.

Remember that every key has a numerical code, including the Enter, Spacebar, Escape, and Control keys. These keys generally have no effect when entering numbers, because the input methods ignore them as leading or trailing input with numerical data. Nor do these keys affect the entry of a single character requested as the first user data to be input, as is the case in Program 9-10. Only when a character is requested after the user has already input some other data, as in Program 9-11, does the usually invisible Enter key become noticeable.

In Section 9.1 you learned some ways to prevent the Enter key from being accepted as a legitimate character input when the getline() method was used. The following approaches can be used when the get() method is used within a program:

- Follow the cin.get() input with the call cin.ignore() before accepting further input.

- Accept the Enter key into a character variable and then don't process it any further.

Program 9-12 applies the first solution to Program 9-11. Ignoring the Enter key immediately after the first character is read and displayed clears the buffer of the Enter key and gets it ready to store the next valid input character as its first character.

Program 9-12

```cpp
#include <iostream>
#include <cctype>
using namespace std;

int main()
{
    char fkey, skey;

    cout << "Type in a character: ";
    cin.get(fkey);
    cout << "The key just accepted is " << (int)fkey << endl;
    cin.ignore();

    cout << "Type in another character: ";
    cin.get(skey);
    cout << "The key just accepted is " << (int)skey << endl;
    cin.ignore();
    return 0;
}
```

9

In reviewing Program 9-12, observe that when the user types an `m` and presses the Enter key, the `m` is assigned to `fkey` and the code for the Enter key is ignored. The next call to `get()` stores the code for the next key pressed in the variable `skey`. From the user's standpoint, the Enter key has no effect except to signal the end of each character input. The following is a sample run for Program 9-12:

```
Type in a character: m
The key just accepted is 109
Type in another character: b
The key just accepted is 98
```

A SECOND LOOK AT USER-INPUT VALIDATION

As mentioned in our first look at user-input validation (Section 4.4), programs that respond effectively to unexpected user input are formally referred to as robust programs and informally as "bullet-proof" programs. Code that validates user input and ensures that a program does not produce unintended results due to unexpected input is a sign of a well-constructed, robust program. One of your jobs as a programmer is to produce such programs. To see how such unintended results can occur, consider the following two code examples. First assume that your program contains the statements:

```
cout << "Enter an integer: ";
cin  >> value;
```

Now assume that, by mistake, a user enters the characters e4. On earlier versions of C++, this would cause the program to unexpectedly terminate, or **crash.** While crashes can still occur with the current ANSI/ISO standard (see, for example, Exercise 9), it will not occur in this case. Rather, a meaningless integer value will be assigned to the variable named `value`. This, of course, will invalidate any results obtained using this variable.

As a second example, consider the following code, which will cause an infinite loop to occur if the user enters a non-numeric value (the program can be halted by pressing the Ctrl and C keys at the same time):

```
double value;

  do
  {
    cout << "Enter a number (enter 0 to exit): ";
    cin  >> value;

    cout << "The square root of this number is: " << sqrt(value) << endl;
  }while (value !=0);
```

The basic technique for handling invalid data input and preventing seemingly innocuous code from producing unintended results, such as that in our two examples, is referred to as **user-input validation**. Essentially this means validating the entered data either during or immediately after data entry and providing the user with a way of re-entering any invalid data. User-input validation is an essential part of any commercially viable program, and if done correctly, it will protect a program from attempting to process data types that can either cause a program to crash, create infinite loops, or produce more invalid results.

The central element in user-input validation is the checking of each entered character to verify that it qualifies as a legitimate character for the expected data type. For example, if an integer is required, the only acceptable characters are a leading plus or minus sign and the digits 0 through 9. These characters can be checked either as they are being typed, which means that the get () function is used to input a character at a time, or all of the characters can be accepted in a string, and then each string character checked for validity. Once all the entered characters have been validated, the entered string can then be converted into the correct data type.

There are two basic means of accomplishing the actual validity of the entered characters. Section 9.5 presents one of these ways, which uses character-by-character checking. A second technique, which encompasses a broader scope of data processing tasks using exception handling, is presented in Appendix C, Section 4.

Exercises 9.2

1. Enter and execute Program 9-8 on your computer.

2. Enter and execute Program 9-9 on your computer.

3. Write and execute a C++ program that counts the number of words in a string. A word is encountered whenever a transition from a blank space to a nonblank character is encountered. Assume that the string contains only words separated by blank spaces.

4. Generate 10 random numbers in the range 0 to 129. If the number represents a printable character, print the character with an appropriate message that:

   The character is a lowercase letter
   The character is an uppercase letter
   The character is a digit
   The character is a space

   If the character is none of these, display its value in integer format.

9

5. a. Write a function named `length()` that determines and returns the length of a string, without using the `string` class's `length()` method.
    b. Write a simple `main()` function to test the `length()` function written for Exercise 5a.

6. a. Write a function named `countlets()` that returns the number of letters in a string passed as an argument. Digits, spaces, punctuation, tabs, and newline characters should not be included in the returned count.
    b. Include the `countlets()` method written for Exercise 6a in an executable C++ program and use the program to test the method.

7. Write a program that accepts a string from the console and displays the hexadecimal equivalent of each character in the string.

8. Write a C++ program that accepts a string from the console and displays the string one word per line.

9. In response to the following code:

    ```
    cout << "Enter an integer: ";
    cin  >> value;
    ```

    suppose a user enters the data 12e4. What value will be stored in the integer variable `value`?

10. a. Write a C++ program that stops reading a line of text when a period is entered and then displays the sentence with correct spacing and capitalization. For this program, correct spacing means that there should only be one space between words and that all letters should be in lowercase, except for the first letter. For example, if the user entered the text i   am going   to   Go   TO   THe moVies, the displayed sentence should be I am going to go to the movies.
    b. Determine what characters, if any, are not displayed correctly by the program you created for Exercise 10a.

11. Write a C++ program that accepts a name as first name-last name and then displays the name as "last name, first name". For example, if the user entered Gary Bronson, the output should be "Bronson, Gary".

12. Modify the program written for Exercise 11 to include an array of five names.

9.3 STRINGS AS CHARACTER ARRAYS

The original method of representing a string in C++ was as an array of characters terminated by a special end-of-string symbolic constant named NULL. The value assigned to the NULL constant is the escape sequence '\0' and is the sentinel that marks the end of every character-array string. As this representation is still used in many C++ programs, and you will certainly encounter it when you are called upon to maintain existing C++ code, it is worthwhile becoming familiar with it. Strings using this original representation are now referred to as both C-strings and strings. This means that when you encounter the word string, you will have to determine whether a C-string or a string class object is being referred to.

Figure 9-11 illustrates how the C-string "Good Morning!" is stored in memory. This C-string uses 14 storage locations, with the last character in the string being the end-of-string marker \0. The double quotes are not stored as part of the string.

FIGURE 9-11
Storing a C-String in Memory

G	o	o	d		M	o	r	n	i	n	g	!	\0

Because a C-string is stored as an array of characters, the individual characters in the array can be input, manipulated, or output using standard array-handling techniques utilizing either subscript or pointer notations.

C-STRING INPUT AND OUTPUT

Inputting a string from a keyboard and displaying a string requires using either a standard library function or class method. In addition to the standard input and output streams, cin and cout, Table 9-6 lists the commonly used library methods for both character-by-character and complete C-string input/output. These are contained in the iostream header file.

Although the character output methods, put() and putback() listed in Table 9-6 are the same as those provided for the string class, the remaining methods derive from the istream and ostream classes.

Program 9-13 illustrates using cin.getline() and cout to input and output a string entered at the keyboard.

9

TABLE 9-6
String and Character I/O Functions
(Require the `iostream` *header file)*

C++ routine	description	example
`cin.getline(str, n, chr)`	C-string input from the keyboard	`cin.getline(str, 81, '\n');`
`cin.get()`	Character input from the keyboard	`nextChar = cin.get();`
`cin.peek()`	Return the next character from the input stream without extracting it from the stream	`key = cin.peek();`
`cout.put(charExp)`	Place the character on the output stream	`cout.put('A');`
`cin.putback(charExp)`	Put a character back onto the input stream	`cin.putback(cKey);`
`cin.ignore(n, char)`	Ignore a maximum of the next n input characters, up to and including the detection of char. If no arguments are specified, ignore the next character on the input stream	`cin.ignore(80,'\n');` `cin.ignore();`

Program 9-13

```cpp
#include <iostream>
using namespace std;

int main()
{
  const int MAXCHARS = 81;
  char message[MAXCHARS];    // an array of characters large
                             // enough storage for a complete line

  cout << "Enter a string:\n";

  cin.getline(message,MAXCHARS,'\n');

  cout << "The string just entered is:\n"
       << message << endl;

  return 0;
}
```

The following is a sample run of Program 9-13:

```
Enter a string:
This is a test input of a string of characters.
The string just entered is:
This is a test input of a string of characters.
```

PROGRAMMING NOTE

Should You Use a string Class Object or a C-String?

The reasons for using a `string` class object are:

- The `string` class does an automatic bounds check on every index used to access string elements. This is not true for C-strings, and using an invalid C-string index can result in a system crash.

- The `string` class automatically expands and contracts storage as needed. C-strings are fixed in length and are subject to overrunning the allocated storage space.

- The `string` class provides a rich set of methods for operating on a string. C-strings almost always require a subsidiary set of functions.

- When necessary, it is easy to convert to a C-string using the `string` class's `c_str()` method. Conversely, a C-string can easily be converted to a `string` class object by assigning it to a string object.

The reasons for using a C-string are:

- The programmer has ultimate control over how the string is stored and manipulated.

- A large number of useful functions exist to input, examine, and process C-strings.

- C-strings are an excellent way to explore advanced programming techniques using pointers (see Chapter 14).

- You will encounter them throughout your programming career, as they are embedded in almost all existing C++ code.

- They are fun to program.

9

PROGRAMMING NOTE

Initializing and Processing C-Strings

Each of the following declarations produces the same result:

```
char test[5] = "abcd";
char test[] = "abcd";
char test[5] = {'a', 'b', 'c', 'd', '\0'};
char test[] = {'a', 'b', 'c', 'd', '\0'};
```

Each declaration creates storage for exactly five characters and initializes this storage with the characters 'a', 'b', 'c', 'd', and '\0'. Since a string literal is used for initialization in the first two declarations, the compiler automatically supplies the end-of-string NULL character.

    String variables declared in any of the ways shown preclude the use of any subsequent assignments, such as test = "efgh";, to the character array. In place of an assignment you can use the strcpy() function, such as strcpy(test, "efgh"). The only restriction on using strcpy() is that the size of the declared array cannot be exceeded, which in this case is five elements. Attempting to copy a larger string value into test causes the copy to overflow the destination array, beginning with the memory area immediately following the last array element. This overwrites whatever was in these memory locations and typically causes a run-time crash when the overwritten areas are accessed via their legitimate identifier name(s).

    The same problem can arise when using the strcat() function. It is your responsibility to ensure that the concatenated string will fit into the original string.

    An interesting situation arises when string variables are defined using pointers (see Programming Note in Section 14.6). In these situations, assignments can be made after the declaration statement.

The cin.getline() method used in Program 9-13 continuously accepts and stores characters typed at the keyboard into the character array named message until either 80 characters are entered (the 81st character is then used to store the end-of-string NULL character, \0), or the Enter key is detected. Pressing the Enter key at the keyboard generates a newline character, \n, which is interpreted by cin.getline() as the end-of-line entry. All the characters encountered by cin.getline(), except the newline character, are stored in the message array. Before returning, the cin.getline() function appends a NULL character, '\0', to the stored set of characters, as illustrated in Figure 9-12. The cout object is then used to display the C-string.

FIGURE 9-12
Inputting a C-String with `cin.getline()`

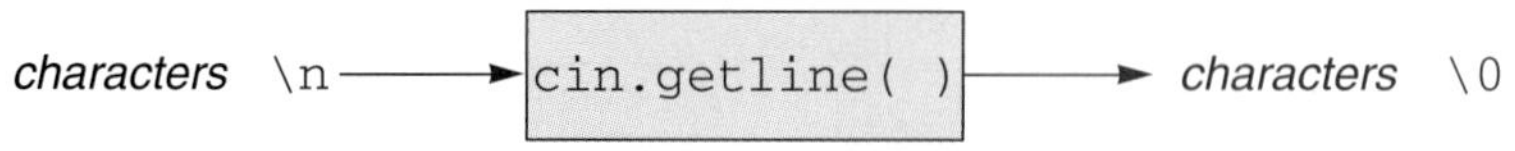

characters   \n ——→ `cin.getline( )` ——→ *characters*   \0

`cin.getline( )` substitutes \0 for the entered \n

Although the `cout` object is used in Program 9-13 for C-string output, `cin` could not be used in place of `cin.getline()` for C-string input. This is because the `cin` object reads a set of characters up to either a blank space or a newline character. The `cin.getline()` function has the syntax

`cin.getline(str, terminatingLength, terminatingChar)`

where *str* is a C-string or character pointer variable (presented in Chapter 14), *terminatingLength* is an integer constant or variable indicating the maximum number of input characters that can be input, and *terminatingChar* is an optional character constant or variable specifying the terminating character. If this optional third argument is omitted, the default terminating character is the newline (`'\n'`) character. Thus, the statement

        `cin.getline(message,MAXCHARS);`

can be used in place of the longer statement

        `cin.getline(message,MAXCHARS,'\n');`

Both of these function calls stop reading characters when the Enter key is pressed or when MAXCHARS characters have been read, whichever comes first. Since `cin.getline()` permits specification of any terminating character for the input stream, a statement such as `cin.getline(message, MAXCHARS, 'x');` is also valid. This particular statement will stop accepting characters whenever the x key is pressed. In all future programs, we will assume that input is terminated by the Enter key, which generates a newline character. As such, the optional third argument passed to `getline()`, which is the terminating character, will be omitted.

C-STRING PROCESSING

C-strings can be manipulated using either standard C-string library functions or standard array-processing techniques. The C-string library functions typically available for use are presented in the next section. For now, we will concentrate on processing a C-string using standard array-processing techniques. This always involves character-by-character processing, and will allow us to understand how the standard library functions are constructed and to create our own library functions. For a specific example, consider the function `strcopy()`, which copies the contents of `string2` to `string1`.

```
// copy string2 to string1
void strcopy(char string1[], char string2[])
{
  int i = 0;                      // i will be used as a subscript

  while (string2[i] != '\0')  // check for the end of string
  {
    string1[i] = string2[i];   // copy the element to string1
    i++;
  }
  string1[i] = '\0';             // terminate the first string
  return;
}
```

Although this C-string copy function can be shortened considerably and written more compactly (as demonstrated at the end of this section), it does illustrate the main features of C-string manipulation. The two C-strings are passed to strcopy() as arrays. Each element of string2 is then assigned to the equivalent element of string1 until the end-of-string marker is encountered. The detection of the NULL character forces the termination of the while loop controlling the copying of elements. Since the NULL character is not copied from string2 to string1, the last statement in strcopy() appends an end-of-string character to string1. Prior to calling strcopy(), the programmer must ensure that sufficient space has been allocated for the string1 array to be able to store the elements of the string2 array. Program 9-14 includes the strcopy() function in a complete program.

Program 9-14

```
#include <iostream>
using namespace std;

int main()
{
  void strcopy(char [], char []); // function prototype

  const int MAXCHARS = 81;
  char message[MAXCHARS];        // enough storage for a complete line
  char newMessage[MAXCHARS];   // enough storage for a copy of message
  int i;

  cout << "Enter a sentence: ";
  cin.getline(message,MAXCHARS);        // get the string
  strcopy(newMessage,message);    // pass two array addresses
  cout << "The copied string is:\n"
       << newMessage << endl;

  return 0;
}
```

(continued on next page)

```
void strcopy(char string1[], char string2[])    // copy string2 to string1
{
  int i = 0;                        // i will be used as a subscript

  while (string2[i] != '\0')       // check for the end.of string
  {
    string1[i] = string2[i];       // copy the element to string1
    i++;
  }
  string1[i] = '\0';               // terminate the first string

  return;
}
```

The following is a sample run of Program 9-14:

```
Enter a sentence: How much wood could a woodchuck chuck.
The copied string is:
How much wood could a woodchuck chuck.
```

DETECTING THE END-OF-STRING NULL CHARACTER

The NULL character that marks the end of each C-string is very important in creating C-string process-ing functions. Frequently, however, it is effectively disguised by C++ programmers. This is because the numerical value of the NULL character is zero, which is treated as `false` in relational expressions.

To understand how the NULL character is typically used by C++ programmers, reconsider Program 9-14's `strcopy()` function, which is repeated below for convenience. This function copies the charac-ters from one array to another array, one character at a time, until the end-of-string NULL is detected.

```
void strcopy(char string1[], char string2[])    // copy string2 to string1
{
  int i = 0;                        // i will be used as a subscript

  while (string2[i] != '\0')       // check for the end of string
  {
    string1[i] = string2[i];       // copy the element to string1
    i++;
  }
  string1[i] = '\0';               // terminate the first string

  return;
}
```

As currently written, the subscript i in the `strcopy()` function is used successively to reference each character in the arrays named `string1` and `string2` by "marching along" the string one character at a time. The `while` statement in `strcopy()` tests each character to ensure that the end of the string has not been reached. As with all relational expressions, the tested expression, `string2[i]` `!= '\0'`, is either `true` or `false`. Using the string `"this is a string"` illustrated in Figure 9-13 as an example, as long as `string2[i]` does not reference the end-of-string character, the value of the expression is nonzero and is considered to be `true`. The expression is only `false` when the value of the expression is zero. This occurs when the last element in the string is accessed.

FIGURE 9-13
The `while` *Test Becomes* `false` *at the End of the String*

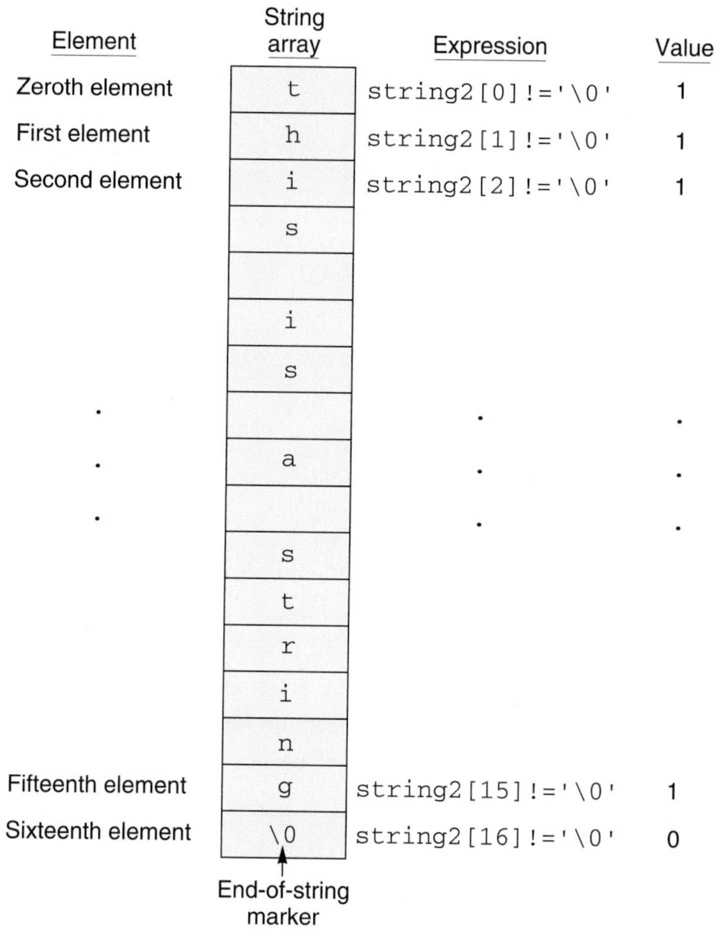

Element	String array	Expression	Value
Zeroth element	t	`string2[0]!='\0'`	1
First element	h	`string2[1]!='\0'`	1
Second element	i	`string2[2]!='\0'`	1
	s		
	i		
	s		
.		.	.
.	a	.	.
.		.	.
	s		
	t		
	r		
	i		
	n		
Fifteenth element	g	`string2[15]!='\0'`	1
Sixteenth element	\0	`string2[16]!='\0'`	0

End-of-string marker

Recall that C++ defines `false` as zero and `true` as anything else. Thus, the expression `string2[i] != '\0'` becomes zero, or `false`, when the end of the string is reached. It is nonzero, or `true`, everywhere else. Since the NULL character has an internal value of zero by itself, the comparison to `'\0'` is not necessary. When `string2[i]` references the end-of-string character, the value of `string2[i]` is zero. When `string2[i]` references any other character, the value of `string2[i]` is the value of the code used to store the character and is nonzero. Figure 9-14 lists the ASCII codes for the C-string `"this is a string"`. As seen in the figure, each element has a nonzero value except for the NULL character.

FIGURE 9-14
The ASCII Codes Used to Store this is a string

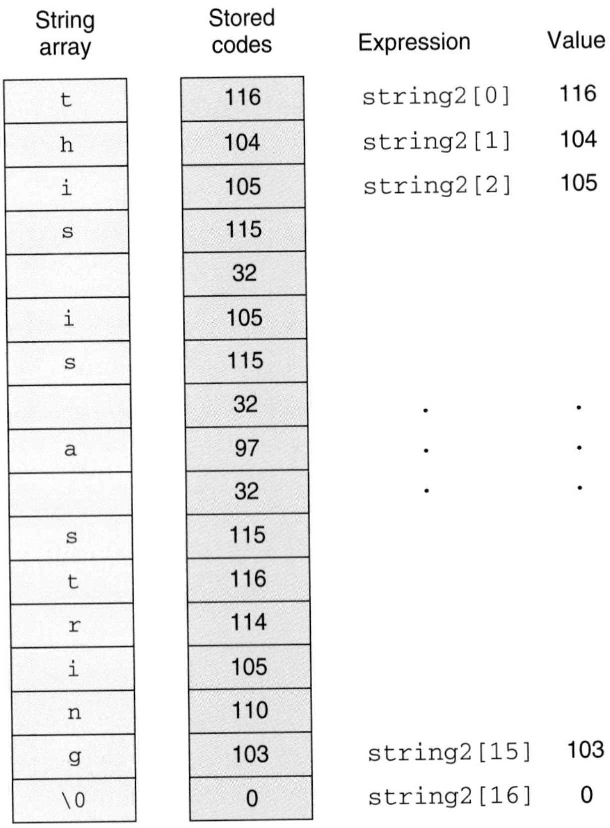

String array	Stored codes	Expression	Value
t	116	string2[0]	116
h	104	string2[1]	104
i	105	string2[2]	105
s	115		
	32		
i	105		
s	115		
	32	.	.
a	97	.	.
	32	.	.
s	115		
t	116		
r	114		
i	105		
n	110		
g	103	string2[15]	103
\0	0	string2[16]	0

Because the expression string2[i] is only zero at the end of a string and nonzero for every other character, the expression while (string2[i] != '\0') can be replaced by the simpler expression while (string2[i]). Although this may appear confusing at first, the revised test expression is certainly more compact than the longer version. Since end-of-string tests are frequently written by professional C++ programmers in this shorter form, it is worthwhile becoming familiar with this expression. Including this expression in strcopy() results in the following version:

```
void strcopy(char string1[], char string2[])    // copy string2 to string1
{
  int i = 0;

  while (string2[i])
  {
    string1[i] = string2[i];    // copy the element to string1
    i++;
  }
  string1[i] = '\0';            // terminate the first string

  return;
}
```

9

The second modification that would be made to this C-string copy function by a professional C++ programmer is to include the assignment inside the test portion of the `while` statement. Our new version of the string copy function is:

```
void strcopy(char string1[], char string2[])    // copy string2 to string1
{
  int i = 0;

  while (string1[i] = string2[i])
    i++;

  return;
}
```

Notice that including the assignment statement within the test part of the `while` statement eliminates the necessity of separately terminating the copied string with the NULL character. The assignment within the parentheses ensures that the NULL character is copied from `string2` to `string1`. The value of the assignment expression only becomes zero after the NULL character is assigned to `string1`, at which point the `while` loop is terminated.

CONVERSION ROUTINES

The last set of standard string library functions, listed in Table 9-7, are used to convert C- strings to and from integer and double-precision data types. The prototypes for each of these routines are contained in the header file `cstdlib`, which must be included in any program that uses these routines.

TABLE 9-7
C-String Conversion Routines
(Require the `cstdlib` header file)

prototype	description	example
`int atoi(stringExp)`	Converts an ASCII string to an integer. Conversion stops at the first noninteger character.	`atoi("1234")`
`double atof(stringExp)`	Converts an ASCII string to a double-precision number. Conversion stops at the first character that cannot be interpreted as a double.	`atof("12.34")`
`char[] itoa(stringExp)`	Converts an integer to an ASCII string. The space allocated for the returned string must be large enough for the converted value.	`itoa(1234)`

Program 9-15a illustrates converting C-strings into integer and floating-point values using the atoi() and atof() functions.

Program 9-15a

```cpp
#include <iostream>
#include <iomanip>   // needed for formatting
#include <cstdlib>   // required for string conversion function library
using namespace std;

int main()
{
   const int MAXELS = 20;
   char str[MAXELS] = "12345";
   int num;
   double dnum;

   num = atoi(str);

   cout << "The string \"" << str << "\" as an integer number is: "
        << num;
   cout << "\nThis number divided by 3 is: " << num / 3 << endl;

   strcat(str, ".96");

   dnum = atof(str);

   cout << "The string \"" << str << "\" as a double number is: "
        << fixed << setprecision(2) << dnum;
   cout << "\nThis number divided by 3 is: " << dnum / 3 << endl;

   return 0;
}
```

The output produced when Program 9-15a is executed is:

```
The string "12345" as an integer number is: 12345
This number divided by 3 is: 4115
The string "12345.96" as a double number is: 12345.96
This number divided by 3 is: 4115.32
```

As this output illustrates, once a string has been converted to either an integer or double-precision value, mathematical operations on the numerical value are valid.

The C-string conversion functions are easily applied to a string class object by first converting the string object into a C-string, using the c_str() string method. Program 9-15b illustrates how this is accomplished, using the same string data as in Program 9-15a. For convenience, the relevant statements distinguishing Program 9-15a from Program 9-15b have been highlighted.

Program 9-15b

```cpp
#include <iostream>
#include <string>
#include <iomanip>  // needed for formatting
#include <cstdlib>  // required for string conversion function library
using namespace std;

int main()
{
    string str = "12345";
    int num;
    double dnum;

    num = atoi(str.c_str());

    cout << "The string \"" << str << "\" as an integer number is: '
         << num;
    cout << "\nThis number divided by 3 is: " << num / 3 << endl;

    str = str + ".96";   // the string automatically expands to
                         // accommodate the additional characters

    dnum = atof(str.c_str());

    cout << "The string \"" << str << "\" as a double number is: "
         << fixed << setprecision(2) << dnum;
    cout << "\nThis number divided by 3 is: " << dnum / 3 << endl;

    return 0;
}
```

The main point to notice in Program 9-15b is the simpler notation contained in the highlighted statements. For example, rather than the more cumbersome expression strcat(str, ".96") needed in the first program to append characters to the original C-string, Program 9-15b uses the more conventional expression str = str + ".96". Also, unlike Program 9-15a, which must declare sufficient array locations to accommodate the additional characters, the string class's object is easily initialized as string str = "12345" and then automatically expands as characters are added. Finally, sufficient C-string space to accommodate the converted string class object is automatically handled by the c_str() method. The output produced by Program 9-15b is identical to that produced by Program 9-15a.

Exercises 9.3

1. Write the following declaration statement in three additional ways: `char string[] = "Hello World"`.

2. a. Write a function named `length()` that returns the length of a C-string, without using any standard library functions. (*Hint*: Count individual characters until the NULL character is encountered.)
   b. Write a simple `main()` function to test the `length()` function written for Exercise 2a.

3. a. The following function can be used to select and display all vowels contained within a user-input C-string:

```
void vowels(char strng[])
{
  int i = 0;
  char c;
  while ((c = strng[i++]) != '\0')
    switch(c)
    {
      case 'a':
      case 'e':
      case 'i':
      case 'o':
      case 'u':
        cout << c;
    } // end of switch
    cout << endl;

  return;
}
```

   Notice that the `switch` statement in `vowels()` uses the fact that selected cases "drop through" in the absence of `break` statements. Thus, all selected cases result in a `cout` object call. Include `vowels()` in a working program that accepts a user-input string and then displays all vowels in the string. In response to the input How much is the little widget worth?, your program should display ouieieieo.
   b. Modify `vowels()` to count and display the total number of vowels contained in the C-string passed to it.

4. Modify the `vowels()` function of Exercise 3 to count and display the individual numbers of each vowel contained in the C-string.

5. Write a program that accepts a C-string from a keyboard and displays the hexadecimal equivalent of each character.

6. Write a function named `trimfrnt()` that deletes all leading blanks from a string. Write the function using pointers so that the function's return type is void.

7. Write a function named `trimrear()` that deletes all trailing blanks from a string. Write the function using pointers so that the function's return type is void.

8. Write a function that reverses the characters in a C-string. (*Hint:* This can be considered as a string copy starting from the back end of the first string.)

9. Write a C++ program that accepts a C-string from a keyboard and displays the string one word per line.

10. a. Write a C++ function named `toUpper()` that converts lowercase letters into uppercase letters. The expression `letter - 'a' + 'A'` can be used to make the conversion for any lowercase character stored in `letter`.
    b. Add a data input check to the function written in Exercise 10a to verify that a valid lowercase letter is passed to the function. A character, in ASCII, is lowercase if it is greater than or equal to `'a'` and less than or equal to 'z'. If the character is not a valid lowercase letter, have the function `toUpper()` return the passed character unaltered.
    c. Write a C++ program that accepts a C-string from the keyboard and converts all lowercase letters in the string to uppercase letters.

11. Write a C++ program that accepts a C-string from the keyboard and converts all uppercase letters in the string to lowercase letters.

12. A palindrome is a word or phrase in which the letters spell the same message (with changes in the white space permitted and punctuation not considered) when written both forward and backward. For example, "Madam I'm Adam" and "A man, a plan, a canal: Panama!" are both palindromes. Write a C++ program that accepts a line of text as a C-string and examines the entered text to determine if it is a palindrome. If the entered text is a palindrome, display the message `This is a palindrome`. If a palindrome was not entered, the message `This is not a palindrome` should be displayed. (*Hint:* This is a rather challenging programming problem. You must first remove all white space and punctuation from the entered string, convert all characters to either lower- or uppercase, make a copy of the string, reverse the copy, and then compare characters between the two strings.)

9.4 THE STANDARD C-STRING LIBRARY

C++ does not provide built-in operations for complete arrays, such as array assignment or array comparisons. Since a C-string is just an array of characters terminated with a `'\0'` character, this means that assignment and relational operations *are not* provided for strings. Extensive collections of C-string-handling functions exist, however, that effectively supply string assignment, comparison, and other very useful string operations. The more commonly used of these are listed in Table 9-8.

TABLE 9-8
C-String Library Functions
(Require the header file `cstring`*)*

name	description	example
`strcpy(stringVar, stringExp)`	Copies `stringExp` to `stringVar`, including the `'\0'`	`strcpy(test, "efgh")`
`strcat(stringVar, stringExp)`	Appends `stringExp` to the end of the string value contained in `stringVar`	`strcat(test,"there")`
`strlen(stringExp)`	Returns the length of the string. Does not include the `'\0'` in the length count	`strlen("Hello World!")`
`strcmp(stringExp1, stringExp2)`	Compares `stringExp1` to `stringExp2`. Returns a negative integer if `stringExp1 < stringExp2`, or if `stringExp1 == stringExp2`, and a positive integer if `stringExp1 > stringExp2`	`strcmp("Bebop", "Beehive")`
`strncpy(string_var, stringExp, n)`	Copies at most n characters of `stringExp` to `string_var`. If `stringExp` has fewer than n characters it will pad `string_var` with `'\0's`	`strncpy(str1, str2, 5)`
`strncmp(stringExp1, stringExp2, n)`	Compares at most n characters of `stringExp1` to `stringExp2`. Returns the same values as `strcmp()` based on the number of characters compared	`strncmp("Bebop", "Beehive", 2)`
`strchr(stringExp, character)`	Locates the position of the first occurrence of the character within the string. Returns the address of the character	`strchr("Hello", 'l')`
`strtok(string1, character)`	Parses `string1` into tokens. Returns the next sequence of characters contained in `string1` up to but not including the delimiting character	`strtok("Hello there World!, ' ')`

C-string library functions are called in the same manner as all C++ functions. This means that the appropriate declarations for these functions, which are contained in the standard header file `<cstring>`, must be included in your program before the function is called.

The most commonly used functions listed in Table 9-8 are the first four. The `strcpy()` function copies a source C-string expression, which consists of either a string literal or the contents of a C-string variable, into a destination C-string variable. For example, in the function call `strcpy(string1, "Hello World!")`, the source string literal `"Hello World!"` is copied into the destination C-string variable `string1`. Similarly, if the source C-string is a C-string variable named `srcString`, the function call `strcpy(string1, srcString)` copies the contents of `srcString` into `string1`. In both cases it is the programmer's responsibility to ensure that `string1` is large enough to contain the source C-string.

The `strcat()` function appends a string expression to the end of a C-string variable. For example, if the contents of a C-string variable named `destString` is `"Hello"`, then the function call `strcat(destString, " there World!")` results in the string value `"Hello there World!"` being assigned to `destString`. As with the `strcpy()` function, it is the programmer's responsibility to ensure that the destination C-string has been defined as large enough to hold the additional concatenated characters.

The `strlen()` function returns the number of characters in its C-string argument but does not include the terminating `NULL` character in the count. For example, the value returned by the function call `strlen("Hello World!")` is 12.

Finally, two C-string expressions may be compared for equality using the `strcmp()` function. When two strings are compared, their individual characters are compared a pair at a time (both first characters, then both second characters, and so on) using the character set in use by the compiler. For example, in both ASCII and UNICODE the digits 0 through 9 are stored using integer codes that are less than the capital letters A through Z, which themselves are stored with codes less than the lowercase letters a through z. If no differences are found between all characters, the strings are equal; if a difference is found, the string with the first lower character is considered the smaller string. For example, "Good Bye" is less than "Hello" because the first `'G'` in `"Good Bye"` is less than the first `'H'` in `"Hello"`, and `"65"` is greater than `"624"` because the second character, the `'5'` in `"65"`, is greater than the second character, the `'2'`, in `"624"`.

Program 9-16 uses these C-string functions within the context of a complete program.

Program 9-16

```
#include <iostream>
#include <cstring>    // required for the c-string function library
using namespace std;

int main()
{
  const int MAXELS = 50;
```

(continued on next page)

```
char string1[MAXELS] = "Hello";
char string2[MAXELS] = "Hello there";
int n;

n = strcmp(string1, string2);

if (n < 0)
  cout << string1 << " is less than " << string2 << endl;
else if (n == 0)
  cout << string1 << " is equal to " << string2 << endl;
else
  cout << string1 << " is greater than " << string2 << endl;

cout << "\nThe length of string1 is " << strlen(string1)
     << " characters" << endl;
cout << "\nThe length of string2 is " << strlen(string2)
     << " characters" << endl;

strcat(string1," there World!");

cout << "\nAfter concatenation, string1 contains "
     << "the string value\n" << string1
     << "\nThe length of this string is "
     << strlen(string1) << " characters" << endl;

cout << "\nType in a sequence of characters for string2: ";
cin.getline(string2, MAXELS);

strcpy(string1, string2);

cout << "After copying string2 to string1, "
     << "the string value in string1 is:\n" << string1
     << "\nThe length of this string is "
     << strlen(string1) << " characters" << endl;

  return 0;
}
```

Following is a sample output produced by Program 9-16:

```
Hello is less than Hello there

The length of string1 is 5 characters
The length of string2 is 11 characters

After concatenation, string1 contains the string value
Hello there World!
The length of this string is 18 characters
```

```
Type in a sequence of characters for string2: It's a wonderful day
After copying string2 to string1, the string value in string1 is:
It's a wonderful day
The length of this string is 20 characters
```

The output of Program 9-16 follows the discussion presented for the C-string library functions. As demonstrated by this output, the extraction operator << displays the contents contained in the variable.

Exercises 9.4

1. Enter and execute Program 9-15a on your computer.

2. Enter and execute Program 9-16 on your computer.

3. Write a function that adds a single character at the end of an existing C-string. The function should replace the existing \0 character with the new character and append a new \0 at the end of the string. The function returns nothing.

4. Write a function that deletes a single character from the end of a C-string. This is effectively achieved by moving the \0 character one position closer to the start of the string. The function returns nothing.

5. Write a function call delChar() that can be used to delete characters from a C-string. The function should take three arguments: the C-string name, the number of characters to delete, and the starting position in the C-string where characters should be deleted. For example, the function call delChar(strng,13,5), when applied to the C-string all enthusiastic people, should result in the C-string all people.

6. Write a function call addChar() to insert one C-string of characters into another C-string. The function should take three arguments: the string to be inserted, the original string, and the position in the original string where the insertion should begin. For example, the call addChar(" for all",message,6) should insert the characters for all in message starting at message[5].

7. a. Include the C-string library functions strlen(), strcat(), and strncat() within a function having the prototype int concat(char string1[], char string2[], int maxlength). The concat() function should perform a complete concatenation of string2 to string1 only if the length of the concatenated string does not exceed maxlength, which is the maximum length defined for string1. If the concatenated string will exceed maxlength, only concatenate the characters in string2 so the maximum combined string length is equal to maxlength - 1, which provides enough room for the end-of-string NULL character.
   b. Write a simple main() function to test the concat() function written for Exercise 7a.

8. a. Write a function named countlets() that returns the number of letters in an entered C-string. Digits, spaces, punctuation, tabs, and newline characters should not be included in the returned count.
   b. Write a simple main() function to test the countlets() function written for Exercise 8a.

9.5 INPUT DATA VALIDATION

One of the major uses of strings in professionally written programs is for user-input validation. Validating user input is necessary because even though a program prompts the user to enter a specific type of data, such as an integer, this does not ensure that the user will comply. What a user enters is, in fact, totally out of the programmer's control. You can control, however, how you deal with the entered data.

It certainly does no good to tell a frustrated user that "The program clearly tells you to enter a number and you entered a date." Rather, professional programmers understand that successful programs always anticipate invalid data and isolate such data from being accepted and processed. This is typically accomplished by first validating that the data is of the correct type. If it is, the data is accepted; otherwise, the user is requested to re-enter the data, with a possible explanation of why the entered data was invalid.

One of the most common means of validating input data is to accept all numbers as strings. Each character in the string can then be checked to ensure that it complies with the data type being requested. Only after this check is made and the data is verified for the correct type is the string converted to either an integer or floating-point value using the conversion functions listed in Table 9-7. (For data accepted using `string` class objects, the `c_str()` method must be applied to the string before the conversion function is invoked.)

As an example, consider the input of an integer number. To be valid, the data entered must adhere to the following conditions:

- The data must contain at least one character.

- If the first character is a + or − sign, the data must contain at least one digit.

- Only digits from 0 to 9 are acceptable following the first character.

The following function, named `isvalidInt()`, can be used to check that an entered string complies with these conditions. This function returns the Boolean value of `true`, if the conditions are satisfied; otherwise, it returns a Boolean `false` value.

```cpp
bool isvalidInt(string str)
{
  int start = 0;
  int i;
  bool valid = true;   // assume a valid
  bool sign = false;   // assume no sign

  // check for an empty string
  if (str.length() == 0)  valid = false;

  // check for a leading sign
  if (str.at(0) == '-'|| str.at(0) == '+')
```

```
    {
       sign = true;
       start = 1;   // start checking for digits after the sign
    }

    // check that there is at least one character after the sign
    if (sign && str.length() == 1) valid = false;

    // now check the string, which we know has at least one non-sign char
    i = start;
    while(valid && i < str.length())
    {
      if(!isdigit(str.at(i))) valid = false;   //found a non-digit character
      i++;   // move to next character
    }

       return valid;
    }
```

In reviewing the code for the isvalidInt() method, pay attention to the conditions that are being checked. These are commented in the code and consist of checking:

- That the string is not empty

- Whether a valid sign symbol (+ or -) is included at the beginning of the string

- That if a sign symbol is present, at least one digit follows it

- That the remaining characters in the string are digits

Only if all of these conditions are met does the function return a Boolean true value. Once this value is returned, the string can be safely converted into an integer with the assurance that no unexpected value will result to hamper further data processing. Program 9-17 uses this method within the context of a complete program.

Program 9-17

```
#include <iostream>
#include <string>
#include <cctype>
using namespace std;

int main()
{
  bool isvalidInt(string);   // function prototype (declaration)
  string value;
  int number;
```

(continued on next page)

```cpp
   cout << "Enter an integer: ";
   getline(cin, value);

   if (!isvalidInt(value))
    cout << "The number you entered is not a valid integer." << endl;
   else
   {
     number = atoi(value.c_str());
     cout << "The number you entered is " << number << endl;
   }

   return 0;
}

bool isvalidInt(string str)
{
   int start = 0;
   int i;
   bool valid = true;   // assume a valid
   bool sign = false;   // assume no sign

   // check for an empty string
   if (str.length() == 0)  valid = false;

   // check for a leading sign
   if (str.at(0) == '-'|| str.at(0) == '+')
   {
       sign = true;
       start = 1;  // start checking for digits after the sign
   }

   // check that there is at least one character after the sign
   if (sign && str.length() == 1) valid = false;

   // now check the string, which we know has at least one non-sign char
   i = start;
   while(valid && i < str.length())
   {
       if(!isdigit(str.at(i))) valid = false;  //found a non-digit character
       i++;   // move to next character
   }

   return valid;
}
```

Two sample runs using Program 9-17 produced the following:

```
Enter an integer: 12e45
The number you entered is not a valid integer.
```

and

```
Enter an integer: -12345
The number you entered is -12345
```

As illustrated by this output, the program successfully determines that an invalid character was entered in the first run.

Rather than accepting and then checking a complete string, you could check each character as it is typed. This is especially useful when a GUI is used for data input, because it permits the user to correct the data as it is being entered, rather than after the complete number has been entered.

A second line of defense is to provide error processing code within the context of exception-handling code. This type of code is typically provided to permit the user to correct a problem such as invalid data entry by re-entering a new value. The means of providing this in C++ using exception handling is presented in Appendix C, Section 4.

Exercises 9.5

1. Write a C++ program that prompts the user to type an integer. Use `cin` to make your program accept the number as an integer and use `cout` to display the value your program actually accepted from the data entered. Run your program five times. The first time you run the program enter a valid integer number, the second time enter a floating-point number, and the third time enter a character. Next, enter the value 12e34 and then 31234.

2. Repeat Exercise 1 but have your program use a floating-point variable. Run the program four times. The first time, enter an integer; the second time, enter a decimal number; the third time, enter a decimal number with an f as the last character entered; and the fourth time, enter a character. Using the output display, keep track of what number your program actually accepted from the data you entered. What happened, if anything, and why?

3. a. Why do you think that successful application programs contain extensive data-input validity checks? (*Hint*: Review Exercises 1 and 2.)
   b. What do you think is the difference between a data type check and a data reasonableness check?
   c. Assume that a program asks the user to enter a month, day, and year. What are some reasonable checks that could be made on the data entered?

4. a. Enter and execute Program 9-17.
   b. Run Program 9-17 five times, using the data referred to in Exercise 1 for each run.

5. Modify Program 9-17 to display any invalid characters that were entered.

6. Modify Program 9-17 to continually request an integer until a valid number is entered.

7. Modify Program 9-17 to remove all leading and trailing spaces from the entered string before it is checked for validity.

8. Write a function that checks each digit as it is entered, rather than checking the completed string, as is done in Program 9-17.

9. Write a C++ function that checks for a valid floating-point number. Such a number can have an optional + or - sign; at most one decimal point, which can be the first character; and at least one digit between 0 and 9, inclusive.

9.6 A CLOSER LOOK: STRINGS AND THE STL

Although the `string` class is not part of the Standard Template Library (STL), it was designed to work directly with STL algorithms. This is not always the case with C-strings because of the end-of-sentinel character. For example, if you reverse a C-string using the STL and are not careful, the `'\0'` terminating character can end up at the front of the array. Thus, if you are dealing with a C-string and want to use an STL function, you are generally better off converting it to a string object first.

Table 9-9 lists the commonly used STL algorithms, previously presented in Section 8.4.

TABLE 9-9
Commonly Used Standard Template Library (STL) Algorithms

algorithm name	description
`accumulate(start, end, initValue)`	Returns the total of `initValue` with the sum of the numbers in the range specified by `start` and `end`.
`binary_search (start, end, value)`	Returns a Boolean value of `true` if the specified value exists within the specified range; otherwise returns `false`. Should only be used on a sorted set of values.
`copy(srcStart, srcEnd, destStart)`	Copies elements from the source range specified by `srcStart` to `srcEnd`, to the range of elements starting at `destStart`
`copy_backward (srcStart, srcEnd, destStart)`	Copies elements from the source range specified by `srcStart` to `srcEnd`, in reverse order, to the range of elements starting at `destStart`
`count (start, end, criterion)`	Returns the number of elements in the specified range that match the specified criterion
`equal(start1, end1, start2)`	Compares the elements in the range of elements specified by the range `start1` to `end1`, element by element, to the elements in the range starting with `start2`

(continued on next page)

9

TABLE 9-9
Commonly Used Standard Template Library (STL) Algorithms (Continued)

algorithm name	description
`fill(start, end, value)`	Assigns every element in the range specified by `start` and `end` with the specified value
`find(start, end, value)`	Returns the position of the first occurrence of an element in a specified range having the specified value, if the value exists. Performs a linear search, starting with the first element in a specified range, and proceeds one element at a time until the complete range has been searched or the specified element has been found
`max_element(start, end, criterion)`	Returns the maximum value of the elements in the specified range that match the specified criterion
`min_element(start, end, criterion)`	Returns the minimum value of the elements in the specified range that match the specified criterion
`random_shuffle(start, end)`	Randomly shuffles element values in the range specified by `start` and `end`
`remove(start, end, value)`	Removes all elements in the range specified by `start` and `end` having the specified value, without changing the order of the remaining elements
`replace (start, end, oldVal, newVal)`	Replaces each element in the range specified by `start` and `end` that has the value `oldVal` with the value `newVal`
`reverse(start, end)`	Reverses elements in the range specified by `start` and `end`
`search (start, end, value)`	Finds the first occurrence of the specified value or sequence of values within a specified range
`sort(start, end)`	Sorts elements in the range specified by `start` and `end` into an ascending order
`swap(srcStart, srcEnd, destStart)`	Swaps elements from the source range specified by `srcStart` to `srcEnd`, to the range of elements starting at `destStart`
`unique (start, end)`	Removes all elements in the range specified by `start` and `end` that are equal to the previous element. When the elements are in sorted order, this will remove all duplicate entries

Typically the ranges required as arguments to all of the algorithms listed in Table 9-9 must be specified as STL iterators. Two of the most useful iterators are returned by the STL iterator functions named `begin()` and `end()`. These are general purpose functions that, for our purposes, return the positions of the first and last elements in a string, respectively.

To clarify this concept, we will apply STL's `reverse()` algorithm to a `string` class object to illustrate how a rather challenging programming problem (see Section 9.3, Exercise 12) is solved very easily using the STL. The programming problem is to determine if a word or line of text is a palindrome.

A palindrome is a word or phrase in which the alphanumeric characters in the text are exactly the same in both the forward and reverse directions. By definition, alphanumeric characters consist of letters and digits only. Thus, all white space, punctuation marks, tabs, and nonprinting characters are not considered in determining if a palindrome exists. For example, the phrase "Madam I'm Adam" is a palindrome, because when the punctuation and white space are removed, the remaining sequence of characters is the same in both the forward and reverse directions.

For our example, we will write a program that accepts a line of text as input and then determines if it is a palindrome. The procedure we will follow to determine if the characters represent a palindrome is:

1.   Remove all nonalphanumeric characters from the string.

2.   Convert all letters to lowercase (uppercase also works).

3.   Make a copy of the resulting string.

4.   Reverse the copy.

5.   Compare the string, element-by-element, with its reversed copy.

A BIT OF BACKGROUND

Anagrams and Palindromes

Some of the most challenging and fascinating word games are played with anagrams and palindromes.

An **anagram** is a rearrangement of the letters in a word or phrase that makes another word or phrase. Although the letters of the word *door* can be rearranged to spell *orod* and *doro,* it is more exciting to discover the words *odor* and *rood.* A word, phrase, or sentence that reads the same forward and backward, such as *top spot* is a **palindrome.**

The origins of most known anagrams and palindromes are lost to anonymity. Here are some collected by Richard Manchester in *The Mammoth Book of Fun and Games* (Hart Publishing Co. Inc., New York City, 1977; pages 229-231):

<u>Apt Anagrams</u>

The Mona Lisa → No hat, a smile
The United States of America → Attaineth its cause: freedom!

<u>Interesting Palindromes</u>

Live not on evil!
'Tis Ivan on a visit.
Yreka Bakery
Able was I ere I saw Elba.
Madam, I'm Adam.
A man, a plan, a canal: Panama!

9

As is shown in Program 9-18, Steps 1 and 2 are accomplished using character operations, Step 3 is accomplished using a one-line `string` class assignment statement, Step 4 is accomplished using the STL `reverse()` algorithm, and Step 5 is accomplished using the `string` class's equality operator.

Program 9-18

```cpp
#include <iostream>
#include <string>
#include <cctype>
#include <algorithm>
using namespace std;

int main()
{
  string text, savetext;
  int i;

  cout << "Enter the text: ";
  getline(cin, text);

  // Steps 1 and 2: remove all non alphanumeric characters
  // and then convert all alphanumerics to lowercase
  for (i = 0; i < text.length(); i++)
    if (isalnum(text.at(i)))
        text.at(i) = tolower(text.at(i));
    else
      {
        text.erase(i,1);
        i--;  // take into account that a character was removed
      }

  savetext = text; // Step 3: Make a copy of the cleaned-up text

  reverse(text.begin(), text.end());  // Step 4: Reverse the cleaned-up text

  if (text == savetext)  // Step 5: Compare forward and reversed texts
    cout << "The entered text is a palindrome." << endl;
  else
    cout << "The entered text is not a palindrome." << endl;

  return 0;
}
```

Program 9-18 illustrates how easily STL algorithms can be used with `string` class objects to complete programming tasks that would otherwise take considerable time and effort, both to program and then verify. Chapter 13 presents an additional set of STL provided classes that also can use the same STL algorithms to solve more advanced programming tasks.

Exercises 9.6

1. Enter and execute Program 9-18. Verify that the program works correctly by entering the following text:

   a. Live not on evil!
   b. 'Tis Ivan on a visit.
   c. Yreka Bakery
   d. Able was I ere I saw Elba.
   e. Madam it's Tim Adam!!
   f. A man, a plan, a canal: Panama!

2. Modify Program 9-18 so that it removes all nondigits, and then displays the entered integer in reverse form. Thus, if the user enters the data 123abc45, the program should display 54321.

3. Modify Program 9-18 to display the entered text after it has been stripped of all nonalpha-numeric characters and all characters have been converted to lowercase.

4. Write a C++ program that consists of either an array or vector of 10 last names. Using STL algorithms, sort the list into alphabetical order.

5. Write a C++ program that swaps the text contained in two strings.

6. Use an STL algorithm to cycle in reverse order through the last names stored in either an array or vector consisting of five names. That is, the program should display the names from the last name in the array or vector up to and including the first name.

7. Write a C++ program that accepts a line of text into a `string` class object and then replaces every occurrence of the letter e with the letter x.

8. Modify the C++ program written for Exercise 7 so that the user can specify both the character that is to be replaced and the replacing character.

9. Write a C++ program that requests a line of text and then removes all the occurrences of a user-specified letter. Display the complete line of text after the removal to see how the order of the remaining elements has been affected. Additionally, display the size of the string both before and after the removal. Discuss why you might want to use the `string` class's `erase()` method rather than the STL's `remove()` algorithm.

9.7 COMMON PROGRAMMING ERRORS

The common errors associated with defining and processing strings are:

1. Forgetting to include the `string` header file when using `string` class objects.

2. Forgetting to convert a `string` class object to a C-string when converting strings to numerical data types.

3. Providing insufficient space for a C-string to be stored. A simple variation of this is not providing space for the end-of-string `NULL` character when a string is defined as an array of characters.

PROGRAMMING NOTE

Conditional Preprocessor Directives

In addition to the `#include` directive, the preprocessor provides a number of other useful directives. Two of the more useful of these are the conditional directives, `#ifndef`, which means "if not defined," and `#ifdef`, which means "if defined." These directives work in almost the same manner as the `if` and `else` statements. For example, the syntax of the `#ifndef` statement is:

```
#ifndef condition
   compile the statements placed here
#else
   compile the statements placed here
#endif
```

As with the `if/else` statement, the `#else` directive is optional.

Both the `#ifndef` and `#ifdef` directives permit *conditional compilation,* in that the statements immediately following these directives, up to either the `#else` or `#endif` directives, are compiled only if the condition is true, while the statements following the `#else` are compiled only if the condition is false.

By far, the `#ifndef` directive is the most frequently used conditional preprocessor directive. The most common usage of this directive is in the form:

```
#ifndef header-file
   #include <header-file>
#endif
```

For example,

```
#ifndef iostream
   #include <iostream>
#endif
```

What this statement does is to check if the `iostream` header file has already been included. Only if it *has not* been previously defined, is the `#include` directive executed. This prevents multiple inclusions of the `iostream` header file.

The `#ifdef` works in a similar way to the `#ifndef`, except that the statements immediately following the `#ifdef`, up to either the `#else` or `#endif` directives, are only executed if the tested condition has been defined.

The relationship between the `#ifdef` and `#ifndef` directives is that `#ifndef condition` performs the same task as `#ifdef !condition`, and these two statements can be used interchangeably.

4. Not including the `'\0'` terminating character when the array is initialized character by character. For example, the definition

```
char string[] = {'H', 'e', 'l', 'l', 'o'};
```

does not create a valid string because a terminating NULL character, `'\0'`, is not included in the initialization.

5. Forgetting that the newline character, `'\n'`, is a valid data input character.

6. Not realizing that the `strcmp()` function returns a value of 0, which is equivalent to false, when the strings being compared are equal. Thus, the condition `!strcmp(string1, string2)` should be used to determine if the strings are equal.

9.8 CHAPTER REVIEW

Key Terms

cctype

cstring

C-string

cin.get()

cin.getline()

getline()

isalpha()

isdigit()

length()

NULL

string()

strlen()

tolower()

toupper()

SUMMARY

1. A string literal is any sequence of characters enclosed in double quotation marks. A string literal is also referred to as a string value, a string constant, and more conventionally, simply as a string.

2. A string can be constructed from either the `string` class or as an array of characters.

3. The `string` class is more commonly used for constructing strings for input and output purposes, such as for prompts and displayed messages. In addition, because of the provided capabilities, this class is also used when strings need to be compared or searched, or individual characters in a string need to be examined or extracted as a substring. It is also used in more advanced situations when characters within a string need to be replaced, inserted, or deleted on a relatively regular basis.

9

4. A string that is constructed as an array of characters is referred to as a C-string and must be terminated by the NULL character, '\0'.

5. A C-string can always be processed using standard array-processing techniques. The input and display of a string, however, always require reliance on a standard library function.

6. The cin object, by itself, tends to be of limited usefulness for string input because it terminates input when a blank is encountered.

7. For string class data input, use the getline() method.

8. For C-string data input, use the cin.getline() function.

9. The cout object can be used to display both string class objects and C-strings.

10. C-strings can be initialized using a string assignment of the form

```
char arrayName[ ] = "text";
```

This initialization is equivalent to

```
char arrayName[ ] = {'t','e','x','t','\0'};
```

Chapter Exercises

1. Write a function to count the number of lines entered using a string class object. Consider a line as any sequence of characters followed by the Enter key.

2. Read a sentence, one character at a time, from the keyboard into a string class object. Entry will terminate with a period (.). Search the array to determine how many times a particular character, specified by the user at the keyboard, occurs in the sentence.

3. Write a function to count the number of sentences entered into a string class object; assume a sentence ends in either a period, question mark, or exclamation point.

4. Modify the function written for Exercise 3 to count the number of words as well as the number of sentences. The function should return the average number of words per sentence.

5. Write a function named remove() that returns nothing and deletes all occurrences of its character argument from a string (use either a string class object or a C-string). The function should take two arguments: the string name and the character to be removed. For example, if message contains the string Happy Holidays, the function call remove(message, 'H') should place the string appy olidays into message.

6. Write a function named addchars() that adds n occurrences of a character to a string (use either a string class object or a C-string). For example, the call addchars(message, 4, '!') should add four exclamation marks at the end of message.

7. Write a function named extract() that accepts two strings, s1 and s2, and two integer numbers, n1 and n2, as arguments (use either a string class object or a C-string). The function should extract n2 characters from s2, starting at position n1, and place the extracted characters into s1. For example, if string s1 contains the characters 05/18/95 D169254 Rotech Systems, the function call extract(s1, s2, 18, 6) should create the string Rotech in s2. Note that the starting position for counting purposes is in position one. If you use a C-string, be sure to close off the returned string with a '\0' and make sure that string s1 is defined in the calling function to be large enough to accept the extracted values.

8. Write and test a function that accepts an array of characters, whose last element is '\0', and then prints the elements in reverse order.

9. Write and test a function that uses an array of characters and returns the position of the first occurrence of a user-specified letter in the array or a −1 if the letter does not occur.

10. Write a C++ program that first initializes a two-dimensional array defined as list [5][30] with the following five strings:

    "04/12/72 74444 Bill Barnes"
    "12/28/65 75255 Harriet Smith"
    "10/17/54 74477 Joan Casey"
    "02/18/48 74470 Deane Fraser"
    "06/15/56 75155 Jan Smiley"

    Your program should include a function named printList() that displays each string in the array.

11. Suppose you work at a company that organizes shipping information as shown in Table 9-10.

TABLE 9-10
Shipping Information for Exercise 11

shipped date	track no.	part no.	first name	last name	company
04/12/05	D50625	74444	James	Lehoff	Rotech Sys.
04/12/05	D60752	75255	Janet	Lezar	Rotech Sys.
04/12/05	D40295	74477	Bill	McHenry	Rotech Sys.
04/12/05	D23745	74470	Diane	Kaiser	Rotech Sys.
04/12/05	D50892	75155	Helen	Richardson	NipNap Inc.

Write a C++ program that creates a character array having five rows, with each row capable of storing 70 characters, and initialize the array with the five records in Table 9-10. (Do not include the table headings.) The format of each line in the array is identical, with fixed-length fields defined as follows:

field position	field name	starting col. no.	ending col. no.	field length
1	Shipped Date	1	8	8
2	Tracking Number	10	15	6
3	Part Number	17	21	5
4	First Name	23	27	5
5	Last Name	29	38	10
6	Company	40	50	11

Using the data in the array, your C++ program should extract the date, part number, first initial, last name, and company name and produce a report listing the extracted data. (*Hint*: Use the `extract()` function created in Exercise 7.)

12. Some prisoners of war devised a system of communicating with each other through the walls of solitary-confinement cells. This system is based on arranging the letters of the alphabet in 5 rows as follows:

> a b c d e
> f g h i j
> l m n o p
> q r s t u
> v w x y z

The prisoners spelled messages to each other by tapping the row and column number of the letters on the wall, substituting c for the omitted k. For example, h would be 2 taps (row 2), a short pause, and then 3 taps (column 3); and help would be '2/3, 1/5, 3/1, 3/5' the digit pairs representing the number of taps for row and column.

Write a program that loads a two-dimensional array with the letters shown in the table. Then write a function to search the array for the letters in a given string and to convert the string to taps, representing the row/column number pairs.

Testing Center

Please visit the Testing Center at www.course.com/testingcenter for more practice on strings and characters.

10

I/O FILE STREAMS
AND DATA FILES

The data for the programs we have used so far has either been assigned internally within the programs or entered by the user during program execution. This data is stored in the computer's main memory, and ceases to exist once the program using it finishes executing. This type of data entry is fine for small amounts of data. But imagine a company having to pay someone to type in the names and addresses of hundreds or thousands of customers every month each time bills are prepared and sent.

As you'll learn in this chapter, it makes more sense to store such data outside of a program on a convenient storage medium. Data that is stored together under a common name on a storage medium other than the computer's main memory is called a data file. Typically data files are stored on disks, tapes, or CD-ROMs. Besides providing permanent storage for the data, another advantage of data files is that they can be shared between programs, so that the data output by one program can be input directly to another program. You'll begin this chapter by learning how data files are created and maintained in C++. One major concern about using data files is ensuring that your programs open and connect correctly to them before any data processing begins. For this reason, you'll also learn how to use exception handling for this task. This type of error detection and correction is a major concern of all professionally written programs.

10.1 I/O FILE STREAM OBJECTS AND METHODS

To store and retrieve data outside a C++ program, you need two things:

- A file

- A file stream object

You'll learn about these important topics in the following two sections.

FILES

A **file** is a collection of data that is stored together under a common name, usually on a disk, magnetic tape, or CD-ROM. For example, the C++ programs that you store on disk are examples of files. The stored data in a program file is the program code that becomes input data to the C++ compiler. In the context of data processing, however, the C++ program is not usually considered data, and the term "file," or "data file," is typically used to refer only to external files that contain the data used in a C++ program.

> **A BIT OF BACKGROUND**
>
> **Privacy, Security, and Files**
>
> Data files were around long before computers were used, but were primarily stored as paper records in filing cabinets. Terms such as *open, close, records,* and *lookup* that are used in handling computer files are reminders of these older techniques for accessing paper files stored in drawers.
>
> Today most files are stored electronically, and the amount of information that is collected and stored proliferates wildly. The ease of sharing large amounts of data electronically has led to increasing problems with privacy and security.
>
> Whenever a person fills out a government form or a credit application, submits a mail order, applies for a job, writes a check, or uses a credit card, an electronic data trail is created. Each time those files are shared among government agencies or private enterprises, the individual loses more privacy.
>
> In order to help protect U.S. citizens' constitutional rights, the Fair Credit Reporting Act was passed in 1970, followed by the Federal Privacy Act in 1974. These acts specify that it is illegal for a business to keep secret files, that you are entitled to examine and correct any data collected about you, and that government agencies and contractors must show justification for accessing your records. Efforts continue to create mechanisms that will serve to preserve an individual's security and privacy.

A file is physically stored on an external medium such as a disk. Each file has a unique file name referred to as the file's **external name.** The external name is how the file is known by the operating system. When you review the contents of a directory or folder (for example, in Windows Explorer) you see files listed by their external names. Each computer operating system has its own specification as to the maximum number of characters permitted for an external file name. Table 10-1 lists these specifications for the more commonly used operating systems.

TABLE 10-1
Maximum Allowable File Name Characters

operating system	maximum file name length
DOS	8 characters plus an optional period and 3-character extension
Windows 98, 2000, XP	255 characters
UNIX Early versions Current versions	 14 characters 255 characters

To ensure that the examples presented in this text are compatible with all of the operating systems listed in Table 10-1, we will generally, but not exclusively, adhere to the more restrictive DOS specifications. If you are using one of the other operating systems, however, you should take advantage of the increased length specification to create descriptive file names. Very long file names should be avoided, however, because they take more time to type and can result in typing errors. A manageable length for a file name is 12 to 14 characters, with an outside maximum of 25 characters.

PROGRAMMING NOTE

Input and Output Streams

A *stream* is a one-way transmission path between a source and a destination. What gets sent down this transmission path is a stream of bytes. A good analogy to this "stream of bytes" is a stream of water that provides a one-way path for water to travel from a source to a destination.

Stream objects are created from stream classes. Two stream objects that we have used extensively are the input stream object named `cin` and the output stream object named `cout`. The `cin` object provides a transmission path from keyboard to program, while the `cout` object provides a transmission path from program to terminal screen. These two objects are created from the stream classes `istream` and `ostream`, respectively, which are parent classes to the `iostream` class. When the `iostream` header file is included in a program using the `#include <iostream>` directive, the `cin` and `cout` stream objects are automatically declared and opened by the C++ compiler for the compiled program.

File stream objects provide the same capabilities as the `cin` and `cout` objects, except they connect a program to a file rather than the keyboard or terminal screen. Also, file stream objects must be explicitly declared. File stream objects that will be used for input must be declared as objects of the class `ifstream`, while file stream objects that will be used for output must be declared as objects of the class `ofstream`. The classes `ifstream` and `ofstream` are made available to a program by inclusion of the `fstream` header file, using the directive `#include <fstream>`. The `fstream` class is derived from both the `ifstream` and `ofstream` classes (see Section 10.7).

Using the DOS convention, the following are all valid computer data file names:

```
prices.dat      records       info.txt
exper1.dat      scores.dat    math.mem
```

Choose file names that indicate both the type of data in the file and the application for which it is used. Frequently, the first eight characters describe the data, and an extension (the characters after the period) describes the application. For example, the Excel spreadsheet program automatically applies an extension of "xls" to all spreadsheet files, Microsoft's Word and the WordPerfect word processing programs use the extensions "doc" and "wp*x*" (where *x* refers to the version number), respectively, and C++ compilers require a program file to have the extension "cpp." When creating your own file names, you should adhere to this practice. For example, using the DOS convention, the name "exper1.dat" is appropriate in describing a file of data corresponding to experiment number 1.

There are two basic types of files: **text files**, which are also known as **character-based files**, and **binary-based files**. Both file types store data using a binary code; the difference is in what the codes represent. Briefly, text-based files store each individual character, such as a letter, digit, dollar sign, decimal point, and so on, using an individual character code (typically ASCII or UNICODE). The use of a character code allows such files to be displayed by a word processing program or text editor so that a person can read them. Binary-based files use the same code as your C++ compiler uses for its primitive data types. This means that numbers appear in their true binary form, while strings retain their ASCII or UNICODE form. The advantage of binary-based files is compactness, because it takes less space to store most numbers using their binary code than as individual character values. In general, the vast majority of files used by programmers are text files, simply because the file's data can be displayed by word processing programs and simple text editors. The default file type in C++ is always a text file, and is the file type presented in this chapter.

FILE STREAM OBJECTS

A **file stream** is a one-way transmission path that is used to connect a file stored on a physical device, such as a disk or CD-ROM, to a program. Each file stream has its own mode, which determines the direction of data on the transmission path—that is, whether the path will move data from a file into a program or whether the path will move data from a program to a file. A file stream that receives or reads data from a file into a program is referred to as an **input file stream.** A file stream that sends or writes data to a file is referred to as an **output file stream.** Notice that the direction, or mode, is always defined in relation to the program and not the file; data that go into a program are considered input data, and data sent out from the program are considered output data. Figure 10-1 illustrates the data flow from and to a file using input and output streams.

FIGURE 10-1
Input and Output File Streams

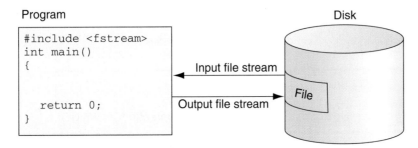

For each file that your program uses, a distinct file stream object must be created. If you are going to read and write to a file, both an input and output file stream object are required.

For each file that your program uses, regardless of the file's type (text or binary), a distinct file stream object must be created. If you want your program to both read and write to a file, both an input and output file stream object are required. Input file stream objects are declared to be of type `ifstream`, while output file streams are declared to be of type `ofstream`. For example, the declaration

```
ifstream inFile;
```

declares an input file stream object named `inFile` to be an object of the class `ifstream`. Similarly, the declaration

```
ofstream outFile;
```

declares an output file stream object named `outFile` to be an object of the class `ofstream`. Within a C++ program, a file stream is always accessed by its appropriate stream object name—one name for reading the file and one name for writing to the file. Object names, such as `inFile` and `outFile`, can be any programmer-selected names that conform to C++'s identifier rules.

File Stream Methods

Each file stream object has access to the methods defined for its respective `ifstream` or `ofstream` class. These methods include connecting a stream object name to an external file name (called **opening a file**), determining if a successful connection has been made, closing a connection (called **closing a file**), getting the next data item into the program from an input stream, putting a new data item from the program onto an output stream, and detecting when the end of a file has been reached.

Opening a file connects each file stream object to a specific external file name. This is accomplished using a file stream's open method, which accomplishes two purposes. First, opening a file establishes the physical connecting link between a program and a file. Since details of this link are handled by the computer's operating system and are transparent to the program, the programmer normally doesn't need to consider them.

From a coding perspective, the second purpose of opening a file is more relevant. Besides establishing the actual physical connection between a program and a data file, opening a file connects the file's external computer name to the stream object name used internally by the program. The method that performs this task is named `open()` and is provided by both the `ifstream` and `ofstream` classes.

In using the `open()` method to connect the file's external name to its internal object stream name, only one argument is required, which is the external file name. For example, the statement

```
inFile.open("prices.dat");
```

connects the external text file named `prices.dat` to the internal program file stream object named `inFile`. This assumes, of course, that `inFile` has been declared as either an `ifstream` or `ofstream` object. If a file has been opened with the preceding statement, the program accesses the file using the internal object name `inFile`, while the computer saves the file under the external name `prices.dat`. Notice that the external file name argument passed to `open()` is a string contained between double quotes. Also notice that calling the `open()` method requires the standard object notation where the name of the desired method, in this case `open()`, is preceded by a period and an object name.

When an existing file is connecting to an input file stream, the file's data is made available for input, starting at the first data item in the file. Similarly, a file connected to an output file stream creates a new file and makes the file available for output. If a file exists with the same name as a file opened in output mode, the old file is erased and all its data is lost.

When opening a file for input or output, good programming practice requires that you check that the connection has been established before attempting to use the file in any way. You can do this via the `fail()` method, which will return a `true` value if the file was unsuccessfully opened (that is, if it is true the open failed), or a `false` value if the open succeeded. Typically the `fail()` method is used in code similar to the following, which attempts to open a file named `prices.dat` for input, checks that a valid connection was made, and reports an error message if the file was not successfully opened for input:

```
ifstream inFile;              // any object name can be used here
inFile.open("prices.dat");   // open the file

// check that the connection was successfully opened
if (inFile.fail())
{
   cout << "\nThe file was not successfully opened"
        << "\n Please check that the file currently exists."
        << endl;
   exit(1);
}
```

If the `fail()` method returns a `true`, which indicates that the open failed, a message is displayed by this code. In addition, the `exit()` function, which is a request to the operating system to end program execution immediately, is called. The `exit()` function requires inclusion of the `cstdlib` header function in any program that uses this function, and `exit()`'s single-integer argument is passed directly to the operating system for possible further operating system program action or user inspection. Throughout the remainder of the text we will include this type of error checking whenever a file is opened. (Section 10.3 shows how to use exception handling for the same type of error checking.)

In addition to the `fail()` method, C++ provides three other methods, all listed in Table 10-2, that can be used to detect a file's status. The use of these additional methods is presented at the end of the next section.

TABLE 10-2
File Status Methods

prototype	description
fail()	Returns a Boolean true if the file has not been successfully opened; otherwise returns a Boolean false value
eof()	Returns a Boolean true if a read has been attempted past the end-of-file; otherwise returns a Boolean false value. The value becomes true only when the first character after the last valid file character is read
good()	Returns a Boolean true value while the file is available for program use. Returns a Boolean false value if a read has been attempted past the end-of-file. The value becomes false only when the first character after the last valid file character is read
bad()	Returns a Boolean true value if a read has been attempted past the end-of-file; otherwise returns a false. The value becomes true only when the first character after the last valid file character is read

Program 10-1 illustrates the statements required to open a file for input, including an error checking routine to ensure that a successful open was obtained. A file opened for input is said to be in **read mode.**

Program 10-1

```cpp
#include <iostream>
#include <fstream>
#include <cstdlib>    // needed for exit()
using namespace std;

int main()
{
  ifstream inFile;

  inFile.open("prices.dat");  // open the file with the
                              // external name prices.dat
  if (inFile.fail())          // check for a successful open
  {
    cout << "\nThe file was not successfully opened"
         << "\n Please check that the file currently exists."
         << endl;
    exit(1);
  }

  cout << "\nThe file has been successfully opened for reading."
       << endl;

  // statements to read data from the file would be placed here

  return 0;
}
```

A sample run using Program 10-1 produced the output:

```
The file has been successfully opened for reading.
```

A slightly different check is required for output files, because if a file exists having the same name as the file to be opened in output mode, the existing file is erased and all its data is lost. To avoid this situation, the file is first opened in input mode to see if it exists. If it does, the user is given the choice of explicitly permitting it to be overwritten when it is later opened in output mode. The code used to accomplish this is highlighted in Program 10-2.

Program 10-2

```cpp
#include <iostream>
#include <fstream>
#include <cstdlib>              // needed for exit()
using namespace std;

int main()
{
  ifstream inFile;
  ofstream outFile;

  inFile.open("prices.dat");   // attempt to open the file for input

  char response;

  if (!inFile.fail())          // if it doesn't fail, the file exists
  {
   cout << "A file by the name prices.dat exists.\n"
        << "Do you want to continue and overwrite it\n"
        << " with the new data (y or n): ";
   cin  >> response;
   if (tolower(response) == 'n')
   {
     cout << "The existing file will not be overwritten." << endl;
     exit(1);                  //terminate program execution
   }
  }
  outFile.open("prices.dat"); // now open the file for writing

  if (inFile.fail())           // check for a successful open
  {
    cout << "\nThe file was not successfully opened"
         << endl;
    exit(1);
  }
```

(continued on next page)

```
cout << "The file has been successfully opened for output."
    << endl;

// statements to write to the file would be placed here

return 0;
}
```

Following are two runs made with Program 10-2:

```
A file by the name prices.dat exists.
Do you want to continue and overwrite it
 with the new data (y or n): n
The existing file will not be overwritten.
```

and

```
A file by the name prices.dat exists.
Do you want to continue and overwrite it
 with the new data (y or n): y
The file has been successfully opened for output.
```

Although Programs 10-1 and 10-2 can be used to open an existing file for reading and writing, respectively, both programs lack statements to actually perform a read or write and close the file. These topics are discussed shortly. Before moving on, however, it is worthwhile noting that it is possible to combine the declaration of either an ifstream or ofstream object and its associated open statement into one statement. For example, the following two statements in Program 10-1

```
ifstream inFile;
inFile.open("prices.dat");
```

can be combined into the single statement

```
ifstream inFile("prices.dat");
```

Embedded and Interactive File Names

Two practical problems with Programs 10-1 and 10-2 are:

1. The external file name is embedded within the program code.

2. There is no provision for a user to enter the desired file name while the program is executing.

As both programs are written, if the file name is to change, a programmer must modify the external file name in the call to open() and recompile the program. Both of these problems can be alleviated by assigning the file name to a string variable.

A string variable as we have used it throughout the text (see especially Chapter 9) is a variable that can hold a string value, which is any sequence of zero or more characters enclosed within double quotes. For example, `"Hello World"`, `"prices.dat"`, and `""` are all strings. Notice that strings are always written with double quotes that delimit the beginning and end of a string, but are not stored as part of the string.

In declaring and initializing a string variable for use in an `open()` method, the string is always considered as a C-string. (See the next Programming Note for precautions that must be understood when using a C-string.) A much safer alternative, and one that we will use throughout this text, is to use a `string` class object and then convert this object to a C-string using the `c_str()` method.

Once a string variable is declared to store a file name, it can be used in one of two ways. First, as shown in Program 10-3a, it can be placed at the top of a program to clearly identify a file's external name, rather than embed it within an `open()` method call.

Program 10-3a

```cpp
#include <iostream>
#include <fstream>
#include <cstdlib>              // needed for exit()
#include <string>
using namespace std;

int main()
{
  string filename = "prices.dat"; // place the file name up front
  ifstream inFile;

  inFile.open(filename.c_str());  // open the file

  if (inFile.fail())              // check for successful open
  {
    cout << "\nThe file named " << filename << " was not successfully opened"
         << "\n Please check that the file currently exists."
         << endl;
    exit(1);
  }

  cout << "\nThe file has been successfully opened for reading.\n";

  return 0;
}
```

In reviewing Program 10-3a, notice that we have declared and initialized the string object named `filename` at the top of `main()` for easy file identification. Next, notice that when a string object is used, as opposed to a string literal, the variable name *is not* enclosed within double quotes in the `open()` method call. Also notice that within the `open()` call, the string object is converted to a C-string using the expression `filename.c_str()`. Finally, notice that in the `fail()` method code the file's external name is displayed by inserting the string object's name in the `cout` output stream. For these reasons, we will continue to identify the external names of files in this manner.

PROGRAMMING NOTE

Using C-Strings as File Names

If you choose to use a C-string to store an external file name, you must be aware of the following restrictions.

The maximum length of the C-string must be specified within brackets immediately after it is declared. For example, in the declaration

```
char filename[21] = "prices.dat";
```

the number 21 limits the number of characters that can be stored in the C-string. The number in brackets, in this example 21, always represents one more than the maximum number of characters that can be assigned to the variable. This is because the compiler always adds a final end-of-string character to terminate the string. Thus the string value `"prices.dat"`, which consists of 10 characters, is actually stored as 11 characters. The extra character is an end-of-string marker supplied by the compiler. In our example, the maximum string value assignable to the string variable file name is a string value consisting of 20 characters.

Another useful role played by string objects is to permit the user to enter the file name as the program is executing. For example, the code

```
string filename;

cout << "Please enter the name of the file you wish to open: ";
cin  >> filename;
```

allows a user to enter a file's external name at run-time. The only restriction in this code is that the user must not enclose the entered string value in double quotes and that the entered string value cannot contain any blanks. The reason is that when using `cin`, the compiler will terminate the string when it encounters a blank. Program 10-3b uses this code in the context of a complete program.

Program 10-3b

```cpp
#include <iostream>
#include <fstream>
#include <cstdlib>    // needed for exit()
#include <string>
using namespace std;
int main()
{
  string filename;
  ifstream inFile;

  cout << "Please enter the name of the file you wish to open: ";
  cin  >> filename;

  inFile.open(filename.c_str());  // open the file

  if (inFile.fail())                      // check for successful open
  {
    cout << "\nThe file named " << filename << " was not successfully opened"
         << "\n Please check that the file currently exists."
         << endl;
    exit(1);
  } cout << "\nThe file has been successfully opened for reading.\n";

  return 0;
}
```

Following is a sample output provided by Program 10-3b:

```
Please enter the name of the file you wish to open: foobar

The file named foobar was not successfully opened
 Please check that the file currently exists.
```

CLOSING A FILE

A file is closed using the `close()` method. This method breaks the connection between the file's external name and the file stream object, which can then be used for another file. For example, the statement

```cpp
        inFile.close();
```

closes the `inFile` stream's connection to its current file. As indicated, the `close()` method takes no argument.

PROGRAMMING NOTE

Using `fstream` Objects

In using both `ifstream` and `ofstream` objects the input or output mode is implied by the object. Thus `ifstream` objects can only be used for input, and `ofstream` objects can only be used for output.

Another means of creating file streams is to use `fstream` objects that can be used for input or output, but this method requires an explicit mode designation. An `fstream` object is declared using the syntax

```
fstream objectName;
```

When using the `fstream` class's `open()` method, two arguments are required: a file's external name and a mode indicator. Permissible mode indicators are:

Indicator	Description
`ios::in`	Open a text file in input mode
`ios::out`	Open a text file in output mode
`ios::app`	Open a text file in append mode
`ios::ate`	Go to the end of the opened file
`ios::binary`	Open a binary file in input mode (default is text file)
`ios::trunc`	Delete file contents if it exists
`ios::nocreate`	If file does not exist, open fails
`ios::noreplace`	If file exists, open for output fails

As with `ofstream` objects, an `fstream` object in output mode creates a new file and makes the file available for writing. If a file exists with the same name as a file opened for output, the old file is erased. For example, assuming that `file1` has been declared as an object of type `fstream` using the statement

```
fstream file1;
```

then the statement

```
file1.open("prices.dat",ios::out);
```

attempts to open the text file named `prices.dat` for output. Once this file has been opened, the program accesses the file using the internal object name `file1`, while the computer saves the file under the external name `prices.dat`.

An `fstream` file object opened in append mode means that an existing file is available for data to be added to the end of the file. If the file opened for appending does not exist, a new file with the designated name is created and made available to receive output from the program. For example, again assuming that `file1` has been declared to be of type `fstream`, the statement

```
file1.open("prices.dat",ios::app);
```

attempts to open a file named `prices.dat` and makes it available for data to be appended to the end of the file.   *(continued on next page)*

PROGRAMMING NOTE

Using `fstream` Objects (Continued from page 641)

Finally, an `fstream` object opened in input mode means that an existing external file has been connected and its data is available as input. For example, assuming that `file1` has been declared to be of type `fstream`, the statement

```
file1.open("prices.dat",ios::in);
```

attempts to open a text file named `prices.dat` for input. The mode indicators can be combined by the bit Or operation (see Section 17.2). For example, the statement

```
file1.open("prices.dat", ios::in | ios::binary)
```

opens the `file1` stream, which can be either an `fstream` or `ifstream`, as an input binary stream. If the mode indicator is omitted as the second argument for an `ifstream` object, the stream is, by default, opened as a text input file; if the mode indicator is omitted for an `ofstream` object, the stream is also opened as a text output file by default.

Because all computers have a limit on the maximum number of files that can be open at one time, closing files that are no longer needed makes good sense. Any open files existing at the end of normal program execution will be automatically closed by the operating system.

PROGRAMMING NOTE

Checking for a Successful Connection

It is important to check that the `open()` method successfully established a connection between a file stream and an external file. This is because the `open()` call is really a request to the operating system that can fail for a variety of reasons. (Chief among these reasons are a request to open an existing file for reading that the operating system cannot locate, or attempting to open a file for output in a nonexistent folder.) If the operating system cannot satisfy the open request, you need to know about it and gracefully terminate your program. Failure to do so almost always results in abnormal program behavior or a subsequent program crash.

There are two styles of coding for checking the return value. The most common method for checking that a fail did not occur when attempting to use a file for input is the one coded in Program 10-1. It is used to clearly distinguish the `open()` request from the check made via the `fail()` call, and is repeated below for convenience:

```
inFile.open("prices.dat");   // request to open the file

if (inFile.fail())        // check for a failed connection
```

(continued on next page)

```
    {
      cout << "\nThe file was not successfully opened"
           << "\n Please check that the file currently
              exists."
           << endl;
      exit(1);
    }
```

Similarly, the check made in Program 10-2 is typically included when a file is being opened in output mode.

Alternatively, you may encounter programs that use `fstream` objects in place of both `ifstream` and `ofstream` objects (see the previous Programming Note). When using `fstream`'s `open()` method, two arguments are required: a file's external name and an explicit mode indication. Using an `fstream` object, the open request and check for an input file typically appear as follows:

```
    fstream inFile;

    inFile.open("external file name", ios::in);
    if (inFile.fail())
    {
      cout << "\nThe file was not successfully opened"
           << "\n Please check that the file currently
              exists."
           << endl;
      exit(1);
    }
```

Many times the conditional expression `inFile.fail()` is replaced by the equivalent expression `!inFile`. Although we will always use `ifstream` and `ofstream` objects, be prepared to encounter the styles that use `fstream` objects.

Exercises 10.1

1. Write individual declaration and open statements that link the following external data file names to their corresponding internal object names. Assume that all the files are text-based.

external name	object name	mode
coba.mem	memo	output
book.let	letter	output
coupons.bnd	coups	append
yield.bnd	yield	append
prices.dat	priFile	input
rates.dat	rates	input

2.   a. Write a set of two statements that first declares the following objects as `ifstream` objects and then opens them as text input files: `inData.txt`, `prices.txt`, `coupons.dat`, and `exper.dat`.

       b. Rewrite the two statements for Exercise 2a using a single statement.

3.   a. Write a set of two statements that first declares the following objects as `ofstream` objects and then opens them as text output files: `outDate.txt`, `rates.txt`, `distance.txt`, and `file2.txt`.

       b. Rewrite the two statements for Exercise 3a using a single statement.

4.   Enter and execute Program 10-1 on your computer.

5.   Enter and execute Program 10-2 on your computer.

6.   a. Enter and execute Program 10-3a on your computer.

       b. Add a `close()` method to Program 10-3a and then execute the program.

7.   a. Enter and execute Program 10-3b on your computer.

       b. Add a `close()` method to Program 10-3b and then execute the program.

8.   Using the reference manuals provided with your computer's operating system, determine:

       a. the maximum number of characters that can be used to name a file for storage by the computer system

       b. the maximum number of data files that can be open at the same time

9.   Would it be appropriate to call a saved C++ program a file? Why or why not?

10.   a. Write individual declaration and open statements to link the following external data file names to their corresponding internal object names. Use only `ifstream` and `ofstream` objects.

external name	object name	mode
coba.mem	memo	binary and output
coupons.bnd	coups	binary and append
prices.dat	priFile	binary and input

       b. Redo Exercise 10a using only `fstream` objects.

       c. Write `close` statements for each of the files opened in Exercise 10a.

10.2 READING AND WRITING CHARACTER-BASED FILES

Reading or writing character-based files involves almost the identical operations for reading input from a keyboard and writing data to a display screen. For writing to a file, the cout object is replaced by the ofstream object name declared in the program. For example, if outFile is declared as an object of type ofstream, the following output statements are valid:

```
outFile << 'a';
outFile << "Hello World!";
outFile << descrip << ' ' << price;
```

The file name in each of these statements, in place of cout, simply directs the output stream to a specific file instead of to the standard display device. Program 10-4 illustrates the use of the insertion operator, <<, to write a list of descriptions and prices to a file.

Program 10-4

```cpp
#include <iostream>
#include <fstream>
#include <cstdlib>    // needed for exit()
#include <string>
#include <iomanip>    // needed for formatting
using namespace std;

int main()
{
  string filename = "prices.dat";  // put the filename up front
  ofstream outFile;

  outFile.open(filename.c_str());

  if (outFile.fail())
  {
    cout << "The file was not successfully opened" << endl;
    exit(1);
  }
  // set the output file stream formats
  outFile << setiosflags(ios::fixed)
          << setiosflags(ios::showpoint)
          << setprecision(2);

  // send data to the file
  outFile << "Mats " << 39.95 << endl
          << "Bulbs " << 3.22 << endl
          << "Fuses " << 1.08 << endl;
```

(continued on next page)

```
    outFile.close();
    cout << "The file " << filename
         << " has been successfully written." << endl;

    return 0;
}
```

When Program 10-4 is executed, a file named `prices.dat` is created and saved by the computer as a text file (which is the default file type). The file is a sequential file consisting of the following data:

```
Mats 39.95
Bulbs 3.22
Fuses 1.08
```

PROGRAMMING NOTE

Formatting Text File Output Stream Data

Output file streams can be formatted in the same manner as the `cout` standard output stream. For example, if an output stream named `fileOut` has been declared, the statement

```
fileOut << setiosflags(ios::fixed)
        << setiosflags(ios::showpoint)
        << setprecision(2);
```

formats all data inserted in the `fileOut` stream in the same way that these parameterized manipulators work for the `cout` stream. The first manipulator parameter, `ios::fixed`, causes the stream to output all numbers as if they were floating-point values. The next parameter, `ios::showpoint`, tells the stream to always provide a decimal point. Thus, a value such as 1.0 will appear as 1.0, and not 1. Finally, the `setprecision` manipulator tells the stream to always display two decimal values after the decimal point. Thus, the number 1.0, for example, will appear as 1.00.

Instead of using manipulators, you can also use the stream methods `setf()` and `precision()`. For example, the previous formatting can also be accomplished using the code:

```
fileOut.setf(ios::fixed);
fileOut.setf(ios::showpoint);
fileOut.precision(2);
```

Which style you select is a matter of preference. In both cases the formats need only be specified once, and remain in effect for every number subsequently inserted into the file stream.

10

The actual storage of characters in the file depends on the character codes used by the computer. Although only 30 characters appear to be stored in the file—corresponding to the descriptions, blanks, and prices written to the file—the file actually contains 36 characters. The extra characters consist of the newline escape sequence at the end of each line that is created by the endl manipulator, which is created as a carriage return character (cr) and linefeed (lf). Assuming characters are stored using the ASCII code, the prices.dat file is physically stored as illustrated in Figure 10-2. For convenience, the character corresponding to each hexadecimal code is listed below the code. A code of 20 represents the blank character. Additionally, both C and C++ append the low-value hexadecimal byte 0x00 as the end-of-file (EOF) sentinel when the file is closed. This end-of-file sentinel is never counted as part of the file.

FIGURE 10-2
The prices.dat *File as Stored by the Computer*

```
4D 61 74 73 20 33 39 2E 39 35 0D 0A 42 75 6C 62 73 20

 M  a  t  s     3  9  .  9  5 cr 1f  B  u  l  b  s


33 2E 32 32 0D 0A 46 75 73 65 73 20 31 2E 30 38 0D 0A

 3  .  2  2 cr 1f  F  u  s  e  s     1  .  0  8 cr 1f
```

PROGRAMMING NOTE

The put() *Method*

All output streams have access to the fstream class's put() method, which permits character-by-character output to a stream. This method works in the same manner as the character insertion operator, <<. The syntax of this method call is:

```
ofstreamName.put(characterExpression);
```

where the *characterExpression* can be either a character variable or literal value. For example, the following code can be used to output an 'a' to the standard output stream:

```
cin.put('a');
```

In a similar manner, if outFile is an ofstream object file that has been opened, the following code outputs the character value in the character variable named keycode to this output:

```
char keycode;
  .
  .
outFile.put(keycode);
```

READING FROM A TEXT FILE

Reading data from a character-based file is almost identical to reading data from a standard keyboard, except that the `cin` object is replaced by the `ifstream` object declared in the program. For example, if `inFile` is declared as an object of type `ifstream` that is opened for input, the input statement

```
inFile >> descrip >> price;
```

will read the next two items in the file and store them in the variables `descrip` and `price`.

The file stream name in this statement, in place of `cin`, simply directs the input to come from the file stream rather than the standard input device stream. Other methods that can be used for stream input are listed in Table 10-3. Each of these methods must, of course, be preceded by a stream object name.

TABLE 10-3
`fstream` *Methods*

method name	description
`get()`	Returns the next character extracted from the input stream as an `int`
`get(charVar)`	Overloaded version of `get()` that extracts the next character from the input stream and assigns it to the specified character variable, `charVar`
`getline(strObj, termChar)`	Extracts characters from the specified input stream, `strObj`, until the terminating character, `termChar`, is encountered. Assigns the characters to the specified `string` class object, `strObj`
`peek()`	Returns the next character in the input stream without extracting it from the stream
`ignore(int n)`	Skips over the next *n* characters. If n is omitted, the default is to skip over the next single character

Program 10-5 illustrates how the `prices.dat` file that was created in Program 10-4 can be read. The program also illustrates one method of detecting the end-of-file (EOF) marker using the `good()` function (See Table 10-2). Because this function returns a Boolean `true` value before the EOF marker has been either read or passed over, it can be used to verify that the data just read is valid file data. Only after the EOF marker has been read or passed over does this function return a Boolean `false`. Thus, the notation `while (inFile.good())` used in Program 10-5 ensures that the data is from the file before the EOF has been read.

10

Program 10-5

```cpp
#include <iostream>
#include <fstream>
#include <cstdlib>                      // needed for exit()
#include <string>
using namespace std;

int main()
{
  string filename = "prices.dat";   // put the filename up front
  string descrip;
  double price;

  ifstream inFile;

  inFile.open(filename.c_str());

  if (inFile.fail())   // check for successful open
  {
    cout << "\nThe file was not successfully opened"
         << "\n Please check that the file currently exists."
         << endl;
    exit(1);
  }

  // read and display the file's contents
  inFile >> descrip >> price;
  while (inFile.good()) // check next character
  {
    cout   << descrip << ' ' << price << endl;
    inFile >> descrip >> price;
  }

  inFile.close();

  return 0;
}
```

The display produced by Program 10-5 is:

```
Mats 39.95
Bulbs 3.22
Fuses 1.08
```

Re-examine the expression inFile.good() used in the while statement. This expression is true as long as the EOF marker has not been read. Thus, as long as the item read was good, the loop continues to read the file. Within the loop, the items just read are first displayed and then a new string and a double-precision number are input to the program. When the EOF has been detected, the expression returns a Boolean value of `false` and the loop terminates. This ensures that data is read and displayed up to, but not including, the end-of-file marker.

PROGRAMMING NOTE

A Way to Clearly Identify a File's Name and Location

During program development, test files are usually placed in the same directory as the program. Therefore, a method call such as `inFile.open("exper.dat")` causes no problems to the operating system. In production systems, however, it is not uncommon for data files to reside in one directory while program files reside in another. For this reason it is always a good idea to include the full path name of any file opened.

For example, if the `exper.dat` file resides in the directory `C:\test\files`, the `open()` call should include the full path name, viz: `inFile.open("c:\\test\\files\\exper.dat")`. Then, no matter where the program is run from, the operating system will know where to locate the file. Note the use of double slashes, which are required.

Another important convention is to list all file names at the top of a program instead of embedding the names deep within the code. This can easily be accomplished by string variables to store each file name. For example, if the statements:

```
string filename = "c:\\test\\files\\exper.dat";
```

are placed at the top of a program file, the declaration statement clearly lists both the name of the desired file and its location. Then, if some other file is to be tested, all that is required is a simple one-line change at the top of the program.

Using a string variable for the file's name is also useful for the `fail()` method check. For example, consider the following code:

```
string filename;
ifstream inFile;

inFile.open(filename.c_str());

if (inFile.fail())
{
  cout << "\n The file named " << filename
       << " was not successfully opened"
       << "\n Please check that this file currently exists."
  exit(1);
}
```

In this code, the name of the file that failed to open is directly displayed within the error message without the name being embedded as a string value.

10

A direct replacement for the statement `while(inFile.good())` is the statement `while(!inFile.eof())`, which is read as "while the end of file *has not* been reached." This works because the `eof()` function returns a `true` only after the EOF marker has been read or passed over. In effect, the relational expression checks that the EOF *has not* been read; hence, the use of the NOT, `!`, operator.

Alternatively, another means of detecting the EOF is to use the fact that the extraction operation, `>>`, returns a Boolean value of `true` if data was extracted from a stream; otherwise, it returns a Boolean `false` value. Using this return value, the following code can be used within Program 10-5 to read the file:

```
// read and display the file's contents
  while (inFile >> descrip >> price) // check next character
    cout << descrip << ' ' << price << endl;
```

Although initially a bit cryptic, this code makes perfect sense when you understand that the expression being tested not only extracts data from the file, but returns a Boolean value to indicate if the extraction was successful or not.

Finally, in either the above `while` statement or in Program10-5, the expression `inFile >> descrip >> price` can be replaced by a `getline()` method (see Section 9.1). For file input, this method has the syntax

```
getline(fileObject, strObj, terminatingChar)
```

where *fileObject* is the name of the `ifstream` file, *strObj* is a `string` class object, and *terminatingChar* is an optional character constant or variable specifying the terminating character. If this optional third argument is omitted, the default terminating character is the newline (`'\n'`) character. Program 10-6 illustrates using `getline()` within the context of a complete program.

Program 10-6

```cpp
#include <iostream>
#include <fstream>
#include <cstdlib>   // needed for exit()
#include <string>
using namespace std;

int main()
{
  string filename = "prices.dat";  // put the filename up front
  string line;
  ifstream inFile;

  inFile.open(filename.c_str());
```

(continued on next page)

```
  if (inFile.fail())    // check for successful open
  {
    cout << "\nThe file was not successfully opened"
        << "\n Please check that the file currently exists."
        << endl;
    exit(1);
  }
  // read and display the file's contents
  while (getline(inFile,line))
    cout << line << endl;

  inFile.close();

  return 0;
}
```

Program 10-6 is really a line-by-line text-copying program, which reads a line of text from the file and then displays it on the terminal. The output of program 10-6, which is the same as program 10-5, is:

```
    Mats 39.95
    Bulbs 3.22
    Fuses 1.08
```

If it were necessary to obtain the description and price as individual variables, either Program 10-5 should be used or the string returned by `getline()` in Program 10-6 must be processed further to extract the individual data items (see Section 10.7 for parsing procedures).

STANDARD DEVICE FILES

The file stream objects we have used have all been logical file objects. A logical file object is a stream that connects a file of logically related data, such as a data file, to a program. In addition to logical file objects, C++ also supports physical file objects. A physical file object is a stream that connects to a hardware device, such as a keyboard, screen, or printer.

The actual physical device assigned to your program for data entry is formally called the **standard input file.** Usually this is the keyboard. When a `cin` object method call is encountered in a C++ program, it is a request to the operating system to go to this standard input file for the expected input. Similarly, when a `cout` object method call is encountered, the output is automatically displayed or "written to" a device that has been assigned as the **standard output file.** For most systems this is a computer screen, although it can be a printer.

PROGRAMMING NOTE

The get() and putback() Methods

All input streams have access to the fstream class's get() method, which permits character-by-character input from an input stream. This method works in a similar manner to character extraction, using the >> operator with two important differences: If a newline character, '\n', or a blank character, ' ', is encountered, these characters are read in the same manner as any other alphanumeric character. The syntax of this method call is:

```
istreamName.get(characterVariable);
```

For example, the following code can be used to read the next character from the standard input stream and store the character into the variable ch:

```
char ch;
cin.get(ch);
```

In a similar manner, if inFile is an ifstream object that has been opened to a file, the following code reads the next character in the stream and assigns it to the character keycode:

```
char keycode;
inFile.get(keycode);
```

In addition to the get() method, all input streams have a putback() method that can be used to put the last character read from an input stream back on the stream. This method has the syntax

```
ifstreamName.putback(characterExpression);
```

where characterExpression can be any character variable or character value.

The putback() method provides an output capability to an input stream. It should be noted that the putback character need not be the last character read; rather, it can be any character. All putback characters, however, have no effect on the data file but only on the open input stream. Thus, the data file characters remain unchanged, although the characters subsequently read from the input stream can change.

When a program is executed, the standard input stream cin is automatically connected to the standard input device. Similarly, the standard output stream cout is automatically connected to the standard output device. These two object streams are always available for programmer use, as are the standard error stream, cerr, and the standard log stream, clog. Both of these streams also connect to the terminal screen.

Other Devices

The keyboard, display, error-reporting, and logging streams are automatically connected to the stream objects named `cin`, `cout`, `cerr`, and `clog`, respectively, when the `iostream` header file is included in a program. Additionally, other devices can be used for input or output if the name assigned by the system is known. For example, most IBM or IBM-compatible personal computers assign the name `prn` to the printer connected to the computer. For these computers, a statement such as `outFile.open("prn")` connects the printer to the `ofstream` object named `outFile`. A subsequent statement such as `outFile << "Hello World!";` would then cause the string `Hello World!` to be output directly on the printer. Notice that as the name of an actual file, `prn` must be enclosed in double quotes in the `open()` function call.

Exercises 10.2

1. a. Enter and execute Program 10-5.

    b. Modify Program 10-5 to use the expression `!inFile.eof()` in place of the expression `inFile.good()`, and execute the program to see that it operates correctly.

2. a. Enter and execute Program 10-6.

    b. Modify Program 10-6 by replacing the identifier `cout` with `cerr`, and verify that the output for the standard error file stream is the screen.

    c. Modify Program 10-6 by replacing the identifier `cout` with `clog`, and verify that the output for the standard log stream is the screen.

3. a. Write a C++ program that accepts lines of text from the keyboard and writes each line to a file named `text.dat` until an empty line is entered. An empty line is a line with no text that is created by pressing the Enter (or Return) key.

    b. Modify Program 10-6 to read and display the data stored in the `text.dat` file created in Exercise 3a.

4. Determine the operating system command provided by your computer to display the contents of a saved file. Compare its operation with the program developed for Exercise 3a. (*Hint*: Typically the operating system command is called list, type, or cat.)

5. a. Create a text file named `employee.dat` containing the following data:

Anthony A	10031	7.82	12/18/62
Burrows W	10067	9.14	6/9/63
Fain B	10083	8.79	5/18/59
Janney P	10095	10.57	9/28/62
Smith G	10105	8.50	12/20/61

    b. Write a C++ program to read the `employee.dat` file created in Exercise 5a and produce a copy of the file named `employee.bak`.

    c. Modify the program written in Exercise 5b to accept the names of the original and duplicate files as user input.

d. The program written for Exercise 5c always copies data from an original file to a duplicate file. What is a better method of accepting the original and duplicate file names, other than prompting the user for them each time the program is executed?

6. **a.** Write a C++ program that opens a file and displays the contents of the file with associated line numbers. That is, the program should print the number 1 before displaying the first line, then print the number 2 before displaying the second line, and so on for each line in the file.
    b. Modify the program written in Exercise 6a to list the contents of the file on the printer assigned to your computer.

7. **a.** Create a text file containing the following data (without the headings):

names	Social Security number	hourly rate	hours worked
B Caldwell	555-88-4182	7.32	37
D Memcheck	555-77-2147	8.32	40
R Potter	555-77-9826	6.54	40
W Rosen	555-99-4263	9.80	35

    b. Write a C++ program that reads the data file created in Exercise 7a and computes and displays a payroll schedule. The output should list the Social Security number, name, and gross pay for each individual, where gross pay is calculated as *Hourly Rate x Hours Worked.*

8. **a.** Create a text file containing the following car numbers, number of miles driven, and number of gallons of gas used in each car (do not include the headings):

car number	miles driven	gallons used
54	250	19
62	525	38
71	123	6
85	1,322	86
97	235	14

    b. Write a C++ program that reads the data in the file created in Exercise 8a and displays the car number, miles driven, gallons used, and the miles per gallon for each car. The output should also contain the total miles driven, total gallons used, and average miles per gallon for all the cars. These totals should be displayed at the end of the output report.

9. **a.** Create a text file with the following data (without the headings):

part number	initial amount	quantity sold	minimum amount
QA310	95	47	50
CM145	320	162	200
MS514	34	20	25
EN212	163	150	160

b. Write a C++ program to create an inventory report based on the data in the file created in Exercise 9a. The display should consist of the part number, current balance, and the amount that is necessary to bring the inventory to the minimum level.

10. a. Create a text file containing the following data (without the headings):

name	rate	hours
Callaway,G.	6.00	40
Hanson,P.	5.00	48
Lasard,D.	6.50	35
Stillman,W.	8.00	50

b. Write a C++ program that uses the information contained in the file created in Exercise 10a to produce the following pay report for each employee:

```
Name     Pay Rate    Hours    Regular Pay    Overtime Pay    Gross Pay
```

Regular pay is to be computed as any hours worked up to and including 40 hours times the pay rate. Overtime pay is to be computed as any hours worked above 40 hours times a pay rate of 1.5 times the regular rate, and the gross pay is the sum of regular and overtime pay. At the end of the report, the program should display the totals of the regular, overtime, and gross pay columns.

11. a. Store the following data in a file:

$$5\ 96\ 87\ 78\ 93\ 21\ 4\ 92\ 82\ 85\ 87\ 6\ 72\ 69\ 85\ 75\ 81\ 73$$

b. Write a C++ program to calculate and display the average of each group of numbers in the file created in Exercise 11a. The data is arranged in the file so that each group of numbers is preceded by the number of data items in the group. Thus, the first number in the file, 5, indicates that the next five numbers should be grouped together. The number 4 indicates that the following four numbers are a group, and the 6 indicates that the last six numbers are a group. (*Hint:* Use a nested loop. The outer loop should terminate when the end-of-file has been encountered.)

10.3 EXCEPTIONS AND FILE CHECKING[1]

Error detection and processing with exception handling is used extensively within C++ programs that use one or more files. For example, if a user deletes or renames a file using an operating system command, this action will cause a C++ program to fail when an `open()` function call attempts to open the file under its original name.

---

[1]This section may be omitted on first reading without loss of subject continuity.

Recall from Section 7.6 that the code for general exception handling looks like this:

```
try
{
  // one or more statements,
  // at least one of which should
  // throw an exception
}
catch(exceptionDataType parameterName)
{
  // one or more statements
}
```

In this code, the `try` block statements are executed. If no error occurs, the `catch` block statements are omitted and processing continues with the statement following the `catch` block. However, if any statement within the `try` block throws an exception, the `catch` block whose exception data type matches the exception is executed. If no `catch` block is defined for a `try` block, a compiler error occurs. If no `catch` block exists that catches a thrown data type, a program crash occurs only if the exception is thrown. Most times, but not always, the `catch` block displays an error message and terminates processing with a call to the `exit()` function. Program 10-7 illustrates the statements required to open a file in read mode that includes exception handling.

Program 10-7

```
#include <iostream>
#include <fstream>
#include <cstdlib>    // needed for exit()
#include <string>
using namespace std;

int main()
{
  string filename = "prices.dat";   // put the filename up front
  string descrip;
  double price;

  ifstream inFile;

  try  // this block tries to open the file, read, and display the file's data
  {
    inFile.open(filename.c_str());

    if (inFile.fail()) throw filename; // this is the exception being checked

    // read and display the file's contents
```

(continued on next page)

```
   inFile >> descrip >> price;
    while (inFile.good()) // check next character
  {
    cout << descrip << ' ' << price << endl;
    inFile >> descrip >> price;
  }
  inFile.close();

  return 0;
}
catch (string e)
{
   cout << "\nThe file "<< e << " was not successfully opened"
        << "\n Please check that the file currently exists."
        << endl;
    exit(1);
  }
}
```

PROGRAMMING NOTE

Checking That a File Was Opened Successfully

Using exception handling, the most common method for checking that the operating system successfully located the designated file is the one coded in Program 10-7, the key coding points of which are repeated here for convenience:

```
    try  // this block tries to open the file, read, and
        // display the file's data
  {
    // open the file, throwing an exception if the open
    // fails
    // perform all required file processing
    // close the file
  }
  catch (string e)
  {
     cout << "\nThe file "<< e << " was not successfully opened"
          << "\n Please check that the file currently exists."
          << endl;
     exit(1);
  }
```

The exception message produced by Program 10-7 when the `prices.dat` file was not found is:

```
The file prices.dat was not successfully opened.
Please check that the file currently exists.
```

Although the exception handling code in Program 10-7 can be used to check for a successful file open for both input and output, a more rigorous check is usually required for output files. This is because, on output, the file is almost guaranteed to be found. If it exists, the file will be found, and if it does not exist, the operating system will create it (unless append mode is specified and the file already exists, or the operating system cannot find the indicated folder). Knowing that the file has been successfully found and opened, however, is insufficient for output purposes when an existing output file *must not* be overwritten. For these cases, the file can first be opened for input, and then, if the file is found, a further check can be made to ensure that the user explicitly provides approval for overwriting it. How this is accomplished is illustrated in highlighted code within Program 10-8.

Program 10-8

```cpp
#include <iostream>
#include <fstream>
#include <cstdlib>    // needed for exit()
#include <string>
#include <iomanip>    // needed for formatting
using namespace std;

int main()
{
  char response;
  string filename = "prices.dat";  // put the filename up front
  ifstream inFile;
  ofstream outFile;

  try // open a basic input stream simply to check if the file exists
  {
    inFile.open(filename.c_str());
    if (inFile.fail()) throw 1; // this means the file doesn't exist
      // only get here if the file was found;
      // otherwise the catch block takes control
    cout << "A file by the name " << filename << " currently exists.\n"
         << "Do you want to overwrite it with the new data (y or n): ";
    cin >> response;
    if (tolower(response) == 'n')
    {
```

(continued on next page)

```
      inFile.close();
      cout << "The existing file has not been overwritten." << endl;
      exit(1);
   }
}
catch(int e) {};   // a do-nothing block that permits
                   // processing to continue
try
{
    // open the file in write mode and continue with file writes
    outFile.open(filename.c_str());
    if (outFile.fail()) throw filename;
    // set the output file stream formats
    outFile << setiosflags(ios::fixed)
            << setiosflags(ios::showpoint)
            << setprecision(2);
    // write the data to the file
    outFile << "Mats " << 39.95 << endl
            << "Bulbs "  << 3.22 << endl
            << "Fuses " << 1.08 << endl;
    outFile.close();
    cout << "The file " << filename
         << " has been successfully written." << endl;

    return 0;
}
catch(string e)
{
    cout << "The file " << filename
         << " was not opened for output and has not been written."
         << endl;
}
}
```

Notice in Program 10-8 that the try blocks are separate. Because a catch block is affiliated with the closest previous try block, there is no ambiguity about unmatched try and catch blocks.

OPENING MULTIPLE FILES

As an example of applying exception handling to the opening of two files at the same time, assume that we wish to read the data from a character-based file named info.txt, one character at a time, and write this data to a file named backup.txt. Essentially, this application is a file-copy program that reads the data from one file in a character-by-character manner and writes them to a second file.

For purposes of illustration, assume that the characters stored in the input file are as shown in Figure 10-3.

FIGURE 10-3
The Data Stored in info.txt

```
Now is the time for all good people
   to come to the aid of their party.
Please call (555) 888-6666 for
   further information.
```

Figure 10-4 illustrates the structure of the streams that are necessary for producing our file copy. For this figure, an input stream object referenced by the variable inFile will be used to read data from the info.txt file, and an output stream object referenced by the variable outFile will be used to write data to the backup.txt file.

FIGURE 10-4
The File Copy Stream Structure

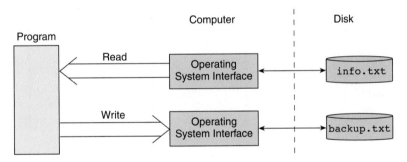

Now consider Program 10-9, which creates the backup.txt file as an exact duplicate of the info.txt file using the procedure illustrated in Figure 10-4.

Program 10-9

```cpp
#include <iostream>
#include <fstream>
#include <cstdlib>    // needed for exit()
#include <string>
using namespace std;

int main()
{
   string fileOne = "info.txt";   // put the filename up front
   string fileTwo = "info.bak";
```

(continued on next page)

```cpp
   char ch;
   ifstream inFile;
   ofstream outFile;

   try   //this block tries to open the input file
   {
      // open a basic input stream
      inFile.open(fileOne.c_str());
         if (inFile.fail()) throw fileOne;
   } // end of outer try block
   catch (string in)   // catch for outer try block
   {
      cout << "The input file " << in
           << " was not successfully opened." << endl
           << " No backup was made." << endl;
      exit(1);
   }

   try   // this block tries to open the output file and
   {     // perform all file processing

      outFile.open(fileTwo.c_str());
      if (outFile.fail())throw fileTwo;
      while ((ch = inFile.get())!= EOF)
         outFile.put(ch);;

      inFile.close();
      outFile.close();
   }
   catch (string out)   // catch for inner try block
   {
      cout << "The backup file " << out
           << " was not successfully opened." << endl;
      exit(1);
   }

   cout << "A successful backup of " << fileOne
        << " named " << fileTwo << " was successfully made." << endl;

   return 0;
}
```

PROGRAMMING NOTE

Nesting try Blocks

When more than one file stream is involved, opening each file stream in its own try block permits exact isolation and identification of which file caused an exception, should one occur. The try blocks can be nested. For example, consider Program 10-9, which is rewritten here using nested try blocks. Notice that in this case the catch block for the inner try block must also be nested in the same block scope as its try block.

```cpp
#include <iostream>
#include <fstream>
#include <cstdlib>    // needed for exit()
#include <string>
using namespace std;

int main()
{
  string fileOne = "prices.dat";  // put the filename up front
  string fileTwo = "C:\\feber\\beeber.bak";
  char c;
  ifstream inFile;
  ofstream outFile;

  try  //this block tries to open the input file
  {
      // open a basic input stream
    inFile.open(fileOne.c_str());
      if (inFile.fail()) throw fileOne;
    try  // this block tries to open the output file and
    {    // perform all file processing

        // open a basic output stream
      outFile.open(fileTwo.c_str());
      if (outFile.fail())throw fileTwo;
      while ((ch = inFile.get()) != EOF)
        outFile.put(c);;

      inFile.close();
      outFile.close();
    }  // end of inner try block
    catch (string out)  // catch for inner try block
    {
      cout << "The backup file " << out
           << " was not successfully opened." << endl;
      exit(1);
    }
  }  // end of outer try block
```

(continued on next page)

PROGRAMMING NOTE

Nesting `try` Blocks (Continued from page 663)

```
catch (string in)   // catch for outer try block
{
  cout << "The input file " << in
       << " was not successfully opened." << endl
       << " No backup was made." << endl;
  exit(1);
}

cout << "A successful backup of " << fileOne
     << " named " << fileTwo << "was successfully made."
     << endl;

return 0;
}
```

The important point to notice in this program is the nesting of the `try` blocks. If the two `try` blocks were not nested and the input stream declaration `if-stream inFile;` was placed in the first block, it could not be used in the second `try` block without producing a compiler error. The reason is that all variables declared in a block of code, which is defined by an opening and closing brace pair, are local to the block in which they are declared.

For simplicity, Program 10-9 attempts to open both the input and output files within separate and non-nested `try` blocks. More generally, the second file would be opened in a nested inner `try` block so that the attempt to open this second file would not be made if the opening of the first file threw an exception. (The Programming Note on nesting `try` blocks explains how this is accomplished.)

In reviewing Program 10-9, pay particular attention to the statement:

```
while((ch = inFile.get())!= EOF)
```

This statement continually reads a value from the input stream until the EOF value is detected. As long as the returned value does not equal the EOF value, the value is written to the output object stream. The parentheses surrounding the expression `(ch = inFile.get())` are necessary to ensure that a value is first read and assigned to the variable `ch` before the retrieved value is compared to the EOF value. In their absence, the complete expression would be `ch = inFile.get() != EOF`. Due to the precedence of operations, the relational expression `inFile.get() != EOF` would be executed first. Because this is a relational expression, its result is either a Boolean `true` or `false` value based on the data retrieved by the `get()` method. Attempting to assign this Boolean result to the character variable `ch` is an invalid conversion across an assignment operator.

Exercises 10.3

1. List two conditions that will cause a fail condition when a file is opened for input.

2. List two conditions that will cause a fail condition when a file is opened for output.

3. If a file that exists is opened for output in write mode, what happens to the data currently in the file?

4. Modify Program 10-7 to use an identifier of your choice, in place of the letter e, for the catch block's exception parameter name.

5. Enter and execute Program 10-8.

6. Determine why the two try blocks in Program 10-8, which are not nested, cause no problems in either compilation or execution. (*Hint:* Place the declaration for the filename within the first try block and compile the program.)

7. a. If the nested try blocks in the Programming Note on nested try blocks are separated into non-nested blocks, the program will not compile. Determine why this is so.
   b. What additional changes would have to be made to the program in Exercise 7a that would allow it to be written with non-nested blocks? (*Hint:* See Exercise 6.)

8. Enter the data for the info.txt file in Figure 10-3 or obtain it from this text's Web site (see the Preface of this book for the URL). Then enter and execute Program 10-9 and verify that the backup file was written.

9. Modify Program 10-9 to use a getline() method in place of the get() method currently in the program.

10.4 RANDOM FILE ACCESS

The term **file access** refers to the process of retrieving data from a file. There are two types of file access: sequential access and random access. To understand file access types, you first need to understand some concepts related to how data is organized within a file.

The term **file organization** refers to the way data is stored in a file. The files we have used, and will continue to use, all have a **sequential organization**. This means that the characters within the file are stored in a sequential manner, one after another.

In addition to being sequentially organized, we have also read each open file in a sequential manner. That is, we have accessed each character sequentially, one after another. This is referred to as sequential access. The fact that the characters in the file are stored sequentially, however, does not force us to access them sequentially. In fact, we can skip over characters and read a sequentially organized file in a non-sequential manner.

In **random access**, any character in the opened file can be read directly, without first having to sequentially read all the characters stored ahead of it. To provide random access to files, each ifstream object automatically creates a file position marker. This marker is a long integer that represents an offset from the beginning of each file and keeps track of where the next character is to be read from or written to. The functions that are used to access and change the file position marker are listed in

Table 10-4. The suffixes g and p in these function names denote get and put, respectively, where get refers to an input (get from) file and put refers to an output (put to) file.

TABLE 10-4
File Position Marker Functions

name	description
seekg(offset, mode)	For input files, move to the offset position as indicated by the mode.
seekp(offset, mode)	For output files, move to the offset position as indicated by the mode.
tellg(void)	For input files, return the current value of the file position marker.
tellp(void)	For output files, return the current value of the file position marker.

The seek() functions allow the programmer to move to any position in the file. To understand this method, you must first clearly understand how data is referenced in the file using the file position marker.

Each character in a data file is located by its position in the file. The first character in the file is located at position 0, the next character at position 1, and so on. A character's position is also referred to as its offset from the start of the file. Thus, the first character has a 0 offset, the second character has an offset of 1, and so on for each character in the file.

The seek() functions require two arguments: the offset, as a long integer, into the file; and where the offset is to be calculated from, as determined by the mode. The three possible alternatives for the mode are ios::beg, ios::cur, and ios::end, which denote the beginning, current position, and the end of the file, respectively. Thus, a mode of ios::beg means the offset is the true offset from the start of the file. A mode of ios::cur means that the offset is relative to the current position in the file, and an ios::end mode means the offset is relative to the end of the file. A positive offset means move forward in the file and a negative offset means move backward. Examples of seek() function calls are shown below. In these examples, assume that inFile has been opened as an input file and outFile as an output file. Notice in these examples that the offset passed to seekg() and seekp() must be a long integer.

```
inFile.seekg(4L,ios::beg);     // go to the fifth character in the input file
outFile.seekp(4L,ios::beg);    // go to the fifth character in the output file
inFile.seekg(4L,ios::cur);     // move ahead five characters in the input file
outFile.seekp(4L,ios::cur);    // move ahead five characters in the output file
inFile.seekg(-4L,ios::cur);    // move back five characters in the input file
outFile.seekp(-4L,ios::cur);   // move back five characters in the output file
inFile.seekg(0L,ios::beg);     // go to start of the input file
outFile.seekp(0L,ios::beg);    // go to start of the output file
inFile.seekg(0L,ios::end);     // go to end of the input file
outFile.seekp(0L,ios::end);    // go to end of the output file
inFile.seekg(-10L,ios::end);   // go to 10 characters before the input file's end
outFile.seekp(-10L,ios::end);  // go to 10 characters before the output file's end
```

10

As opposed to the `seek()` functions that move the file position marker, the `tell()` functions simply return the offset value of the file position marker. For example, if 10 characters have already been read from an input file named `inFile`, the function call

```
inFile.tellg();
```

returns the long integer 10. This means that the next character to be read is offset 10 byte positions from the start of the file, and is the eleventh character in the file.

Program 10-10 illustrates the use of `seekg()` and `tellg()` to read a file in reverse order, from last character to first. As each character is read it is also displayed.

Program 10-10

```cpp
#include <iostream>
#include <fstream>
#include <string>
#include <cstdlib>
using namespace std;

int main()
{
  string filename = "test.dat";
  char ch;
  long offset, last;

  ifstream inFile(filename.c_str());

  if (inFile.fail())    // check for successful open
  {
    cout << "\nThe file was not successfully opened"
      << "\n Please check that the file currently exists"
      << endl;
    exit(1);
  }

  inFile.seekg(0L,ios::end);    // move to the end of the file
  last = inFile.tellg();        // save the offset of the last character

  for(offset = 1L; offset <= last; offset++)
  {
    inFile.seekg(-offset, ios::end);
    ch = inFile.get();
    cout << ch << " : ";
  }
}
```

(continued on next page)

```
    inFile.close();

    cout << endl;

    return 0;
}
```

Assuming the file test.dat contains the following data:

```
    The grade was 92.5
```

the output of Program 10-10 is:

```
5 : . : 2 : 9 :    : s : a : w :    : e : d : a : r : g :    : e : h : T :
```

Program 10-10 initially goes to the last character in the file. The offset of this character, which is the end-of-file character, is saved in the variable last. Since tellg() returns a long integer, last has been declared as a long integer.

Starting from the end of the file, seekg() is used to position the next character to be read, referenced from the end of the file. As each character is read, the character is displayed and the offset adjusted in order to access the next character. It should be noted that the first offset used is -1, which represents the character immediately preceding the EOF marker.

Exercises 10.4

1. a. Create a file named test.dat that contains the data in the test.dat file used in Program 10-10. You can do this by using a text editor or by copying the file test.dat on the data disk provided with this book.

    b. Enter and execute Program 10-10 on your computer.

2. Rewrite Program 10-10 so that the origin for the seekg() function used in the for loop is the start of the file rather than the end.

3. Modify Program 10-10 to display an error message if seekg() attempts to reference a position beyond the end of the file.

4. Write a program that will read and display every second character in a file named test.dat.

5. Using the seek() and tell() functions, write a function named fileChars() that returns the total number of characters in a file.

6. a. Write a function named readBytes() that reads and displays n characters starting from any position in a file. The function should accept three arguments: a file object name, the offset of the first character to be read, and the number of characters to be read. (*Note:* The prototype for readBytes() should be void readBytes(fstream&, long, int.))

b. Modify the `readBytes()` function written in Exercise 6a to store the characters read into a string or an array. The function should accept the address of the storage area as a fourth argument.

10.5   FILE STREAMS AS FUNCTION ARGUMENTS

A file stream object can be used as a function argument. The only requirement is that the function's formal parameter be a reference (see Section 7.4) to the appropriate stream, either as `ifstream&` or `ofstream&`. For example, in Program 10-11 an `ofstream` object named `outFile` is opened in `main()` and this stream object is passed to the function `inOut()`. Notice that the function prototype and header line for `inOut()` both declare the formal parameter as a reference to an `ostream` object type. The `inOut()` function is then used to write five lines of user-entered text to the file.

Program 10-11

```cpp
#include <iostream>
#include <fstream>
#include <cstdlib>
#include <string>
using namespace std;

int main()
{
  string fname = "list.dat";   // here is the file we are working with

  void inOut(ofstream&);       // function prototype

  ofstream outFile;

  outFile.open(fname.c_str());
  if (outFile.fail())          // check for a successful open
  {
    cout << "\nThe output file " << fname << " was not successfully opened"
         << endl;
    exit(1);
  }

  inOut(outFile);   // call the function

  return 0;
}

void inOut(ofstream& fileOut)
{
```

(continued on next page)

```
  const int NUMLINES = 5;   // number of lines of text
  string line;
  int count;

  cout << "Please enter five lines of text:" << endl;
  for (count = 0; count < NUMLINES; count++)
  {
    getline(cin,line);
    fileOut << line << endl;
  }

  cout << "\nThe file has been successfully written." << endl;
  return;
}
```

Within `main()` the file is an `ostream` object named `outFile`. This object is passed to the `inOut()` function and is accepted as the formal parameter named `fileOut`, which is declared to be a reference to an `ostream` object type. The function `inOut()` then uses its reference parameter `outFile` as an output file stream name in the same manner as `main()` would use the `fileOut` stream object. Notice also that Program 10-11 uses the `getline()` method introduced in Section 10.2 (see Table 10-3).

In Program 10-12, we have expanded on Program 10-11 by adding a `getOpen()` function to perform the open. Notice that `getOpen()`, like `inOut()`, accepts a reference argument to an `ofstream` object. After the `getOpen()` function completes execution, this reference is passed to `inOut()`, as it was in Program 10-11. Although you might be tempted to write `getOpen()` to return a reference to an `ofstream`, this will not work because it ultimately results in an attempt to assign a returned reference to an existing one.

Program 10-12

```
#include <iostream>
#include <fstream>
#include <cstdlib>
#include <string>
using namespace std;

int main()
{
  int getOpen(ofstream&);   // pass a reference to an fstream
  void inOut(ofstream&);    // pass a reference to an fstream

  ofstream outFile;         // filename is an fstream object
```

(continued on next page)

```
    getOpen(outFile);   // open the file
    inOut(outFile);     // write to it

    return 0;
}

int getOpen(ofstream& fileOut)
{
    string name;

    cout << "\nEnter a file name: ";
    getline(cin,name);

    fileOut.open(name.c_str());     // open the file

    if (fileOut.fail())             // check for successful open
    {
        cout << "Cannot open the file" << endl;
        exit(1);
    }
    else
        return 1;
}

void inOut(ofstream& fileOut)
{
    const int NUMLINES = 5;   // number of lines
    int count;
    string line;

    cout << "Please enter five lines of text:" << endl;
    for (count = 0; count < NUMLINES; ++count)
    {
        getline(cin,line);
        fileOut << line << endl;
    }
    cout << "\nThe file has been successfully written.";
    return;
}
```

Program 10-12 is simply a modified version of Program 10-11 that now allows the user to enter a file name from the standard input device and then opens the ofstream connection to the external file. If the name of an existing data file is entered, the file will be destroyed when it is opened for output. A useful trick that you may employ to prevent this type of mishap is to open the entered file using an input file stream. If the file exists, the fail() method will indicate a successful open (i.e., the open does not fail), which indicates that the file is available for input. This can be used to alert the user that a file with the entered name currently exists in the system, and to request confirmation that the data in the file can be destroyed and the file opened for output. Before the file is reopened for output, the input file stream should be closed. The implementation of this algorithm is left as an exercise.

Exercises 10.5

1. A function named `pFile()` is to receive a file name as a reference to an `ifstream` object. What declarations are required to pass a file name to `pFile()`?

2. Write a function named `fcheck()` that checks whether a file exists. The function should accept an `ifstream` object as a formal reference parameter. If the file exists, the function should return a value of 1; otherwise the function should return a value of zero.

3. Assume that a data file consisting of a group of individual lines has been created. Write a function named `printLine()` that will read and display any desired line of the file. For example, the function call `printLine(fstream& fName,5);` should display the fifth line of the passed object stream.

4. Rewrite the function `getOpen()` used in Program 10-12 to incorporate the file-checking procedures described in this section. Specifically, if the entered file name exists, an appropriate message should be displayed. The user should then be presented with the option of entering a new file name or allowing the program to overwrite the existing file. Use the function written for Exercise 2 in your program.

10.6 PROGRAM DESIGN AND DEVELOPMENT: CREATING AND USING A HOLIDAY DATE TABLE

A common real-world programming requirement is creating and maintaining a small file of constants, reading and storing these constants into a list, and then providing methods for checking data against the constants in the list. For example, a scientific program might require a set of temperatures at which various elements freeze or change state, or an engineering program might require a set of material densities for various grades of steel and iron ore. In financial and scheduling programs, this requirement takes the form of reading in a set of holiday dates and then checking a date against the data in the table. This determination is important in many applications to ensure that contractual settlement dates and delivery dates are not scheduled on a holiday.

Our objective in this section is to create a `Date` class method that determines if a given date is a holiday, using concepts that are equally applicable to any program that needs to check data against a list of constants, such as temperatures, densities, or other parameters. Specifically, two methods are developed that complete the `Date` class that was constructed in Section 5.6. The first method constructs a list of holidays, which is referred to as a holiday table, and consists of legal holiday dates that have previously been stored in a file. The second method compares any given `Date` object to the dates in the table and determines if there is a match.

The creation of a list of holidays requires reading data from a file that contains the necessary dates. Because these dates change each year, a separate maintenance class is created to maintain the holiday dates. Typically, toward the latter part of December, a method would automatically send a reminder to the user to update the holiday dates.

In this program, we will use the North American holidays listed in Table 10-5 for the dates that our Date class will store in its holiday table.

TABLE 10-5
North American Government Holidays

holiday	date
New Year's Day	1/1/2005
Martin Luther King Jr.'s Birthday	1/17/2005
Presidents' Day	2/21/2005
Good Friday	4/25/2005
Easter	4/27/2005
Cinco de Mayo	5/5/2005
Victoria Day	5/23/2005
Memorial Day	5/30/2005
Canada Day	7/1/2005
Independence Day	7/4/2005
Labor Day	9/5/2005
Columbus Day	10/10/2005
Canadian Thanksgiving	10/10/2005
United States Thanksgiving	11/24/2005
Christmas	12/25/2005

The holiday dates listed in Table 10-5 have been stored in a file named Holidays.txt. Such a file can be created using either a text editor, copying the file from the Web site provided for this text, or writing a program that accepts the dates, as strings, from a user and writes the dates to a file, one line per date. Table 10-6 illustrates the 15 holiday dates, one per line, as they are stored in the Holidays.txt file.

TABLE 10-6
The Holidays.txt File

```
1/1/2005
1/17/2005
2/21/2005
4/25/2005
4/27/2005
```

(continued on next page)

```
5/5/2005
5/23/2005
5/30/2005
7/1/2005
7/4/2005
9/5/2005
10/10/2005
10/10/2005
11/24/2005
12/25/2005
```

Our first task will be to develop a method, which we will name getHolidays(), that reads the dates in the Holidays.txt file and stores them in a table. We then develop a method named isHoliday() to compare a date to each entry in the holiday table. If the date matches an entry in the table, the method will return a Boolean value of true, which indicates that the date corresponds to a holiday; otherwise, the method will return a Boolean value of false, which indicates that the date is not a holiday. The getHolidays() method is constructed first.

THE getHolidays() METHOD

The purpose of the getHolidays() method is to read the Holidays.txt file and construct a table of dates. For our purposes, we will construct the table as an STL vector, which was presented in detail in Section 8.6. This is the container of choice for this application because it automatically expands to fit the number of objects being stored, which can change over time as new holidays are declared, and vary for each country.[2] Thus, the fact that the United States has a different number of official holidays than Canada or Mexico does not matter. We simply let the vector expand, if necessary, as a date is read from the Holidays.txt file, and when the last date has been stored, we trim the list to the exact number of dates, using the size() method.

For convenience, we will read each line in the file as a string, and then parse the string to extract its month, day, and year values. Once these individual values have been extracted, they can be used as arguments in the Date class's setDate() method to modify an existing Date object, which is then appended to the vector. We will name this vector hTable. Because only one instance of hTable is needed, which must be available to all Date objects, it will be declared as a static variable in the Date class's data declaration section using the following statement.

---

[2]An alternative is to use an array. The disadvantage of using arrays is that, unless the number of dates is stored at the start of the file or a larger-than-necessary array is declared, two file reads are required. The first determines the number of dates in the file. An array of Dates can then be declared using this number, and the file read a second time, at which point each date is stored in the array.

```
static vector<Date> hTable;  // this is a declaration
```

Assuming that `hTable` has been correctly declared and created, the pseudocode describing the algorithm for reading the `Holidays` file is:

getHolidays() **Algorithm**
Instantiate a Date **object**
Open the Holidays.txt **file, checking that a successful open occurred**
While there are Dates **in the file**
    Read a line as a string value
    Parse the string object into a month, day, and year value (use the / as a delimiter)
    Assign the parsed month, day, and year values to the instantiated Date **object**
    Add the Date **object to the** hTable **vector**
Close the file

Following is the C++ code that corresponds to this pseudocode:

```cpp
void Date::getHolidays()
{
  string filename = "c:\\cpcode\\Holidays.txt"; // <-- change this to the path
  ifstream inFile;      // name where the Holiday.txt
  string line;          // file is stored on your computer

  int month, day, year, firstdel, secdel;
  Date a;  // create a single Date object

  inFile.open(filename.c_str());  // open the file
  // check that the connection was successfully opened
  if (inFile.fail())
  {
    cout << "\nThe file was not successfully opened"
         << "\n Please check that the file currently exists."
         << endl;
    exit(1);
  }

  // read and store each Date
  while (getline(inFile,line))
  {
    cout << line << endl;
    // parse the string
    firstdel = line.find("/");
    secdel = line.find("/",firstdel + 1);
```

(continued on next page)

```
    month = atoi(line.substr(0,firstdel).c_str());
    day = atoi(line.substr(firstdel + 1, secdel - (firstdel + 1)).c_str());
    year = atoi(line.substr(secdel + 1, line.length() - (secdel + 1)).c_str());
    a.setDate(month, day, year);      // convert to a Date object
    hTable.put_back(a);               // add the holiday into the vector
  }
  inFile.close();


}
```

The coding of getHolidays() is rather straightforward once its underlying algorithm is understood. The first important point to notice is that the separation of a date into a month, day, and year depends on the stored dates within the Holidays.txt file being written in the form month/day/year, which uses a forward slash to delimit the individual values. Thus, in parsing these values from the input date, the slash, /, is designated as the delimiter. Specifically, this information is used in determining the position of the first and second slashes (required as a string value for the find() method) within the statements

```
        firstdel = line.find("/");
        secdel = line.find("/",firstdel + 1);
```

Because the first find() method does not include a second argument, the method returns the first occurrence of the slash. The second argument in the second statement starts the search for the next slash at one position beyond where the first slash was found. Thus, for a date such as 12/25/2005 the value of firstdel is 3 and the value of secdel is 6.

The next point to note is that the getHolidays() method must be declared as static within the Date class's declaration section. This means that the method is a general-purpose one that is not preceded by a specific object's name when it is invoked. (Formally, the static designation means that the method *does not* use an implied object.) This designation is appropriate because getHolidays() will be called only once, independent of any specific object, to populate the holiday vector with the dates in the Holidays.txt file.

VERIFYING THE getHolidays() METHOD

Once the getHolidays() method has been included within the Date class, we can test its operation. To perform this testing we can add the following code at the end of the method, after the inFile.close() statement:

```
cout << "The Holiday file was successfully read and stored." << endl;
cout << "\nThe vector initially has a size of "
     << hTable.size() << ",\n and contains the elements:\n";
     for (int i = 0; i < hTable.size(); i++)
       hTable[i].showDate();
```

Assuming that this code has been placed in the `getHolidays()` method, the method has been included in the `Date` class code, the `Date` class has been recompiled, and the `Holidays.txt` file listed in Table 10-6 has been created, Program 10-13 can be used to provide a quick verification of the `getHolidays()` performance.

Program 10-13

```
#include <c:\\cpcode\\Date.cpp>   // change this to be the path where
int main()                        // Date.cpp is stored on your computer
{
  Date::getHolidays();

  return 0;
}
```

The output produced by Program 10-13 is:

```
The Holiday file was successfully read and stored.

The vector initially has a size of 15,
 and contains the elements:

01/01/05
01/17/05
02/21/05
04/25/05
04/27/05
05/05/05
05/23/05
05/30/05
07/01/05
07/04/05
09/05/05
10/10/05
10/10/05
11/24/05
12/25/05
```

As indicated by this output, the file's data have been successfully read, parsed, and stored in the `hTable` vector by `getHolidays()`.

THE isHoliday() METHOD

The requirement for this method is that it accepts a Date object as an implied parameter and checks it against the dates stored in the class's static holiday vector. If a matching date is found, the method should return a Boolean value of true; otherwise, it should return a Boolean value of false. Before the check is made, however, the method must first determine if the table is empty; if it is, the getHolidays() method should be called to create a valid table. The algorithm describing this process, in pseudocode, is

> **If the holiday table is empty,**
> > **Call** getHolidays()
>
> **For all** Holidays **in the table**
> > **Retrieve the holiday from the table**
> > **Retrieve the holiday's month, day, and year**
>
> **Compare the holiday's month, day, and year to the implicit object's month, day, and year**
> > **If there is a match**
> > > **Return** true
>
> **EndFor**
>
> **Return** false

Written in C++, this algorithm becomes

```cpp
bool Date::isHoliday()
{
    int i, mm, dd, yy;
    Date holiday;

    // read the Holiday file if the Holiday table is empty
    if (hTable.empty())
        getHolidays();

    // search the Holiday table for the given date
    for(i = 0; i < hTable.size(); i++)
    {
        holiday = hTable[i];   // retrieve a holiday
        mm = holiday.getMonth();
        dd = holiday.getDay();
        yy = holiday.getYear();
        if ( month == mm && day == dd && year == yy )
            return true;
    }
    return false;
}
```

In reviewing this code, notice that the object retrieved from the vector is a Date object. The three accessor methods, getMonth(), getDay(), and getYear(), which have yet to be written, are then applied to this `Date` object so that the individual values can be compared to the implied object's instance variables. If there is a match, the method breaks out of the loop and returns a Boolean `true` value. If the loop exits normally, indicating that no match was found, a Boolean `false` value is returned. Class 10-1 includes the `isHoliday()` method and the three new accessor methods within the context of a complete `Date` class. For ease of reading, this new code has been highlighted, the display lines within the `getHolidays()` method have been removed, and the `dayOfWeek()` and `isLeapYear()` codes have been omitted.

Class 10-1

```cpp
#include <iostream>
#include <fstream>
#include <string>
#include <iomanip>
#include <cctype>
#include <vector>
#include <algorithm>
using namespace std;

class Date
{
    // data declaration section
    private:
        static vector<Date> hTable; // not stored with each instantiated object
        int month;
        int day;
        int year;

    // methods declaration
    public:
        Date(){setDate(7, 4, 2005);};  // default constructor
        Date(int mm, int dd, int yyyy){setDate(mm, dd, yyyy);} // overloaded constructor
        void setDate(int mm, int dd, int yyyy){month = mm; day = dd; year = yyyy;};
        void showDate();   // accessor
        static void getHolidays();
        int getMonth() {return month;};
        int getDay() {return day;};
        int getYear() {return year;};
        bool isHoliday();
};

vector<Date> Date::hTable;   // instantiate hTable;
```

(continued on next page)

```cpp
// methods implementation section

  void Date::showDate()
  {
    cout << setfill('0')
              << setw(2) << month << '/'
              << setw(2) << day << '/'
              << setw(2) << year % 100; // extract the last 2 year digits
    cout << endl;
  }

  void Date::getHolidays()
  {1
    string filename = "c:\\cpcode\\Holidays.txt"; // <-- change this to the path
    ifstream inFile;                        // name where the Holidays.txt
    string line;                            // file is stored on your computer

    int month, day, year, firstdel, secdel;
    Date a;   // create a single Date object

    inFile.open(filename.c_str());  // open the file
    // check that the connection was successfully opened
    if (inFile.fail())
    {
      cout << "\nThe file was not successfully opened"
           << "\n Please check that the file currently exists."
           << endl;
      exit(1);
    }

    // read and store each Date
    while (getline(inFile, line))
    {
      // parse the string
      firstdel = line.find("/");
      secdel = line.find("/",firstdel + 1);
      month = atoi(line.substr(0,firstdel).c_str());
      day = atoi(line.substr(firstdel + 1, secdel - (firstdel + 1)).c_str());
      year = atoi(line.substr(secdel + 1, line.length() - (secdel + 1)).c_str());

      a.setDate(month, day, year);  //convert to a Date object
      hTable.put_back(a);  // add the holiday into the vector
    }
    inFile.close();

  }
```

(continued on next page)

```cpp
bool Date::isHoliday()
{
   int i, mm, dd, yy;
   Date holiday;

   // read the Holiday file if the Holiday table is empty
   if (hTable.empty())
      getHolidays();

   // search the Holiday table for the given Date
   for(i = 0; i < hTable.size(); i++)
   {
      holiday = hTable[i];   // retrieve a holiday
      mm = holiday.getMonth();
      dd = holiday.getDay();
      yy = holiday.getYear();
      if ( month == mm && day == dd && year == yy )
         return true;
   }
   return false;
}
```

VERIFYING THE isHoliday() METHOD

A simple verification of the isHoliday() method is obtained by including the class within Program 10-14. The program also implicitly tests the getHolidays() method, because this method is explicitly called from within the isHoliday() method whenever the holiday table has not been initialized. Program 10-14 verifies isHoliday() by testing for one holiday and one nonholiday date.

Program 10-14

```
#include <c:\\cpcode\\Class10-1.cpp> // change this to be the path where
int main()                           // Date.cpp is stored on your computer
{
  Date a(1,5,2005);     // this is not a holiday
  Date b(12,25,2005);   // this is a holiday

  a.showDate();
  if (a.isHoliday())
    cout << " is a holiday." << endl;
  else
    cout << " is not a holiday." << endl;
  b.showDate();
  if (b.isHoliday())
    cout << " is a holiday." << endl;
  else
    cout << " is not a holiday." << endl;

  return 0;
}
```

The output produced by Program 10-14 is:

```
01/05/05
 is not a holiday.
12/25/05
 is a holiday.
```

As indicated by this output, the isHoliday() method appears to be working correctly.

Exercises 10.6

1. Explain why the class named Date is required in Program 10-13's call to getHolidays().

2. Enter, compile, and execute Program 10-13.

3. Enter and compile the Date class presented in Class 10-1.

4. Enter and execute Program 10-14 on your computer. To accomplish this successfully, you will have to complete Exercise 3.

5. Replace the following statements in the `isHoliday()` method with a call to a method named `isEqual()`.

```
mm = holiday.getMonth();
dd = holiday.getDay();
yy = holiday.getYear();
if ( month == mm && day == dd && year == yy )
    return true;
```

The method header for `isEqual()` should be

```
bool isEqual(Date secDate)
```

6. Program 10-13's `getHolidays()` method is actually one of three methods typically used in creating, maintaining, and using a list of constants stored in a file. Thus, this method can be defined in its own class, which would contain all of the necessary file-related methods. For this exercise, place the `getHolidays()` method within a class named `Holidays` and make all of the necessary adjustments to the `Date` class to ensure that all class methods work correctly when Program 10-14 is executed.

7. a. Add a method named `setHolidays()` to either Class 10-1 or the `Holidays` class created in Exercise 6. This new method should read and display the current list of `Holidays`, and then let the user change, add, or delete `Holidays` from the list. After a holiday has been modified, deleted, or added, the method should sort the `Holidays` and display the new list. Finally, the method should ask the user whether the new list should be saved; if the user responds affirmatively, the method should write the new data to the existing `Holidays.txt` file, overwriting the contents of the existing file.

   b. Add a method named `createHolidays()` to either Class 10-1 or the `Holidays` class created in Exercise 6. This new method should be used to create a completely new `Holidays.txt` file and overwrite the existing file when the user provides positive confirmation that the file should be written.

8. a. A file named `Polar.dat` contains the polar coordinates needed in a graphics program. Currently, this file contains the following data:

Distance (inches)	Angle (degrees)
2	45
6	30
10	45
4	60
12	55
8	15

Write a C++ program to create this file on your computer system (do not include the headings in the file).

b. Using the `Polar.dat` file created in Exercise 8a, write a C++ program that accepts distance and angle data from the user and adds the data to the end of the file.

c. Using the `Polar.dat` file created in Exercise 8a, write a C++ program that reads this file and creates a second file named `xyCoord.dat`. The entries in the new file should contain the rectangular coordinates corresponding to the polar coordinates in the `Polar.dat` file. Polar coordinates are converted to rectangular coordinates using the equations:

$$x = r \cos \theta$$
$$y = r \sin \theta$$

where r is the distance coordinate and θ is the radian equivalent of the angle coordinate in the `Polar.dat` file.

9. Pollen count readings, which are taken from August through September in the northeastern region of the United States, measure the number of ragweed pollen grains in the air. Pollen counts in the range of 10 to 200 grains per cubic meter of air are typical during this time of year. Pollen counts above 10 begin to affect a small percentage of hay fever sufferers, counts in the range of 30 to 40 will noticeably bother approximately 30% of hay fever sufferers, and counts between 40 and 50 adversely affect more than 60% of all hay fever sufferers.

Write a C++ program that updates a file containing the 10 most recent pollen counts. Add each new count to the end of the file. As you add a new count to the end of the file, delete the oldest count, which is the first value in the file. Your program should also calculate and display the averages of the data for the old and new files.

To test your program, first create a file named `Pollen.dat` that contains the following pollen count data: 30, 60, 40, 80, 90, 120, 150, 130, 160, 170. Here the first value, 30, corresponds to the oldest pollen count, and the last value, 170, corresponds to the most recent pollen count. The pseudocode for the file update program is

Display a message indicating what the program does
Request the name of the data file
Request a new pollen count reading
Open the data file as an input file
Do for ten data items
    Read a value into an array
    Add the value to a total
EndDo
Close the file
Open the file as an output file
Calculate and display the old ten-day average
Calculate and display the new ten-day average
Write the nine most recent pollen counts from the array to the file
Write the new pollen count to the file
Close the file

10.7 A CLOSER LOOK: THE IOSTREAM CLASS LIBRARY

As we have seen, the classes contained within the `iostream` class library access files using entities called streams. For most systems, the data bytes transferred on a stream represent either ASCII characters or binary numbers.

The mechanism for reading a byte stream from a file or writing a byte stream to a file is always hidden when using a high-level language such as C++. Nevertheless, it is useful to understand this mechanism so that we can place the services provided by the `iostream` class library in their appropriate context.

FILE STREAM TRANSFER MECHANISM

The mechanism for transferring data between a program and a file is illustrated in Figure 10-5. As shown, transferring data between a program and a file involves an intermediate file buffer contained in the computer's memory. Each opened file is assigned its own file buffer, which is simply a storage area that is used by the data as it is transferred between the program and the file.

FIGURE 10-5
The Data Transfer Mechanism

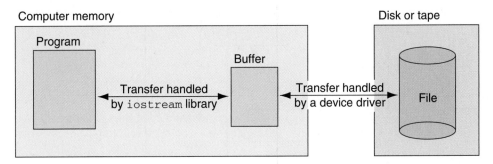

From its side, the program either writes a set of data bytes to the file buffer or reads a set of data bytes from the file buffer using a stream object. On the other side of the buffer, the transfer of data between the device storing the actual data file (usually a tape, disk, or CD-ROM) and the file buffer is handled by special operating system programs that are referred to as **device drivers**. Device drivers are not stand-alone programs but are an integral part of the operating system. Essentially a device driver is a section of operating system code that accesses a hardware device, such as a disk unit, and handles the data transfer between the device and the computer's memory. As such it must correctly synchronize the speed of the data transferred between the computer and the device sending or receiving the data. This is because the computer's internal data transfer rate is generally much faster than any device connected to it.

Typically a disk device driver will only transfer data between the disk and file buffer in fixed sizes, such as 1024 bytes at a time. Thus, the file buffer provides a convenient means of permitting a device driver to transfer data in blocks of one size while the program can access them using a different size (typically as individual characters or as a fixed number of characters per line).

COMPONENTS OF THE iostream CLASS LIBRARY

The iostream class library consists of two primary base classes, the streambuf class and the ios class. The streambuf class provides the file buffer illustrated in Figure 10-5 and a number of general routines for transferring binary data. The ios class contains a pointer to the file buffers provided by the streambuf class and a number of general routines for transferring text data. From these two base classes a number of other classes are derived and included in the iostream class library.

Figure 10-6 illustrates an inheritance diagram for the ios family of classes as it relates to the ifstream, ofstream, and fstream classes. The inheritance diagram for the streambuf family of classes is shown in Figure 10-7. The convention adopted for inheritance diagrams is that the arrows point from a derived class to a base class.

FIGURE 10-6
The Base Class ios *and Its Derived Classes*
(Not all derived classes are shown)

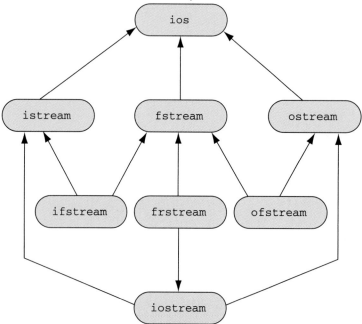

FIGURE 10-7
The Base Class streambuf *and Its Derived Classes*
(Not all derived classes are shown)

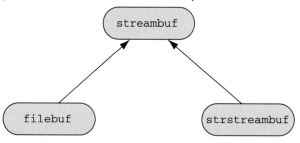

The correspondence between the classes illustrated in Figures 10-6 and 10-7, including the header files that define these classes, is listed in Table 10-7.

TABLE 10-7
Correspondence Between Classes Illustrated in Figures 10-6 and 10-7

ios class	streambuf class	header file
iostream ostream iostream	streambuf	iostream **or** fstream
ifstream ofstream fstream	filebuf	fstream

Thus, the `ifstream`, `ofstream`, and `fstream` classes that we have used for file access all use a buffer provided by the `filebuf` class that is defined in the `fstream` header file. Similarly, the `cin`, `cout`, `cerr`, and `clog` `iostream` objects that we have been using throughout the text use a buffer provided by the `streambuf` class and defined in the `iostream` header file.

IN-MEMORY FORMATTING

In addition to the classes illustrated in Figure 10-6, a class named `strstream` is also derived from the `ios` class. This class uses the `strstreambuf` class illustrated in Figure 10-7, requires the `strstream` header file, and provides capabilities for writing and reading strings to and from in-memory defined streams.

As an output stream, such streams are typically used to "assemble" a string from smaller pieces until a complete line of characters is ready to be written, either to `cout` or to a file. Attaching a `strstream` object to a buffer for this purpose is done in a similar manner as attaching an `fstream` object to an output file. For example, the statement

```
strstream inmem(buf, 72, ios::out);
```

attaches a `strstream` object to an existing buffer of 72 bytes in output mode. Program 10-15 illustrates how this statement is used within the context of a complete program.

Program 10-15

```cpp
#include <iostream>
#include <strstream>
#include <iomanip>
using namespace std;

int main()
{
  const int MAXCHARS = 81;  // one more than the maximum characters in a line
  int units = 10;
  double price = 36.85;
  char buf[MAXCHARS];

  strstream inmem(buf, MAXCHARS, ios::out);   // open an in-memory stream

    // write to the buffer through the stream
    inmem << "No. of units = "
          << setw(3) << units
          << "  Price per unit = $"
          << setw(6) << setprecision(2) << fixed << price << '\0';

  cout << '|' << buf << '|';

  cout << endl;

  return 0;
}
```

The output produced by Program 10-15 is:

```
|No. of units =   10   Price per unit = $   36.85|
```

As illustrated by this output, the character buffer has been correctly filled in by insertions to the inmem stream (note that the end-of-string NULL, '\0', which is the last insertion to the stream, is required to correctly close off the C-string). Once the desired character array has been filled, it would typically be written out to a file as a single string.

In a similar manner, a strstream object can be opened in input mode. Typically such a stream would be used as a working storage area, or buffer, for storing a complete line of text from either a file or standard input. Once the buffer has been filled, the extraction operator would be used to "disassemble" the string into component parts and convert each data item into its designated data type. Doing this permits inputting data from a file on a line-by-line basis prior to assigning individual data items to their respective variables.

10.8 COMMON PROGRAMMING ERRORS

The common programming errors with respect to files are:

1. Using a file's external name in place of the internal file stream object name when accessing the file. The only stream method that uses the data file's external name is the `open()` function. As always, all stream methods presented in this chapter must be preceded by a stream object name and the dot operator.

2. Opening a file for output without first checking that a file with the given name already exists. Not checking for a pre-existing file name ensures that the file will be overwritten.

3. Not understanding that the end of a file is detected only after the EOF sentinel has either been read or passed over.

4. Attempting to detect the end of a file using character variables for the EOF marker. Any variable used to accept the EOF must be declared as an integer variable. For example, if `ch` is declared as a character variable, the expression

   ```
   while ( (ch = in.file.peek()) != EOF )
   ```

   produces an infinite loop.[3] This occurs because a character variable can never take on an EOF code. EOF is an integer value (usually -1) that has no character representation. This ensures that the EOF code can never be confused with any legitimate character encountered as normal data in the file. To terminate the loop created by the above expression, the variable `ch` must be declared as an integer variable.

5. Using an integer argument with the `seekg()` and `seekp()` functions. This offset must be a long integer constant or variable. Any other value passed to these functions can result in an unpredictable effect.

---

[3]This will not occur on UNIX systems, where characters are stored as signed integers.

10.9 CHAPTER REVIEW

Key Terms

binary file

character-based file

close()

data file

external file name

file access

file organization

input file stream object

open()

output file stream object

physical file

random access

sequential organization

text file

SUMMARY

1. A data file is any collection of data stored together in an external storage medium under a common name.

2. A data file is connected to a file stream using `fstream`'s `open()` method. This function connects a file's external name with an internal object name. After the file is opened, all subsequent accesses to the file require the internal object name.

3. A file can be opened in input or output mode. An opened output file stream either creates a new data file or erases the data in an existing opened file. An opened input file stream makes an existing file's data available for input. An error condition results if the file does not exist and can be detected using the `fail()` method.

4. All file streams must be declared as objects of either the `ifstream` or `ofstream` classes. This means that a declaration similar to either

```
ifstream inFile;
ofstream outFile;
```

    must be included with the declarations in which the file is opened. The stream object names `in-File` and `outFile` can be replaced with any user-selected object name.

5. In addition to any files opened within a function, the standard stream objects `cin`, `cout`, and `cerr` are automatically declared and opened when a program is run. `cin` is the object name of an input file stream used for data entry (usually from the keyboard), `cout` is the object name of an output file stream used for default data display (usually the computer screen), and `cerr` is the object name of an output file stream used for displaying system error messages (usually the computer screen).

6. Data files can be accessed randomly using the `seekg()`, `seekp()`, `tellg()`, and `tellp()` methods. The `g` versions of these functions are used to alter and query the file position marker for input file streams, while the `p` versions do the same for output file streams.

7. Table 10-8 lists the methods supplied by the `fstream` class for file manipulation.

TABLE 10-8
`fstream` *Methods*

method name	description
`get()`	Extract the next character from the input stream and return it as an `int`
`get(chrVar)`	Extract the next character from the input stream and assign it to `chrVar`
`getline(fileObj, string, termChar)`	Extract the next string of characters from the input file stream object and assign them to `string` until the specified terminating character is detected. If omitted, the default terminating character is a newline
`getline(C-stringVar, int n, '\n')`	Extract and return characters from the input stream until either `n-1` characters are read or a newline is encountered (terminates the input with a `'\0'`)
`peek()`	Return the next character in the input stream without extracting it from the stream
`put(chrExp)`	Put the character specified by `chrExp` on the output stream
`putback(chrExp)`	Push the character specified by `chrExp` back onto the input stream. Does not alter the data in the file

TABLE 10-8
fstream *Methods (Continued)*

ignore(int n)	Skip over the next n characters; if n is omitted, the default is to skip over the next single character
eof()	Returns a Boolean true value if a read has been attempted past the end-of-file; otherwise returns a Boolean false value. The value becomes true only when the first character after the last valid file character is read
good()	Returns a Boolean true value while the file is available for program use. Returns a Boolean false value if a read has been attempted past the end-of-file. The value becomes false only when the first character after the last valid file character is read
bad()	Returns a Boolean true value if a read has been attempted past the end-of-file; otherwise returns a false. The value becomes true only when the first character after the last valid file character is read
fail()	Returns a Boolean true if the file has not been opened successfully; otherwise returns a Boolean false value

Chapter Exercises

1. You are to write a C++ program that allows the user to enter the following information from the keyboard for each of up to 20 students in a class:

    Name   Exam-1-Grade   Exam-2-Grade   Homework-Average   Final-Exam-Grade

    For each student, your program should first calculate a final grade, using the formula:

    Final Grade = 0.20 * Exam-1-Grade + 0.20 * Exam-2-Grade
                 + 0.35 * Homework-Average + 0.25 * Final-Exam-Grade

    and assign a letter grade on the scale 90–100 = A, 80–89 = B, 70–79 = C, 60–69 = D, less than 60 = F. All of the information, including the final grade and the letter grade, should then be displayed and written to a file.

2. Write a C++ program that permits a user to enter the following information about your small company's 10 employees, sorts the information in decreasing value by years with the company, and writes the following sorted information to a file.

ID No.	Sex (M/F)	Hourly Wage	Years with the Company

3. Write a C++ program that allows you to read the file created in Exercise 2, change the hourly wage or years for any employee, and create a new, updated file.

4. Write a C++ program that reads the file created in Exercise 2, one record at a time, asks for the number of hours worked by that employee each month, and calculates and displays each employee's total pay for the month.

5. a. You have collected information about cities in your state. You decide to store each city's name, population, and the name of its mayor in a file. Write a C++ program to accept the data for a number of cities from the keyboard and store the data in a file in the order in which they are entered.

   b. Read the file created in Exercise 5a, sort the data alphabetically by city name, and display the data.

6. A bank's customer records are to be stored in a file and read into a set of arrays so that an individual's record can be accessed randomly by account number. Create the file by entering five customer records, with each record consisting of an integer account number (starting with account number 1000), a first name having a maximum of 10 characters, a last name having a maximum of 15 characters, and a floating-point balance.

   Once the file is created, write a C++ program that reads the records into four separate arrays. The starting address of any element in the account array can then be calculated as the *address of the first record in the array + (account number - 1000) * sizeof(int)*. Using this information, your program should request a user-entered account number and display the corresponding name and account balance.

7. Create an ASCII file with the following data or use the file named shipped.txt on the data disk provided with this text. (*Note:* The headings are not part of the file but indicate what the data represent.)

shipped date	tracking number	part number	first name	last name	company
04/12/05	D50625	74444	James	Lehoff	Rotech Systems
04/12/05	D60752	75255	Janet	Lezar	Rotech Systems
04/12/05	D40295	74477	Bill	McHenry	Rotech Systems
04/12/05	D23745	74470	Diane	Kaiser	Rotech Systems
04/12/05	D50892	75155	Helen	Richardson	NipNap Inc.

The format of each line in the file is identical with fixed-length fields defined as follows:

field position	field name	starting column number	ending column number	field length
1	Shipped Date	1	8	8
2	Tracking Number	10	15	6
3	Part Number	17	21	5
4	First Name	23	32	10
5	Last Name	34	48	15
6	Company	50	63	14

Using this data file, write a C++ program that reads the file; extracts the date, part number, first name, last name, and company name; and produces a report listing the extracted data.

8.   a. Write a C++ program to create a data file containing the following information:

student ID number	student name	course code	course credits	course grade
2333021	BOKOW, R.	NS201	3	A
2333021	BOKOW, R.	MG342	3	A
2333021	BOKOW, R.	FA302	1	A
2574063	FALLIN, D.	MK106	3	C
2574063	FALLIN, D.	MA208	3	B
2574063	FALLIN, D.	CM201	3	C
2574063	FALLIN, D.	CP101	2	B
2663628	KINGSLEY, M.	QA140	3	A
2663628	KINGSLEY, M.	CM245	3	B
2663628	KINGSLEY, M.	EQ521	3	A
2663628	KINGSLEY, M.	MK341	3	A
2663628	KINGSLEY, M.	CP101	2	B

b. Using the file created in Exercise 8a, write a C++ program that creates student grade reports. The grade report for each student should contain the student's name and identification number, a list of courses taken, the credits and grade for each course, and a semester grade point average. For example, the grade report for the first student is:

```
Student name: BOKOW, R.
Student ID Number: 2333021

Course      Course      Course
Name        Credits     Grade

------      -------     ------

NS201          3           A
MG342          3           A
FA302          1           A
Total Semester Course Credits Completed: 7
Semester Grade Point Average: 4.0
```

The semester grade point average is computed in two steps. First, each course grade is assigned a numerical value (A = 4, B = 3, C = 2, D = 1, F = 0) and the sum of each course's grade value times the credits for each course is computed. This sum is then divided by the total number of credits taken during the semester.

9. **a.** Write a C++ program to create a data file containing the following information:

student ID number	student name	course credit	grade point average
2333021	BOKOW, R.	48	4.0
2574063	FALLIN, D.	12	1.8
2663628	KINGSLEY, M.	36	3.5

b. Using the file created in Exercise 9a as a master file and the file created in Exercise 8a as a transactions file, write a file update program to create an updated master file.

Testing Center

Please visit the Testing Center at www.course.com/testingcenter for more practice on I/O file streams and data files.

PART 4

ADDITIONAL CLASS CAPABILITIES

11

CLASS FUNCTIONS AND CONVERSIONS

In this chapter we continue our construction of classes by providing more advanced capabilities. These include the creation of class operators (such as assignment, comparison, and addition operators) as they apply to objects; conversion capabilities similar to those provided for C++'s built-in type; and additional special purpose methods. With these additions, our user-defined types will have all the functionality of built-in types. As an illustration of how classes can be used in practice, a simulation program is presented that relies on two user-defined classes. Finally, we show how both the cin and cout standard stream objects can be adapted to deal directly with the input and output of objects.

11.1 ASSIGNMENT

In Chapter 4 we saw how C++'s assignment operator, =, performs assignment between variables. In this section we see how assignment works when it is applied to objects, and how to define our own assignment operator to override the default provided for user-defined classes.

For a specific assignment example, consider the `main()` function of Program 11-1. To help you understand the central point being illustrated, only the relevant `Date` class methods are used (the complete `Date` class can be found in Section 5.6 as Class 5-2). Also, the class is highlighted to help you distinguish it from `main()`.

Notice that the implementation section of the `Date` class in Program 11-1 contains no assignment function. Nevertheless, we would expect the assignment statement `a = b;` in `main()` to assign `b`'s data member values to their counterparts in `a`. This is, in fact, the case and is verified by the output produced when Program 11-1 is executed:

```
The date stored in a is originally 07/04/05
After assignment the date stored in a is 12/18/08
```

Program 11-1

```cpp
#include <iostream>
#include <iomanip>
using namespace std;

class Date
{
  // data declaration section
  private:
    int month;
    int day;
    int year;

  // method declarations
  public:
    Date(int = 7, int = 4, int = 2005); // constructor with default
                                        // arguments

    void showDate();                    // accessor
};

// methods implementation section
```

(continued on next page)

```
Date::Date(int mm, int dd, int yyyy)
{
  month = mm;
  day = dd;
  year = yyyy;
}

void Date::showDate()
{
  cout << setfill('0')
       << setw(2) << month << '/'
       << setw(2) << day << '/'
       << setw(2) << year % 100 << endl;
}
```

```
int main()
{
  Date a, b(12,18,2008); // declare two objects
  cout << "The date stored in a is originally ";
  a.showDate();  // display the original date
  a = b;         // assign b's value to a
  cout << "After assignment the date stored in a is ";
  a.showDate();  // display a's values

  return 0;
}
```

The type of assignment illustrated in Program 11-1 is referred to as a **memberwise assignment**. In the absence of any specific instructions to the contrary, the C++ compiler builds this type of default assignment operator for each class. If the class *does not* contain any pointer data members, this default assignment operator is adequate and can be used without further consideration. Before considering the problems that can occur with pointer data members, let's see how to construct our own explicit assignment operators.

Assignment operators, like all class members, are declared in the class declaration section and defined in the class implementation section. For the declaration of operators, however, the keyword operator must be included in the declaration. Using this keyword, a simple **assignment operator declaration** has the form:

```
void operator=(className&);
```

Here the keyword void indicates that the assignment returns no value, the term operator= indicates that we are overloading the assignment operator with our own version, and the class name and ampersand within the parentheses indicates that the argument to the operator is a reference to a class. For example, to declare a simple assignment operator for our Date class, the declaration:

```
void operator=(Date&);
```

can be used.

The actual implementation of the assignment operator is defined in the implementation section. For our declaration, a suitable implementation is:

```cpp
void Date::operator=(Date& newdate)
{
    day = newdate.day;       // assign the day
    month = newdate.month;   // assign the month
    year = newdate.year;     // assign the year
}
```

The use of the reference parameter in the definition of this operation is not accidental. In fact, one of the primary reasons for adding reference variables to C++ was to facilitate the construction of over-loaded operators and make the notation more natural.[1] In this definition, newdate is defined as a reference to a Date class. Within the body of the definition the day member of the object referenced by newdate is assigned to the day member of the current object, which is then repeated for the month and year members. Assignments such as a.operator=(b); can then be used to call the overloaded assignment operator and assign b's member values to a. For convenience, the expression a.operator=(b) can be replaced with a = b;. Program 11-2 contains our new assignment operator within the context of a complete program.

Except for the addition of the overloaded assignment operator declaration and definition, Program 11-2 is identical to Program 11-1 and produces the same output. Its usefulness to us is that it illustrates how we can explicitly construct our own assignment definitions. In Section 12.5, when we introduce pointer data members, we will see how C++'s default assignment can cause troublesome errors that are circumvented by constructing our own assignment operators. Before moving on, however, two simple modifications to our assignment operator need to be made.

Program 11-2

```cpp
#include <iostream>
#include <iomanip>
using namespace std;

class Date
{
    // data declaration section
    private:
        int month;
        int day;
        int year;

    // method declarations
```

(continued on next page)

---

[1] Passing a reference is preferable to passing an object by value because it reduces the overhead required in making a copy of each object's data values.

```cpp
  public:
    Date(int = 7, int = 4, int = 2005); // constructor with default
                                         // arguments

    void showDate();                     // accessor
    void operator=(Date &);              // define assignment of a date
};

// methods implementation section
Date::Date(int mm, int dd, int yyyy)
{
  month = mm;
  day = dd;
  year = yyyy;
}

void Date::showDate()
{
  cout << setfill('0')
       << setw(2) << month << '/'
       << setw(2) << day << '/'
       << setw(2) << year % 100 << endl;
}
void Date::operator=(Date& newdate)
{

  day = newdate.day;        // assign the day
  month = newdate.month;    // assign the month
  year = newdate.year;      // assign the year
}
```

```cpp
int main()
{
  Date a, b(12,18,2008); // declare two objects

  cout << "The date stored in a is originally ";
  a.showDate();  // display the original date
  a = b;         // assign b's value to a
  cout << "After assignment the date stored in a is ";
  a.showDate();  // display a's values

  return 0;
}
```

First, to preclude any inadvertent alteration to the object used on the right side of the assignment, a constant reference argument should be used. For our Date class, this takes the form:

```cpp
        void Date::operator=(const Date& secdate);
```

The final modification concerns the operation's return value. As constructed, our simple assignment operator returns no value, which precludes us from using it in multiple assignments such as a = b = c. The reason for this is that overloaded operators retain the same precedence and associativity as their equivalent built-in versions. Thus, an expression such as a = b = c is evaluated in the order a = (b = c). As we have defined assignment, unfortunately, the expression b = c returns no value, making subsequent assignment to a an error. To provide for multiple assignments, a more complete assignment operation would return a reference to its class type. As the implementation of such an assignment requires a special class pointer, the presentation of this more complete assignment operator is deferred until the material presented in the next chapter is introduced. Until then, our simple assignment operator will be more than adequate for our needs.

COPY CONSTRUCTORS

Although assignment looks similar to initialization, it is worthwhile noting that they are two entirely different operations. In C++ an initialization occurs every time a new object is created. In an assignment, no new object is created; the value of an existing object is simply changed. Figure 11-1 illustrates this difference.

FIGURE 11-1
Initialization and Assignment

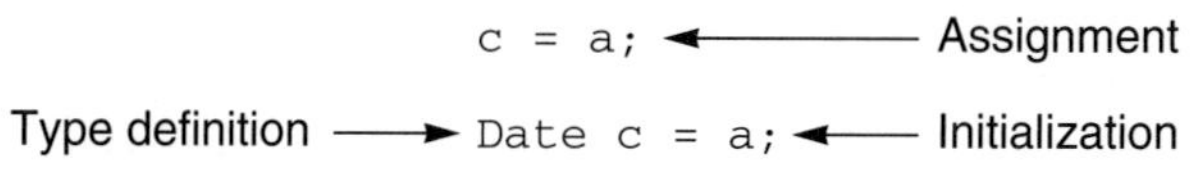

```
                     c = a;  ◄─────────  Assignment
Type definition ────►  Date c = a; ◄─────  Initialization
```

One type of initialization that closely resembles assignment occurs in C++ when one object is initialized using another object of the same class. For example, in the declaration

```
    Date b = a;
```

or its entirely equivalent form

```
    Date b(a);
```

the b object is initialized to a previously declared a object. The constructor that performs this type of initialization is called a **copy constructor** and, if you do not declare one, the compiler will construct one for you. The compiler's default copy constructor performs in a similar manner to the default assignment operator by doing a memberwise copy between objects. Thus, for the declaration Date b = a; the default copy constructor sets b's month, day, and year values to their respective counterparts in a. As with default assignment operators, default copy constructors work just fine unless the class contains pointer data members. Before considering the complications that can occur with pointer data members and how to handle them, it will be helpful to see how to construct our own copy constructors.

Copy constructors, like all class functions, are declared in the class declaration section and defined in the class implementation section. The declaration of a copy constructor has the general form:

```
    className(const className&);
```

As with all constructors, the function name must be the class name. As further illustrated by the declaration, the argument is a reference to the class, which is a characteristic of all copy constructors.[2] To ensure that the argument is not inadvertently altered, it is always specified as a const. Applying this general form to our Date class, a copy constructor can be explicitly declared as:

```
Date(const Date&);
```

The actual implementation of this constructor, if it were to perform the same **memberwise initialization** as the default copy constructor, would take the form:

```
Date:: Date(const Date& olddate)
{
   month = olddate.month;
   day = olddate.day;
   year = olddate.year;
}
```

As with the assignment operator, the use of a reference parameter for the copy constructor is no accident: the reference argument again facilitates a simple notation within the body of the function. Program 11-3 contains this copy constructor within the context of a complete program.

Program 11-3

```
#include <iostream>
#include <iomanip>
using namespace std;

class Date
{
   // data declaration section
   private:
      int month;
      int day;
      int year;

   // method declarations
   public:
      Date(int = 7, int = 4, int = 2005); // constructor with default arguments
      void showDate();                     // accessor
      Date(const Date &);                  // copy constructor
};
```

(continued on next next page)

---

[2] A copy constructor is frequently defined as a constructor whose first argument is a reference to its class type, with any additional arguments being defaults.

```cpp
// methods implementation section
Date::Date(int mm, int dd, int yyyy)
{
   month = mm;
   day = dd;
   year = yyyy;
}

void Date::showDate()
{
  cout << setfill('0')
       << setw(2) << month << '/'
       << setw(2) << day << '/'
       << setw(2) << year % 100 << endl;
}
Date::Date(const Date& olddate)
{
  month = olddate.month;
  day = olddate.day;
  year = olddate.year;
}
```

```cpp
int main()
{
  Date a(4,1,2007), b(12,18,2008); // use the constructor
  Date c(a);   // use the copy constructor
  Date d = b;  // use the copy constructor

  cout << "The date stored in a is ";
  a.showDate();
  cout << "The date stored in b is ";
  b.showDate();
  cout << "The date stored in c is ";
  c.showDate();
  cout << "The date stored in d is ";
  d.showDate();

  return 0;
}
```

The output produced by Program 11-3 is:

```
The date stored in a is 04/01/07
The date stored in b is 12/18/08
The date stored in c is 04/01/07
The date stored in d is 12/18/08
```

As illustrated by this output, c's and d's data members have been initialized by the copy constructor to a's and b's values, respectively. Although the copy constructor defined in Program 11-3 adds nothing to the functionality provided by the compiler's default copy constructor, it does provide us with the fundamentals of defining copy constructors. In the next section, we will see how to modify this basic copy constructor to handle cases that are not adequately managed by the compiler's default.

BASE/MEMBER INITIALIZATION[3]

Except for the reference names `olddate` and `newdate`, a comparison of Program 11-3's copy constructor to Program 11-2's assignment operator shows them to be essentially the same function. The difference in these functions is that the copy constructor first creates an object's data members before the body of the constructor uses assignment to specify member values. Thus, the copy constructor does not perform a true initialization, but rather a creation followed by assignment.

A true initialization would have no reliance on assignment whatsoever and is possible in C++ using a **base/member initialization list**. Such a list can only be applied to constructor functions and may be written in two ways.

The first way to construct a base/member initialization list is within a class's declaration section using the form:

```
className(argument list) : list of data members(initializing values) {}
```

For example, using this form, a default constructor that performs true initialization is:

```
// class declaration section

public:
   Date(int mo=4, int da=1, int yr=2006) : month(mo), day(da), year(yr) {}
```

The second method is to declare a prototype in the class's declaration section, followed by the initialization list in the implementation section. For our `Date` constructor, this takes the form:

```
// class declaration section

public:
   Date(int = 4, int = 1, int = 2006);   // prototype with default arguments

// class implementation section

Date::Date(int mo, int da, int yr) : month(mo), day(da), year(yr) {}
```

---

[3]This section may be omitted on first reading without loss of subject continuity.

Notice that in both forms the body of the constructor function is empty. This is not a requirement, and the body can include any subsequent operations that you would like the constructor to perform. The interesting feature of this type of constructor is that it clearly differentiates between the initialization tasks performed in the member initialization list contained between the colon and the braces, and any subsequent assignments that might be contained within the function's body. Although we will not be using this type of initialization subsequently, it is required whenever there is a `const` class instance variable.

Exercises 11.1

1. Describe the difference between assignment and initialization.

2. **a.** Construct a class named `Time` that contains three integer data members named `hours, mins,` and `secs`, which will be used to store hours, minutes, and seconds. Class methods should include a constructor that provides default values of 0 for each instance variable, a display method that prints an object's data values, and an assignment operator that performs a memberwise assignment between two time objects.

   b. Include the `Time` class developed in Exercise 2a in a working C++ program that creates and displays two time objects, the second of which is assigned the values of the first object.

3. **a.** Construct a class named `Complex` that contains two floating-point data members named `real` and `imag`, which will be used to store the real and imaginary parts of a complex number. Class methods should include a constructor that provides default values of 0 for each instance variable, a display method that prints an object's data values, and an assignment operator that performs a memberwise assignment between two complex number objects.

   b. Include the class written for Exercise 3a in a working C++ program that creates and displays the values of two complex objects, the second of which is assigned the values of the first object.

4. **a.** Construct a class named `Car` that contains the following three data members: a floating-point variable named `engineSize`, a character variable named `bodyStyle`, and an integer variable named `colorCode`. Class methods should include a constructor that provides default values of 0 for each numeric data member and an 'X' for each character variable; a display method that prints the engine size, body style, and color code; and an assignment operator that performs a memberwise assignment between two car objects for each instance variable except the pointer member.

   b. Include the program written for Exercise 4a in a working C++ program that creates and displays two car objects, the second of which is assigned the values of the first object.

11.2 ADDITIONAL CLASS FEATURES

This section presents additional features pertaining to classes. These include creating static class members, and granting access privileges to nonmember functions. Each of these topics may be read independently of the others.

STATIC CLASS MEMBERS

As each class object is created, it gets its own block of memory for its data members. In some cases, however, it is convenient for every instantiation of a class to share the *same* memory location for a specific variable. For example, consider a class consisting of employee records, where each employee is subject to the same state sales tax. Clearly we could make the sales tax a global variable, but this is not very safe. Such data could be modified anywhere in the program or could conflict with an identical variable name within a function, and using a global variable certainly violates C++'s principle of data hiding.

This type of situation is handled in C++ by declaring a class variable to be `static`. Static data members share the same storage space for all objects of the class; as such, they act as global variables for the class and provide a means of communication between objects.

C++ requires that `static` variables be declared as such within the class's declaration section. Since a static data member requires only a single storage area, regardless of the number of class instantiations, it is defined in a single place outside of the class definition. This is typically done within the class implementation section. For example, assuming the class declaration:

```
//class declaration

class Employee
{
  private:
    static double taxRate;
    int idNum;
  public:
    Employee(int);    //constructor
    void display();
};
```

the definition and initialization of the `static` variable `taxRate` is accomplished using a statement such as

```
double Employee::taxRate = 0.0025;
```

Here the scope resolution operator (`::`) is used to identify `taxRate` as a member of the class `Employee` and the keyword `static` is not included. Program 11-4 uses this definition within the context of a complete program.

Program 11-4

```cpp
#include <iostream>
using namespace std;

class Employee
{
  // data declaration section
  private:
    static double taxRate;
    int idNum;

  // method declarations
  public:
    Employee(int);    // constructor
    void display();   // access function
};

// static member definition
double Employee::taxRate = 0.0025;

// implementation section

Employee::Employee(int num = 0)
{
  idNum = num;
}

void Employee::display()
{
  cout << "Employee number " << idNum
       << " has a tax rate of " << taxRate << endl;
}
```

```cpp
int main()
{
  Employee emp1(11122), emp2(11133);

  emp1.display();
  emp2.display();

return 0;
}
```

The output produced by Program 11-4 is:

```
Employee number 11122 has a tax rate of 0.0025
Employee number 11133 has a tax rate of 0.0025
```

Although it might appear that the initialization of `taxRate` is global, it is not. Once the definition is made, any other definition will result in an error. Thus, the actual definition of a `static` member remains the responsibility of the class creator. A compiler error will occur if this definition is omitted. The storage sharing produced by the `static` data member and the objects created in Program 11-4 is illustrated in Figure 11-2.

FIGURE 11-2
Sharing the Static Data Member `taxRate`

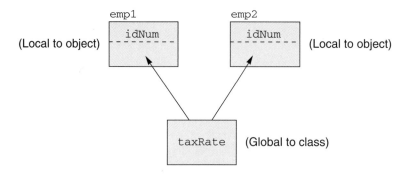

In addition to `static` data members, `static` member methods can also be created. Such methods apply to a class as a whole rather than for individual objects and can only access `static` data members and other `static` class methods.[4] An example of such a method is provided by Program 11-5.

Program 11-5

```
#include <iostream>
using namespace std;

class Employee
{
  // data declaration section
  private:
    static double taxRate;
    int idNum;

  // method declarations
  public:
    Employee(int);     // constructor
    void display();        // access function
    static void disp();  // static function
};
```

(continued on next page)

---

[4]The reason for this is that the `this` pointer, discussed next, is not passed to static member functions.

```
// static member definition
double Employee::taxRate = 0.0025;

// implementation section

Employee::Employee(int num = 0)
{
  idNum = num;
}

void Employee::display()
{
  cout << "Employee number " << idNum
       << " has a tax rate of " << taxRate << endl;
}

void Employee::disp()
{
  cout << "The static tax rate is " << taxRate << endl;
}
```

```
int main()
{
  Employee::disp();    // call the static functions
  Employee emp1(11122), emp2(11133);

  emp1.display();
  emp2.display();

  return 0;
}
```

The output produced by Program 11-5 is:

```
The static tax rate is 0.0025
Employee number 11122 has a tax rate of 0.0025
Employee number 11133 has a tax rate of 0.0025
```

In reviewing Program 11-5, notice that the keyword static is used only when static data and methods are declared: it is not included in the definition of these members. Also notice that the static class method is called using the resolution operator with the method's class name. Finally, since static methods access only static variables that are not contained within a specific object, static methods may be called before any instantiations are declared.

FRIEND FUNCTIONS

The only method we currently have for accessing and manipulating a class' private variables is through the class's methods. Conceptually, this arrangement can be viewed as illustrated in Figure 11-3A.

There are times, however, when it is useful to provide such access to selected nonmember functions.

FIGURE 11-3A
Direct Access Is Provided to Member Methods

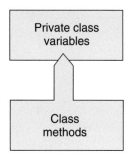

FIGURE 11-3B
Access Provided to Nonmember Functions

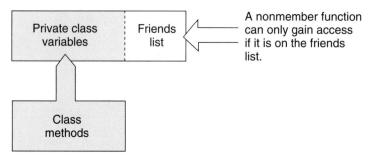

The procedure for providing this external access is rather simple—the class maintains its own approved list of nonmember functions that are granted the same privileges as a class method. The nonmember functions on the list are called friend functions, and the list is referred to as a friends list.

Figure 11-3B conceptually illustrates the use of such a list for nonmember access. Any function attempting access to an object's private variables is first checked against the friends list. If the function is on the list, access is approved; otherwise access is denied.

From a coding standpoint, the friends list is simply a series of function prototype declarations that are preceded by the word `friend` and included in the class's declaration section. For example, if the functions named `addreal()` and `addimag()` are to be allowed access to the private members of a class named `Complex`, the following prototypes would be included within `Complex`'s declaration section.

```
friend double addreal(Complex&, Complex&);
friend double addimag(Complex&, Complex&);
```

Here the friends list consists of two declarations. The prototypes indicate that each function returns a double-precision number and expects two references to objects of type `Complex` as arguments. Program 11-6 includes these two friend declarations in a complete program.

11

Program 11-6

```cpp
#include <iostream>
#include <math.h>
using namespace std;

class Complex
{
  // friends list
  friend double addreal(Complex&, Complex&);
  friend double addimag(Complex&, Complex&);
  // data declarations section
  private:
    double real;
    double imag;
  // method declarations
  public:
    Complex(double, double);   // constructor
    void display();

};

// implementation section

Complex::Complex(double rl = 0, double im = 0)
{
  real = rl;
  imag = im;
}

void Complex::display()
{
  char sign = '+';

  if(imag < 0) sign = '-';
  cout << real << sign << fabs(imag) << 'i';

  return;
}

// friend implementations

double addreal(Complex &a, Complex &b)
{
  return(a.real + b.real);
}
```

(continued on next page)

```
double addimag(Complex &a, Complex &b)
{
   return(a.imag + b.imag);
}

int main()
{
   Complex a(3.2, 5.6), b(1.1, -8.4);
   double re, im;

   cout << "\nThe first complex number is ";
   a.display();
   cout << "\nThe second complex number is ";
   b.display();

   re = addreal(a,b);
   im = addimag(a,b);
   Complex c(re,im);   // create a new Complex object
   cout << "\n\nThe sum of these two complex numbers is ";
   c.display();
   cout << endl;

   return 0;
}
```

The output produced by Program 11-6 is:

```
The first complex number is 3.2+5.6i
The second complex number is 1.1-8.4i

The sum of these two complex numbers is 4.3-2.8i
```

In reviewing Program 11-6, notice the following important points. First, because friends are not class members, they are unaffected by the access section in which they are declared. In other words, *they may be declared anywhere within the declaration section.* The convention we have followed is to include all friend declarations immediately following the class header. Also notice that the keyword friend (like the keyword static) is used only within the class declaration and not in the actual function definition. Third, because a friend function is intended to have access to an object's private variables at least one of the friend's arguments should be a reference to an object of the class that has made it a friend. Finally, as illustrated by Program 11-6, it is the class that grants friend status to a function and not the other way around. The function can never confer friend status on itself, because to do so would violate the concepts of data hiding and access provided by a class.

Exercises 11.2

1. **a.** Rewrite Program 11-5 to include an integer static variable named `numemps`. This variable should act as a counter that is initialized to zero and is incremented by the class constructor each time a new object is declared. Rewrite the static function `disp()` to display the value of this counter.

   b. Test the program written for Exercise 1a. Have the `main()` function call `disp()` after each `Employee` object is created.

2. **a.** Construct a class named `Circle` that contains two integer instance variables named `xCenter` and `yCenter`, and a double-precision instance variable named `radius`. Additionally, the class should contain a static variable named `scaleFactor`. Here the `xCenter` and `yCenter` values represent the center point of a circle, `radius` represents the circle's actual radius, and `scaleFactor` represents a scale factor that will be used to scale the circle to fit on a variety of display devices.

   b. Include the program written for Exercise 2a in a working C++ program.

3. **a.** Consider the following three statements in Program 11-6:

   ```
   re = addreal(a,b);
   im = addimag(a,b);
   complex c(re,im);   // create a new complex object
   ```

   Could they be replaced by the single statement below?
   ```
   complex(addreal(a,b), addimag(a,b));
   ```

   b. Verify your answer to Exercise 3a by running Program 11-6 with the suggested replacement statement.

4. **a.** Rewrite the program written for Exercise 2a, but include a friend function that multiples an object's radius by the static scale factor and then displays the actual radius value and the scaled value.

   b. Include the program written for Exercise 4a in a working C++ program.

5. Rewrite Program 11-6 to have only one friend function named `addcomplex()`. This function should accept two complex objects and return a complex object. The real and imaginary parts of the returned object should be the sum of the real and imaginary parts, respectively, of the two objects passed to `Complex()`.

11.3 OPERATOR FUNCTIONS

A simple assignment operator was constructed in Section 11.1. In this section, we extend this capability and show how to broaden C++'s built-in operators to work with class objects. As we will discover, class operators are themselves either member or friend functions.

The only symbols permitted for user-defined purposes are the subset of C++'s built-in symbols listed in Table 11-1. Each of these symbols may be adopted for class use with no limitation as to its meaning.[5] This is done by making each operation a function that can be overloaded like any other function.

The operation of the symbols listed in Table 11-1 can be redefined as we see fit for our classes, subject to the following restrictions:

- Symbols not in Table 11-1 cannot be redefined. For example, the ., ::, and ?: symbols cannot be redefined.

- New operator symbols cannot be created. For example, because %% is not an operator in C++, it cannot be defined as a class operator.

- Neither the precedence nor the associativity of C++'s operators can be modified. Thus, you cannot give the addition operator a higher precedence than the multiplication operator.

- Operators cannot be redefined for C++'s built-in types.

- A C++ operator that is unary cannot be changed to a binary operator, and a binary operator cannot be changed to a unary operator.

- The operator must either be a member of a class or be defined to take at least one class member as an operand.

The first step in providing a class with operators from Table 11-1 is to decide which operations make sense for the class and how they should be defined. As a specific example, we continue to build on the Date class introduced in Section 5.6. For this class a small, meaningful set of class operations is defined.

Clearly the addition of two dates is not meaningful. The addition of a date with an integer, however, does make sense if the integer is taken as the number of days to be added to the date. Likewise, the subtraction of an integer from a date makes sense. Also, the subtraction of two dates is meaningful if we define the difference to mean the number of days between the two dates. Similarly, it makes sense to compare two dates and determine if the dates are equal or if one date occurs before or after another date. Let's now see how these operations can be implemented using C++'s operator symbols.

---

[5]The only limitation is that the syntax of the operator cannot be changed. Thus, a binary operator must remain binary and a unary operator must remain unary. Within this syntax restriction an operator symbol can be used to produce any operation, whether or not the operation is consistent with the symbol's accepted usage. For example, we could redefine the addition symbol to provide multiplication. Clearly this violates the intent and spirit of making these symbols available to us. We shall be very careful to redefine each symbol in a manner consistent with its accepted usage.

11

TABLE 11-1
Operators Available for Class Use

operator	description
( )	Function call
[ ]	Array element
->	Structure member pointer reference
new	Dynamically allocate memory
delete	Dynamically deallocate memory
++	Increment
--	Decrement
-	Unary minus
!	Logical negation
~	One's complement
*	Indirection
*	Multiplication
/	Division
%	Modulus (remainder)
+	Addition
-	Subtraction
<<	Left shift
>>	Right shift
<	Less than
<=	Less than or equal to
>	Greater than
>=	Greater than or equal to
==	Equal to
!=	Not equal to
&&	Logical AND
||	Logical OR
&	Bitwise AND
^	Bitwise exclusive OR
|	Bitwise inclusive OR
=	Assignment
+= -= *=	Assignment
/= %= &=	Assignment
^= |=	Assignment
<<= >>=	Assignment
,	Comma

A user-defined operation is created as a function that redefines C++'s built-in operator symbols for class use. Functions that define operations on class objects and use C++'s built-in operator symbols are referred to as **operator functions**.

Operator functions are declared and implemented in the same manner as all class methods, with one exception: it is the function's name that connects the appropriate operator symbol to the operation defined by the function. An operator function's name is always of the form `operator<symbol>` where `<symbol>` is one of the operators listed in Table 11-1. For example, the function name `operator+` is the name of the addition function, while the function name `operator==` is the name of the equal to comparison function.

Once the appropriate function name is selected, the process of writing the function simply amounts to having it accept the desired inputs and produce the correct returned value.[6] For example, in comparing two `Date` objects for equality we would select C++'s equality operator. Thus, the name of our function becomes `operator==`. We would want our comparison operation to accept two `Date` objects, internally compare them, and return an integer value indicating the result of the comparison: `true` for equality and `false` for inequality. A suitable prototype for a member function that could be included in the class declaration section is:

```
bool operator==(Date&);
```

This prototype indicates that the function is named `operator==`, that it returns a Boolean value, and that it accepts a reference to a `Date` object.[7] Only one `Date` object is required here because the second `Date` object will be the explicit object that calls the function. Let's now write the function definition to be included in the class implementation section. Assuming our class is named `Date`, a suitable definition is:

```
bool Date::operator==(Date& Date2)
{
   if(day == date2.day && month == date2.month && year == date2.year)
     return true;
   else
     return false;
}
```

Once this function has been defined, it may be called using the same syntax as for C++'s built-in types. For example, if a and b are objects of type `Date`, the expression `if (a == b)` is valid. Program 11-7 includes the call as well as the declaration and definition of this operator function within the context of a complete program.

---

[6]As previously noted, this implies that the specified operator can be redefined to perform any operation. Good programming practice, however, dictates against such redefinitions.

[7]The prototype `bool operator==(Date)` also works. Passing a reference, however, is preferable to passing an object because it reduces the function call's overhead. This is because passing an object means that a copy of the object must be made for the called function, while passing a reference gives the function direct access to the object whose address is passed.

Program 11-7

```cpp
#include <iostream>
using namespace std;

class Date
{
  // data declaration section
  private:
    int month;
    int day;
    int year;

  // method declarations
  public:
    Date(int = 7, int = 4, int = 2006);   // constructor
    bool operator==(Date &);              // declare the operator== function
};

// implementation section

Date::Date(int mm, int dd, int yyyy)
{
  month = mm;
  day = dd;
  year = yyyy;
}

bool Date::operator==(Date &date2)
{
  if(day == date2.day && month == date2.month && year == date2.year)
    return true;
  else
    return false;
}

int main()
{
  Date a(4,1,2007), b(12,18,2008), c(4,1,2007); // declare 3 objects

  if (a == b)
    cout << "Dates a and b are the same." << endl;
  else
    cout << "Dates a and b are not the same." << endl;

  if (a == c)
    cout << "Dates a and c are the same." << endl;
```

(continued on next page)

```
    else
      cout << "Dates a and c are not the same." << endl;

    return 0;
}
```

The output produced by Program 11-7 is:

```
      Dates a and b are not the same.
      Dates a and c are the same.
```

The first new feature to be illustrated in Program 11-7 is the declaration and implementation of the function named `operator==()`. Except for its name, this operator function is constructed in the same manner as any other class method: it is declared in the declaration section and defined in the implementation section. The second new feature is how the function is called. Operator functions may be called using their associated symbols. They may also be called in the traditional manner, by specifying their name and including appropriate arguments. Thus, in addition to being called by the expression `a == b` in Program 11-7, the call `a.operator==(b)` could also have been used.

Let's now create an addition operator for our `Date` class. As before, creating this operator requires that we specify three items:

1.   The name of the operator function

2.   The processing that the function is to perform

3.   The data type, if any, that the function is to return

Naturally, for addition we will use the operator function named `operator+`. Having selected the function's name, we must now determine what we want this function to do as it relates specifically to `Date` objects. As we noted previously, the sum of two dates makes no sense. Adding an integer to a date is meaningful, however, when the integer represents the number of days either before or after the given date. Here the sum of an integer to a `Date` object is simply another `Date` object, which should be returned by the addition operation. Thus, a suitable prototype for our addition function is:

```
      Date operator+(int);
```

This prototype would be included in the class declaration section. It specifies that an integer is to be added to a class object and the operation returns a `Date` object. Thus, if a is a `Date` object, the function call `a.operator+(284)`, or its more commonly used alternative, `a + 284`, would cause the addition of the number `284` and the value currently assigned to the `Date` object named a, and return the sum of these two values as a new `Date` object. We must now construct the function to accomplish this.

Constructing the function requires that we first select a specific date convention. For simplicity we will adopt the financial date convention that considers each month to consist of 30 days and each year to consist of 360 days. Using this convention, our function will first add the integer number of days to the

11

Date object's day value and then adjust the resulting day value to lie within the range 1 to 30 and the month value to lie within the range 1 to 12. A function that accomplishes this is:

```
Date Date::operator+(int days)
{
  Date temp;                  // a temporary Date to store the result

  temp.day = day + days;    // add the days
  temp.month = month;
  temp.year = year;
  while (temp.day > 30)     // now adjust the months
  {
    temp.month++;
    temp.day -= 30;
  }
  while (temp.month > 12)   // adjust the years
  {
    temp.year++;
    temp.month -= 12;
  }
  return temp;                // the values in temp are returned
}
```

The important feature to notice here is the use of the `temp` object. The purpose of this object is to ensure that none of the function's arguments, which become the operator's operands, are altered. To understand this, consider a statement such as `b = a + 284;` that uses this operator function, where a and b are `Date` objects. This statement should never modify a's value. Rather, the expression a + 284 should yield a `Date` value that is then assigned to b. The result of the expression is, of course, the temp `Date` object returned by the `operator+()` function. Program 11-8 uses this function within the context of a complete program.

Program 11-8

```cpp
#include <iostream>
#include <iomanip>
using namespace std;

class Date
{
  // data declaration section
  private:
    int month;
    int day;
    int year;
```

(continued on next page)

```cpp
// method declarations
  public:
    Date(int = 7, int = 4, int = 2005);  // constructor with default
    Date operator+(int);                  // overload the + operator
    void showDate();                      // accessor

};

// methods implementation section
Date::Date(int mm, int dd, int yyyy)
{
  month = mm;
  day = dd;
  year = yyyy;
}

Date Date::operator+(int days)
{
  Date temp;  // a temporary date to store the result

  temp.day = day + days;                  // add the days
  temp.month = month;
  temp.year = year;
  while (temp.day > 30)                   // now adjust the months
  {
    temp.month++;
    temp.day -= 30;
  }
  while (temp.month > 12)                 // adjust the years
  {
    temp.year++;
    temp.month -= 12;
  }
  return temp;                            // the values in temp are returned
}

void Date::showDate()
{
  cout << setfill('0')
       << setw(2) << month << '/'
       << setw(2) << day << '/'
       << setw(2) << year % 100 << endl;
}
```

(continued on next page)

11

```
int main()
{
  Date a(4,1,2007), b;   // declare two objects

  cout << "The initial date is ";
  a.showDate();
  b = a + 284;           // add in 284 days = 9 months and 14 days
  cout << "The new date is ";
  b.showDate();

return 0;
}
```

The output produced by Program 11-8 is:

```
The initial date is 04/01/07
The new date is 01/15/08
```

OPERATOR FUNCTIONS AS FRIENDS

The operator functions in Programs 11-7 and 11-8 have been constructed as class members. An interesting feature of operator functions is that, except for the operator functions =, (), [], and ->, they may also be written as friend functions. For example, if the operator+() function used in Program 11-8 were written as a friend, a suitable declaration section prototype is:

```
friend Date operator+(Date& , int);
```

Notice that the friend version contains a reference to a Date object that is not contained in the member function version. In all cases, the equivalent friend version of a member operator function *must* contain an additional class reference that is not required by the member function.[8] This equivalence is listed in Table 11-2 for both unary and binary operators.

TABLE 11-2
Operator Function Argument Requirements

	member function	friend function
unary operator	1 implicit	1 explicit
binary operator	1 implicit	2 explicit and 1 explicit

---

[8]This extra argument is necessary to identify the correct object. This argument is not needed when using a member function because the member function "knows" which object it is operating on. The mechanism of this "knowing" is supplied by an implied member function argument named this, which is explained in detail in Section 12.3.

Program 11-8's `operator+()` function, written as a friend function, is:

```
Date operator+(Date& op1, int days)
{
   Date temp;   // a temporary Date to store the result

   temp.day = op1.day + days;   // add the days
   temp.month = op1.month;
   temp.year = op1.year;
   while (temp.day > 30)          // now adjust the months
   {
      temp.month++;
      temp.day -= 30;
   }
   while (temp.month > 12)        // adjust the years
   {
      temp.year++;
      temp.month -= 12;
   }
   return temp;                   // the values in temp are returned
}
```

The only difference between this version and the member version is the explicit use of a `Date` argument named `op1` (the choice of this name is entirely arbitrary) in the friend version. This means that within the body of the friend function the first three assignment statements explicitly reference `op1`'s data members as `op1.day`, `op1.month`, and `op1.year`, whereas the member function simply refers to its arguments as `day`, `month`, and `year`.

In making the determination to overload a binary operator as either a friend or member operator function, the following convention can be applied:

- Friend functions are more appropriate for binary operators that modify neither of their operands, such as `==`, `+`, `-`, `*`, and `/`..

- Member functions are more appropriate for binary operators, such as `=`, `+=`, and `-=` , when they are used to modify one of their operands.

Exercises 11.3

1. **a.** Define a *greater than* relational operator function named `operator>()` that can be used with the `Date` class declared in Program 11-7.
    b. Define a *less than* operator function named `operator<()` that can be used with the `Date` class declared in Program 11-7.
    c. Include the operator functions written for Exercises 1a and 1b in a working C++ program.

2. **a.** Define a subtraction operator function named `operator-()` that can be used with the `Date` class defined in Program 11-7. The subtraction should accept a long integer argument that represents the number of days to be subtracted from an object's date and return a `Date`. For the subtraction, use the financial assumption that all months consist of 30 days and all years of 360 days. Additionally, an end-of-month adjustment should be made, if necessary, that converts any resulting day of 31 to a day of 30, except if the month is February. If the resulting month is February and the day is either 29, 30, or 31, the day should be changed to 28.

    b. Define another subtraction operator function named `operator-()` that can be used with the `Date` class defined in Program 11-7. The subtraction should yield a long integer that represents the difference in days between two dates. In calculating the day difference, use the financial day-count basis that assumes that all months have 30 days and all years have 360 days.

    c. Include the overloaded operators written for Exercises 2a and 2b in a working C++ program.

3. **a.** Determine if the following addition operator function provides the same result as the function used in Program 11-8.

```
Date Date::operator+(int days)          // return a Date object
{
    Date temp;

    temp.day = day + days;              // add the days in
    temp.month = month + int(day/30);   // determine total months
    temp.day = temp.day % 30;           // determine actual day
    temp.year = year + int(temp.month/12);  // determine total years
    temp.month = temp.month % 12;       // determine actual month

    return temp;
}
```

    b. Verify your answer to Exercise 3a by including the function in a working C++ program.

4. **a.** Rewrite the equality relational operator function in Program 11-7 as a friend function.

    b. Verify the operation of the friend operator function written for Exercise 4a by including it within a working C++ program.

5. **a.** Rewrite the addition operator function in Program 11-8 to account for the actual days in a month, neglecting leap years.

    b. Verify the operation of the operator function written for Exercise 5a by including it within a working C++ program.

6. **a.** Construct an addition operator for the `Complex` class declared in Program 11-6. This should be a member function that adds two complex numbers and returns a complex number.

    b. Add a member multiplication operator function for the program written for Exercise 6a that multiplies two complex numbers and returns a complex number.

    c. Verify the operation of the operator functions written for Exercises 6a and 6b by including them within a working C++ program.

11.4 TWO USEFUL ALTERNATIVES: OPERATOR() AND OPERATOR[]

There are times when it is convenient to define an operation having more than two arguments, which is the limit imposed on all binary operator functions. For example, each of our Date objects contains three integer data members: month, day, and year. For such an object we might want to add an integer value to any of these three members, instead of just the day member as was done in Program 11-8. C++ provides for this possibility by supplying the parentheses operator function, operator(), which has no limits on the number of arguments that may be passed to it.

On the other end of the spectrum, the case illustrated by Program 11-8, where only a single nonobject argument is required, occurs so frequently that C++ also provides an alternative means of achieving it. For this special case, C++ supplies the subscript operator function, operator[], which permits a maximum of one argument. The only restriction imposed by C++ on the operator() and operator[] functions is that they must be defined as member (not friend) functions. For simplicity, we consider the operator[] function first.

The subscript operator function, operator[], is declared and defined in the same manner as any other operator function, but is called differently from the normal function and operator call. For example, if we wanted to use this operator function to accept an integer argument and return a Date object, the following prototype is valid:

```
Date operator[](int);  // declare the subscript operator
```

Except for the operator function's name, this is similar in construction to any other operator function prototype. Assuming we want this function to add its integer argument to a Date object, a suitable function implementation is:

```
Date Date::operator[](int days)
{
  Date temp;                  // a temporary Date to store the result

  temp.day = day + days;    // add the days
  temp.month = month;
  temp.year = year;
  while (temp.day > 30)     // now adjust the months
  {
    temp.month++;
    temp.day -= 30;
  }
  while (temp.month > 12)   // adjust the years
  {
    temp.year++;
    temp.month -= 12;
  }
  return temp;              // the values in temp are returned
}
```

Again, except for the initial header line, this is similar in construction to other operator function definitions. Once the function is created, however, it can only be called by passing the required argument through the subscript brackets. For example, if a is a Date object, the function call a[284] calls the subscript operator function and causes the function to operate on the a object using the integer value 284. This call is illustrated in Program 11-9.

Program 11-9

```cpp
#include <iostream>
#include <iomanip>
using namespace std;

class Date
{
  // data declaration section
  private:
    int month;
    int day;
    int year;

  // method declarations
  public:
    Date(int = 7, int = 4, int = 2006);    // constructor
    Date operator[](int);      // overload the subscript operator
    void showDate();           // accessor
};
// methods implementation section

Date::Date(int mm, int dd, int yyyy)
{
  month = mm;
  day = dd;
  year = yyyy;
}

Date Date::operator[](int days)
{
  Date temp;                       // a temporary date to store the result

  temp.day = day + days;       // add the days
  temp.month = month;
  temp.year = year;
  while (temp.day > 30)        // now adjust the months
```

(continued on next page)

```
  {
    temp.month++;
    temp.day -= 30;
  }
  while (temp.month > 12)   // adjust the years
  {
    temp.year++;
    temp.month -= 12;
  }
  return temp;              // the values in temp are returned
}

void Date::showDate()
{
  cout << setfill('0')
       << setw(2) << month << '/'
       << setw(2) << day << '/'
       << setw(2) << year % 100 << endl;
}
```

```
int main(){
  Date a(4,1,2006), b;      // declare two objects

  cout << "The initial date is ";
  a.showDate();
  b = a[284];               // add in 284 days = 9 months and 14 days
  cout << "The new date is ";
  b.showDate();

  return 0;
}
```

Program 11-9 is identical in every way to Program 11-8, except that we have used an overloaded sub-script operator function in place of an overloaded addition operator function. Both Programs 11-9 and 11-8 produce the identical output.[9]

The parentheses operator function, `operator()`, is almost identical in construction and calling to the subscript function, `operator[]`, with the substitution of the parentheses, `()`, for the brackets, `[]`. The difference between these two operator functions is in the number of allowable arguments. Whereas the subscript operator permits passing zero or one argument, the parentheses operator has no limit on the number of its arguments. For example, a suitable operator prototype for adding an integer number of months, days, or years to a `Date` object is:

```
        Date operator()(int, int, int);
```

---

[9]If you are familiar with arrays, notice that the expression `a[284]` used in Program 11-9 *appears* to indicate that `a` is an array, but it is not. It is simply the notation that is required to call an overloaded subscript function.

Once such a function is implemented (which is left as an exercise), a call such as a(2,4,3) can be used to add 2 months, 4 days, and 3 years to the Date object named a.

These two extra functions provide a great deal of programming flexibility. In the case where only one argument is needed, they permit two different overloaded functions to be written, both of which have the same argument type. For example, we could use the operator[] to add an integer number of days to a Date object and the operator() to add an integer number of months. Because both functions have the same argument type, one function name could not be overloaded for both of these cases.

These two functions also permit us the flexibility to restrict the other operator functions to class member arguments and use these two functions for any other argument types or operations, such as adding an integer to a Date object.

Exercises 11.4

1. Replace the subscript operator[] function in Program 11-9 with the parentheses operator() function.

2. a. Replace the subscript operator[] function in Program 11-9 with a member operator() function that accepts an integer month, day, and year count. Have the function add the input days, months, and years to the object's date and return the resulting date. For example, if the input is 3, 2, 1 and the object's date is 7/16/2008, the function should return the date 10/18/2009. Make sure that your function correctly handles an input such as 37 days and 15 months, and adjusts the calculated day to be within the range 1 to 30 and the month within the range 1 to 12.
    b. Include the operator function written for Exercise 2a in a working C++ program and verify its operation.

3. a. Construct a class named student consisting of the following private data members: an integer ID number, an integer count, and four double-precision grades. The constructor for this class should set all data member values to zero. The class should also include a method that displays all valid member grades, as determined by the grade count, and calculates and displays the average of the grades. Include the class in a working C++ program that declares three class objects named a, b, and c.
    b. Include a member operator[] function in the class constructed for Exercise 3a that has a double-precision grade argument. The function should check the gradecount data member, and if fewer than four grades have been entered the function should store its argument into the next grade slot available. If four grades have already been entered, the function should return an error message indicating that the new grade cannot be accepted. Additionally, a new grade should force an increment to the count data member.
    c. Include a member operator() function in the class constructed for Exercise 3a that has a grade identification number and grade value as arguments. The function should force a change to the grade corresponding to the identification number and update the count if necessary. For example, an argument list of 4,85 should change the fourth test grade value to 85.

4. **a.** Add a member `operator[]` function to Program 11-9 that multiples an object's complex number (both the real and imaginary parts) by a real number and returns a complex number. For example, if the real number is 2 and the complex number is 3+4i, the result is 6+8i.
   b. Verify the operation of the operator function written for Exercise 4a by including it within a working C++ program.

11.5 DATA TYPE CONVERSIONS

The conversion from one built-in data type to another was previously described in Section 4.1. With the introduction of user-defined data types, the possibilities for conversion between data types expand to the following cases:

- Conversion from built-in type to built-in type

- Conversion from built-in type to class (user-defined) type

- Conversion from class (user-defined) types to built-in types

- Conversion from class (user-defined) types to user-defined (class) types

The first conversion is handled either by C++'s built-in implicit conversion rules or its explicit cast operator. The second conversion type is made using a **type conversion constructor**. The third and fourth conversion types are made using a **conversion operator function**. The specific means of performing each of these conversions is presented in this section.

BUILT-IN TO BUILT-IN CONVERSION

The conversion from one built-in data type to another has already been presented in Section 4.1. To review this case briefly, this type of conversion is either implicit or explicit.

An implicit conversion occurs in the context of one of C++'s operations. For example, when a double-precision value is assigned to an integer variable, only the integer portion of the value is stored. The conversion is implied by the operation and is performed automatically by the compiler.

An explicit conversion occurs whenever a cast is used. Two compile-time cast notations exist in C++. Using the older C notation, a compile-time cast has the form `(dataType) expression` while the newer C++ notation uses the form `dataType(expression)`. For example, both of the expressions `(int)24.32` and `int(24.32)` cause the double-precision value 24.32 to be truncated to the integer value 24.

Built-In to Class Conversion

User-defined casts for converting a built-in to a user-defined data type are created using constructor functions. A constructor whose first argument is not a member of its class and whose remaining arguments, if any, have default values is a **type conversion constructor**. If the first argument of a type conversion constructor is a built-in data type, the constructor can be used to cast the built-in data type to a class object. Clearly, one restriction of such functions is that, as constructors, they must be member functions.

Although this type of cast occurs when the constructor is invoked to initialize an object, it is actually a more general cast than might be evident at first glance. This is because a constructor function can be explicitly invoked after all objects have been declared, whether or not it was invoked previously as part of an object's declaration. Before exploring this further, let's first construct a type conversion constructor. We will then see how to use it as a cast independent of its initialization purpose.

The cast we will construct will convert a long integer into a Date object. Our Date object will consist of dates in the form month/day/year and will use our standard Date class. The long integer will be used to represent dates in the form year * 10000 + month * 100 + day. For example, using this representation the date 12/31/2008 becomes the long integer 20081231. Dates represented in this fashion are very useful for two reasons. First, it permits a date to be stored as a single value, and second, such numerical dates can be arranged in ascending or descending order, making sorting easy. For example, the date 1/2/2009, which occurs after 12/31/2008, becomes the integer 20090102, which is larger than 20081231.

A suitable constructor function for converting from a long integer date to a date stored as a month, day, and year is:

```
// type conversion constructor from long to Date

Date::Date(long findate)
{
  year = int(findate/10000.0);
  month = int((findate - year * 10000.0)/100.0);
  day = int(findate - year * 10000.0 - month * 100.0);
}
```

Program 11-10 uses this type conversion constructor both as an overloaded constructor when an object is defined and as an explicit cast later on in the program. In calling this function it is essential that the single argument be explicitly designated as a long; it if is not, the compiler considers the argument as an integer and calls the constructor with the default integer arguments to fill in the two remaining integer arguments.

Program 11-10

```cpp
#include <iostream>
#include <iomanip>
using namespace std;

class Date
{
  // data declaration section
  private:
    int month, day, year;

  // method declarations
  public:
    Date(int = 7, int = 4, int = 2006);   // constructor
    Date(long);              // overloaded constructor - type conversion
    void showDate();         // accessor
};

//methods implementation section
Date::Date(int mm, int dd, int yyyy)
{
  month = mm;
  day = dd;
  year = yyyy;
}

Date::Date(long findate)
{
  year = int(findate/10000);
  month = int((findate - year * 10000)/100);
  day = int(findate - year * 10000 - month * 100);
}

void Date::showDate()
{
  cout << setfill('0')
       << setw(2) << month << '/'
       << setw(2) << day << '/'
       << setw(2) << year % 100 << endl;
}
```

(continued on next page)

```
int main()
{
  Date a, b(20061225L), c(4,1,2007);  // declare 3 objects
                                       // initialize 2 of them

  cout << "Dates a, b, and c are " << endl;
  a.showDate();
  b.showDate();
  c.showDate();
  cout << endl;

  a = Date(20080101L);  // cast a long to a date

  cout << "Date a is now ";
  a.showDate();
  cout << endl;

  return 0;
}
```

The output produced by Program 11-10 is:

```
Dates a, b, and c are
07/04/06
12/25/06
04/01/07

Date a is now 01/01/08
```

The change in a's date value illustrated by this output is produced by the assignment expression
a = Date(20080101L), which uses a type conversion constructor to perform the cast from long to
Date.

CLASS TO BUILT-IN CONVERSION

Conversion from a user-defined data type to a built-in data type is accomplished using a conversion
operator function. A **conversion operator function** is a member operator function having the name of a
built-in data type or class. When the operator function has a built-in data type name, it is used to convert from a class to a built-in data type. For example, a conversion operator function for casting a class
object to a long integer would have the name operator long(). Here the name of the operator
function indicates that a conversion to a long will take place. If this function were part of a Date class it
would be used to cast a Date object into a long integer. This usage is illustrated by Program 11-11.

Program 11-11

```cpp
#include <iostream>
#include <iomanip>
using namespace std;

class Date
{
  // data declaration section
  private:
    int month, day, year;
  // method declarations
  public:
    Date(int, int, int);      // constructor
    operator long();          // conversion operator function
    void showDate();
};

// methods implementation section

// constructor
Date::Date(int mm = 7, int dd = 4, int yyyy = 2006)
{
  month = mm;
  day = dd;
  year = yyyy;
}

// conversion operator function converting from Date to long
Date::operator long()         // must return a long
{
  long yyyymmdd;

  yyyymmdd = year * 10000.0 + month * 100.0 + day;

  return(yyyymmdd);
}

void Date::showDate()
{
  cout << setfill('0')
       << setw(2) << month << '/'
       << setw(2) << day << '/'
       << setw(2) << year % 100 << endl;
}
```

(continued on next page)

```
int main()
{
  Date a(4,1,2007);       // declare and initialize one object of type date
  long b;                 // declare an object of type long

  b = a;                  // a conversion takes place here

  cout << "a's date is ";
  a.showDate();
  cout << "\nThis date, as a long integer, is " << b << endl;

  return 0;
}
```

The output produced by Program 11-11 is:

```
a's date is 04/01/07

This date, as a long integer, is 20070401
```

The change in a's date value to a long integer is produced by the assignment expression b = a. This assignment, which also could have been written as b = long(a), calls the conversion operator function long() to perform the cast from Date to long.

Notice that the conversion operator has no explicit argument and has no explicit return type. This is true of all conversion operators: Its implicit argument will always be an object of the class being cast from, and the return type is implied by the name of the function. Additionally, as previously indicated, a conversion operator function *must be* a member function.

Class to Class Conversion

Converting from a user-defined data type to a user-defined data type is performed in the same manner as a cast from a user-defined to built-in data type; it is done using a member conversion operator function. In this case, however, the operator function uses the class name being converted to, rather than a built-in data name. For example, if two classes named Date and IntDate exist, the operator function named operator IntDate() could be placed in the Date class to convert a Date object to an IntDate object. Similarly, the operator function named Date() could be placed in the IntDate class to convert an IntDate object to a Date object.

Notice that as before, in converting from a user-defined data type to a built-in data type, the operator function's name determines the result of the conversion; the class containing the operator function determines the data type being converted from.

Before providing a specific example of a class to class conversion, one additional point must be noted. Converting between classes clearly implies that we have two classes, one of which is always defined first and one of which is defined second. Having, within the second class, a conversion operator function with the name of the first class poses no problem because the compiler knows of the first class' existence. However, including a conversion operator function with the second class's name in the first class does pose a problem because the second class has not yet been defined. This is remedied by including a declaration for the second class prior to the first class's definition. This declaration, which is formally referred to as a forward declaration, is illustrated in Program 11-12, which also includes conversion operators between the two defined classes.

Program 11-12

```cpp
#include <iostream>
#include <iomanip>
using namespace std;

// forward declaration of class IntDate
class IntDate;

// class declaration for Date
class Date
{
  private:
    int month, day, year;
  public:
    Date(int, int, int);     // constructor
    operator IntDate();      // conversion operator Date to IntDate
    void showDate(void);
};
// class declaration for IntDate
class IntDate
{
  private:
    long yyyymmdd;
  public:
    IntDate(long);           // constructor
    operator Date();         // conversion operator intdate to date
    void showint(void);
};

// implementation section for Date
Date::Date(int mm = 7, int dd = 4, int yyyy = 2006)   // constructor
{
  month = mm;
  day = dd;
  year = yyyy;
}
// conversion operator function converting from Date to IntDate class
Date::operator IntDate()     // must return an IntDate object
{
```

(continued on next page)

```cpp
  long temp;

  temp = year * 10000.0 + month * 100.0 + day;
  return(IntDate(temp));
}
// member function to display a Date
void Date::showDate()
{
  cout << setfill('0')
       << setw(2) << month << '/'
       << setw(2) << day << '/'
       << setw(2) << year % 100 << endl;
}

// method implementation section for IntDate
IntDate::IntDate(long ymd = 0)   // constructor
{
  yyyymmdd = ymd;
}
// conversion operator function converting from IntDate to Date class
IntDate::operator Date()         // must return a Date object
{
  int mo, da, yr;

  yr = int(yyyymmdd/10000);
  mo = int((yyyymmdd - yr * 10000)/100);
  da = int(yyyymmdd - yr * 10000 - mo * 100);
  return(Date(mo,da,yr));
}
// member function to display an IntDate
void IntDate::showint()
{
  cout << yyyymmdd << endl;
  return;
}
int main()
{
  Date a(4,1,2007), b;         // declare two Date objects
  IntDate c(20081215), d;      // declare two IntDate objects

  b = Date(c);                 // cast c into a Date object
  d = IntDate(a);              // cast a into an IntDate object

  cout << " a's date is ";
```

(continued on next page)

```
    a.showDate();
    cout << "   as an IntDate object this date is ";
    d.showint();

    cout << "\n c's date is ";
    c.showint();
    cout << "   as a Date object this date is ";
    b.showDate();
    cout << endl;

    return 0;
}
```

The output produced by Program 11-12 is:

```
        a's date is 04/01/07
            as an IntDate object this date is 20070401

        c's date is 20081215
            as a Date object this date is 12/15/08
```

As illustrated by Program 11-12, the cast from `Date` to `IntDate` is produced by the assignment `b = Date(c)` and the cast from `IntDate` to `Date` is produced by the assignment `d = IntDate(a)`. Alternatively, the assignments `b = c` and `d = a` would produce the same results. Notice also the forward declaration of the `IntDate` class prior to the `Date` class's declaration. This is required so that the `Date` class can reference `IntDate` in its operator conversion function.

Exercises 11.5

1. a. Define the four data type conversions available in C++ and the method of accomplishing each conversion.
    b. Define the terms "type conversion constructor" and "conversion operator function" and describe how they are used in user-defined conversions.

2. Write a C++ program that declares a class named `Time` having integer data members named `hours`, `minutes`, and `seconds`. Include in the program a type conversion constructor that converts a long integer, representing the elapsed seconds from midnight into an equivalent representation as hours:minutes:seconds. For example, the long integer 30336 should convert to the time 8:25:36. Use a military representation of time so that 2:30 pm is represented as 14:30:00. The relationship between time representations is:

    *elapsed seconds = hours * 3600 + minutes * 60 + seconds*

3. A Julian date is a date represented as the number of days from a known base date. One algorithm for converting from a Gregorian date, in the form month/day/year, to a Julian date with a base date of 0/0/0 is given below. All of the calculations in this algorithm use integer arithmetic, which means

that the fractional part of all divisions must be discarded. In this algorithm M = month, D = day, and Y = year.

> **If M is less than or equal to 2**
>   **set the variable MP = 0 and YP = Y-1**
> **Else**
>   **set MP = int(0.4 * M + 2.3) and YP = Y**
> **T = int(YP/4) - int(YP/100) + int(YP/400)**
> **Julian date = 365 * Y + 31 * (M - 1) + D + T - MP**

Using this algorithm, modify Program 11-11 to cast from a Gregorian date object to its corresponding Julian representation as a long integer. Test your program using the Gregorian dates 1/31/2005 and 3/16/2006, which correspond to the Julian dates 38381 and 38790, respectively.

4. Modify the program written for Exercise 2 to include a member conversion operator function that converts an object of type `Time` into a long integer representing the number of seconds from twelve midnight.

5. Write a C++ program that has a `Date` class and a `Julian` class. The `Date` class should be the same `Date` class as that used in Program 11-12, while the `Julian` class should represent a date as a long integer. For this program include a member conversion operator function within the `Date` class that converts a `Date` object to a `Julian` object, using the algorithm presented in Exercise 3. Test your program by converting the dates 1/31/2006 and 3/16/2007, which correspond to the Julian dates 38746 and 39155, respectively.

6. Write a C++ program that has a `Time` class and an `Ltime` class. The `Time` class should have integer data members named `hours`, `minutes`, and `seconds`, while the `Ltime` class should have a long data member named `elsecs`, which represents the number of elapsed seconds since midnight. For the `Time` class, include a member conversion operator function named `Ltime()` that converts a `Time` object to an `Ltime` object. For the `Ltime` class, include a member conversion operator function named `Time()` that converts an `Ltime` object to a `Time` object.

11.6 PROGRAM DESIGN AND DEVELOPMENT

In this section we present a complete development of a simulation that uses two separate classes. The first class models a gas pump, while the second class models the arrival of a customer and various requests for differing amounts of gas to be pumped. The complete simulation is based on the following requirements:

- We have been requested to write a program that simulates the operation of a gas pump. At any time during the simulation we should be able to determine, from the pump, the price per gallon of gas and the amount remaining in the supply tank from which the gas is pumped. If the amount of gas in the supply tank is greater than or equal to the amount of gas requested, the request should be filled; otherwise, only the available amount in the supply tank should be used. Once the gas is pumped, the total price of the gallons pumped should be displayed and the amount of gas in gallons that was pumped should be subtracted from the amount in the supply tank.

- For the simulation, assume that the pump is randomly idle between 1 to 15 minutes between customer arrivals and that a customer randomly requests between 3 and 20 gallons of gas. Although the default supply tank capacity is 500 gallons, assume that the initial amount of gas in the tank for this simulation is only 300 gallons. Initially, the program should simulate a one-half hour time frame.

- Additionally, for each arrival and request for gas, we want to know the idle time before the customer arrived, how many gallons of gas were pumped, and the total price of the transaction. The pump itself must keep track of the price per gallon of gas and the amount of gas remaining in the supply tank. Typically, the price per gallon is $1.80, but the price for the simulation should be $2.00.

APPLICATION 1: A SINGLE-CLASS GAS PUMP SIMULATION

In developing this application, first notice that it involves two distinct object types. The first is a person who can arrive randomly between 1 and 15 minutes and can randomly request between 3 and 20 gallons of gas. The second object type is the gas pump. In this application, our goal will be to create a suitable gas pump class that can be used in the final simulation, which is completed in the next application.

The model for constructing a gas pump class that meets the requirements of the simulation is described in pseudocode as:

> **Put Pump in Service**
>   *Initialize the amount of gas in the supply tank*
>   *Initialize the price per gallon of gas*
>
> **Display Values**
>   *Display the amount of gas in the supply tank*
>   *Display the price per gallon*
>
> **Pump an Amount of Gas**
>   *If the amount in the supply tank is greater than or equal to the requested amount*
>   *Set the pumped amount of gas equal to the requested amount*
>   *Else*
>   *Set the pumped amount equal to the amount in the supply tank*
>   *EndIf*
>   *Subtract the pumped amount from the amount in the supply tank*
>   *Calculate the total price as the price per gallon times the pumped amount*
>   *Display the gallons of gas requested*
>   *Display the gallons of gas pumped*
>   *Display the amount remaining in the supply tank*
>   *Display the total price for the amount of gas pumped*

From the pseudocode description, the implementation of a Pump class is rather straightforward. The attributes of interest for the pump are the amount of gallons in the supply tank and the price per gallon. The required operations include supplying initial values for the pump's attributes, interrogating the pump for its attribute values, and satisfying a request for gas. The UML diagram for this class is shown as Figure 11-4.

FIGURE 11-4
Pump *Class UML Diagram*

Pump
− amtInTank: double − price: double − AMOUNT_IN_TANK: static double = 500.0; − DEFAULT_PRICE: static double = 1.80;
+ Pump( ) + Pump(todaysPrice, amountInTank) + request(gallons) + getValues( )

Because the two attributes, the amount in the tank and the price per gallon, can have fractional values, it is appropriate to make them double-precision values. Additionally, three services need to be provided. The first consists of initializing a pump's attributes, which consists of setting values for the amount in the supply tank and the price per gallon. The second consists of satisfying a request for gas, while the third service simply provides a reading of the pump's current attribute values. A suitable class definition that provides these services is:

Pump.cpp

```cpp
#include <iostream>
#include <iomanip>
using namespace std;

const double AMOUNT_IN_TANK = 500;   // default gallons in the tank
const double DEFAULT_PRICE = 1.80;   // default price per gallon

class Pump
{
  // data declaration section
  private:
    double amtInTank;
    double price;

  // method declarations
```

(continued on next page)

```cpp
  public:
    Pump(double = DEFAULT_PRICE, double = AMOUNT_IN_TANK);   // constructor
    void getValues();
    void request(double);
}

// methods implementation section

Pump::Pump(double todaysPrice, double amountInTank)
{
  amtInTank = amountInTank;
  price = todaysPrice;
}

void Pump::getValues()
{
  cout << "\nThe gas tank has " << amtInTank << " gallons of gas." << endl;
  cout << "The price per gallon of gas is $" << setiosflags(ios::showpoint)
       << setprecision(2) << setiosflags(ios::fixed) << price << endl;
}

void Pump::request(double pumpAmt)
{
  double pumped;

  if (amtInTank >= pumpAmt)
     pumped = pumpAmt;
  else
     pumped = amtInTank;

  amtInTank -= pumped;
  cout << pumpAmt << " gallons were requested " << endl;
  cout << pumped << " gallons were pumped" << endl;
  cout << amtInTank << " gallons remain in the tank" << endl;
  cout << "The total price is $" << setiosflags(ios::showpoint)
       << setprecision(2) << (pumped * price) << endl;

  return;
}
```

Let's analyze this class by individually inspecting both its data and method members. First, notice that we have declared two symbolic constants and two private instance variables. As private members, these data attributes can only be accessed through the class's member methods: `Pump()`, `getValues()`, and `request()`. These methods provide the external services available to each `Pump` object.

The constructor function is straightforward. When a `Pump` object is declared it will be initialized to a given amount of gas in the supply tank and a given price per gallon. If no values are given, the defaults of $1.80 per gallon and 500 gallons are used; if only the price per gallon is provided, the constructor uses the default value of 500 for the missing second argument.

The `getvalues()` function defined in the implementation section simply provides a readout of the current attribute values. It is the `request()` function that is the most complicated because it provides the primary `Pump` service. The code follows the requirements of the pump, which is to provide all of the gas required unless the amount remaining in the supply tank is less than the requested amount. Finally, it subtracts the amount pumped from the amount in the tank and calculates the total dollar value of the transaction.

To test the `Pump` class requires testing each class operation, as shown in Program 11-13.

Program 11-13

```
#include <c:\\cpcode\\Pump.cpp>
int main()
{
  Pump a(2.00, 300), b;    // declare 2 objects of type Pump

  a.getValues();
  cout << endl;
  a.request(20.0);
  cout << endl;
  a.request(290.0);
  b.getValues();

  return 0;
}
```

Notice that in Program 11-13 we have included the `Pump` class using the statement:

```
#include <c:\\cpcode\\Pump.cpp>
```

This assumes that the `Pump` class resides in the folder named `cpcode` on the C drive, and is saved as the file named `Pump.cpp`. An equivalent statement is:

```
#include "c:\\cpcode\\Pump.cpp"
```

In both include statements the double slashes are required, as a single slash would be interpreted as an escape character.

Within the `main()` method eight statements are included. The first statement creates two objects of type `Pump`. The supply tank for the first `Pump` object contains 300 gallons and the price per gallon is set to $2.00, while the second `Pump` object uses the default values AMOUNT_IN_TANK and DEFAULT_PRICE, which are 500 and 1.80, respectively.

A call is then made to `getValues()` to display the first pump's attribute values. The next statement is a request for gas of 20 gallons from the first `Pump` object. This is followed by a request for 290 gallons, which exceeds the remaining gas in the supply tank. Finally, the attribute values for the second pump are displayed. The output produced by Program 11-13 is:

```
The gas tank has 300 gallons of gas.
The price per gallon of gas is $2.00

20.00 gallons were requested
20.00 gallons were pumped
280.00 gallons remain in the tank
The total price is $40.00

290.00 gallons were requested
280.00 gallons were pumped
0.00 gallons remain in the tank
The total price is $560.00

The gas tank has 500 gallons of gas.
The price per gallon of gas is $1.80
```

As indicated by this output, all of the Pump class methods provide the correct functionality. Specifically, both Pump objects are initialized correctly by the constructor, and the request() method supplies the requested amount of gas, at the correct price, until the supply tank has been emptied.

APPLICATION 2: A MULTI-CLASS GAS PUMP SIMULATION

Having constructed a Pump class to model the operation of a gas pump, we can now use this class within the context of a complete simulation. We do so by first providing a Customer class and then controlling the interaction between these two classes using a main() method.

For this simulation, there are multiple instances of customers arriving randomly between 1 and 15 minutes and requesting gas in amounts that vary randomly between 3 and 20 gallons. From an object viewpoint, however, we are not interested in storing the arrival time of customers and number of gallons requested by each customer. We simply need a Customer object to present us with an arrival time and a request for gas in gallons. Thus, our Customer object type needs no attributes but must provide two operations. The first operation, which we will name arrive(), will provide a random arrival time between 1 and 15 minutes. The second operation, which we will call gallons(), will provide a random request of between 3 and 20 gallons of gas. The UML class diagram for this class is presented in Figure 11-5.

FIGURE 11-5
Customer *Class UML Diagram*

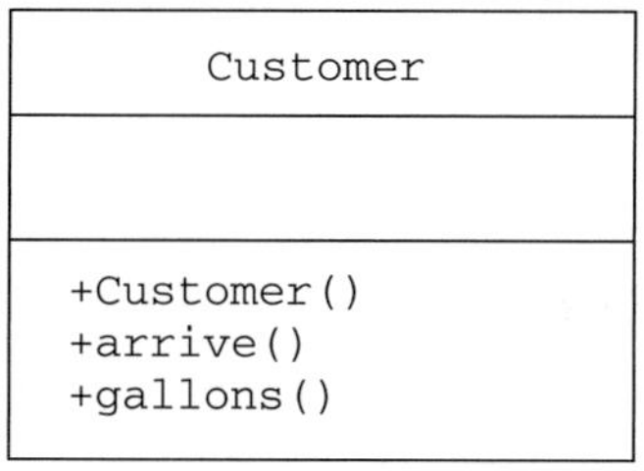

```
┌─────────────────────────┐
│        Customer         │
├─────────────────────────┤
│                         │
├─────────────────────────┤
│ +Customer()             │
│ +arrive()               │
│ +gallons()              │
└─────────────────────────┘
```

The actual class implementation can be coded as:

```cpp
#include <ctime>
#include <cmath>
using namespace std;

//class declaration and implementation
class Customer
{
  public:
    Customer() {srand(time(NULL));};
    int arrive() {return(1 + rand() % 15);};
    int gallons() {return(3 + rand() % 18);};
};
```

In reviewing this code notice that the class constructor is used to randomize the `rand()` function. (Review Section 6.7 if you are unfamiliar with either the `srand()` or `rand()` functions.) The `arrive()` function simply returns a random integer between 1 and 15, while the `gallons()` function returns a random integer between 3 and 20 (we leave it as an exercise for you to rewrite the `gallons()` function to return a noninteger value). Since all of the methods are single-line, we have included their definitions within the declaration section as inline methods.

Again, for later convenience in writing the complete simulation program, assume that the code for the `Customer` class is placed in a file named `Customer.cpp` within a folder named `cpcode` on the C drive. Once this is done, including the `Customer` class within a program requires the statement:

```cpp
#include <c:\\cpcode\\Customer.cpp
```

Having analyzed and defined the two classes that we will be using, we still need to analyze and define the logic to correctly control the interaction between `Customer` and `Pump` objects for a valid simulation.

PROGRAMMING NOTE

Program and Class Libraries

The concept of a program library began with FORTRAN, which was the first commercial high-level language, introduced in 1954. The FORTRAN library consisted of a group of completely tested and debugged mathematical routines that were provided with the compiler. Since that time every programming language has provided its own library of functions. In both C and C++, this library is referred to as the standard program library, and includes more than 12,000 functions declared in 15 different header files. Examples of standard library functions include `sqrt()`, `pow()`, `abs()`, `rand()`, `srand()`, and `time()`. The advantage of library functions is that they significantly enhance program development and design by providing code that is known to work correctly without the need for additional testing and debugging.

With the introduction of object-oriented languages, the concept of a program library has been extended to include class libraries. A *class library* is a library of tested and debugged classes.

One of the key practical features of class libraries is that they help realize the goal of code reuse in a significant way. By providing tested and debugged code consisting of both data and methods, class libraries furnish large sections of prewritten and reusable code ready for incorporation within new applications. This shifts the focus of writing application programs from the creation of new code to understanding how to use predefined objects and stitch them together in a cohesive and useful way.

In this particular case, the only interaction between a `Customer` object and a `Pump` object is that a customer's arrival, followed by a request, determines when the `Pump` is activated and how much gas is requested. Thus, each interaction between a `Customer` and a `Pump` can be expressed by the pseudocode:

> ***Obtain a Customer arrival time***
> ***Obtain a Customer request for gas***
> ***Activate the Pump with the request***

Although this repetition of events takes place continuously over the course of a day, we are only interested in a one-half hour period. Therefore, we must place these three events in a loop that is executed until the required simulation time has elapsed.

Having developed and coded the two required classes, `Pump` and `Customer`, what remains to be developed is the control logic within the `main()` function for correctly activating class events. This will require a loop controlled by the total arrival time for all customers. A suitable control structure for `main()` is described by the algorithm:

> **Create a Pump object with the required initial supply of gas**
> **Display the values in the initialized Pump**
> **Set the total time to 0**
> **Obtain a Customer arrival time   // first arrival**
> **Add the arrival time to the total time**
> **While the total time does not exceed the simulation time**
> > **Display the total time**
> > **Obtain a Customer request for gas**
> > **Activate the Pump with the request**
> > **Obtain a Customer arrival time // next arrival**
> > **Add the arrival time to the total time**
>
> **EndWhile**
> **Display a message indicating that the simulation is over**

C++ code corresponding to this algorithm is listed as Program 11-14.

Program 11-14

```cpp
#include <c:\\cpcode\\Pump.cpp>        // note use of full path name here
#include <c:\\cpcode\\Customer.cpp>    // again - a full path name is used

const double SIMTIME = .5;             // simulation time in hours
const int MINUTES = 60;                // number of minutes in an hour

int main()
{
  Pump a(2.00, 300);                   // declare 1 object of type Pump
  Customer b;                          // declare 1 object of type Customer
  int totalTime = 0;
  int idleTime;
  int amtRequest;
  int SimMinutes;                      // simulation time in minutes
  SimMinutes = SIMTIME * MINUTES;
  cout << "\nStarting a new simulation - simulation time is "
       << SimMinutes << " minutes" << endl;
  a.getValues();

  // get the first arrival
  idleTime = b.arrive();
  totalTime += idleTime;
```

(continued on next page)

```
while (totalTime <= SimMinutes)
{
    cout << "\nThe idle time is " << idleTime << " minutes" << endl
         << "    and we are " << totalTime
         << " minutes into the simulation." << endl;
    amtRequest = b.gallons();
    a.request(double(amtRequest));

    // get the next arrival
    idleTime = b.arrive();
    totalTime += idleTime;
}
cout << "\nThe idle time is " << idleTime << " minutes." << endl
     << "As the total time now exceeds the simulation time, " << endl
     << "    this simulation run is over." << endl;

return 0;
}
```

Assuming that the Pump and Customer classes have been thoroughly tested and debugged, testing and debugging Program 11-14 is really restricted to testing and debugging the main() function. This specificity of testing is one of the great advantages of an object-oriented approach. Using previously written and tested class definitions allows us to focus our attention on the remaining code that controls the flow of events between objects, which in Program 11-14 centers on the main() function.

By itself, the main() function in Program 11-14 is a straightforward while loop where the Pump idle time corresponds to the time between customer arrivals. The output of a sample run, shown below, verifies that the loop is operating correctly:

```
Starting a new simulation - simulation time is 30 minutes

The gas tank has 300 gallons of gas.
The price per gallon of gas is $2.00

The idle time is 2 minutes
    and we are 2 minutes into the simulation.
7.00 gallons were requested
7.00 gallons were pumped
293.00 gallons remain in the tank
The total price is $14.00

The idle time is 1 minutes
    and we are 3 minutes into the simulation.
15.00 gallons were requested
15.00 gallons were pumped
278.00 gallons remain in the tank
The total price is $30.00
```

```
The idle time is 11 minutes
    and we are 14 minutes into the simulation.
13.00 gallons were requested
13.00 gallons were pumped
265.00 gallons remain in the tank
The total price is $26.00

The idle time is 8 minutes
    and we are 22 minutes into the simulation.
20.00 gallons were requested
20.00 gallons were pumped
245.00 gallons remain in the tank
The total price is $40.00

The idle time is 9 minutes.
As the total time now exceeds the simulation time,
    this simulation run is over.
```

In reviewing the operation of Program 11-14, realize that we have used the same `Customer` object for each arrival and request. In Section 12.4 we will see how to dynamically create a new `Customer` object for each arrival and destroy the created object when it has completed its designated task.

Exercises 11.6

1. Enter Program 11-13 on your computer and execute it.

2. Enter Program 11-14 on your computer and execute it.

3. a. Remove the inline methods in the `Customer` class declaration and implementation section by constructing individual declaration and implementation sections. Discuss which form of the `Customer` class you prefer and why.
    b. Rewrite the `gallons()` method in the `Customer` class so that it returns a double-precision number between 3.0 and 20.0 gallons.

4. In place of the `main()` function used in Program 11-14, a student proposed the following:

```
const double SIMTIME = .5;          // simulation time in hours
const int MINUTES = 60;             // number of minutes in an hour

int main()
{
  Pump a(2.00, 300);    // declare 1 object of type Pump
  Customer b;           // declare 1 object of type Customer
  int totalTime = 0;
  int idleTime;
  int amtRequest;
  int SimMinutes;       // simulation time in minutes
```

```
  SimMinutes = SIMTIME * MINUTES;
  cout << "\nStarting a new simulation - simulation time is "
        << SimMinutes << " minutes" << endl;
  a.getValues();

  do
  {
    idleTime = b.arrive();
    totalTime += idleTime;
    if (totalTime > (SIMTIME * MINUTES))
    {
      cout << "\nThe idle time is " << idleTime << " minutes." << endl
            << "As the total time now exceeds the simulation time, " << endl
            << "    this simulation run is over." << endl;
      break;
    }
    else
    {
      cout << "\nThe idle time is " << idleTime << " minutes" << endl
            << "    and we are " << totalTime
            << " minutes into the simulation." << endl;
      amtRequest = b.gallons();
      a.request(double(amtRequest));
    }
  } while (1);   // always true

  return 0;
}
```

Determine if this main() function produces a valid simulation. If it does not, explain why. If it does, discuss which version you prefer and why.

5. Using the Elevator class created in Section 6.7 (Class 6-2) and defining a new class named Person, construct a simulation whereby a person randomly arrives at any time from 1 to 10 minutes on any floor and calls the elevator. If the elevator is not on the same floor as the person, it must move to the floor that the person is on. Once inside the elevator, the person can select any floor except the current one. Run the simulation for three randomly arriving people and have the simulation display the movement of the elevator.

11.7 A CLOSER LOOK: ADAPTING COUT AND CIN FOR OBJECTS

For all of the class examples seen so far, a class method has been used to output an object's attribute values. Since a user-defined type should provide all of the functionality of a built-in type, we should be able to input and output object values using `cin` and `cout`, respectively. This, in fact, is the case.

As has already been noted, `cin` is the name of an input stream object of the class `istream` that connects data sent from the standard input device, which is the keyboard, to a program. Similarly, `cout` is an output stream object of class `ostream` that connects output from the program to the standard output device, which is the screen.

For our current purposes we only need to know that the insertion, or "put to", operator `<<` is both defined and overloaded in the `ostream` class to handle the output of built-in types, while the extraction, or "get from", operator `>>` is both defined and overloaded in the `istream` class to handle input of built-in types. The capabilities of both the `ostream` and `istream` classes are available to the `iostream` class (through the process of inheritance explained in the next chapter). Thus, we have access to the `cin` and `cout` streams, and the insertion and extraction operators through the `iostream` class that we have been including in all of our programs. This access permits us to create our own overloaded versions of the `<<` and `>>` operator functions to specifically handle user-defined object types.

Specifically, the process of making `cin` extractions and `cout` insertions available to a user-defined class consists of:

1. Making each overloaded operator function a friend of the user-defined class (this ensures that these overloaded functions will have access to a class's private data members).

2. Constructing an overloaded version for each operator function that is appropriate to the user-defined class.

What makes overloading the insertion and extraction operators so easy is that the function prototypes and header lines for each overloaded function can be created by following a series of straightforward steps. To understand how this is accomplished in practice, consider Program 11-15, which overloads the insertion and extraction operators to handle objects of type `Date`.

Program 11-15

```cpp
#include <iostream>
using namespace std;

class Date
{
   friend ostream& operator<<(ostream&, const Date&);  // overloaded insertion
                                                        // operator
   friend istream& operator>>(istream&, Date&);         // overloaded extraction
                                                        // operator

   // data declaration section
   private:
      int month;
      int day;
      int year;

   // method declarations
   public:
      Date(int = 7, int = 4, int = 2006);               // constructor
}

// methods implementation section

// overloaded insertion operator function
ostream& operator<<(ostream& out, const Date& adate)
{
   out << adate.month << '/' << adate.day << '/' << adate.year;

   return out;
}

// overloaded extraction operator function
istream& operator>>(istream& in, Date& somedate)
{
   in >> somedate.month;    // accept the month part
   in.ignore(1);            // ignore 1 character, the /
   in >> somedate.day;      // get the day part
   in.ignore(1);            // ignore 1 character, the /
   in >> somedate.year;     // get the year part

   return in;
}
```

(continued on next page)

11

```
Date::Date(int mm, int dd, int yyyy)     // constructor
{
    month = mm;
    day = dd;
    year = yyyy;
}

int main()
{
    Date a;

    cout << "Enter a date: ";
    cin  >> a;          // accept the date using cin
    cout << "The date just entered is " << a << endl;

    return 0;
}
```

Following is a sample run using Program 11-15:

```
Enter a date: 1/15/2008
The date just entered is 1/15/2008
```

In reviewing Program 11-15 first notice that within the `main()` function a `Date` object is entered using `cin` and is output using `cout`. Now take a look at the class declaration for `Date` and notice that two friend functions have been included in the friend's list using the function prototype declarations:

```
friend ostream& operator<<(ostream&, const Date&);
friend istream& operator>>(istream&, Date&);
```

The first declaration makes the overloaded insertion operator function (`<<`) a friend of the `Date` class, while the second statement does the same for the overloaded extraction operator function (`<<`). In the first declaration, the `<<` operator has been declared to return a reference to the `ostream` object and to have two formal parameters, a reference to an `ostream` object and a reference to a `Date` class, which is a constant. Similarly, in the second declaration the `>>` operator has been declared to return a reference to an `istream` object and to have two formal parameters, a reference to an `istream` object and a reference to a `Date` object. By simply changing the class name `Date` to the name of any other class and including these declarations within the class's declaration section, these two prototypes can be used in any user-defined class. Thus, the general syntax of these declarations, applicable to any class are:

```
friend ostream& operator<<(ostream&, const className&);
friend istream& operator>>(istream&, className&);
```

Now consider the implementations of these overloaded functions. Consider first the overloaded insertion operator function, which for convenience we repeat below:

```
ostream& operator<<(ostream& out, const Date& adate)
{
  out << adate.month << '/' << adate.day << '/' << adate.year;

  return out;
}
```

Although the name of the reference to a `Date` object has been named `adate`, any user-selected name would do. Similarly, the argument named `out`, which is a reference to an `ostream` object, can be any user-selected name. Within the body of the function we insert the month, day, and year members of the `Date` object to the `out` object, which is then returned from the function. As required in the header line, `out` is a reference to an `ostream` object. Also notice the notation used in inserting the month, day, and year to `out`:

```
adate.month
adate.day
adate.year
```

This notation follows the notation introduced in Section 7.1 that includes both the object name and attribute name, with the names separated by a period. This was the reason for making the overloaded operator function a friend of the `Date` class. By doing so, the overloaded insertion operator has direct access to a `Date` object's month, day, and year data members.

Now consider the implementations of the overloaded extraction operator function, which for convenience is repeated below:

```
// overloaded extraction operator function
istream& operator>>(istream& in, Date& somedate)
{
  in >> somedate.month;    // accept the month part
  in.ignore(1);            // ignore 1 character, the /
  in >> somedate.day;      // get the day part
  in.ignore(1);            // ignore 1 character, the /
  in >> somedate.year;     // get the year part

  return in;
}
```

11

The header line for this function declares that it will return a reference to an `istream` object and has two reference arguments: a reference to an `istream` object and a reference to a `Date` object. The argument names, `in` and `somedate`, can be replaced by any other user-selected names.

The body of the function first extracts a value for the `month` variable of the `Date`, then uses the `ignore member` function of `istream` to ignore the next input character, which is usually a slash,(/). The value for the `day` variable is then extracted, the next character is ignored, and finally the value for the `year` variable is extracted. Thus, if the user typed in the data 1/15/2008 or the date 1-15-2008, the overloaded extractor function would extract 1, 15, and 2008 as the month, day, and year values, respectively. Although this same effect is produced by the single line

```
in >> somedate.month >> '/' >> somedate.day >> '/' >> somedate.year;
```

the coding used in Program 11-15 makes it clear that we are ignoring the delimiting character.

Exercises 11.7

1. **a.** Modify the overloaded insertion operator function in Program 11-15 so that it displays dates in the form day-month-year, which is the European standard.
   b. Modify the overloaded insertion operator function in Program 11-15 to accept a third character argument. If the actual argument is an E, the displayed date should be in European format of day-month-year; otherwise it should be in the American standard form of month/day/year.

2. Rewrite the overloaded extraction operator in Program 11-15 so that it will display a date, such as 1/15/2008 in the form 01/15/08.

3. For the `Time` class constructed in Exercise 2 of Section 11.1, remove the display method and include overloaded extraction and insertion extraction operator functions for the input and output of `Time` objects using `cin` and `cout`, respectively. Times should be displayed in the form hrs:min:sec.

4. For the `Complex` class constructed in Exercise 3 of Section 11.1, remove the display method and include overloaded extraction and insertion extraction operator functions for the input and output of `Complex` objects using `cin` and `cout`, respectively.

11.8 COMMON PROGRAMMING ERRORS

The following are some common errors related to creating class operator functions and conversion methods:

1. Using the keyword `static` when defining either a `static` data or method member. Here, the `static` keyword should be used only within a class declaration section.

2. Failing to instantiate `static` data members before creating class objects that attempt to access these data members.

3. Using a user-defined assignment operator, which has not been defined, in a multiple-assignment expression to return an object.

4. Using the keyword `friend` when defining a `friend` function. The `friend` keyword should be used only within a class declaration section.

5. Attempting to redefine an operator's meaning as it applies to C++'s built-in data types.

6. Redefining an overloaded operator to perform a function not indicated by its conventional meaning. Although this will work, it is an example of poor programming practice.

7. Attempting to make a conversion operator function a friend, rather than a member function.

8. Attempting to specify a return type for a member conversion operator function.

11.9 CHAPTER REVIEW

Key Words

assignment operator

copy constructor

data type conversions

friend functions

inheritance

operator functions

operator()

operator[]

static method

static variable

SUMMARY

1. An assignment operator may be declared for a class with the function prototype:

   ```
   void operator=(className&);
   ```

   Here, the argument is a reference to the class name. The return type of `void` precludes using this operator in multiple assignment expressions such as `a = b = c`.

2. A type of initialization that closely resembles assignment occurs in C++ when one object is initialized using another object of the same class. The constructor that performs this type of initialization is called a *copy constructor* and has the function prototype:

   ```
   className(const className&);
   ```

   This is frequently represented using the notation `X(X&)`.

3. For each class object a separate set of memory locations is reserved for all data members, except those declared as `static`. A `static` variable is shared by all class objects and provides a means of communication between objects. Static data members must be declared as such within the class declaration section and are defined outside of the declaration section.

4. Static class methods apply to the class as a whole, rather than individual objects. As such, a `static` method can access only `static` data members and other `static` methods. Static methods must be declared as such within the class declaration section and are defined outside of the declaration section.

5. A nonmember function may access a class's private data members if it is granted `friend` status by the class. This is accomplished by declaring the function as a `friend` within the class's declaration section. Thus, it is always the class that determines which nonmember functions are friends; a function can never confer `friend` status on itself.

6. User-defined operators can be constructed for classes using member operator functions. An operator function has the form `operator<symbol>`, where `<symbol>` is one of the following:

   ```
   ()   []   ->   new   delete   ++   --   !   ~   *   /   %   +   -
   <<   >>   <   <=   >   >=   ++   !=   &&   ||   &   ^   |   =   +=
   -=   *=   /=   %=   &=   ^=   |=   <<=   >>=   ,
   ```

   For example, the function prototype `Date operator+(int);` declares that the addition operator will be defined to accept an integer and return a `Date` object.

7. User-defined operators may be called in either of two ways—as a conventional function with arguments or as an operator expression. For example, for an operator having the header line

   ```
   Date Date::operator+(int)
   ```

if `dte` is an object of type `Date`, the following two calls produce the same effect:

```
dte.operator+(284)
dte + 284
```

8. Operator functions may also be written as `friend` functions. The equivalent `friend` version of a member operator function will always contain an additional class reference that is not required by the member function.

9. The subscript operator function, `operator[]`, permits a maximum of one nonclass argument. This function can only be defined as a member function.

10. The parentheses operator function, `operator()`, has no limits on the number of arguments. This function can only be defined as a member function.

11. There are four categories of data type conversions:

   - from built-in types to built-in types

   - from built-in types to class (user-defined) types

   - from class (user-defined) types to built-in types

   - from class (user-defined) types to class (user-defined) types

   Built-in to built-in type conversions are done using C++'s implicit conversion rules or by explicitly using casts. Built-in to user-defined type conversions are done using type conversion constructors. Conversions from user-defined types to either built-in or other user-defined types are accomplished using conversion operator functions.

12. A type conversion constructor is a constructor whose first argument is not a member of its class and whose remaining arguments, if any, have default values.

13. A conversion operator function must be a member function. It has no explicit arguments or return type; rather, the return type is the name of the function.

14. The `cout` insertion operator (`<<`) and the `cin` extraction operator (`>>`) can be overloaded to work with any class objects as follows:

   a. Make each overloaded operator function a `friend` of the user-defined class (this ensures that these overloaded functions will have access to a class's private instance variables).
   b. Construct an overloaded version for each operator function that is appropriate to the user-defined class.

   The general function prototype syntax for providing these operator functions with `friend` status is:

```
friend ostream& operator<<(ostream&, const ClassName&);
friend istream& operator>>(istream&, ClassName&);
```

   These prototypes should be placed in the declaration section of the desired class and the `ClassName` in each declaration should be changed to the actual class name.

Chapter Exercises

1. **a.** Construct a class named `Cartesian` that contains two double-precision data members named x and y, which will be used to store the x and y values of a point in rectangular coordinates. The function members should include a constructor that initializes the x and y values of an object to 0, and functions to input and display an object's x and y values. Additionally, include an assignment function that performs a memberwise assignment between two `Cartesian` objects.
    b. Include the class written for Exercise 1a in a working C++ program that creates and displays the values of two `Cartesian` objects, the second of which is assigned the values of the first object.

2. **a.** Construct a class named `Savings` that contains three double-precision data members named `balance`, `rate`, and `interest`, and a constructor that initializes each of these members to 0. Additionally, include a member function that inputs a balance and rate and then calculates an interest. The rate should be stored as a percent, such as 6.5 for 6.5%, and the interest computed as *interest = balance x rate/100*. Include a member function to display all member values.
    b. Include the class written for Exercise 2a in a working C++ program that tests each member function.

3. **a.** Redo Exercise 2, except make `rate` a static data member and include a static member function to input and alter `rate`'s value.
    b. Include the class written for Exercise 3a in a working C++ program that tests each member function.

4. **a.** Construct a class named `Coord` that contains two double-precision instance variables named `xval` and `yval`, which will be used to store the x and y values of a point in rectangular coordinates. Class methods should include appropriate constructor and display methods and a `friend` function named `conv_pol()`. The `conv_pol()` function should accept two double-precision numbers that represent a point in polar coordinates and convert them into rectangular coordinates. For conversion from polar to rectangular coordinates use the formulas:

    $$x = r \cos\theta$$
    $$y = r \sin\theta$$

    b. Include the program written for Exercise 4a in a working C++ program.

5. **a.** Construct two classes named `Rec_coord` and `Pol_coord`. The class named `Rec_coord` should contain two double-precision instance variables named `xval` and `yval`, which will be used to store the x and y values of a point in rectangular coordinates. The class methods should include appropriate constructor and display methods and a friend function named `conv_pol()`.

    The class named `Pol_coord` should contain two double-precision instance variables named `dist` and `theta`, which will be used to store the distance and angle values of a point represented in polar coordinates. The class methods should include appropriate constructor and display methods and a friend function named `conv_pol()`.

The friend function should accept an integer argument named `dir`; two double-precision arguments named `val1` and `val2`; and two reference arguments named `recref` and `polref`, the first of which should be a reference to an object of type `rec_coord`, and the second to an object of type `pol_coord`. If the value of `dir` is 1, `val1` and `val2` are to be considered as x and y rectangular coordinates that are to be converted to polar coordinates; if the value of `dir` is any other value, `val1` and `val2` are to be considered as distance and angle values that are to be converted to rectangular coordinates. For conversion from rectangular to polar coordinates, use:

$$r = \sqrt{x^2 + y^2}$$

$$\theta = tan^{-1}\,(y/x)$$

For conversion from polar to rectangular coordinates, use the formulas:

$$x = r\,cos\theta$$
$$y = r\,sin\theta$$

b. Include the program written for Exercise 5a in a working C++ program.

6. List three C++ operators that cannot be overloaded.

7. **a.** Create a class named `Fractions` having two integer data members named for a fraction's numerator and denominator. The class's default constructor should provide both data members with default values of 1 if no explicit user initialization is provided. The constructor must also prohibit a 0 denominator value. Additionally, provide member functions for displaying an object's data values. Also provide the class with overloaded operators that are capable of adding, subtracting, multiplying, and dividing two `Fraction` objects according to the following formulas:

$$\text{Sum of two fractions:}\quad \frac{a}{b} + \frac{c}{d} = \frac{ad + cb}{bd}$$

$$\text{Difference of two fractions:}\quad \frac{a}{b} - \frac{c}{d} = \frac{ad - cb}{bd}$$

$$\text{Product of two fractions:}\quad \frac{a}{b} \times \frac{c}{d} = \frac{ac}{bd}$$

$$\text{Division of two fractions:}\quad \frac{a}{b} \Big/ \frac{c}{d} = \frac{ad}{bc}$$

b. Include the class written for Exercise 7a within a working C++ program that tests each of the class's member functions.

11

8.   a. Include a member function named `gcd()` in the `Fraction` class constructed in Exercise 7a that reduces a fraction to its lowest common terms. Thus, a fraction such as 2/4 would be reduced to 1/2. The means of doing this is to divide both the numerator and denominator values by their greatest common divisor (see Exercise 5 in the Chapter Exercises of Chapter 7 for a description of obtaining the greatest common divisor of two numbers).

  b. Modify the constructor written for Exercise 7a to include a call to `gcd()` so that every initialized fraction is in lowest common terms. Also make sure that each overloaded operator function also uses `gcd()` to return a fraction in lowest common terms.

  c. Replace the display function with an overloaded insertion operator so that a `Fraction` object can be inserted directly into the `cout` stream. Also include an overloaded extraction operator that will use the `cin` stream with a Fraction object.

Testing Center

Please visit the Testing Center at www.course.com/testingcenter for more practice on class functions and conversions.

12

INHERITANCE, POLYMORPHISM, AND DYNAMIC MEMORY ALLOCATION

The ability to create new classes from existing ones is the underlying motivation and power behind class- and object-oriented programming techniques. Doing so facilitates re-using existing code in new ways without the need for retesting and validation. It permits the designers of a class to make it available to other programmers without relinquishing control over existing class features, while at the same time allowing other programmers to make additions and extensions.

Constructing one class from another is accomplished using a capability called inheritance. Related to this capability is an equally important feature named polymorphism. Polymorphism provides the ability to invoke appropriate versions of a method depending on the type of class object being referenced. In fact, for a programming language to be classified as an object-oriented language it must provide the features of classes, inheritance, and polymorphism.

In this chapter you will learn about inheritance and polymorphism. Additionally, you'll learn how to create and delete objects dynamically—that is, while a program is executing.

12.1 CLASS INHERITANCE

In this section we describe the inheritance and polymorphism features provided in C++. **Inheritance** is the capability of deriving one class from another class. The initial class used as the basis for the derived class is referred to as either the **base**, **parent**, or **superclass**. The **derived** class is referred to as the **child**, or **subclass**.

A derived class is a completely new class that incorporates all of the variables and methods of its base class. It can, and usually does, however, add its own new variables and methods and can override any base class method.

As an example of inheritance, consider three geometric shapes consisting of a circle, cylinder, and sphere. All of these shapes share a common characteristic, a radius. Thus, for these shapes we can make the circle a base type for the other two shapes, as illustrated in Figure 12-1. Reformulating these shapes as class types, we would make `Circle` the base class and derive `Cylinder` and `Sphere` classes from it.

PROGRAMMING NOTE

Object-Based Versus Object-Oriented Languages

An object-*based* language is one in which data and operations can be incorporated together in such a way that data values can be isolated and accessed through the specified class methods. The ability to bind the data members with operations in a single unit is referred to as **encapsulation**. The class capability of C++ makes encapsulation possible.

For a language to be classified as object-*oriented* it must also provide inheritance and polymorphism. Inheritance is the capability to derive one class from another. A derived class is a completely new data type that incorporates all of the variables and methods of the original class with any new variables and methods unique to itself. The class used as the basis for the derived type is referred to as the base or parent class and the derived data type is referred to as the derived or child class.

Polymorphism permits the same method name to invoke one operation in objects of a parent class and a different operation in objects of a derived class.

C++, which provides encapsulation, inheritance, and polymorphism, is a true object-oriented language. Because C, which is C++'s predecessor, does not provide these features, it is neither an object-based nor an object-oriented language.

FIGURE 12-1
Relating Object Types

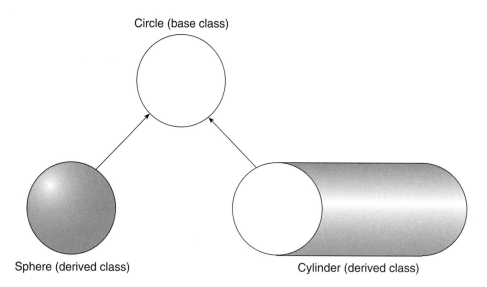

The relationships illustrated in Figure 12-1 are examples of simple inheritance. In **simple inheritance** each derived type has only one immediate base type. The complement to simple inheritance is multiple inheritance. In **multiple inheritance** a derived type has two or more base types. Figure 12-2 illustrates an example of multiple inheritance. In this text we will only consider simple inheritance.

FIGURE 12-2
An Example of Multiple Inheritance

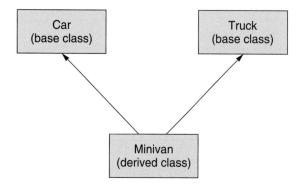

The class derivations illustrated in both Figures 12-1 and 12-2 are formally referred to as **class hierarchies**, because they illustrate the hierarchy, or order, in which one class is derived from another. Let's now see how to derive one class from another.

A derived class has the same form as any other class, in that it consists of both a declaration and an implementation. The only difference is in the first line of the declaration section. For a derived class this line is extended to include an access specification and a base class name and has the form:

```
class  DerivedClassName : ClassAccess  BaseClassName
```

For example, if `Circle` is the name of an existing class, a new class named `Cylinder` can be derived as follows:

```
class Cylinder : public Circle
{
    // add any additional data and
    // function members here
};  // end of Cylinder class declaration
```

Except for the class-access specifier after the colon and the base class name, there is nothing inherently new or complicated about the construction of the `Cylinder` class. Before providing a description of the `Circle` class and adding data and function members to the derived `Cylinder` class, we will need to re-examine access specifiers and how they relate to derived classes.

ACCESS SPECIFICATIONS

Until now we have only used private and public access specifiers within a class. Giving all data members private status ensured that they can only be accessed by either class member methods or friends. This restricted access prevents access by any nonclass functions (except friends), *which also precludes access by any derived class functions.* This is a sensible restriction because if it did not exist anyone could "jump around" the private restriction by simply deriving a class.

To retain a restricted type of access across derived classes, C++ provides a third access specification— protected access. Protected access behaves identically to private access in that it only permits member or friend function access, but it permits this restriction to be inherited by any derived class. The derived class then defines the type of inheritance it is willing to take on, subject to the base class's access restrictions. This is done by the class-access specifier, which is listed after the colon at the start of its declaration section. Table 12-1 lists the resulting derived class member access based on the base class member specifications and the derived class-access specifier.

TABLE 12-1
Inherited Access Restrictions

base class member	derived class access	derived class member
private ⟶	: private ⟶	inaccessible
protected ⟶	: private ⟶	private
public ⟶	: private ⟶	private
private ⟶	: public ⟶	inaccessible
protected ⟶	: public ⟶	protected
public ⟶	: public ⟶	public
private ⟶	: protected ⟶	inaccessible
protected ⟶	: protected ⟶	protected
public ⟶	: protected ⟶	protected

As you can see in the highlighted rows of Table 12-1, if the base class member has a protected access and the derived class specifier is public, then the derived class member will be protected to its class. Similarly, if the base class has a public access and the derived class specifier is public, the derived class member will be public. As this is the most commonly used type of specification for base class data and function members, respectively, it is the one we will use. This means that for all classes intended for use as a base class, we will use a protected data member access in place of a private designation.

AN EXAMPLE

To illustrate the process of deriving one class from another, we will derive a `Cylinder` class from a base `Circle` class. The definition of the `Circle` class is:

```
// class declaration
class Circle
{
  protected:
    double radius;
  public:
    Circle(double);  // constructor
    double calcval();
};

// class implementation
// constructor
Circle::Circle(double r = 1.0)  // constructor
```

12

```
{
   radius = r;
}

// calculate the area of a Circle
double Circle::calcval(void)
{
   return(PI * radius * radius);
}
```

Except for the substitution of the `protected` specification in place of the usual `private` specification for the data member, this is a standard class definition. The only variable not defined is PI, which is used in the `calcval()` function. We will define this as:

```
const double PI = 2.0 * asin(1.0);
```

This is simply a "trick" that forces the computer to return the value of PI accurate to as many decimal places as allowed by your computer. This value is obtained by taking the arcsin of 1.0, which is $\pi/2$, and multiplying the result by 2.

Having defined our base class, we can now extend it to a derived class. The definition of the derived class is:

```
// class declaration where
// Cylinder is derived from Circle

class Cylinder : public Circle
{
  protected:
    double length;   // add one additional data member and
  public:            // two additional function members
    Cylinder(double r = 1.0, double l = 1.0) : Circle(r), length(l) {}
    double calcval();
};

// class implementation
double Cylinder::calcval(void)          // this calculates a volume
{
   return (length * Circle::calcval()); // note the base function call
}
```

This definition encompasses several important concepts relating to derived classes. First, as a derived class, `Cylinder` contains all of the data and function members of its base class, `Circle`, plus any additional members that it may add. In this particular case the `Cylinder` class consists of a radius data member, inherited from the `Circle` class, plus an additional `length` member. Thus, each `Cylinder` object contains *two* data members, as is illustrated in Figure 12-3.

FIGURE 12-3
Relationship Between Circle *and* Cylinder *Data Members*

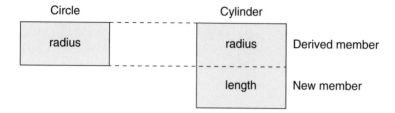

In addition to having two data members, the Cylinder class also inherits Circle's function members. This is illustrated in the Cylinder constructor, which uses a base member initialization list (see Section 11.1) that specifically calls the Circle constructor. It is also illustrated in Cylinder's calcval() function, which makes a call to Circle::calcval().

In both classes the same function name, calcval(), has been specifically used to illustrate the overriding of a base function by a derived function. When a Cylinder object calls calcval() it is a request to use the Cylinder version of the function, while a Circle object call to calcval() is a request to use the Circle version. In this case the Cylinder class can only access the class version of calcval() using the scope resolution operator, as is done in the call Circle::calcval(). Program 12-1 uses these two classes within the context of a complete program.

Program 12-1

```cpp
#include <iostream>
#include <cmath>
using namespace std;

const double PI = 2.0 * asin(1.0);

class Circle
{
  // data declaration section
  protected:
    double radius;
  // methods declaration section
  public:
    Circle(double);            // constructor
    double calcval();
};

// methods implementation section for Circle
```

(continued on next page)

12

```cpp
Circle::Circle(double r= 1.0)   // constructor
{
  radius = r;
}

// calculate the area of a Circle
double Circle::calcval(void)
{
  return(PI * pow(radius,2));
}
// the Cylinder class is derived from Circle
class Cylinder : public Circle
{
  //data declaration section
  protected:
    double length;   // add one additional data member
  // methods declaration section
  public:            // two additional member methods
    Cylinder(double r = 1.0, double l = 1.0) : Circle(r), length(l) {}
    double calcval();
};

// methods implementation section for Cylinder

double Cylinder::calcval(void)              // this calculates a volume
{
  return (length * Circle::calcval()); // note the base function call
}

int main()
{
  Circle CircleOne, CircleTwo(2);   // create two Circle objects
  Cylinder CylinderOne(3,4);        // create one Cylinder object

  cout << "The area of CircleOne is " << CircleOne.calcval() << endl;
  cout << "The area of CircleTwo is " << CircleTwo.calcval() << endl;
  cout << "The volume of CylinderOne is " << CylinderOne.calcval() << endl;

  CircleOne = CylinderOne;          // assign a Cylinder to a Circle

  cout << "\nThe area of CircleOne is now " << CircleOne.calcval() << endl;

  return 0;
}
```

The output produced by Program 12-1 is:

```
The area of CircleOne is 3.14159
The area of CircleTwo is 12.5664
The volume of CylinderOne is 113.097

The area of CircleOne is now 28.2743
```

The first three output lines are all straightforward and are produced by the first three `cout` statements in the program. As the output shows, a call to `calcval()` using a `Circle` object activates the `Circle` version of this method, while a call to `calcval()` using a `Cylinder` object activates the `Cylinder` version.

The assignment statement `CircleOne = CylinderOne;` introduces another important relationship between a base and derived class: *A derived class object can be assigned to a base class object.*

This should not be surprising because both base and derived classes share a common set of data member types. In this type of assignment it is only this set of data members, which consist of all the base class data members, that are assigned. Thus, as illustrated in Figure 12-4, our `Cylinder` to `Circle` assignment results in the following member-wise assignment:

```
CircleOne.radius = CylinderOne.radius;
```

The `length` member of the `Cylinder` object is not used in the assignment because it has no equivalent variable in the `Circle` class. The reverse cast, from base to derived class, is not as simple and requires a constructor to correctly initialize the additional derived class members not in the base class.

FIGURE 12-4
Assignment from Derived to Base Class

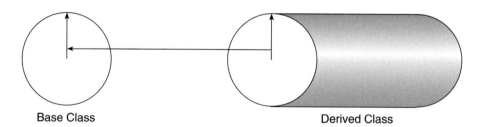

Circle = Cylinder

Base Class   Derived Class

Before leaving Program 12-1 one additional point should be made. Although the `Circle` constructor was explicitly called using a base-member initialization list for the `Cylinder` constructor, an implicit call could also have been made. In the absence of an explicit derived class constructor, the compiler will automatically call the default base class constructor first, before the derived class constructor is called. This works because the derived class contains all of the base class data members. In a similar fashion the destructor methods are called in the reverse order—the derived class first and then the base class.

Exercises 12.1

1. Define the following terms:

    a. inheritance
    b. base class
    c. derived class
    d. simple inheritance
    e. multiple inheritance
    f. class hierarchy

2. Describe the difference between a private and a protected class member.

3. What three features must a programming language provide for it to be classified as an object-oriented language?

4. a. Modify Program 12-1 to include a derived class named Sphere from the base Circle class. The only additional class members of sphere should be a constructor and a calcval() function that returns the volume of the sphere. (*Note:* For volume, use the formula *4/3 π radius³.*)
    b. Include the class constructed for Exercise 4a in a working C++ program. Have your program call all of the member methods in the Sphere class.

12.2 POLYMORPHISM

Overriding a base member method using an overloaded derived member method, as was illustrated by the calcval() function in Program 12-1, is an example of polymorphism. **Polymorphism** permits the same function name to invoke one response in objects of a base class and another response in objects of a derived class. In some cases, however, this method of overriding does not work as one might desire. To understand why this is so, consider Program 12-2:

Program 12-2

```
#include <iostream>
#include <cmath>
using namespace std;

// this is the base class
class One
{
  protected:
    double a;
  public:
    One(double);    // constructor
```

(continued on next page)

```cpp
    double f1(double);        // a member method
    double f2(double);        // another member method
};

// methods implementation section for class One
One::One(double val = 2)      // constructor
{
  a = val;
}

double One::f1(double num)    // a member method
{
  return(num/2);
}
double One::f2(double num)    // another member method
{
  return( pow(f1(num),2) );   // square the result of f1()
}
```

```cpp
// this is the derived class
class Two : public One
{
  public:
    double f1(double);        // this overrides class One's f1()
};

// methods implementation section for class Two

double Two::f1(double num)
{
  return(num/3);
}
```

```cpp
int main()
{
  One objectOne;   // objectOne is an object of the base class
  Two objectTwo;   // objectTwo is an object of the derived class

    // call f2() using a base class object call
  cout << "The computed value using a base class object call is "
       << objectOne.f2(12) << endl;

    // call f2() using a derived class object call
  cout << "The computed value using a derived class object call is "
       << objectTwo.f2(12) << endl;

  return 0;
}
```

The output produced by this program is:

```
The computed value using a base class object call is 36
The computed value using a derived class object call is 36
```

As this output shows, the same result is obtained no matter which object type calls the `f2()` method. This result is produced because the derived class does not have an override to the base class `f2()` method. Thus, both calls to `f2()` result in the base class `f1()` method being called.

Once invoked, the base class `f2()` method will always call the base class version of `f1()` rather than the derived class override version. This behavior is due to a process referred to as **function binding**. There are two types of function binding: static and dynamic.

In normal function calls static binding is used. In **static binding** the determination of which method is called is made at compile time. Thus, when the compiler first encounters the `f1()` method in the base class it makes the determination that whenever `f2()` is called, either from a base or derived class object, it will subsequently call the base class `f1()` method.

In place of static binding, what is required is a binding method that is capable of determining which method should be invoked at run-time, based on the object type making the call. This type of binding is referred to as **dynamic binding**. To achieve dynamic binding, C++ provides virtual functions.

A **virtual method**, which is also referred to as a virtual function, tells the compiler to create a pointer to a method, but not fill in the value of the pointer until the method is actually called. Then, at run-time, *and based on the object making the call*, the appropriate method address is used. Creating a virtual method is easy—all that is required is that the keyword `virtual` be placed before the method's return type in the declaration section. For example, consider Program 12-3, which is identical to Program 12-2 except for the virtual declaration of the `f1()` method.

Program 12-3

```cpp
#include <iostream>
#include <cmath>
using namespace std;

// this is the base class
class One
{
  protected:
    double a;
  public:
    One(double);                  // constructor
    virtual double f1(double);    // a member method
    double f2(double);            // another member method
};

// methods implementation section for class One
One::One(double val = 2)          // constructor
```

(continued on next page)

```
{
  a = val;
}

double One::f1(double num)        // a member method
{
  return(num/2);
}

double One::f2(double num)        // another member method
{
  return( pow(f1(num),2) );       // square the result of f1()
}
```

```
// this is the derived class
class Two : public One
{
  public:
    virtual double f1(double);   // this overrides class One's f1()
};

// methods implementation for class Two
double Two::f1(double num)
{
  return(num/3);
}
```

```
int main()
{
  One objectOne;   // objectOne is an object of the base class
  Two objectTwo;   // objectTwo is an object of the derived class

    // call f2() using a base class object call
  cout << "The computed value using a base class object call is "
       << objectOne.f2(12) << endl;
    // call f2() using a derived class object call
  cout << "The computed value using a derived class object call is "
       << objectTwo.f2(12) << endl;

  return 0;
}
```

The output produced by Program 12-3 is:

```
The computed value using a base class object call is 36
The computed value using a derived class object call is 16
```

12

As illustrated by this output the f2() function now calls different versions of the overloaded f1() function, based on the object type making the call. This selection, based on the object making the call, is the classic definition of polymorphic function behavior and is caused by the dynamic binding imposed on f1() by virtue of its being a virtual function.

Once a function is declared as virtual *it remains virtual for the next derived class with or without a virtual declaration in the derived class*. Thus, the second virtual declaration in the derived class is not strictly needed, but should be included both for clarity and to ensure that any subsequently derived classes correctly inherit the function. Consider the inheritance diagram illustrated in Figure 12-5, where class C is derived from class B and class B is derived from class A. In this situation, if function f1() is virtual in class A, but is not declared in class B, it will not be virtual in class C.

The only other requirement is that once a function has been declared as virtual, the return type and parameter list of all subsequent derived class override versions *must be* the same.

FIGURE 12-5
Simple Inheritance Diagram

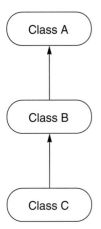

Exercises 12.2

1. Enter and execute Programs 12-2 and 12-3 on your computer so that you understand the relationship between method calls in each program.

2. Describe the two methods C++ provides for implementing polymorphism.

3. Describe the difference between static binding and dynamic binding.

4. Describe the difference between a virtual function and a nonvirtual function.

5. Describe what polymorphism is and provide an example of polymorphic behavior.

6. Discuss whether the multiplication operator provided for both the integer and double built-in types is an example of overloading or polymorphism.

12.3 THE THIS POINTER

Except for static data members, which are shared by all class objects, each object maintains its own set of instance variables. This permits each object to have its own clearly defined state as determined by the values stored in its instance variables.

For example, consider the Date class previously defined in Program 11-1 and repeated below for convenience:

```cpp
#include <iostream>
#include <iomanip>
using namespace std;

class Date
{
  // data declaration section
  private:
    int month;
    int day;
    int year;

    // method declarations
    public:
      Date(int = 7, int = 4, int = 2007); // constructor with default arguments
      void showDate(); // accessor
};

// methods implementation section

Date::Date(int mm, int dd, int yyyy)
{
  month = mm;
  day = dd;
  year = yyyy;
}

void Date::showDate()
{
  cout << setfill('0')
       << setw(2) << month << '/'
       << setw(2) << day << '/'
       << setw(2) << year % 100 << endl;
}
```

12

Each time an object is created from this class, a distinct area of memory is set aside for its instance variables. For example, if two objects named a and b are created from this class, the memory storage for these objects would be as illustrated in Figure 12-6. Notice that each set of instance variables has its own starting address in memory, which corresponds to the address of the first instance variable for the object.

FIGURE 12-6
The Storage of Two Date *Objects in Memory*

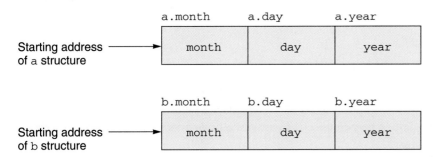

This replication of data storage is not implemented for class methods. In fact, for each class *only one copy of all methods is retained in memory,* and each object uses these same methods.

Sharing methods requires providing a means of identifying which specific object a method should be operating on. This is accomplished by providing address information to the method indicating where in memory the particular object is located. This address is provided by the name of the object, which is in fact a reference name. For example, again using our Date class and assuming a is an object of this class, the statement a.showDate() passes the address of the a object into the showDate() member method.

An obvious question at this point is how this address is passed to showDate() and where it is stored. The answer is that the address is stored in a special parameter named this, which is automatically supplied as a hidden parameter to each nonstatic class method when the method is called.

Unlike a reference parameter, which is effectively a named constant for an address, the this parameter is a pointer. Pointer parameters provide much more flexibility in using addresses than reference parameters. For our current purposes, all we need to know is that to gain access to the object whose address is provided by the this pointer, we must apply either the indirection operator, *, or the arrow operator (->) to this.

Before proceeding to use the this pointer in a "cookbook" manner, let's take a moment to compare the differences between a pointer's address and a reference address. Recall from Section 7.4 that whenever a reference parameter is encountered it is always *the content of the reference address* that is accessed. This type of access is referred to as automatic or implicit dereferencing of the address, and effectively hides the fact that a reference parameter is fundamentally a named constant for an address. In using a pointer parameter, dereferencing is not automatic. To access the contents of the address provided by the this pointer, the notation *this or its equivalent this-> must be used. This formally provides a means of obtaining the referenced variable. This is also known as **explicit dereferencing** because the extra operation involved in using the pointer parameter (in this case named `this`) to locate the final value being accessed is explicitly indicated.

Returning now to our `Date` class, which has three member methods, the actual argument list of the constructor `Date()` method is equivalent to

```
Date(Date *this, int mm, int dd, int yy)
```

where the declaration `Date *this` means that the `this` pointer contains the address of a specific `Date` object. Similarly, the actual parameter list of `showDate()` is equivalent to

```
showDate(Date *this)
```

The important point here is to understand that when a member method is called it actually receives an extra, hidden parameter that is the address of a `Date` object. Although it is usually not necessary to do so, a `this` pointer data member can be explicitly used within all class methods. For example, consider Program 12-4, which uses the hidden parameter `this` within the body of each class method to access the appropriate instance variables.

Program 12-4

```cpp
#include <iostream>
#include <iomanip>
using namespace std;

class Date
{
  // data declaration section
  private:
    int month;
    int day;
    int year;

  // methods declaration section
  public:
    Date(int = 7, int = 4, int = 2007); // constructor with default arguments
    void showDate();                     // accessor
};

// methods implementation section
Date::Date(int mm, int dd, int yyyy)
{
  (*this).month = mm;
  (*this).day = dd;
```

(continued on next page)

```
  (*this).year = yyyy;
}

void Date::showDate()
{
  cout << setfill('0')
       << setw(2) << (*this).month << '/'
       << setw(2) << (*this).day << '/'
       << setw(2) << (*this).year % 100 << endl;
}
```

```
int main()
{
  Date a(4,1,2007), b(12,18,2008);  // declare two objects

  cout << "The date stored in a is originally ";
  a.showDate();                     // display the original date
  a = b;                            // assign b's value to a
  cout << "After assignment the date stored in a is ";
  a.showDate();                     // display a's values

  return 0;
}
```

The output produced by Program 12-4 is:

```
The date stored in a is originally 4/1/07
After assignment the date stored in a is 12/18/08
```

This is the same output produced by Program 11-1, which omits using the this pointer to access the data members. Clearly, using the this pointer in Program 12-4 is unnecessary and simply clutters the member method code. There are times, however, when an object must pass its address on to other methods. In these situations, one of which we now consider, the address stored in the this pointer must explicitly be used.

THE ASSIGNMENT OPERATOR REVISITED

A simple assignment operator function was defined in Program 11-2 and is repeated below for convenience:

```
void Date::operator=(Date& newdate)
{
  day = newdate.day;       // assign the day
  month = newdate.month;   // assign the month
  year = newdate.year;     // assign the year
}
```

The drawback of this function is that it does not return a value, making multiple assignments such as `dateThree = dateTwo = dateOne` impossible. Now that we have the `this` pointer at our disposal, we can fix our simple assignment operator function to provide an appropriate return type. In this case the return value should be a `Date` rather than a `void`. Making this change in the function's prototype for our assignment operator yields:

```
Date operator=(const Date&);
```

Notice also that we have declared the function's argument to be a `const`, which ensures that this operand cannot be altered by the function. A suitable function definition for this prototype is:

```cpp
Date  Date::operator=(const Date& newdate)
{

  day = newdate.day;        // assign the day
  month = newdate.month;    // assign the month
  year = newdate.year;      // assign the year

  return *this;
}
```

In the case of an assignment such as `b = c`, or its equivalent form `b.operator=(c)`, the function first alters b's member values from within the function and then returns the value of this object, which may be used in a subsequent assignment. Thus, a multiple assignment expression such as `a = b = c` is possible and is illustrated in Program 12-5.

Program 12-5

```cpp
#include <iostream>
#include <iomanip>
using namespace std;

class Date
{
  // data declaration section
  private:
    int month;
    int day;
    int year;
  // methods declaration section
  public:
    Date(int = 7, int = 4, int = 2007); // constructor
    Date operator=(const Date&);        // define assignment of a date
    void showDate();                    // member method to display a date
};
```

(continued on next page)

```cpp
// methods implementation section
Date::Date(int mm, int dd, int yy)
{
   month = mm;
   day = dd;
   year = yy;
}

Date Date::operator=(const Date& newdate)
{
   day = newdate.day;        // assign the day
   month = newdate.month;    // assign the month
   year = newdate.year;      // assign the year

   return *this;
}

void Date::showDate()
{
   cout << setfill('0')
        << setw(2) << month << '/'
        << setw(2) << day << '/'
        << setw(2) << year % 100 << endl;
}
```

```cpp
int main()
{
   Date a(4,1,2007), b(12,18,2008), c(1,1,2009); // declare three objects

   cout << "Before assignment a's date value is ";
   a.showDate();
   cout << "Before assignment b's date value is ";
   b.showDate();
   cout << "Before assignment c's date value is ";
   c.showDate();

   a = b = c;   // multiple assignment

   cout << "\nAfter assignment a's date value is ";
   a.showDate();
   cout << "After assignment b's date value is ";
   b.showDate();
   cout << "After assignment c's date value is ";
   c.showDate();

   return 0;
}
```

The output produced by Program 12-5 is:

```
Before assignment a's date value is 4/1/07
Before assignment b's date value is 12/18/08
Before assignment c's date value is 1/1/09

After assignment a's date value is 1/1/09
After assignment b's date value is 1/1/09
After assignment c's date value is 1/1/09
```

The only restriction on the assignment operator function is that it can only be overloaded as a member method. It cannot be overloaded as a friend function.

Exercises 12.3

1. Discuss the difference between the automatic dereferencing that occurs when a reference parameter is used and the explicit dereferencing that occurs using either the indirection operator, *, or the arrow operator, -> with the `this` parameter.

2. Modify Program 12-4 so that the notation `this->` is used in place of the notation `*this` within the body of both the constructor and `showDate()` methods. In doing so notice that the -> symbol is constructed using a minus sign, –, followed by a greater-than symbol, >.

3. Rewrite the `Date()`, `setDate()`, and `showDate()` class methods in Program 11-2 to explicitly use the `this` pointer when referencing all data members. Run your program and verify that the same output as produced by Program 11-2 is achieved.

4. A problem with the assignment operator defined in this section is that it does not return a suitable l-value (recall from Section 4.1 that an l-value is a value that can be used on the left side of an assignment statement). Although Program 12-5 defines a return type for the `Date` assignment operator, the return type is not used as an l-value because the expression a = b = c is evaluated as a = (b = c). Thus, in both the initial assignment b = c and the subsequent assignment a = b, the return value of the assignment operator is used as an r-value (that is, it is used on the right side of an assignment). Modify the assignment operator so that the expression returns a correct l-value. This means that in the evaluation of the expression (a = b) = c, the initial l-value returned should be a.

12.4 PROGRAM DESIGN AND DEVELOPMENT

In addition to inheritance and polymorphism, another feature of object-oriented programs is the ability to both create and destroy objects while a program is executing. This feature, which is referred to as dynamic object creation and deletion, is presented in this section. To understand how dynamic creation and deletion is accomplished, we present an initial application that takes a first look at the dynamic allocation and deallocation of memory storage. This is followed by an extension of the multi-object simulation presented in Section 11.6. In that simulation the same `Customer` object was re-used to simulate multiple `Customer` arrivals. In the problem presented in this chapter, different `Customer` objects are dynamically created as they are needed and deleted once their task has been completed.

You will encounter dynamic allocation a third time, when we look at linked lists, including stacks and queues, in Chapter 13, and one final time as they apply to the dynamic creation and destruction of arrays, in Chapter 14. Each presentation can be read independently.

APPLICATION 1: DYNAMIC OBJECT CREATION AND DELETION

As each variable or object is defined in a program, sufficient storage for it is designated by the compiler and assigned from a pool of computer memory locations before the program is executed. Once specific memory locations have been assigned, they remain fixed for the lifetime of the variable and object or until the program has finished executing. For example, if a function requests storage for three nonstatic integers and five objects of a user-defined class, the storage for these integers and objects remains fixed from the point of their definition until the function finishes executing.

An alternative to this fixed allocation of memory is a dynamic allocation. Under dynamic allocation, the amount of allocated storage is determined and assigned as the function is executing, rather than being fixed prior to execution.

Although dynamic allocation of memory is most useful when dealing with lists, where it allows the list to expand as new items are added and contracted as items are deleted, it can also be useful in simulation programs. For example, in simulating the arrival and departure of `Customer`s, it is helpful to have a mechanism whereby a new `Customer` can be randomly created and then removed after being serviced. Two C++ operators, `new` and `delete`, provide this capability as described in Table 12-2.

TABLE 12-2
The Dynamic Allocation and Deallocation Operators

operator name	description
`new`	Reserves the correct number of bytes for the variable or object type requested by the declaration. Returns the address of the first reserved location or a NULL value if sufficient memory is not available.
`delete`	Releases previously reserved memory

From an operational viewpoint, dynamically allocated variables and objects created using the `new` operator are only accessible using the address returned by `new`. This means that, like the `this` pointer, the address of the newly created variable or object must be stored in a pointer variable. The mechanism for doing this is rather simple. For example, the statement `int *num = new int;` both reserves a memory area sufficient to hold one integer and places the address of this storage area into a pointer

---

PROGRAMMING NOTE
Using a `typedef` Statement

Among other uses, a `typedef` statement can be used to create a new and shorter name for pointer definitions. The syntax for a `typedef` statement is:

```
typedef dataType newTypeName;
```

For example, to make the name `PtrToInt` a synonym for the term `int *`, the following statement can be used:

```
typedef int *PtrToInt;
```

Such a statement would normally be placed at the top of a program file immediately after all `#include`s. If this is done, the term `PtrToInt` can be used in place of the notation `int *`. Thus, for example, the declaration

```
PtrToInt   pointerOne;
```

can replace the statement

```
int *pointerOne;
```

Both statements declare that `pointerOne` is a pointer to an integer value.

By convention all `typedef` names are written in either initial cap or all uppercase letters, but this is not mandatory. The names used in a `typedef` statement can be any name that conforms to C++'s identifier naming rules.

---

variable named `num`. This same dynamic allocation can also be made in two steps; the first step is to declare a pointer variable using a declaration statement followed by a statement requesting dynamic allocation. Using this two-step process, the single statement `int *num = new int;` can be replaced by the sequence of statements

```
int *num;        // this declares a pointer variable that can
                 // store the address of an integer
num = new int;   // this reserves memory for an integer and
                 // puts the address of the memory area into num
```

In either case, the allocated storage area comes from the computer's free storage area.[1] Dynamically creating an object is accomplished using the same technique as dynamically creating a variable for a built-in data type. How this is accomplished and understanding why the dynamic creation of objects is so useful is addressed next.

---

[1]The free storage area of a computer is formally referred to as the heap. The heap consists of unallocated memory that can be allocated to a program, as requested, while the program is running.

> **PROGRAMMING NOTE**
>
> **Pointers Versus References**
>
> The distinguishing characteristic of a pointer, either as a formal parameter or variable, is that every pointer contains a value that is an address. Whereas a pointer is a variable or argument *whose content is an address*, a reference is an address. As such, a reference can be thought of as a named constant, where the constant is a value that happens to be a valid memory address.
>
> From an advanced programming viewpoint, pointers are much more flexible than references. This is because a pointer's contents can be manipulated in much the same manner as any other variable's value. For example, if foo is a pointer, the statement cout << foo; displays the value stored in the pointer variable. This is identical to the operation of displaying the value of an integer or floating-point variable. That the value stored in a pointer happens to be an address is irrelevant as far as cout is concerned.
>
> The disadvantage of pointers is that their very flexibility makes them more complicated to understand and use than reference parameters or variables. Since references can only be used as a named address, they are easier to use. Thus, when the compiler encounters a reference it automatically dereferences the address to obtain the contents of the address. This is not the case with pointers. If you use a pointer's name, as we have noted, you access the pointer's contents. To correctly dereference the address stored in a pointer you must explicitly use C++'s dereference operator, *, in front of the pointer name. This informs the compiler that what you want is the item whose address is in the pointer variable.

For example, the declaration

```
Customer *anotherCust;
```

declares anotherCust as a pointer variable that can be used to store the address of a Customer object. The actual creation of a new Customer object is completed by the statement

```
anotherCust = new Customer;
```

This statement both creates a new Customer object and stores the address of the first reserved memory location into the pointer variable anotherCust. Program 12-6 illustrates this sequence of code within the context of a complete program.

Program 12-6

```
#include <iostream>
#include <ctime>
#include <cmath>
using namespace std;
```

(continued on next page)

```cpp
// Customer class
// precondition: srand() must be called once before any member methods
// postcondition: arrive() returns a random integer between 1 and 15
//               : gallons() returns a random integer between 3 and 20

class Customer
{
  public:
    Customer() {cout << "\n**** A new Customer has been created ****" << endl;};
    ~Customer() {cout << "!!!! This Customer object has been deleted !!!!" << endl;};
    int arrive() {return(1 + rand() % 15);};
    int gallons() {return(3 + rand() % 18);};
};
```

```cpp
int main()
{
    Customer *anotherCust; // declare a pointer to an object of type Customer
    int i, howMany;
    int interval, request;

    cout << "Enter the number of Customers to be created: ";
    cin  >> howMany;
    srand(time(NULL));
    for(i = 1; i <= howMany; i++)
    {
        // create a new object of type Customer
        anotherCust = new Customer;

        // use the pointer to access the member methods
        interval = anotherCust->arrive();
        request = anotherCust->gallons();
        cout << "The arrival interval is " << interval << " minutes" << endl;
        cout << "The new Customer requests " << request << " gallons" << endl;
        cout << "The memory address of this object is: "<< int(anotherCust) << endl;

        // delete the created object
        // delete anotherCust;
    }

return 0;
}
```

Before looking at a sample output produced by Program 12-6 and analyzing how this output was produced by the `main()` function, consider the declaration of the `Customer` class. Notice that we have included an in-line constructor function to display the message

```
**** A new Customer has been created ****
```

whenever an object is created and an in-line destructor function to display the message

```
!!!! This Customer object has been deleted !!!!
```

whenever an object is deleted. These messages are only used to help you monitor the creation and deletion of an object when the program is executed. Also notice that we have not included the `srand()` function call within the constructor as we did in our original `Customer` class implementation presented in Section 11.6. Rather, we have made the calling of `srand()` a precondition to using any member method.

The primary reason for not including an `srand()` call in the `Customer` class constructor is that inclusion of this function would mean that it is called each time an object is created, when a single initial call to `srand()` is really all that is necessary for any single program execution. For large simulation runs where hundreds or even thousands of `Customer` objects can be created and deleted, execution times can be excessive and the savings in run times by careful placement of both function calls and calculations within repetitive loops can be dramatic.

Following is a sample output produced by Program 12-6:

```
Enter the number of Customers to be created: 4

**** A new Customer has been created ****
The arrival interval is 7 minutes
The new Customer requests 6 gallons
The memory address of this object is: 3279920

**** A new Customer has been created ****
The arrival interval is 10 minutes
The new Customer requests 9 gallons
The memory address of this object is: 3280040

**** A new Customer has been created ****
The arrival interval is 13 minutes
The new Customer requests 9 gallons
The memory address of this object is: 3280048

**** A new Customer has been created ****
The arrival interval is 4 minutes
The new Customer requests 13 gallons
The memory address of this object is: 3280136
```

As illustrated by this output, we can make the decision as to how many objects are to be created by Program 12-6 while the program is executing. Figure 12-7 illustrates the allocation of memory space corresponding to this sample output just before the program completes execution.

FIGURE 12-7
The Memory Allocation Produced by the Sample Execution of Program 12-6

1st allocation at `3279920`

2nd allocation at `3280040`

3rd allocation at `3280048`

4th allocation at `3280136`

Now look at the `main()` function to see how this output was produced. First notice that new `Customer` objects are created using the statements:

```
Customer *anotherCust;
anotherCust = new Customer;
```

The first statement defines a single pointer variable named `anotherCust`. Each time the second statement is executed, a new object is created and its address is stored in the `anotherCust` variable (the old address is lost).[2] Notice also that this stored address can be displayed by inserting the pointer variable name in the `cout` stream as we have done in the last executable statement contained within `main()`'s body. Since the content of a pointer variable is a value, this value, even though it happens to be an address, can be displayed using the `cout` stream. Each time the value is displayed it simply represents the current address stored in the variable. Notice also that the last line in the `main()` function comments out the statement `delete anotherCust;`. This was done intentionally to force each newly created object into a new memory area. If a `delete` had been used to release the previously allocated block of storage, the operating system would simply provide the same locations right back for the next allocation. In this case you would not see the assigned address change while the programming is executing.[3] In practice, however, it is very important to delete dynamically created objects

---

[2]In practice, the object whose address is currently in the pointer variable would have been deleted prior to re-using the pointer variable, so that the address being overwritten would be of no use anyway.

[3]The allocated storage would automatically be returned to the heap when the program completed execution. It is, however, good practice to formally restore the allocated storage back to the heap using `delete` when the memory is no longer needed. This is especially true for larger programs that make numerous requests for additional storage areas.

when their usefulness ends. As you can see by the sample output, if you don't, the computer system starts to effectively "eat up" available memory space.

Finally, notice the notation used to access the member methods of each dynamically created object. For example, the notation `anotherCust->arrive()` calls the `arrive()` function of the object whose address resides in the pointer variable `anotherCust`. Since dynamically created objects do not have symbolic names, they can only be accessed using the address information contained within the pointer variable. This can be done using the notation `pointerName->methodName()` shown in Program 12-6 or by using the equivalent notation `(*pointerName).methodName()`.

APPLICATION 2: A DYNAMIC GAS PUMP SIMULATION

In the multi-object simulation presented in Section 11.6, one `Customer` object was used repeatedly to simulate multiple `Customer` arrivals. Using the information presented in the previous application, we now can write this simulation using dynamically created new and different `Customer` objects that are deleted once their request for gas has been fulfilled.

As with all dynamic allocations, at least one pointer variable must be available to store the address of the newly created object. The `new` operator is used to actually reserve this memory space and return the address, which should be assigned to the pointer variable. For example, the declaration

```
Customer *anotherCust;
```

declares a pointer variable named `anotherCust` that can be used to store an address of a `Customer` object.[4] Once this pointer has been defined, it can be used in an assignment statement such as `anotherCust = new Customer;` that both allocates new storage and stores the address of the allocated area into the pointer variable.

For our simulation we will require both a `Pump` class and a `Customer` class. The `Customer` class, which is identical to that used in Program 12-6 except for the message displayed by the constructor, is:

```
#include <iostream>
#include <cmath>
using namespace std;

// Customer class declaration
// precondition: srand() must be called once before any function methods
// postcondition: arrive() returns a random integer between 1 and 15
//              : gallons() returns a random integer between 3 and 20
```

---

[4]It should be noted that the width of all addresses is the same, be they addresses of `Customer` objects, `Pump` objects, or integer variables. Typically an address is either 32 or 48 bits wide. The reason for specifying the type of object is to inform the compiler of how many bytes must be accessed when the address is dereferenced. The actual allocation of memory for the object depends on how many data members it has, plus a fixed minimum size, which is typically 8 or 16 bytes.

```cpp
class Customer
{
  public:
     Customer() {cout << "\n**** A new Customer has arrived ****"
                      << endl;};
    ~Customer() {cout << "!!!! The Customer has departed !!!!" << endl;};
    int arrive() {return(1 + rand() % 15);};
    int gallons() {return(3 + rand() % 18);};
};
```

For convenience we assume that this class is stored as NewCustomer.cpp in the Classes directory of a C drive.

The Pump class is exactly the same as that used in Chapter 11, and is repeated below for convenience.

```cpp
// class declaration

#include <iostream>
#include <iomanip>
using namespace std;

const double AMOUNT_IN_TANK = 500;   // initial gallons in the tank
const double DEFAULT_PRICE = 1.80;    // price per gallon

class Pump
{
  // data declaration section
  private:
    double amtInTank;
    double price;

  // method declarations
  public:
    Pump(double = DEFAULT_PRICE, double = AMOUNT_IN_TANK);   // constructor
    void getValues();
    void request(double);
};

// methods implementation section

Pump::Pump(double todaysPrice, double amountInTank)
{
  amtInTank = amountInTank;
  price = todaysPrice;
}
```

```
void Pump::getValues()
{
  cout << "\nThe gas tank has " << amtInTank << " gallons of gas." << endl;
  cout << "The price per gallon of gas is $" << setiosflags(ios::showpoint)
       << setprecision(2) << setiosflags(ios::fixed) << price << endl;
}

void Pump::request(double pumpAmt)
{
  double pumped;

  if (amtInTank >= pumpAmt)
     pumped = pumpAmt;
  else
     pumped = amtInTank;

  amtInTank -= pumped;
  cout << pumpAmt << " gallons were requested " << endl;
  cout << pumped << " gallons were pumped" << endl;
  cout << amtInTank << " gallons remain in the tank" << endl;
  cout << "The total price is $" << setiosflags(ios::showpoint)
       << setprecision(2) << (pumped * price) << endl;

  return;
}
```

We assume that this class has been thoroughly tested and has been stored on a C drive in the Classes directory as Pump.cpp. In using these pre-existing Pump and Customer classes, all that remains to be developed is the control logic within the main() function for correctly creating Pump and Customer objects, and controlling the interaction between objects by appropriately activating class methods. A suitable control structure for main() is described by the following pseudocode:

> **Create a Pump object with the required initial gallons of gas**
> **Display the values in the initialized Pump**
> **Set the total time to 0**
>
> **Create the first Customer object**
> **Obtain the Customer's interval arrival time**
> **Add the arrival time to the total time**
>
> **While the total time does not exceed the simulation time**
>   **Display the total time**
>   **Obtain a Customer request for gas**
>   **Activate the Pump with the request**
>   **Delete this Customer object**

> *Create a new Customer // next arrival*
> *Obtain the Customer's interval arrival time*
> *Add the arrival time to the total time*
> *EndWhile*
>
> *Display a message that the simulation is over*

The C++ code corresponding to our design is illustrated in Program 12-7.

Program 12-7

```cpp
#include <c:\Classes\Pump.cpp>          // note use of full path name here
#include <c:\Classes\NewCustomer.cpp>   // again a full path name is used
#include <ctime>

const double SIMTIME = .5;              // simulation time in hours
const int MINUTES = 60;                 // number of minutes in an hour

int main()
{
  Pump a(2.00, 300);      // declare 1 object of type Pump
  Customer *anotherCust;  // declare a pointer to an object of type Customer
  int totalTime = 0;
  int idleTime;
  int amtRequest;
  int SimMinutes;         // simulation time in minutes

  SimMinutes = SIMTIME * MINUTES;
  cout << "\nStarting a new simulation - simulation time is "
       << SimMinutes << " minutes" << endl;
  a.getValues();

  srand(time(NULL));

  // create a new object of type Customer
  anotherCust = new Customer;

  // get the Customer's arrival time
  idleTime = anotherCust->arrive();
  totalTime += idleTime;

  while (totalTime <= SimMinutes)
  {
```

(continued on next page)

```
    cout << "The idle time is " << idleTime << " minutes" << endl
         << "   and we are " << totalTime
         << " minutes into the simulation." << endl;
    amtRequest = anotherCust->gallons();
    a.request(double(amtRequest));

    // delete this Customer
    delete anotherCust;

    // create the next Customer
    anotherCust = new Customer;
    // get the next arrival
    idleTime = anotherCust->arrive();
    totalTime += idleTime;
  }
  cout << "The idle time is " << idleTime << " minutes." << endl
       << "\nAs the total time now exceeds the simulation time, " << endl
       << "   this simulation run is over." << endl;

  return 0;
}
```

Because the Pump and Customer classes are known to correctly meet their respective specifications, testing and debugging Program 12-7 can be restricted to testing and debugging the main() function. By itself, the main() function in Program 12-7 uses a straightforward while loop that creates and deletes Customer objects within a simulated time span of SimMinutes. Within the program the Pump idle time corresponds to the time between Customer arrivals. Notice that the notation used to dereference the address in the pointer variable anotherCust and activate the arrive() method is anotherCust->arrive(). In place of this notation, the alternative notation (*anotherCust).arrive() can be used. The output of a sample run, shown below, verifies that the loop is operating correctly:

```
    Starting a new simulation - simulation time is 30 minutes

    The gas tank has 300 gallons of gas.
    The price per gallon of gas is $2.00

    **** A new Customer has arrived ****
    The idle time is 2 minutes
        and we are 2 minutes into the simulation.
    19.00 gallons were requested
    19.00 gallons were pumped
    281.00 gallons remain in the tank
    The total price is $38.00
    !!!! The Customer has departed !!!!
```

```
**** A new Customer has arrived ****
The idle time is 14 minutes
    and we are 16 minutes into the simulation.
9.00 gallons were requested
9.00 gallons were pumped
272.00 gallons remain in the tank
The total price is $18.00
!!!! The Customer has departed !!!!

**** A new Customer has arrived ****
The idle time is 12 minutes
    and we are 28 minutes into the simulation.
14.00 gallons were requested
14.00 gallons were pumped
258.00 gallons remain in the tank
The total price is $28.00
!!!! The Customer has departed !!!!

**** A new Customer has arrived ****
The idle time is 1 minutes
    and we are 29 minutes into the simulation.
11.00 gallons were requested
11.00 gallons were pumped
247.00 gallons remain in the tank
The total price is $22.00
!!!! The Customer has departed !!!!

**** A new Customer has arrived ****
The idle time is 3 minutes.

As the total time now exceeds the simulation time,
    this simulation run is over.
```

Exercises 12.4

1. a. Explain how dynamic allocation of memory works.
    b. Describe the process of creating a dynamically allocated object. Specifically, discuss the roles of a pointer variable and the `new` operator in creating a dynamically allocated object.
    c. Discuss the importance of deleting dynamically allocated objects and explain what can happen if such objects are not deleted.

2. Programs 11-13 and 12-7 both produce a valid simulation. Discuss the advantages and disadvantages of using multiple `Customer` objects in Program 12-7 as opposed to using a single `Customer` object in Program 11-13.

3. a. Modify Program 12-7 to use the `Customer` class defined in Program 11-13 (that is, put the `srand()` function call back into the constructor function). Now run the program and notice that the same arrival times are obtained for each newly created `Customer` object. What do you think causes this effect?
    b. To correct the problem noticed in Exercise 3a, place the following loop in the constructor function. (*Note*: After you add the loop, the constructor can no longer take the form of an in-line function.)

    ```
    for(int i = 0; i < 500000; i++);
    ```

    What does this loop accomplish? Run the program and notice that the randomness of `Customer` arrivals has been restored. What do you notice about the time it takes to execute a complete simulation? Comment about the efficiency of your modified program as compared to Program 12-7.

4. a. Describe what a pointer is.
    b. For each of the following pointer declarations, identify the name of the pointer variable and the data type of the object that will be accessed when the address in the pointer variable is dereferenced.

    ```
    Customer *a;
    Pump *pointer1;
    Pump *addr_of_aPump;
    int *addr_of_int;
    double *b;
    ```

    c. If the asterisks were removed from the declarations in Exercise 4b, what would the names immediately preceding the semicolon represent?

12.5 COMMON PROGRAMMING ERRORS

The following common programming errors are associated with inheritance, pointers, and dynamic memory allocation:

1. Attempting to override a virtual function without using the same type and number of arguments as the original function.

2. Using the keyword `virtual` in the class implementation section. Functions are only declared as virtual in the class declaration section.

3. Using the default copy constructor and default assignment operators with classes containing pointer members. Since these default functions do a member-wise copy, the address in the source pointer is copied to the destination pointer. Typically this is not what is wanted, since both pointers end up pointing to the same memory area.

4. Forgetting that `this` is a pointer that must be dereferenced using either `*this` or `this->`.

12.6 CHAPTER REVIEW

Key Terms

base class

class hierarchy

derived class

dynamic binding

inheritance

multiple inheritance

polymorphism

simple inheritance

static binding

this pointer

virtual function

SUMMARY

1. Inheritance is the capability of deriving one class from another class. The initial class used as the basis for the derived class is referred to as the base, parent, or superclass. The class created from the base class is referred to as either the derived class, child, or subclass.

2. Base class methods can be overridden by derived class methods with the same name. The override method is simply an overloaded version of the base class method defined in the derived class.

3. Polymorphism is the capability of having the same method name invoke different responses based on the object making the method call. Polymorphism can be achieved via override methods or virtual methods, also know as virtual functions.

4. In static binding, the determination of which method actually is invoked is made at compile-time. In dynamic binding, the determination is made at run-time.

5. A virtual method specification designates that dynamic binding should take place. The specification is made in the method's declaration by placing the keyword `virtual` before the method's return type. Once a method has been declared as virtual, it remains so for all derived classes as long as there is a continuous trail of method declarations through the derived chain of classes.

6. For each class, only one copy of a class' methods is retained in memory, and each object uses the same method. The address of an object is provided to the class method by passing a hidden parameter corresponding to the memory address of the selected object to the method. The address is passed in a special pointer parameter named `this`. The `this` pointer may be used explicitly by a class method to access the object's variables.

7. Pointers may be included as instance variables.

8. The default copy constructor and default assignment operators are typically not useful with classes containing pointer instance variables. This is because these default functions do a member-wise copy in which the address in the source pointer is copied to the destination pointer, resulting in both pointers "pointing to" the same memory area. For these situations you must define your own copy constructor and assignment operator.

Chapter Exercises

1. Describe the difference between static and dynamic binding.

2. a. Create a base class named `Point` that consists of an x- and y-coordinate. From this class, derive a class named `Circle` that has an additional instance variable named `radius`. For this derived class, the `x` and `y` instance variables represent the center coordinates of a `Circle`. The methods of the first class should consist of a constructor, an area method named `area` that returns zero, and a distance method that returns the distance between two points, where

$$distance = \sqrt{(x2 - x1)^2 + (y2 - y1)^2}$$

   Additionally, the derived class should have a constructor and an override method named `area` that returns the area of `Circle`.

   b. Include the classes constructed for Exercise 2a in a working C++ program. Have your program call all of the methods in each class. In addition, call the base class distance method with two `Circle` objects and explain the result returned by the method.

3. a. Using the classes constructed for Exercise 2a, derive a class named `Cylinder` from the derived `Circle` class. The `Cylinder` class should have a constructor and an override method named `area` that determines the surface area of the `Cylinder`. For this method use the algorithm *surface area = 2 π r (l + r)*, where `r` is the radius of the `Cylinder` and *l* is the length.

   b. Include the classes constructed for Exercise 3a in a working C++ program. Have your program call all of the member methods in the `Cylinder` class.

   c. What do you think might be the result if the base class distance method was called with two `Cylinder` objects?

4. a. Create a base class named `Rectangle` that contains `length` and `width` instance variables. From this class, derive a class named `Box` having an additional instance variable named `depth`. The methods of the base `Rectangle` class should consist of a constructor and an area method. The derived `Box` class should have a constructor and an override method named `area` that returns the surface area of the box and a method named `volume` that returns the volume of the box.

   b. Include the class written for Exercise 4a in a working C++ program that tests each class' method.

5. a. Construct a class named `TelBook` that contains instance variables capable of holding a last name, first name, and telephone number. The constructor should set each of these variables to a `'\0'`. Additionally, there should be class methods to input data values, display data values, and to assign one object's data values to another object.

    b. Include the class written for Exercise 5a in a working C++ program that tests each class method.

Testing Center

Please visit the Testing Center at www.course.com/testingcenter for more practice on inheritance, polymorphism, and dynamic memory allocation.

13

THE STANDARD TEMPLATE LIBRARY

As we have seen in Section 8.5, C++ provides a vector class for storing, ordering, and retrieving objects that permits the list to expand or contract as objects are added or removed from it. In this chapter we present two additional types of list maintenance classes, both of which are supported by the same Standard Template Library (STL) from which vectors are derived. You'll learn about these two new classes by studying three specific list-handling applications: linked lists, stacks, and queues. You will also study the underlying algorithm for a linked list. The advantage of using STL classes is that the advanced programming capabilities underlying linked lists, stacks, and queues are all provided as part of the STL class implementations.

This chapter is intended as an introduction to the Standard Template Library. A full textbook would be required to cover the complete set of classes and capabilities provided by the STL. Additionally, the applications presented in this chapter represent a very small subset of those that can be addressed using the STL. Typically, the second course in a computer science curriculum is specifically devoted to presenting advanced applications that can be programmed using either the STL or similarly constructed classes.

13.1 THE STANDARD TEMPLATE LIBRARY

You have already worked with one kind of list, an array, which is the list of choice for a fixed-length set of related data. Many programming applications, however, require variable-length lists that must constantly be expanded and contracted as items are added to and removed from the list. Although expanding and contracting an array can be accomplished by creating, copying, and deleting arrays, this solution tends to be costly in terms of initial programming, maintenance, and testing time.

In all but the simplest situations, it is more efficient to use the Standard Template Library (STL) to create and manipulate lists. One purpose of the STL is to provide a fully tested and generic set of easily used lists that can be maintained in various configurations. This is accomplished by calling either prewritten class methods or generalized algorithms applicable to all STL-created list types. The STL is one component of the larger Standard Library of header files and classes. It provides a broad range of generic capabilities for rapidly constructing and manipulating lists of elements that consist of either built-in variables or objects. These STL capabilities allow you to maintain lists and perform operations on them, such as sorting and searching, without having to fully understand or program the advanced and frequently complicated underlying algorithms.

Currently the STL provides seven different types of lists, each supported by its own class. These seven list types are summarized in Table 13-1.

TABLE 13-1
STL Lists

list type	classification	usage
vector	sequence	Dynamic arrays
list	sequence	Linked lists
deque	sequence	Stacks and queues
set	associative	Binary trees without duplicate elements
multiset	associative	Binary trees that may have duplicate elements
map	associative	Binary trees with a unique key that does not permit duplicate elements
multimap	associative	Binary trees with a unique key that permits duplicate elements

As listed in Table 13-1, the seven different list types are classified as either sequence or associative. A **sequence list** is one in which a list element is determined solely by its position in the list—that is, by where the element was placed in the list and how it may have been subsequently moved. For example, both arrays and vectors are sequence lists, where an element's position in the list is determined by the exact order in which it was added into the array or vector or subsequently moved. An **associative list** is automatically maintained in a sorted order. An element's position in an associative list depends on its value and a selected sorting criterion. For example, an alphabetical list of names depends on the name and a sorting criterion, rather than on the exact order that individual names were entered into the list. In this chapter we will only address STL's sequence types. You already learned about one kind of sequence list, the vector type, in Section 8.6.

Before you begin working with lists and the STL, it's helpful to understand the difference between the lists provided by the STL and arrays. An array is a built-in list type. By contrast, the lists provided by the STL are class types. Although arrays are most often used to directly store built-in numerical data types, they still retain general characteristics common to the more advanced lists provided by the STL. For example, like an array, an STL list can be empty, which means that it currently holds no items. When discussing both arrays and lists provided by the STL, a list is considered to be a container that can hold a collection of zero or more items, each of which is of the same type. For this reason, STL lists and arrays are referred to as both **containers** and **collections**, and we will use these terms interchangeably. Additionally, a list must provide a means for accessing individual elements. When a list provides this individual data location capability, it becomes a data structure. In an array this location ability is provided by the position of each element in the array, which is designated using an integer index value.

Although STL lists can also store built-in data types, they are more commonly used to store and maintain objects. When used in commercial applications, the stored objects are usually referred to as records. Once an object's structure has been defined, we require some means of collecting all of the objects into a single list. For example, the objects that we may be storing could be students' academic records. In addition to the individual records, a means is needed to store all of the records in some order so that records can be located, displayed, printed, and updated.

Before describing specific types of applications in detail, however, it is worthwhile emphasizing that only objects—and not a class's methods—are stored in a list. The methods, which apply to the class as a whole, simply provide a means of initializing each object before it is placed into the list, and a means of reporting and modifying an object either before it is inserted into, or after it has been extracted from, the list. Figure 13-1 illustrates the complete process of creating and using both objects and lists.

FIGURE 13-1
The List Creation Process

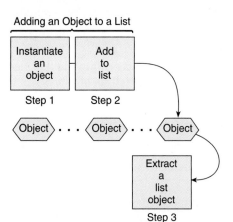

Adding an Object to a List

Extracting an Object from a List

PROGRAMMING NOTE

Homogeneous and Heterogeneous Data Types

Both lists and objects are data structures. Formally, a data structure is a container of data organized in a way that facilitates the insertion, retrieval, and deletion of data. The difference between a list and an object relates to the types of elements they contain. A list is a **homogeneous** data structure, which means that its components must be of the same data type. An object is a **heterogeneous** data structure, which means that each of its internal elements can be of different data types. For example, an object could contain a name, stored as a string data type, a pay rate, stored as a double-precision data type, and an identification number, stored as an integer data type. Because an object can be composed of different data types, it is a heterogeneous data structure. However, the list holding all of the objects is a homogeneous data structure, where each object has the same heterogeneous structure.

Each STL class provides its own set of methods, as was illustrated by the `vector` class presented in Section 8.6. Additionally, the STL provides a general set of methods, referred to as algorithms, which can be applied to any range of objects stored in any STL-created list. These algorithms, previously introduced in Section 9.6, are repeated in Table 13-2 for convenience.

TABLE 13-2
Commonly Used STL Algorithms

algorithm name	description
accumulate	Returns the sum of the numbers in a specified range
binary_search	Returns a Boolean value of `true` if the specified value exists within the specified range; otherwise returns `false`. Can only be used on a sorted set of values
copy	Copies elements from a source range to a destination range
copy_backward	Copies elements from a source range to a destination range in a reverse direction
count	Returns the number of elements in a specified range that match a specified value
equal	Compares the elements in one range of elements, element by element, to the elements in a second range
fill	Assigns every element in a specified range to a specified value
find	Returns the position of the first occurrence of an element in a specified range having a specified value, if the value exists. Performs a linear search, starting with the first element in a specified range, and proceeds one element at a time until the complete range has been searched or the specified element has been found
max_element	Returns the maximum value of the elements in the specified range
min_element	Returns the minimum value of the elements in the specified range
random_shuffle	Randomly shuffles element values in a specified range
remove	Removes a specified value within a specified range without changing the order of the remaining elements
replace	Replaces each element in a specified range having a specified value with a newly specified value
reverse	Reverses elements in a specified range
search	Finds the first occurrence of a specified value or sequence of values within a specified range
sort	Sorts elements in a specified range into an ascending order
swap	Exchanges element values between two objects
unique	Removes duplicate adjacent elements within a specified range

Finally, the last major set of components provided as part of the STL are iterators. Iterators provide a means of specifying the elements in a container and operate in a similar manner as indices do for an array.

The steps for creating and using an STL list are:

1.   Use an STL class to construct the desired container type.

2.   Store objects within the list.

3.   Apply either the STL class's methods or the more general STL algorithms to the stored objects.

These steps will be put into practice in the following sections, as we construct three kinds of lists: linked lists, stacks, and queues.

Exercises 13.1

1. Define the following terms:

   a. container
   b. collection
   c. data field
   d. data structure
   e. iterator
   f. list
   g. object
   h. STL

2. What sequential container types are supported in STL?

3. What associative container types are supported in STL?

4. For each of the following, define a class that contains only a data declaration section and which can be used to create the objects described:

   a. an object, known as a student record, containing a student identification number, the number of credits completed, and a cumulative grade point average
   b. an object, known as a student record, capable of holding a student's name, date of birth, number of credits completed, and cumulative grade point average
   c. a mailing list containing a title field, last-name field, first-name field, two street-address fields, a city field, a state field, and a zip code field.
   d. a stock object containing the stock's name, the price of the stock, and the date of purchase
   e. an inventory object containing an integer part number, a string part description, an integer number of parts in inventory, and an integer re-order value.

5. For each of the individual classes declared in Exercise 4, add a suitable constructor and accessor method. Test each method to initialize and display the following data:

   a. `Identification Number: 4672`
   `Number of Credits Completed: 68`
   `Grade Point Average: 3.01`

   b. `Name: Rhona Karp`
   `Date of Birth: 8/4/60`
   `Number of Credits Completed: 96`
   `Grade Point Average: 3.89`

   c. `Title: Dr.`
   `Last Name: Kingsley`
   `First Name: Kay`
   `Street Address: 614 Freeman Street`
   `City: Indianapolis`
   `State: IN`
   `Zip Code: 07030`

d. `Stock: IBM`
   `Price Purchased: 134.5`
   `Date Purchased: 10/1/86`

e. `Part Number: 16879`
   `Description: Battery`
   `Number in Stock: 10`
   `Re-order Number: 3`

6. **a.** Write a C++ program that prompts a user to input the current month, day, and year. Store the data entered in a suitably defined object and display the date in an appropriate manner.

   b. Modify the program written in Exercise 6a to use an object that accepts the current time in hours, minutes, and seconds.

7. Define a class capable of creating objects that can store a business's name, description of the business's product or services, address, number of employees, and annual revenue.

8. Define a class capable of creating objects for various screw types held in inventory. Each object should contain a field for an integer inventory number, double-precision screw length, double-precision diameter, kind of head (Phillips or standard slot), material (steel, brass, other), and cost.

9. Write a C++ program that defines a class capable of creating objects for storing the name of a stock, its estimated earnings per share, and its estimated price-to-earnings ratio. Have the program prompt the user to enter these items for five different stocks. When the data has been entered for a particular stock, have the program compute and display the anticipated stock price based on the entered earnings and price-per-earnings values. For example, if a user entered the data XYZ 1.56 12, the anticipated price for a share of XYZ stock is (1.56)*(12) = $18.72.

13.2 LINKED LISTS

A classic data-handling problem is making additions or deletions to existing objects that are maintained in a specific order. This is best illustrated by considering the alphabetical telephone list shown in Figure 13-2. Starting with this initial set of names and telephone numbers, assume that we now need to add new objects to the list such that the alphabetic ordering of the objects is always maintained.

Although the insertion or deletion of ordered objects can be accomplished using an array or vector, these containers are not efficient representations for adding or deleting objects internal to the list, because deleting an object creates an empty slot that requires shifting up all objects below the deleted object to close the empty slot. Similarly, adding an object internally to the list requires that all elements after the addition be shifted down to make room for the new entry. Thus, either adding or deleting objects in an array or a vector requires restructuring elements within the container—an inherently inefficient practice even though it is handled automatically by the `vector` class.

FIGURE 13-2
A Telephone List in Alphabetical Order

```
Acme, Sam
(555) 898-2392
Dolan, Edith
(555) 682-3104
Lanfrank, John
(555) 718-4581
Mening, Stephen
(555) 382-7070
Zebee, Frank
(555) 219-9912
```

A linked list provides a convenient method for maintaining a constantly changing list without the need for continually reordering and restructuring. In a **linked list**, each object contains one variable that specifies the location of the next object in the list. Thus, with a linked list it is not necessary to physically store each object in the proper order; instead, each new object is physically stored in whatever memory space is currently free. If an object is inserted into the list, it is only necessary to update the location variables for the objects immediately preceding and following the newly inserted object with the new location information. Thus, from a programming standpoint, information is always contained within one object that permits location of the next object, no matter where this next object is actually stored.

A linked list is illustrated in Figure 13-3, where each element consists of a name and telephone number, plus an additional variable that stores the address of the next object in the list. Although the actual data for the Lanfrank object illustrated in the figure may be physically stored anywhere in the computer, the variable included at the end of the Dolan object maintains the proper alphabetical order and provides the location of the Lanfrank object. A variable used in this way is formally called a **pointer variable**, and is described in the next chapter. All that you need to know at this point is that each object in a linked list must contain information to locate the next object.

FIGURE 13-3
Using Pointer Variables to Link Objects

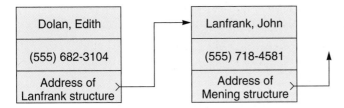

To see the usefulness of the pointer variable in the Dolan object, let us add a telephone number for June Hagar to the alphabetical list shown in Figure 13-3. The data for June Hagar is stored in a data object using the same type as that used for the existing objects. To ensure that the telephone number for Hagar is correctly displayed after the Dolan telephone number, the value in the pointer variable in the Dolan object must be altered to locate the Hagar object, and the pointer variable in the Hagar object must be set to the location of the Lanfrank object. This is illustrated in Figure 13-4. Notice that the pointer variable in each object simply locates the object in the list, even if that object is not physically located in the correct order. Removal of an object from a linked list is the reverse process of adding an object. The actual object is logically removed from the list by simply changing the pointer variable's value in the object preceding it, to the location of the object immediately following the deleted object.

FIGURE 13-4
Adjusting Addresses to Point to Appropriate Objects

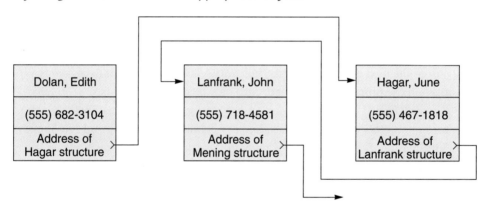

There are two fundamentally different approaches to actually constructing a linked list. The first approach is to use the STL list class; the second approach is to "make your own," in which the programmer provides a class that includes an object's declaration and the code for creating and maintaining the list.

The usefulness of the STL list class is that the linked list shown in Figure 13-4 can be constructed without the programmer either having to understand or program the internal details of the pointer variables. The programmer doesn't even have to understand the details of how the STL list is created and maintained. This is, of course, the major benefit of object-oriented programming using existing classes.

Thus, except for specialized cases, you should almost always use the STL list class, which is described next. However, because it is useful to understand what is actually being provided by this class and the concepts underlying it, we will also illustrate the basics of creating your own linked lists after the list class is described.

13

STL list CLASS IMPLEMENTATION

Figure 13-5 presents the internal structure used by the list class to maintain a list of linked objects. The important point to notice is that the access through the list only occurs via the link variables that contain location information for successive and previous objects. This structure makes it possible to insert a new object into the list simply by storing the new object in any available memory location and adjusting the location information in, at most, two link variables. That is, unlike an array implementation, it is not necessary to store list objects in contiguous memory locations. Similarly, an object can be removed by adjusting the link information in two link variables. As explained earlier, this means that expansion and contraction of the list is more efficient than the same operations using a vector approach.

FIGURE 13-5
Internal Structure Used by the list *Class Showing the Link Variables*

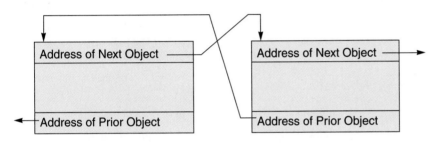

Table 13-3 lists the methods provided by the list class. These methods deal with adding, removing, and locating objects from the front and rear of the list. Note that linked lists provide no random access methods. To get to any internal object the list must be traversed sequentially, object-by-object, starting at either the front or back of the list.

Also note that the list class provides no method for returning any object except the first and last objects. Instead, to access an internal object, not only must the list be traversed from one end, but all objects before the desired object must be removed from the list. Technically, when an item is removed in this fashion it is referred to as popping the object from the list. Generally, so as not to lose the removed objects, a copy of the list is made, either as a complete list or object-by-object as each object is removed.

TABLE 13-3
Summary of list *Class Methods and Operations*

methods and operations	type	description
list<DataType> name	constructor	Creates an empty list named name with compiler-dependent initial size
list<DataType> name(source)	constructor	Creates a copy of the source list
list<DataType> name(n)	constructor	Creates a list of size n

(continued on next page)

TABLE 13-3

Summary of `list` *Class Methods and Operations (Continued)*

methods and operations	type	description
`list<DataType> name(n, elem)`	constructor	Creates a list of size n with each object initialized as `elem`
`list<DataType> name(src.beg, src.end)`	constructor	Creates a list initialized with objects from a source container beginning at `src.beg` and ending at `src.end`
`~list<DataType>()`	destructor	Destroys the list and all objects it contains
`name.front()`	accessor	Returns the first object at the front of the list, with no check for the existence of a first object
`name.pop_front()`	mutator	Removes, but does not return, the first object at the front of the list
`name.push_front(object)`	mutator	Inserts `object` at the front of the list
`name.back()`	accessor	Returns the object at the back of the list, with no check for the existence of a last object
`name.pop_back()`	mutator	Removes, but does not return, the last object at the back of the list
`name.push_back(object)`	mutator	Inserts `object` at the back of the list
`name.insert(itr, object)`	mutator	Inserts `object` at iterator position `itr`
`name.insert(itr, src.beg, src.end)`	mutator	Inserts copies of objects from a source container, beginning at `src.beg` and ending at `src.end`, at iterator position `itr`
`name.insert(itr, n, object)`	mutator	Inserts n copies of `object` at iterator position `itr`
`name.assign(n, object)`	mutator	Assigns n copies of `object`
`name.(src.begin, src.end)`	mutator	Assigns the objects of the `src` container (need not be a list) between the range `src.begin` and `src.end`, to the named list
`name.erase(pos)`	mutator	Removes the object at the specified position
`name.erase(begin, end)`	mutator	Removes the objects within the specified range
`name.resize(value)`	mutator	Resizes the list to a larger size, with new objects instantiated using the default constructor
`name.resize(value, object)`	mutator	Resizes the list to a larger size, with new objects instantiated as `object`
`name.clear()`	mutator	Removes all objects from the list
`name.swap(nameB)`	mutator	Swaps the objects of `nameA` and `nameB` lists; can be performed using the `swap()` algorithm
`name.begin()`	accessor	Returns an iterator to the first object in the list
`name.end()`	accessor	Returns an iterator to the position after the last object in the list

(continued on next page)

13

TABLE 13-3

Summary of `list` *Class Methods and Operations (Continued)*

methods and operations	type	description
`name.rbegin()`	accessor	Returns a reverse iterator for the first object in the list to be used in a reverse list iteration
`name.rand()`	accessor	Returns a reverse iterator for the position after the last object in the list after a reverse list iteration
`name.unique()`	mutator	Removes consecutive duplicate objects
`name.merge(name2)`	mutator	Merges the sorted objects of `name2` into the sorted objects of `name`, creating a final sorted list
`name.reverse()`	mutator	Reverses the objects in the list
`name.splice(itr, name1)`	mutator	Inserts `name1` objects into `name` at position `itr`
`name.splice(itr, name2, beg, end)`	mutator	Inserts `name2` objects in the position range from `beg` to `end` into `name` at position `itr`
`name.sort()`	mutator	Sorts the objects in the list
`nameA == nameB`	relational	Returns a Boolean `true` if `nameA` objects all equal `nameB` objects; otherwise, returns `false`
`nameA != nameB`	relational	Returns a Boolean `false` if `nameA` objects all equal `nameB` objects; otherwise, returns `true`; same as `!(nameA == nameB)`
`nameA < nameB`	relational	Returns a Boolean `true` if `nameA` is less than `nameB`; otherwise, returns `false`
`nameA > nameB`	relational	Returns a Boolean `true` if `nameA` is greater than `nameB`; otherwise, returns `false`; same as `nameB < nameA`
`nameA <= nameB`	relational	Returns a Boolean `true` if `nameA` is less than or equal to `nameB`
`nameA >= nameB`	relational	Returns a Boolean `true` if `nameA` is greater than or equal to `nameB`
`name.size()`	capacity	Returns the number of objects in the list, as an `int`
`name.empty()`	capacity	Returns a Boolean `true` if list is empty; otherwise, returns `false`
`name.max_size()`	capacity	Returns the maximum possible objects as an integer
`name.capacity()`	capacity	Returns the maximum possible objects, as an integer, without relocation of the list

Now consider the following two example programs. Program 13-1 creates and displays a single linked list of names, stored as strings, while Program 13-2 shows how to store and retrieve programmer-created objects. Because of the STL's structure, the two applications are virtually the same.

Program 13-1

```cpp
#include <iostream>
#include <list>
#include <algorithm>
#include <string>
using namespace std;

int main()
{
   list<string> names, addnames;
   string n;

   // add names to the original list
   names.push_front("Dolan, Edith");
   names.push_back("Lanfrank, John");

   // create a new list
   addnames.push_front("Acme, Sam");
   addnames.push_front("Zebee, Frank");

   names.sort();
   addnames.sort();

   // merge the second list into the first
   names.merge(addnames);
   cout << "The first list size is: " <<  names.size() << endl;
   cout << "This list contains the names:\n";

   while (!names.empty())
   {
      cout << names.front() << endl;
      names.pop_front();   // remove the element
   }
}
```

The output produced by Program 13-1 is:

```
The first list size is: 4
This list contains the names:
Acme, Sam
Dolan, Edith
Lanfrank, John
Zebee, Frank
```

PROGRAMMING NOTE

List Application Considerations

Vectors are the preferred list type whenever you need random access to objects without performing many insertions or deletions. The reason is that an index value can be used to go directly to the desired object. Insertions and deletions require modifying the underlying array supporting the vector, and can be costly in terms of overhead time required to perform these operations when many insertions and deletions are required.

Because the only way to get to an element in the middle of a list is by traversing all of the elements before it or by traversing elements from the back of the list toward the desired element, attempts at random access tend to be costly in terms of access time. Thus, a list is the preferred list type whenever many object insertions and deletions need to be made *and* object access tends to be sequential.

Finally, if you only need to store primitive data types, such as integers or double-precision values, a simple array should be your first choice.

USING USER-DEFINED OBJECTS

In practice, the majority of real-life applications using linked lists require a programmer-defined object consisting of a combination of data types. For example, consider the problem of creating a linked list for the simplified telephone objects class illustrated in Figure 13-6.

FIGURE 13-6
UML Class Diagram for a Telephone Directory Object

NameTele
-name: string -phoneNum: string
+NameTele(name, phoneNum) +string getName(): return name +string getPhone(): return phoneNum

A suitable class definition corresponding to Figure 13-6's UML diagram is shown in Class 13-1:

Class 13-1

```
class NameTele
{
  // data declaration section
  private:
    string name;
    string phoneNum;
```

(continued on next page)

```
                        // methods declaration and implementation section
  public:
    NameTele(string nn, string phone)   // constructor
    {
      name = nn;
      phoneNum = phone;
    }
    string getName(){return name;}
    string getPhone(){return phoneNum;}
};
```

This class permits constructing objects consisting of name and phoneNum instance variables using a constructor, as well as accessor methods for setting and retrieving these variables. Program 13-2 instantiates four objects of this class and stores them within a linked list. After it is created, the complete list is displayed.

Program 13-2

```
#include <iostream>
#include <list>
#include <string>
using namespace std;

class NameTele
{
  // data declaration section
  private:
      string name;
      string phoneNum;

  // methods declaration and implementation section
  public:
    NameTele(string nn, string phone)   // constructor
    {
      name = nn;
      phoneNum = phone;
    }
    string getName(){return name;}
    string getPhone(){return phoneNum;}
};

  int main()
  {
```

(continued on next page)

```
   // instantiate a list and initialize the list
   // using the objects in the array
   list<NameTele> employee;

   employee.push_front( NameTele("Acme, Sam", "(555) 891-2392"));
   employee.push_back( NameTele("Dolan, Edith", "(555) 682-3104"));
   employee.push_back( NameTele("Mening, Stephen", "(555) 382-7070"));
   employee.push_back( NameTele("Zeman, Harold", "(555) 219-9912"));

   // retrieve all list objects
   // use accessor methods to extract the name and pay rate
   cout <<"The size of the list is " << employee.size() << endl;
   cout <<"\n     Name               Telephone";
   cout <<"\n--------------        --------------\n";

   while (!employee.empty())
   {
     cout << employee.front().getName()
          << "\t     " << employee.front().getPhone() << endl;
     employee.pop_front();   // remove the object
   }
}
```

The output produced by Program 13-2 is:

```
The size of the list is 4

     Name               Telephone
--------------        --------------
Acme, Sam             (555) 891-2392
Dolan, Edith          (555) 682-3104
Mening, Stephen       (555) 382-7070
Zeman, Harold         (555) 219-9912
```

Notice in Program 13-2 that after each object is retrieved from the list, the underlying class's accessor methods extract individual name and telephone values. Because the dot operator has a left-to-right associativity, an expression such as `employee.front().getName()` is interpreted as `(employee.front()).getName()`. Thus, the STL's `list` class's `front()` method is used to return the front object from the list, which is then further processed by the `NameTele` class's `getName()` method.

CONSTRUCTING YOUR OWN LINKED LIST[1]

The key to constructing a linked list is to provide each object with at least one pointer variable. For example, to use the `NameTele` class (Class 13-1) in a programmer-created linked list, we first have to

---

[1]This topic can be omitted without loss of subject continuity.

provide a link from one object to the next. This is accomplished by adding an extra variable to each object. As this variable must be capable of storing the address value of a NameTele object, a suitable declaration for the required instance variable is:

```
NameTele *link; // create a pointer variable to a NameTele object
```

The inclusion of a pointer variable in a data declaration section should not be surprising, because an object is permitted to contain any C++ data type. In this case, the variable named link will be used to locate an object of type NameTele. In addition to this new variable, we will need to supply the class with a set of constructor, mutator, and accessor methods that include setting and retrieving the value stored in link. Class 13-2 provides a complete class definition to meet these additional requirements.

Class 13-2

```cpp
#include <iostream>
#include <string>
using namespace std;

class NameTele
{

  // data declaration section
  private:
    string name;
    string phoneNum;
    NameTele *link;

  // methods declaration and implementation section
  public:
    NameTele(string nn, string phone)   // constructor
    {
      name = nn;
      phoneNum = phone;
      link = NULL;
    }
    string getName(){return name;}
    string getPhone(){return phoneNum;}
    NameTele *getLink(){return link;}
    void setLink(NameTele *ll){link = ll;}
};
```

Because each element in a linked list has the same format, it is clear that the last object cannot have a pointer value that points to another object, since there is none. To satisfy this requirement, the last object in the list will always have a Null value in its pointer variable. The Null value is interpreted as a sentinel indicating the end of the list has been reached. Similarly, an initial pointer variable must be available for storing the address of the first object in the list.

13

Program 13-3 illustrates using the `NameTele` class by specifically defining four objects having this form, which have been named `head`, `r1`, `r2`, and `r3`, respectively. The names and telephone numbers of three of these objects are initialized with actual names and telephone numbers when the objects are defined.

Program 13-3

```cpp
#include <iostream>
#include <string>
using namespace std;

class NameTele
{
  // data declaration section
  private:
    string name;
    string phoneNum;
    NameTele *link;

  // methods declaration and implementation section
  public:
    NameTele(string nn, string phone)   // constructor
    {
      name = nn;
      phoneNum = phone;
      link = NULL;
    }
    string getName(){return name;}
    string getPhone(){return phoneNum;}
    NameTele *getLink(){return link;}
    void setLink(NameTele *ll){link = ll;}
};

int main()
{
  NameTele head = NameTele("xx", "xx");  // create an empty object

  // create three objects
  NameTele r1 = NameTele("Acme, Sam", "(555) 898 2392");
  NameTele r2 = NameTele("Dolan, Edith", "(555) 682 3104");
  NameTele r3 = NameTele("Lanfrank, John", "(555) 718 4581");

  // link all of the objects
  head.setLink(&r1);  // have the head link point to the first object;
  r1.setLink(&r2);
  r2.setLink(&r3);
```

(continued on next page)

```
    // retrieve each object using the link from the prior object
    cout << head.getLink()->getName() << endl
        << r1.getLink()->getName() << endl
        << r2.getLink()->getName() << endl;
}
```

The output produced by executing Program 13-3 is:

```
Acme, Sam
Dolan, Edith
Lanfrank, John
```

The important concept illustrated by Program 13-3 is the use of a pointer variable in one object to access the next object in the list, as illustrated in Figure 13-7.

FIGURE 13-7
The Relationship Between Objects in Program 13-3

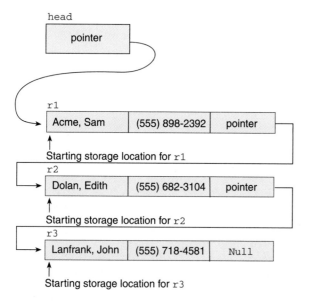

The initialization of the names and telephone numbers for each of the objects defined in Program 13-3 is straightforward. Although each object consists of three variables, only the first two variables in each are explicitly initialized when an object is instantiated. The remaining variable, which is a pointer, is only assigned an explicit address after the next object is placed in the list.

The three assignment statements in Program 13-3 perform the correct pointer assignments. The expression head.setLink(&r1); stores the address of the first telephone object in the pointer variable of the object named head. The expression r1.setLink(&r2); stores the address of the r2 object into the pointer member of the r1 object. Similarly, the expression r2.setLink(&r3); stores the address of the r3 object in the pointer member of the r2 object.

Once name and telephone values have been assigned to each object, and correct location information has been stored in the appropriate pointers, the pointers are then used to access each object's name member. For example, the expression `head.getLink()->getName()` is used to locate the `r1` object and then extract its `name` value. More generally, the links in a linked list of objects can be used to loop through the complete list. As each object is accessed, it can be either examined to select a specific value or used to print a complete list. Equally important is that a linked list can easily expand as new objects are added, and contract as objects are deleted.

For objects that need to be inserted internally within a list, the new object's link would also have to be set to locate the next object in the list; the prior object's link would also have to be adjusted to correctly locate the inserted object. Deleting an object is accomplished by removing the link to the object and adjusting the prior object's link to locate the next valid object in the list.

To actually program all of the required insertion and deletion methods takes time and care. Using the STL's `list` class eliminates this programming effort, while providing a complete set of tested methods for performing all the maintenance tasks associated with a linked list.

Exercises 13.2

1. Modify Program 13-3 to prompt the user for a name. Have the program search the existing list for the entered name. If the name is in the list, display the corresponding phone number; otherwise display this message:

    ```
    The name is not in the current phone list.
    ```

2. Write a C++ program containing a linked list of 10 integer numbers. Have the program display the numbers in the list.

3. Using the linked list of objects illustrated in Figure 13-4, write the sequence of steps necessary to delete the object for John Lanfrank from the list.

4. Generalize the description obtained in Exercise 3 to describe the sequence of steps necessary to remove the *n*th object from a list of linked objects. The *n*th object is preceded by the (*n*-1)-listed object and followed by the (*n*+1)-listed object.

5. Determine the output of the following program:

    ```cpp
    #include <iostream>
    #include <list>
    using namespace std;

    int main()
    {
        int intValue;
        double sum = 0.0;
        double average;
    ```

(continued on next page)

```
// create an array of integer values
int nums[] = {1, 2, 3, 4, 5 };

// instantiate a list of ints using a constructor that
// initializes the list with values from the array
list<int> x(nums, nums + 4);

cout <<"\nThe list x initially has a size of " << x.size()
     << "," << "\n  and contains the elements: " ;

while (!x.empty())
{
  cout << x.front() << "   ";
  x.pop_front();
}
cout << endl;
}
```

13.3 STACKS

A stack is a special type of list in which objects can only be added and removed from the top of the list. As such, it is a last-in, first-out (LIFO) list—that is, a list in which the last item added to the list is the first item that can be removed. An example of this type of operation is a stack of dishes in a cafeteria, where the last dish placed on top of the stack is the first dish removed. Another example is the "in basket" on a desk, where the last paper placed in the basket is typically the first one removed. In computer programming, stacks, among other uses, are used in all function calls to store and retrieve data to and from the function.

As a specific stack example, consider Figure 13-8, which illustrates an existing list of three last names. As shown, the top name on this list is Barney.

FIGURE 13-8
A List of Last Names

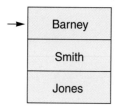

If we now restrict access to the list so that names can only be added and removed from the top of the list, then the list becomes a stack. This requires that we clearly designate which end of the list is the top and which is the bottom. Since the name Barney is physically placed above the other names in Figure 13-8, by implication, this is considered the top of the list. To explicitly signify this, however, we have used an arrow to clearly indicate the list's top.

Figure 13-9 (which consists of six parts, labeled a through f) illustrates how the stack expands and contracts as names are added and deleted. For example, in part b, the name Ventura has been added to the list. By part c, a total of two new names have been added and the top of the list has changed accordingly. By removing the top name, Lanfrank, from the list in part c, the stack shrinks to that shown in part d, where Ventura now resides at the top of the stack. As names continue to be removed from the list (parts e and f), the stack continues to contract.

A BIT OF BACKGROUND

Dr. Lukasiewicz and RPN

Dr. Jan Lukasiewicz, born in 1878, studied and taught mathematics at the University of Lvov, in Poland, before becoming a respected professor at the University of Warsaw. He received an appointment in 1919 to the post of Minister of Education in Poland and, with Stanislaw Lesniewski, founded the Warsaw School of Logic.

After World War II, Dr. Lukasiewicz and his wife, Regina, found themselves exiled in Belgium. When he was offered a professorship at the Royal Academy in Dublin, they moved to Ireland, where they remained until his death in 1956.

In 1951, Dr. Lukasiewicz developed a new set of postfix algebraic notation, which was critical in the design of early microprocessors in the 1960s and 1970s.

The actual implementation of postfix algebra was done using stack arithmetic, in which data were pushed on a stack and popped off when an operation needed to be performed. Such stack handling instructions require no address operands and made it possible for very small computers to handle large tasks effectively.

Stack arithmetic, which is based on Dr. Lukasiewicz's work, reverses the more commonly known prefix algebra, and became known as Reverse Polish Notation (RPN). Early pocket calculators developed by the Hewlett-Packard Corporation were especially notable for their use of RPN and made stack arithmetic the favorite of many scientists and engineers.

FIGURE 13-9
An Expanding and Contracting Stack of Names

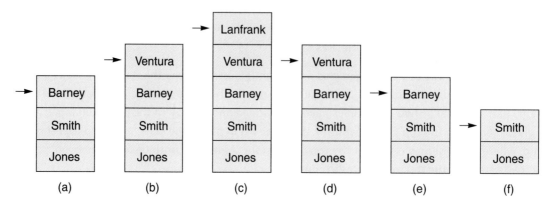

Although Figure 13-9 is an accurate representation of a list of names, it contains additional information that is not provided by a true stack object. When adding names to a stack or removing them, no count is kept of how many names have been added or deleted, or of how many items the stack actually contains at any one time.

For example, in examining each part of Figure 13-9, you can determine how many names are on the list. In a true stack, the only item that can be seen and accessed is the top item on the list. To find out how many items the list contains would require continual removal of the top item until no more items exist.

STACK CLASS IMPLEMENTATION

Creating a stack requires the following four components:

- A container for holding items in the list

- A method of designating the current top stack item

- An operation for placing a new item on the stack

- An operation for removing an item from the stack

By convention, the operation of placing a new item on the top of a stack is called a **push**, and the operation of removing an item from a stack is called a **pop**. How each of these operations is actually implemented depends on the container-type used to represent a stack. In C++, a stack can be easily created using the STL's deque class. This class creates a double-ended list, where objects can be pushed and popped from either end of the list. To create a stack, only the front end of the deque is used. A summary of the deque class' methods and operations is listed in Table 13-4.

A BIT OF BACKGROUND

Stacking the Deque

Stacks and queues are two special forms of a more general data object called a *deque* (pronounced "deck"). Deque stands for *double-ended queue*.

In a deque, data can be handled in one of four ways:

1. Insert at the beginning and remove from the beginning. This is the last-in, first-out (LIFO) stack.
2. Insert at the beginning and remove from the end. This is the first-in, first-out (FIFO) queue.
3. Insert at the end and remove from the end, which represents an inverted LIFO technique.
4. Insert at the end and remove from the beginning, which represents an inverted FIFO queue.

Implementation 1 (a stack) is presented in this section and implementation 2 (a queue) is presented in the next section. Implementations 3 and 4 are sometimes used for keeping track of memory addresses, such as when programming is done in machine language or when objects are handled in a file. When a high-level language, such as C++, manages the data area automatically, users may not be aware of where the data are being stored or of which type of deque is being applied.

TABLE 13-4
Summary of Deque *Class Methods and Operations*

methods and operations	type	description
`deque<DataType> name`	constructor	Creates an empty deque named name with compiler-dependent initial size
`deque<DataType> name(source)`	constructor	Creates a copy of the source deque
`deque<DataType> name(n)`	constructor	Creates a deque of size n
`deque<DataType> name(n, object)`	constructor	Creates a deque of size n with each object initialized as `object`
`deque<DataType> name(src.beg, src.end)`	constructor	Creates a deque initialized with objects from a source container beginning at `src.beg` and ending at `src.end`
`~deque<DataType>()`	destructor	Destroys the deque and all objects it contains
`name.at(index)`	accessor	Returns the object at the designated index, and throws an exception if the index is out of bounds
`name.front()`	accessor	Returns the first object at the front of the deque, with no check for the existence of a first object

(continued on next page)

TABLE 13-4

Summary of Deque *Class Methods and Operations (Continued)*

methods and operations	type	description
name.pop_front()	mutator	Removes, but does not return, the first object at the front of the deque
name.push_front(object)	mutator	Inserts object at the front of the deque
name.back()	accessor	Returns the object at the back of the deque, with no check for the existence of a last object
name.pop_back()	mutator	Removes, but does not return, the last object at the back of the deque
name.push_back(object)	mutator	Inserts object at the back of the deque
name.insert(itr, object)	mutator	Inserts object at iterator position itr
name.insert(itr, src.beg, src.end)	mutator	Inserts copies of objects from a source container, beginning at src.beg and ending at src.end, at iterator position itr
name.insert(itr, n, object)	mutator	Inserts n copies of object at iterator position itr
name2.assign(n, object)	mutator	Assigns n copies of object
name2.(src.begin, src.end)	mutator	Assigns the objects of the src container (need not be a deque) between the range src.begin and src.end, to the named deque
name.erase(pos)	mutator	Removes the object at the specified position
name.erase(begin, end)	mutator	Removes the objects within the specified range
name.resize(value)	mutator	Resizes the deque to a larger size, with new objects instantiated using the default constructor
name.resize(value, object)	mutator	Resizes the deque to a larger size, with new objects instantiated as object
name.clear()	mutator	Removes all objects from the deque
name.swap(nameB)	mutator	Swaps the objects of nameA and nameB deques; can be performed using the swap() algorithm
name.begin()	accessor	Returns an iterator to the first object in the deque
name.end()	accessor	Returns an iterator to the position after the last object in the deque
name.rbegin()	accessor	Returns a reverse iterator for the first object in the deque to be used in a reverse list iteration
name.rand()	accessor	Returns a reverse iterator for the position after the last object in the deque after a reverse list iteration

(continued on next page)

TABLE 13-4

Summary of Deque *Class Methods and Operations (Continued)*

methods and operations	type	description
nameA == nameB	relational	Returns a Boolean true if nameA objects all equal nameB objects; otherwise, returns false
nameA != nameB	relational	Returns a Boolean false if nameA objects all equal nameB objects; otherwise, returns true; same as !(nameA == nameB)
nameA < nameB	relational	Returns a Boolean true if nameA is less than nameB; otherwise, returns false
nameA > nameB	relational	Returns a Boolean true if nameA is greater than nameB; otherwise, returns false; same as nameB < nameA
nameA <= nameB	relational	Returns a Boolean true if nameA is less than or equal to nameB
nameA >= nameB	relational	Returns a Boolean true if nameA is greater than or equal to nameB
name.size()	capacity	Returns the number of objects in the deque, as an int
name.empty()	capacity	Returns a Boolean true if deque is empty; otherwise, returns false
name.max_size()	capacity	Returns the maximum possible objects as an integer
name.capacity()	capacity	Returns the maximum possible objects, as an integer, without relocation of the deque

Program 13-4 uses the deque class to implement a stack. The program is straightforward in that only one stack is instantiated, and user-entered names are pushed onto the front of the deque until the sentinel value of x is entered. Upon detection of this sentinel string value, the names are popped from the front of the deque as long as the deque is not empty.

Program 13-4

```
#include <iostream>
#include <deque>
#include <string>
#include <cctype>
using namespace std;

int main()
{
    string name;
    deque<string> stack;
```

```
cout << "Enter as many names as you wish, one per line" << endl;
cout << " To stop, enter a single x" << endl;
while(true)
{
   cout << "Enter a name (or x to stop): " ;
   getline(cin, name);
   if (toupper(name.at(0)) == 'X') break;
   stack.push_front(name);
}

cout << "\nThe names in the stack are:\n";

  // pop names from the stack
while(!stack.empty())
{
   name = stack.front();  // retrieve the name
   stack.pop_front();  // pop name from the stack
   cout << name << endl;
}
}
```

Following is a sample run using Program 13-4:

```
Enter as many names as you wish, one per line
 To stop, enter a single x
Enter a name (or x to stop): Jane Jones
Enter a name (or x to stop): Bill Smith
Enter a name (or x to stop): Jim Robinson
Enter a name (or x to stop): x

The names in the stack are:
Jim Robinson
Bill Smith
Jane Jones
```

Exercises 13.3

1. State whether a stack is appropriate for each of the following tasks. Indicate why or why not.

    a. A word processor must remember a line of up to 80 characters. Pressing the Backspace key deletes the previous character, and pressing CTRL and Backspace deletes the entire line. Users must be able to undo deletion operations.

    b. Customers must wait one to three months for delivery of their new automobiles. The dealer creates a list that will determine the "fair" order in which customers should get their cars; the list is to be prepared in the order in which customers placed their requests for a new car.

c. You are required to search downward in a pile of magazines to locate the issue for last January. Each magazine was placed on the pile as soon as it was received.

d. A programming team accepts jobs and prioritizes them on the basis of urgency.

e. A line formed at a bus stop.

2. Modify Program 13-4 to implement a stack of integers rather than a stack of strings.

3. Modify Program 13-4 to instantiate three stacks of digits named `digits1`, `digits2`, and `digits3`. Initialize `digits1` to contain the digits 9, 8, 5, and 2, which is the number 2589 in reverse-digit order. Similarly, the `digits2` stack should be initialized to contain the digits 3, 1, 4, and 7, which is the number 7413 in reverse-digit order. Calculate and place the sum of these two numbers in the `digits3` stack. This sum should be obtained by popping respective elements from `digits1` and `digits2` and adding them together with a variable named `carry`, which is initialized to 0. If the sum of the two popped elements and `carry` does not exceed 10, the sum should be pushed onto `digits3` and `carry` set to 0; otherwise, `carry` should be set to 1, and the units digit of the sum pushed onto the `digits3` stack.

4. Write a C++ program that permits a user to enter a maximum of 100 integers into a stack object. Then have your program do the following:

a. Reverse the stack contents into a second stack of integers.

b. Using two additional stacks, reverse the contents in the original stack. Thus, if the stack originally contains the integers 1, 2, 3, and 4, at the end of your program it should contain the integers 4, 3, 2, and 1.

5. Write a C++ program that permits a user to enter a maximum of 50 characters into a stack object. Then have your program sort the stack contents into increasing order. Thus, if the contents of the stack are initially D, E, A, and B, the final contents of the stack will be A, B, D, and E.

13.4 QUEUES

A queue (pronounced *cue*) is a list in which items are added to one end of the list, called the top, and removed from the other end of the list, called the bottom. This arrangement ensures that items are removed from the list in the exact order in which they were entered. This means that the first item placed on the list is the first item to be removed, the second item placed on the list is the second item to be removed, and so on. Thus, a queue is a first-in, first-out (FIFO) list—a list in which the first item added to the list is the first item that can be removed.

As an example of a queue, consider a list of people waiting to purchase season tickets to a professional football team. The first person on the list should be called when the first set of tickets becomes available, the second person should be called for the second available set, and so on. The names of the people currently on the list are shown in Figure 13-10.

FIGURE 13-10
A Queue with Its Pointers

```
Harriet Wright <----- last name on the queue (head)
Jim Robinson
Bill Smith
Jane Jones <----- first name on the queue (tail)
```

As illustrated in Figure 13-10, the names have been added in the same fashion as on a stack; that is, as new names are added to the list, they have been stacked on top of the existing names. The difference in a queue relates to how the names are popped off the list. Clearly, the people on this list expect to be serviced in the order that they were placed on the list—that is, first-in, first-out. Thus, unlike a stack, the most recently added name to the list *is not* the first name removed. Rather, the oldest name still on the list is always the next name removed.

To keep the list in proper order, where new names are added to one end of the list and old names are removed from the other end, it is convenient to use two link variables: one that locates the front of the list for the next person to be serviced and one that locates the end of the list where new people will be added. The link variable that points to the front of the list where the next name is to be removed is referred to as the tail pointer, or tail, for short. The second link variable, which locates the last person in the list and indicates where the next person entering the list is to be placed, is called the head pointer, or head, for short. Thus, for the list shown in Figure 13-10, the tail points to Jane Jones and the head points to Harriet Wright. If Jane Jones were now removed from the list and Lou Hazlet and Teresa Filer were added, the queue and its associated position indicators would appear as in Figure 13-11.

FIGURE 13-11
The Updated Queue References

```
Teresa Filer <----- head
Lou Hazlet
Harriet Wright
Jim Robinson
Bill Smith  <----- tail
```

deque CLASS IMPLEMENTATION

A queue is easily derived using the STL deque container. The operation of placing a new item on the queue is formally referred to as **enqueuing** and more causally referred to as a **push** operation, while removing an item from a queue is formally referred to as **serving** and casually as a **pop** operation. Operationally, enqueuing is an operation similar to pushing on one end of a stack, and serving from a queue is an operation similar to popping from the other end of a stack. How each of these operations is implemented depends on the list used to represent a queue.

13

Because we will use the deque class as our base class, we can easily create the push and pop operations using the deque class's push_front() and pop_back() methods (see Table 13-4). Program 13-5 illustrates using the deque class to construct a queue within the context of a complete program, where names are pushed onto the front of the deque and popped from the back. This creates the first-in, first-out ordering that characterizes a queue.

Program 13-5

```cpp
#include <iostream>
#include <deque>
#include <string>
#include <cctype>
using namespace std;

int main()
{
  string name;
  deque<string> queue;

  cout << "Enter as many names as you wish, one per line" << endl;
  cout << " To stop, enter a single x" << endl;

  // push names on the queue
  while(true)
  {
    cout << "Enter a name (or x to stop): " ;
    getline(cin, name);
    if (toupper(name.at(0)) == 'X') break;
    queue.push_front(name);
  }

  cout << "\nThe names in the queue are:\n";

  // pop names from the queue
  while(!queue.empty())
  {
    name = queue.back();  // retrieve the name
    queue.pop_back();  // pop name from the queue
    cout << name << endl;
  }
}
```

A sample run using Program 13-5 produced the following:

```
Enter as many names as you wish, one per line
 To stop, enter a single x
Enter a name (or x to stop): Jane Jones
Enter a name (or x to stop): Bill Smith
Enter a name (or x to stop): Jim Robinson
Enter a name (or x to stop): x

The names in the queue are:
Jane Jones
Bill Smith
Jim Robinson
```

A BIT OF BACKGROUND

Artificial Intelligence

One of the major steps toward creating programs that "learn" as they work is the development of dynamic data objects.

In 1950, Alan Turing proposed a test in which an expert enters questions at an isolated terminal. Presumably, artificial intelligence (AI) is achieved when the expert cannot discern whether the answers returned to the screen have been produced by a human or by a machine. Although there are problems with the Turing test, its concepts have spawned numerous research efforts.

By the mid-1960s, many AI researchers believed the efforts to create "thinking machines" were futile. Today, however, much lively research and development focus on topics such as dynamic problem solving, computer vision, parallel processing, natural language processing, and speech and pattern recognition—all of which are encompassed within the field of artificial intelligence.

The development of techniques that allow machines to emulate humans has proliferated in recent years with the development of computers that are smaller, faster, more powerful, and less expensive. Most people agree that computers could never replace all human decision making. There is also general agreement that society must remain alert and in control of important decisions that require human compassion, ethics, and understanding.

Exercises 13.4

1. State whether a queue, a stack, or neither object would be appropriate for each of the following tasks. Indicate why or why not.

   a. a list of customers waiting to be seated in a restaurant
   b. a group of student tests waiting to be graded
   c. an address book listing names and telephone numbers in alphabetical order
   d. patients waiting for examinations in a doctor's office

2. Modify Program 13-5 to use a queue of integers rather than a queue of strings.

3. Write a C++ program that permits a user to enter a maximum of 50 double-precision values into a queue. Then have your program sort the queue contents into increasing order. Thus, if the contents of the queue are initially 99.5, 106.25, 10.5, and 150.75, the final contents of the queue will be 10.5, 99.5, 106.25, and 150.75.

4. Write a queue program that accepts an object consisting of an integer identification number and a floating-point hourly pay rate.

5. Add a menu method to Program 13-5 that gives the user a choice of adding a name to the queue, removing a name from the queue, or listing the contents of the queue without removing any objects from it.

6. A group of people have arrived at a bus stop and are lined up in this order:

1. Chaplin	4. Laurel	7. Oliver	10. Garland
2. West	5. Smith	8. Hardy	11. Wayne
3. Taylor	6. Grisby	9. Burton	12. Stewart

   Read the names from an input file into a queue and display the order in which the passengers board the bus, assuming that they board in the same order as they arrived.

13.5 COMMON PROGRAMMING ERRORS

Two common programming errors related to using STL's `list` and `deque` classes are:

1. Inserting objects instantiated from different classes into the same list.

2. Attempting to use indices rather than iterators when using STL class methods and algorithms.

The five most common programming errors related to linked lists, stacks, and queues (which occur when programmers attempt to construct their own lists) are:

1. Not checking the return pointer provided by the `new` operator when constructing a non-STL list. If this operator returns a `NULL` value, the user should be notified that the allocation did not take place and the normal program operation must be altered in an appropriate way. You simply cannot assume that all calls to `new` result in the requested allocation of memory space.

2. Not correctly updating all relevant pointer addresses when adding or removing records from dynamically created stacks and queues. Unless extreme care is taken in updating all addresses, each of these dynamic data structures can quickly become corrupted.

3. Forgetting to free previously allocated memory space when the space is no longer needed. This is typically only a problem in a large application program that is expected to run continuously and which can make many requests for allocated space based on user demand.

4. Not preserving the integrity of the addresses contained in the top-of-stack pointer when dealing with a stack and the queue-in and queue-out pointers when dealing with a queue. As each of these pointers locates a starting position in their respective data structures, the complete list will be lost if the starting addresses are incorrect.

5. Not correctly updating internal record pointers when inserting and removing records from a stack or queue. This is related to the preceding error and can be equally disastrous. Once an internal pointer within these lists contains an incorrect address, it is almost impossible to locate and reestablish the missing set of objects.

13.6 CHAPTER REVIEW

Key Terms

deque

enqueuing

first-in, first-out

last-in, last-out

linked list

pop

push

queue

serving

stack

STL

SUMMARY

1. An object permits individual data items to be stored under a common variable name. These objects can then be stored together in a list.

2. A linked list is a list of objects in which each object contains a pointer variable that locates the next object in the list. Additionally, each linked list must have a pointer to locate the first object in the list. The last object's pointer variable is set to NULL to indicate the end of the list.

3. Linked lists can be automatically constructed using the Standard Template Library's `list` class.

4. A stack is a list consisting of objects that can only be added and removed from the top of the list. Such an object is a last-in, first-out (LIFO) list, which means the last object added to the list is the first object removed. Stacks can be implemented using the STL's `deque` class.

5. A queue is a list consisting of objects that are added to the top of the list and removed from the bottom of the list. Such an object is a first-in, first-out (FIFO) list, which means objects are removed in the order in which they were added. Queues can be implemented using the STL's `deque` class.

Chapter Exercises

1. Modify Program 13-2 to list the names and phone numbers in reverse order.

2. Stacks can be used to efficiently determine whether the parentheses in an expression are correctly balanced. This means that each left-facing parenthesis is matched by a right-facing parenthesis. For example, consider the string

        (a + b) / ((x + y) * z)

   Using a stack, each character in this string, starting from the left, is examined. If the character is a left-facing parenthesis, it is pushed onto the stack. Whenever a right-facing parenthesis is encountered, the top stack element is popped. An unbalanced expression results if a right-facing parenthesis is encountered and the stack is empty or if the stack is not empty when the end of the string is encountered. Using this information, write a C++ program that permits the user to type a string and determines if the string contains a balanced set of parentheses.

3. The program written for Exercise 2 can be expanded to include braces, {}, and brackets, [], as well as parentheses. For example, consider the string:

        { (a + b) / [(x + y) * z] }

   To use a stack to determine if such a string contains balanced pairs of braces, brackets, and parentheses, each left-facing delimiter is pushed onto a stack of characters starting from the left-most character. Whenever a right-facing delimiter is encountered, the top stack element is popped. An unbalanced expression results if a right-facing delimiter is encountered and the popped element is not its matching left-facing delimiter, or if the stack is not empty when the end of the string is encountered. Using this information, write a C++ program that permits the user to type a string and determines if the string contains balanced sets of braces, brackets, or parentheses.

4. A group of people have arrived at a bus stop and are lined up in the order indicated:

1. Chaplin	4. Laurel	7. Oliver	10. Garland
2. West	5. Smith	8. Hardy	11. Wayne
3. Taylor	6. Grisby	9. Burton	12. Stewart

   Read the names from an input file into a stack and display the order in which they board the bus, assuming that they board in the reverse order that they lined up.

5. Write a single-line word processor. As characters are typed, they are to be pushed onto a stack. Some characters have special meanings:

#	Erase the previous character (pop it from the stack).
@	Kill the entire line (empty the stack).
?, !, ., or Enter	Terminate line entry. Move the characters to an array and write the contents of the array to the screen.

6. In recursive methods, the parameters are usually stored on a stack. For example, when the method

```
int factorial(int n)
{
    int fact;

    if (n = 0)
        fact = 1;
    else
        fact = n * factorial(n - 1);
    return (fact);
}
```

is called, the successive values of the parameter *n* are stored on a stack. For example, if the initial call were `value = factorial(5)`, then 5 would be pushed onto the stack for *n*. The next call to `factorial` would push 4, then 3, and so on, until the last parameter value of 0. Then the values would be popped one at a time and multiplied by the previous product until the stack is empty.

Using this information, write a C++ program that performs the same operation as the `factorial` procedure for a given value of *n* entered by the user. After each push, the contents of the stack should be displayed. After each pop, the contents of the stack and the value of `factorial` should be displayed. Once the display indicates that your method works properly, stop the display and have the method return the correct `factorial` value.

7. Write a queue-handling program that asks customers for their names as they place orders at a fast-food restaurant. Each object in the queue should consist of a name field with a maximum of 20 characters, and an integer field that keeps track of the total number of customers served. The value in the integer field should be provided automatically by the program each time a name is entered. Orders are processed in the same sequence as they are placed. The order taker examines the queue and calls the names when the order is ready. When the queue is empty, print a message telling the staff to take a break.

8. Descriptions of print jobs waiting in a computer for the printer are generally kept in a queue. Write a C++ program that keeps track of printing jobs, objected by user name and anticipated printer time (in seconds) for the job. Add jobs to the queue as printouts

are requested and remove them from the queue as they are serviced. When a user adds a job to the queue, display a message giving an estimate of how long it will be before the job is printed. The estimate should consist of the sum of all the prior jobs in the queue. (*Hint:* Store the accumulated times in a separate variable.)

9. **a.** On your electronic mail terminal, you receive notes to call people. Each message contains the name and phone number of the caller as well as a date (in the form month/day/year) and a 24-hour integer clock (in the form hours:minutes) that records the time that the message was received. A `latest-attempt` field is initially set to 0, indicating that no attempt has yet been made to return the call. For example, a particular object may appear as

    ```
    Jan Williamson (555)666-7777   8/14/2005   17:05   0
    ```

    Write a C++ program to store these objects in a queue as they arrive and to feed them to you, one at a time, upon request. If you cannot reach a person when you try to call, place that object at the end of the queue and fill the `latest-attempt` field with the time you tried to return the call, in the form (days later/hours:minutes). Thus, if your last unsuccessful attempt to return Jan Williamson's call was on 8/16/2005 at 4:20, the new enqueued object would be:

    ```
    Jan Williamson (555)666-7777   8/14/2005   17:05   2/16:20
    ```

    b. Modify the program written for Exercise 9a so that the time and date fields are automatically filled in using system calls to time and date methods provided by your compiler.

 Testing Center

Please visit the Testing Center at www.course.com/testingcenter for more practice on the Standard Template Library.

14

ADDRESSES, POINTERS, AND ARRAYS

Languages such as C, C++, and Java all provide a feature called pointers, which permit the construction of dynamically linked lists (see Section 13.2). One of C++'s advantages is that it also allows the programmer to directly access the addresses of variables and manipulate them using pointer arithmetic; that is, addresses can be added, subtracted, and compared. This is a feature that is not provided in other high-level languages.

This chapter presents the basics of declaring pointer variables to store addresses. Additionally, methods of using pointer variables to access and use their stored addresses in meaningful ways are presented.

14.1 INTRODUCTION

As we saw in Section 4.6, we can use C++'s **address operator**, &, to display the address of a variable. When used in a nondeclarative statement, the address operator placed in front of a variable's name refers to the address of the variable.[1] For example, in a nondeclarative statement, &num means *the address of* num, &miles means *the address of* miles, and &foo means *the address of* foo. Program 14-1, which is a copy of Program 4-15, uses the address operator, casts the result into an integer, and then displays the address of the variable num.

Program 14-1

```cpp
#include <iostream>
using namespace std;

int main()
{
    int num;

    num = 22;
    cout << "num = " << num << endl;
    cout << "The address of num = " << int(&num) << endl;

    return 0;
}
```

The output of Program 14-1, when run on the author's computer, is:

```
num = 22
The address of num = 1244884
```

Figure 14-1 illustrates both the contents and address of the num variable provided by the output of Program 14-1.

---

[1]As we have seen in Chapter 6, when used in declaring reference arguments the ampersand refers to the data type *preceding* it. Thus, both the declarations double& num and double # are read as "num is the address of a float," or more commonly as "num is a reference to a double."

FIGURE 14-1
A More Complete Picture of the Variable num

FIGURE 14-1
A More Complete Picture of the Variable num

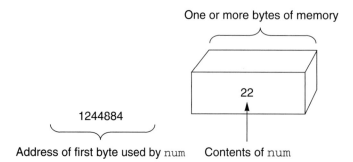

As mentioned in Section 4.6, address information will change depending on what computer is executing the program and how many other programs are currently loaded into memory.

STORING ADDRESSES

Besides displaying the address of a variable, as in Program 14-1, we can also store addresses in suitably declared variables. For example, the statement

```
numAddr = &num;
```

stores the address corresponding to the variable num in the variable numAddr, as illustrated in Figure 14-2. Similarly, the statements

```
d = &m;
tabPoint = &list;
chrPoint = &ch;
```

store the addresses of the variables m, list, and ch in the variables d, tabPoint, and chrPoint, respectively, as illustrated in Figure 14-3.

FIGURE 14-2
Storing num's *Address into* numAddr

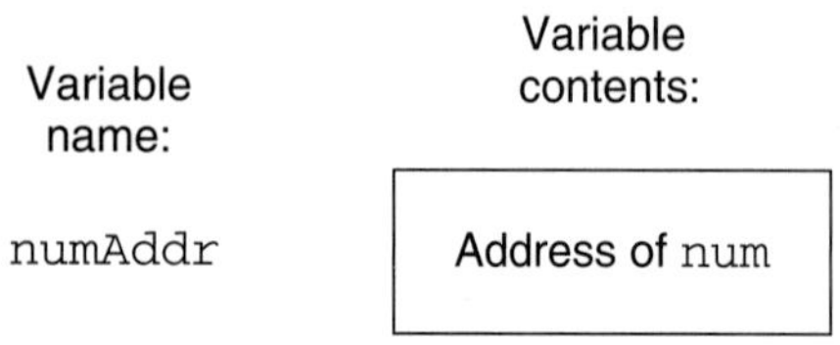

Variable
name:

Variable
contents:

numAddr   Address of num

14

FIGURE 14-3
Storing More Addresses

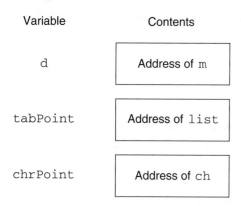

Variable | Contents

d — Address of m

tabPoint — Address of list

chrPoint — Address of ch

The variables numAddr, d, tabPoint, and chrPoint are formally called pointer variables, or pointers for short. **Pointers** are simply variables that are used to store the addresses of other variables.

USING ADDRESSES

To use a stored address, you must employ the **indirection operator, ***. The * symbol, when followed by a pointer (with a space permitted both before and after the *), means *the variable whose address is stored in*. Thus, if numAddr is a pointer (remember that a pointer is a variable that stores an address), *numAddr means *the variable whose address is stored in* numAddr. Similarly, *tabPoint means *the variable whose address is stored in* tabPoint and *chrPoint means *the variable whose address is stored in* chrPoint. Figure 14-4 shows the relationship between the address contained in a pointer variable and the variable ultimately addressed.

FIGURE 14-4
Using a Pointer Variable

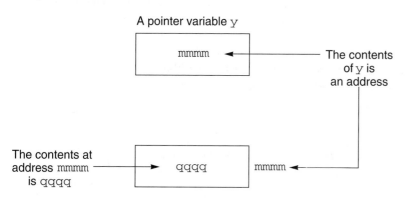

A pointer variable y

mmmm ← The contents of y is an address

The contents at address mmmm is qqqq → qqqq   mmmm ←

Although *d literally means *the variable whose address is stored in* d, this is commonly shortened to the statement *the variable pointed to by* d. Similarly, referring to Figure 14-4, *y can be read as *the variable pointed to by* y. The value ultimately obtained, as shown in Figure 14-4, is qqqq.

To obtain a value from a pointer variable, a program must first look in the pointer variable (or pointer, for short) for an address. The address contained in the pointer is then used to get the desired contents. Certainly, this is a rather indirect way of getting to the final value; therefore the term **indirect addressing** is used to describe this procedure.

Because a pointer requires a computer to do a double lookup (first the address is retrieved, then the address is used to retrieve the actual data), you may wonder why you would want to store an address in the first place. The answer rests on the intimate relationship between pointers and arrays and the necessity of using pointers when creating and deleting new variable storage locations dynamically, as a program is running. Both of these topics are presented later in this chapter. For now, however, given that each variable has a memory address associated with it, the idea of actually storing an address should not seem overly strange.

DECLARING POINTERS

Like all variables, pointers must be declared before they can be used to store an address. When we declare a pointer variable, C++ requires that we also specify the type of variable that is pointed to. For example, if the address in the pointer numAddr is the address of an integer, the correct declaration for the pointer is:

```
int *numAddr;
```

This declaration is read as *the variable pointed to by* numAddr (from the *numAddr in the declaration) *is an integer*.[2]

Notice that the declaration int *numAddr; specifies two things: first, that the variable pointed to by numAddr is an integer; second, that numAddr must be a pointer (because it is used with the indirection operator *). Similarly, if the pointer tabPoint points to (contains the address of) a double-precision number and chrPoint points to a character variable, the required declarations for these pointers are:

```
double *tabPoint;
char *chrPoint;
```

---

[2]Pointer declarations may also be written in the form dataType* pointerName;, where a space is placed between the indirection operator symbol and the pointer variable name. This form, however, becomes error prone when multiple pointer variables are declared in the same declaration statement and the asterisk symbol is inadvertently omitted after the first pointer name is declared. For example, the declaration int* num1, num2; declares num1 as a pointer variable and num2 as an integer variable. In order to more easily accommodate multiple pointers in the same declaration and clearly mark a variable as a pointer, we will adhere to the convention that places an asterisk directly in front of each pointer variable name. This possible error rarely occurs with reference declarations because references are almost exclusively used as formal parameters and single declarations of parameters are mandatory.

These two declarations can be read, respectively, as *the variable pointed to by* `tabPoint` *is a* `double` and *the variable pointed to by* `chrPoint` *is a* `char`. Because all addresses appear the same, this additional information is needed by the compiler to know how many storage locations to access when it uses the address stored in the pointer. Further examples of pointer declarations are:

```
char *inKey;
int *numPt;
double *distAddr;
double *nm1Ptr;
```

To understand pointer declarations, it is helpful to read them "backwards," starting with the indirection operator, the asterisk, *, and translating it either as *the variable whose address is stored in* or *the variable pointed to by*. Applying this to pointer declarations, the declaration `char *inKey;`, for example, can be read as either *the variable whose address is stored in* `inKey` *is a character* or *the variable pointed to by* `inKey` *is a character*. Both of these statements are frequently shortened as follows: `inKey` *points to a character*. Because all three interpretations of the declaration statement are correct, you can select and use whichever description makes more sense to you. We now put this together to construct a program using pointers. Consider Program 14-2.

Program 14-2

```cpp
#include <iostream>
using namespace std;

int main()
{
  int *numAddr;         // declare a pointer to an int
  int miles, dist;      // declare two integer variables

  dist = 158;           // store the number 158 into dist
  miles = 22;           // store the number 22 into miles
  numAddr = &miles;     // store the 'address of miles' in numAddr

  cout << "The address stored in numAddr is " << int(numAddr) << endl;
  cout << "The value pointed to by numAddr is " << *numAddr << "\n\n";

  numAddr = &dist;      // now store the address of dist in numAddr
  cout << "The address now stored in numAddr is " << int(numAddr) << endl;
  cout << "The value now pointed to by numAddr is " << *numAddr << endl;

  return 0;
}
```

The output of Program 14-2 is:

```
The address stored in numAddr is 1244872
The value pointed to by numAddr is 22

The address now stored in numAddr is 1244860
The value now pointed to by numAddr is 158
```

The only use for Program 14-2 is to help us understand "what gets stored where." Let's review the program to see how the output was produced.

The declaration statement int *numAddr; declares numAddr to be a pointer variable used to store the address of an integer variable. The statement numAddr = &miles; stores the address of the variable miles into the pointer numAddr. The first cout statement causes this address to be displayed. The second activation of cout in Program 14-2 uses the indirection operator to retrieve and print *the value pointed to by* numAddr, which is, of course, the value stored in miles.

Because numAddr has been declared as a pointer to an integer variable, we can use this pointer to store the address of any integer variable. The statement numAddr = &dist illustrates this by storing the address of the variable dist in numAddr. The last two cout statements verify the change in numAddr's value and that the new stored address does point to the variable dist. As illustrated in Program 14-2, only addresses should be stored in pointers.

It certainly would have been much simpler if the pointer used in Program 14-2 could have been declared as pointer numAddr;. Such a declaration, however, conveys no information as to the storage used by the variable whose address is stored in numAddr. This information is essential when the pointer is used with the indirection operator, as it is in the second cout statement in Program 14-2. For example, if the address of an integer is stored in numAddr, then only four bytes of storage are typically retrieved when the address is used. If the address of a character is stored in numAddr, only one byte of storage would be retrieved, and a double typically requires the retrieval of eight bytes of storage. The declaration of a pointer must, therefore, include the type of variable being pointed to. Figure 14-5 illustrates this concept.

FIGURE 14-5
Addressing Different Data Types Using Pointers

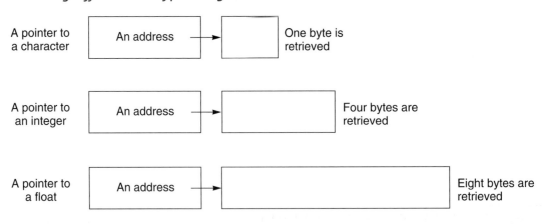

14

REFERENCES AND POINTERS

At this point you might be asking what the difference is between a pointer and a reference. Essentially, a reference is a named constant for an address; hence, the address named as a reference cannot be altered. But because a pointer is a variable, the address in the pointer can be changed. For simple applications, the use of references over pointers is easier and clearly preferred. Another difference is that references don't require the indirection operator to locate the final value being accessed, whereas pointers do. Technically, this is designated by saying that references are **automatically dereferenced** or **implicitly dereferenced** (the terms are synonymous), whereas pointers must be **explicitly dereferenced**.

In passing a scalar variable's address as a function argument, references provide a simpler notational interface and are usually preferred. The same is true when we consider references to structures, which is the topic of the next section. For other situations, such as dynamically allocating new sections of memory for additional variables as a program is running or using alternatives to array notation (both topics are presented in this chapter), pointers are required.

Reference Variables[3]

References are used almost exclusively as formal function parameters and return types. Nevertheless, reference variables are also available in C++. For completeness, we now show how such variables can be declared and used.

Once a variable has been declared it may be given additional names. This is accomplished using a reference declaration, which has the form:

```
dataType& newName = existingName;
```

For example, the reference declaration

```
double& sum = total;
```

equates the name `sum` to the name `total`; both now refer to the same variable, as illustrated in Figure 14-6.

FIGURE 14-6
sum *Is an Alternative Name for* total

Two names for the
same memory area

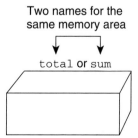

total **or** sum

---

[3]This section may be omitted without loss of subject continuity.

Once another name has been established for a variable using a reference declaration, the new name, which is referred to as an **alias**, can be used in place of the original name. For example, consider Program 14-3:

Program 14-3

```
#include <iostream>
using namespace std;

int main()
{
  double total = 20.5;     // declare and initialize total
  double& sum = total;     // declare another name for total

  cout << "sum =" << sum << endl;
  sum = 18.6;                // this changes the value in total
  cout << "total =" << total << endl;

  return 0;
}
```

The following output is produced by Program 14-3:

```
        sum = 20.5
        total = 18.6
```

Since the variable sum is simply another reference to the variable total, it is the value stored in total that is obtained by the first cout object in Program 14-3. Changing the value in sum then changes the value in total, which is displayed by the second cout object in Program 14-3.

In constructing references, two considerations must be kept in mind. First, the reference must be of the same data type as the variable it refers to. For example, the sequence of declarations

```
    int num = 5;
    double& numref = num;   // INVALID - CAUSES A COMPILER ERROR
```

does not equate numref to num; rather it causes a compiler error. Secondly, a compiler error is also produced when an attempt is made to equate a reference to a constant. For example, the declaration

```
    int& val = 5;   // INVALID - CAUSES A COMPILER ERROR
```

is also invalid.

Once a reference name has been correctly equated to one variable name, the reference cannot be changed to refer to another variable.

As with all declaration statements, multiple references may be declared in a single statement as long as each reference name is preceded by the ampersand symbol. Thus, the declaration

```
double& sum = total, &  average;
```

creates two reference variables named `sum` and `average`.[4]

Another way of looking at references is to consider them as pointers with restricted capabilities that implicitly hide a lot of referencing that is explicitly required with pointers.

For example, consider the statements:

```
int b;          // b is an integer variable
int& a = b;     // a is a reference variable that stores b's address
a = 10;         // this changes b's value to 10
```

Here, `a` is declared as a reference variable that is effectively a named constant for the address of the `b` variable. Since the compiler knows from the declaration that `a` is a reference variable, it automatically assigns the address of `b` (rather than the contents of `b`) to `a` in the declaration statement. Finally, in the statement `a = 10;` the compiler uses the address stored in `a` to change the value stored in `b` to 10. The advantage of using the reference is that it automatically performs an indirect access of `b`'s value without the need for explicitly using the indirection symbol, `*`. As we have noted previously, this type of access is referred to as an automatic dereference.

Implementing this same correspondence between `a` and `b` using pointers is done by the following sequence of instructions:

```
int b;          // b is an integer variable
int *a = &b;    // a is a pointer - store b's address in a
*a = 10;        // this changes b's value to 10 by explicit
                // dereference of the address in a
```

Here, `a` is defined as a pointer that is initialized to store the address of `b`. Thus, `*a`, which can be read as either "the variable whose address is in `a`" or "the variable pointed to by `a`", is `b`, and the expression `*a = 10` changes `b`'s value to 10. Notice in the pointer case that the stored address can be altered to point to another variable; in the reference case the reference variable cannot be altered to refer to any variable except the one it is initialized to. Also notice that to dereference `a`, we must explicitly use the indirection operator, `*`. As you might expect, the `*` is also referred to as the **dereferencing operator**.

---

[4]Reference declarations may also be written in the form `dataType &newName = existingName;`, where a space is placed before the ampersand symbol and the reference variable name. This form is not used often, however, probably to distinguish reference variable address notation from that used in assigning addresses to pointer variables.

Exercises 14.1

1. If `average` is a variable, what does `&average` mean?

2. For the variables and addresses illustrated in Figure 14-7, determine `&temp`, `&dist`, `&date`, and `&miles`.

FIGURE 14-7
Memory Bytes for Exercise 2

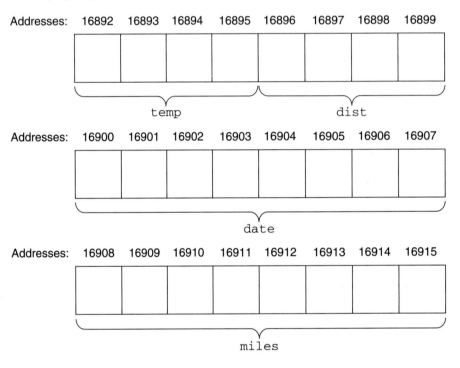

3. a. Write a C++ program that includes the following declaration statements. Have the program use the address operator and the `cout` object to display the addresses corresponding to each variable.

```
char key, choice;
int num, count;
long date;
double yield;
double price;
```

   b. After running the program written for Exercise 3a, draw a diagram of how your computer has set aside storage for the variables in the program. On your diagram, fill in the addresses displayed by the program.

c. Modify the program written in Exercise 3a to display the amount of storage your computer reserves for each data type (use the `sizeof()` operator). With this information and the address information provided in Exercise 3b, determine if your computer set aside storage for the variables in the order in which they were declared.

4. If a variable is declared as a pointer, what must be stored in the variable?

5. Using the indirection operator, write expressions for the following:

a. The variable pointed to by `xAddr`
b. The variable whose address is in `yAddr`
c. The variable pointed to by `ptYld`
d. The variable pointed to by `ptMiles`
e. The variable pointed to by `mptr`
f. The variable whose address is in `pdate`
g. The variable pointed to by `distPtr`
h. The variable pointed to by `tabPt`
i. The variable whose address is in `hoursPt`

6. Write declaration statements for the following:

a. The variable pointed to by `yAddr` is an integer.
b. The variable pointed to by `chAddr` is a character.
c. The variable pointed to by `ptYr` is a long integer.
d. The variable pointed to by `amt` is a double-precision variable.
e. The variable pointed to by `z` is an integer.
f. The variable pointed to by `qp` is a floating-point variable.
g. `datePt` is a pointer to an integer.
h. `yldAddr` is a pointer to a double-precision variable.
i. `amtPt` is a pointer to a floating-point variable.
j. `ptChr` is a pointer to a character.

7. a. What are the variables `yAddr`, `chAddr`, `ptYr`, `amt`, `z`, `qp`, `datePt`, `yldAddr`, `amtPt`, and `ptChr` used in Exercise 6 called?
b. Why are the variable names `amt`, `z`, and `qp` used in Exercise 6 not good choices for pointer variable names?

8. Write English sentences that describe what is contained in the following declared variables:

a. `char *keyAddr;`
b. `int *m;`
c. `double *yldAddr;`
d. `long *yPtr;`
e. `double *pCou;`
f. `int *ptDate;`

9. Which of the following are declarations for pointers?

    a. `long a;`
    b. `char b;`
    c. `char *c;`
    d. `int x;`
    e. `int *p;`
    f. `double w;`
    g. `double *k;`
    h. `double l;`
    i. `double *z;`

10. For the following declarations,

    ```
    int *xPt, *yAddr;
    long *dtAddr, *ptAddr;
    double *pt_z;
    int a;
    long b;
    double c;
    ```

    determine which of the following statements are valid.

    a. `yAddr = &a;`   **b.** `yAddr = &b;`   **c.** `yAddr = &c;`
    d. `yAddr = a;`   **e.** `yAddr = b;`   **f.** `yAddr = c;`
    g. `dtAddr = &a;`   **h.** `dtAddr = &b;`   **i.** `dtAddr = &c;`
    j. `dtAddr = a;`   **k.** `dtAddr = b;`   **l.** `dtAddr = c;`
    m. `pt_z = &a;`   **n.** `ptAddr = &b;`   **o.** `ptAddr = &c;`
    p. `ptAddr = a;`   **q.** `ptAddr = b;`   **r.** `ptAddr = c;`
    s. `yAddr = xPt;`   **t.** `yAddr = dtAddr;` **u.** `yAddr = ptAddr;`

11. For the variables and addresses illustrated in Figure 14-8, fill in the appropriate data as determined by the following statements:

    a. `ptNum = &m;`
    b. `amtAddr = &amt;`
    c. `*zAddr = 25;`
    d. `k = *numAddr;`
    e. `ptDay = zAddr;`
    f. `*ptYr = 1987;`
    g. `*amtAddr = *numAddr;`

14

FIGURE 14-8
Memory Locations for Exercise 11

Variable: `ptNum`
Address: 500

Variable: `amtAddr`
Address: 564

Variable: `zAddr`
Address: 8024

20492

Variable: `numAddr`
Address: 10132

18938

Variable: `ptDay`
Address: 14862

Variable: `ptYr`
Address: 15010

694

Variable: `years`
Address: 694

Variable: `m`
Address: 8096

Variable: `amt`
Address: 16256

Variable: `firstnum`
Address: 18938

154

Variable: `balance`
Address: 20492

Variable: `k`
Address: 24608

12. Using the `sizeof()` operator, determine the number of bytes used by your computer to store the address of an integer, character, and double-precision number. (*Hint:* `sizeof(*int)` can be used to determine the number of memory bytes used for a pointer to an integer.) Would you expect the size of each address to be the same? Why or why not?

A BIT OF BACKGROUND

Admiral Grace Hopper, USN

Grace Hopper received a Ph.D. from Yale University and joined the Naval Reserve in 1943, eventually achieving the rank of Commodore. In her assignment to the Bureau of Ordinance Computation Project at Harvard University she programmed the Mark I, the first large-scale, electro-mechanical, digital computer. Later she applied her outstanding talents in mathematics as senior programmer of the UNIVAC I.

Commodore Hopper became a pioneer in the development of computer languages and served on the Conference of Data Systems Languages (CODASYL) committee. She helped develop COBOL and is credited with producing the first practical program in that language. In 1959 she developed a COBOL compiler, which allowed programs written in a standardized language to be transported between different computers for the first time.

An interesting sidelight to her career was her entry into her log book, dated September 19, 1945, at 15:45 hours, which recorded "First actual case of bug being found." It was an actual insect that had shorted a relay in the Mark I. This was the first known use of the word bug to denote a computing error.

Admiral Hopper remained a colorful figure in the computing community after her retirement from active duty in the U.S. Navy in August 1986 at the age of 79.

14.2 ARRAY NAMES AS POINTERS

Although pointers are simply, by definition, variables used to store addresses, there is also a direct and intimate relationship between array names and pointers. In this section we describe this relationship in detail.

Figure 14-9 illustrates the storage of a single-dimensional array named grade, which contains five integers. Assume that each integer requires four bytes of storage.

FIGURE 14-9
The grade *Array in Storage*

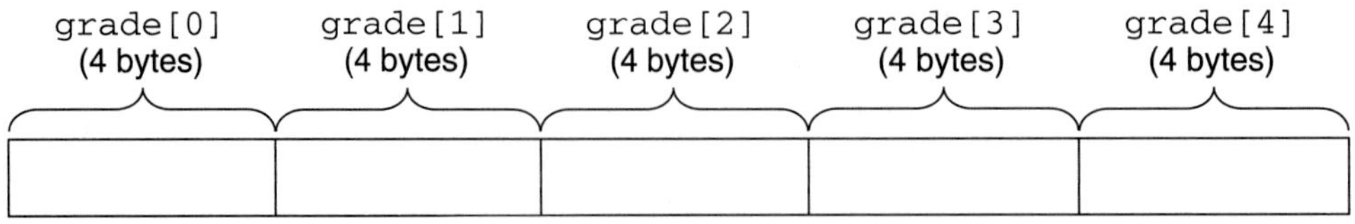

grade[0] (4 bytes)	grade[1] (4 bytes)	grade[2] (4 bytes)	grade[3] (4 bytes)	grade[4] (4 bytes)

Using subscripts, the fourth element in the `grade` array is referred to as `grade[3]`. The fact that subscripts are used to specify positions in an array might make you think that addresses have nothing to do with arrays. But in fact, the computer uses the subscript to calculate the address of the desired element based on both the starting address of the array and the amount of storage used by each element. Calling the fourth element `grade[3]` forces the compiler, internally, to make the address computation

```
&grade[3] = &grade[0] + (3 * sizeof(int))
```

Remembering that the address operator, &, means "the address of," this last statement is read "the address of `grade[3]` equals the address of `grade[0]` plus 12." Figure 14-10 illustrates the address computation used to locate `grade[3]`.

FIGURE 14-10
Using a Subscript to Obtain an Address

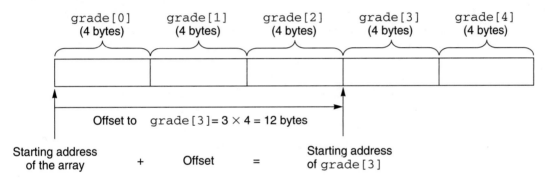

Recall that a pointer is a variable used to store an address. If we create a pointer to store the address of the first element in the `grade` array, we can mimic the operation used by the computer to access the array elements. Before we do this, let us first consider Program 14-4.

Program 14-4

```cpp
#include <iostream>
using namespace std;

int main()
{
const int ARRAYSIZE = 5;

  int i, grade[ARRAYSIZE] = {98, 87, 92, 79, 85};

  for (i = 0; i < ARRAYSIZE; i++)
    cout << "\nElement " << i << " is " << grade[i];
  cout << endl;

  return 0;
}
```

When Program 14-4 is run, the following display is obtained:

```
Element 0 is 98
Element 1 is 87
Element 2 is 92
Element 3 is 79
Element 4 is 85
```

Program 14-4 displays the values of the array `grade` using standard subscript notation. Now, let us store the address of array element `0` in a pointer. Then, using the indirection operator, `*`, we can use the address in the pointer to access each array element. For example, if we store the address of `grade[0]` into a pointer named `gPtr` (using the assignment statement `gPtr = &grade[0];`), then, as illustrated in Figure 14-11, the expression `*gPtr`, which means "the variable pointed to by `gPtr`," references `grade[0]`.

FIGURE 14-11
The Variable Pointed to by `*gPtr` *Is* `grade[0]`

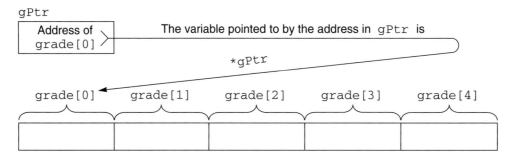

One unique feature of pointers is that they can be used to designate **offsets**, which are the positions of elements in an array relative to the element being designated by a pointer. For example, the 1 in the expression `* (gPtr + 1)` is an offset. The complete expression references the integer that is one beyond the variable pointed to by `gPtr`. Similarly, as illustrated in Figure 14-12, the expression `* (gPtr + 3)` references the variable that is three integers beyond the variable pointed to by `gPtr`. This is the variable `grade[3]`.

FIGURE 14-12
An Offset of 3 from the Address in `gPtr`

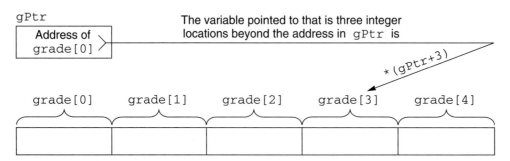

14

Table 14-1 lists the complete correspondence between elements referenced by subscripts and by pointers and offsets. The relationships listed in Table 14-1 are illustrated in Figure 14-13.

TABLE 14-1
Array Elements May Be Referenced in Two Ways

element	referenced by subscripts	referenced by pointers
Element 0	grade[0]	*gPtr and *(gPtr + 0)
Element 1	grade[1]	*(gPtr + 1)
Element 2	grade[2]	*(gPtr + 2)
Element 3	grade[3]	*(gPtr + 3)
Element 4	grade[4]	*(gPtr + 4))

FIGURE 14-13
The Relationship Between Array Elements and Pointers

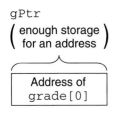

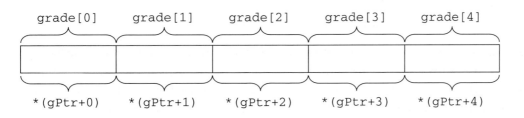

Using the correspondence between pointers and subscripts illustrated in Figure 14-13, the array elements previously accessed in Program 14-4 using subscripts can now be accessed using pointers. This is done in Program 14-5.

Program 14-5

```
#include <iostream>
using namespace std;

int main()
{
  const int ARRAYSIZE = 5;

  int *gPtr;                  // declare a pointer to an int

  int i, grade[ARRAYSIZE] = {98, 87, 92, 79, 85};

  gPtr = &grade[0];       // store the starting array address
  for (i = 0; i < ARRAYSIZE; i++)
    cout << "\nElement " << i << " is " << *(gPtr + i);
  cout << endl;

  return 0;
}
```

The following display is obtained when Program 14-5 is run:

```
    Element 0 is 98
    Element 1 is 87
    Element 2 is 92
    Element 3 is 79
    Element 4 is 85
```

Notice that this is the same display produced by Program 14-4.

The method used in Program 14-5 to access individual array elements simulates how the compiler internally references all array elements. Any subscript used by a programmer is automatically converted to an equivalent pointer expression by the compiler. In this case, since the declaration of gPtr included the information that integers are pointed to, any offset added to the address in gPtr is automatically scaled by the size of an integer. Thus, *(gPtr + 3), for example, refers to the address of grade[0] plus an offset of 12 bytes (3 * 4), where we have assumed that the sizeof(int) = 4. This is the address of grade[3] illustrated in Figure 14-13.

The parentheses in the expression *(gPtr + 3) are necessary to correctly reference the desired array element. Omitting the parentheses results in the expression *gPtr + 3. Due to the precedence of the operators, this expression adds 3 to "the variable pointed to by gPtr." Since gPtr points to grade[0], this expression adds the value of grade[0] and 3 together. Note also that the expression *(gPtr + 3) does not change the address stored in gPtr. Once the computer uses the offset to locate the correct variable from the starting address in gPtr, the offset is discarded and the address in gPtr remains unchanged.

Although the pointer gPtr used in Program 14-5 was specifically created to store the starting address of the grade array, this was unnecessary. When an array is created, the compiler automatically creates an internal pointer constant for it and stores the starting address of the array in this pointer. In almost all respects, a pointer constant is identical to a pointer variable created by a programmer; but, as we shall see, there are some differences.

For each array created, the name of the array becomes the name of the pointer constant created by the compiler for the array, and the starting address of the first location reserved for the array is stored in this pointer. Thus, declaring the `grade` array in both Program 14-4 and Program 14-5 actually reserved enough storage for five integers, created an internal pointer named `grade`, and stored the address of `grade[0]` in the pointer. This is illustrated in Figure 14-14.

FIGURE 14-14
Creating an Array Also Creates a Pointer

grade

&grade[0]

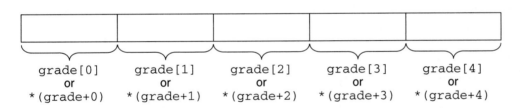

grade[0]	grade[1]	grade[2]	grade[3]	grade[4]
or	or	or	or	or
*(grade+0)	*(grade+1)	*(grade+2)	*(grade+3)	*(grade+4)

The implication is that every reference to `grade` using a subscript can be replaced by an equivalent reference using `grade` as a pointer. Thus, wherever the expression `grade[i]` is used, the expression `*(grade + i)` can also be used. This is illustrated in Program 14-6, where `grade` is used as a pointer to reference all of its elements.

Program 14-6

```cpp
#include <iostream>
using namespace std;

int main()
{
  const int ARRAYSIZE = 5;

  int i, grade[ARRAYSIZE] = {98, 87, 92, 79, 85};

  for (i = 0; i < ARRAYSIZE; i++)
    cout << "\nElement " << i << " is " << *(grade + i);
  cout << endl;

  return 0;
}
```

Executing Program 14-6 produces the same output previously produced by Program 14-4 and Program 14-5. However, using `grade` as a pointer made it unnecessary to declare and initialize the pointer `gPtr` used in Program 14-5.

In most respects, an array name and pointer can be used interchangeably. A true pointer, however, is a variable and the address stored in it *can* be changed by an assignment statement. An array name is a pointer constant and the address stored in the pointer *cannot* be changed by an assignment statement. Thus, a statement such as `grade = &grade[2];` is invalid. This should come as no surprise. Since the whole purpose of an array name is to correctly locate the beginning of the array, allowing a programmer to change the address stored in the array name would defeat this purpose and lead to havoc whenever array elements were referenced. Also, expressions taking the address of an array name are invalid because the pointer created by the compiler is internal to the computer, not stored in memory as are pointer variables. Thus, trying to store the address of `grade` using the expression `&grade` results in a compiler error.

An interesting sidelight to the observation that elements of an array can be referenced using pointers is that a pointer reference can always be replaced with a subscript reference. For example, if `numPtr` is declared as a pointer variable, the expression `* (numPtr + i)` can also be written as `numPtr[i]`. This is true even though `numPtr` is not created as an array. As before, when the compiler encounters the subscript notation, it replaces it internally with the pointer notation.

DYNAMIC ARRAY ALLOCATION[5]

As each variable is defined in a program, sufficient storage for it is assigned from a pool of computer memory locations made available to the compiler. Once specific memory locations have been reserved for a variable, these locations are fixed for the life of that variable, whether they are used or not. For example, if a function requests storage for an array of 500 integers, the storage for the array is allocated and fixed from the point of the array's definition. If the application requires less than 500 integers, the unused allocated storage is not released back to the system until the array goes out of existence. If, on the other hand, the application requires more than 500 integers, the size of the integer array must be increased and the function defining the array recompiled.

An alternative to this fixed or static allocation of memory storage locations is the dynamic allocation of memory. Under a dynamic allocation scheme, the amount of storage to be allocated is determined and adjusted as the program is run, rather than being fixed at compile time.

The dynamic allocation of memory is useful when dealing with lists, because it allows the list to expand as new items are added and contract as items are deleted. For example, in constructing a list of grades, the exact number of grades ultimately needed may not be known. Rather than creating a fixed array to store the grades, it is useful to have a mechanism whereby the array can be enlarged and shrunk as necessary. Two C++ operators, `new` and `delete`, that provide this capability are described in Table 14-2. (These operators require the `<iostream>` header file.)

---

[5]This topic may be omitted on first reading with no loss of subject continuity.

TABLE 14-2
Dynamic Allocation and Deallocation Operators
(Requires the `<iostream>` header file)

operator name	description
new	Reserves the number of bytes requested by the declaration. Returns the address of the first reserved location or NULL if sufficient memory is not available
delete	Releases a block of bytes previously reserved. The address of the first reserved location is passed as an argument to the operator

Explicit dynamic storage requests for scalar variables or arrays are made either as part of a declaration or assignment statement.[6] For example, the declaration statement `int *num = new int;` reserves an area sufficient to hold one integer and places the address of this storage area into the pointer num. This same dynamic allocation can be made by first declaring the pointer using the declaration statement `int *num;` and then subsequently assigning the pointer an address with the assignment statement `num = new int;`. In either case, the allocated storage area comes from the computer's free storage area.[7]

A similar technique, which is more useful, is the dynamic allocation of arrays. For example, the declaration

```
int *grades = new int[200];
```

reserves an area sufficient to store 200 integers and places the address of the first integer into the pointer grades. Although we have used the constant 200 in this example declaration, a variable dimension can be used. For example, consider the sequence of instructions

```
cout << "Enter the number of grades to be processed: ";
cin  >> numgrades;
int *grades = new int[numgrades];
```

In this sequence, the actual size of the array that is created depends on the number input by the user. Since pointer and array names are related, each value in the newly created storage area can be accessed using standard array notation, such as `grades[i]`, rather than the equivalent pointer notation `*(grades + i)`. Program 14-7 illustrates this sequence of code in the context of a complete program.

---

[6]It should be noted that the compiler automatically provides this dynamic allocation and deallocation from the stack for all auto variables.

[7]The free storage area of a computer is formally referred to as the *heap*. The heap consists of unallocated memory that can be allocated to a program, as requested, while the program is running.

Program 14-7

```cpp
#include <iostream>
using namespace std;
int main()
{
  int numgrades, i;

  cout << "Enter the number of grades to be processed: ";
  cin  >> numgrades;

  int *grades = new int[numgrades];   // create the array

  for(i = 0; i < numgrades; i++)
  {
    cout << "  Enter a grade: ";
    cin  >> grades[i];
  }
  cout << "\nAn array was created for " << numgrades << " integers\n";
  cout << " The values stored in the array are:";
  for (i = 0; i < numgrades; i++)
    cout << "\n    " << grades[i];
  cout << endl;

  delete [] grades;    // return the storage to the heap

  return 0;
}
```

Notice in Program 14-7 that the delete operator is used with braces whenever the new operator was used to create an array. The delete [] statement restores the allocated block of storage back to the operating system while the programming is executing.[8] The only address required by delete is the starting address of the block of storage that was dynamically allocated. Thus, any address returned by new can subsequently be used by delete to restore the reserved memory back to the computer. The delete operator does not alter the address passed to it, but simply removes the storage that the address references. Following is a sample run using Program 14-7:

```
Enter the number of grades to be processed: 4
  Enter a grade: 85
  Enter a grade: 96
  Enter a grade: 77
  Enter a grade: 92
```

[8]The allocated storage should automatically be returned to the heap, by the operating system, when the program has completed execution. The term **memory leak** is used to describe the condition that occurs when dynamically allocated memory has no pointers that can access it for de-allocation, and as a consequence this allocated memory can no longer be utilized until the program terminates.

```
An array was created for 4 integers
The values stored in the array are:
    85
    96
    77
    92
```

Exercises 14.2

1. Replace each of the following references to a subscripted variable with a pointer reference.

   a. `prices[5]`   **b.** `grades[2]`   **c.** `yield[10]`
   d. `dist[9]`   **e.** `mile[0]`   **f.** `temp[20]`
   g. `celsius[16]`   **h.** `num[50]`   **i.** `time[12]`

2. Replace each of the following references using a pointer with a subscript reference.

   a. `*(message + 6)`   **b.** `*amount`   **c.** `*(yrs + 10)`
   d. `*(stocks + 2)`   **e.** `*(rates + 15)`   **f.** `*(codes + 19)`

3. **a.** List the three things that the declaration statement `double prices[5];` causes the compiler to do.
   b. If each double-precision number uses eight bytes of storage, how much storage is set aside for the `prices` array?
   c. Draw a diagram similar to Figure 14-14 for the `prices` array.
   d. Determine the byte offset relative to the start of the `prices` array, corresponding to the offset in the expression `*(prices + 3)`.

4. **a.** Write a declaration to store the C-string "`This is a sample`" into an array named `samtest`. Include the declaration in a program that displays the values in `samtest` using a `for` loop and pointer to access each element in the array.
   b. Modify the program written in Exercise 4a to display only array elements 10 through 15 (these are the letters s, a, m, p, l, and e).

5. Write a declaration to store the following values into an array named `rates`: 12.9, 18.6, 11.4, 13.7, 9.5, 15.2, 17.

6. Include the declaration written in Exercise 5 in a program that displays the values in the array using pointer notation.

14.3 POINTER ARITHMETIC

Pointer variables, like all variables, contain values. The value stored in a pointer is, of course, an address. Thus, by adding and subtracting numbers to pointers we can obtain different addresses. Additionally, the addresses in pointers can be compared using any of the relational operators (==, !=, < , >, etc.) that are valid for comparing other variables. In performing arithmetic on pointers we must be careful to produce addresses that point to something meaningful. In comparing pointers we must also make comparisons that make sense. Consider the declarations:

```
const int ARRAYSIZE = 100;
int nums[ARRAYSIZE];
int *nPt;
```

To set the address of nums[0] into nPt, either of the following two assignment statements can be used:

```
nPt = &nums[0];
nPt = nums;
```

The two assignment statements produce the same result because nums is a pointer constant that contains the address of the first location in the array. This is, of course, the address of nums[0]. Figure 14-15 illustrates the allocation of memory resulting from the previous declaration and assignment statements, assuming that each integer requires four bytes of memory and that the location of the beginning of the nums array is at the decimal address 18934.

FIGURE 14-15
The nums *Array in Memory*

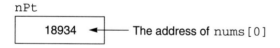

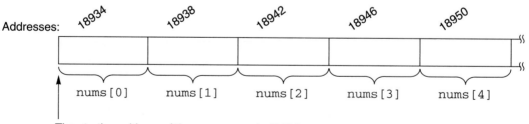

The starting address of the nums array is 18934

A BIT OF BACKGROUND

Numerosophy

The ancient Greeks attached great philosophical and religious significance
to numbers. They considered the natural (counting) numbers, 1, 2, 3, ..., to
be examples of perfection, and ratios of whole numbers (fractions) as somewhat suspect. Diophantus (third century B.C.) called negative numbers
"absurd."

According to tradition, Hipparchus (second century B.C.) was
drowned when he discussed the scandalous irrational nature of the square
root of 2 outside of the Pythagorean Society. The first mention of the
square root of a negative number was by Heron of Alexandria (third century
A.D.). Such concepts were treated with disbelief and even considered
wicked. Today, of course, it is not unusual to use negative, irrational, "artificial," and complex numbers all at once to represent such concepts as vectors
and points in a plane. The Greeks of that Golden Age would probably regard our modern mathematics as truly degenerate.

Once nPt contains a valid address, values can be added and subtracted from the address to produce
new addresses. When adding or subtracting numbers to pointers, the computer automatically
adjusts the number to ensure that the result still "points to" a value of the correct type. For example, the statement nPt = nPt + 3; forces the computer to scale the 3 by the correct number to
ensure that the resulting address is the address of an integer. Assuming that each integer requires
four bytes of storage, as illustrated in Figure 14-15, the computer multiplies the 3 by 4 and adds the
result, 12, to the address in nPt. The resulting address is 18946, which is the correct address of
nums[3].

This automatic scaling by the computer ensures that the expression nPt + i, where i is any positive
integer, correctly points to the ith element beyond the one currently being pointed to by nPt. Thus, if
nPt initially contains the address of nums[0], nPt + 4 is the address of nums[4], nPt + 50 is the
address of nums[50], and nPt + i is the address of nums[i]. Although we have used actual addresses in Figure 14-15 to illustrate the scaling process, the programmer need never know or care
about the actual addresses used by the computer. The manipulation of addresses using pointers generally does not require knowledge of the actual address.

Addresses can also be incremented or decremented using both prefix and postfix increment and
decrement operators. Adding 1 to a pointer causes the pointer to point to the next element of the
type being pointed to. Decrementing a pointer causes the pointer to point to the previous element.

For example, if the pointer variable p is a pointer to an integer, the expression p++ causes the address in the pointer to be incremented to point to the next integer. This is illustrated in Figure 14-16.

FIGURE 14-16
Increments Are Scaled When Used with Pointers

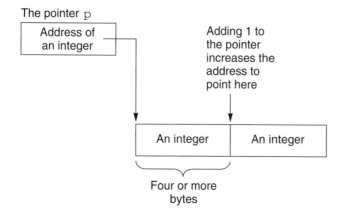

In reviewing Figure 14-16, notice that the increment added to the pointer is correctly scaled to account for the fact that the pointer is used to point to integers. It is, of course, up to the programmer to ensure that the correct type of data is stored in the new address contained in the pointer.

The increment and decrement operators can be applied as both prefix and postfix pointer operators. All of the following combinations using pointers are valid:

```
*ptNum++      // use the pointer and then increment it
*++ptNum      // increment the pointer before using it
*ptNum--      // use the pointer and then decrement it
*--ptNum      // decrement the pointer before using it
```

Of the four possible forms, the most commonly used is the form *ptNum++. This is because such an expression allows each element in an array to be accessed as the address is "marched along" from the starting address of the array to the address of the last array element. The use of the increment operator is shown in Program 14-8. In this program each element in the nums array is retrieved by successively incrementing the address in nPt.

Program 14-8

```cpp
#include <iostream>
using namespace std;

int main()
{
  const int NUMS = 5;
  int nums[NUMS] = {16, 54, 7, 43, -5};
  int i, total = 0, *nPt;

  nPt = nums;     // store address of nums[0] in nPt
  for (i = 0; i < NUMS; i++)
    total = total + *nPt++;
  cout << "The total of the array elements is " << total << endl;

  return 0;
}
```

The output produced by Program 14-8 is:

```
The total of the array elements is 115
```

The expression `total = total + *nPt++` used in Program 14-8 accumulates the values "pointed to" by the `nPt` pointer variable. Within this expression, the term `*nPt++` first causes the computer to retrieve the integer pointed to by `nPt`. This is done by the `*nPt` part of the term. The postfix increment, `++`, then adds 1 to the address in `nPt` so that `nPt` now contains the address of the next array element. The increment is, of course, scaled by the computer so that the actual address in `nPt` is the correct address of the next integer element.

Pointers may also be compared. This is particularly useful when dealing with pointers that point to elements in the same array. For example, rather than using a counter in a `for` loop to access each element in an array correctly, the address in a pointer can be compared to the starting and ending address of the array itself. The expression

```
nPt <= &nums[4]
```

is `true` as long as the address in `nPt` is less than or equal to the address of `nums[4]`. Since `nums` is a pointer constant that contains the address of `nums[0]`, the term `&nums[4]` can be replaced by the equivalent term `nums + 4`. Using either of these forms, Program 14-8 can be rewritten in Program 14-9 to continue adding array elements while the address in `nPt` is less than or equal to the address of the last array element.

Program 14-9

```cpp
#include <iostream>
using namespace std;

int main()
{
  const int NUMS = 5;
  int nums[NUMS] = {16, 54, 7, 43, -5};
  int total = 0, *nPt;

  nPt = nums;     // store address of nums[0] in nPt
  while (nPt < nums + NUMS)
    total += *nPt++;
  cout << "The total of the array elements is " << total << endl;

  return 0;
}
```

Notice that in Program 14-9 the compact form of the accumulating expression, `total += *nPt++`, was used in place of the longer form, `total = total + *nPt++`. Also, the expression `nums + NUMS` does not change the address in `nums`. Since `nums` is an array name and not a pointer variable, its value cannot be changed. The expression `nums + NUMS` first retrieves the address in `nums`, adds 4 to this address (appropriately scaled) and uses the result for comparison purposes. Expressions such as `*nums++`, which attempt to change the address, are invalid. Expressions such as `*nums` or `*(nums + i)`, which use the address without attempting to alter it, are valid.

POINTER INITIALIZATION

Like all variables, pointers can be initialized when they are declared. When initializing pointers, how-ever, you must be careful to set an address in the pointer. For example, an initialization such as

```cpp
int *ptNum = &miles;
```

is only valid if `miles` was declared as an integer variable prior to `ptNum`. Here we are creating a pointer to an integer and setting the address in the pointer to the address of an integer variable. No-tice that if the variable `miles` is declared subsequently to `ptNum`, as follows,

```cpp
int *ptNum = &miles;
int miles;
```

an error occurs. This is because the address of `miles` is used before `miles` has even been defined. Since the storage area reserved for `miles` has not been allocated when `ptNum` is declared, the ad-dress of `miles` does not yet exist.

Pointers to arrays can also be initialized within their declaration statements. For example, if `prices` has been declared an array of double-precision numbers, either of the following two declarations can be used to initialize the pointer named `zing` to the address of the first element in `prices`:

```
double *zing = &prices[0];
double *zing = prices;
```

The last initialization is correct because `prices` is itself a pointer constant containing an address of the proper type. (The variable name `zing` was selected in this example to reinforce the idea that any variable name can be selected for a pointer.)

Exercises 14.3

1. Replace the `while` statement in Program 14-9 with a `for` statement.

2. a. Write a program that stores the following numbers in the array named `rates`: 6.25, 6.50, 6.8, 7.2, 7.35, 7.5, 7.65, 7.8, 8.2, 8.4, 8.6, 8.8, 9.0. Display the values in the array by changing the address in a pointer called `dispPt`. Use a `for` statement in your program.
   b. Modify the program written in Exercise 2a to use a `while` statement.

3. a. Write a program that stores the C-string `"Hooray for All of Us"` into an array named `strng`. Use the declaration `strng[] = "Hooray for All of Us";`, which ensures that the end-of-string escape sequence `\0` is included in the array. Display the characters in the array by changing the address in a pointer called `messPt`. Use a `for` statement in your program.
   b. Modify the program written in Exercise 3a to use the `while` statement `while (*messPt++ != '\0')`.
   c. Modify the program written in Exercise 3a to start the display with the word `All`.

4. Write a program that stores the following numbers in an array named `miles`: 15, 22, 16, 18, 27, 23, 20. Have your program copy the data stored in `miles` to another array named `dist` and then display the values in the `dist` array.

5. Write a program that stores the following sentence in an array named `message`: `This is a test`. Have your program copy the data stored in `message` to another array named `mess2` and then display the letters in the `mess2` array.

14.4 PASSING ADDRESSES

We have already seen one method of passing addresses to a function. This was accomplished using reference variables, as described in Section 6.3. Although passing reference variables to a function provides the function with the address of the passed variables, it is an implied use of addresses because the function call does not reveal the fact that reference variables are being used. For example, the function call `swap(firstnum, secnum);` does not reveal whether `firstnum` or `secnum` is a reference variable. Only by looking at the declaration for these variables or by examining the function header line for `swap()` are the data types of `firstnum` and `secnum` revealed.

In contrast to implicitly passing addresses using reference variables, addresses can be explicitly passed using pointer variables. Let us see how this is accomplished.

To explicitly pass an address to a function, all that needs to be done is to place the address operator, &, in front of the variable being passed. For example, the function call

```
swap(&firstnum, &secnum);
```

passes the addresses of the variables `firstnum` and `secnum` to `swap()`, as illustrated in Figure 14-17. Explicitly passing addresses using the address operator effectively is a **call by reference** because the called function can reference, or access, variables in the calling function using the passed addresses. As we saw in Section 6.3, calls by reference are also accomplished using reference variables. Here we will use the passed addresses and pointers to directly access the variables `firstnum` and `secnum` from within `swap()` and exchange their values—a procedure that was previously accomplished using classes in Program 3-4.

FIGURE 14-17
Explicitly Passing Addresses to `swap()`

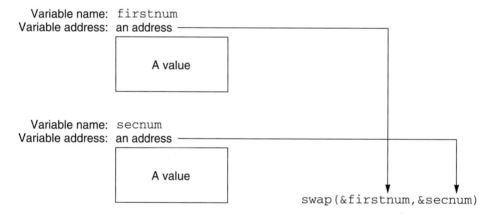

One of the first requirements in writing `swap()` is to construct a function header line that correctly receives and stores the passed values, which in this case are two addresses. As we saw in Section 14.1, addresses are stored in pointers, which means that the arguments of `swap` must be declared as pointers.

Assuming that `firstnum` and `secnum` are double-precision variables, and that `swap()` returns no value, a suitable function header line for `swap` is

```
void swap(double *nm1Addr, double *nm2Addr)
```

The choice of the argument names `nm1Addr` and `nm2Addr` is, as with all parameter names, up to the programmer. The declaration double *nm1Addr, however, declares that the parameter named `nm1Addr` will be used to store the address of a double-precision value. Similarly, the declaration double *nm2Addr declares that `nm2Addr` will also store the address of a double-precision value.

Before writing the body of `swap()` to exchange the values in `firstnum` and `secnum`, let's first check that the values accessed using the addresses in `nm1Addr` and `nm2Addr` are correct. This is done in Program 14-10.

14

Program 14-10

```
#include <iostream>
using namespace std;

int main()
{
    void swap(double *, double *);       // function prototype

    double firstnum = 20.5, secnum = 6.25;

    swap(&firstnum, &secnum);            // call swap

    return 0;
}

// this function illustrates passing pointer arguments
void swap(double *nm1Addr, double *nm2Addr)
{
    cout << "The number whose address is in nm1Addr is "
         << *nm1Addr << endl;
    cout << "The number whose address is in nm2Addr is "
         << *nm2Addr << endl;

    return;
}
```

The output displayed when Program 14-10 is run is:

```
The number whose address is in nm1Addr is 20.5
The number whose address is in nm2Addr is 6.25
```

In reviewing Program 14-10, note two things. First, the function prototype for swap():

```
void swap(double *, double *)
```

declares that swap() returns no value directly and that its arguments are two pointers that "point to" double-precision values. As such, when the function is called it will require that two addresses be passed, and that each address is the address of a double-precision value.

The second item to notice is that within swap() the indirection operator is used to access the values stored in firstnum and secnum. swap() itself has no knowledge of these variable names, but it does have the address of firstnum stored in nm1Addr and the address of secnum stored in nm2Addr. The expression *nm1Addr used in the first cout statement means "the variable whose address is in nm1Addr." This is of course the variable firstnum. Similarly, the second cout statement obtains the value stored in secnum as "the variable whose address is in nm2Addr." Thus, we have successfully used pointers to allow swap() to access variables in main(). Figure 14-18 illustrates the concept of storing addresses in parameters.

FIGURE 14-18
Storing Addresses in Arguments

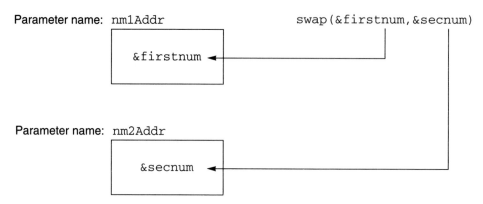

Having verified that swap() can access main()'s local variables firstnum and secnum, we can now expand swap() to exchange the values in these variables. The values in main()'s variables firstnum and secnum can be interchanged from within swap() using the three-step interchange algorithm previously described in Section 3.4, which for convenience is again listed below:

1. Store firstnum's value in a temporary location.

2. Store secnum's value in firstnum.

3. Store the temporary value in secnum.

Using pointers from within swap(), this takes the form:

1. Store the value of the variable pointed to by nm1Addr in a temporary location.

    The statement temp = *nm1Addr; does this (see Figure 14-19).

FIGURE 14-19
Indirectly Storing firstnum's value

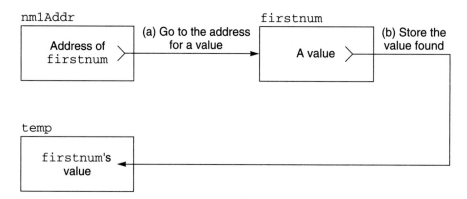

2. Store the value of the variable whose address is in `nm2Addr` in the variable whose address is in `nm1Addr`.

    The statement `*nm1Addr = *nm2Addr;` does this (see Figure 14-20).

FIGURE 14-20
Indirectly Changing `firstnum`*'s Value*

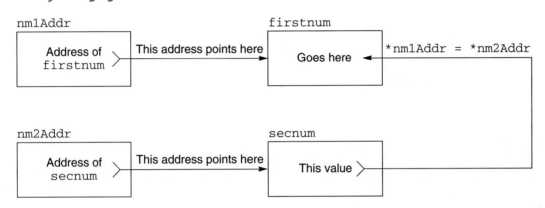

3. Move the value in the temporary location into the variable whose address is in `nm2Addr`.

    The statement `*nm2Addr = temp;` does this (see Figure 14-21).

FIGURE 14-21
Indirectly Changing `secnum`*'s Value*

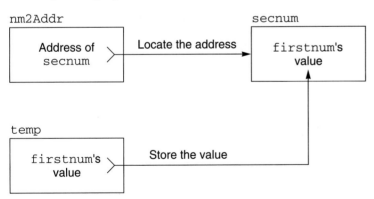

Program 14-11 contains the final form of `swap()`, written according to our description.

Program 14-11

```cpp
#include <iostream>
using namespace std;

int main()
{
    void swap(double *, double *);     // function prototype

    double firstnum = 20.5, secnum = 6.25;


    cout << "The value stored in firstnum is: " << firstnum << endl;
    cout << "The value stored in secnum is: " << secnum << "\n\n";

    swap(&firstnum, &secnum);          // call swap

    cout << "The value stored in firstnum is now: "
        << firstnum <<  endl;
    cout << "The value stored in secnum is now: "
        << secnum << endl;

    return 0;
}

// this function swaps the values in its two arguments
void swap(double *nm1Addr, double *nm2Addr)
{
  double temp;

  temp = *nm1Addr;          // save firstnum's value
  *nm1Addr = *nm2Addr;      // move secnum's value in firstnum
  *nm2Addr = temp;          // change secnum's value
}

  return;
```

The following sample run was obtained using Program 14-11:

```
The value stored in firstnum is: 20.5
The value stored in secnum is: 6.25

The value stored in firstnum is now: 6.25
The value stored in secnum is now: 20.5
```

As illustrated in this output, the values stored in `main()`'s variables have been modified from within `swap()`.

PASSING ARRAYS

When an array is passed to a function, its address is the only item actually passed. By this we mean the address of the first location used to store the array, as illustrated in Figure 14-22. Since the first location reserved for an array corresponds to element 0 of the array, the "address of the array" is also the address of element 0.

FIGURE 14-22
The Address of an Array Is the Address of the First Location Reserved for the Array

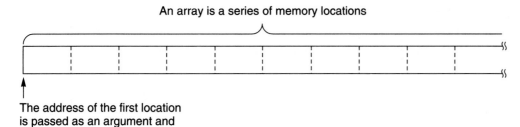

An array is a series of memory locations

The address of the first location
is passed as an argument and
stored in a pointer parameter

For a specific example in which an array is passed to a function, consider Program 14-12. In this program, the `nums` array is passed to the `findMax()` function using conventional array notation.

Program 14-12

```cpp
#include <iostream>
using namespace std;

int main()
{
  int findMax(int [], int);    // function prototype

  const int NUMPTS = 5;
  int nums[NUMPTS] = {2, 18, 1, 27, 16};

  cout << "\nThe maximum value is "
       << findMax(nums,NUMPTS) << endl;

  return 0;
}

// this function returns the maximum value in an array of ints
int findMax(int vals[], int numels)
{
  int i, max = vals[0];

  for (i = 1; i < numels; i++)
   if (max < vals[i])
     max = vals[i];

  return max;
}
```

The output displayed when Program 14-12 is executed is:

```
The maximum value is 27
```

The parameter named `vals` in the header line declaration for `findMax()` actually receives the address of the array `nums`. As such, `vals` is really a pointer, since pointers are variables (or parameters) used to store addresses. Since the address passed into `findMax()` is the address of an integer, another suitable header line for `findMax()` is:

```cpp
int findMax(int *vals, int numels) // here vals is declared as
                                   // a pointer to an integer
```

The declaration `int *vals` in the header line declares that `vals` is used to store an address of an integer. The address stored is, of course, the location of the beginning of an array. The following is a rewritten version of the `findMax()` function that uses the new pointer declaration for `vals`, but retains the use of subscripts to refer to individual array elements:

14

```
int findMax(int *vals, int numels)    // find the maximum value
{
  int i, max = vals[0];

  for (i = 1; i < numels; i++)
    if (max < vals[i])
      max = vals[i];

  return max;
}
```

Regardless of how `vals` is declared in the function header or how it is used within the function body, it is truly a pointer variable. Thus, the address in `vals` may be modified. This is not true for the name `nums`. Since `nums` is the name of the originally created array, it is a pointer constant. As described in Section 14-2, this means that the address in `nums` cannot be changed and that the address of `nums` itself cannot be taken. No such restrictions, however, apply to the pointer variable named `vals`. All the address arithmetic that we learned in the previous section can be legitimately applied to `vals`.

We shall write two additional versions of `findMax()`, both using pointers instead of subscripts. In the first version we simply substitute pointer notation for subscript notation. In the second version we use address arithmetic to change the address in the pointer.

As previously stated, access to an array element using the subscript notation `arrayName[i]` can always be replaced by the pointer notation `*(arrayName + i)`. In our first modification to `findMax()`, we make use of this correspondence by simply replacing all references to `vals[i]` with the equivalent expression `*(vals + i)`.

```
int findMax(int *vals, int numels)    // find the maximum value
{
  int i, max = *vals;

  for (i = 1; i < numels; i++)
    if (max < *(vals + i) )
      max = *(vals + i);

  return max;
}
```

Our next version of `findMax()` makes use of the fact that the address stored in `vals` can be changed. After each array element is retrieved using the address in `vals`, the address itself is incremented by 1 in the altering list of the `for` statement. The expression `max = *vals` previously used to set `max` to the value of `vals[0]` is replaced by the expression `max = *vals++`, which adjusts the address in `vals` to point to the second element in the array. The element assigned to `max` by this expression is the array element pointed to by `vals` before `vals` is incremented. The postfix increment, `++`, does not change the address in `vals` until after the address has been used to retrieve the first array element.

```
int findMax(int *vals, int numels)   // find the maximum value
{
  int i, max = *vals++;    // get the first element and increment

  for (i = 1; i < numels; i++, vals++)
  {
    if (max < *vals)
      max = *vals;
  }
  return max;
}
```

Let us review this version of findMax(). Initially the maximum value is set to "the thing pointed to by vals." Since vals initially contains the address of the first element in the array passed to findMax(), the value of this first element is stored in max. The address in vals is then incremented by 1. The 1 that is added to vals is automatically scaled by the number of bytes used to store integers. Thus, after the increment, the address stored in vals is the address of the next array element. This is illustrated in Figure 14-23. The value of this next element is compared to the maximum and the address is again incremented, this time from within the altering list of the for statement. This process continues until all the array elements have been examined.

FIGURE 14-23
Pointing to Different Elements

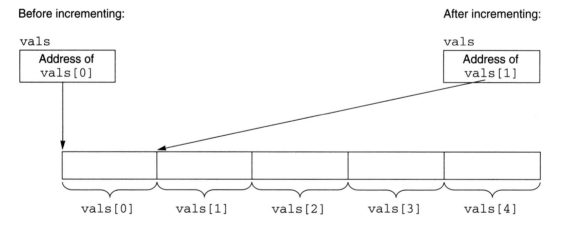

The version of findMax() that you should choose is a matter of personal style and taste. Generally, beginning programmers feel more at ease using subscripts rather than using pointers. Also, if the program uses an array as the natural storage structure for the application and data at hand, an array reference using subscripts is more appropriate to clearly indicate the intent of the program. However, for C-strings and data structures (see Chapter 15), the use of pointers becomes an increasingly useful and powerful tool in its own right. In these instances there is no simple or easy equivalence to the use of subscripts.

One further "neat trick" can be gleaned from our discussion. Since passing an array to a function really involves passing an address, we can just as well pass any valid address. For example, the function call `findMax(&nums[2],3)` passes the address of `nums[2]` to `findMax()`. Within `findMax()` the pointer `vals` stores the address and the function starts the search for a maximum at the element corresponding to this address. Thus, from `findMax()`'s perspective, it has received an address and proceeds appropriately.

ADVANCED POINTER NOTATION[9]

Access to multidimensional arrays can also be made using pointer notation, although the notation becomes more and more cryptic as the array dimensions increase. An extremely useful application of this notation occurs with two-dimensional character arrays, one of the topics of the next chapter. Here we consider pointer notation for two-dimensional numeric arrays. For example, consider the declaration

```
int nums[2][3] = { {16,18,20},
                   {25,26,27} };
```

This declaration creates an array of elements and a set of pointer constants named `nums`, `nums[0]`, and `nums[1]`. The relationship between these pointer constants and the elements of the `nums` array is illustrated in Figure 14-24.

FIGURE 14-24
Storage of the nums *Array and Associated Pointer Constants*

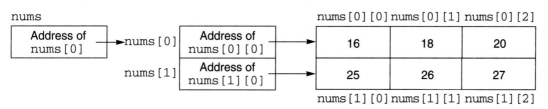

The availability of the pointer constants associated with a two-dimensional array allows us to reference array elements in a variety of ways. One way is to consider the two-dimensional array as an array of rows, where each row is itself an array of three elements. Considered in this light, the address of the first element in the first row is provided by `nums[0]` and the address of the first element in the second row is provided by `nums[1]`. Thus, the variable pointed to by `nums[0]` is `nums[0][0]` and the variable pointed to by `nums[1]` is `nums[1][0]`. Once the nature of these constants is understood, each element in the array can be accessed by applying an appropriate offset to the appropriate pointer. Thus, the notations listed in Table 14-3 are equivalent.

[9]This topic may be omitted without loss of subject continuity.

TABLE 14-3
Equivalence Between Pointer and Subscript Notation

pointer notation	subscript notation	value
*nums[0]	nums[0][0]	16
*(nums[0] + 1)	nums[0][1]	18
*(nums[0] + 2)	nums[0][2]	20
*nums[1]	nums[1][0]	25
*(nums[1] + 1)	nums[1][1]	26
*(nums[1] + 2)	nums[1][2]	27

We can now go even further and replace nums[0] and nums[1] with their respective pointer nota-tions, using the address of nums itself. As illustrated in Figure 14-24, the variable pointed to by nums is nums[0]. That is, *nums is nums[0]. Similarly, *(nums + 1) is nums[1]. Using these relationships leads to the equivalences listed in Table 14-4.

TABLE 14-4
Equivalence Between Pointer and Subscript Notation

pointer notation	subscript notation	value
*(*nums)	nums[0][0]	16
*(*nums + 1)	nums[0][1]	18
*(*nums + 2)	nums[0][2]	20
((nums + 1))	nums[1][0]	25
((nums + 1) + 1)	nums[1][1]	26
((nums + 1) + 2)	nums[1][2]	27

The same notation applies when a two-dimensional array is passed to a function. For example, assume that the two-dimensional array nums is passed to the function calc() using the call calc(nums);. Here, as with all array passes, an address is passed. A suitable function header line for the function calc() is:

```
calc(int pt[2][3])
```

As we have already seen, the argument declaration for pt can also be:

```
calc(int pt[][3])
```

Using pointer notation, another suitable declaration is:

```
calc(int (*pt)[3])
```

In this last declaration, the inner parentheses are required to create a single pointer to arrays of three integers. Each array is, of course, equivalent to a single row of the nums array. By suitably offsetting the pointer, each element in the array can be accessed. Notice that without the parentheses the declaration becomes

```
int *pt[3]
```

which creates an array of three pointers, each one pointing to a single integer.

Once the correct declaration for pt is made (any of the three valid declarations can be used), the notations within the function calc() that are listed in Table 14-5 are all equivalent.

TABLE 14-5
Equivalence Between Pointer and Subscript Notation

pointer notation	subscript notation	value
*(*pt)	pt[0][0]	16
*(*pt + 1)	pt[0][1]	18
*(*pt + 2)	pt[0][2]	20
((pt + 1))	pt[1][0]	25
((pt + 1) + 1)	pt[1][1]	26
((pt + 1) + 2)	pt[1][2]	27

The last two notations using pointers are encountered in more advanced C++ programs. The first of these occurs because functions can return any valid C++ scalar data type, including pointers to any of these data types. If a function returns a pointer, the data type being pointed to must be declared in the function's declaration. For example, the declaration

```
int *calc()
```

declares that calc() returns a pointer to an integer value. This means that an address of an integer variable is returned. Similarly, the declaration

```
double *taxes()
```

declares that taxes() returns a pointer to a double-precision value. This means that an address of a double-precision variable is returned.

In addition to declaring pointers to integers, floating-point numbers, and C++'s other data types, pointers can also be declared that point to (contain the address of) a function. Pointers to functions are possible because function names, like array names, are themselves pointer constants. For example, the declaration

```
int (*calc)()
```

declares calc to be a pointer to a function that returns an integer. This means that calc will contain the address of a function, and the function whose address is in the variable calc returns an integer value. If, for example, the function sum() returns an integer, the assignment calc = sum; is valid.

Exercises 14.4

1. The following declaration was used to create an array named `prices`:

    ```
    const int SIZE = 500
    double prices[SIZE];
    ```

    Write three different declarations for a function named `sortArray()` that accepts the `prices` array as an argument named `inArray`.

2. The following declaration was used to create an array named `keys`:

    ```
    const int SIZE = 256;
    char keys[SIZE];
    ```

    Write three different declarations for a function named `findKey()` that accepts the `keys` array as an argument named `select`.

3. The following declaration was used to create an array named `rates`:

    ```
    const int SIZE = 100;
    double rates[SIZE];
    ```

    Write three different declarations for a function named `prime()` that accepts the `rates` array as an argument named `rates`.

4. Modify the `findMax()` function presented in this section to locate the minimum value of the passed array. Rename the function `findMin()` and code it using pointers.

5. In the last version of `findMax()` presented in this section, the parameter `vals` was incremented inside the altering list of the `for` statement. Instead, suppose that the incrementing was done within the condition expression of the `if` statement, as follows:

    ```
    int findMax(int *vals, int numels)     // incorrect version
    {
      int i, max = *vals++;    // get the first element and increment

      for (i = 1; i < numels; i++)
        if (max < *vals++)
          max = *vals;
      return (max);
    }
    ```

    This version produces an incorrect result. Determine why.

6. a. Write a program that has a declaration in `main` to store the following numbers into an array named `rates`: 6.5, 7.2, 7.5, 8.3, 8.6, 9.4, 9.6, 9.8, 10.0. There should be a call to a function named `show()` that accepts `rates` in an argument named `rates` and then displays the numbers using the pointer notation `*(rates + i)`.

    b. Modify the `show()` function written in Exercise 6a to alter the address in `rates`. In this function, use the expression `*rates` rather than `*(rates + i)` to retrieve the correct element.

14.5 POINTERS AND C-STRING LIBRARY FUNCTIONS

Pointers are exceptionally useful in constructing functions that manipulate C-strings. (Recall that the term "C-string" is short for "character string." A character string consists of text stored in a character array whose last character is `'\0'`.) When pointer notation is used in place of subscripts to access individual characters in a C-string, the resulting statements are both more compact and more efficient. In this section we describe the relationship between subscripts and pointers when accessing individual characters in a C-string.

Consider the final version of the `strcopy()` function introduced in Section 9.3. This function copies the characters of one C-string to a second string. For convenience, this function is repeated below:

```
void strcopy(char string1[], char string2[])   // copy string2 to string1
{
  int i = 0;

  while (string1[i] = string2[i])
    i++;
  return;
}
```

The conversion of `strcopy()` from subscript notation to pointer notation is now straightforward. Although each subscript version of `strcopy()` can be rewritten using pointer notation, the following is the equivalent of the final subscript version:

```
void strcopy(char *string1, char *string2)   // copy string2 to string1
{
  while (*string1 = *string2)
  {
    string1++;
    string2++;
  }
  return;
}
```

In both subscript and pointer versions of strcopy(), the function receives the name of the array being passed. Recall that passing an array name to a function actually passes the address of the first location of the array. In our pointer version of strcopy() the two passed addresses are stored in the pointer arguments string1 and string2, respectively.

The declarations char *string1; and char *string2; used in the pointer version of strcopy() indicate that string1 and string2 are both pointers containing the address of a character, and stress the treatment of the passed addresses as pointer values rather than array names. These declarations are equivalent to the declarations char string1[] and char string2[], respectively.

Internal to strcopy(), the pointer expression *string1, which refers to "the element whose address is in string1," replaces the equivalent subscript expression string1[i]. Similarly, the pointer expression *string2 replaces the equivalent subscript expression string2[i]. The expression *string1 = *string2 causes the element pointed to by string2 to be assigned to the element pointed to by string1. Since the starting addresses of both strings are passed to strcopy() and stored in string1 and string2, respectively, the expression *string1 initially refers to string1[0] and the expression *string2 initially refers to string2[0].

Consecutively incrementing both pointers in strcopy() with the expressions string1++ and string2++ simply causes each pointer to "point to" the next consecutive character in the respective C-string. As with the subscript version, the pointer version of strcopy() steps along, copying element by element, until the end of the C-string is copied. One final change to the C-string copy function can be made by including the pointer increments as postfix operators within the test part of the while statement. The final form of the C-string copy function is:

```
void strcopy(char *string1, char *string2)    // copy string2 to string1
{
   while (*string1++ = *string2++)
     ;
   return;
}
```

There is no ambiguity in the expression *string1++ = *string2++ even though the indirection operator, *, and the increment operator, ++, have the same precedence. Here the character pointed to is accessed before the pointer is incremented. Only after completion of the assignment *string1 = *string2 are the pointers incremented to correctly point to the next characters in the respective strings.

The C-string copy function included in the standard library supplied with C++ compilers is typically written exactly like our pointer version of strcopy().

Exercises 14.5

1. Determine the value of `*text`, `*(text + 3)`, and `*(text + 10)`, assuming that `text` is an array of characters and the following has been stored in the array:

   a. now is the time
   b. rocky raccoon welcomes you
   c. Happy Holidays
   d. The good ship

2. a. The following function, `convert()`, "marches along" the C-string passed to it and sends each character in the C-string one at a time to the `toUpper()` function until the `Null` character is encountered.

   ```
   void   convert(char strng[])    // convert a C-string to uppercase letters
   {
     int i = 0;
     while (strng[i] != '\0')
     {
       strng[i] = toUpper(strng[i]);
       i++;
     }
     return;
   }

   char toUpper(char letter)   // convert a character to uppercase
   {
     if( (letter >= 'a') && (letter <= 'z') )
       return (letter - 'a' + 'A');
     else
       return (letter);
   }
   ```

   The `toUpper()` function takes each character passed to it and first examines it to determine if the character is a lowercase letter (a lowercase letter is any character between a and z, inclusive). Assuming that characters are stored using the standard ASCII character codes, the expression `letter − 'a' + 'A'` converts a lowercase letter to its uppercase equivalent. Rewrite the `convert()` function using pointers.

   b. Include the `convert()` and `toUpper()` functions in a working program. The program should prompt the user for a C-string and echo the C-string back to the user in uppercase letters.

3.   Using pointers, repeat Exercise 3 from Section 9.3.

4.   Using pointers, repeat Exercise 4 from Section 9.3.

5.   Using pointers, repeat Exercise 5 from Section 9.3.

6.   Write a function named `remove()` that returns nothing and deletes all occurrences of a character from a C-string. The function should take two arguments: the C-string name and the character to be removed. For example, if `message` contains the C-string `Happy Holidays`, the function call `remove(message, 'H')` should place the C-string `appy olidays` into `message`.

7.   Using pointers, repeat Exercise 9 from Section 9.3.

8.   Write a function that uses pointers to add a single character at the end of an existing C-string. The function should replace the existing `'\0'` character with the new character and append a new `'\0'` at the end of the C-string. The function returns nothing.

9.   Write a function that uses pointers to delete a single character from the end of a C-string. This is effectively achieved by moving the `'\0'` character one position closer to the start of the string. The function returns nothing.

10. Determine the C-string-handling functions that are provided by the standard C++ library. For each function list the data types of the arguments expected by the function and the data type of any returned value.

14.6 C-STRING DEFINITIONS AND POINTER ARRAYS

The definition of a C-string automatically involves a pointer. For example, the definition `char message1[80];` both reserves storage for 80 characters and automatically creates a pointer constant, `message1`, which contains the address of `message1[0]`. As a pointer constant, the address associated with the pointer cannot be changed; it must always "point to" the beginning of the created array.

Instead of creating a C-string as an array, however, it is also possible to create a C-string using a pointer. For example, the definition `char *message2;` creates a pointer to a character. In this case, `message2` is a true pointer variable. Once a pointer to a character is defined, assignment statements, such as `message2 = "this is a string";`, can be made. In this assignment, `message2`, which is a pointer, receives the address of the first character in the string.

The main difference in the definitions of `message1` as an array and `message2` as a pointer is the way the pointer is created. Defining `message1` using the declaration `char message1[80]` explicitly calls for a fixed amount of storage for the array. This causes the compiler to create a pointer constant.

Defining `message2` using the declaration `char *message2` explicitly creates a pointer variable first. This pointer is then used to hold the address of a C-string when the C-string is actually specified. This difference in definitions has both storage and programming consequences.

From a programming perspective, defining `message2` as a pointer to a character allows C-string assignments, such as `message2 = "this is a string";`, to be made within a program. Similar assignments are not allowed for C-strings defined as arrays. Thus, the statement `message1 = "this is a string";` is not valid. Both definitions, however, allow initializations to be made using a C-string assignment. For example, both of the following initializations are valid:

```
char message1[80] = "this is a string";
char *message2 = "this is a string";
```

From a storage perspective, the allocation of space for `message1` and `message2` is quite different. As illustrated in Figure 14-25, both initializations cause the computer to store the same C-string internally. In the case of `message1`, a specific set of 80 storage locations is reserved and the first 17 locations are initialized. For `message1`, different strings can be stored, but each C-string will overwrite the previously stored characters. The same is not true for `message2`.

FIGURE 14-25
C-String Storage Allocation

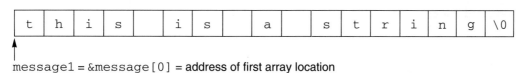

`message1 = &message[0]` = address of first array location

a. Storage allocation for a C-string defined as an array

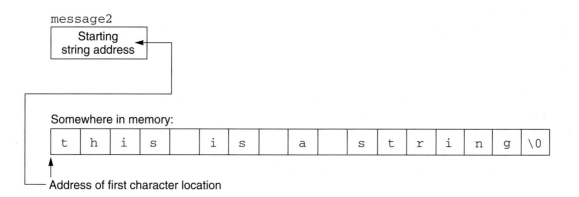

b. Storage of a C-string using a pointer

The definition of message2 reserves enough storage for one pointer. The initialization then causes the C-string to be stored in memory and the address of the string's first character, in this case the address of the t, to be loaded into the pointer. If a later assignment is made to message2, the initial C-string remains in memory and new storage locations are allocated to the new C-string. For example, consider the sequence of instructions

```
char *message2 = "this is a string";
message2 = "a new message";
```

The first statement defines message2 as a pointer variable, stores the initialization C-string in memory, and loads the starting address of the C-string (the address of the t in this) into message2. The next assignment statement causes the computer to store the second C-string and change the address in message2 to point to the starting location of this new string.

It is important to realize that the second C-string assigned to message2 does not overwrite the first C-string, but simply changes the address in message2 to point to the new C-string. As illustrated in Figure 14-26, both strings are stored inside the computer. Any additional C-string assignment to message2 would result in the additional storage of the new C-string and a corresponding change in the address stored in message2. Doing so also means that we no longer have access to the original C-string memory location.

FIGURE 14-26
Storage Allocation for Figure 14-25

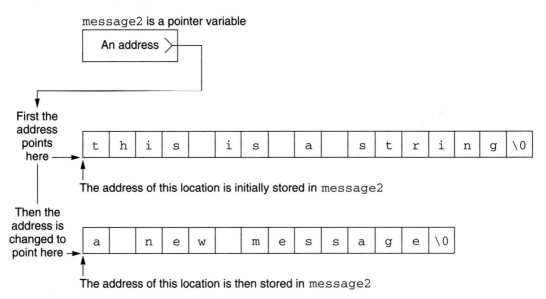

PROGRAMMING NOTE

Allocating Space for a String

Although the two declarations

```
char test[5] = "abcd";
```

and

```
char *test = "abcd";
```

both create storage for the characters `'a'`, `'b'`, `'c'`, `'d'`, and `'\0'`, there is a subtle difference between the two declarations and how values can be assigned to `test`. An array declaration, such as `char test[5];` precludes the use of any subsequent assignment expression, such as `test = "efgh"`, to assign values to the array. The use of a `strcpy()`, such as `strcpy(test,"efgh")`, however, is subsequently valid. The only restriction on the `strcpy()` is the size of the array, which in this case is five elements. This situation is reversed when a pointer is created. A pointer declaration, such as `char *test;` precludes the use of a `strcpy()` to initialize the memory locations pointed to by the pointer, but it does allow assignments. For example, the following sequence of statements is valid:

```
char *test;
test = "abcd";
test = "here is a longer string";
```

Once a string of characters has been assigned to `test`, a `strcpy()` can be used, provided the copy uses no more elements than are currently contained in the string.

The difference in usage is explained by the fact that the compiler automatically allocates sufficient new memory space for any C-string pointed to by a pointer variable, but does not do so for an array of characters. The array size is fixed by the definition statement.

Formally, any expression that yields a value that can be used on the left side of an assignment expression is said to be an **lvalue**. (Similarly, any expression that yields a value that can be used on the right side of an assignment statement is said to be an **rvalue**.) Thus, a pointer variable can be an lvalue but an array name cannot.

POINTER ARRAYS

The declaration of an array of character pointers is a useful extension to single C-string pointer declarations. For example, the declaration

```
const int NUMSEASONS = 4;
char *seasons[NUMSEASONS];
```

creates an array of four elements, where each element is a pointer to a character. As individual pointers, each pointer can be assigned to point to a C-string using assignment statements. Thus, the statements

```
seasons[0] = "Winter";
seasons[1] = "Spring";
seasons[2] = "Summer";
seasons[3] = "Fall";   // note: the C-string lengths may differ
```

set appropriate addresses into the respective pointers. Figure 14-27 illustrates the addresses loaded into the pointers for these assignments.

FIGURE 14-27
The Addresses Contained in the seasons[] *Pointers*

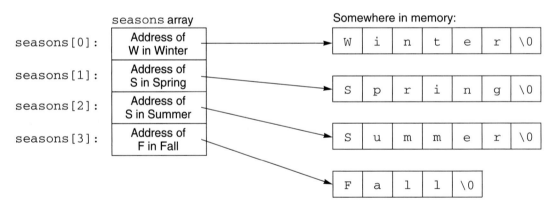

As illustrated in Figure 14-27, the seasons array does not contain the actual strings assigned to the pointers. These C-strings are stored elsewhere in the computer, in the normal data area allocated to the program. The array of pointers contains only the addresses of the starting location for each C-string.

The initializations of the seasons array can also be incorporated directly within the definition of the array, as follows:

```
char *seasons[4] = {"Winter",
                    "Spring",
                    "Summer",
                    "Fall"};
```

This declaration both creates an array of pointers and initializes the pointers with appropriate addresses. Once addresses have been assigned to the pointers, each pointer can be used to access its corresponding string. Program 14-13 uses the seasons array to display each season using a for loop.

Program 14-13

```cpp
#include <iostream>
using namespace std;

int main()
{
    const int NUMSEASONS = 4;
    int n;
    char *seasons[] = {"Winter",
                       "Spring",
                       "Summer",
                       "Fall"};

    for( n = 0; n < NUMSEASONS; n++)
       cout << "\nThe season is " << seasons[n];
       cout << endl;

    return 0;
}
```

The output obtained for Program 14-13 is:

```
The season is Winter
The season is Spring
The season is Summer
The season is Fall
```

The advantage of using a list of pointers is that logical groups of data headings can be collected together and accessed with one array name. For example, the months in a year can be collectively grouped in one array called months, and the days in a week collectively grouped in an array called days. The grouping of like headings allows the programmer to access and print an appropriate heading by simply specifying the correct position of the heading in the array. Program 14-14 uses the seasons array to correctly identify and display the season corresponding to a user-input month.

Program 14-14

```cpp
#include <iostream>
using namespace std;

int main()
{
    int n;
    char *seasons[] = {"Winter",
                       "Spring",
                       "Summer",
                       "Fall"};

    cout << "\nEnter a month (use 1 for Jan., 2 for Feb., etc.): ";
    cin  >> n;
    n = (n % 12) / 3;    // create the correct subscript
    cout << "The month entered is a "<< seasons[n]
         << " month." << endl;

    return 0;
}
```

Except for the expression n = (n % 12) / 3, Program 14-14 is rather straightforward. The program requests the user to input a month and accepts the number corresponding to the month using a cin object call.

The expression n = (n % 12) / 3 uses a common programming "trick" to scale a set of numbers into a more useful set. Using subscripts, the four elements of the seasons array must be accessed using a subscript from 0 through 3. Thus, the months of the year, which correspond to the numbers 1 through 12, must be adjusted to correspond to the correct season subscript. This is done using the expression n = (n % 12) / 3. The expression n % 12 adjusts the month entered to lie within the range 0 through 11, with 0 corresponding to December, 1 for January, and so on. Dividing by 3 causes the resulting number to range between 0 and 3, corresponding to the possible seasons elements. The result of the division by 3 is assigned to the integer variable n. The months 0, 1, and 2, when divided by 3, are set to 0; the months 3, 4, and 5 are set to 1; the months 6, 7, and 8 are set to 2; and the months 9, 10, and 11 are set to 3. This is equivalent to the following assignments:

months	season
December, January, February	Winter
March, April, May	Spring
June, July, August	Summer
September, October, November	Fall

The following is a sample output obtained for Program 14-14:

```
Enter a month (use 1 for Jan., 2 for Feb., etc.): 12
The month entered is a Winter month.
```

Exercises 14.6

1. Write two declaration statements that can be used in place of the declaration `char text[] = "Hooray!";`.

2. Determine the value of `*text`, `*(text + 3)`, `*(text + 7)` for each of the following sections of code:

   a. `char *text;`
   `char message[] = "the check is in the mail";`
   `text = message;`

   b. `char *text;`
   `char formal[] = {'t','h','i','s',' ','i','s',' ','a','n',' ',`
   `                 'i','n','v','i','t','a','t','i','o','n','\0'};`
   `text = &formal[0];`

   c. `char *text;`
   `char more[] = "Happy Holidays";`
   `text = &more[4];`

   d. `char *text, *second;`
   `char blip[] = "The good ship";`
   `second = blip;`
   `text = ++second;`

3. Determine the error in the following program:

```cpp
#include <iostream>
using namespace std;

int main()
{
  int i = 0;
  char message[] = {'H','e','l','l','o','\0'};

  for( ; i < 5; i++)
  {
    cout << *message;
    ++message;
  }


  return 0;
}
```

4. a. Write a C++ function that displays the day of the week corresponding to a user-entered input number between 1 and 7. That is, in response to an input of 2, the program displays the name "Tuesday." Use an array of pointers in the function.

    b. Include the function written for Exercise 4a in a complete working program.

5. Modify the function written in Exercise 4a so that the function returns the address of the character string containing the proper day to be displayed.

6. Write a function that will accept 10 lines of user-input text and store the entered lines as 10 individual strings. Use a pointer array in your function.

14.7 POINTERS AS CLASS MEMBERS

As we saw in Section 7.2, a class can contain any C++ data type. Thus, the inclusion of a pointer variable in a class should not seem surprising. For example, the following class:

```
class Test
  {
    private:
      int idNum;
      double *ptPay;
    public:
      Test(int = 0, double * = NULL); //constructor
      void setVals(int a, double *b);
      void display();
  };
```

declares a class consisting of two instance variables and three member methods. The first instance variable is an integer variable named idNum, and the second instance variable is a pointer named ptPay, which is a pointer variable to a double-precision number. We will use the setVals() member method to store values into the private member variables and the display() method for output purposes. The implementation of these two methods along with the constructor method Test() is contained in the class implementation section:

```
// methods implementation section
Test::Test(int id = 0, double *pt = NULL)
{
  idNum = id;
  ptPay = pt;
}
void Test::setVals(int a, double *b)
{
  idNum = a;
  ptPay = b;

  return;
}
void Test::display()
{
  cout << "\nEmployee number " << idNum << " was paid $"
       << setiosflags(ios::showpoint)<< setiosflags(ios::fixed)
       << setw(6) << setprecision(2)
       << *ptPay << endl;

  return;
}
```

In this implementation, the Test() constructor initializes its idNum data member to its first argument and its pointer member to its second argument; if no arguments are given these variables are initialized to a 0 and NULL, respectively. The display function simply outputs the value pointed to by its pointer member. As defined in this implementation, the setVals() function is very similar to the constructor and is used to alter member values after the object has been declared. The function's first argument (an integer) is assigned to idNum and its second argument (an address) is assigned to ptPay.

The main() function in Program 14-15 illustrates the use of the Test class by first creating one object, named emp, which is initialized using the constructor's default arguments. The setVals() function is then used to assign the value 12345 and the address of the variable pay to the data members of this emp object. Finally, the display() function is used to display the value whose address is stored in emp.ptPay. As illustrated by Program 14-15, the pointer member of an object is used like any other pointer variable.

Program 14-15

```cpp
#include <iostream>
#include <iomanip>
using namespace std;

class Test
{

  private:
    int idNum;
    double *ptPay;
  public:
    Test(int, double *);          // constructor
    void setVals(int, double *);  // accessor function
    void display();               // accessor function
};

// methods implementation section
Test::Test(int id = 0, double *pt = NULL)
{
  idNum = id;
  ptPay = pt;
}

void Test::setVals(int a, double *b)
{
  idNum = a;
  ptPay = b;

  return;
}

void Test::display()
{
  cout << "\nEmployee number " << idNum << " was paid $"
       << setiosflags(ios::showpoint)<< setiosflags(ios::fixed)
       << setw(6) << setprecision(2)
       << *ptPay << endl;

  return;
}
```

(continued on next page)

```
int main()
{
    Test emp;
    double pay = 456.20;
    emp.setVals(12345, &pay);
    emp.display();

    return 0;
}
```

The output produced by executing Program 14-15 is:

```
Employee number 12345 was paid $456.20
```

Figure 14-28 illustrates the relationship between the data members of the `emp` object defined in Program 14-15 and the variable named `pay`. The value assigned to `emp.idNum` is the number 12345 and the value assigned to `pay` is 456.20. The address of the `pay` variable is assigned to the object member `emp.ptPay`. Since this member has been defined as a pointer to a double-precision number, placing the address of the double-precision variable `pay` in it is a correct use of this data member.

FIGURE 14-28
Storing an Address in a Data Member

Object `emp`'s data members:

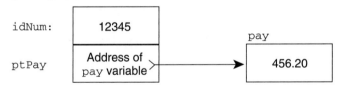

Although the pointer defined in Program 14-15 has been used in a rather trivial fashion, the program does illustrate the concept of including a pointer in a class.

Clearly it would be more efficient to include the `pay` variable directly as a data member of the `Test` class rather than using a pointer to it. In some cases, however, pointers are advantageous. For example, assume we need to store a list of book titles. Rather than use a C-string to hold each title, which initially allocates a fixed amount of space for each title, we will use a pointer member to a character array. This will allow us to easily allocate the exact array size, as it is needed, for each book title. This arrangement is illustrated in Figure 14-29, which shows two objects, a and b, each of which consists of a single pointer data member. As depicted, object a's pointer contains the address of ("points to") a character array containing the characters `Windows Primer`, while object b's pointer contains the address of a character array containing the characters `A Brief History of Western Civilization`.

FIGURE 14-29
Two Objects Containing Pointer Data Members

Object a's data member:

Object b's data member:

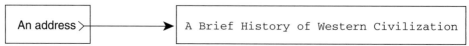

A suitable class for a list of book titles that are to be accessed as illustrated in Figure 14-29 is:

```
class Book
{
  private:
    char *title;    // a pointer to a book title
  public:
    Book(char *);   // constructor
    void showtitle();    // display the title
};
```

The definition of the constructor method, `Book()`, and the display method, `showtitle()`, are defined in the implementation section as:

```
// methods implementation section

Book::Book(char *name = NULL)
{
    title = new char[strlen(name)+1];   // allocate memory
    strcpy(title,name);                 // store the string
}

void Book::showtitle()
{

    cout << title << endl;
}
```

The body of the `Book()` constructor contains two statements. The first statement, `title = new char[strlen(name)+1];`, performs two tasks: first, the right side of the statement allocates enough storage for the length of the `name` argument plus 1, to accommodate the end of C-string null character, `'\0'`. Next, the address of the first allocated character position is assigned to the pointer

14

variable `title`. These operations are illustrated in Figure 14-30. The second statement in the constructor copies the characters in the `name` argument to the newly created memory allocation. If no argument is passed to the constructor, then `title` is the empty string; that is, `title` is set to NULL. Program 14-16 uses this class definition within the context of a complete program.

FIGURE 14-30
Allocating Memory for `title = new char[strlen(name)+1]`

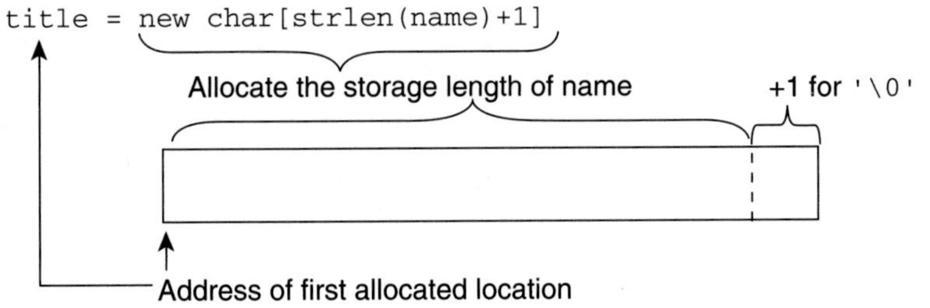

Program 14-16

```cpp
#include <iostream>
using namespace std;

class Book
{
  private:
    char *title;    // a pointer to a book title
  public:
    Book(char *);  // constructor
    void showtitle();   // display the title
};

// class implementation

Book::Book(char *strng = NULL)
{
  title = new char[strlen(strng)+1];  // allocate memory
  strcpy(title,strng);                // store the string
}

void Book::showtitle()
{
  cout << title << endl;

  return;
}
```

(continued on next page)

```
int main()
{
  Book   book1("Windows Primer");    // create 1st title
  Book   book2("A Brief History of Western Civilization");  // 2nd title

  book1.showtitle();   // display book1's title
  book2.showtitle();   // display book2's title

  return 0;
}
```

The output produced by Program 14-16 is:

```
Windows Primer
A Brief History of Western Civilization
```

ASSIGNMENT OPERATORS AND COPY CONSTRUCTORS RECONSIDERED[11]

When a class contains no pointer data members, the compiler-provided defaults for the assignment operator and copy constructor adequately perform their intended tasks. Both of these defaults provide a member-by-member operation that produces no adverse side effects. This is not the case when a pointer member is included in the class declaration. Let's see why this is so.

Figure 14-31a illustrates the arrangement of pointers and allocated memory produced by Program 14-16 just before it completes execution. Let's now assume that we insert the assignment statement book2 = book1; before the closing brace of the main() function. Since we have not defined an assignment operation, the compiler's default assignment is used. As we know, this assignment produces a memberwise copy (that is, book2.title = book1.title) and means that the address in book1's pointer is copied into book2's pointer. Thus, both pointers now "point to" the character array containing the characters Windows Primer, and the address of A Brief History of Western Civilization has been lost. This situation is illustrated in Figure 14-31b.

Because the memberwise assignment illustrated in Figure 14-31b results in the loss of the address of A Brief History of Western Civilization, there is no way for the program to release this memory storage (it will be cleaned up by the operating system when the program terminates). Worse, however, is the case where a destructor attempts to release the memory. Once the memory pointed to by book2 is released (again, referring to Figure 14-31b), book1 points to an undefined memory location. If this memory area is subsequently reallocated before book1 is deleted, the deletion will release memory that another object is using. The results of this can wreak havoc on a program.

---

[11]The material in this section pertains to the problems that occur when using the default assignment, copy constructor, and destructor functions with classes containing pointer members, and how to overcome these problems. On first reading, this section can be omitted without loss of subject continuity.

FIGURE 14-31A
Before the Assignment `book2 = book1;`

book1's Pointer

book2's Pointer

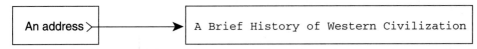

FIGURE 14-31B
The Effect Produced by Default Assignment

book1's Pointer

book2's Pointer

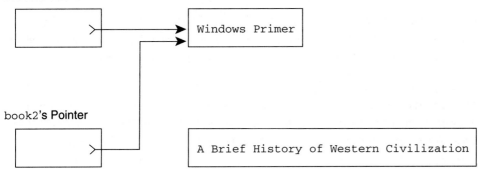

FIGURE 14-31C
The Desired Effect

book1's Pointer

book2's Pointer

What is typically desired is that the book titles themselves be copied, and their pointers left alone. This situation also removes all of the side effects of a subsequent deletion of any book object. To achieve the desired assignment, we must explicitly write our own assignment operator. A suitable definition for this operator is:

```
void Book::operator=(Book& oldbook)
{
  if(oldbook.title != NULL)   // check that it exists
    delete(title);            // release existing memory
  title = new char[strlen(oldbook.title) + 1];   // allocate new memory
  strcpy(title, oldbook.title);  // copy the title
}
```

This definition cleanly releases the memory previously allocated for the object and then allocates sufficient memory to store the copied title.

The problems associated with the default assignment operator also exist with the default copy constructor, because it also performs a memberwise copy. As with assignment, these problems are avoided by writing our own copy constructor. For our Book class such a constructor is:

```
Book::Book(Book& oldbook)
{
  title = new char[strlen(oldbook.title) + 1];   // allocate new memory
  strcpy(title, oldbook.title);  // copy the title
}
```

Comparing the body of this copy constructor to the assignment operator's function body reveals they are identical except for the de-allocation of memory performed by the assignment operator. This is because the copy constructor does not have to release the existing array prior to allocating a new one, since none exists when the constructor is called.

Exercises 14.7

1. Include the copy constructor and assignment operator presented in this section in Program 14-16 and run the program to verify their operation.

2. Write a suitable destructor function for Program 14-16.

3. a. Construct a class named Car that contains the following four data members: a floating-point variable named engineSize, a character variable named bodyStyle, an integer variable named colorCode, and a character pointer named vinPtr to a vehicle identification code. Class methods should include a constructor that provides default values of 0 for each numeric instance variable, an 'X' for each character variable, and a NULL for each pointer; a display method that prints the engine size, body style, color code, and vehicle identification number; and an assignment operator that performs a memberwise assignment between two car objects that correctly handles the pointer member.

b. Include the class written for Exercise 3a in a working C++ program that creates two car objects, the second of which is assigned the values of the first object.

4. Modify Program 14-16 to include the assignment statement `b = a;`, then run the modified program to assess the error messages, if any, that occur.

5. Using Program 14-16 as a start, write a program that creates five `Book` objects. The program should allow the user to enter the five book titles interactively and then display the titles entered.

6. Modify the program written in Exercise 5 so that the program sorts the entered book titles in alphabetical order before it displays them. (*Hint:* You will have to define a sort routine for the titles.)

14.8 COMMON PROGRAMMING ERRORS

In using the material presented in this chapter, be aware of the following possible programming errors:

1. Attempting to store an address in a variable that has not been declared as a pointer.

2. Using a pointer to access nonexistent array elements. For example, if `nums` is an array of 10 integers, the expression `*(nums + 15)` points six integer locations beyond the last element of the array. Because C++ does not do any bounds checking on array accesses, this type of error is not caught by the compiler. This is the same error, disguised in pointer notation form, that occurs when using a subscript to access an out-of-bounds array element.

3. Incorrectly applying the address and indirection operators. For example, if `pt` is a pointer variable, the expressions

```
pt = &45
pt = &(miles + 10)
```

are both invalid because they attempt to take the address of a value. Notice that the expression `pt = &miles + 10`, however, is valid. Here, 10 is added to the address of `miles`. Again, it is the programmer's responsibility to ensure that the final address "points to" a valid data element.

4. Taking addresses of pointer constants. For example, given the declarations

```
int nums[25];
int *pt;
```

the assignment

```
pt = &nums;
```

is invalid. `nums` is a pointer constant that is itself equivalent to an address. The correct assignment is `pt = nums`.

5. Taking addresses of a reference argument or reference variable. The reason for this is that reference arguments and variables are essentially the same as pointer constants, in that they are named address values.

6. Initializing pointer variables incorrectly. For example, the initialization

```
int *pt = 5;
```

is invalid. Since `pt` points to an integer, it must be initialized with a valid address.

7. Becoming confused about whether a variable *contains* an address or *is* an address. Pointer variables and pointer arguments contain addresses. Although a pointer constant is synonymous with an address, it is useful to treat pointer constants as pointer variables with two restrictions:

- The address of a pointer constant cannot be taken.
- The address "contained in" the pointer constant cannot be altered.

Except for these two restrictions, pointer constants and variables can be used almost interchangeably. Therefore, when an address is required, any of the following can be used:
- a pointer variable name
- a pointer argument name
- a pointer constant name
- a nonpointer variable name preceded by the address operator (e.g., `&variable`)
- a nonpointer argument name preceded by the address operator (e.g., `&argument`)

Some of the confusion surrounding pointers is caused by the cavalier use of the word "pointer." For example, the phrase "a function requires a pointer argument" is more clearly understood when it is realized that the phrase really means "a function requires an address as an argument." Similarly, the phrase "a function returns a pointer" really means "a function returns an address."

If you are ever in doubt as to what is really contained in a variable or how it should be treated, use the `cout` object to display the contents of the variable, the "thing pointed to," or "the address of the variable." Seeing what is displayed frequently helps sort out what is really in the variable.

8. Using the pointer to "point to" a nonexistent array element. This error is, of course, the same error we have already seen using subscripts. Since C++ compilers do not perform bounds checking on arrays, it is the programmer's responsibility to ensure that the address in the pointer is the address of a valid data element.

9. Misunderstanding the casual use of terminology. For example, if `text` is defined as

```
char *text;
```

the variable `text` might be referred to as a character string, or C-string for short. Thus, you might, for example, hear a programmer say something like "store the characters `Hooray for the Hoosiers` in the `text` string." Strictly speaking, calling `text` a character string or a C-string variable is incorrect. The variable `text` is a pointer that contains the address of the first character in the string. Nevertheless, referring to a character pointer as a C-string occurs frequently enough that you should be aware of it.

10. Using the default copy constructor and default assignment operators with classes containing pointer members. Since these default functions do a memberwise copy, the address in the source pointer is copied to the destination pointer. Typically this is not what is wanted since both pointers end up pointing to the same memory area.

11. Forgetting to use the bracket set, [], following the `delete` operator when dynamically deallocating memory that was previously allocated using the `new` [] operator.

14.9 CHAPTER REVIEW

Key Terms

address
address operator
indirection
indirection operator
offset
pointer variable
scaling

SUMMARY

1. Every variable has a data type, an address, and a value. In C++ the address of a variable can be obtained by using the address operator `&`.

2. A pointer is a variable that is used to store the address of another variable. Pointers, like all C++ variables, must be declared. The indirection operator, `*`, is used both to declare a pointer variable and to access the variable whose address is stored in a pointer.

3. An array name is a pointer constant. The value of the pointer constant is the address of the first element in the array. Thus, if `val` is the name of an array, `val` and `&val[0]` can be used interchangeably.

4. Any access to an array element using subscript notation can always be replaced using pointer notation. That is, the notation `a[i]` can always be replaced by the notation `*(a + i)`. This is true whether `a` is initially declared explicitly as an array or as a pointer.

5. Arrays can be dynamically created as a program is executing. For example, the sequence of statements:

```
cout << "Enter the array size: ";
cin  >> num;
int *grades = new int[num];
```

creates an array named `grades` of size `num`. The area allocated for the array can be dynamically destroyed using the `delete []` expression. For example, the statement `delete [] grades;` returns the allocated area for the `grades` array back to the computer.

6. Arrays are passed to functions as addresses. The called function always receives direct access to the originally declared array elements.

7. When a single-dimensional array is passed to a function, the argument declaration for the function can be either an array declaration or a pointer declaration. Thus, the following argument declarations are equivalent:

```
double a[];
double *a;
```

8. Pointers can be incremented, decremented, compared, and assigned. Numbers added to or subtracted from a pointer are automatically scaled. The scale factor used is the number of bytes required to store the data type originally pointed to.

Chapter Exercises

1. Repeat Exercise 6 in Section 8.2, but use pointer references to access all array elements.

2. Repeat Exercise 7 in Section 8.2, but use pointer references to access all array elements.

3. Write a C++ program that asks for two lowercase characters. Pass the two entered characters using pointers to a function named `capit()`. The `capit()` function should capitalize the two letters and return the capitalized values to the calling function through its pointer arguments. The calling function should then display all four letters.

4. Write a program that declares three single-dimensional arrays named `miles`, `gallons`, and `mpg`. Each array should be capable of holding 10 elements. In the `miles` array, store the numbers 240.5, 300.0, 189.6, 310.6, 280.7, 216.9, 199.4, 160.3, 177.4, 192.3. In the `gallons` array, store the numbers 10.3, 15.6, 8.7, 14, 16.3, 15.7, 14.9, 10.7, 8.3, 8.4. Each element of the `mpg` array should be calculated as the corresponding element of the `miles` array divided by the equivalent element of the `gallons` array; for example,

```
mpg[0] = miles[0] / gallons[0]
```

Use pointers when calculating and displaying the elements of the `mpg` array.

5. a. Write a program that has a declaration in `main` to store the C-string `Vacation is near` into an array named `message`. There should be a function call to display that accepts `message` in an argument named `strng` and then displays the message using the pointer notation `*(strng + i)`.

    b. Modify the display function written in Exercise 5a to alter the address in `message`. Also use the expression `*strng` rather than `*(strng + i)` to retrieve the correct element.

6. Write a program that declares three single-dimensional arrays named `price`, `quantity`, and `amount`. Each array should be declared in `main` and be capable of holding 10 double-precision numbers. The numbers to be stored in `price` are 10.62, 14.89,

14

13.21, 16.55, 18.62, 9.47, 6.58, 18.32, 12.15, 3.98. The numbers to be stored in `quantity` are 4, 8.5, 6, 7.35, 9, 15.3, 3, 5.4, 2.9, 4.8. Have your program pass these three arrays to a function called `extend()`, which calculates the elements in the `amount` array as the product of the equivalent elements in the `price` and `quantity` arrays; for example, `amount[1] = price[1] * quantity[1]`.

After `extend()` has put values into the `amount` array, display the values in the array from within `main()`. Write the `extend()` function using pointers.

7.   **a.** Determine the output of the following program:

```
#include <iostream>
using namespace std;

const int ROWS = 2;
const int COLS = 3;

int main()
{
  void arr(int [ROWS][COLS]);    //function prototype
  int nums[ROWS][COLS] = { {33,16,29},
                           {54,67,99}};

  arr(nums);

  return 0;
}

void arr(int val[ROWS][COLS])
{
  cout << endl << *(*val);
  cout << endl << *(*val + 1);
  cout << endl << *(*(val + 1) + 2);
  cout << endl << *(*val) + 1;
  cout << endl;

  return;
}
```

b. Given the declaration for `val` in the `arr()` function, would the reference `val[1][2]` be valid within the function?

8.   Define an array of 10 pointers to floating-point numbers. Then read 10 numbers into the individual locations referenced by the pointers. Now add all of the numbers and store the result in a pointer-referenced location. Display the contents of all of the locations.

**Testing
Center**

Please visit the Testing Center at www.course.com/testingcenter for more practice on addresses, pointers, and arrays.

DATA STRUCTURES

15

A structure is a historical holdover from C. From a programmer's perspective, a structure can be thought of as a class that has all public instance variables and no member methods. In commercial applications a structure is referred to, and is the same thing as, a record. In both C and C++, a structure provides a means of storing values that have different data types (such as a string name, an integer part number, and a real price) together under a common name. To get a better sense of what this means, consider Figure 15-1, which shows the data items that might be stored for an address label.

Each of the individual data items listed in Figure 15-1 is an entity by itself, and is referred to as a **data field**. Taken together, all the data fields form a single unit that is referred to as a **record**. In the C language, a record is referred to as a **structure**, and the two terms are used interchangeably. The same is true in C++, with one major difference. C++ permits methods to be included in a structure. When methods are added, the only real difference between a C++ structure and a class is the default access used by each. In a structure the default for variables is public, while in a class this default is private. The implication is that a structure can be used to create a class and a class can be made to create a structure. This, however, is rarely if ever done.

Structures are now primarily used for their historical purpose, which is to create a publicly available record. This chapter presents the C++ statements required to create, use, and manipulate structures, in their role as records.

FIGURE 15-1
Typical Mailing List Components

Name:
Street Address:
City:
State:
Zip Code:

15.1 STRUCTURES

A **structure** can be considered as a class that has no methods and whose variables are all public. In dealing with structures, as such, it is important to distinguish between form and content.

A structure's form consists of the symbolic names, data types, and arrangement of individual data items that form its elements. The structure's contents refer to the actual data values in the symbolic names. For example, Figure 15-2 shows acceptable contents for the structure whose form was illustrated in Figure 15-1.

FIGURE 15-2
The Form and Contents of a Structure

Name: Ronda Bronson-Karp
Street Address: 614 Freeman Street
City: Orange
State: NJ
Zip Code: 07052

Creating and using a structure requires the same two steps needed for creating and using any variable. First the structure's type must be declared. Then specific values can be assigned to the individual structure elements. Declaring a structure requires listing the data types, data names, and arrangement of data items. For example, the statement

```
struct
{
   int month;
   int day;
   int year;
}  birth;
```

declares the form of a structure named `birth` and reserves storage for the individual data items listed in the structure. The `birth` structure consists of three data items or fields, which are called members of the structure.

Assigning actual data values to the data items of a structure is called **populating the structure**, and is a relatively straightforward procedure. Each member of a structure is accessed by giving both the structure name and individual data item name, separated by a period. Thus, `birth.month` refers to the first member of the `birth` structure, `birth.day` refers to the second member of the structure, and `birth.year` refers to the third member. Program 15-1 illustrates assigning values to the individual members of the `birth` structure.

Program 15-1

```
// a program that defines and populates a record
#include <iostream>
using namespace std;

int main()
{
   struct
```

(continued on next page)

15

```
    {
        int month;
        int day;
        int year;
    } birth;

    birth.month = 12;
    birth.day = 28;
    birth.year = 86;

    cout << "My birth date is "
         << birth.month << '/'
         << birth.day   << '/'
         << birth.year  << endl;

    return 0;
}
```

The output produced by Program 15-1 is:

```
    My birth date is 12/28/86
```

As in most C++ statements, the spacing of a structure definition is not rigid. For example, the `birth` structure could just as well have been defined as:

```
    struct {int month; int day; int year;} birth;
```

Also, as with all C++ definition statements, multiple variables can be defined in the same statement. For example, the definition statement

```
    struct
    {
        int month;
        int day;
        int year;
    } birth, current;
```

creates two structure variables having the same form. The members of the first structure are referenced by the individual names `birth.month`, `birth.day`, and `birth.year`, while the members of the second structure are referenced by the names `current.month`, `current.day`, and `current.year`. Notice that the form of this particular structure definition statement is identical to the form used in defining any program variable: The data type is followed by a list of variable names.

A helpful and commonly used modification for defining structure types is to list the form of the structure with no following variable names. In this case, however, the list of structure members must be preceded by a user-selected data-type name. For example, in the declaration

```
struct BirthDate
{
  int month;
  int day;
  int year;
};
```

the term `BirthDate` is a structure type name: It defines a new data type that is a data structure of the declared form. By convention the first letter of a user-selected data-type name is uppercase, as in the name `BirthDate`. This helps to identify a data-type name when it is used in subsequent definition statements. Here, the declaration for the `BirthDate` structure creates a new data type without actually reserving any storage locations. As such it is not a definition statement. It simply declares a `BirthDate` structure type and describes how individual data items are arranged within the structure. Actual storage for the members of the structure is reserved only when specific variable names are assigned. For example, the definition statement

```
BirthDate birth, current;
```

reserves storage for two `BirthDate` structure variables named `birth` and `current`, respectively. Each of these individual structures has the form previously declared for the `BirthDate` structure.

The declaration of a structure data type, like all declarations, may be global or local. Program 15-2 illustrates the global declaration of a `BirthDate` data type. Internal to `main()`, the variable `birth` is defined as a local variable of `BirthDate` type.

Program 15-2

```
#include <iostream>
using namespace std;

struct BirthDate     // this is a global declaration
{
  int month;
  int day;
```

(continued on next page)

15

```
  int year;
};

int main()
{
  BirthDate birth;

  birth.month = 12;
  birth.day = 28;
  birth.year = 86;

  cout << "My birth date is " << birth.month << '/'
                             << birth.day   << '/'
                             << birth.year  << endl;

  return 0;
}
```

The output produced by Program 15-2 is identical to the output produced by Program 15-1.

The initialization of structures follows the same rules as for the initialization of arrays; structures may be initialized by following the definition with a list of initializers. For example, the definition statement

```
    BirthDate  birth = {12, 28, 86};
```

can be used to replace the first four statements internal to main() in Program 15-2. Notice that the initializers are separated by commas, not semicolons.

The individual members of a structure are not restricted to integer data types, as illustrated by the BirthDate structure. Any valid C++ data type can be used. For example, consider an employee record consisting of the following data items:

Name:
Identification Number:
Regular Pay Rate:
Overtime Pay Rate:

A suitable declaration for these data items is:

```
    struct PayRec
    {
      string name;
      int idNum;
      double regRate;
      double otRate;
    };
```

Once the `PayRec` data type is declared, a specific structure variable using this type can be defined and initialized. For example, the definition

```
PayRec employee = {"H. Price",12387,15.89,25.50};
```

creates a structure named `employee` of the `PayRec` data type. The individual members of `employee` are initialized with the respective data listed between braces in the definition statement.

Notice that a single structure is simply a convenient method for combining and storing related items under a common name. Although a single structure is useful in explicitly identifying the relationship among its members, the individual members could be defined as separate variables. One of the real advantages to using structures is only realized when the same data type is used in a list many times over. Creating lists with the same data type is the topic of the next section.

Before leaving single structures, it is worth noting that the individual members of a structure can be any valid C++ data type, including arrays, strings, and structures. A string was used as a member of the `employee` structure defined previously. Accessing an element of a member array requires giving the structure's name, followed by a period, followed by the array designation.

Including a structure within a structure follows the same rules for including any data type in a structure. For example, assume that a structure is to consist of a name and a birth date, where a `BirthDate` structure has been declared as:

```
struct BirthDate
{
   int month;
   int day;
   int year;
};
```

A suitable definition of a structure that includes a name and a `BirthDate` structure is:

```
struct
{
   string name;
   BirthDate birth;
} person;
```

Notice that in declaring the `BirthDate` structure, the term `BirthDate` is a data type name; thus it appears before the braces in the declaration statement. In defining the `person` structure variable, `person` is a variable name; thus it is the name of a specific structure. The same is true of the variable named `birth`. This is the name of a specific `BirthDate` structure. Individual members in the `person` structure are accessed by preceding the desired member with the structure name followed by a period. For example, `person.birth.month` refers to the `month` variable in the `birth` structure contained in the `person` structure.

15

Exercises 15.1

1. Declare a structure data type named STemp for each of the following records:

   a. a student record consisting of a student identification number, number of credits completed, and cumulative grade point average

   b. a student record consisting of a student's name, date of birth, number of credits completed, and cumulative grade point average

   c. a mailing list consisting of a person's name and address (street, city, state, and zip code)

   d. a stock record consisting of the stock's name, the price of the stock, and the date of purchase

   e. an inventory record consisting of an integer part number, part description, number of parts in inventory, and an integer reorder number

2. For the individual data types declared in Exercise 1, define a suitable structure variable name, and initialize each structure with the appropriate following data:

   a. Identification Number: 4682
      Number of Credits Completed: 68
      Grade Point Average: 3.01

   b. Name: Rhona Karp
      Date of Birth: 8/4/60
      Number of Credits Completed: 96
      Grade Point Average: 3.89

   c. Name: Kay Kingsley
      Street Address: 614 Freeman Street
      City: Indianapolis
      State: IN
      Zip Code: 07030

   d. Stock: IBM
      Price Purchased: 134.5
      Date Purchased: 10/1/86

   e. Part Number: 16879
      Description: Battery
      Number in Stock: 10
      Reorder Number: 3

3. a. Write a C++ program that prompts a user to input the current month, day, and year. Store the data entered in a suitably defined record and display the date in an appropriate manner.

   b. Modify the program written in Exercise 3a to use a record that accepts the current time in hours, minutes, and seconds.

4. Write a C++ program that uses a structure for storing the name of a stock, its estimated earnings per share, and its estimated price-to-earnings ratio. Have the program prompt the user to enter these items for five different stocks, each time using the same structure to store the entered data. When the data have been entered for a particular stock, have the program compute and display the anticipated stock price based on the entered earnings and price-per-earnings values. For example, if a user entered the data XYZ 1.56 12, the anticipated price for a share of XYZ stock is (1.56)*(12) = $18.72.

5. Write a C++ program that accepts a user-entered time in hours and minutes. Have the program calculate and display the time one minute later.

6. a. Write a C++ program that accepts a user-entered date. Have the program calculate and display the date of the next day. For purposes of this exercise, assume that all months consist of 30 days.

    b. Modify the program written in Exercise 6a to account for the actual number of days in each month.

15.2 ARRAYS OF STRUCTURES

The real power of structures is realized when the same structure is used for lists of data. For example, assume that the data shown in Figure 15-3 must be processed.

FIGURE 15-3
A List of Employee Data

employee number	employee name	employee pay rate
32479	Abrams, B.	6.72
33623	Bohm, P.	7.54
34145	Donaldson, S.	5.56
35987	Ernst, T.	5.43
36203	Gwodz, K.	8.72
36417	Hanson, H.	7.64
37634	Monroe, G.	5.29
38321	Price, S.	9.67
39435	Robbins, L.	8.50
39567	Williams, B.	7.20

15

Clearly, the employee numbers can be stored together in an array of integers, the names in an array of strings, and the pay rates in an array of double-precision numbers. In organizing the data in this fashion, each column in Figure 15-3 is considered as a separate list, which is stored in its own array. The correspondence between items for each individual employee is maintained by storing an employee's data in the same array position in each array.

The separation of the complete list into three individual arrays is unfortunate, since all of the items relating to a single employee constitute a natural organization of data into structures, as illustrated in Figure 15-4. Using a structure, the integrity of the data organization as a record can be maintained and reflected by the program. Under this approach, the list illustrated in Figure 15-4 can be processed as a single array of 10 structures.

FIGURE 15-4
A List of Structures

	employee number	employee name	employee pay rate
1st structure ⟶	32479	Abrams, B.	6.72
2nd structure ⟶	33623	Bohm, P.	7.54
3rd structure ⟶	34145	Donaldson, S.	5.56
4th structure ⟶	35987	Ernst, T.	5.43
5th structure ⟶	36203	Gwodz, K.	8.72
6th structure ⟶	36417	Hanson, H.	7.64
7th structure ⟶	37634	Monroe, G.	5.29
8th structure ⟶	38321	Price, S.	9.67
9th structure ⟶	39435	Robbins, L.	8.50
10th structure ⟶	39567	Williams, B.	7.20

Declaring an array of structures is the same as declaring an array of any other variable type. For example, if the data type `PayRec` is declared as

```
struct PayRec {int idnum; string name; double rate;};
```

then an array of 10 such structures can be defined as

```
PayRec employee[10];
```

This definition statement constructs an array of 10 elements, each of which is a structure of the data type `PayRec`. Notice that the creation of an array of 10 structures has the same form as the creation of any other array. For example, creating an array of 10 integers named `employee` requires the declaration:

```
int employee[10];
```

In this declaration the data type is `integer`, while in the former declaration for `employee` the data type is `PayRec`.

Once an array of structures is declared, a particular data item is referenced by giving the position of the desired structure in the array followed by a period and the appropriate structure member. For example, the variable `employee[0].rate` references the `rate` member of the first `employee` structure in the `employee` array. Including structures as elements of an array permits a list of structures to be processed using standard array programming techniques. Program 15-3 displays the first five employee structures illustrated in Figure 15-4.

Program 15-3

```cpp
#include <iostream>
#include <string>
#include <iomanip>
using namespace std;

const int NUMRECS = 5;               // maximum number of records

struct PayRec                        // this is a global declaration
{
  int id;
  string name;
  double rate;
};

int main()
{
  int i;
  PayRec employee[NUMRECS] = {
                               {32479, "Abrams, B.", 6.72},
                               {33623, "Bohm, P.", 7.54},
                               {34145, "Donaldson, S.", 5.56},
                               {35987, "Ernst, T.", 5.43},
                               {36203, "Gwodz, K.", 8.72}
                             };

  cout << endl;                       // start on a new line
  cout << setiosflags(ios::left);     // left justify the output
  for (i = 0; i < NUMRECS; i++)
    cout << setw(7)  << employee[i].id
         << setw(15) << employee[i].name
         << setw(6)  << employee[i].rate << endl;

  return 0;
}
```

The output displayed by Program 15-3 is:

```
32479   Abrams, B.      6.72
33623   Bohm, P.        7.54
34145   Donaldson, S.   5.56
35987   Ernst, T.       5.43
36203   Gwodz, K.       8.72
```

In reviewing Program 15-3, notice the initialization of the array of structures. Although the initializers for each structure have been enclosed in inner braces, these are not strictly necessary because all members have been initialized. As with all external and static variables, in the absence of explicit initializers, the numeric elements of both static and external arrays or structures are initialized to zero and their character elements are initialized to NULLs. The setiosflags(ios::left) manipulator inserted into the cout object forces each name to be displayed left-justified in its designated field width.

Exercises 15.2

1. Define arrays of 100 structures for each of the data types described in Exercise 1 of the previous section.

2. a. Using the data type

   ```
   struct MonthDays
   {
     string name;
     int days;
   };
   ```

   define an array of 12 structures of type MonthDays. Name the array convert[], and initialize the array with the names of the 12 months in a year and the number of days in each month.

   b. Include the array created in Exercise 2a in a program that displays the names and number of days in each month.

3. Using the data type declared in Exercise 2a, write a C++ program that accepts a month from a user in numerical form and displays the name of the month and the number of days in the month. Thus, in response to an input of 3, the program would display March has 31 days.

4. a. Declare a single-structure data type suitable for an employee structure of the type illustrated below:

number	name	rate	hours
3462	Jones	4.62	40
6793	Robbins	5.83	38
6985	Smith	5.22	45
7834	Swain	6.89	40
8867	Timmins	6.43	35
9002	Williams	4.75	42

b. Using the data type declared in Exercise 4a, write a C++ program that interactively accepts the above data into an array of six structures. Once the data have been entered, the program should create a payroll report listing each employee's name, number, and gross pay. Include the total gross pay of all employees at the end of the report.

5. **a.** Declare a single-structure data type suitable for a car structure of the type illustrated:

car number	miles driven	gallons used
25	1,450	62
36	3,240	136
44	1,792	76
52	2,360	105
68	2,114	67

b. Using the data type declared for Exercise 5a, write a C++ program that interactively accepts the above data into an array of five structures. Once the data have been entered, the program should create a report listing each car number and the miles per gallon achieved by the car. At the end of the report, include the average miles per gallon achieved by the complete fleet of cars.

15.3 STRUCTURES AS FUNCTION ARGUMENTS

Individual structure members may be passed to a function in the same manner as any scalar variable. For example, given the structure definition

```
struct
{
  int idNum;
  double payRate;
  double hours;
} emp;
```

the statement

```
display(emp.idNum);
```

passes a copy of the structure member `emp.idNum` to a function named `display()`. Similarly, the statement

```
calculatePay(emp.payRate,emp.hours);
```

passes copies of the values stored in structure members `emp.payRate` and `emp.hours` to the function `calculatePay()`. Both functions, `display()` and `calculatePay()`, must declare the correct data types of their respective arguments.

Complete copies of all members of a structure can also be passed to a function by including the name of the structure as an argument to the called function. For example, the function call

```
calculateNet(emp);
```

passes a copy of the complete emp structure to calculateNet(). Internal to calculateNet(), an appropriate declaration must be made to receive the structure. Program 15-4a declares a global data type for an Employee structure. This type is then used by both the main() and calculateNet() functions to define specific structures with the names emp and temp, respectively.

Program 15-4a

```cpp
#include <iostream>
#include <iomanip>
using namespace std;

struct Employee
{
  int idNum;
  double payRate;
  double hours;
};

int main()
{
  double calculateNet(Employee);    // function prototype

  Employee emp = {6786, 8.93, 40.5};
  double netPay;

  netPay = calculateNet(emp);        // pass copies of the values in emp

    // set output formats
  cout << setw(10)
       << setiosflags(ios::fixed)
       << setiosflags(ios::showpoint)
       << setprecision(2);

  cout << "The net pay for employee " << emp.idNum
       << " is $" << netPay << endl;;

  return 0;
}

double calculateNet(Employee temp) // temp is of data type Employee
{
  return(temp.payRate * temp.hours);
}
```

The output produced by Program 15-4a is:

```
The net pay for employee 6786 is $361.66
```

In reviewing Program 15-4a, observe that both `main()` and `calculateNet()` use the same data type to define their individual structure variables. The structure variable defined in `main()` and the structure variable defined in `calculateNet()` are two completely different structures. Any changes made to the local `temp` variable in `calculateNet()` are not reflected in the `emp` variable of `main()`. In fact, since both structure variables are local to their respective functions, the same structure variable name could have been used in both functions with no ambiguity.

When `calculateNet()` is called by `main()`, copies of `emp`'s structure values are passed to the `temp` structure. `calculateNet()` then uses two of the passed member values to calculate a number, which is returned to `main()`. An alternative to the pass-by-value function call illustrated in Program 15-4a, in which the called function receives a copy of a structure, is a pass-by reference that passes a reference to a structure. Passing a reference to a function permits the called function to directly access and alter values in the calling function's structure variable. For example, referring to Program 15-4a, the prototype of `calculateNet()` can be modified to:

```
double calculateNet(Employee &);
```

If this function prototype is used and the `calculateNet()` function is rewritten to conform to it, the `main()` function in Program 15-4a may be used as is. Program 15-4b illustrates these changes within the context of a complete program.

Program 15-4b

```cpp
#include <iostream>
#include <iomanip>
using namespace std;

struct Employee                      // declare a global type
{
  int idNum;
  double payRate;
  double hours;
};

int main()
{
  double calculateNet(Employee &);   // function prototype

  Employee emp = {6786, 8.93, 40.5};
  double netPay;

  netPay = calculateNet(emp);        // pass a reference
```

(continued on next page)

```
   // set output formats
  cout << setw(10)
       << setiosflags(ios::fixed)
       << setiosflags(ios::showpoint)
       << setprecision(2);

  cout << "The net pay for employee " << emp.idNum
       << " is $" <<  netPay << endl;

  return 0;
}

double calculateNet(Employee &temp)    // temp is a reference variable
{
  return(temp.payRate * temp.hours);
}
```

Program 15-4b produces the same output as Program 15-4a, except that the `calculateNet()` function in Program 15-4b receives direct access to the `emp` structure rather than a copy of it. This means that the variable name `temp` within `calculateNet()` is an alternate name for the variable `emp` in `main()`, and any changes to `temp` are direct changes to `emp`. Although the same function call, `calculateNet(emp)`, is made in both programs, the call in Program 15-4b passes a reference while the call in Program 15-4a passes values.

PASSING A POINTER

In place of passing a reference, a pointer can be used. Using a pointer requires, in addition to modifying the function's prototype and header line, that the call to `calculateNet()` in Program 15-4a be modified to

```
      calculateNet(&emp);
```

Here the function call clearly indicates that an address is being passed (which is not the case in Program 15-4b). The disadvantage, however, is in the dereferencing notation required internal to the function. However, as pointers are widely used in practice, it is worthwhile to become familiar with the notation used.

To correctly store the passed address `calculateNet()` must declare its argument as a pointer. A suitable function definition for `calculateNet()` is:

```
      calculateNet(Employee *pt)
```

Here, the declaration for `pt` declares this argument as a pointer to a structure of type `Employee`. The pointer variable, `pt`, receives the starting address of a structure whenever `calculateNet()` is called. Within `calculateNet()`, this pointer is used to directly reference any member in the structure. For example, `(*pt).idNum` refers to the `idNum` member of the structure, `(*pt).payRate` refers to the `payRate` member of the structure, and `(*pt).hours` refers to the `hours` member of the structure. These relationships are illustrated in Figure 15-5.

FIGURE 15-5
A Pointer Can Be Used to Access Structure Members

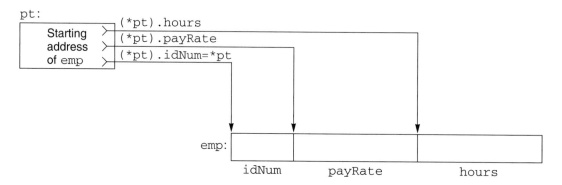

The parentheses around the expression `*pt` in Figure 15-5 are necessary to initially access "the structure whose address is in `pt`." This is followed by an identifier to access the desired member within the structure. In the absence of the parentheses, the structure member operator takes precedence over the indirection operator. Thus, the expression `*pt.hours` is another way of writing `*(pt.hours)`, which would refer to "the variable whose address is in the `pt.hours` variable." This last expression clearly makes no sense because there is no structure named `pt` and `hours` does not contain an address.

As illustrated in Figure 15-5, the starting address of the `emp` structure is also the address of the first member of the structure.

The use of pointers in this manner is so common that a special notation exists for it. The general expression `(*pointer).member` can always be replaced with the notation `pointer->member`, where the `->` operator is constructed using a minus sign followed by a greater-than symbol. Either expression can be used to locate the desired member. For example, the following expressions are equivalent:

`(*pt).idNum`	can be replaced by	`pt->idNum`
`(*pt).payRate`	can be replaced by	`pt->payRate`
`(*pt).hours`	can be replaced by	`pt->hours`

Program 15-5 illustrates passing a structure's address and using a pointer with the new notation to directly reference the structure.

Program 15-5

```cpp
#include <iostream>
#include <iomanip>
using namespace std;

struct Employee
{
  int idNum;
  double payRate;
  double hours;
};

int main()
{
  double calculateNet(Employee *);    // function prototype

  Employee emp = {6786, 8.93, 40.5};
  double netPay;

  netPay = calculateNet(&emp);        // pass an address

  // set output formats
  cout << setw(10)
       << setiosflags(ios::fixed)
       << setiosflags(ios::showpoint)
       << setprecision(2);

  cout << "The net pay for employee " << emp.idNum
       << " is $" << netPay << endl;

  return 0;
}

double calculateNet(Employee *pt)    // pt is a pointer to a
{                                    // structure of Employee type
  return(pt->payRate * pt->hours);
}
```

The name of the pointer argument declared in Program 15-5 is, of course, selected by the programmer. When calculateNet() is called, emp's starting address is passed to the function. Using this address as a reference point, individual members of the structure are accessed by including their names with the pointer.

As with all C++ expressions that access a variable, the increment and decrement operators can also be applied to them. For example, the expression

    `++pt->hours`

adds 1 to the `hours` member of the `emp` structure. Because the `->` operator has a higher priority than the increment operator, the `hours` member is accessed first and then the increment is applied. Alternatively, the expression `(++pt)->hours` uses the prefix increment operator to increment the address in `pt` before the `hours` member is accessed. Similarly, the expression `(pt++)->hours` uses the post-fix increment operator to increment the address in `pt` after the `hours` member is accessed. In both of these cases, however, there must be sufficient defined structures to ensure that the incremented pointers actually point to legitimate structures.

As an example, Figure 15-6 illustrates an array of three structures of type `Employee`. Assuming that the address of `emp[1]` is stored in the pointer variable `pt`, the expression `++pt` changes the address in `pt` to the starting address of `emp[2]`, while the expression `--pt` changes the address to point to `emp[0]`.

FIGURE 15-6
Changing Pointer Addresses

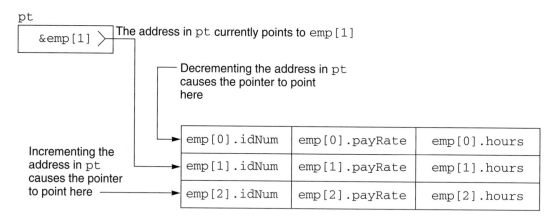

RETURNING STRUCTURES

In practice, most structure-handling functions receive direct access to a structure by receiving a structure reference. Then any changes to the structure can be made directly from within the function. If you want to have a function return a separate structure, however, you must follow the same procedures for returning complete data structures as for returning scalar values. These procedures include declaring the function appropriately and alerting any calling function to the type of data structure being returned. For example, the function `getValues()` in Program 15-6 returns a complete structure to `main()`.

15

Program 15-6

```cpp
#include <iostream>
#include <iomanip>
using namespace std;

struct  Employee
{
  int idNum;
  double payRate;
  double hours;
};

int main()
{
  Employee getValues();    // function prototype

  Employee emp;

  emp = getValues();
  cout << "\nThe employee id number is " << emp.idNum
       << "\nThe employee pay rate is $" << emp.payRate
       << "\nThe employee hours are " << emp.hours << endl;

  return 0;
}

Employee getValues()       // returns an employee structure
{
  Employee next;

  next.idNum = 6789;
  next.payRate = 16.25;
  next.hours = 38.0;

  return(next);
}
```

The following output is displayed when Program 15-6 is run:

```
The employee id number is 6789
The employee pay rate is $16.25
The employee hours are 38
```

Since the getValues() function returns a structure, the function header for getValues() must specify the type of structure being returned. Because getValues() does not receive any arguments, the function header has no argument declarations and consists of the line:

```
Employee getValues();
```

Within `getValues()`, the variable `next` is defined as a structure of the type to be returned. After values have been assigned to the `next` structure, the structure values are returned by including the structure name within the parentheses of the return statement.

On the receiving side, `main()` must be alerted that the function `getValues()` will be returning a structure. This is handled by a function declaration for `getValues()` in `main()`. Notice that these steps for returning a structure from a function are identical to the normal procedures for returning scalar data types previously described in Chapter 7.

Exercises 15.3

1. Write a C++ function named `days()` that determines the number of days from the turn of the century for any date passed as a structure. Use the `Date` structure:

   ```
   struct Date
   {
       int month;
       int day;
       int year;
   };
   ```

   In writing the `days()` function, use the convention that all years have 360 days and each month consists of 30 days. The function should return the number of days for any `Date` structure passed to it.

2. Write a C++ function named `difDays()` that calculates and returns the difference between two dates. Each `Date` is passed to the function as a structure using the following global type:

   ```
   struct Date
   {
       int month;
       int day;
       int year;
   };
   ```

   The `difDays()` function should make two calls to the `days()` function written for Exercise 1.

3. a. Rewrite the `days()` function written for Exercise 1 to receive a reference to a `Date` structure, rather than a copy of the complete structure.
   b. Redo Exercise 3a using a pointer rather than a reference.

4. a. Write a C++ function named `larger()` that returns the later date of any two dates passed to it. For example, if the dates 10/9/05 and 11/3/05 are passed to `larger()`, the second date would be returned.
   b. Include the `larger()` function that was written for Exercise 4a in a complete program. Store the `Date` structure returned by `larger()` in a separate `Date` structure and display the member values of the returned `Date`.

5. **a.** Modify the function `days()` written for Exercise 1 to account for the actual number of days in each month. Assume, however, that each year contains 365 days (that is, do not account for leap years).

b. Modify the function written for Exercise 5a to account for leap years.

15.4 DYNAMIC DATA STRUCTURE ALLOCATION

We have already encountered the concept of explicitly allocating and deallocating memory space using the `new` and `delete` operators (see section 14.2). For convenience the descriptions of these operators are repeated in Table 15-1.

TABLE 15-1
Dynamic Memory Allocation Operators

operator name	description
new	Reserves the number of bytes required by the requested data type. Returns the address of the first reserved location or `NULL` if sufficient memory is not available.
delete	Releases a block of bytes previously reserved. The address of the first reserved location is passed as an argument to the function.

This dynamic allocation of memory is especially useful when dealing with a list of structures, because it permits the list to expand as new records are added and contract as records are deleted.

In requesting additional storage space, the user must provide the `new` function with an indication of the amount of storage needed. This is done by requesting enough space for a particular type of data. For example, the expression `new(int)` or `new int` (the two forms may be used interchangeably) requests enough storage to store an integer number. A request for enough storage for a data structure is made in the same fashion. For example, using the declaration

```
struct TeleType
{
  string name;
  string phoneNo;
};
```

the function calls `new TeleType` and `new(TeleType)` both reserve enough storage for one `TeleType` data structure.

In allocating storage dynamically, we have no advance indication as to where the computer system will physically reserve the requested number of bytes, and we have no explicit name to access the newly created storage locations. To provide access to these locations, new returns the address of the first location that has been reserved. This address must be assigned to a pointer. The return of an address by new is especially useful for creating a linked list of data structures. As each new structure is created, the address returned by new to the structure can be assigned to a member of the previous structure in the list.

Program 15-7 illustrates using new to create a structure dynamically in response to a user-input request.

Program 15-7

```cpp
// a program illustrating dynamic structure allocation
#include <iostream>
#include <string>
using namespace std;
struct TeleType
{
  string name;
  string phoneNo;
};
int main()
{
  void populate(TeleType *);         // function prototype needed by main()
  void dispOne(TeleType *);          // function prototype needed by main()

  char key;
  TeleType *recPoint;                    // recPoint is a pointer to a
                                         // structure of type TeleType

  cout << "Do you wish to create a new record (respond with y or n): ";
  key = cin.get();
  if (key == 'y')
  {
    key = cin.get();                   // get the Enter key in buffered input
    recPoint = new TeleType;
    populate(recPoint);
    dispOne(recPoint);
  }
  else
    cout << "\nNo record has been created.";
  return 0;
}
```

(continued on next page)

```
// input a name and phone number
void populate(TeleType *record)   // record is a pointer to a
{                                 // structure of type TeleType
  cout << "Enter a name: ";
  getline(cin, record->name);
  cout << "Enter the phone number: ";
  getline(cin, record->phoneNo);

  return;
}

// display the contents of one record
void dispOne(TeleType *contents)  // contents is a pointer to a
{                                 // structure of type TeleType
  cout << "\nThe contents of the record just created is:"
       << "\nName: " << contents->name
       << "\nPhone Number: " << contents->phoneNo << endl;

  return;
}
```

A sample session produced by Program 15-7 is:

```
Do you wish to create a new record (respond with y or n): y
Enter a name: Monroe, James
Enter the phone number: (555) 555-1817

The contents of the record just created is:
Name: Monroe, James
Phone Number: (555) 555-1817
```

In reviewing Program 15-7, notice that only two variable declarations are made in main(). The variable key is declared as a character variable and the variable recPoint is declared as being a pointer to a structure of the TeleType type. Since the declaration for the type TeleType is global, TeleType can be used within main() to define recPoint as a pointer to a structure of the TeleType type.

If a user enters y in response to the first prompt in main(), a call to new is made for the required memory to store the designated structure. Once recPoint has been loaded with the proper address, this address can be used to access the newly created structure. The function populate() is used to prompt the user for data needed in filling the structure and to store the user-entered data in the correct members of the structure. The argument passed to populate() in main() is the pointer recPoint. Like all passed arguments, the value contained in recPoint is passed to the function. Since the value in recPoint is an address, populate() receives the address of the newly created structure and can directly access the structure members.

Within `populate()`, the value received by it is stored in the argument named `record`. Since the value to be stored in `record` is the address of a structure, `record` must be declared as a pointer to a structure. This parameter declaration is provided by the statement `TeleType *record`. The statements within `populate()` use the address in `record` to locate the respective members of the structure.

The `dispOne()` function in Program 15-7 is used to display the contents of the newly created and populated structure. The address passed to `dispOne()` is the same address that was passed to `populate()`. Since this passed value is the address of a structure, the argument name used to store the address is declared as a pointer to the correct structure type.

Exercises 15.4

1. Enter and execute Program 15-7.

2. As described in Table 15-1, the `new` operator returns either the address of the first new storage area allocated, or NULL if insufficient storage is available. Modify Program 15-7 to check that a valid address has been returned before a call to `populate()` is made. Display an appropriate message if sufficient storage is not available.

3. Write a C++ function named `modify()` that can be used to modify the name and phone number members of a structure of the type created in Program 15-7. The argument passed to `modify()` should be the address of the structure to be modified. The `modify()` function should first display the existing name and phone number in the selected structure and then request new data for these members.

15.5 COMMON PROGRAMMING ERRORS

Two common errors are often made when using structures.

1. Attempting to compare two structures, as complete entities, in a relational expression. For example, even if `TeleType` and `PhoneType` are two structures of the same type, the expression `TeleType == PhoneType` is invalid. Individual members of a structure can, of course, be compared if they are of the same data type, using any of C++'s relational operators.

2. Using a pointer to access either a structure or a member of a structure without ensuring that the address in the pointer is declared for the appropriate data type being accessed.

15.6 CHAPTER REVIEW

Key Terms

data field

record

structure

structure member

SUMMARY

1. A structure allows individual variables to be grouped under a common variable name. Each variable in a structure is accessed by its structure variable name, followed by a period, followed by its individual variable name. Another term for a data structure is a record. One form for declaring a structure is:

    ```
    struct
    {
        individual member declarations;
    } structureName;
    ```

2. A data type can be created from a structure using the declaration form

    ```
    struct DataTypeName
    {
        individual member declarations;
    };
    ```

    Individual structure variables may then be defined as this `DataTypeName`. By convention, the first letter of the `DataTypeName` is always capitalized.

3. Structures are particularly useful as elements of arrays. Used in this manner, each structure becomes one record in a list of records.

4. Complete structures can be used as function arguments, in which case the called function receives a copy of each element in the structure. The address of a structure may also be passed, either as a reference or a pointer, which provides the called function with direct access to the structure.

5. Structure members can be any valid C++ data type, including other structures, arrays, and pointers. When a pointer is included as a structure member, a linked list can be created. Such a list uses the pointer in one structure to "point to" (contain the address of) the next logical structure in the list.

Chapter Exercises

1. Define a structure data type and member variables for a business, including fields for the business name, description of the product or services, address, number of employees, and annual revenue.

2. Define a structure data type and member variables for a single kind of screw in your parts inventory, with fields for inventory number, screw length, diameter, kind of head (Phillips or standard slot), material (steel, brass, other), and cost.

3. A structure type is defined as:

    ```
    struct Inventory
    {
       char description[50];
       int prodnum;
       int quantity;
       double price;
    };
    ```

    Write the following:

    a. a declaration for an array of 100 structures of type `Inventory`
    b. an assignment of product number 4355 to the 83rd `Inventory` item
    c. a statement that reads the price of the 15th `Inventory` item

4. Define an array of structures for up to 50 factory employees, in which each structure contains fields for name, age, social security number, hourly wage, and years with the company. Write the following:

    a. statements that display the name and number of years with the company for the 25th employee in the array
    b. a loop that, for every employee, adds 1 to the number of years with the company and that adds 50 cents to the hourly wage

5. a. In two dimensions a mathematical vector is a pair of numbers that represent directed arrows in a plane, as shown by the mathematical vectors v1 and v2 in Figure 15-7.

FIGURE 15-7
Vectors v1 and v2

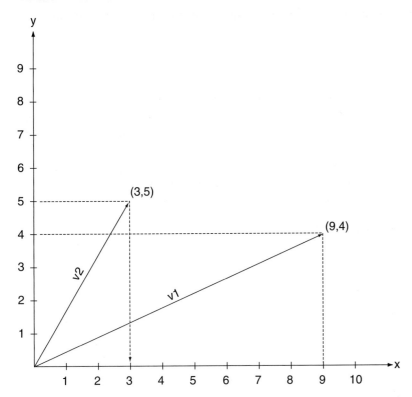

Two-dimensional mathematical vectors can be written in the form (a, b), where a and b are called the x and y components of the vector. For example, for the vectors illustrated in Figure 15-7, v1 = (9, 4) and v2 = (3, 5). For vectors, the following operations apply:

If
  v1 = (a,b) and v2 = (c,d)
then
  v1 + v2 = (a,b) + (c,d) = (a + c, b + d)
  v1 − v2 = (a,b) − (c,d) = (a − c, b − d)

Using this information, write a C++ program that defines an array of two vector structures, where each structure consists of two double-precision components a and b. Your program should permit a user to enter two vectors, call two functions that return the sum and difference of the entered vectors, and display the results calculated by these functions.

b. In addition to the operations defined in Exercise 5a, two additional vector operations are negation and absolute value. For a vector v1 with components (a,b), these operations are defined as follows:

negation: $-v1 = -(a,b) = (-a,-b)$
absolute value: $|v1| = sqrt(a * a + b * b)$

Using this information, modify the program that you wrote for Exercise 5a to display the negation and absolute values of both vectors input by a user, as well as the negation and absolute value of the sum of the two input vectors.

Testing Center

Please visit the Testing Center at www.course.com/testingcenter for more practice on data structures.

INDEX